WOMEN AS SUBJECTS IN STREET ART AROUND THE WORLD

Dr. Katja Fleischmann and Robert H. Mann

WOMEN ON THE WALLS

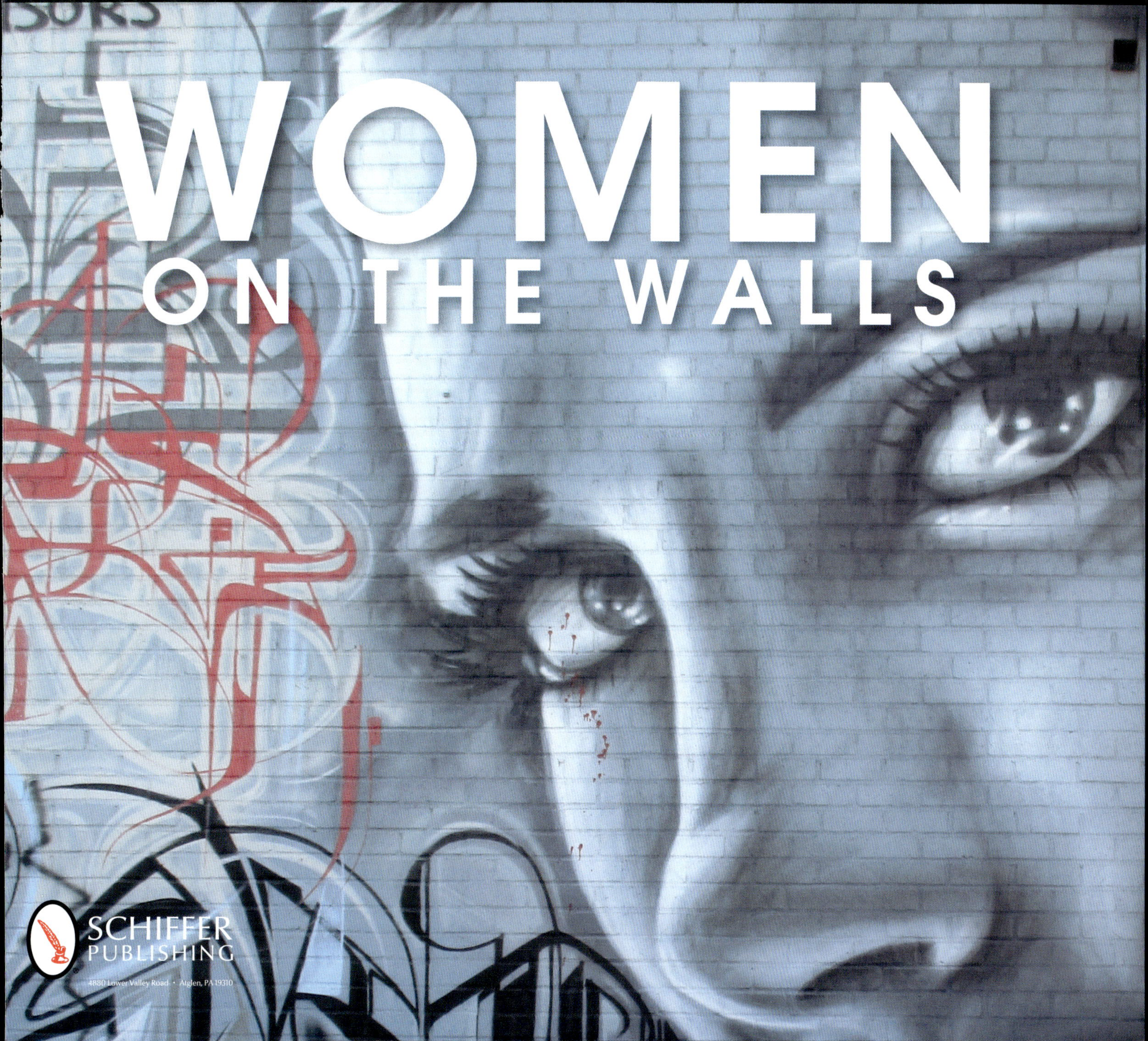

SCHIFFER PUBLISHING
4880 Lower Valley Road · Atglen, PA 19310

Library of Congress Control Number: 2021948643

Designed by Brenda McCallum
Cover design by Molly Shields
Cover art by "ROY," Costa Rica
Previous page: Detail of *Her Eyes Like Emotional Sensors* by Starfighter, Ease One, Sek, and Mar
All photos by Katja Fleischmann and Robert H. Mann unless otherwise noted.
Costa Rica interview translations by Robert H. Mann.

ISBN: 978-0-7643-6403-7
Printed in Serbia

Published by Schiffer Publishing, Ltd.
4880 Lower Valley Road
Atglen, PA 19310
Phone: (610) 593-1777; Fax: (610) 593-2002
Email: Info@schifferbooks.com
Web: www.schifferbooks.com

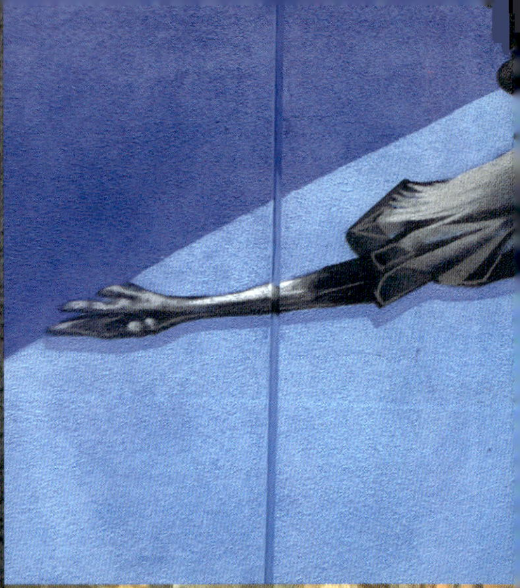

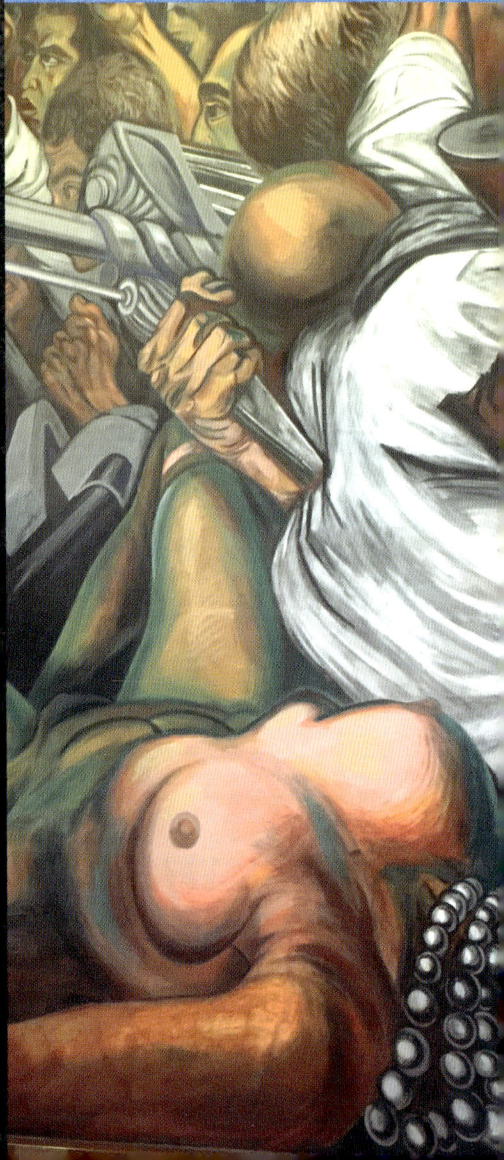

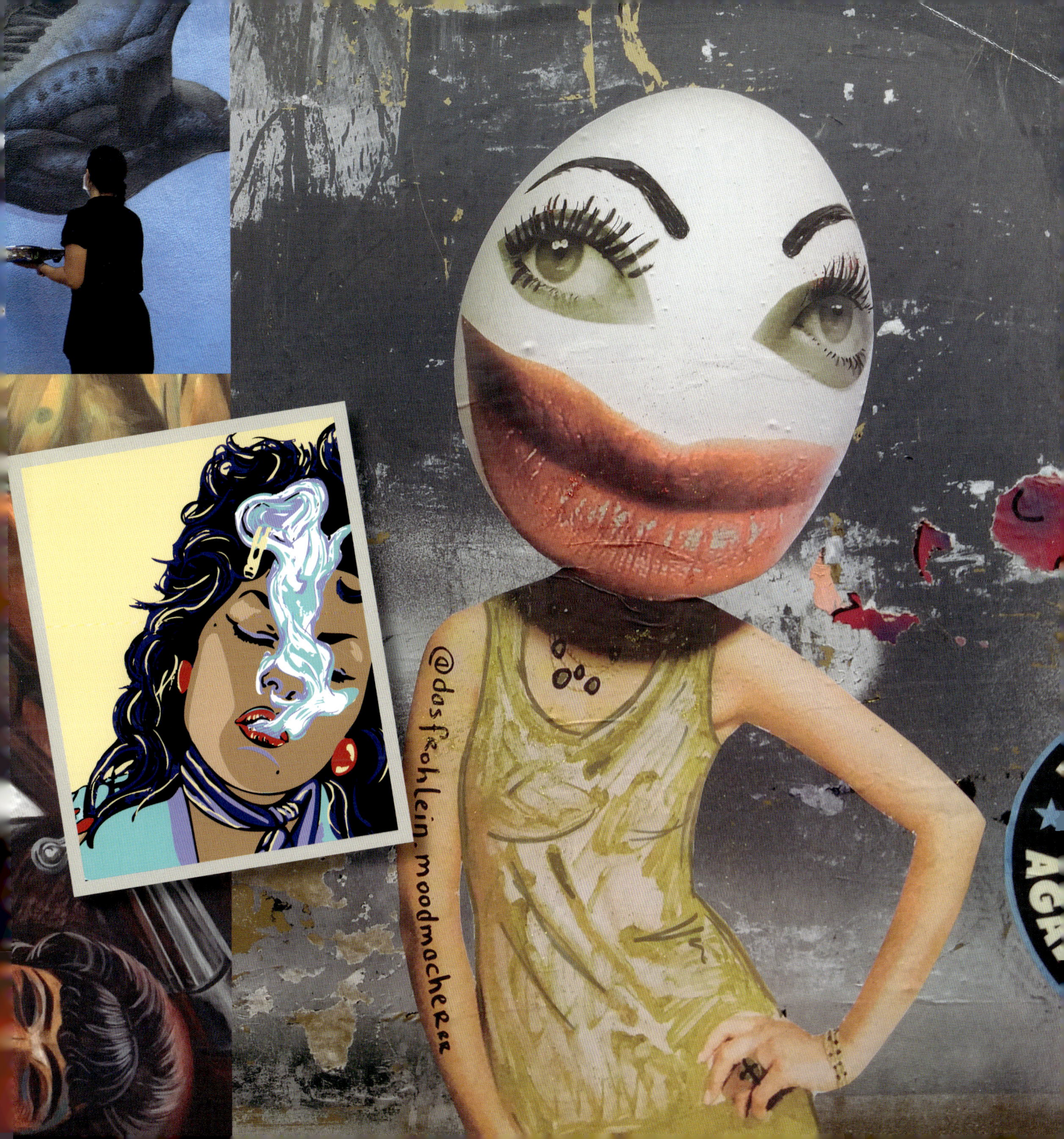
@dasfrohlein_moodmacherer

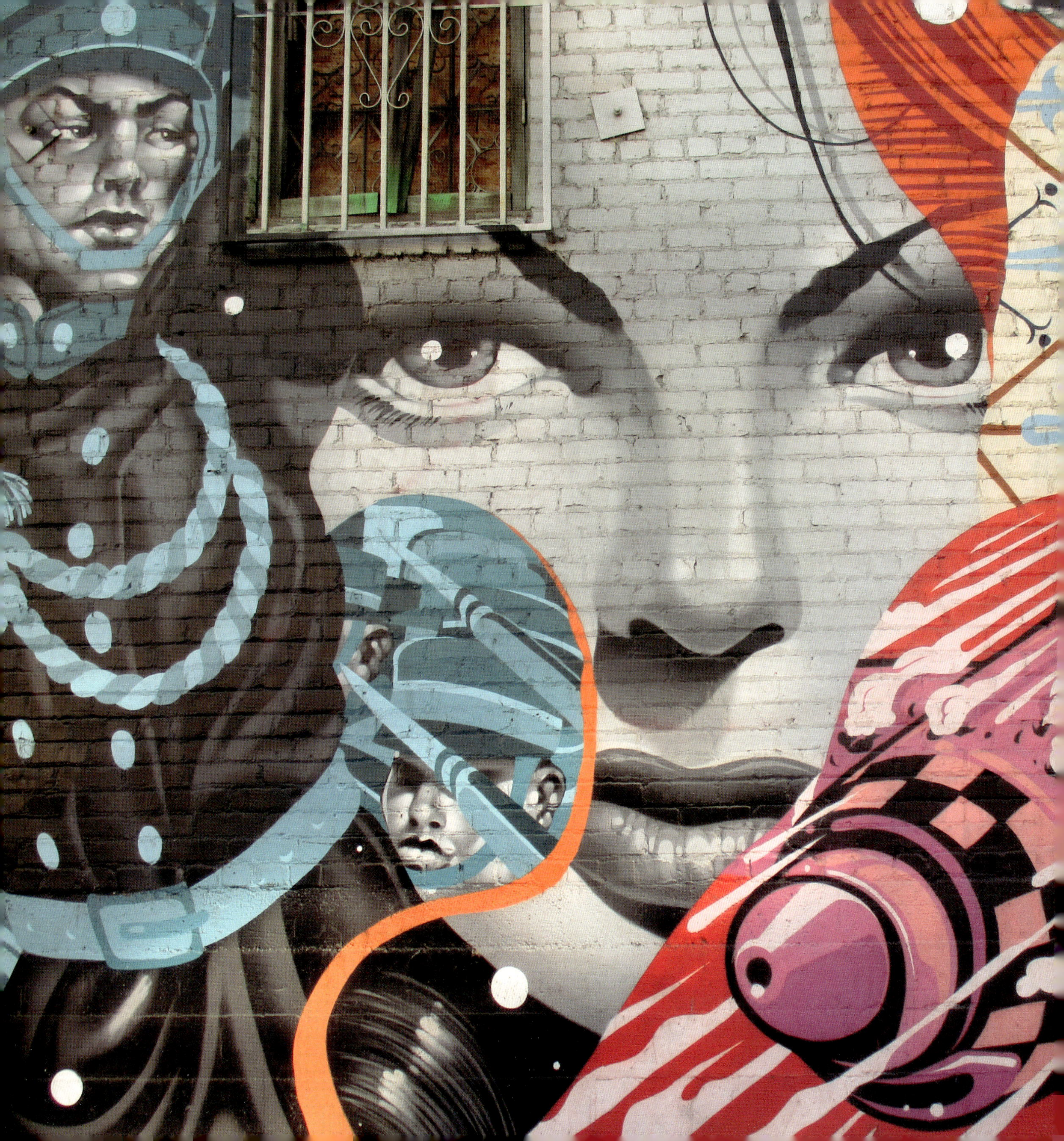

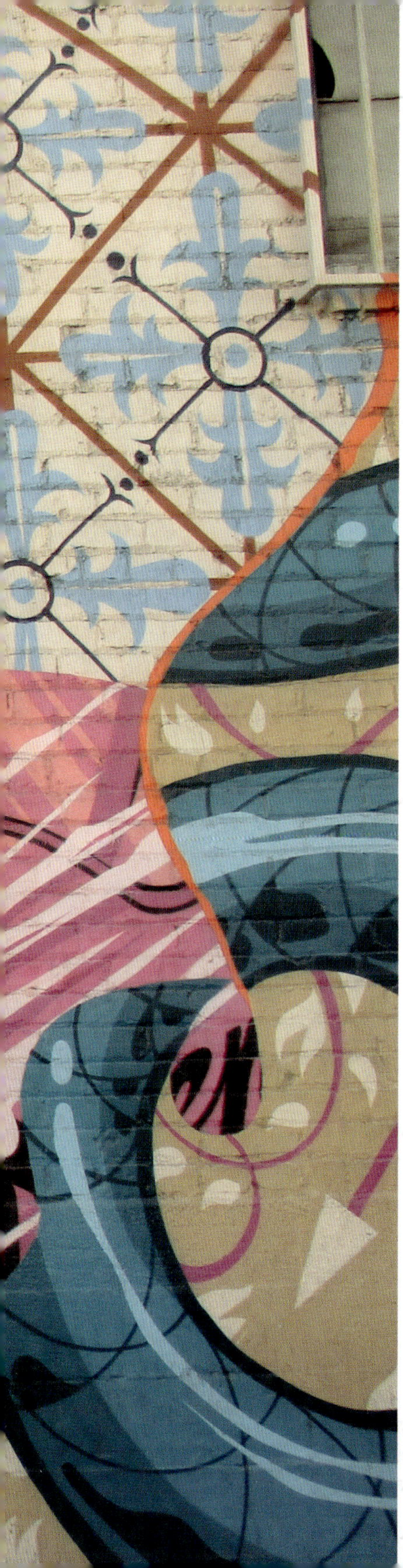

FOREWORD

The Transformative Power of Women on the Walls: The Story behind the Book

The genesis of this book was brought about by my interest in typography and signage and how it can change a city's landscape. The signs and letters can be historical windows to culture and politics. I travel a lot, and I began expanding this interest to women subjects, who can be found in most cities I traveled to. I began taking photos of women on walls, and I began asking myself: Who are the artists behind this wall art, and what are they trying to say about their women subjects? The next step was to obviously ask the artists themselves, and the results were surprisingly candid.

There is no question that women are spearheading a new political power movement that is changing the perception of how we see them, and this is reflected in some of the wall art that is overtly political in nature. Wall art is a fascinating expression of frustrations and newfound power to speak up in a bold, graphic way. In our journey we experienced a public expression of artistic freedom, embodied by women on the walls found in various countries. Just as the Statue of Liberty greeted immigrants with the promise of endless opportunity, the artwork found on the outdoor walls of cities and towns is symbolic of the need we have as people to display our individual vision. That many of these walls feature women as subjects is a testament to women's strength and beauty.

The women on the walls are the outgrowth of a rebellious spirit that runs contrary to conventionalism and advertising. The fact that many of these pieces are done without permission demonstrates a certain urgency in the artwork itself. Some of it has an unfinished or raw quality, and that piques my interest.

There is a never-ending gallery of opportunities for the people who pick up a spray can and say to us, "Look at me." This declaration may be as much about ego as it is about expanding artistic vision and making a point. As long as there are walls, there will be women adorning them. It is up to us, as viewers, to support these expressions of freedom by the simple act of viewing them.

—Dr. Katja Fleischmann

I like asking questions and investigating intentions, so it was a natural fit for me to find out as much as I could about the motivations behind a particular piece of wall art. Tracking down the artists was no easy task, but I was able to put those investigative skills to good use to ask the questions that form the heart of this book. Street artists are notoriously difficult to pin down. They are gypsies by their very nature, particularly the international artists who parachute into a city, do their work, and then disappear. It's not as if you are walking into the middle of dozens of amateur watercolorists painting a seascape from a bluff.

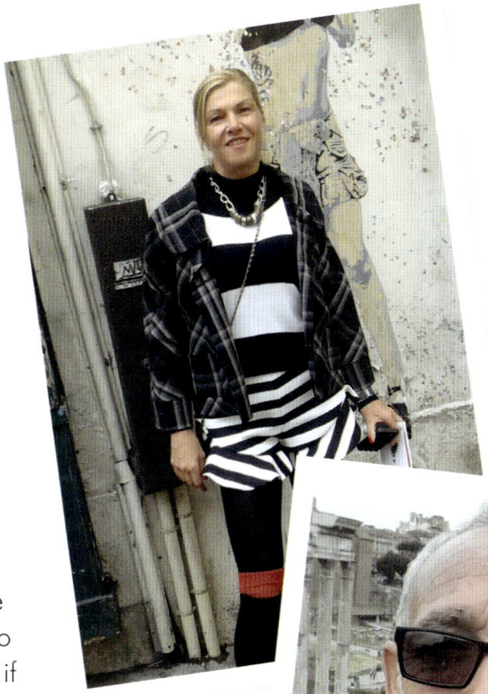

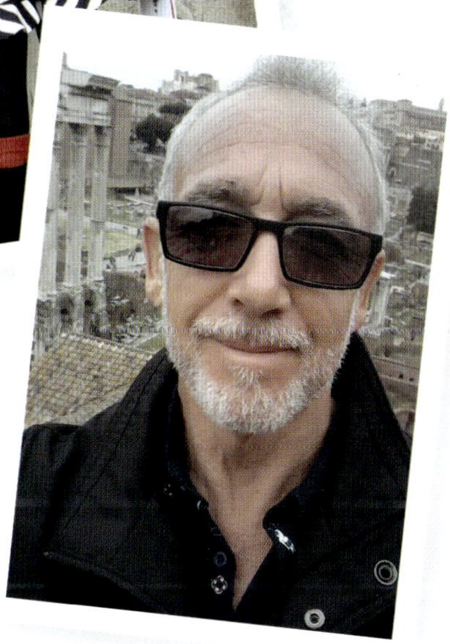

What I found on this journey was a huge variety of street art styles and scales that stretch a viewer's idea of women as subjects. The artists we spoke to are thoughtful and driven. They define a passion that comes across in their work from a sub rosa tradition where the streets are often the schools. It is decidedly not an elitist type of art.

There is no one way you can sum up the women on the walls. There is no well defined school or style, which makes it interesting and speculative by nature. "What did the artist mean to say?" Maybe nothing at all. Maybe they just like the idea of painting on walls illegally and getting away with it. So this mystery and answer remains in the question, your interpretation, and the art itself, until you speak directly with the artists. This book has been a labor of love that hopefully comes across for you, the observer/reader. Maybe your eyes will open just a crack after taking our tour. I certainly know mine have, so have fun looking for the women on the walls wherever you live in the world.

—Robert H. Mann

Author Dr. Katja Fleischmann poses in front of Sobr's fan dancer in the Marais District in Paris.

Author Robert H. Mann at the Roman Forum

Acknowledgments

The authors would like to thank all the wall artists who graciously donated their time to explain the vision behind their wall art of women. The list includes Dr. Judy Baca, Erin Yoshi, Colette Miller, Vhils (Alexandre Farto), JUST, PUCHO, and Faith47.

The authors also wish to thank Costa Rican filmmaker Federico Peixoto, who chronicled the rise of street art throughout Central America; his invaluable insights during our interview illuminated the street art scene in the region. Thanks also to Elena Martinez, Co-Artistic Director of the Bronx Music Heritage Center City Lore in New York City, for graciously putting the authors in touch with renowned photographer Henry Chalfant, who allowed us to use his seminal photographs documenting the early days of graffiti writers on New York subways. Thanks also Beatriz Navarro Soto of Santiago de Chile for her photographs of Valparaíso.

The authors made every attempt to identify the wall artists pictured in this book. Some were easy to find and identify; others we couldn't name simply because their works are obscure, had no signature, or the signatures were too hard to read. Wherever possible, we attributed the work we photographed. (You will find more information on the artists we identified in the "Artist Information" section at the end of the book.)

To every street artist who appears in this book, a heartfelt "thank you" from the authors for sharing your work on public walls and seeding the idea for this book with your art.

Keep spraying, stenciling, rolling, printing, and pasting. You are making the world a more interesting place.

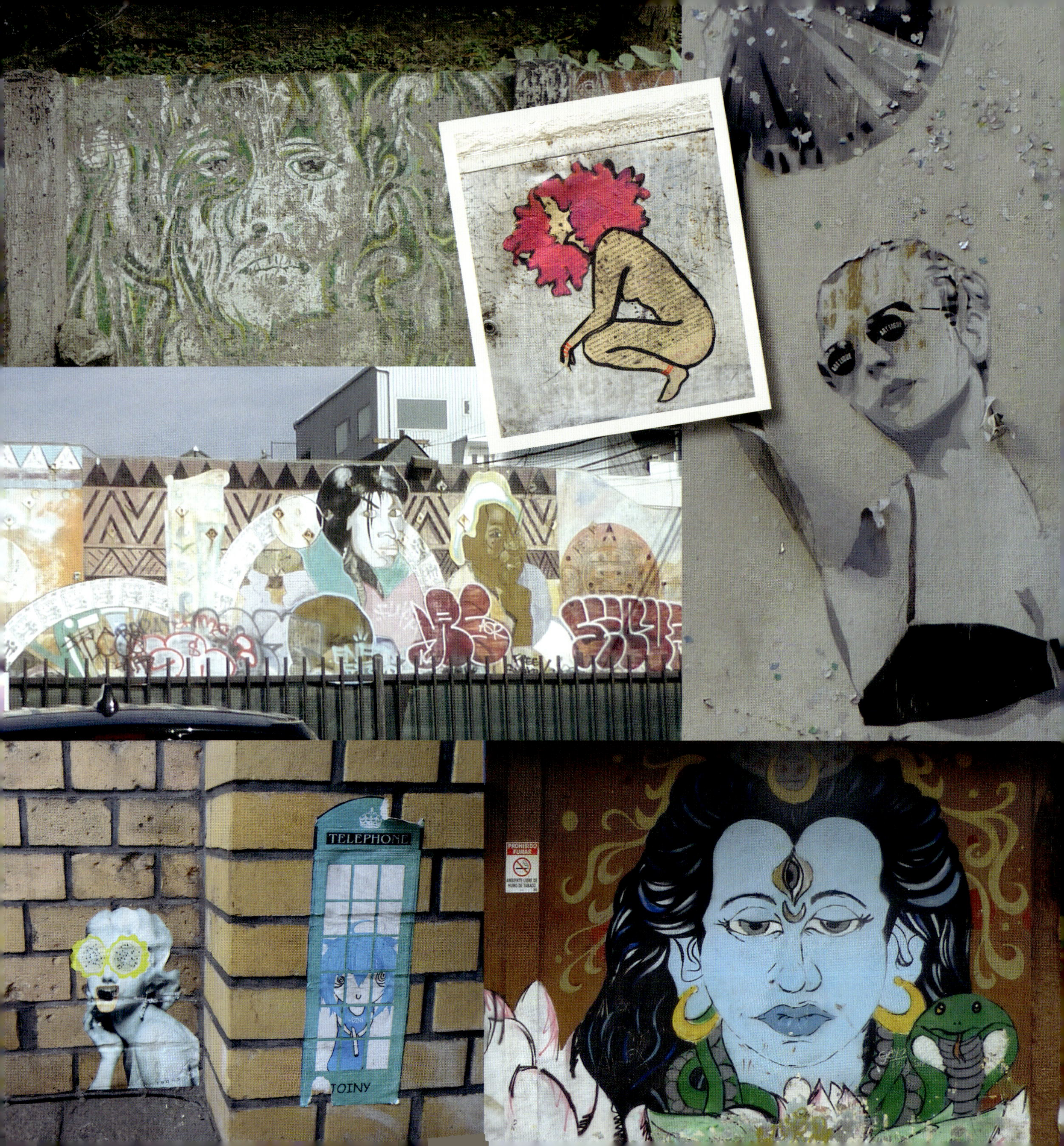
TELEPHONE
TOINY

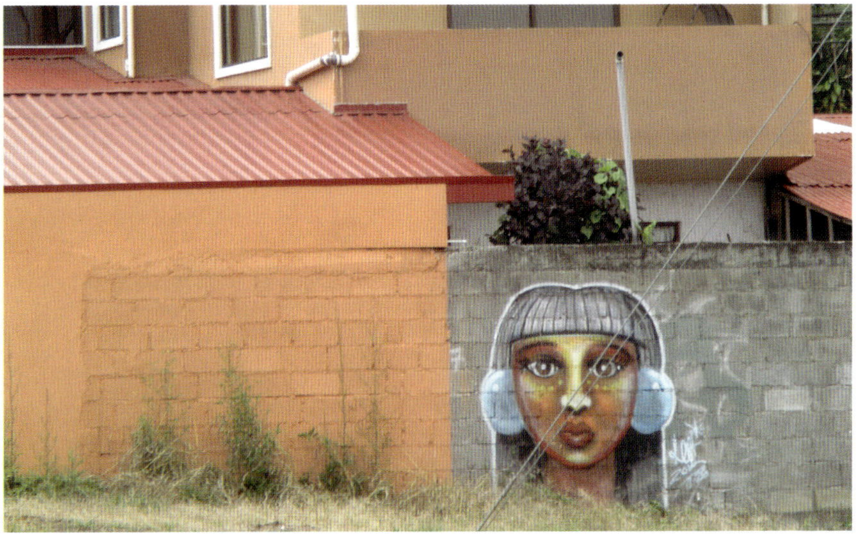

I

Portrait by Costa Rican wall artist, Kaat, one of the few women wall artists in the country.

WELCOME to the World of Women on the Walls

Women on the walls throughout the world reflect the diversity of artistic styles: Examples from Los Angeles, Paris, Palermo, Berlin, and Costa Rica. Photo of woman with pink hair by John Harris.

They dance; they play; they act coy; they stare right through you from broken surfaces; they exude power, eroticism, and a mystery that many have tried to capture. They are the women on the walls, and they speak to us from the subconscious of the artists who have portrayed women in all their guises. Wherever you go in the world, these street galleries often turn to women as a source of inspiration, whether the message is politically freighted, cultural jamming, or a way of expressing appreciation of feminine rhythm, power, and beauty.

Today's wall artists use relatively quick ways of expressing themselves, yet their subject matter reflects ancient motifs that were painstakingly carved from stone or painted in meticulous detail on canvases. In one sense, wall art connects our collective history and storytelling, from ancient Greece vases to famous works of Renaissance art, such as Botticelli's *Primavera*. The thematic thread found in modern wall art of women is woven from the tapestry of the past; both examples of the Roman relief and Botticelli celebrate the role of women as unifying figures, often holding hands and dancing.

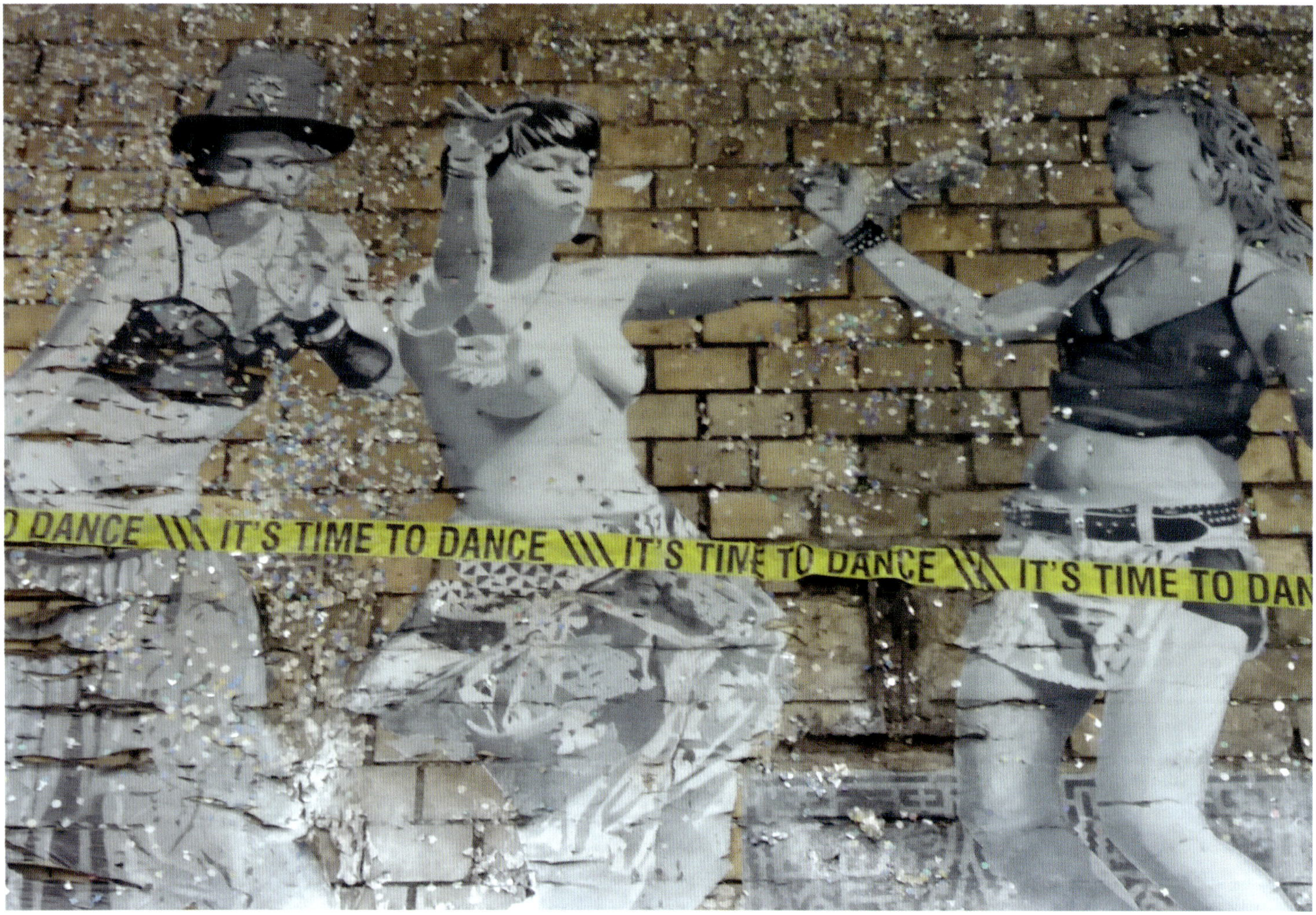

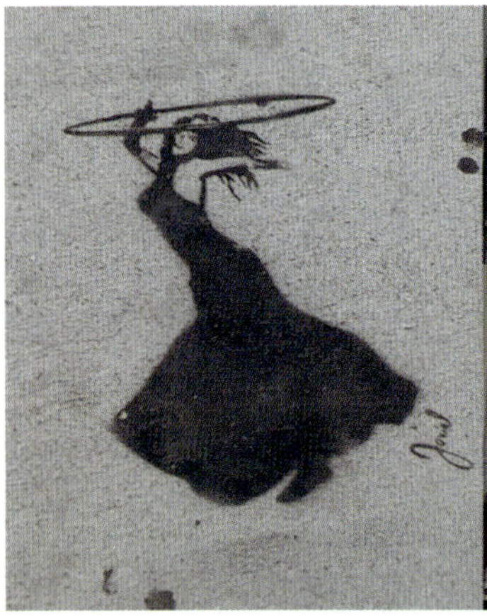

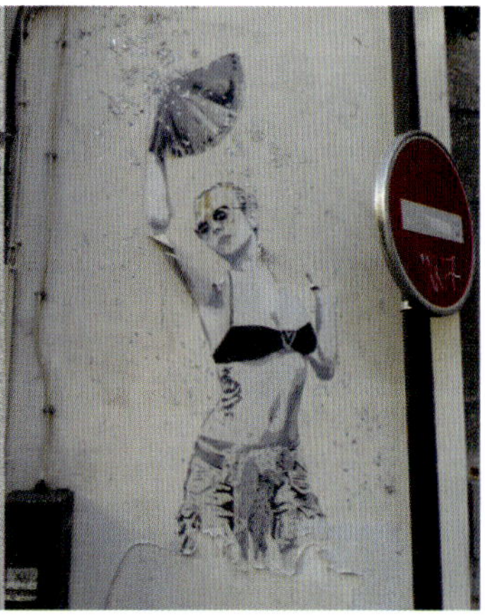

Women in motion: Hula-Hoop stencil by Jovial on a Venice Beach, California, sidewalk. A woman dancing with a fan in Paris and a group of women dancers from Berlin by Sobr, whose paste-ups are part of his A Time to Dance series.

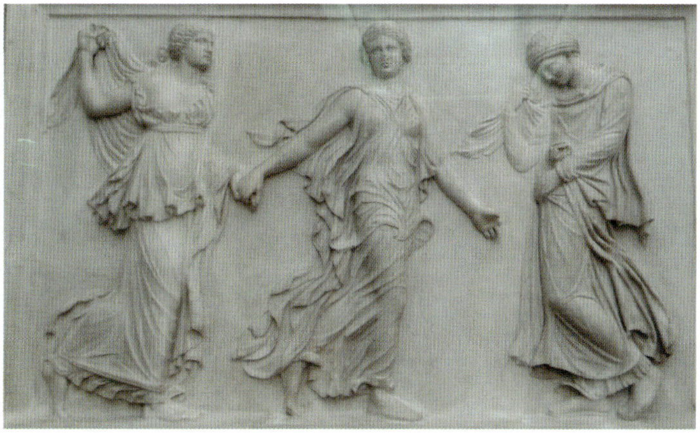

This historical connection is what makes women on the wall a continuing story that unites all wall art of women no matter what technique is employed or historical era it represents. The current representations of women can be as simple as a stencil on a sidewalk, a peeling poster down an alleyway, or giant murals covering sides of buildings. Once you enter this world on foot, it is easy to become entranced by the variations of artists and their women subjects.

As a subgenre of studio art, wall art is much more than a passing object of curiosity. It asks the viewer to participate because of its openly urban context. In fact, street art tours are now popular

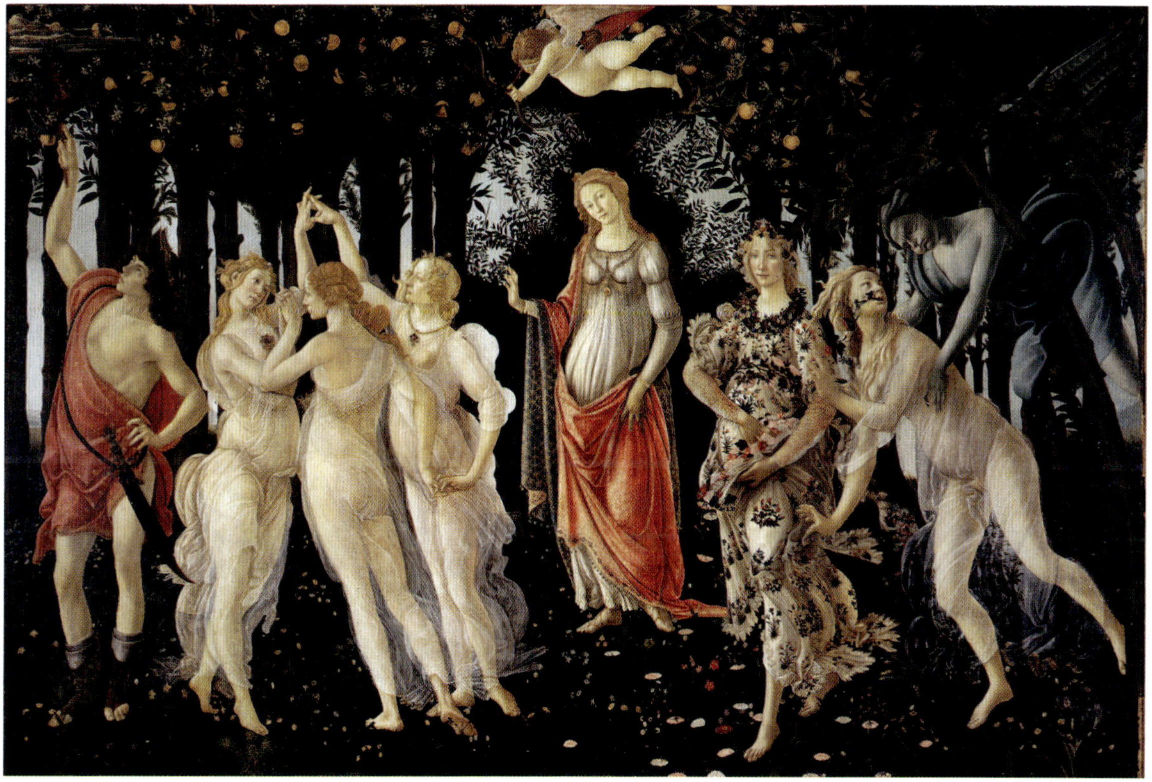

ABOVE *A relief from the time of Hadrian's rule, based on Hellenistic vase art, depicts the dance of the Horai, who personified the seasons. Uffizi Gallery, Florence.*

BELOW *Sandro Botticelli's Primavera, the Renaissance masterpiece where the Three Graces gracefully join hands. Uffizi Gallery, Florence.*

options for tourist treks in major cities from Berlin to Los Angeles, where wall art has become the darling of travel bloggers who map out walking tours that showcase outdoor galleries throughout the world. A handful of street artists have been catapulted into public awareness through these tours, and some have become international stars such as Banksy, whose secretive stencil works have made him a media celebrity worth millions.

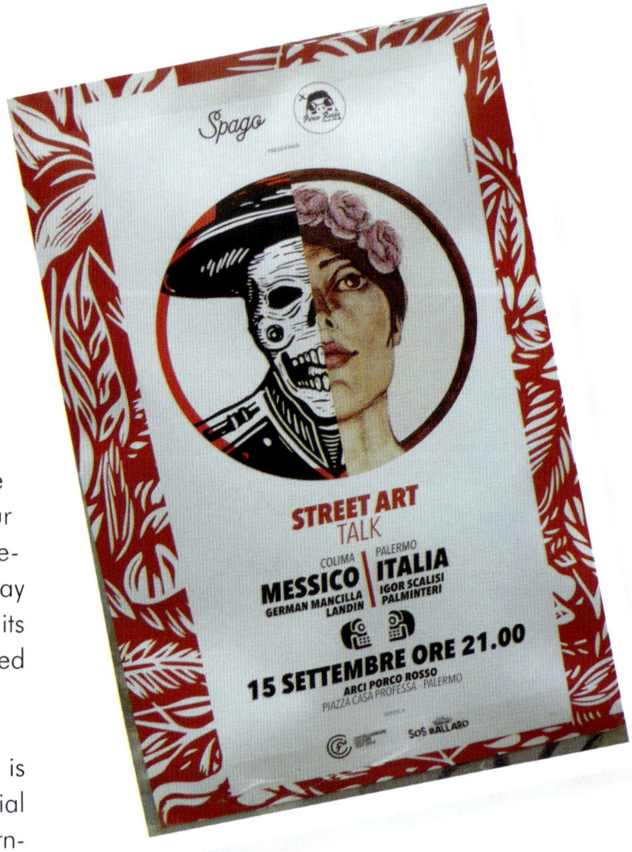

Poster advertising a street art talk in Palermo, Sicily

All street art, whether the work of obscure, unknown "bombers" or gallery-quality muralists, is in a sense owned by the public; you don't need to buy a ticket and queue up to observe it—wall art is part of a free, open-air gallery guided by your feet and curiosity. Some street art is still tagged by law enforcement as the work of graffiti vandals, and some of it is spray painted illegally on public walls. And that is the heart of its original power—it's often raw and confronting, uninhibited quality and dubious legality.

But some of that rebellious spirit is changing as street art is becoming less of an act of defiance and more of a commercial enterprise often sanctioned and commissioned by local governments. Street artists need to make a living, and some are doing so by hiring agents and selling their work through online galleries offering frameable prints and merchandising their images on t-shirts and hoodies. Some street artists are even suing major corporations in courtroom copyright battles to protect their brand.

With or without fame or approval, the shadow artists keep working with spray cans and guns, mosaics, stencils, and paste-up posters. Their subjects often maintain a rebel spirit that defines their wall art. And their favorite subjects, more often than not, are women.

In this guided tour—part travelogue and part exposition—you will meet some of the artists behind the street art of women and learn what motivated them to select their subject matter and the viewpoints they want to share about their women subjects. Women street artists from LA who were interviewed are determined to challenge the often sexualized male stereotypes of women on the wall. In Costa Rica, the authors met young men whose street art forms an important part of their identity and who paint women in the context of nature and as symbols of inspiration and beauty. You will also hear from an artist from Portugal whose unconventional sculpting techniques and subject matter define a humanist approach to wall art, while a woman artist from South Africa adopts a nurturing feminist vision as a visual counterpoint to violence against women in her homeland.

You will also see the huge variety of women on the wall in Chile, Peru, Mexico, Paris, Palermo, Berlin, and South Africa.

The Attraction of Walls as Surfaces

Why take to the walls? First, it is their texture. Often found on neglected, industrial, and abandoned public places, walls are grand canvases on which to practice your art. The pitted, uneven surfaces require not small brushes and a palette knife, but spray cans, cherry picker cranes, rollers, and powered chisels. This is not a finely etched art form created on a studio canvas painted in a garret, but almost an industrial approach to art made by bold strokes of imagination and technique. By their very nature, walls are also viewed by everyone who walks by them, particularly in well trafficked pedestrian areas of cities. Street art featuring women is not only discovered in the intensely urban global cities such as Paris, but also in small market towns in Mexico, where it is commissioned to beautify rundown neighborhoods. In Palermo, Sicily, the wall art women defiantly gaze at you from an impasto of peeling paint and plaster.

This type of public art is a chance for wall artists to share their peculiar visions and style. Like all art, street art reflects a grand arc of evolution and experience that mirrors the culture, history, and politics of a given time period. But unlike art curators, who divide museums into neat galleries reflecting styles and historical periods, the curators of wall art are you and me as we walk past. Wall art can appear and disappear overnight; its practitioners are traveling in the fast lane of cultural whims, swerving to avoid conformity and still maintain some originality.

Wall art of women has gone well beyond the cartoonish and unsophisticated—although examples of that tattoo body art style of women are plentiful. At times, it is often hard to tell where the personal expression of wall art begins and self-promotion ends. Suddenly large-scale murals have become part of a civic pride movement in commissioned pieces by internationally well known artists found on monolithic building-size pieces in Paris. Conversely, wall art can be part of an artscape of a city, like Valparaíso in Chile, where the homes themselves are like colored confetti spilling down steep mountainside streets to the historic port.

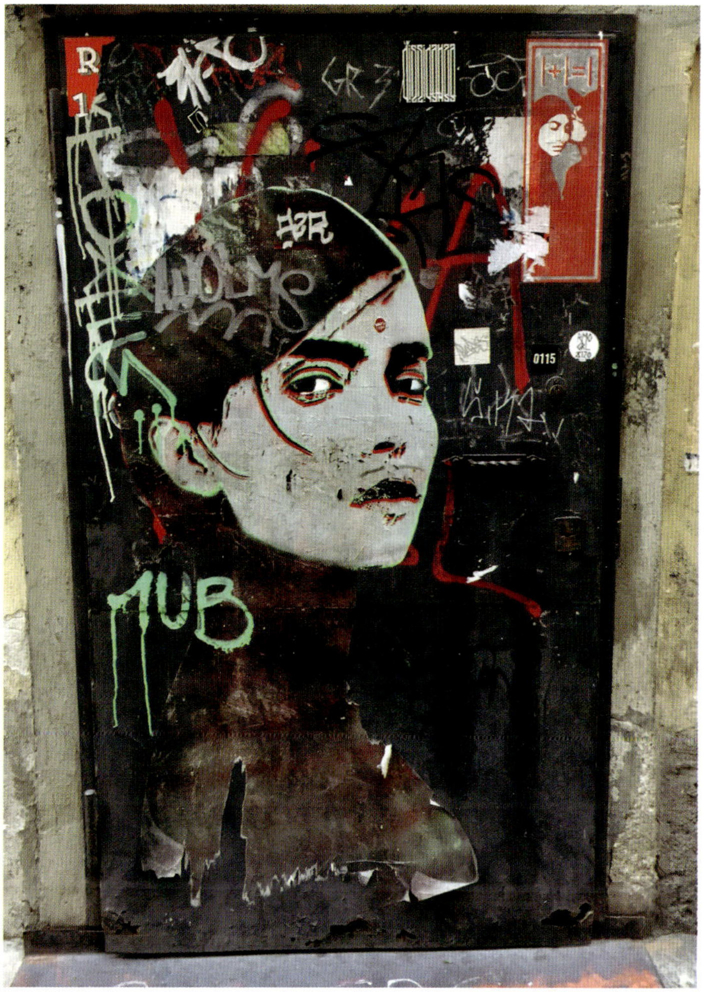

A woman's defiant gaze challenges you in Palermo, Sicily, possibly the work of street artist 7ub. Photo: John Harris

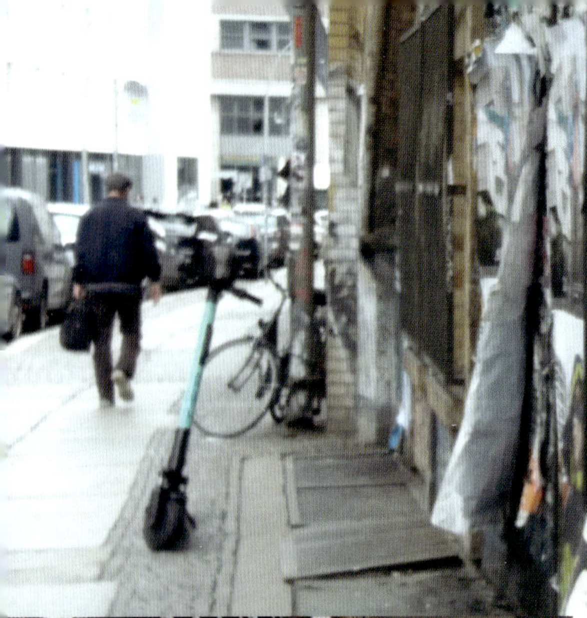

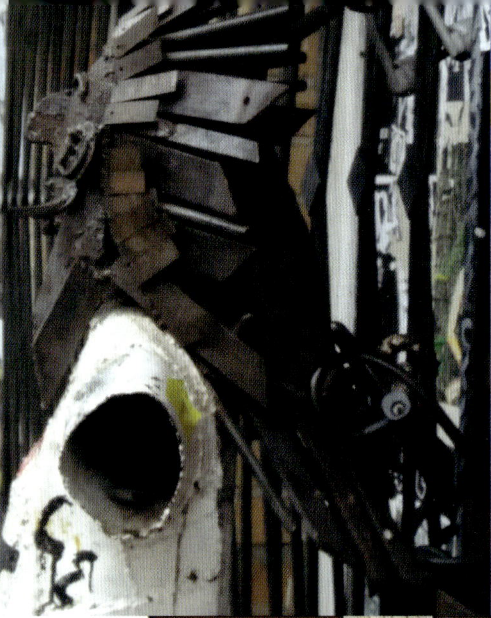

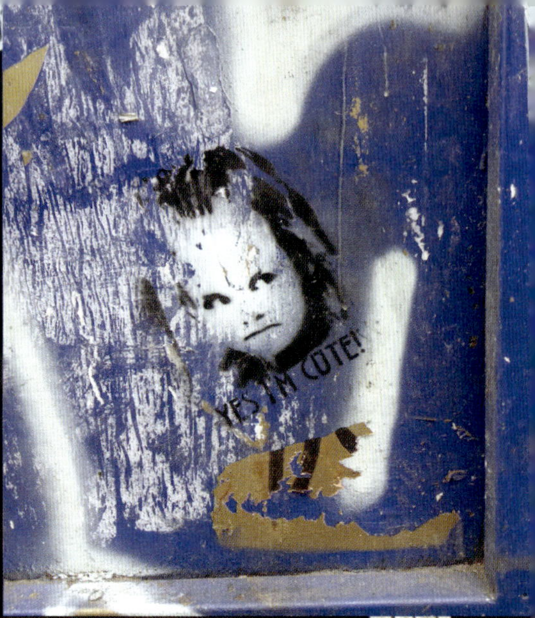

YES I'M CUTE!

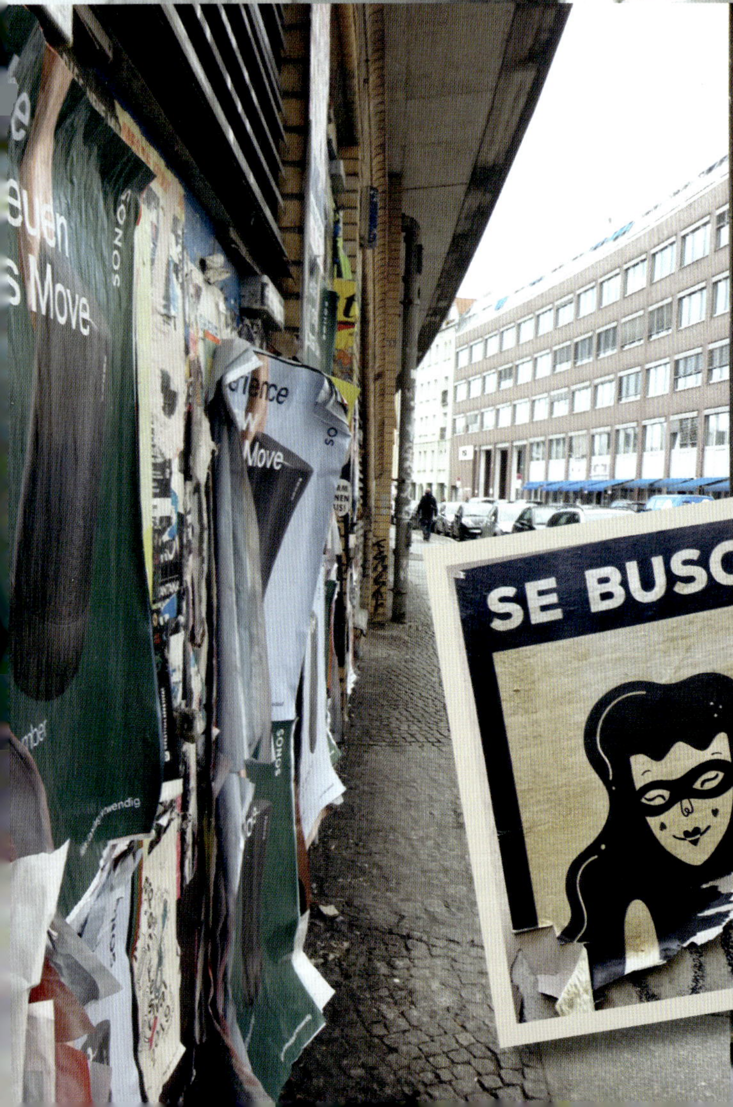

SONOS
Move
SE BUSCA

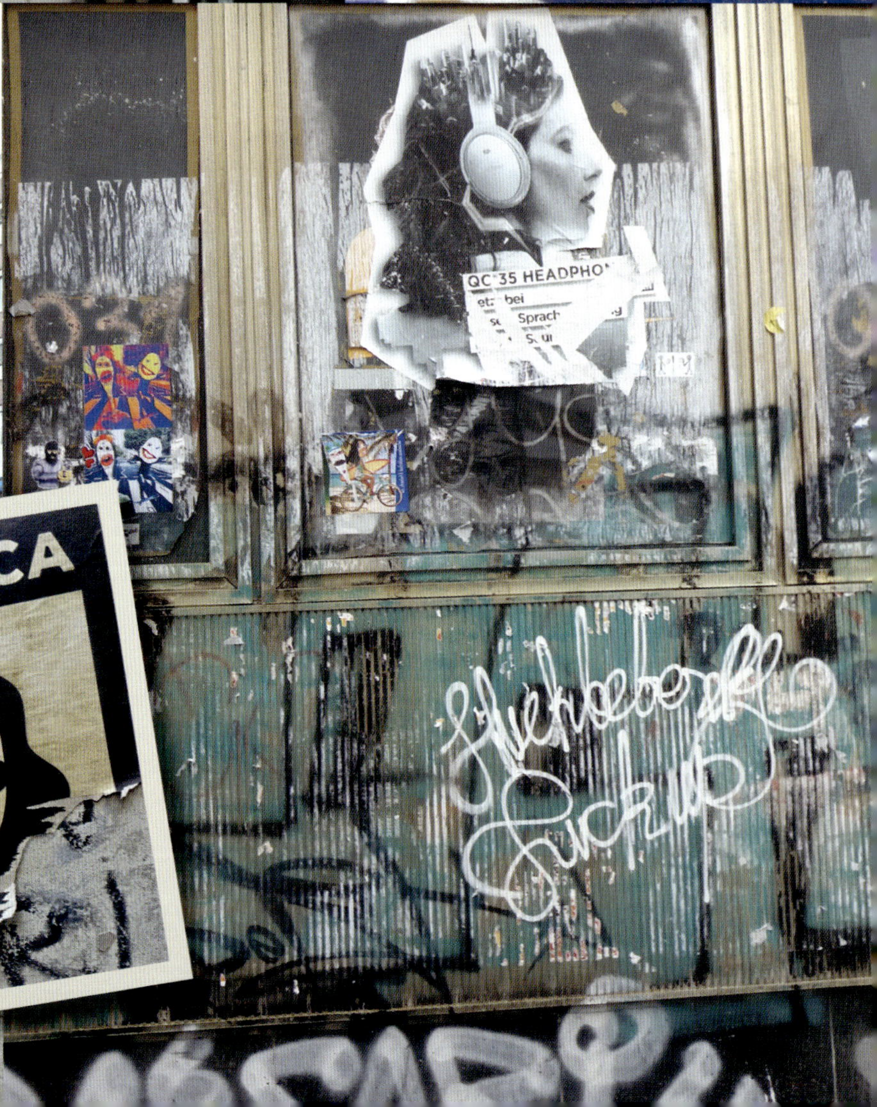

Wall art of women here can be found on corrugated roller doors of local workshops. In many cases the artists are not paid—their work is compelled by making themselves heard through a public visual language. In a sense, wall art of women is now part of our quotidian visual field, much as it was on the amphora of Greece and Roman temple facades.

This layered, organic appearance often defines street art's spontaneous, replaceable quirkiness; it invites comparison to a tree shedding its bark, where your gaze peels off the layers. There are artists' signatures hidden in many of these sketch pad pieces overlaid with graffiti, which are difficult to decipher. In many cases it is often impossible to tell who created the art, which requires the archeological skills of an Egyptologist to decode the hieroglyphic signature. [Note: The authors have attempted wherever possible to identify and credit the wall artists in this book, and we apologize if we couldn't read the signatures.]

Women on the Wall as Protest Art and Parody

Wall art has always been a political messaging medium and continues to play a very important role in public protest. Women wall artists are also part of these spontaneous street rebellions. Some are currently painting their messages of female empowerment in dangerous streets, where they fight religious orthodoxy and bigotry with portraits of women pursuing education and independence. Other wall artists rely on visual puns to satirize women in power.

These peeling layers of posters on Dircksenstraße, Berlin often conceal hidden wall art treasures. The street is a well-known street art gallery running under a railway line.

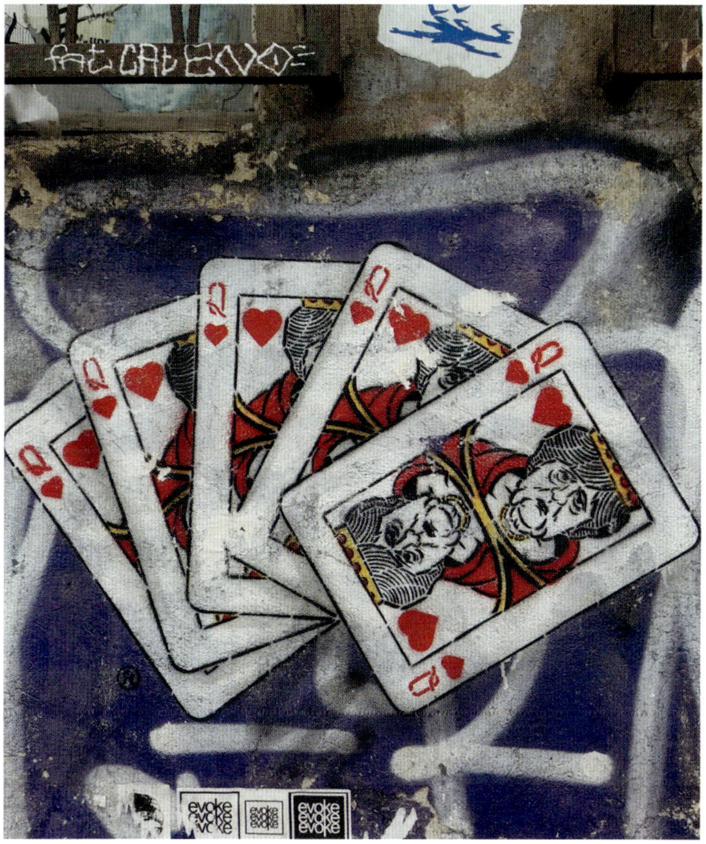

The deck is stacked in favor of Germany's leader Angela Merkel in this satirical wall art from Berlin. Artist unknown.

The examples of wall art as political commentary, parody, and satire do not require an elaborate analysis of artistic viewpoint. But not all wall art of women is so transparent. As an observer of street art of women, you can often only draw an outline around artistic intentions unless you speak directly to the artists. The authors have traveled the world looking for examples of women on the wall, walking outdoor galleries, and interviewing some of the artists to reveal their purpose behind the art you'll find in these pages.

Street artists, like their women, are sui generis—who subscribe to the idea of the fleeting nature of their art. Some of the wall art of women is derivative and some of it original. No matter

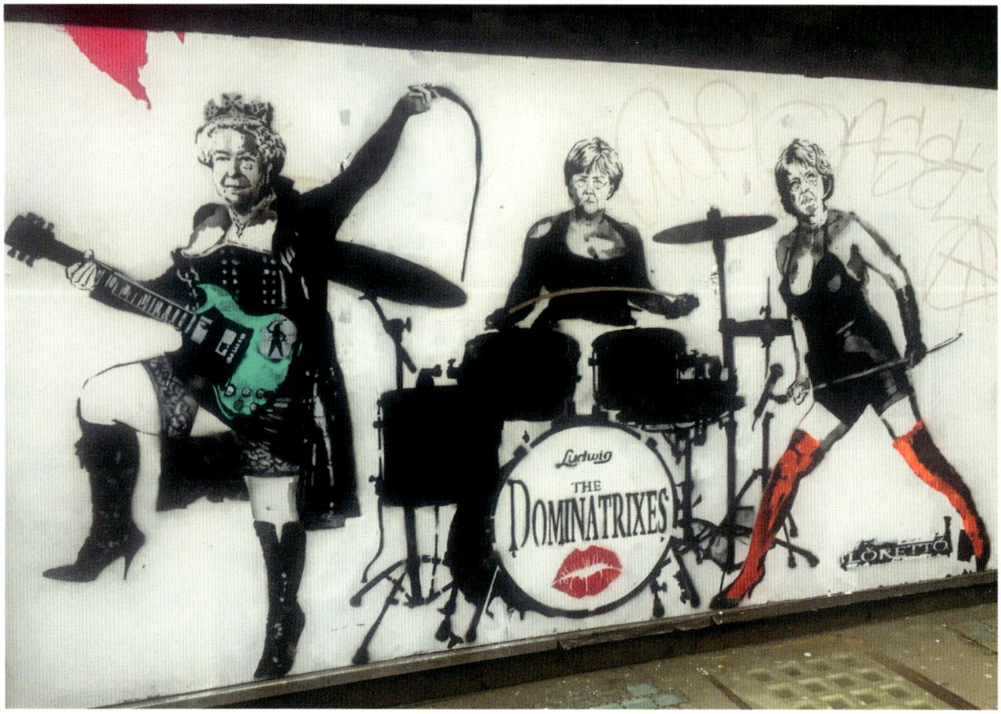

The Dominatrixes by Loretto, a London-based wall artist who has created a supergroup with Queen Elizabeth on lead guitar, Angela Merkel on drums, and perhaps Theresa May as the lead singer. Photo: John Harris

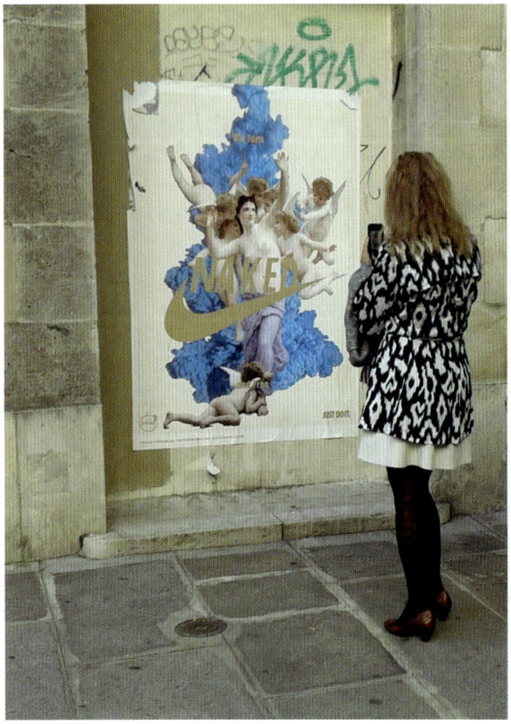

what its inspiration, if there is an unspoken consensus, it's that women are more interesting subjects because they can simultaneously convey political and social power and sensuality. This book is a rough sketch, then, of how important women are to street artists who have graduated from the "University of Tagging and Bombing," into the realm of displaying their talents in more considered large and small-scale pieces on public walls.

A patron of Parisian street art in the Marais District studies a satiric poster using classical art images coupled with Nike's tagline: Just Do It.

Venice Reconstituted is a building-size mural along the boardwalk in Venice Beach, California, which borrows liberally from Botticelli's The Birth of Venus with the twentieth-century tagline "History Is Myth." Mural by Rip Cronk, 1989.

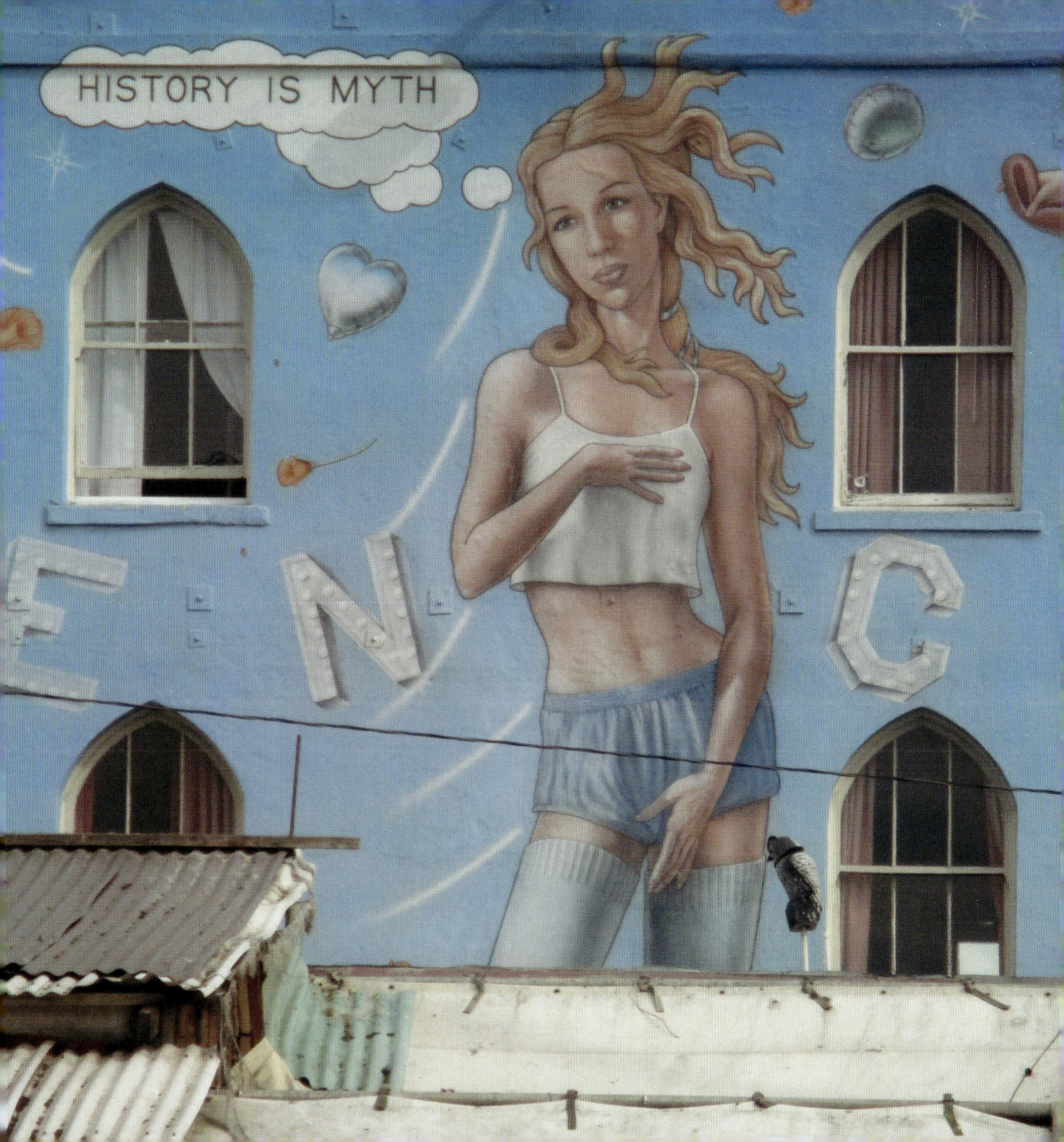
HISTORY IS MYTH
E N C

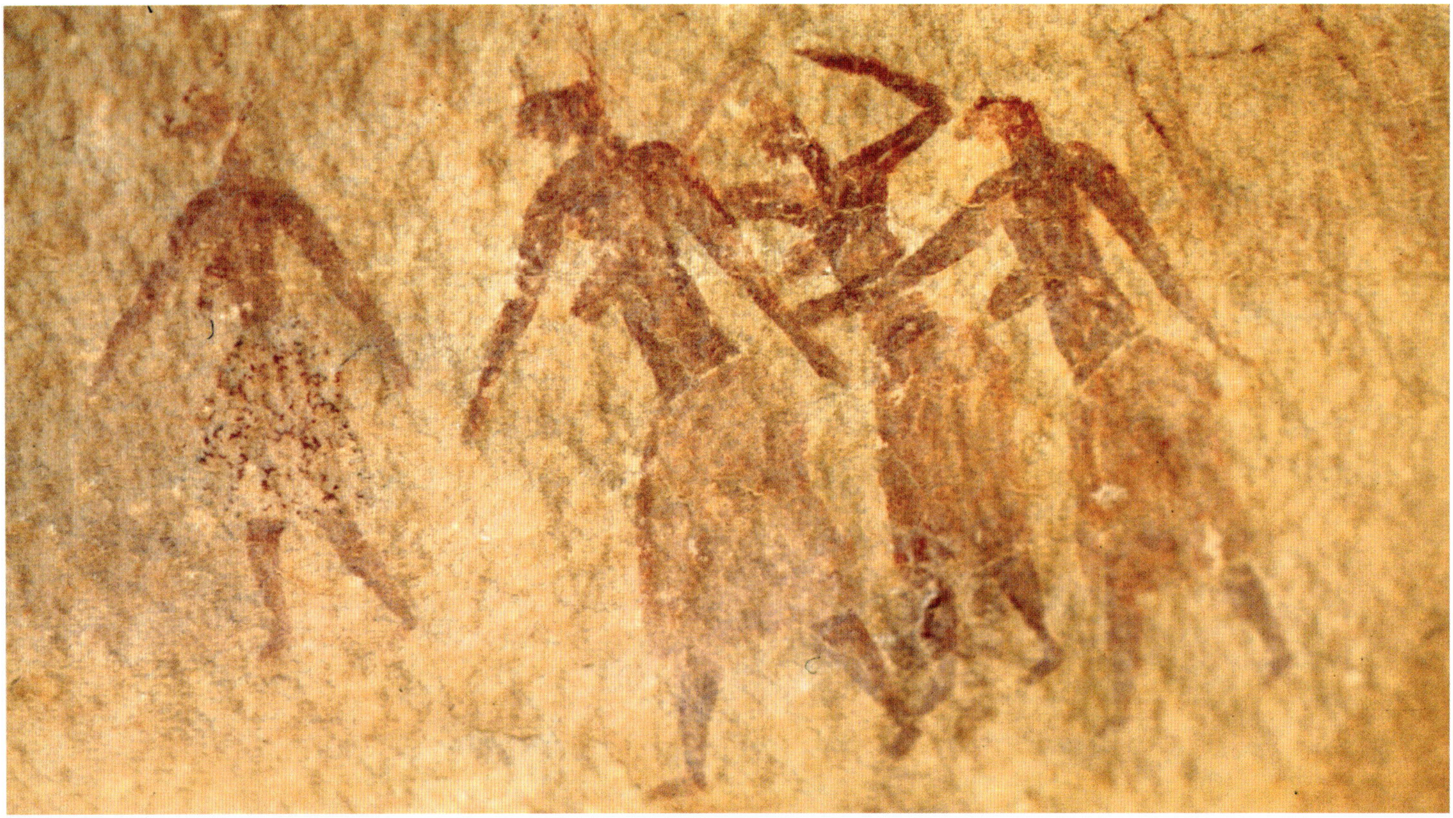

The Genesis of Wall Art: Roman Bathhouses and Train Tagging

Historically, you can make a case that cave paintings are early examples of wall art. There are many surviving examples of Neolithic hunters who told stories on rock overhangs or cave walls, and women feature in the storytelling narrative. At its most basic, wall art is another form of visual communication and storytelling that has evolved with humanity. The aesthetic antecedents of women as public subjects had their origins on the vases of Greece, the carvings on Doric columns, and the interior walls of Roman Italy in decorative frescoes. The Roman art was designed to brighten the interior of dark homes without windows and could be considered the painterly forerunner of feature walls inspired by the Greeks, who painted their heroic stories on vases. These classical representations of women as goddesses and mortals formed the basis of a mythology that to this day informs wall art of women on a much larger scale.

When sexually explicit graffiti was uncovered on brothel and bar walls in Pompeii, it revealed the vox populi heart of graffiti, the hastily scribbled precursor to wall art.[1] The scratches in stone walls boasted of sexual prowess, while just down the street from

Women in Tassili prehistoric cave painting, southeastern Algeria. Photo: Patrick Gruban, licensed through CC BY-SA 2

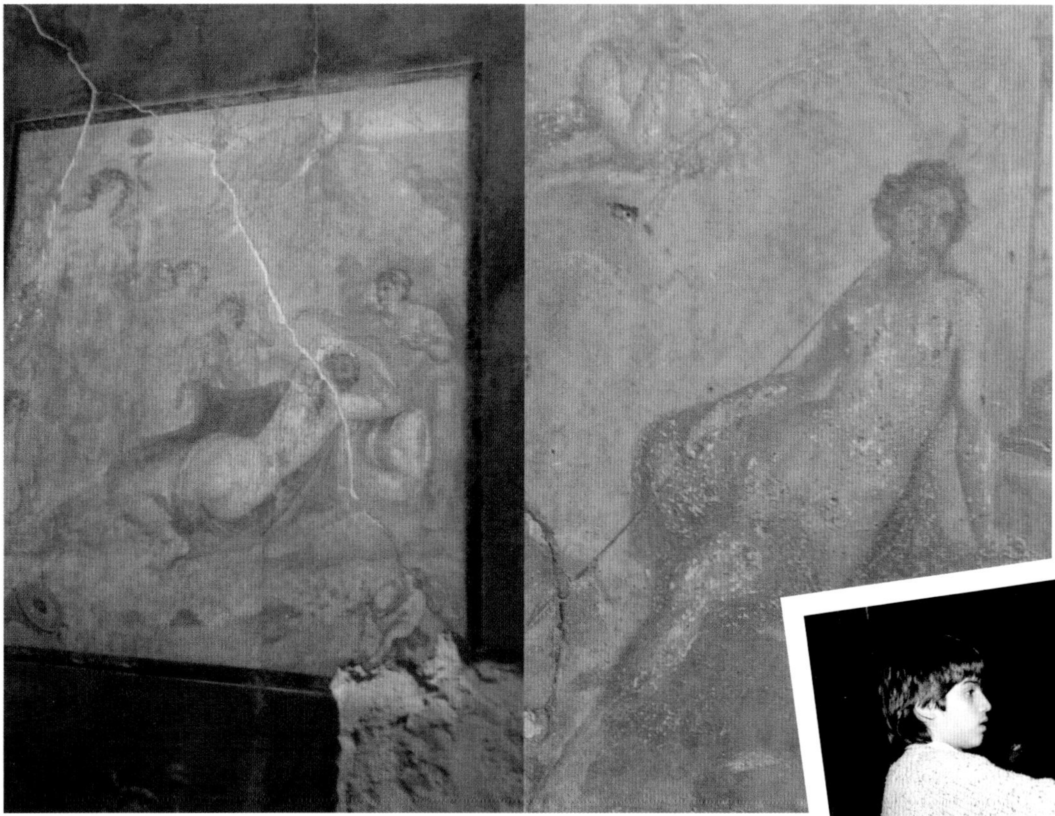

Women on the wall in Pompeii's restored frescoes

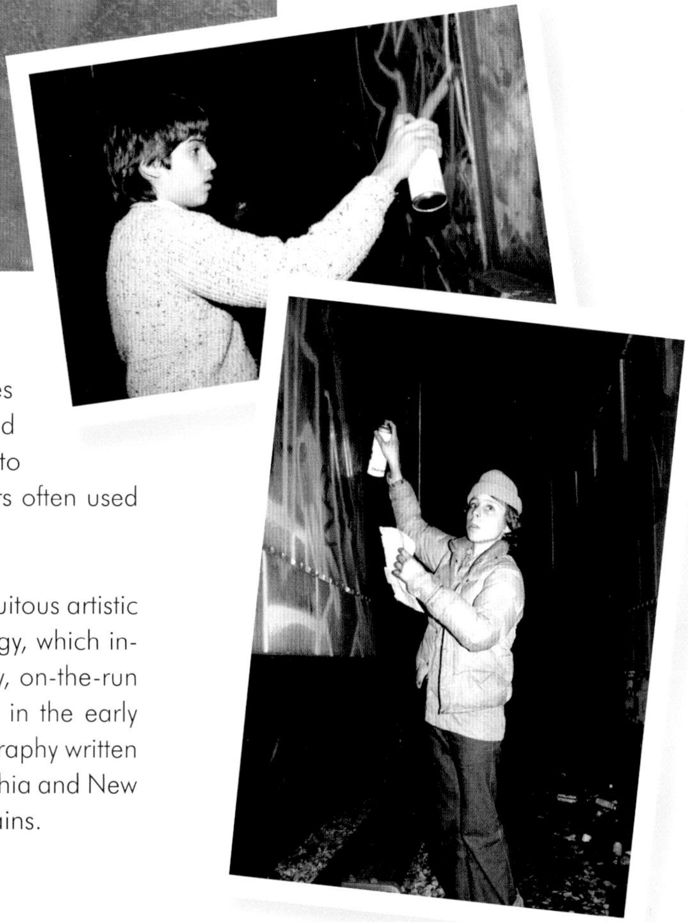

Early New York subway taggers Mare and Min One doing their "spray paint" thing, 1981. Photos: Henry Chalfant

the brothel were more studied forms of wall art. The restored examples of women on the wall in Pompeii are displayed inside the well preserved Roman homes; artists were hired to brighten up the windowless walls to make the living areas more cheery. These ancient interior decorators often used women from Greek and Roman mythology as their subjects.[2]

From the frescoes of Pompeii to urban America has been a long, circuitous artistic journey marked by social upheavals and rapid changes in technology, which included the spray can. The modern era of street art began with hasty, on-the-run tactics of graffitists or "writers," who first gained national attention in the early 1970s. The outlaw history of wall art started with a new form of typography written through the nozzle of spray cans that appeared overnight in Philadelphia and New York along railroad lines and was scrawled on subway tracks and trains.

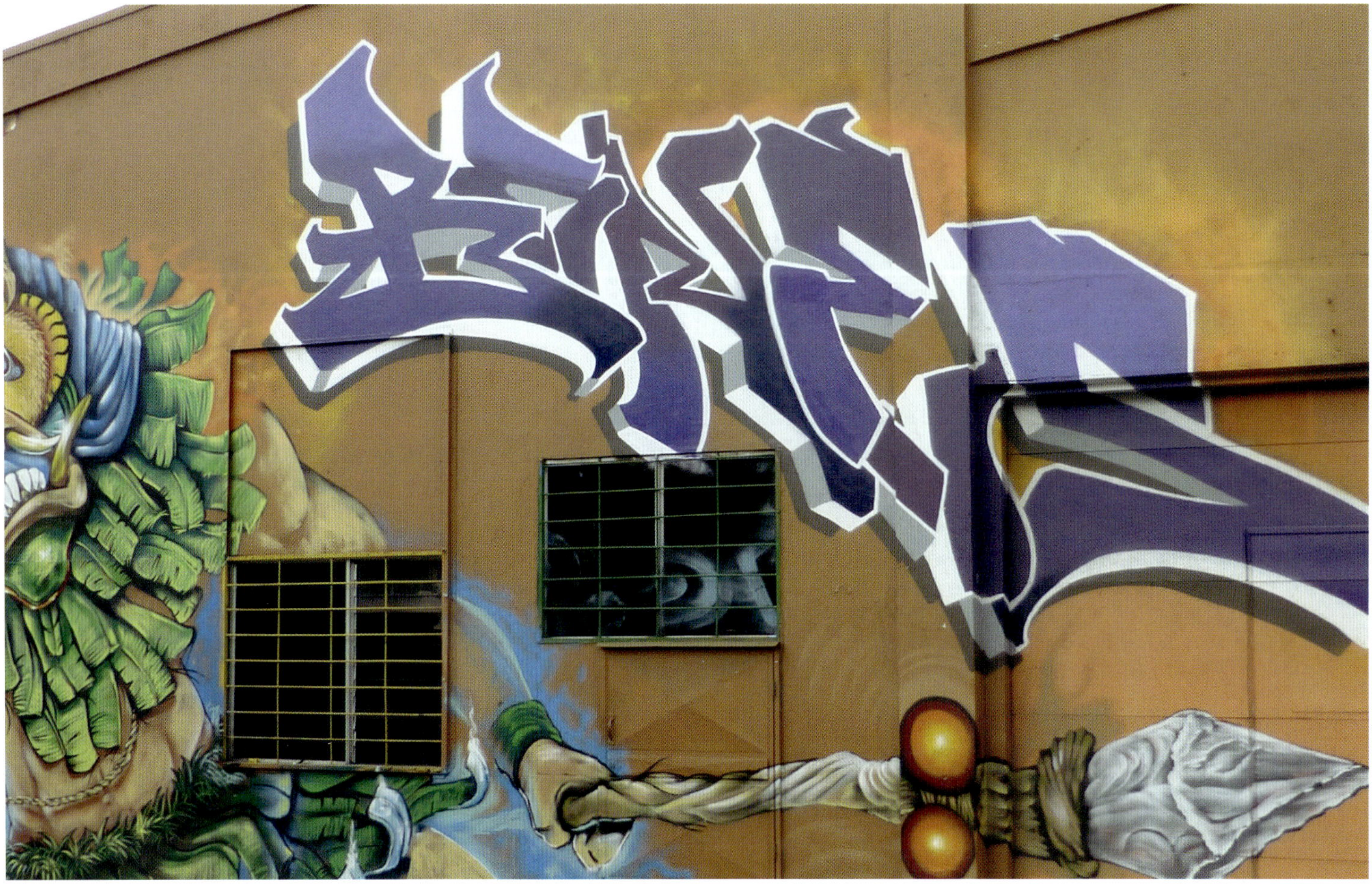

Wall Art's New Language

The subculture of wall art invented its own language to describe the illegal trespasses of hit-and-paint tactics. "Tagging," for example, is a quickly spray painted signature meant to stand out and mark territory. "Bombing" is painting as many surfaces in an area as possible, either with "tags" or "throw-ups," fast drawings or elaborate tags that can be sprayed on in minutes to avoid detection. Tagging and bombing have evolved into "paste-ups," pieces that are created and printed in a studio and literally pasted to a wall surface like posters, often with wheat paste. Stencils, which are a thin piece of metal or plastic with a cutout pattern, are also used in combination with spray paint for a fast wall art job. In contrast, large-scale, elaborate murals are often painstakingly planned and completed over a period of days, not minutes. The wall artists who paint large wall murals are often suspended from baskets at the end of hydraulic cranes with their spray cans; these large-scale works often carry the imprimatur of local governments and businesses, but some are still done illegally on off-limit decayed walls.

Tagging's close cousin is bombing, which has evolved into strange bubble letters, wild colors, and cryptic typographic shapes that are still considered an illegal defacement of public

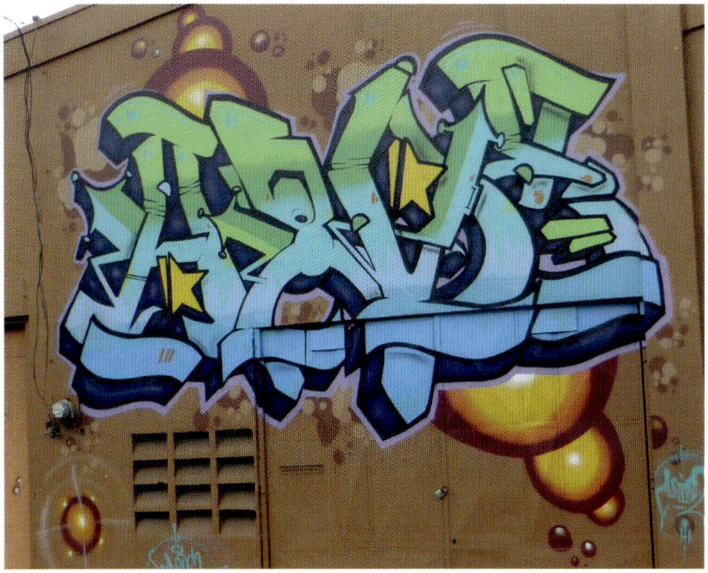

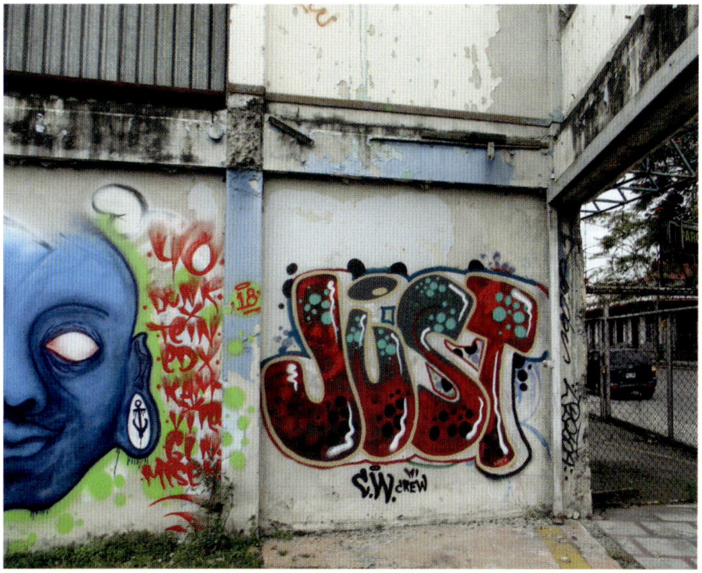

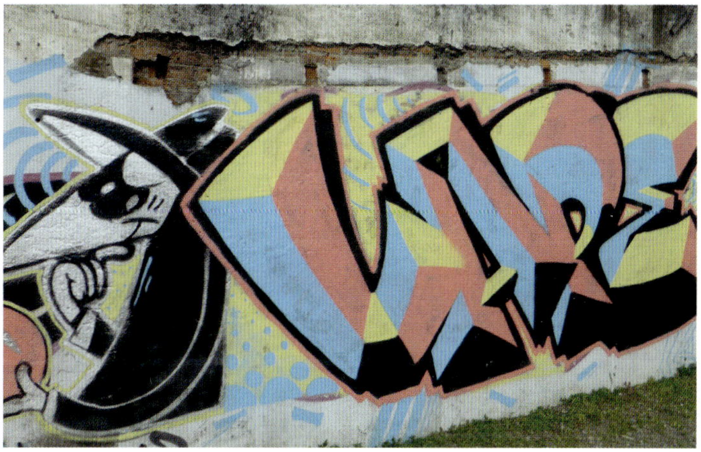

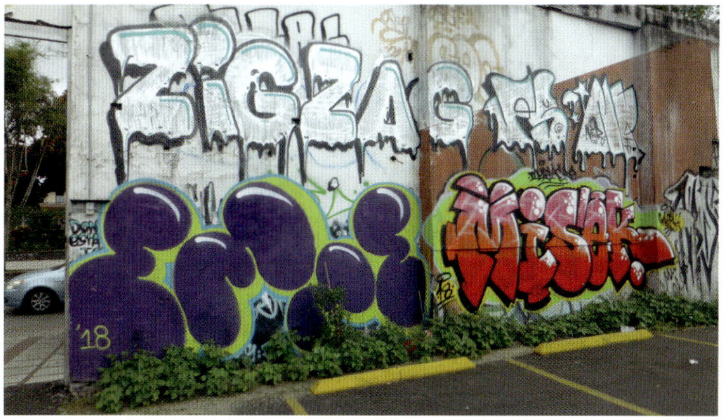

property, an urban eyesore to be whitewashed or scrubbed into oblivion. Chances are you've seen many examples of bombs and tags along highway overpasses or on abandoned buildings and fence lines. The practitioners of tagging and bombing are often involved in spray-and-run trespassing, avoiding police by practicing their marking at night. Sometimes tags are painted in the open—a defiant gesture to the authorities sprayed by gang members who also want to establish their territory. On the streets, tagging and bombing are often practiced with your "crew," the people you hang with in the neighborhood; tagging and bombing, then, are a uniting, social activity usually among young men who want to display their courage and creativity. Bombing examples are from the walls of San José, Costa Rica.

Tagging or bombing are akin to a sport for young graffiti artists, who are declaring their identity by spray painting their mark, often close to where they live. It is a personal signature declaring, "I am here!" Tagging can be crude and aggressive, more of a male marking experience. Murals, by contrast, are often transformative and, by their very nature and their size, give artists more latitude to express and communicate their feelings and viewpoints. The bridge from vandalism to "acceptable" artistic

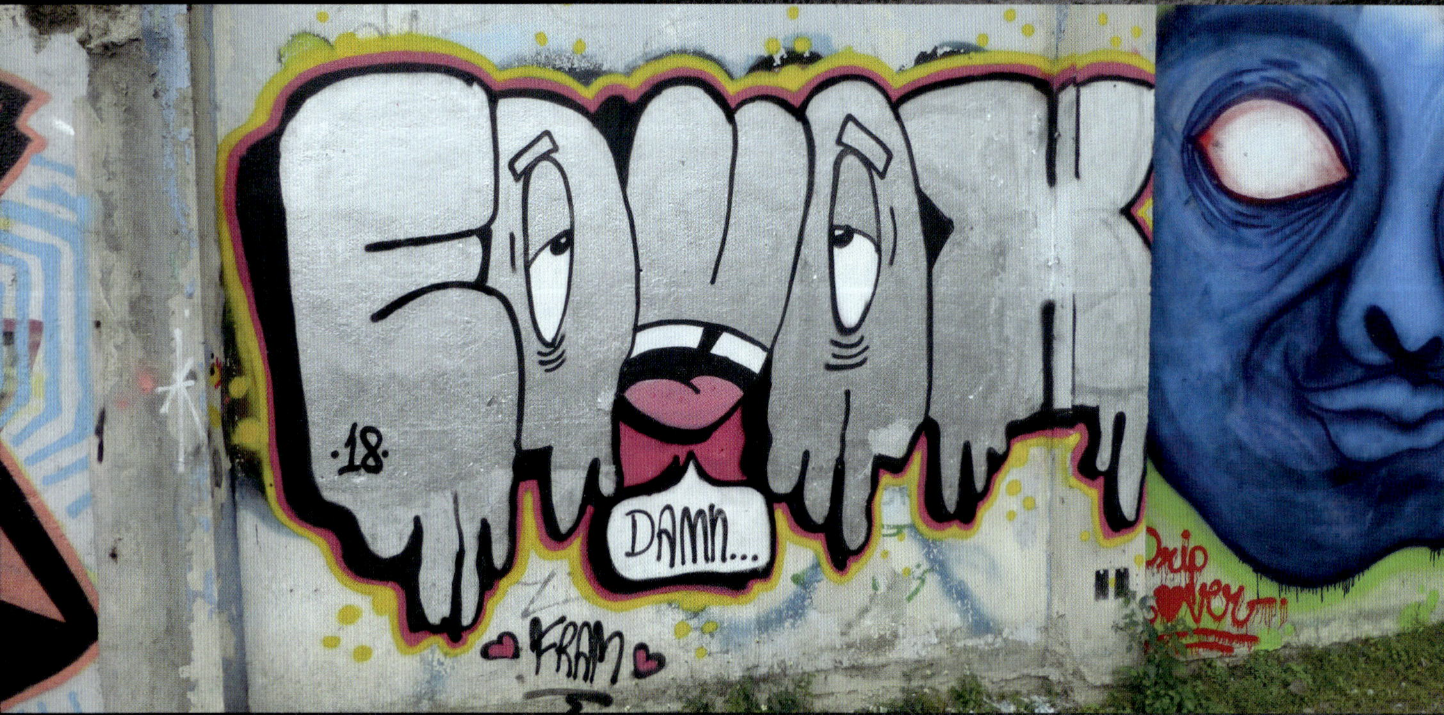
·18·
DAMN...

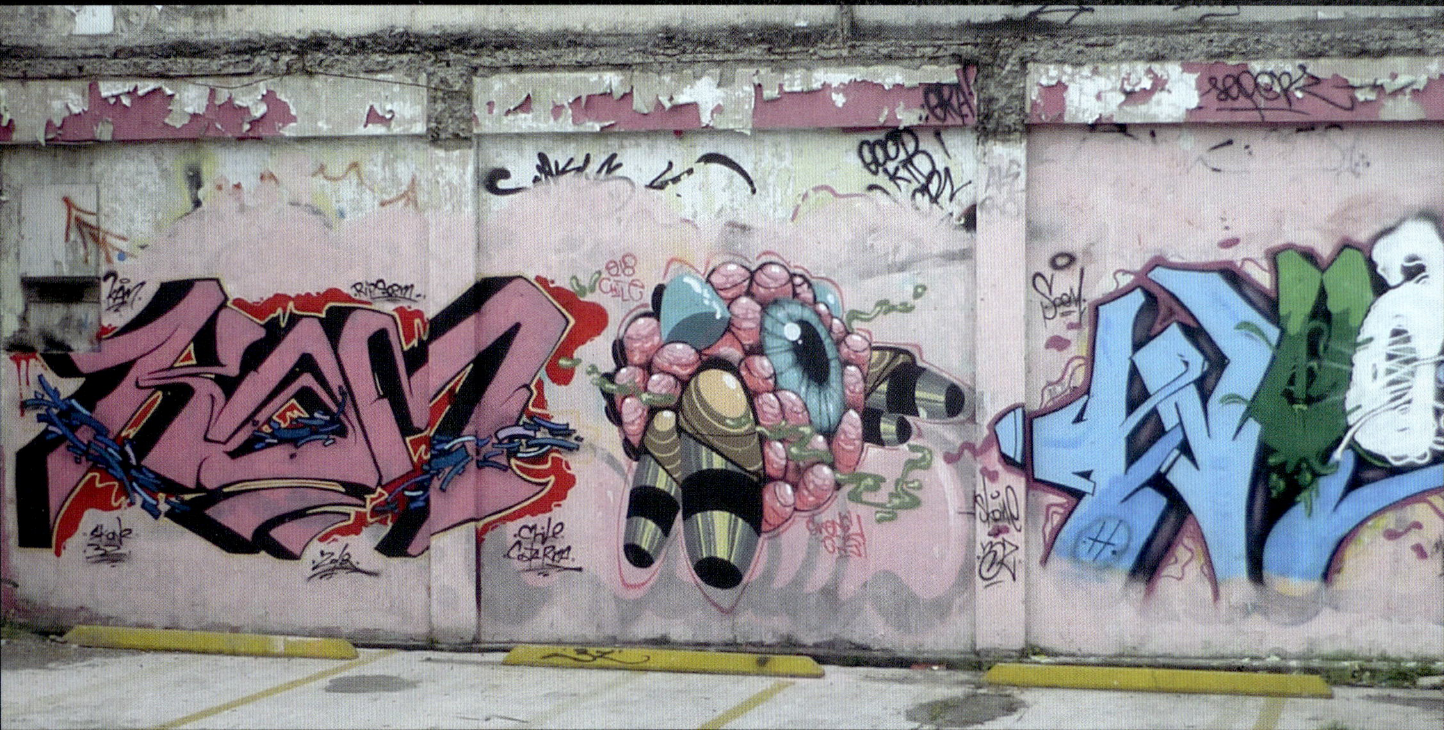

expression in the world of wall art is uneven at best, always swaying in the crosswinds blowing between hip culture and conformity.

Women as Subjects and Artists

Like all art, street art, and the portraits of women as subjects, is as varied as the artists themselves. Whether they are practicing on the wrong side of the tracks in Cape Town, South Africa, struggling to make a living in Costa Rica, or painting in the upscale art district of LA or the back alleys of Paris, the perishable nature of their artwork is what defines the women on the wall. They are not portraits to hang in museums, but they belong to you and me. We are all critics in these outdoor galleries.

This book is a journey of discovery, a visual snapshot that surveys a highly perishable commodity that has the power to transform the everyday into the extraordinary. You will find in this journey the works of known and unknown artists who are compelled to make their voices known. Street art as a democratic process is what you will discover in this book.

This book is by no means a comprehensive visual dictionary of street art of women. In a literal sense, the authors have just scratched the surface. But it is a good starting point to examine the importance of women as subjects and painters in this important and evolving genre of art.

The Women on the Wall Tour

Our guided tour begins in chapter 2 in Los Angeles. LA is often derided as a city without a center, an endless suburb created by visionaries who built an entertainment empire from a dusty pueblo of dirt streets watered by man-made rivers. This land of make-believe conceals a stark reality behind the two-dimensional edifices of Hollywood's tilt-up movie sets and its pop culture. We take a walking tour of the LA Arts District, where well known international wall artists present large-scale works of women. We also speak to a well known artist-activist, Dr. Judy Baca, who grew up in one of the roughest neighborhoods in LA and helped create a public institution in a former jailhouse in Venice Beach, the Social and Public Art Resource Center (SPARC). Her mural *The Great Wall of Los Angeles* is now a national landmark and speaks to the power of wall art to liberate the imagination of kids who grew up in a milieu of violence and gang warfare. One of Baca's protégées is Erin Yoshi, whose street murals celebrate older women and the natural world. Yoshi's wall art wake-up call came in Colombia, where she painted a politically dangerous mural outside a university. You will also meet Colette Miller, whose view of wall art finds expression in "interactive" angel wings meant to unify a vision of our common humanity.

Berlin's Uncle Sam signing you up for street art in this stencil based on the World War I and II recruiting poster in the US

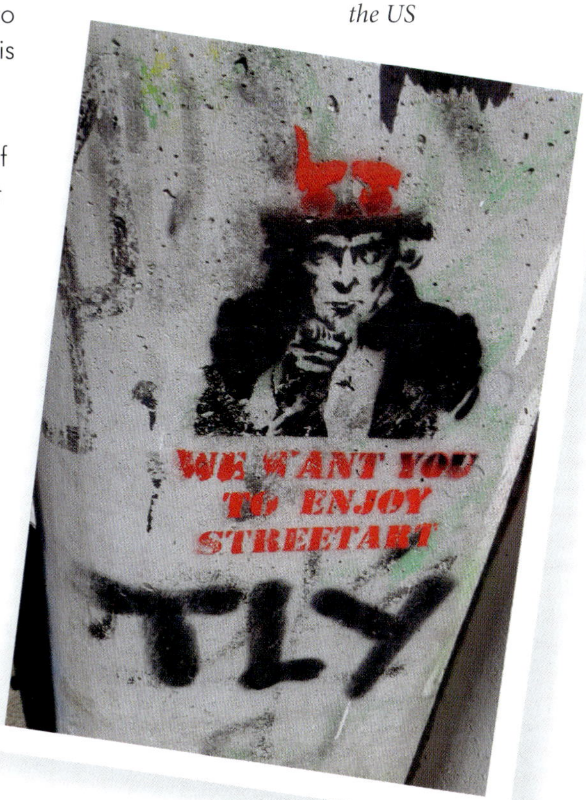

In chapter 3, we travel to Mexico City to pay homage to arguably the most famous muralists in the world—Diego Rivera, David Alfaro Siqueiros, and José Clemente Orozco—whose views of women are more allegorical and symbolic than portraits of feminist empowerment. In the World Heritage city of Oaxaca, we sample the walls of artist collectives who present a unified vision of street art as protest and social activism. Nearby, the market town of Tlacolula reveals remarkable examples of women on the wall that are also the work of wall artist collectives, one of which has strong ties to LA. All of their subjects are women, whose faces often manifest the history of the region. We also take a tour of wall art that is part of an ocean awareness campaign in the cruise ship destination of Cozumel. And we touch on the connection between Mexico's iconic Day of the Dead imagery and its expressions of women on the walls.

In chapter 4, we continue our journey south to a young country that venerates its natural heritage: Costa Rica. This land of volcanoes, rainforests, and a large expat community is home to a vibrant street art scene where women are featured. We speak with a documentary filmmaker, Federico Peixoto, who reflects the melting pot of Costa Rica's citizens. Peixoto is a DJ and documentary filmmaker whose film *Tlacuilos* follows the development and work of graffiti artists in Central America; the film debuted at the Bronx World Film festival in 2018 and was a Golden Award winner at the Asia Pacific International Filmmaker Festival in 2019. We also meet two young wall artists, "JUST" and "PUCHO," whose depictions of women reflect a veneration of their beauty and homage to the magic side of women whose spirits are rooted in myth and nature.

Chapter 5 finds our "walking" tour winding through the streets of Valparaíso, Chile, where the wall art of women becomes part of the colorful city's geographic proximity to the rocky and boiling waters of the Pacific. This historic port city was home to one of the world's greatest contemporary poets, Pablo Neruda, whose words intertwine with the city's sensual, artistic reputation. In Peru, the authors take you to a mecca for surfing, Huanchaco, a dusty town near ancient Incan ruins of Chan Chan that hosts an unusually active street art scene with surprising surreal references alongside the reed fishing craft that have been surfing waves for millennia.

In chapter 6, we cross the Atlantic to Europe, where our tour skips the world famous museums of European capitals; instead we wind through the galleries of street art in Paris, Berlin, and Palermo, where an observer can appreciate the wildly different depictions of women from some of the best and least known street artists in the world. We also speak to internationally acclaimed street artist Vhils, whose technique has more in common with a sculptor than a wall artist. Vhils (real name, Alexandre Farto) cultivates a humanist view of his subjects that is expressed by removing bricks on walls and revealing expressive faces hidden underneath.

In chapter 7, we hear from a self-taught and successful woman muralist who developed her craft in the violent neighborhoods of Cape Town, South Africa. Faith47/ Faith XLVII's wall art is an often subtle meditation on the strengths and vulnerabilities of her women subjects. Her art is an antidote to the violence that plagues her homeland. We also consider the idea of whether or not wall art of women is outgrowing its "street cred" by becoming a vehicle for merchandising and making money. Many street artists have become more entrepreneurial and are using skills they developed in the commercial art world. So it is no surprise that their street murals may have more to do with marketing and promotion than rebellion.

So, let's take the advice of Uncle Sam exhorting you to enter the wonderful world of women on the wall: "We want you to enjoy street art."

2

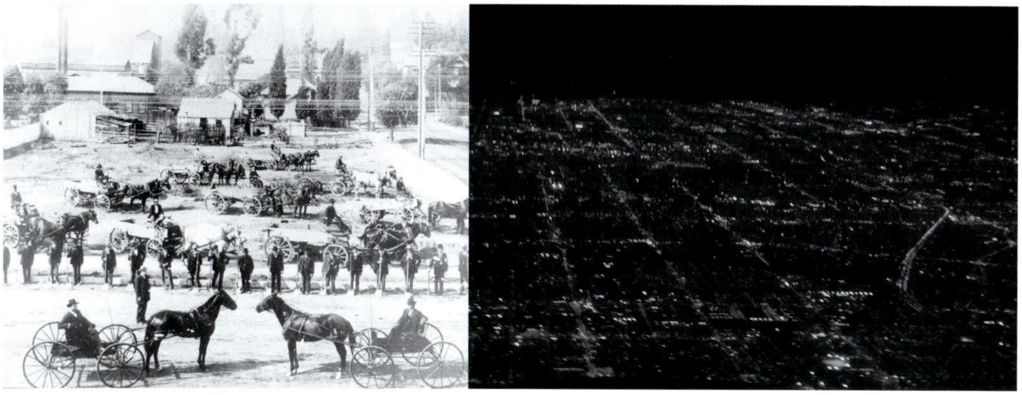

Los Angeles, early 1900s (left) (exbt-LAS-61), by Fæunder CC BY 2.0. Publisher (of the digital version): University of Southern California Libraries. Landing at LAX at night, 2018.

LOS ANGELES AND CELEBRITY POWER

The Real Deal in a Land of Make-Believe

LA is less of a well-defined city and more of an idea built on the dreams of migrants that stretches for miles in an artificial landscape.

The reality of Los Angeles really hits you at night when you are flying over the city and looking out of the airplane window. Stretching before you is an endless carpet of lights, a constellation of crisscrossing six-lane roads and eight-lane freeways dividing up the landscape into two-dimensional grids on what could be a computer chip streaming endless permutations.

This otherworldly landscape of freeways, shopping malls, and giant roads that stretch from downtown to the beach is home to ten million people who spill into the valleys beyond the city center. LA's suburbs are built on shaky ground prone to earthquakes; its satellite cities are often ravaged by fast-moving bushfires fanned by the ferociously hot Santa Ana desert winds sweeping flames over its hills; following the fires, the torrential winter rains often trigger mudslides. As nature dictates, nothing is permanent in LA other than its impermanence, the perfect ingredients for concocting wall art on flat surfaces.

At its decentralized heart, Los Angeles, and the greater Southland, is a series of interconnected cultures divided and tied together by a vast network of concrete ribbons and roads marking off suburban territories based on class and ethnic divisions: Hollywood's elite-by-the-beach and in the hills; Latinos in East LA;

African Americans in Watts and Pacoima. The Asia-Pacific cultures are also well represented; Japanese, Koreans, Vietnamese, Chinese, and Pacific Islanders all call the greater LA area their home and represent its migrant heritage. LA is less a city than a stitched together polyglot, polycultural world—a sprawling, untidy place that is difficult to characterize because it is constantly re-inventing ethnic and class boundaries. This shape-shifting quality is what makes LA what it is: a man-made desert oasis at the edge of the Pacific, reflecting the multicultural and linguistic tumult of today's modern America with roots dug deeply in the Spanish past. There are historical reasons why most of the highway signs in California are written in Spanish.

A Brief History of LA: From Missions to Mavericks

Before the Spanish colonial period, about a third of all Native Americans in the US lived in the greater California region, divided among an estimated 500 tribes covering a territory that overlapped parts of Arizona and Mexico's Baja Peninsula.[1] For roughly 19,000 years, these Indigenous Californians enjoyed the abundance of the land and friendly climate until the Spanish came in 1796 and built their adobe missions from San Diego to San Francisco and began to convert the state's first peoples to Catholicism.[2]

Mexico's considerable influence in California history and culture began in 1821, when it took over California after winning its independence from Spain. The missions were closed down and California was left to a few thousand people, some military outposts, and what was left of the Indigenous tribes. But the Pax Mexicana didn't last long. Mexico and the US went to war in 1846, resulting in the defeat of Mexico. The Treaty of Guadalupe Hidalgo, which ended the Mexican-American War in 1848, granted the US more than 500,000 square miles, which included the territories of California, Arizona, Texas, New Mexico, Utah, and Wyoming.[3] Gold rush fever soon swept the state in the late 1840s, resulting in the decimation of California's Indigenous peoples through disease and violence and made San Francisco merchants rich by supplying the miners with tools, food, and clothes. Gold fever may have bypassed LA by an accident of geography and geological forces, but the small "pueblo de Los Angeles" would soon get its day in the spotlight.

Difficult though it may be to imagine, central LA during this period was a small town with horse-drawn carriages; the population was dependent on water drawn from the Los Angeles River, which was dry for much of the year. The LA most people know as the mega-city today began as a dusty pueblo of 5,000 in 1870 and grew quickly as gold miners from Mexico heading north made Los Angeles their home. The California dream was irrigated when water was pumped over the Tehachapi Mountains from the Sacramento River delta in the massive California Aqueduct system of channels and tunnels.

With the water and rail lines came the East Coasters living in the ghettos of big cities such as New York, who were enticed to move to California by real estate agents promising a life among the orange groves fringed by snow-capped mountains; the truth about Southern California is you *can* ski in the morning and surf in the afternoon. The Dust Bowl and Depression in the 1930s brought thousands of midwestern farmers to California's central valley to start over in the Golden State. The movie studios weren't far behind. Land was cheap, and you could realize your back-lot dreams in LA and start movie studios from scratch. Mickey Mouse found a home nearby; Disneyland was built near pepper fields in Orange County, just south of LA, which soon turned into housing tracts as far as the eye can see, dominated by giant shopping malls and tilt-up business parks. Southern California soon became a land of big dreams interlaced by freeways. Its beachside communities built the piers that jut into the Pacific, and became emblematic of the surf way of life and casting out fishing lines and waiting for a bite from lawn chairs.

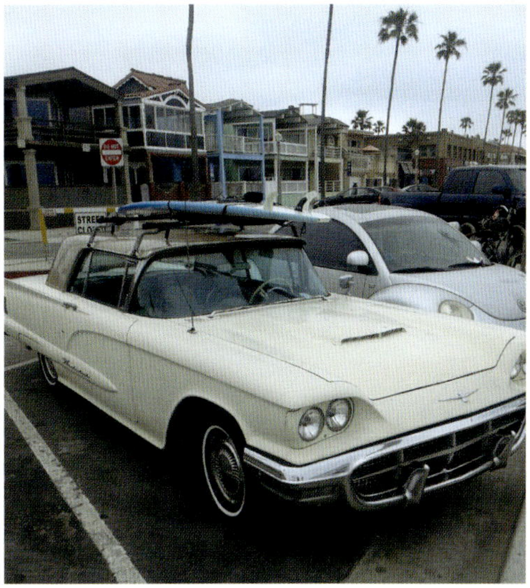
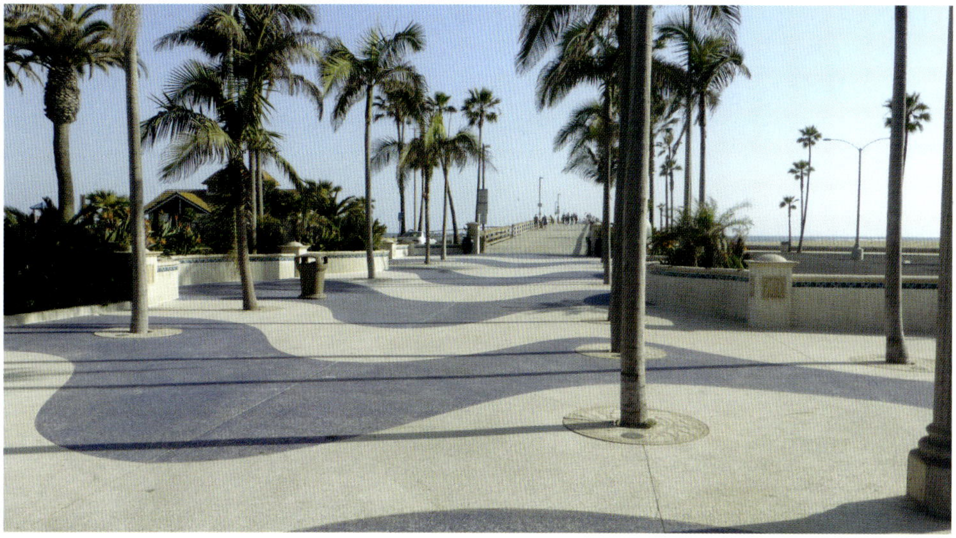
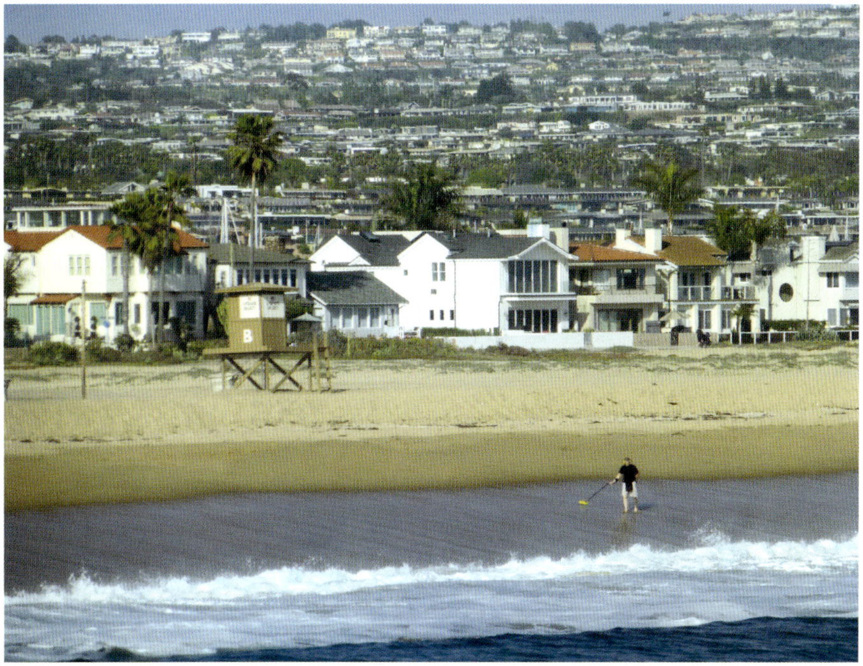
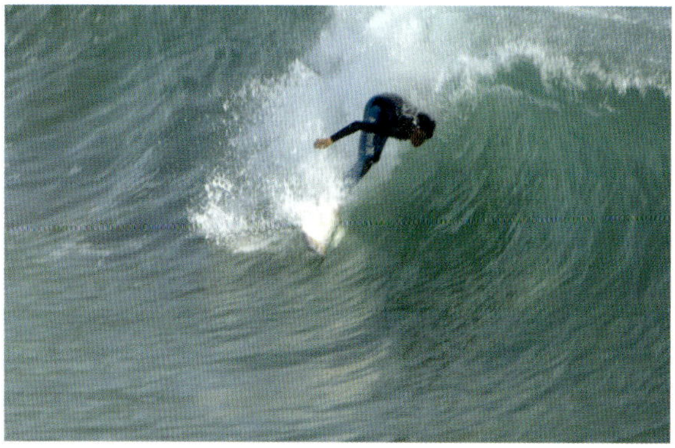
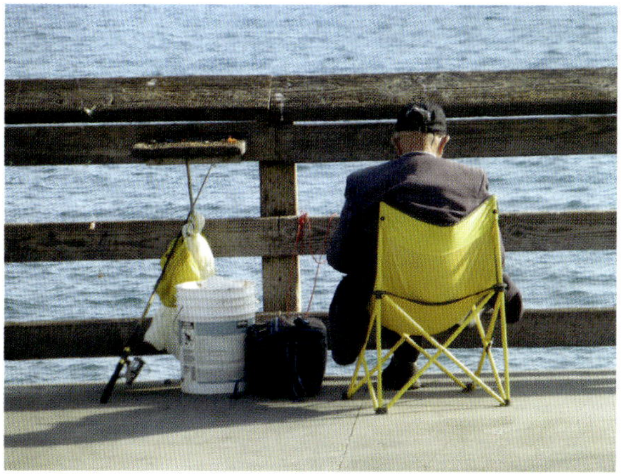

Life by the Pacific in Newport Beach. Surfers and fishermen at the Balboa pier enjoy the Southern California sun.

The City of Angels became an inspiration for writers and artists who found in its endless suburbs by the beach a wellspring of ideas based on what is essentially a desert mirage watered by the California Aqueduct and Colorado River. This shimmering heatstroke of a city—which revolves around a mythic fantasy of the perfect climate and endless opportunity—is also gritty and real, which makes it an ideal subject for the many writers, painters, musicians, and poets who have lived on the city's palm-lined streets and explored the world behind its glittery facade. Even a partial list of LA's artistic luminaries is impressive: David Hockney, Nathaniel West, Joan Didion, Raymond Chandler, the Doors, and the poet Charles Bukowski, all working on the fringes of the great movie industry empire. But there is a dark reality lurking behind the stage props that is often expressed in street art that crosses racial, economic, and cultural barriers.

LA is home to gangland tagging in its ghettos, grand statements and portraits on display near downtown, and hastily painted works along the boardwalk of Venice Beach. Street artists from around the world who work in LA often make visually bold statements, perhaps taking a cue from Hollywood's artifice of back lots that re-created Egypt, the Wild West, and New York's tenements. LA's wall artists seem to live by this credo: If you can imagine it, you can create it. Like Hollywood's make-believe movie sets, LA is an artistic blank wall on which street artists can project their visions of women, which are expressions as diverse as the city's neighborhoods. A good example of that diversity is concentrated in the LA Arts District, a warren of old brick buildings and warehouses with loading docks near downtown, where street art of women has gone mainstream. You will see examples of artists who have wildly different ideas and styles of representing women in the Arts District.

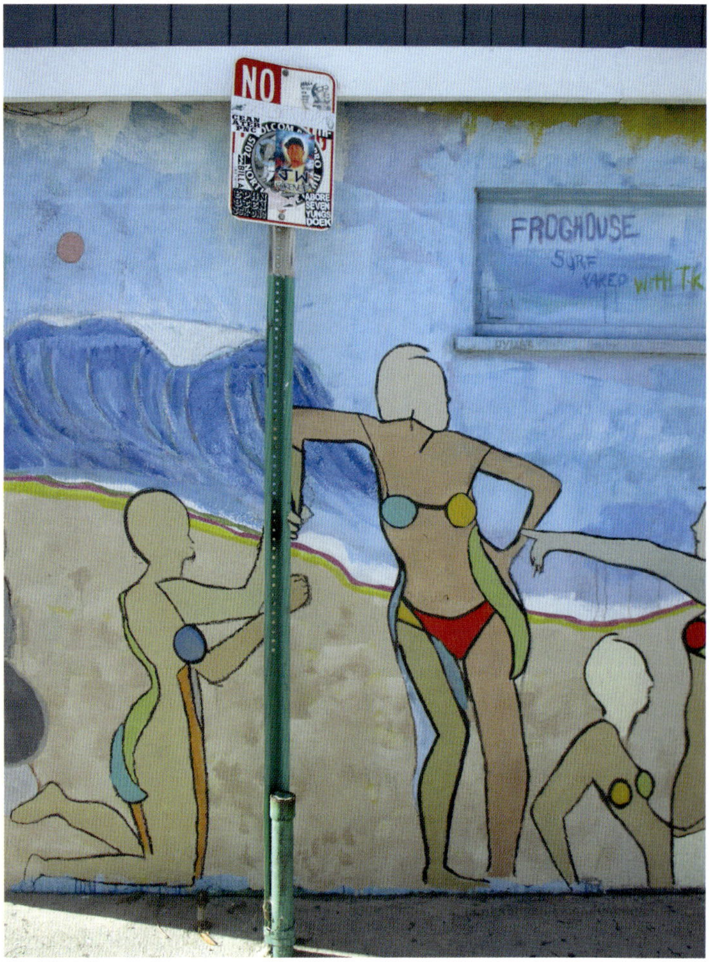

Women on the walls are everywhere in the LA basin, such as in these highly stylized examples from Newport Beach, an affluent beachside community south of downtown LA in Orange County. Portrait of the purple-tinted woman by James Haunt.

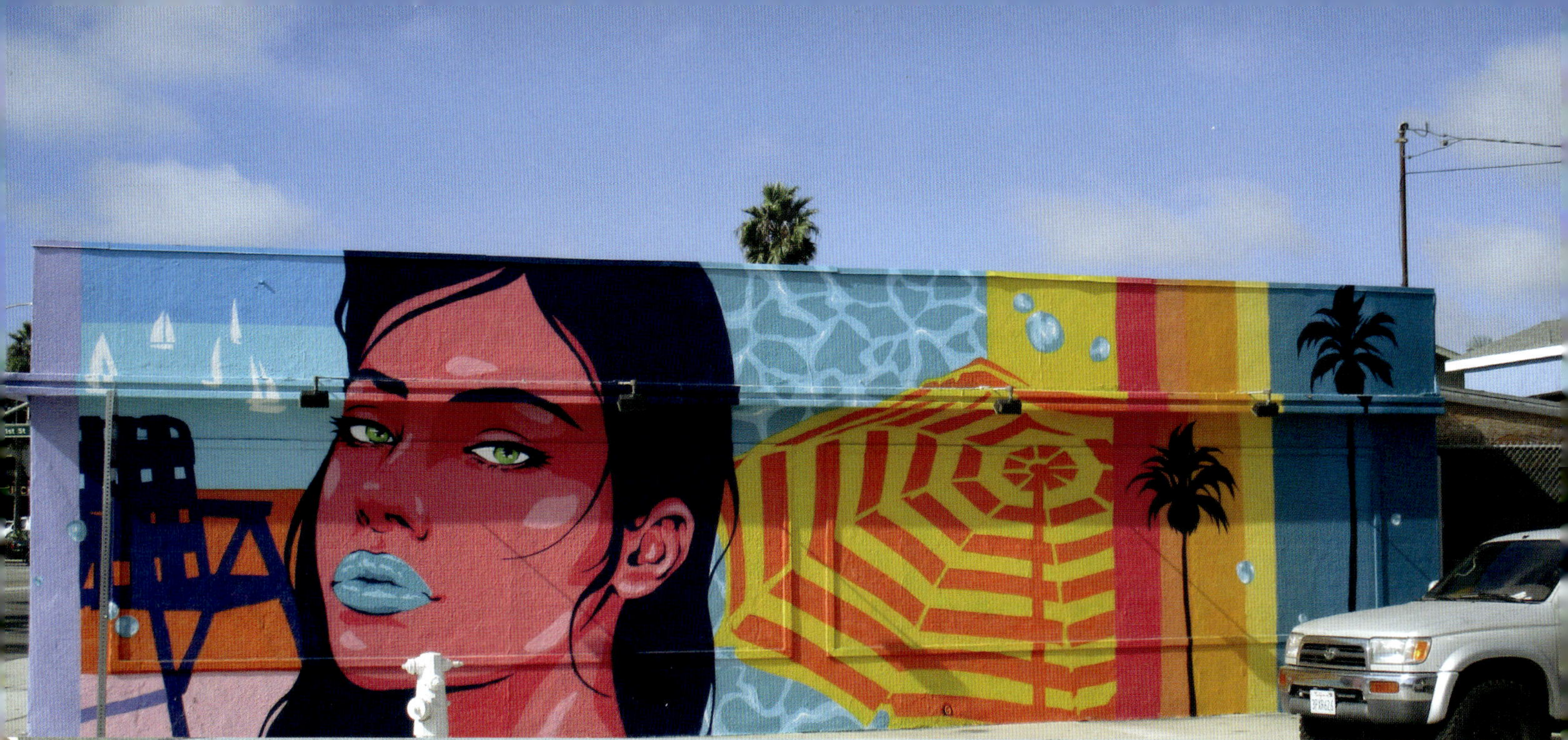

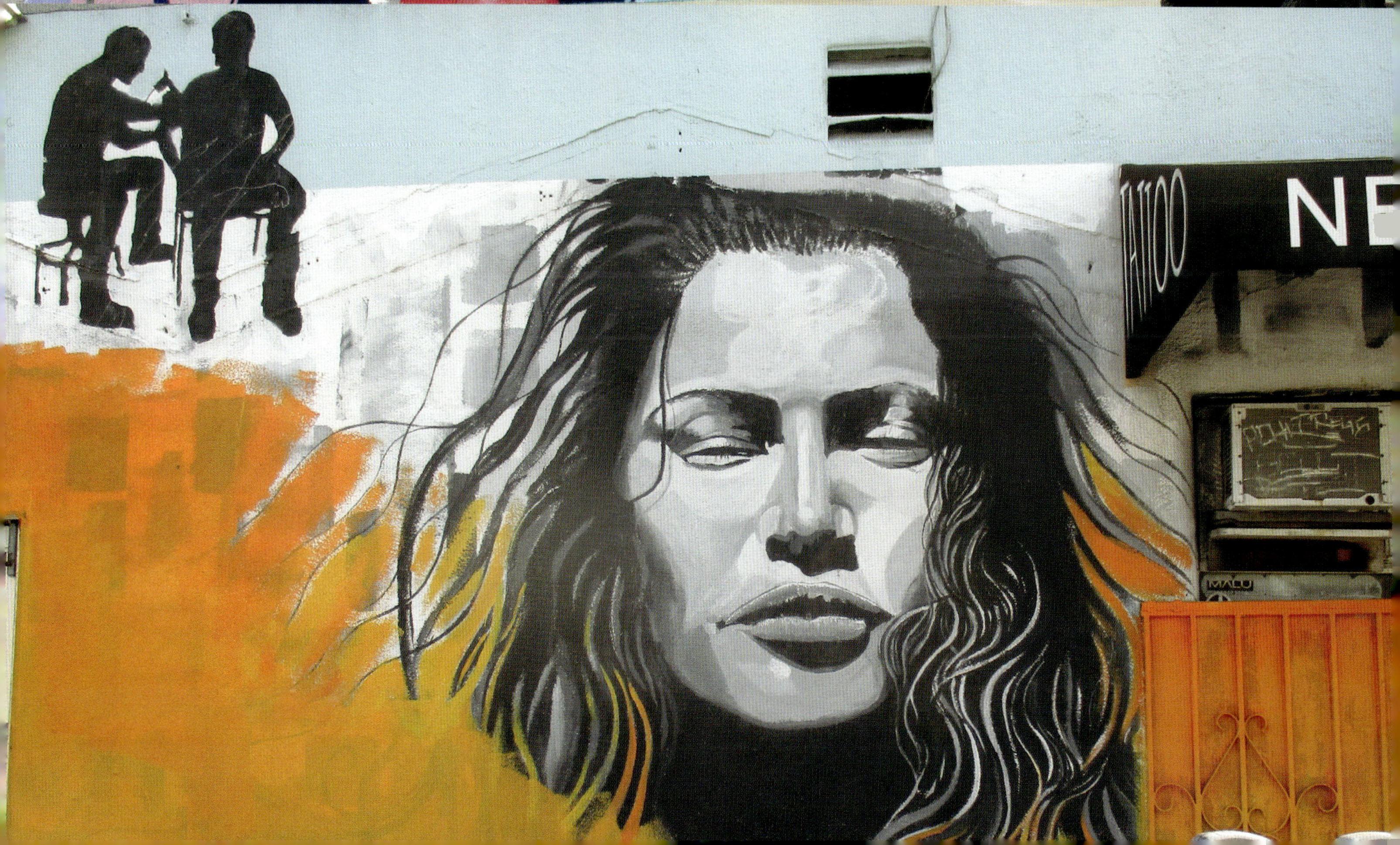
TATTOO
NE

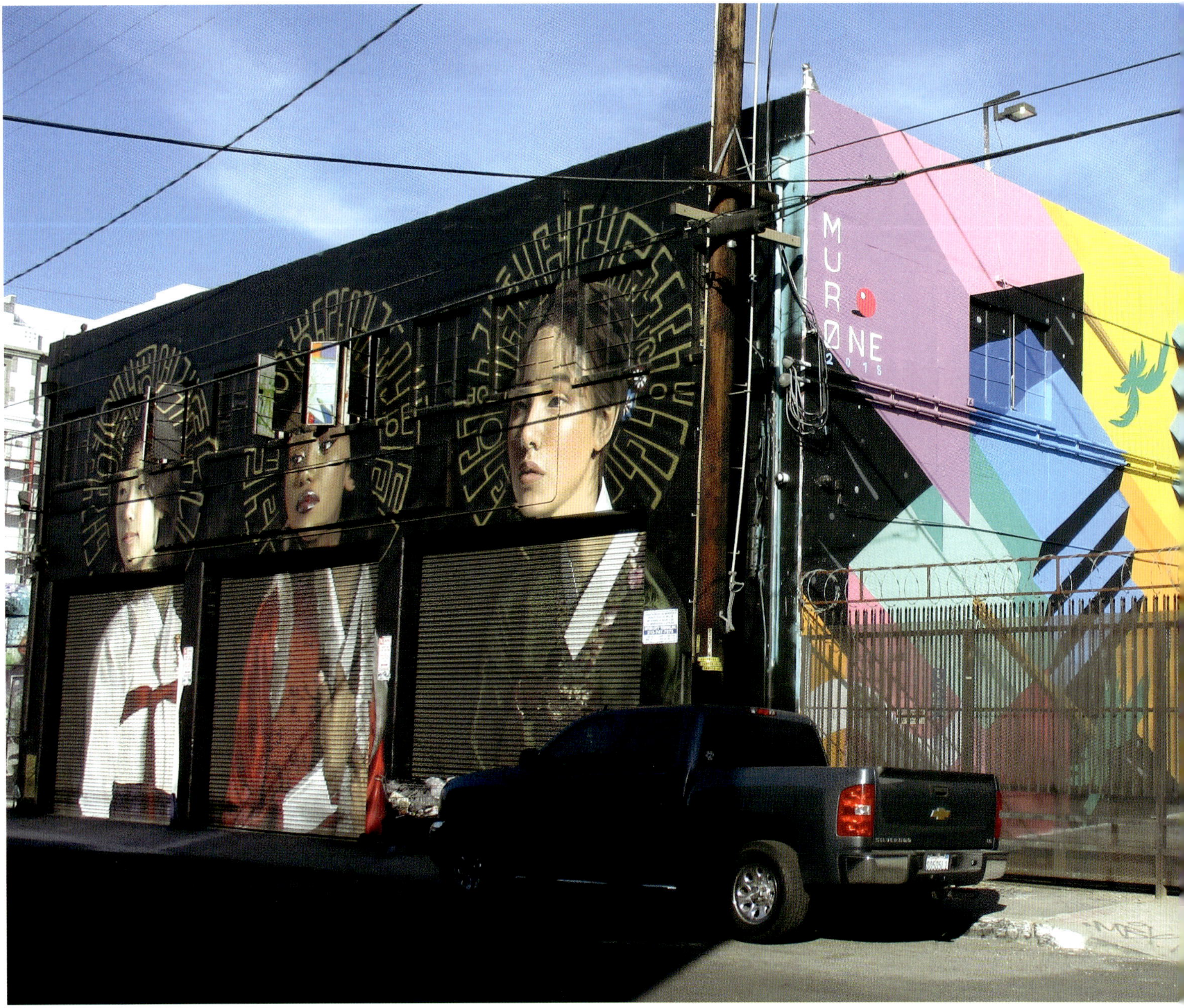

The LA Arts District features large-scale murals that wrap around the sides of buildings.

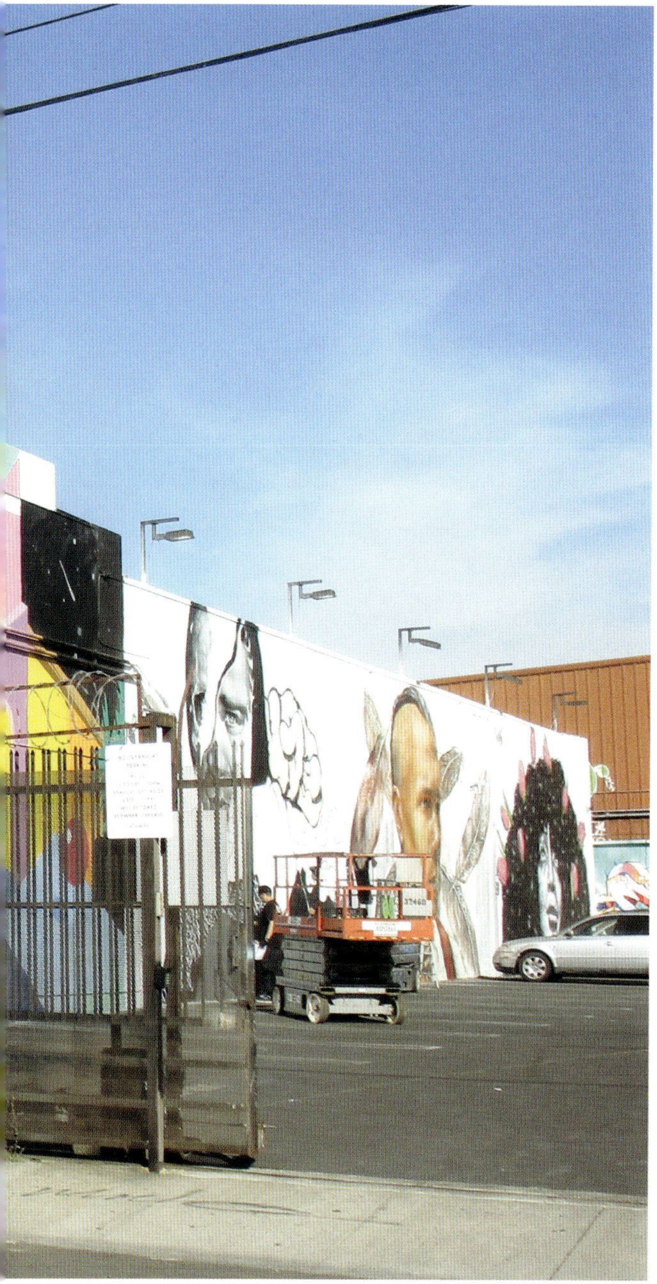

Not far from the impressive Arts District murals, there are other wall artists who take a more politically activist stance in their interpretation of women. The first is Dr. Judy Baca, whose *Great Wall of Los Angeles* portrays the history of California through the champions of social justice and equality. The Wall unspools a half mile down a concrete drainage ditch like a roll from a documentary film—each mural panel or frame depicting important moments in the state's political history by honoring in wall art the women and men who took a stand against racial and economic injustice. *The Great Wall* is now on the National Register of Historic Places and is as much a landmark of Los Angeles as the Hollywood sign, albeit a bit more hidden. *The Great Wall* launched Dr. Baca's career as a sought-after academic and mentor who embodies a new vision of the historical role of women in the founding of California.

Dr. Baca mentored Erin Yoshi, our next artistic exemplar, who draws on inspiration from older women, preserving the natural world, and whose past work encompassed politically dangerous wall art in Colombia. Yoshi grew up in East LA, a notorious Mexican gang neighborhood, where her parents encouraged her to paint.

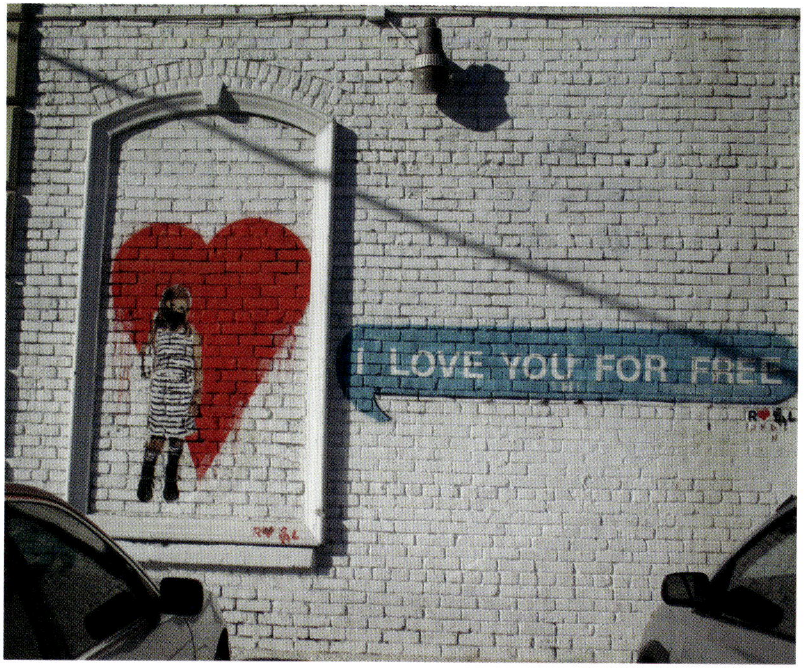

Royal painted the girl with the heart as a love letter to the Arts District and its visitors.

While Dr. Judy Baca and Erin Yoshi focus on a new way to portray women subjects, Colette Miller paints pictures of large angel wings on walls not far from where Yoshi grew up. Miller's Global Angel Wings project has gained her international recognition; her latest work involved painting her "interactive" wings in Dubai's landmark skyscraper, the Burj Kahlifa.

LA's wall artists interviewed in this chapter embody the creative drive to reflect the world around them with their unique visions of women. Before we hear from the artists, we're going to put on our walking shoes and take a tour of the LA Arts District, where women on the wall are on full display in the works of well known street artists.

LA Arts District

Street artists can paint legally here, without the spray-and-run tactics of the street outlaws who climb chain-link fences and paint in the shadows under freeway overpasses. The LA Arts District really came into its own with the city's Artist in Residence Ordinance in the 1980s, which legitimized the work/living space in this commercially zoned district.[4] The District, which you can walk to from downtown LA, is now home to large-scale works by internationally known artists who display their talents to curious tourists.

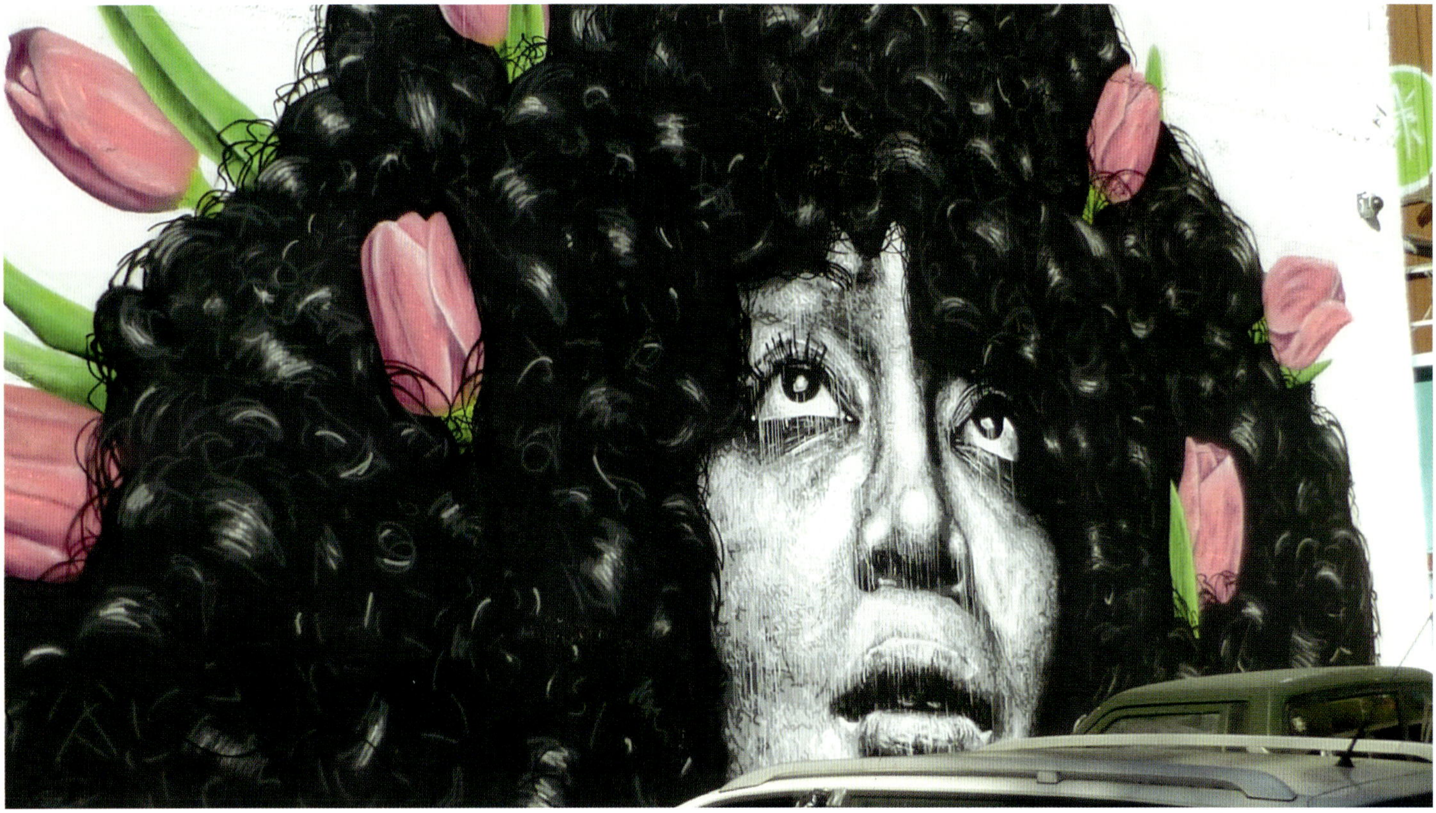

Artists from around the world display their ideas of women on the walls in the LA Arts District.

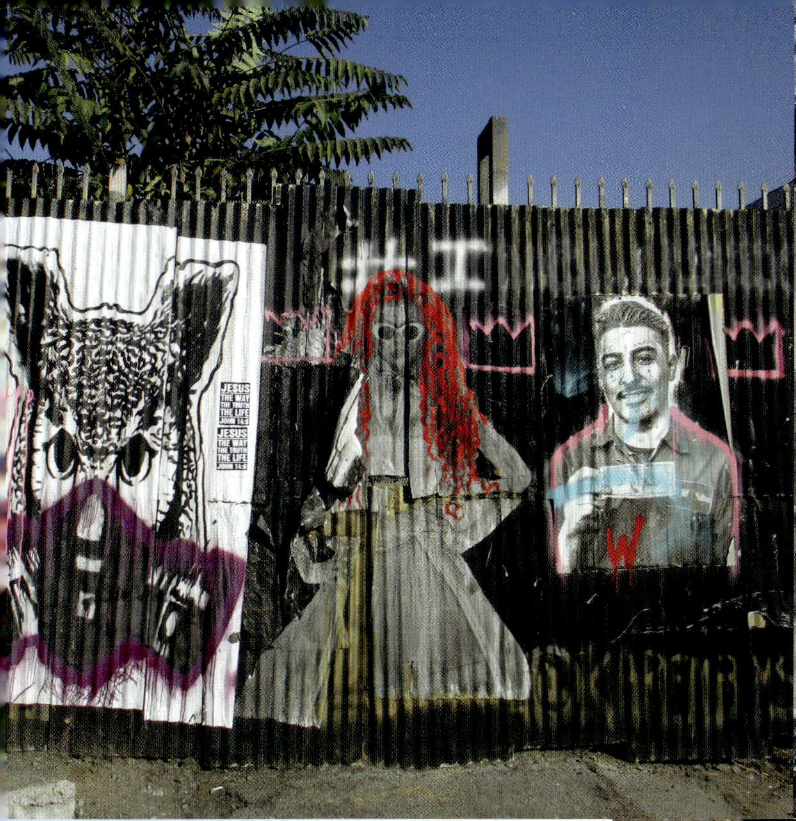

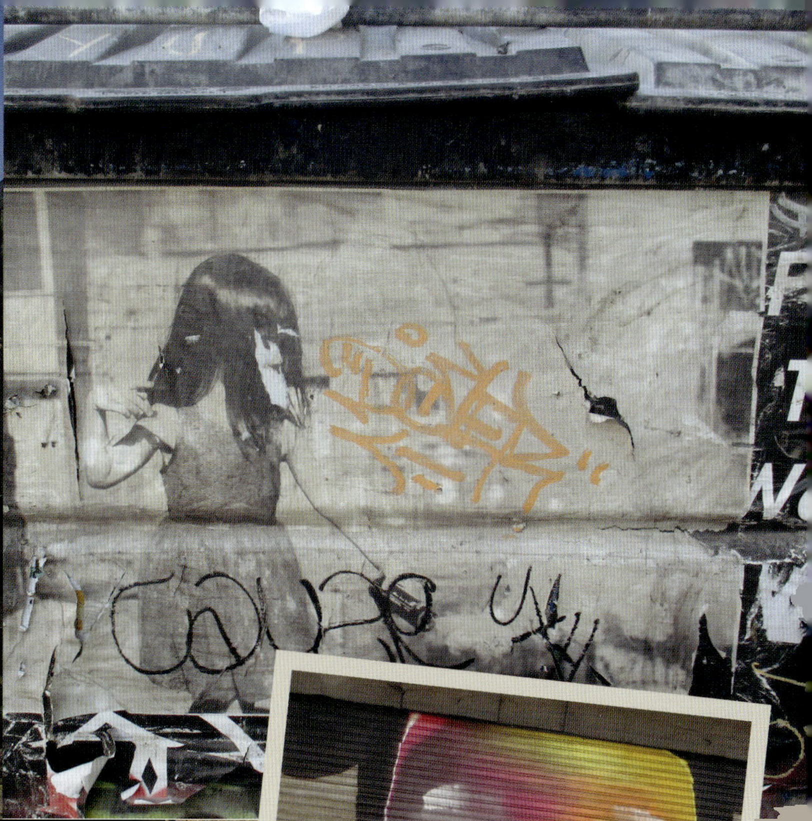

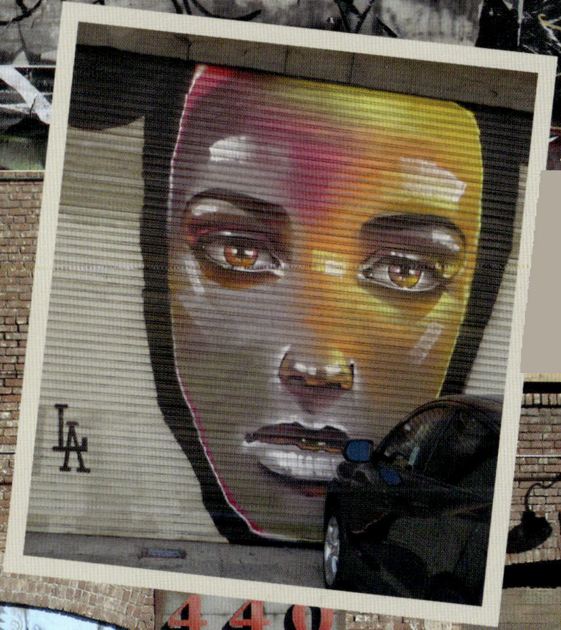
LA

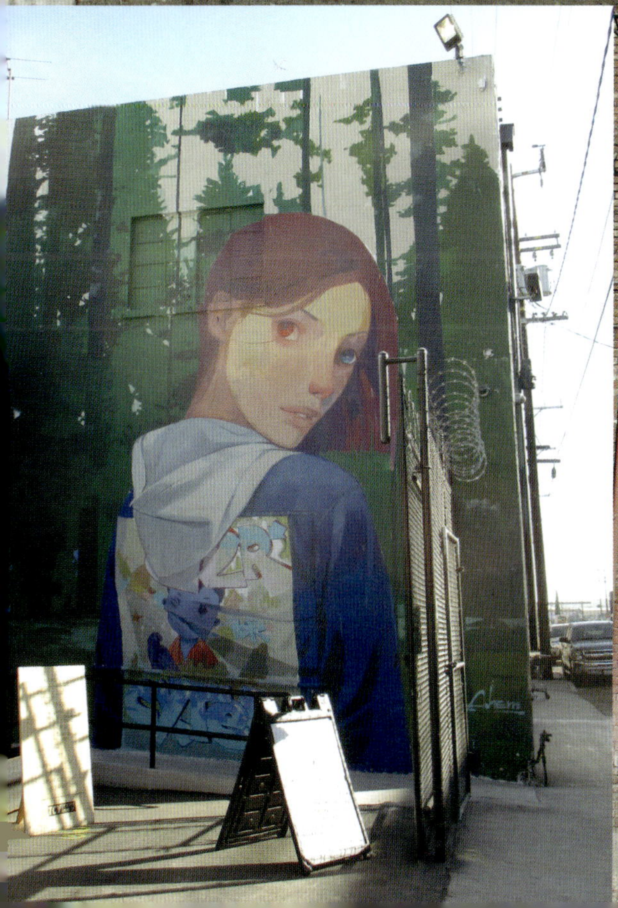

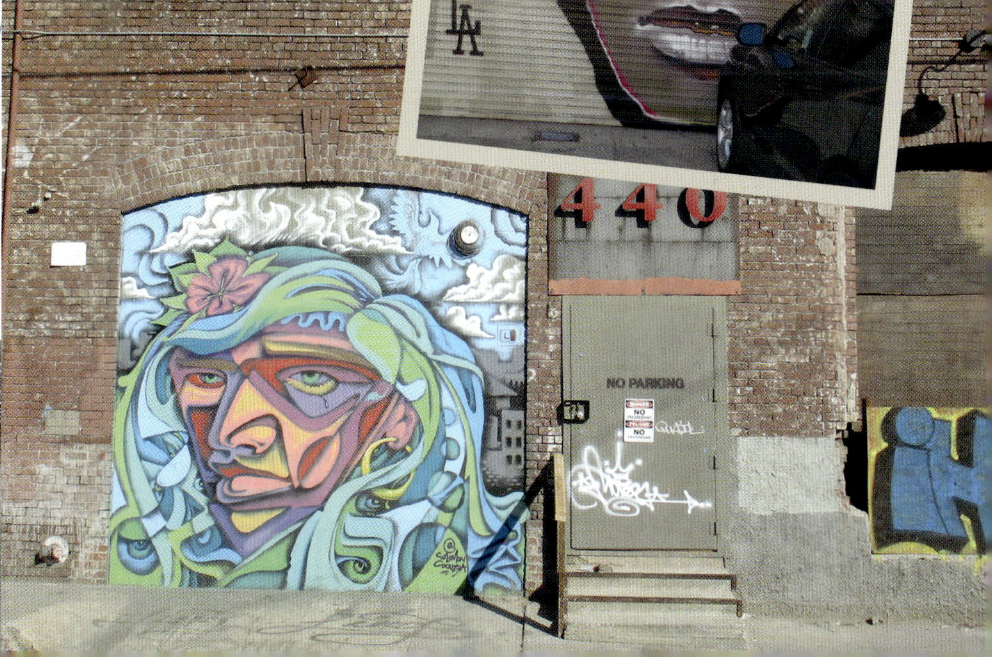
440
NO PARKING

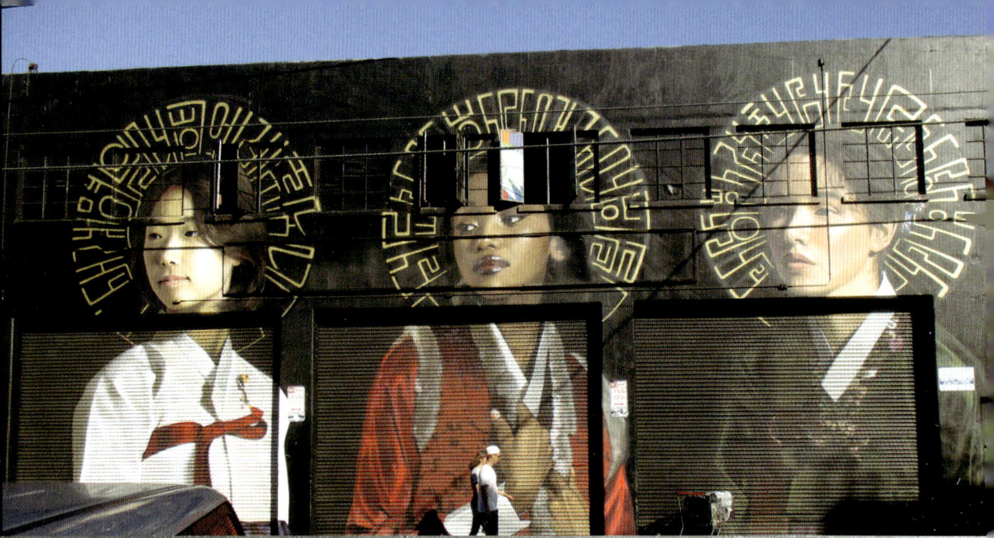

Royyal Dog's striking work of LA women in traditional Korean robes was done entirely with spray cans.

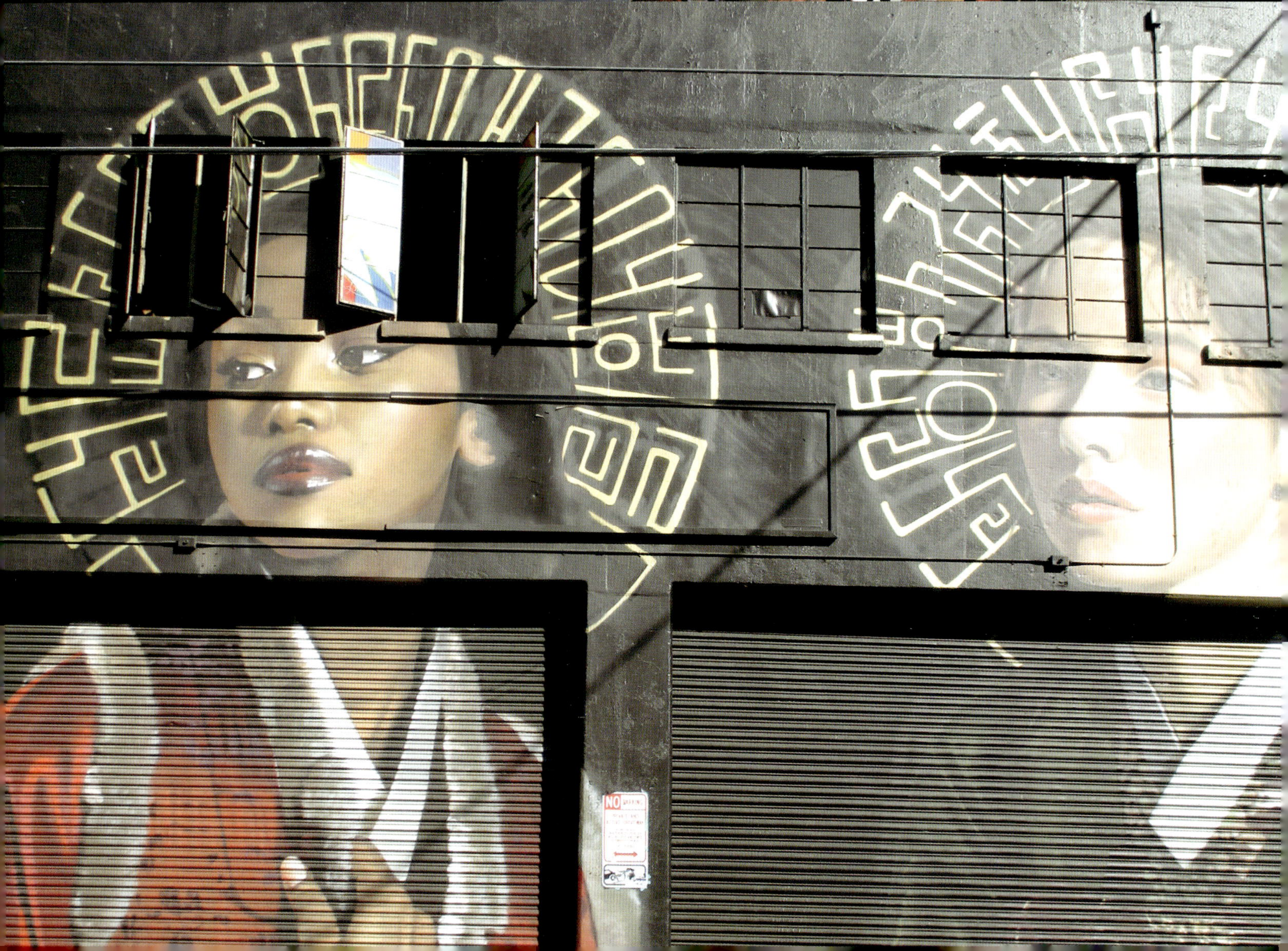

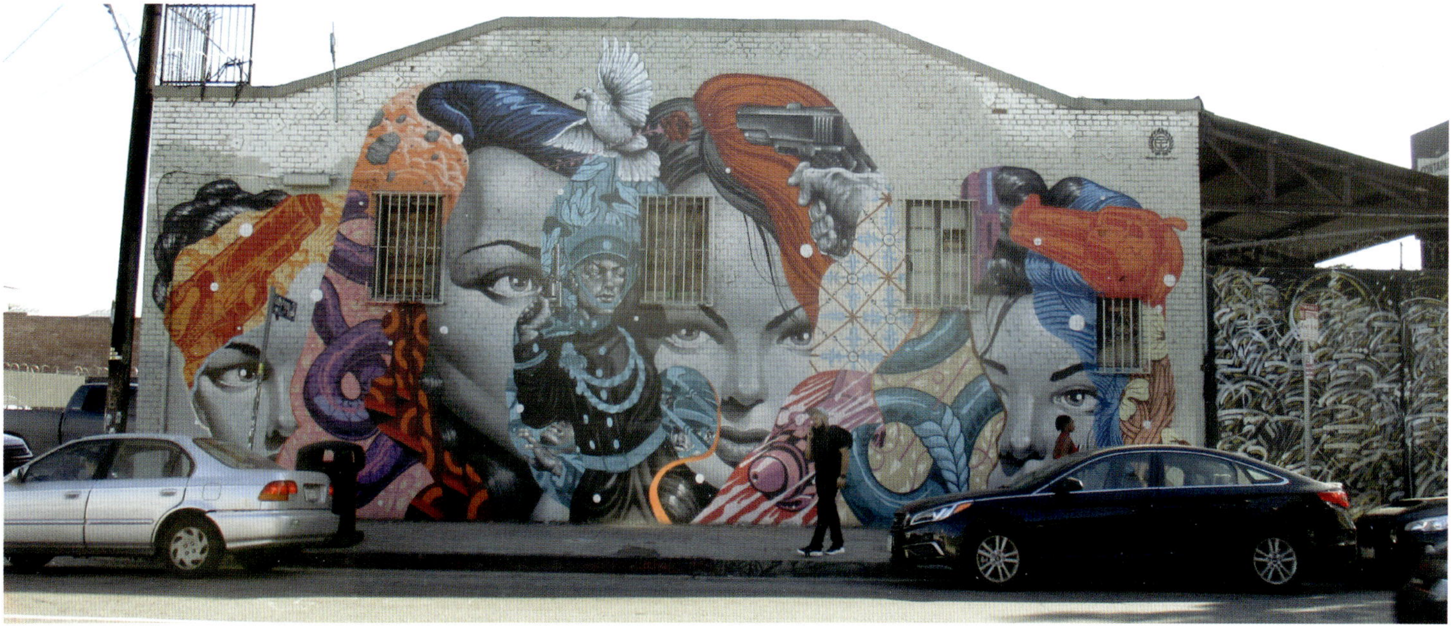

The diversity of women on the wall in the LA Arts District is on full display in a high-density grid of streets. Royyal Dog, a South Korean street artist whose given name is Chris Changyang Shim, is known for painting women in traditional Korean robes called *hanbok* to reflect the cultural diversity of LA. There are also collaborative works in *Her Eyes Like Emotional Sensors* by Christina Angelina, Ease, Sek, and Mar. World-renowned movie poster artist Tristan Eaton's work is also part of the District.

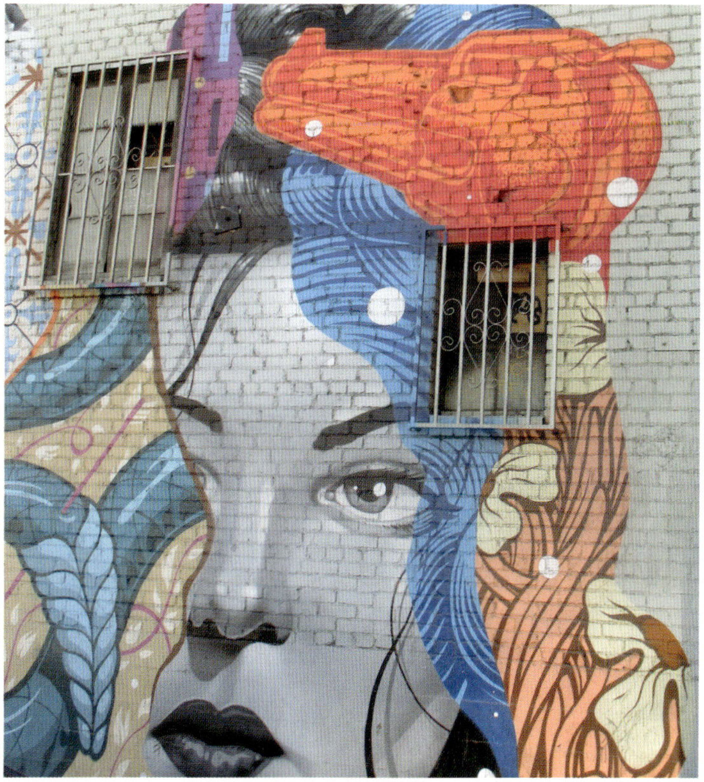

Tristan Eaton's landmark wall features his strong and original graphic design images of women. His artwork can also be found at the New York's Museum of Modern Art (MOMA). Mural details on following pages.

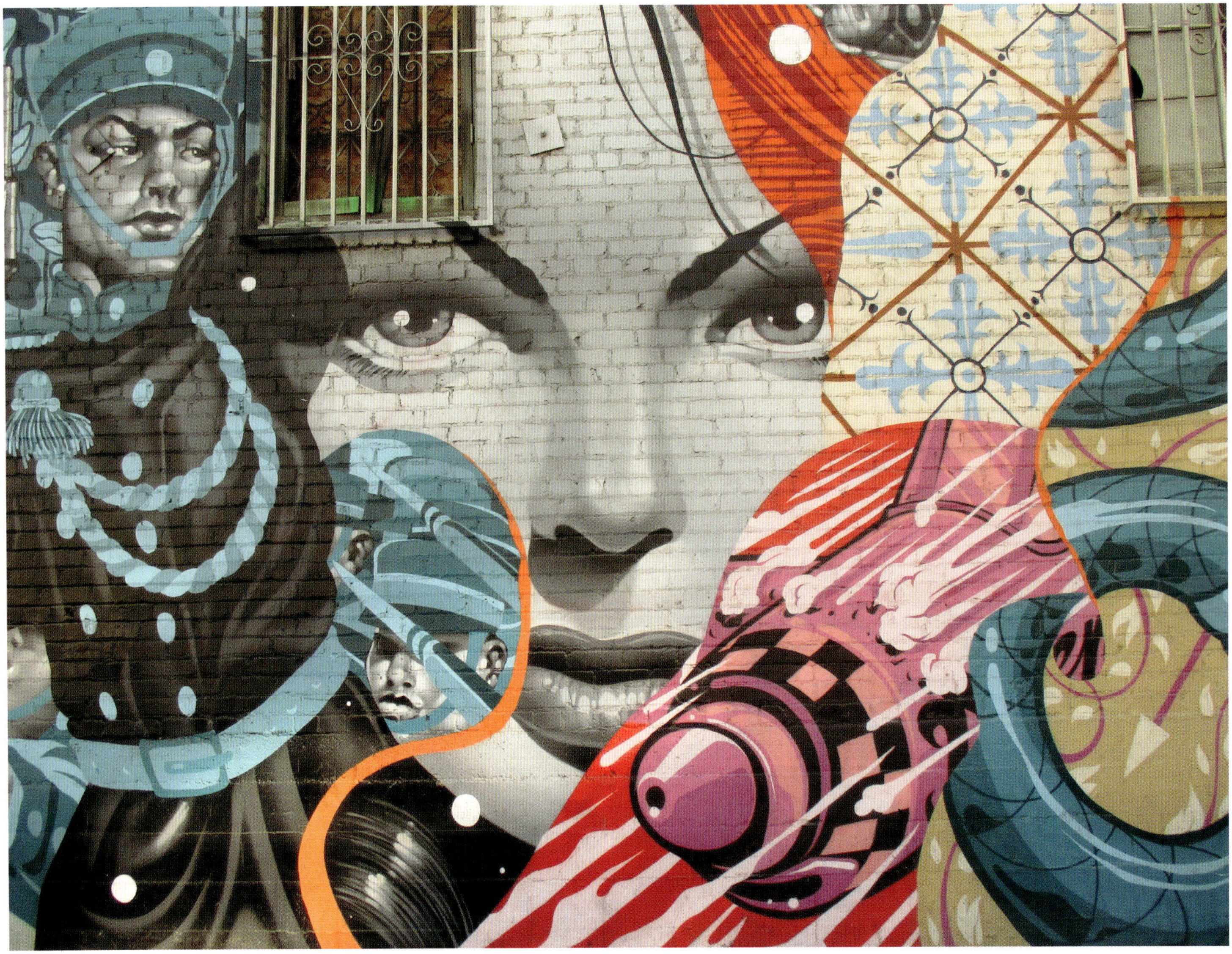

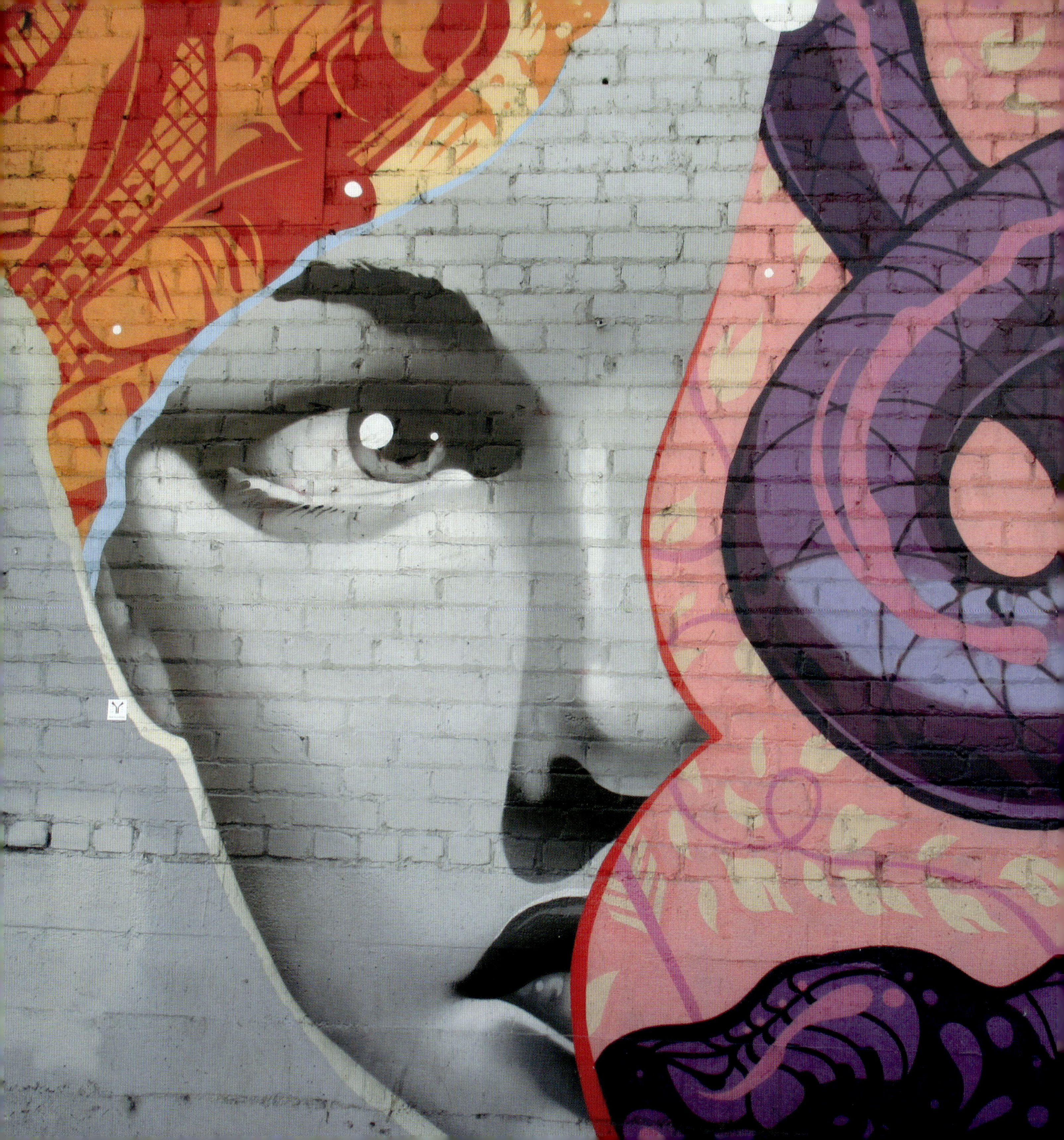

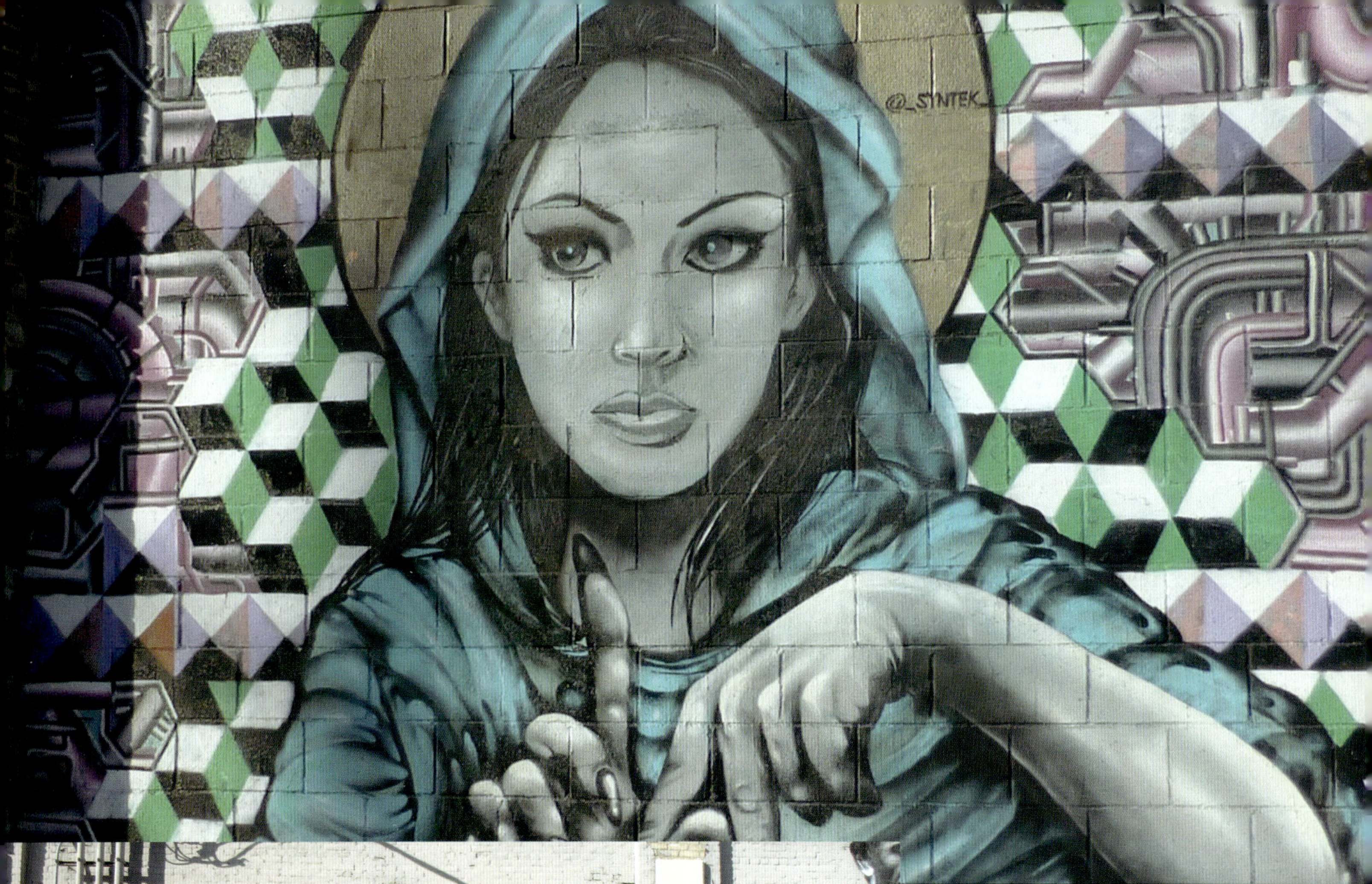

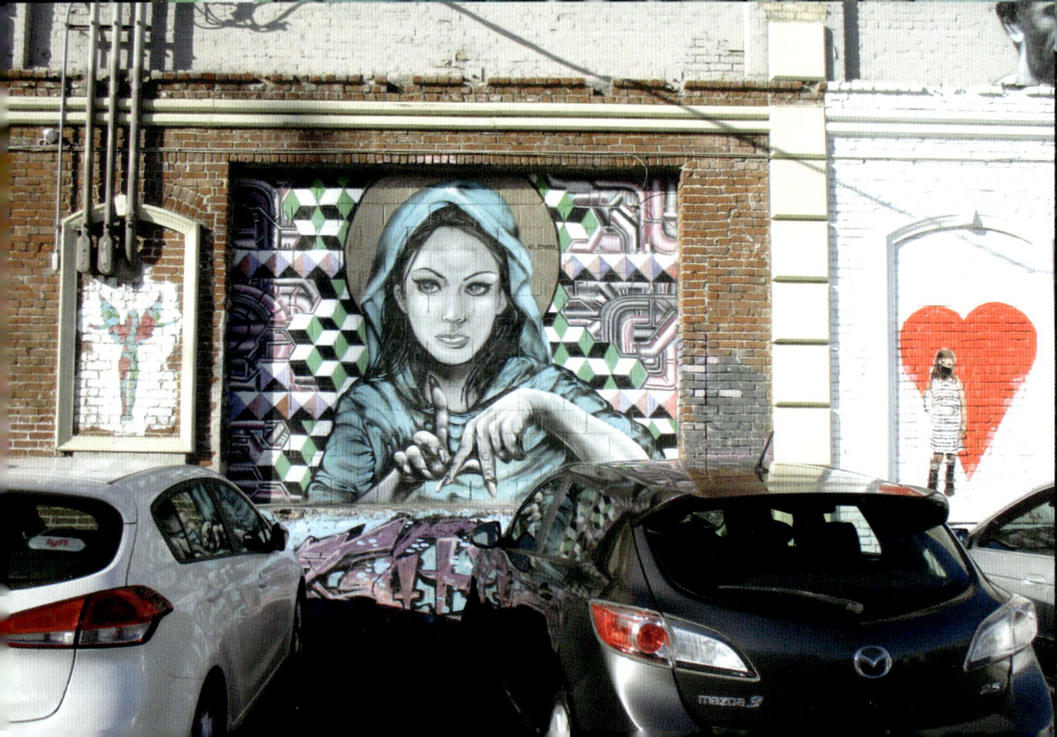

Syntek is the artist behind the woman with the turquoise cowl surrounded by geometric forms. According to one blogger, he wears a mask when he paints because he doesn't like to be photographed. The woman's hands spell LA.

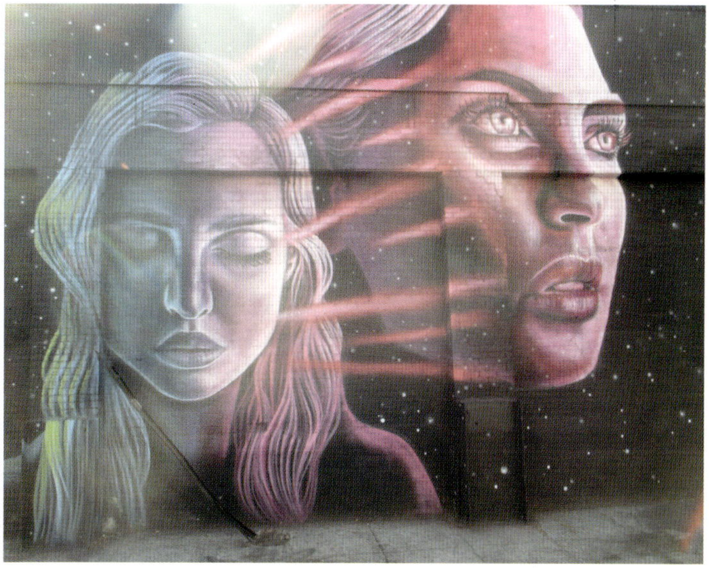

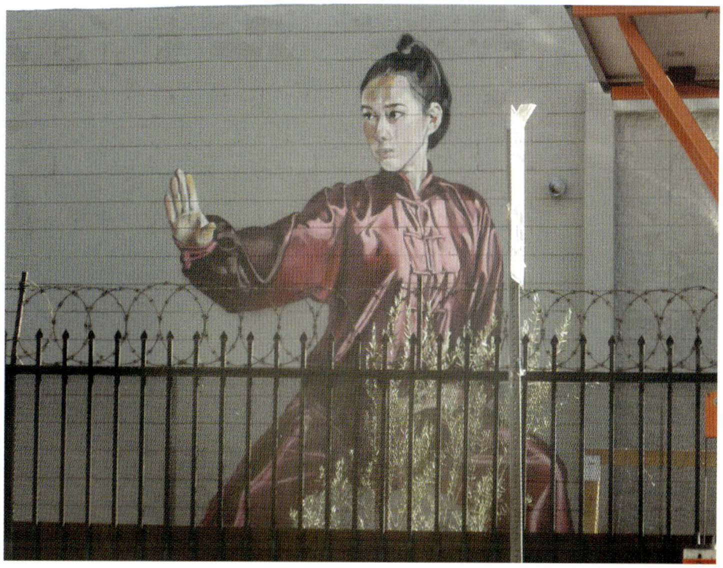

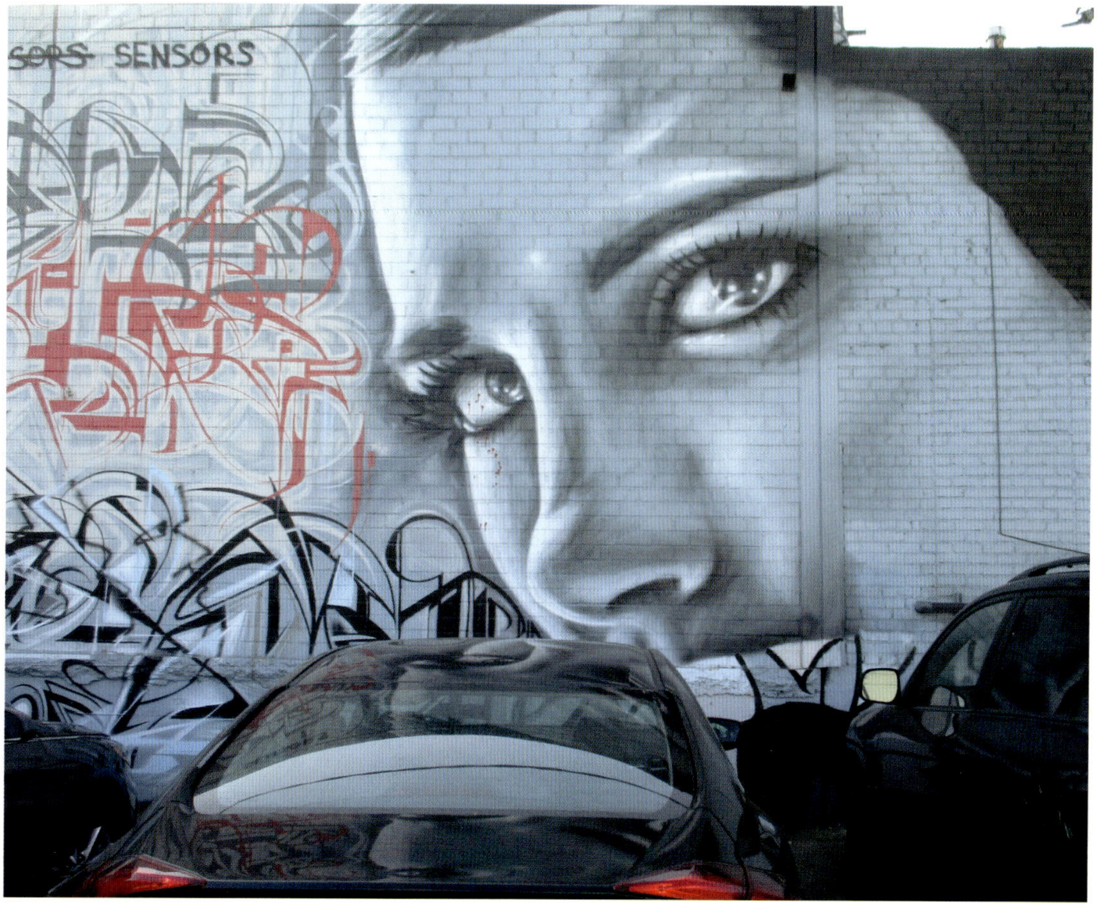

Carley Ealey, a street artist from San Diego, depicts women in the context of celestial objects. The woman practicing tai chi shows the scale of the Arts District murals.

RIGHT *Muralists often collaborate, such as this example by Starfighter (a.k.a. Christina Angelina), Ease One, Sek, and Mar in their work Her Eyes Like Emotional Sensors.*

The SPARC That Ignited the Great Wall of LA: Dr. Judy Baca

If there's a beachside promenade that defines the LA image, it's Venice Beach. The brainchild of developer Abbott Kinney, Venice used to be laced with canals like its Italian namesake, and a few weed-choked waterways still exist. Its quaint cottages on tidy laneways were once affordable, so a young rock band, the Doors, could get their start here. Now the few people who can afford to live there are the entertainment industry elite and the homeless, who set up shop on the sand and push their mobile homes in shopping carts along the streets and the Venice Beach boardwalk.

If you drive inland from the narrow beachside streets of Venice Beach, away from the homeless and mentally marginalized who camp out openly on the sand during the day, you'll find a white art deco building that was once a jailhouse that still has intact cells. It is the home of SPARC—the Social and Public Art Resource Center[5]—an LA landmark that celebrates the rebellious and contrarian spirit of street art in Los Angeles. SPARC was born from the vision of a street artist and a political maverick who makes no secret of her affiliation with the radical Chicano movement of the 1960s and 1970s.

Dr. Judy Baca was one of SPARC's founders and remains an outspoken street artist and political gadfly who carries the honorific Dr. Judy Baca, an emeritus professor of world arts and culture and Chicano studies at the University of California at

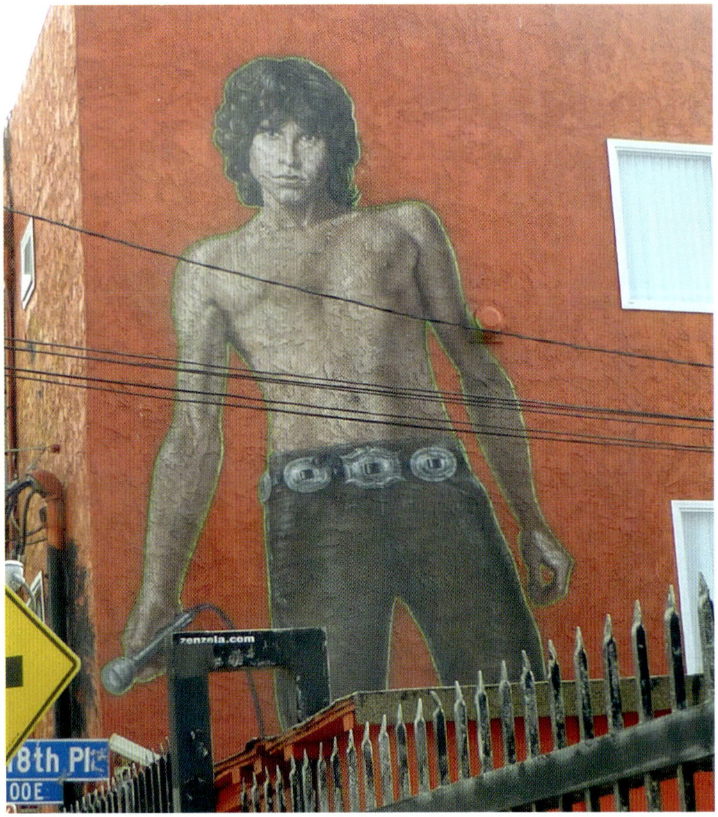

Rip Cronk's version of the young Jim Morrison of the Doors overlooks the Venice Beach boardwalk.

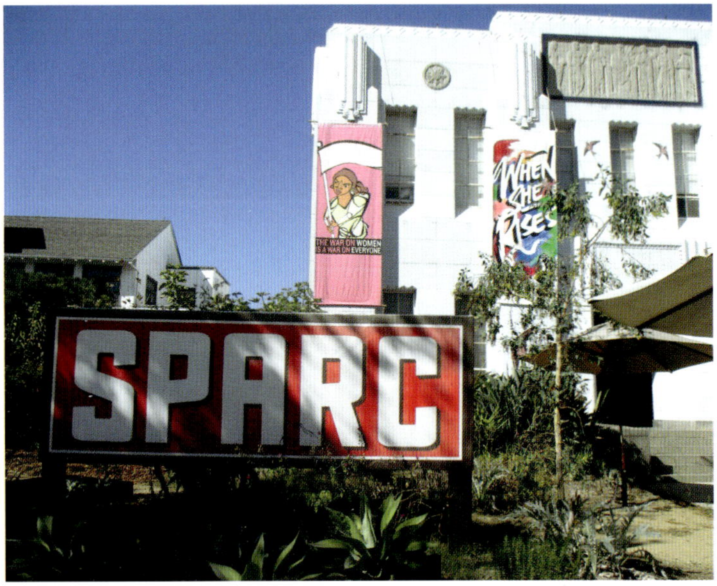

The Social and Public Art Resource Center (SPARC) encourages mural art as activism while training and mentoring future LA muralists on the art and techniques of the mural arts.

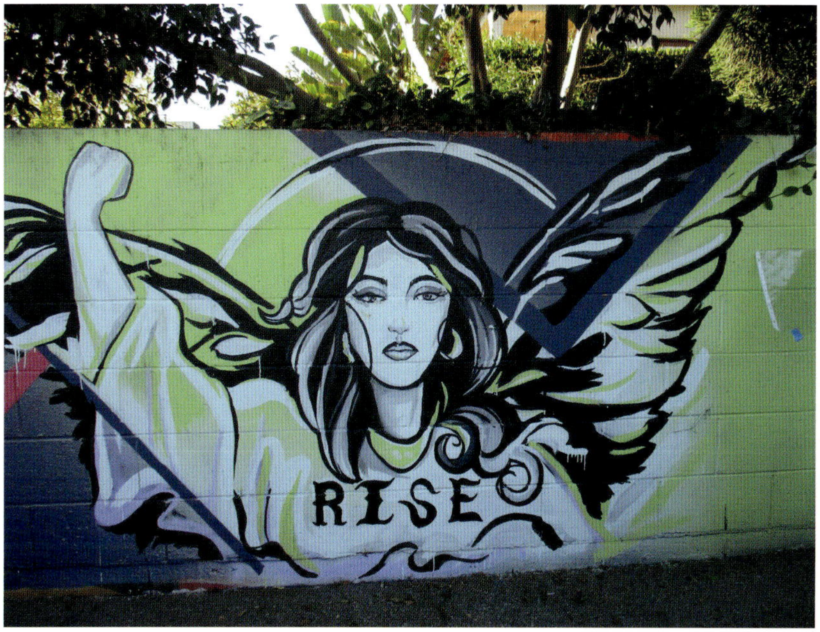

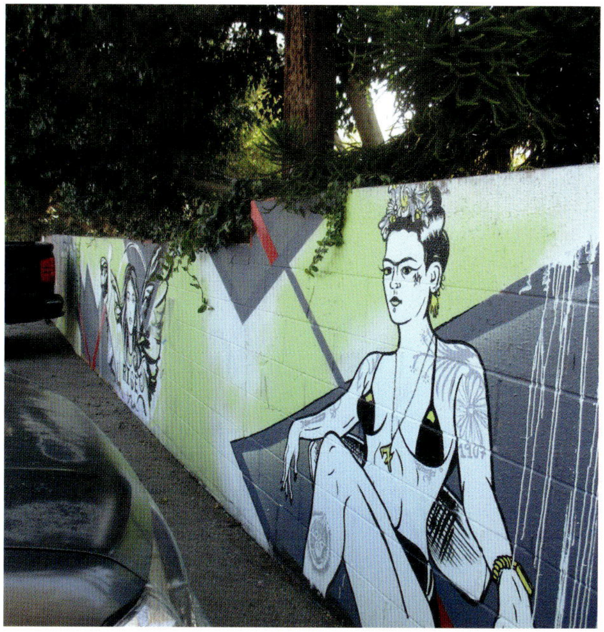

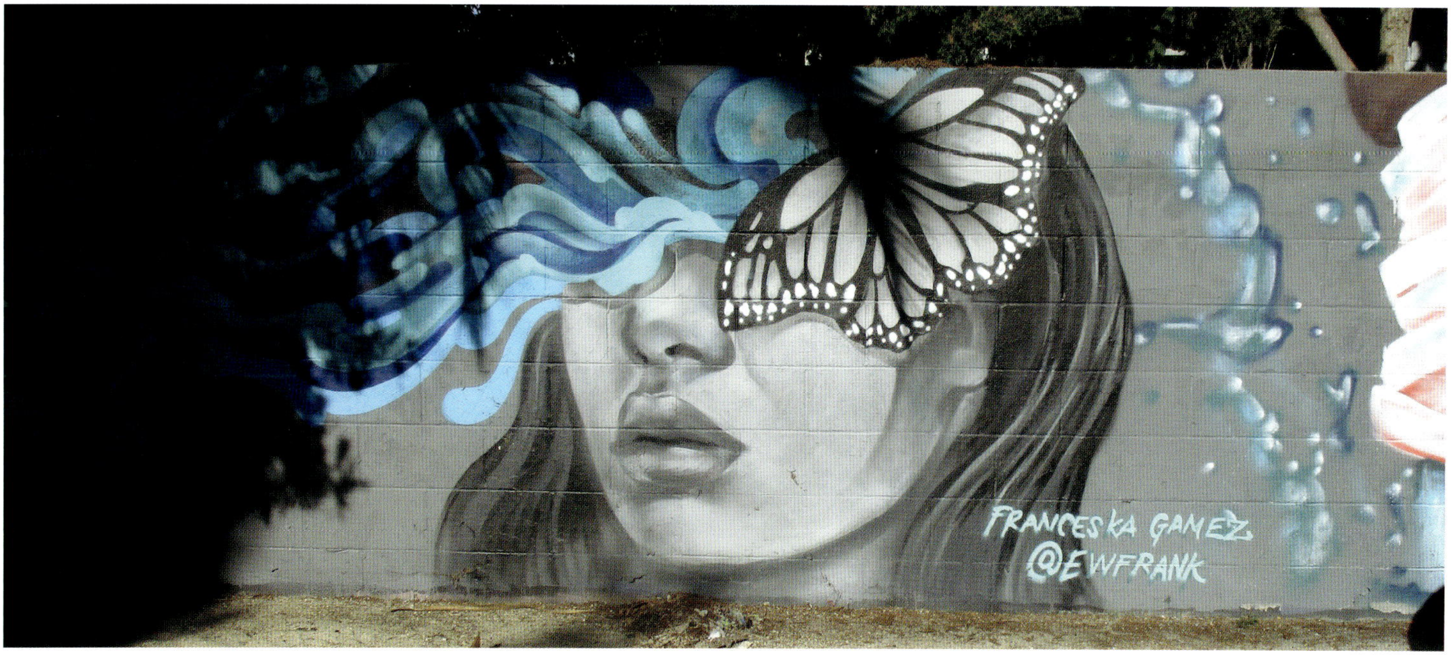

The SPARC parking lot is a living mural project with examples by young wall artists.

Los Angeles. Dr. Baca was the only woman to be invited to take part in a workshop to learn the techniques of the great Mexican muralist David Alfaro Siqueiros in 1977. Baca's workshop experience made her realize that the epic images painted by the Mexican muralists did not have room for a woman's perspective of inclusion, their historical importance, and mythical power. She brings a fierce intellectual independence to her rebellious, contrarian work, which was cemented during the Siqueiros workshop.

The "Big Three" Mexican muralists—Diego Rivera, José Clemente Orozco, and David Alfaro Siqueiros—inspired a generation of wall artists, among them Judy Baca, a *muralista*, who also drew inspiration from the magic of Native American *curanderas* from northern Mexico and the Chicano movement that came to define the Mexican diaspora in LA. Students often question their teachers, and Judy Baca was no exception. She rejected the Mexican muralists' Marxist didactic and instead adapted the muralist tradition in a community-based movement of art-as-activism. Street art became a way of lifting young Angelenos out of a spiral of violence into a world of recognizing the power of history and the role of women who have shaped California and the greater Southwest. That view was given expression in *The Great Wall of Los Angeles*, where street gang members with police records picked up the spray can. *The Great Wall of Los Angeles* [6] was an opportunity for young people who were in trouble to learn about their cultural identity through street art.

Today Dr. Baca's perspective is in high demand. She mentors and fosters young women street artists struggling for recognition and money to finance their works and who want to go beyond stereotypical images and tap into their highly personal visions of women. Judy Baca understands struggle. She was born in Watts, the African American ghetto near downtown LA that was the center of a bloody riot in 1965 that resulted in thirty-four deaths and heavy property damage. The riot was the expression of a long-held belief that LA cops targeted African Americans and Mexicans, a mistrust that is still bubbling below the surface of LA. The city again erupted in racial violence following the acquittal of police who were filmed beating motorist Rodney King in 1992.

This uneasiness, this racial tension, has always been a part of LA's modern history. And it has often served as the blank canvas for gang-tagging drug territory, which to Baca also served as the handwriting on the wall to embrace LA's dismissed and dispossessed. It was fertile ground for Judy Baca, whose volunteer masterwork *The Great Wall of Los Angeles* was an attempt to use street art to help bridge those deep community divisions that are part of LA's cultural and racial geography. In order to work on the internationally recognized *Great Wall of Los Angeles*, some of the young artists had to have been arrested. This was no accident, but a strategy by Judy Baca to get money out of the local and state government, which had funds to teach ex-prisoners the skills that would reduce the state's recidivism rate.

Judy Baca spoke to the authors about her work, her life, and the future of street art. She is truly one of LA's founding women street artists, promoting activism and inspiring a younger generation of street artists.

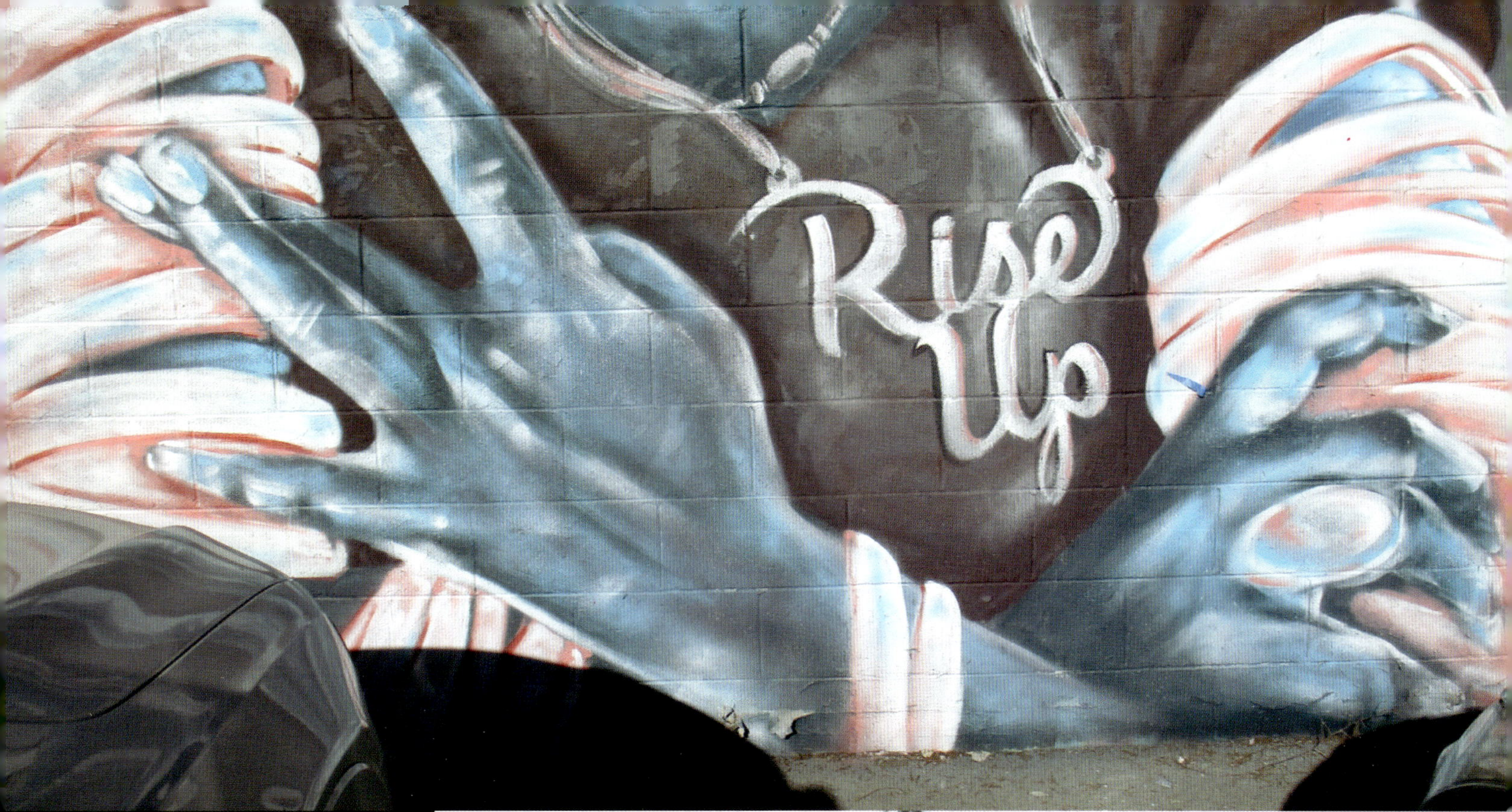

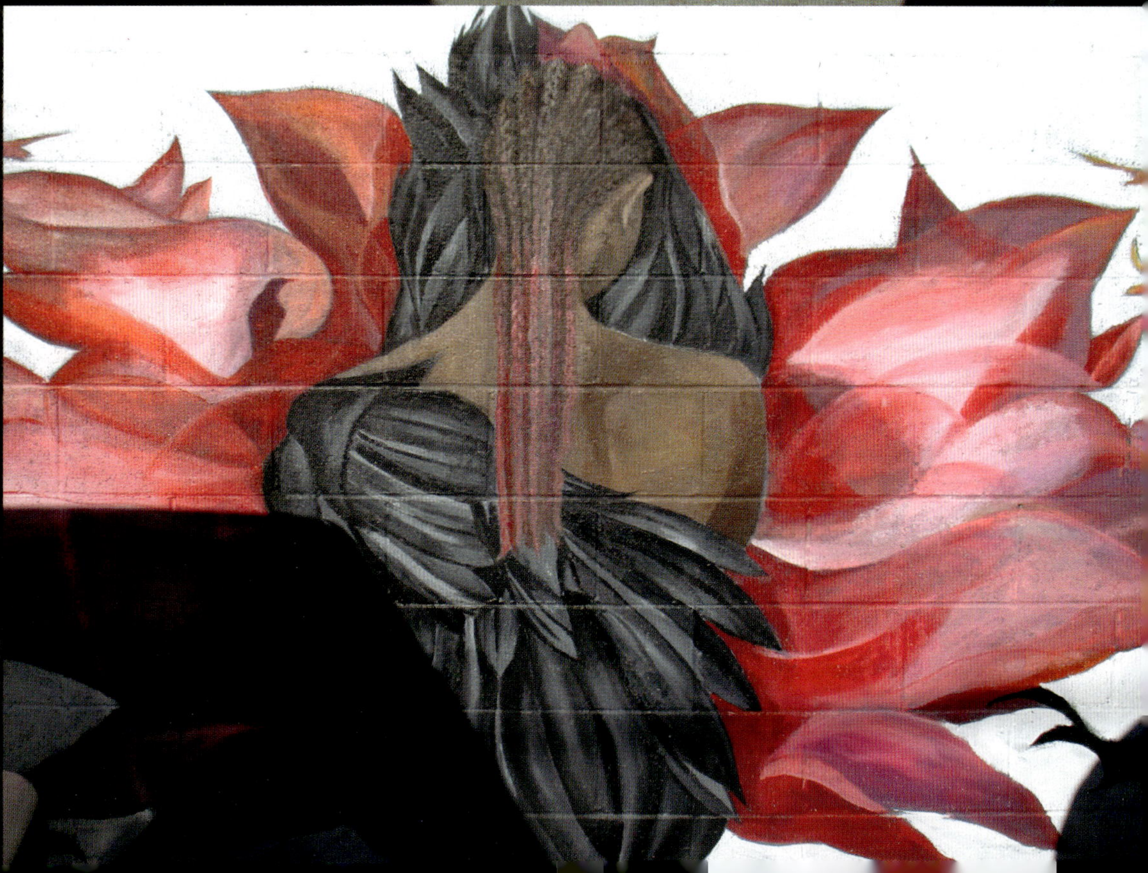

The wall art done by practicing muralists at SPARC reflects the activist ethos of SPARC and its focus on women subjects.

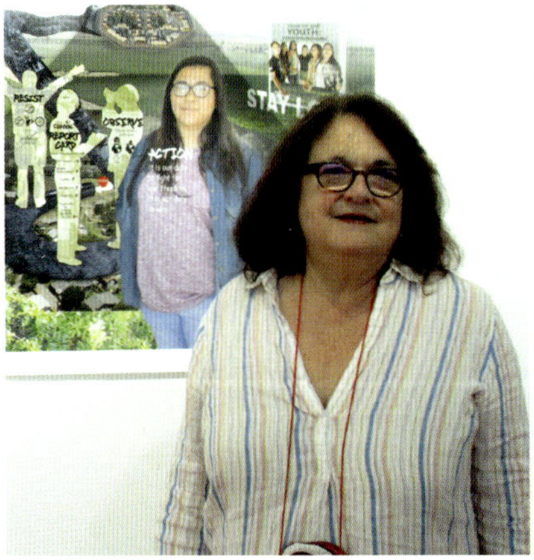

INTERVIEW WITH DR. JUDY BACA

From "Pachuca" to Activist

In 1969, when I came out of the university with a degree in art, I was coming out in the midst of a revolution, particularly in the Southwest. In Los Angeles, there was a movement for civil rights that was a profound movement that affected my community, the Chicano community. I don't know whatever possessed me to become an artist. It was a crazy idea for a person from my background, born in Watts, growing up in a place called Pacoima, living in a community that had no examples of Latina women artists. I also did a degree that included education, so I saw my work as perhaps transformative—a way of working to organize communities and beginning to work on civil rights issues. So, I stepped out of the university at a moment when I was totally useless as a minimalist painter, understanding Op art and the gestural mark, which was pointless. I could speak to five people and there was a revolution going on. I wanted to be helpful to that. I began to look very closely at the writings on the wall. And that's what actually inspired me.

Dr. Judy Baca's vision of women on the walls takes in the importance of history and a strong feminist approach to wall art.

RIGHT *Judith F. Baca © 2008, Absolutely Chicana. SPARC Archives, SPARCinLA.org.*

From Tagging to a New Visual Language Celebrating Chicano Heritage

I was interested in looking at the narrative on the wall; for me, it was a roll call narrative. The young people were using the walls to record their neighborhood and their associations with one another. You could see something like "Soy Flaco" (I'm a skinny guy), and I hang with these people and I'm from this territorial place. People fear that. They thought it was intense gang marking and these were very dangerous individuals. And probably in the intervening years the gangs have become more and more violent and involved with drugs. But in the early seventies, when I began to work, it was pretty much about defining your neighborhood and defining your "Chicanoness." So, I was very interested in the creation of an alternative narrative. What if we actually made those pieces say more than "Soy Flaco"? How about "I'm from a grand heritage, a family that actually helped build the Southwest."

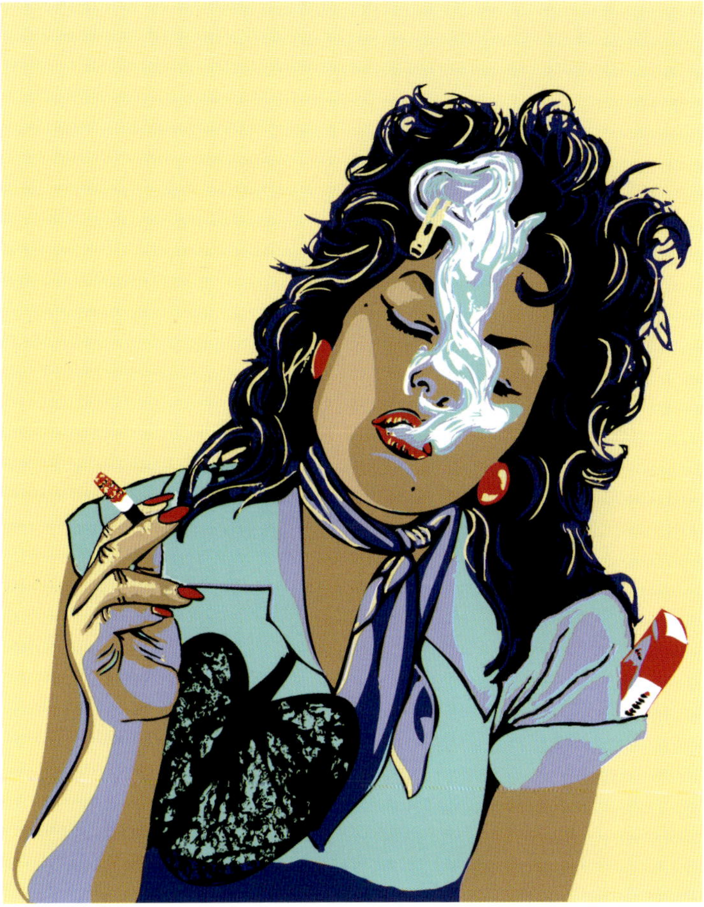

The Curandera

My grandmother was an Indigenous woman who was a healer, a *curandera*. Much of my work is really based on her ideas and her notion of land and memory. My images of women are very much the people whom I know: my grandmother, my mother, my *tías* (aunts); they're my *compañeras* in the struggle, people I knew.

On the Founding of SPARC

SPARC began as a program run by women, developed by a feminist positionality. There were two members of my founding group, both of whom came from the upper class. They were progressives, one of them educated at Berkeley. The other was a daughter of one of America's greatest historians, Arthur Schlesinger. And because of her, I had access to Arthur Schlesinger. And that's how I learned a lot about the history of the WPA (Works Progress Administration). [President Franklin Roosevelt's governmental program to create jobs during the Great Depression, which employed thousands of actors, musicians, writers, and other artists.]

So here's this kid from Pacoima and Watts getting to know a side of American history that was profound and gave me a sense of how we could configure this place. I was running this program when I made a call for muralists and had a city-funded program where we could sponsor murals and commission art—less than 15 percent of applicants would be women.

The Great Wall Project

The Great Wall was a self-initiated piece, financed by me and this organization that began to develop it. It was never censored because I never submitted it for approvals. It was absolutely an act of defiance.

> Why did we pick an LA drainage wash to do it? Because nobody cared. It's a sewer. Where else could you go to get an endless wall below ground level where you could not be shot in a drive-by shooting? I mean that's the kind of thing I had to think about because I was bringing gangs together from different neighborhoods.

I was balancing boys and girls; I was trying to develop a space that was a space apart from the daily lives of these kids from the ghettos of Los Angeles. They were coming in from South Central; they were the most difficult kids. The first segment of the wall, eighty kids came on, and all of them had to have been arrested once to be on the mural. The only monies I could get was recidivism monies from the juvenile justice system.

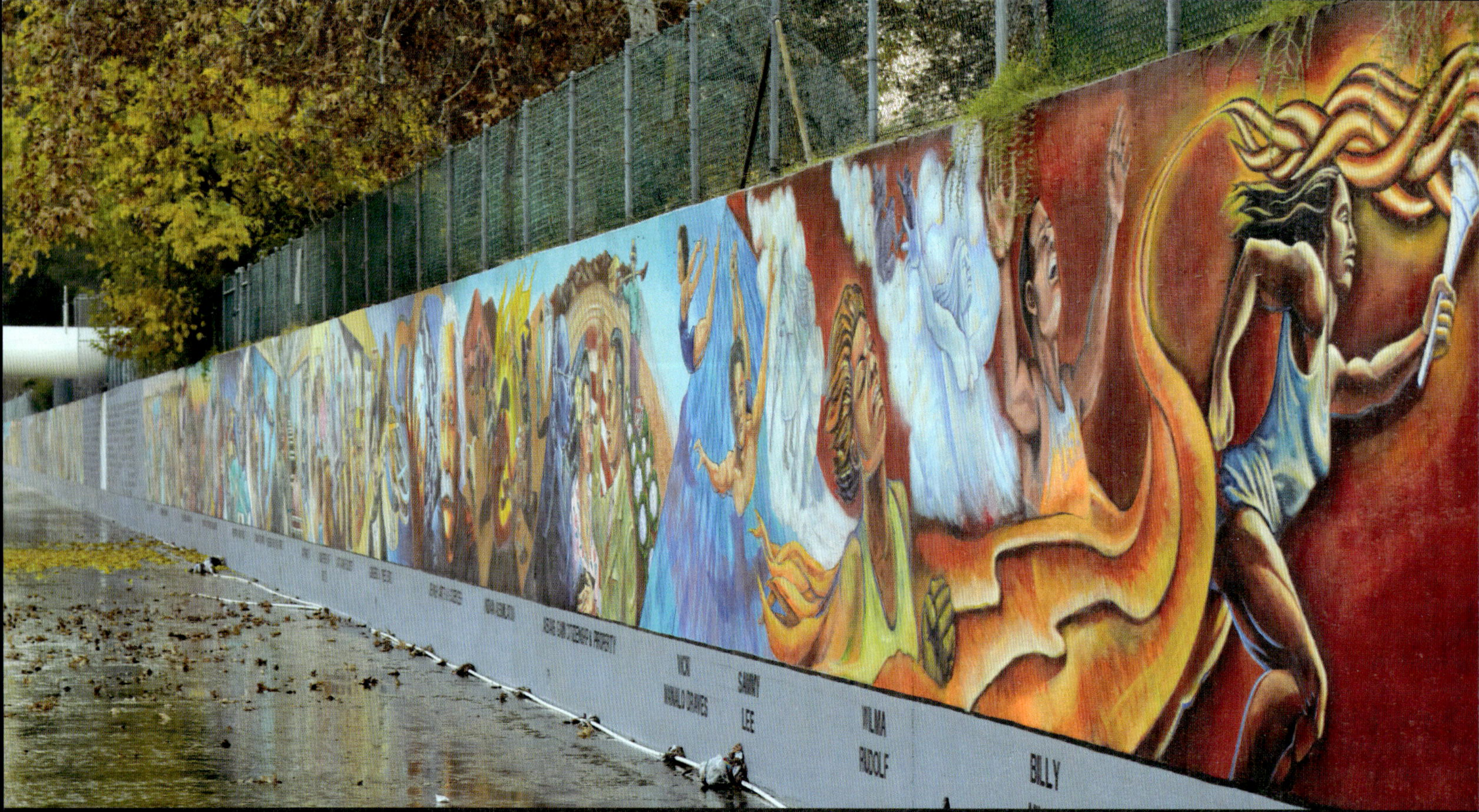

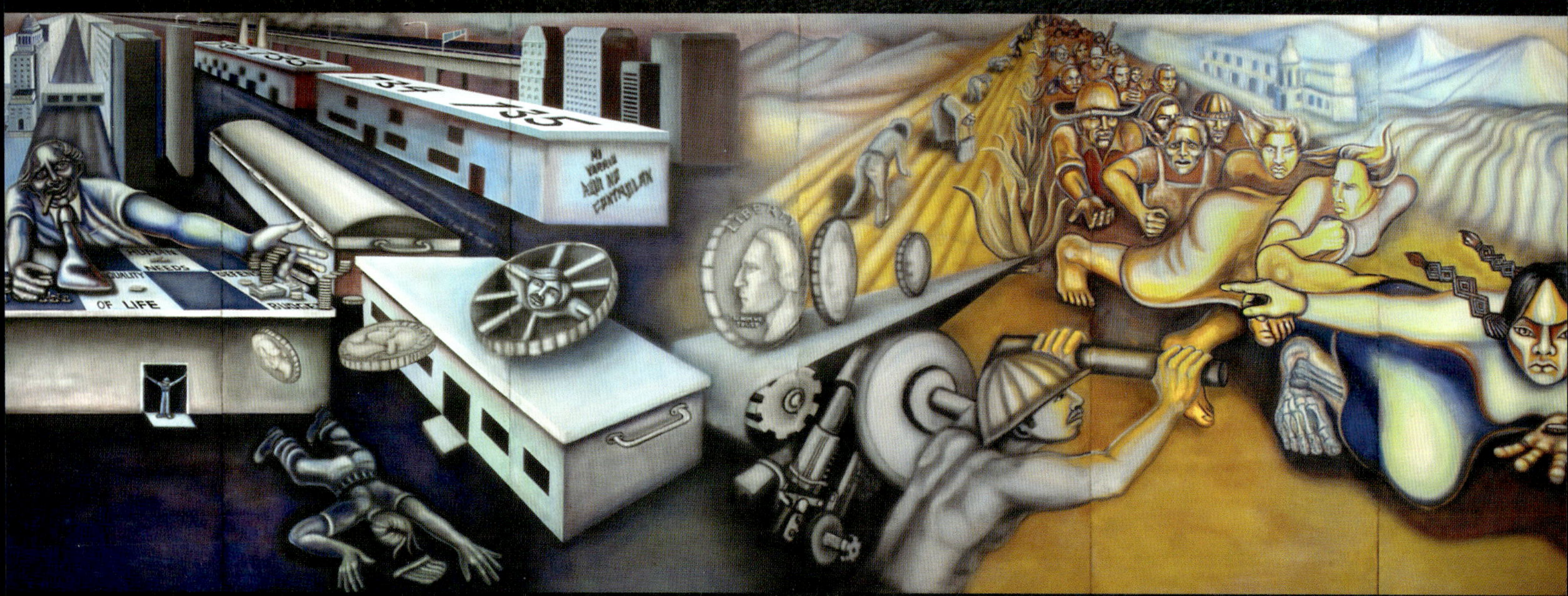

TOP *Judith F. Baca, © 1976, Olympic Champions, detail from the 1950s section of the Great Wall of Los Angeles. SPARC Archives, SPARCinLA.org*

BELOW *Uprising of the Mujeres, 1976 SPARC Archives, SPARCinLA.org*

On Being a Woman Muralist

> I think it's a public voice when you're a muralist. It's a different thing than the private voice in the studio, which is one where you're exploring some kind of internal dream or a kind of thought about yourself.

We're working on resurrecting a piece I started in the '80s and never finished because it never got funded. The piece is called When God Was Woman. It's a series I did with thirteen women in a workshop. The figures are all about the power of women. So these women stand in volcanic eruptions. They are nude but making symbols with their hands, and they are unscathed by the lava and they are unscathed about what is happening around them. And as the panels revolve, the back end is them basically as Gaia, the earth, the land. It is very spiritual in that sense. So I lived between these two worlds: the highly political that was also highly spiritual. The coming out of my mother's Apache background. The driving of my family out of Mexico during the Mexican Revolution. And my grandmother's love of Pancho Villa. My grandfather's hatred of Pancho Villa. He was more of a Spaniard, and she was an Indigenous woman. Her family lived in a hacienda, and the revolution freed the Indigenous, right? So there is this tension within the family.

> Very early, in the Uprising Ahead the central figure is a woman leading workers out of the fields, and she is mythological, she is spiritual, and she's Indigenous. And she's incredibly powerful. So it was the opposite of the reticent woman with the little rebozo saying, "Sí, señor." These women were dangerous, powerful, and to be reckoned with.

A Counternarrative to the Mexican Muralists

> I was also interested in the creation of absolutely beautiful and exquisite women because I thought there was enough denigration. You know, the cha cha, the hot tamale, the kinds of things I was experiencing as a young woman being cast in a particular vision. It was a counternarrative to those things.

I was in a sense in a dialogue, countering the Mexican painters who were the most inspirational of the twentieth century, I think the most important muralists probably ever. What they were doing was a completely male-dominated form. The man was the maestro; he was the leader, and the minions who worked under him followed his direction. They achieved a really high art form as a result of that, but David Alfaro Siqueiros, José Clemente Orozco, Diego Rivera—they were really powerful influences in California and all through the United States. Each in a different city. In Los Angeles it was Siqueiros; in San Francisco it was Rivera; in Dartmouth and the East Coast it was Orozco. The Dartmouth murals are a wonder. You're looking at how each of these artists who came and stayed left their mark.

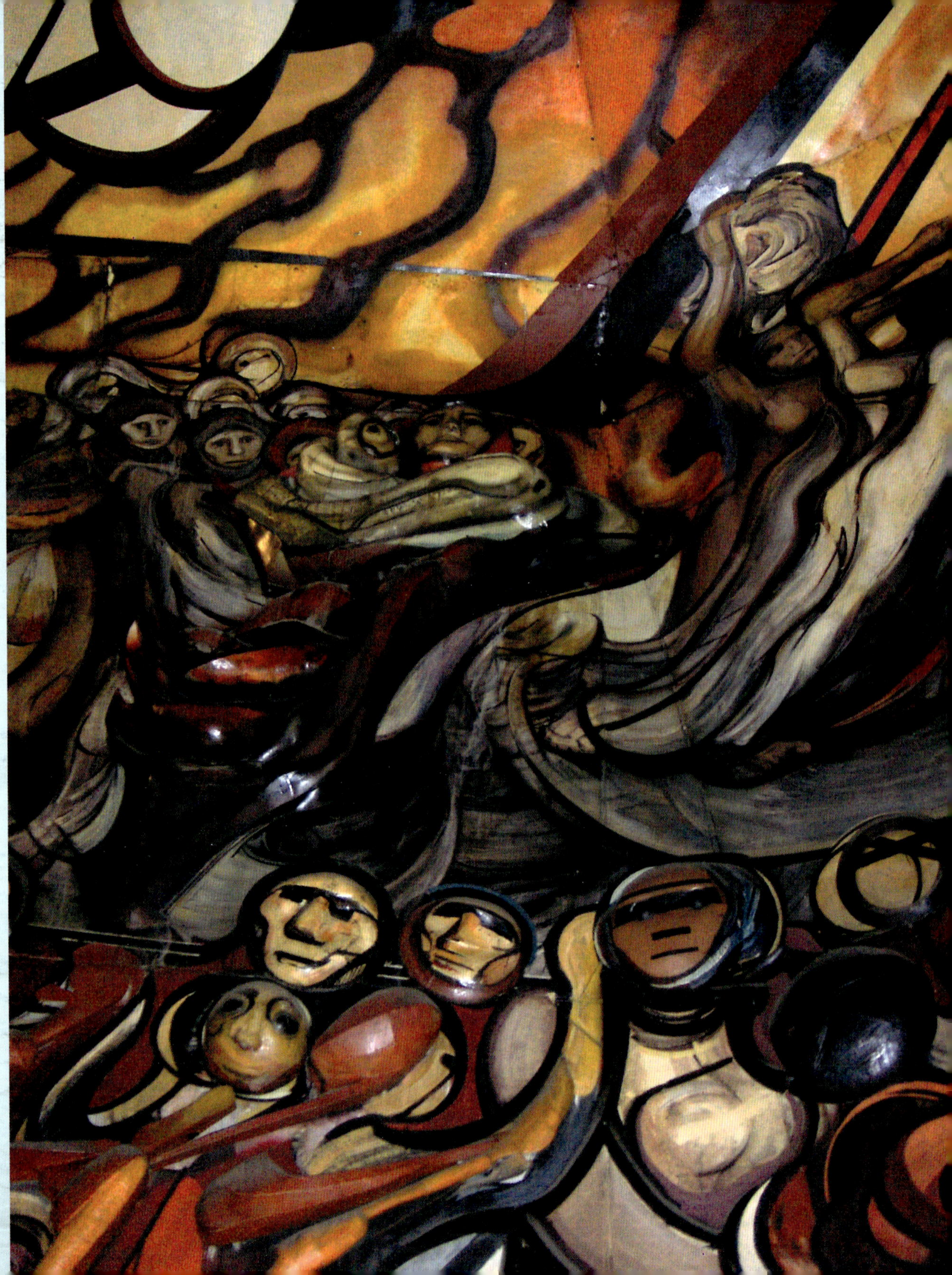

But all of them had one thing in common, which is they were patriarchal. Their view of the world was a male view completely dominated by their notion of what a Mexican woman was.

And my notion of a Mexican woman was completely informed by a single mother, by an Indigenous grandmother who looked like an Apache with braids down to her waist— you know, walking around under a parasol in Los Angeles. We were an anathema; we were "other" and at the same time we were the original people.

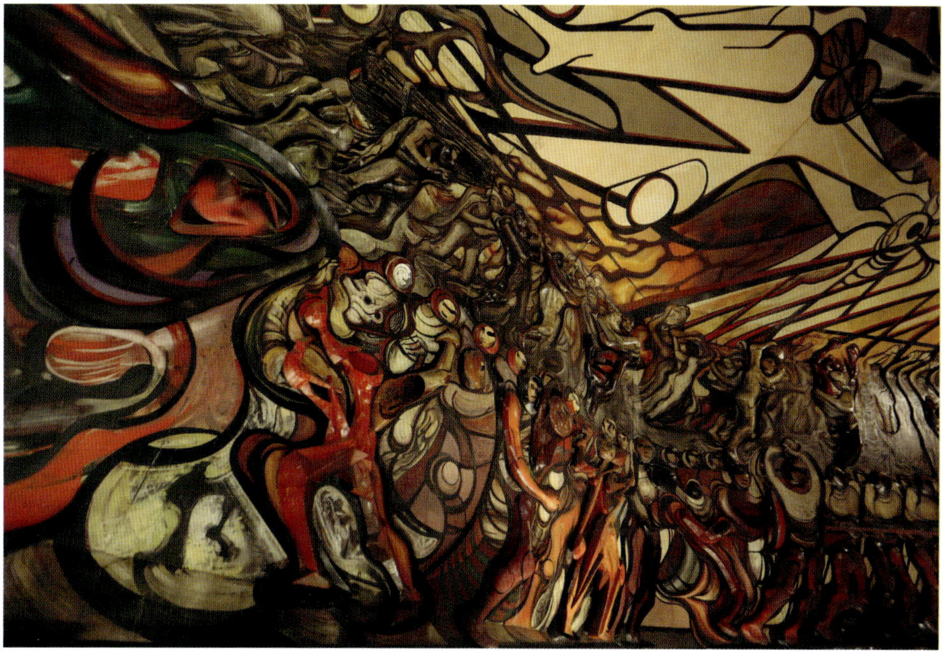

Siqueiros's Polyforum mural, which is part of the World Trade Center in Mexico City. Photo: Carl Campbell, licensed under CC BY-SA 3.0

The Siqueiros Workshop

I was the only woman in the workshop. There were twenty-six men. They were from Russia; they were from Chile. The Chilean coup had occurred. It was a very transformative moment for my own work. I was learning the polyangular theory, the divisions of space, which was really much more about composition. There was nowhere else to be trained.

At one point they broke us up into teams, and they said because you are the woman on the team you are going to deal with the "Woman's Question." It was the Marxist way of women being a question. Why were women a question?

That was part of my problem with the Communist Party as well. So I'm in the Women's Question group —the piece upstairs in the hallway is my drawing that I submitted to the men. I came back with this drawing that was this incredible Indigenous woman who came out of the mural and was leading all these people as a sort of spiritual leader and a mythological character. But I'd seen her on the street. I saw a woman who looked like she might have been twenty-five years old, and her hair had turned completely gray. And she was Indigenous and just incredibly beautiful, but what was happening to this person? She was living in two worlds. And they rejected it. Instead they wanted to do this funnel into the mouth of the woman with all these products that were being poured into her. Which I thought was essentially a rape image. The denigration of the woman.

RIGHT *At the Polyforum Center, viewers of Siqueiros's mural can stand on a rotating platform to view the mural in its entirety. Photo: government of Mexico City, license CC0 1.0*

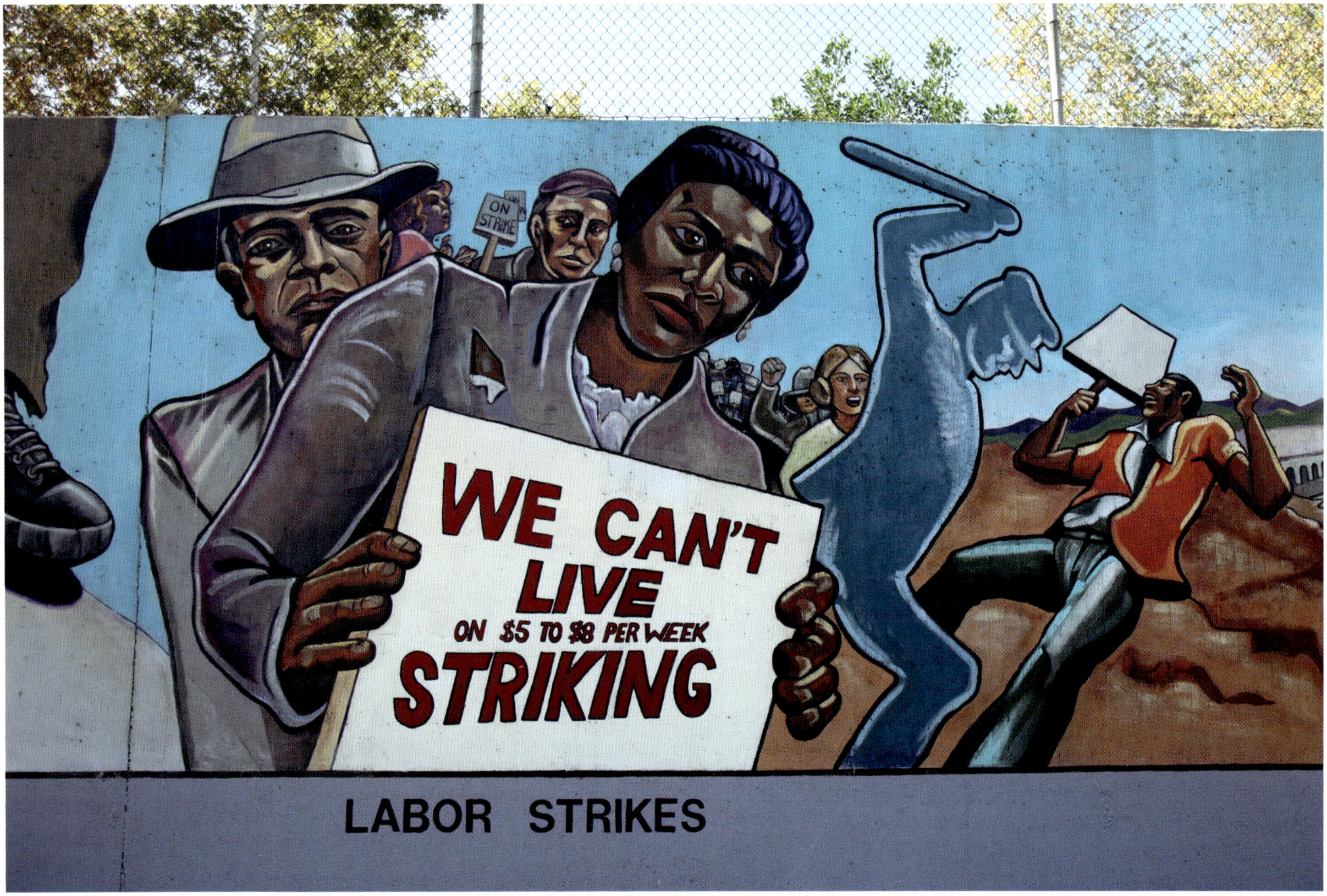

Judith F. Baca, © 1976, Labor Strikes detail from the 1930s section of the Great Wall of Los Angeles. SPARC Archives, SPARCinLA.org

Muralism: Breaking the Sex Barrier

> Muralism is hand-to-hand training. There's no other way to learn muralism but to paint alongside a painter who's experienced. So the men were passing their knowledge along to the men. They literally would not give women an opportunity.

You take some of the early, classic Chicano murals like those in Chicano Park in San Diego, which is a hundred murals on the pillars of the Coronado Bridge. In the place where the sheriff's department decided to put a substation. It was a community park. The people took the park over. It was an incredible movement of strength. And the panels, which are some 50 feet tall, were painted by men. There was one women's piece, that was by Cecilia Muñoz, and she just restored it now some twenty-five years later. And like the *Great Wall of Los Angeles* it's been declared a national historic site. So what I was interested in was transforming that narrative. Moving from the male dominance.

Women as Sexual Objects—the Spray Painted Pin-Ups

Spray can artists do a lot of highly sexualized images of women. You look at the culture within the prisons, the kind of art that comes out of the prisons, and it's highly sexualized. The work of spray can artists has a close relationship with tattoo art. The images that are done by spray can, that's a particular genre of work. And then there are those sorts of young men who think they are elevating women by doing these beautiful portraits of their girlfriend on a two-story building, who just annoy the hell out of me, right? It's like, Who cares about this? I don't. It's a pretty young girl; it's a piece that's really a vanity piece in the sense he's painting a self-portrait: "This is what I own. This is mine." Claiming the territory with my woman.

On the Future of Murals in LA

The last ten years in LA has been a very bad time for murals. We finally got an ordinance passed recently that allowed people to paint again. It's quite restrictive and there is no funding. So what you're seeing is pretty much throw-ups. In other words, if you don't have money and there is not a sponsorship, then you're relegated to putting up works in a fast way. You have to get them up with probably a little bit of money with a spray can, with a short time on the street. Many of these works aren't permissioned. If they are permissioned, you probably have a little bit more time, but if they're not permissioned you're doing this in twenty or thirty minutes so you're seeing the denigration of the whole mural form in Los Angeles. So what used to be the mural capital of the United States I would say is no longer that. Philadelphia is probably the mural capital. But a lot of the murals done in Philadelphia are by the women trained here at SPARC. Jane Golden, for example. She had to make deals with the devil in a sense, which is something I never did with our program. We had a different opinion. Her point was to use city monies and amplify them with other donors, which is essentially sound thinking, so her program was like $3 million and mine's gone. There's the two different women's point of view. One could argue that my point of view was not so good. Her program readily and quickly became "official art."

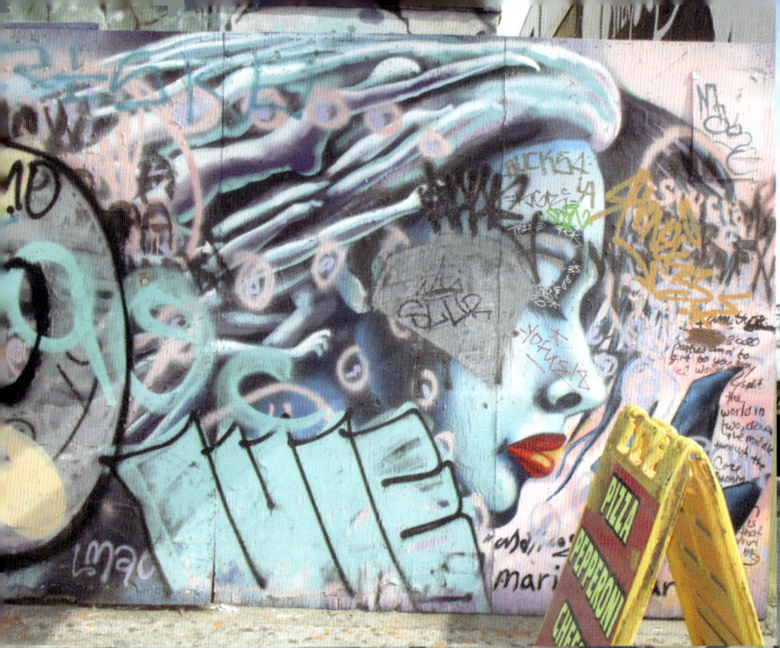
PIZZA
PEPPERONI

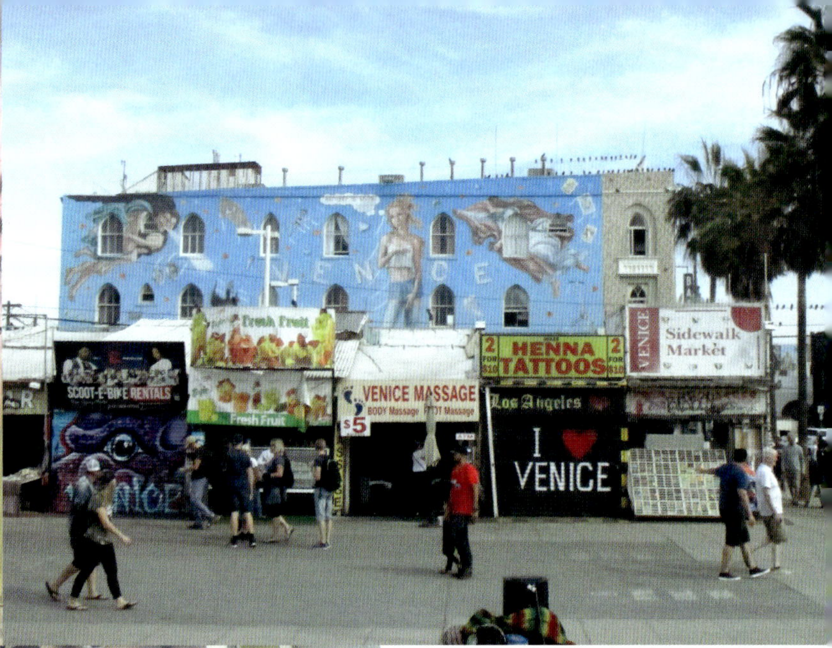
SCOOT-E-BIKE RENTALS
Fresh Fruit
VENICE MASSAGE
$5
HENNA TATTOOS
VENICE
Sidewalk Market
Los Angeles
I ♥ VENICE

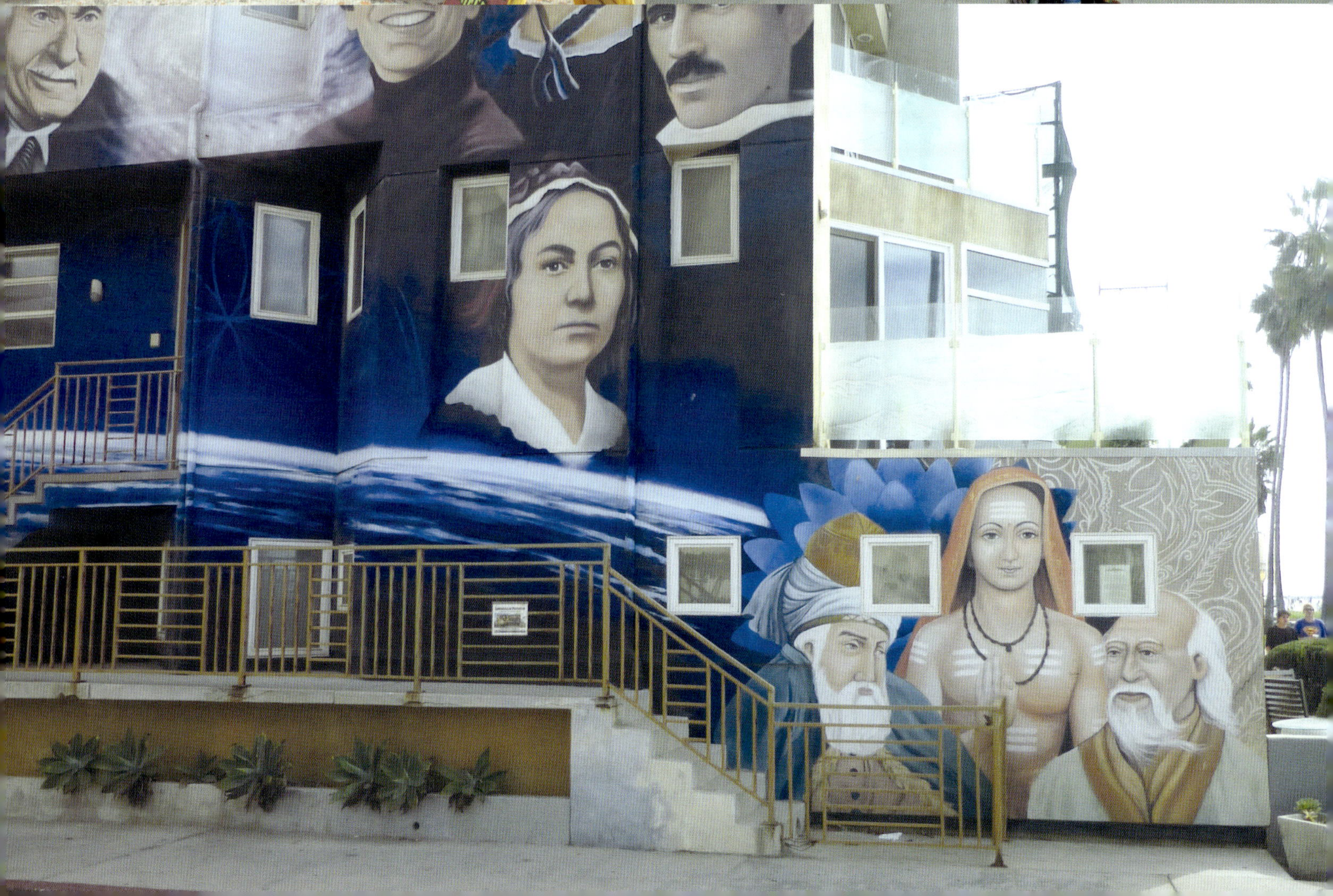

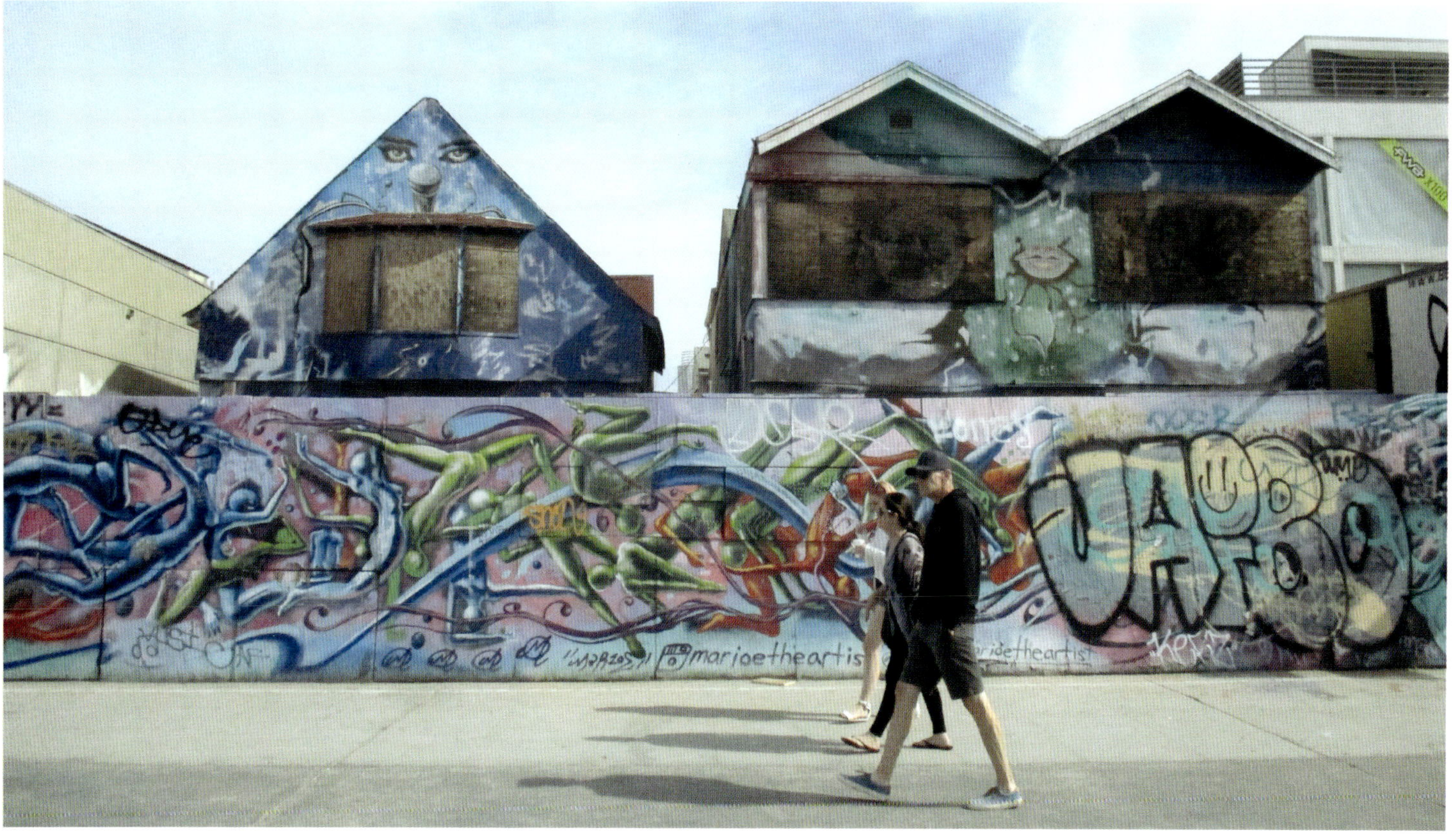

The Venice Beach Boardwalk

After the interview with Judy Baca, the authors wandered the famed Venice Beach boardwalk, full of fast-buck tourist shops and home to roller bladers and skateboarders. As you approach the waterfront of Venice Beach and walk its backstreets and ocean promenade, you begin to gain an appreciation of the variety of street artists at work here. As Baca alluded to, much of the artwork on the edge of the Pacific is throw-ups, and many of the walls are overwritten in sloppy graffiti; there are also examples of considered and thoughtful murals such as those of Levi Ponce, exploring the history of influential women.

Tucked away in the alleys just off the often messy jumble of images on the boardwalk, you'll also find examples that speak to a finer interpretation of women on the wall. One of the artists is Jules Muck, who moved to Venice Beach from the UK, whose green-tinged works explore a range of emotions between families and women.

UPPER LEFT *The Venice Beach boardwalk is a self-propelled conveyor belt of street art largely dominated by tags. In the midst of the graffiti, you get pop-up women, like this profile by "marioetheartist."*

Levi Ponce's murals (lower left) are often treated as public works, where he enlists volunteers to help paint his wall art.

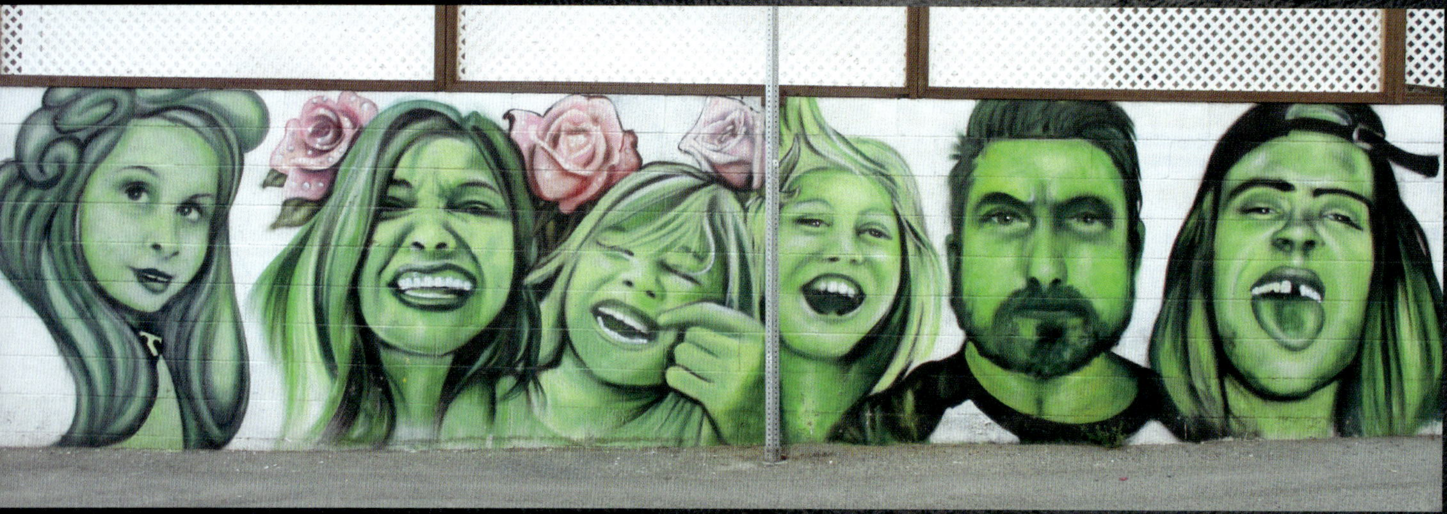
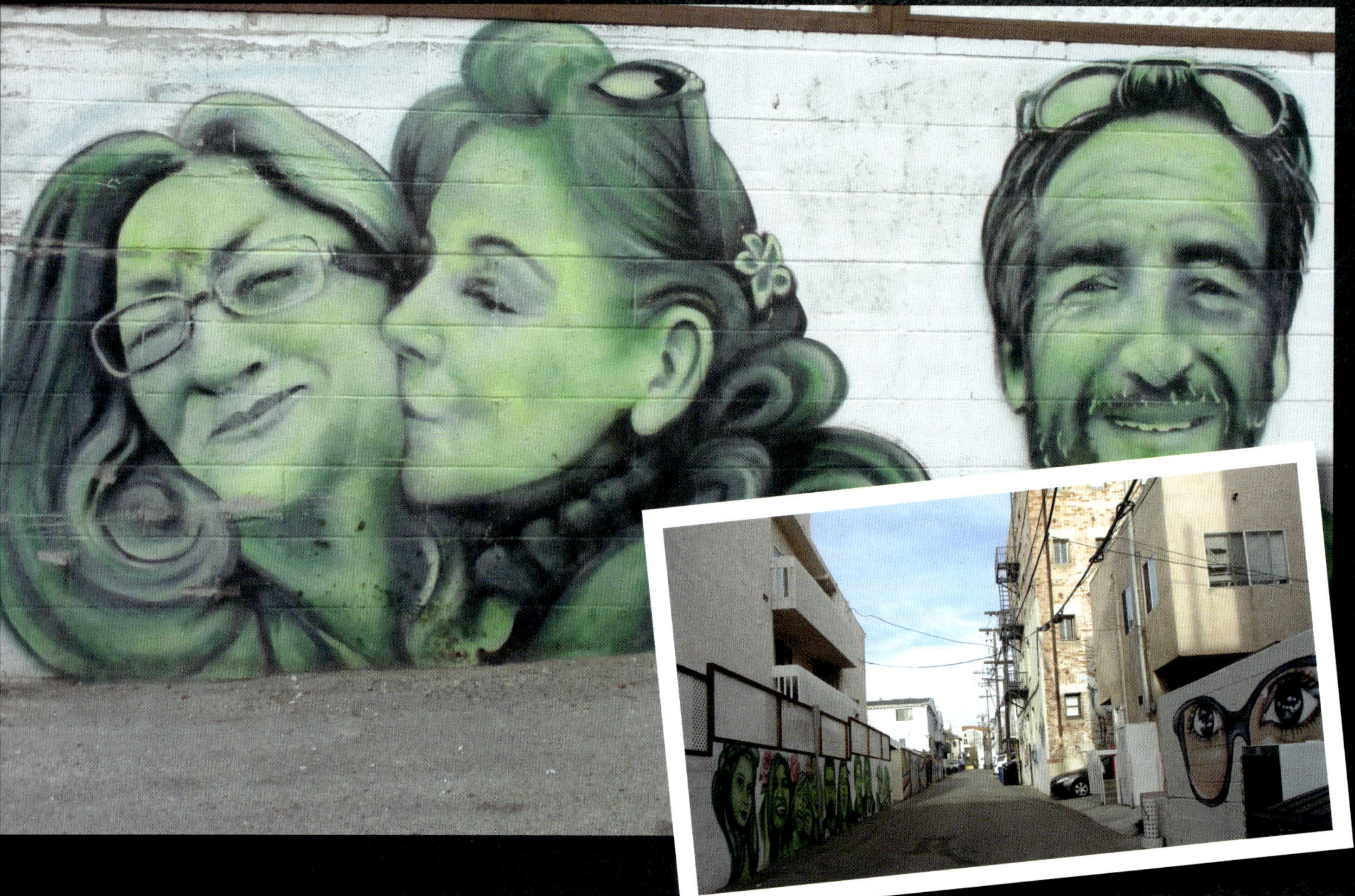

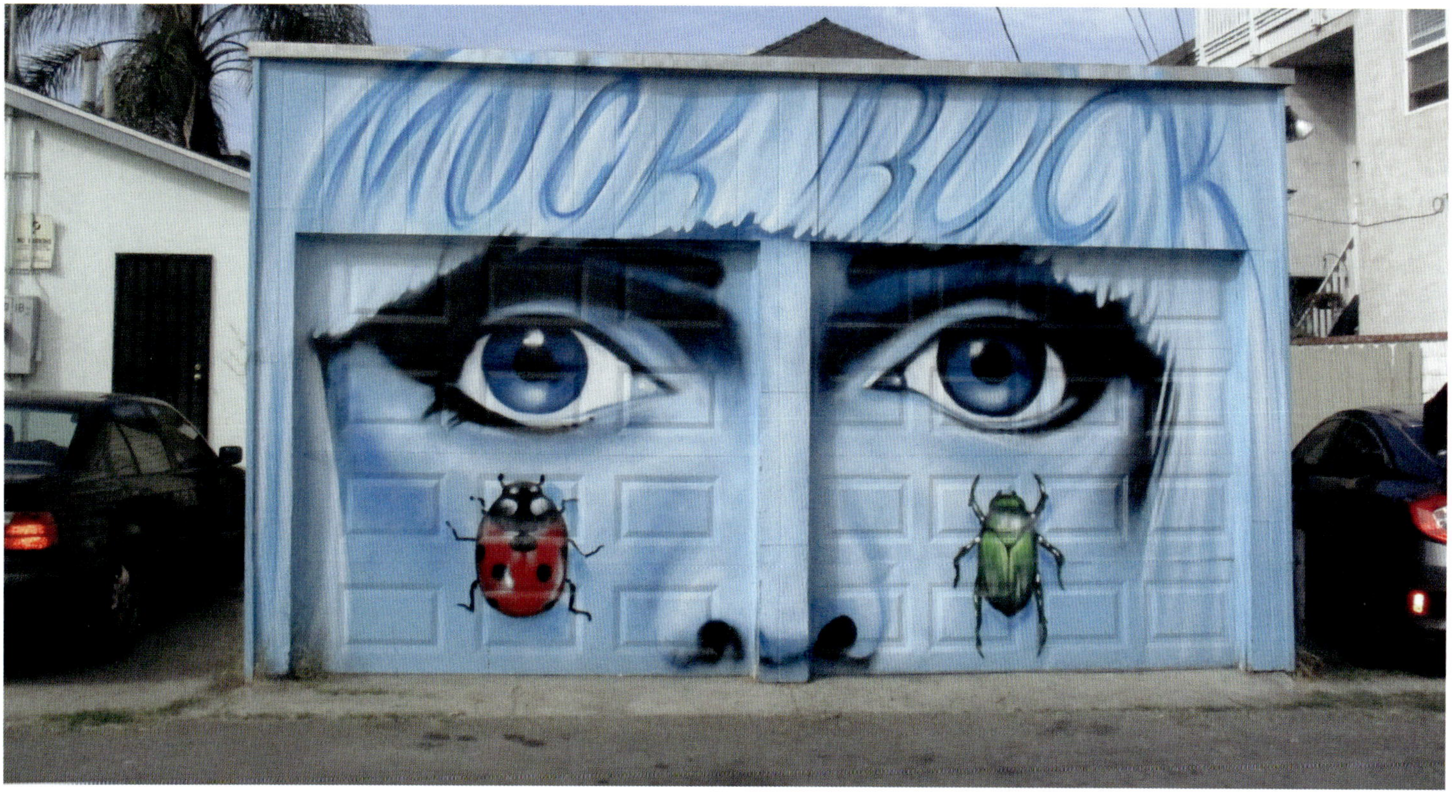

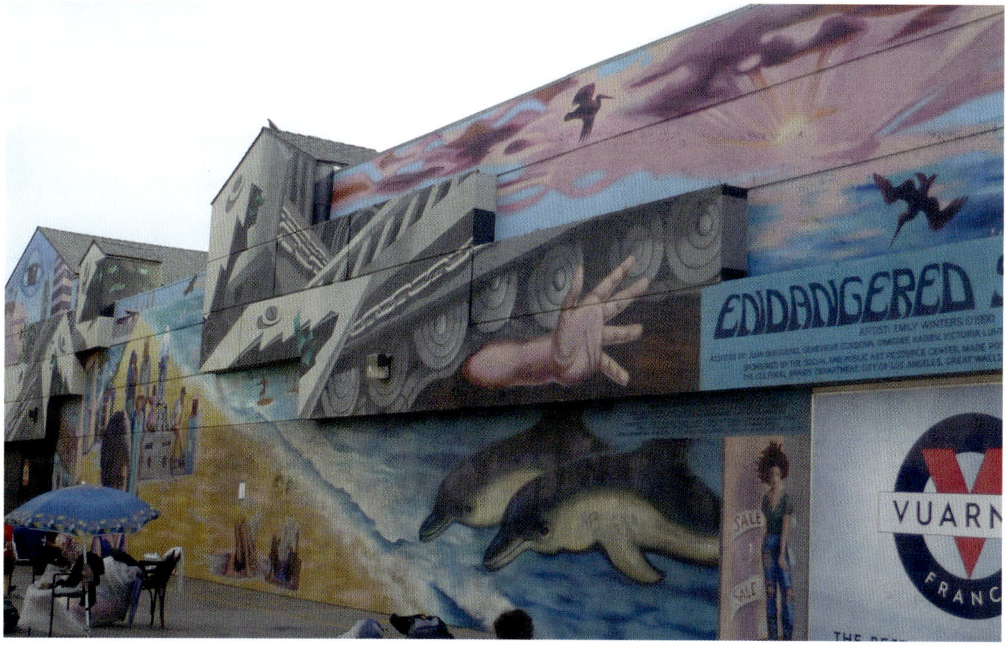

The alleyways of Venice Beach off the boardwalk are the canvases for Jules Muck, whose work brings together the intergenerational faces of Venice, tinted in green. Her other work stares at you from a garage.

LOWER RIGHT *Emily Winters is another woman wall artist who captures the street life of Venice Beach, particularly the gaps between rich and poor in her Endangered Species mural.*

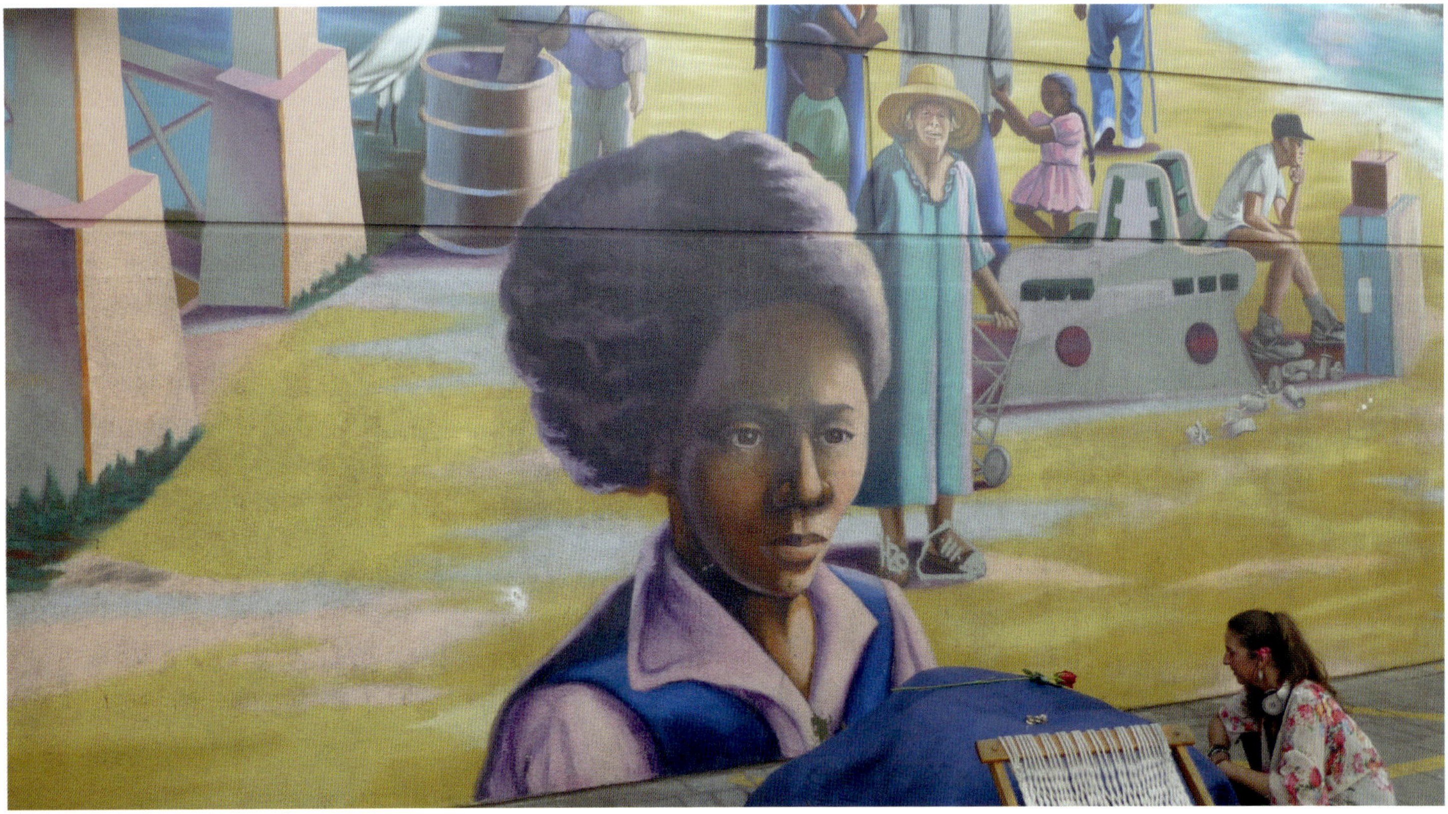

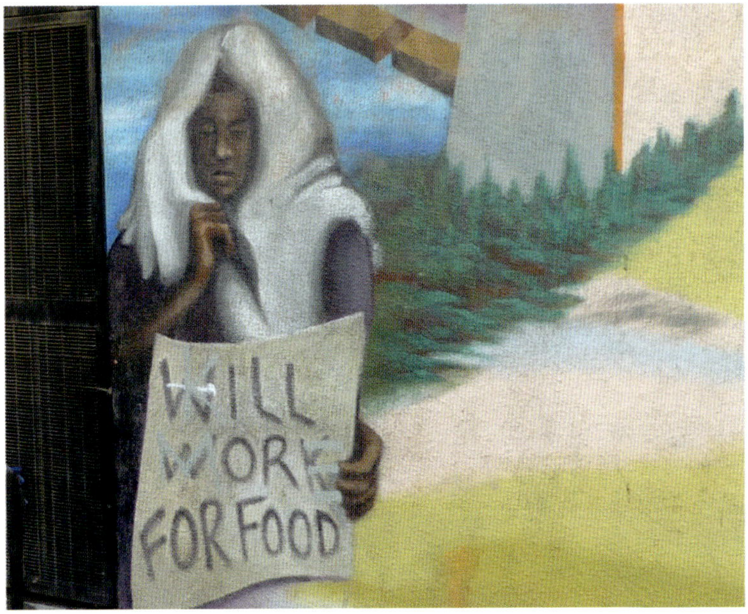

Endangered Species
by Emily Winters

Venice Beach is a wall art voyeur's visual feast and is emblematic of the California people-watching that intrigues tourists who imagine the Southern California as a hedonistic paradise where you can see movie stars cavorting in the sand like the *Bay Watch* TV series. But as anybody who has dipped their toe into the Pacific Ocean will tell you, the water can be very cold. So not all is what it seems in Venice Beach.

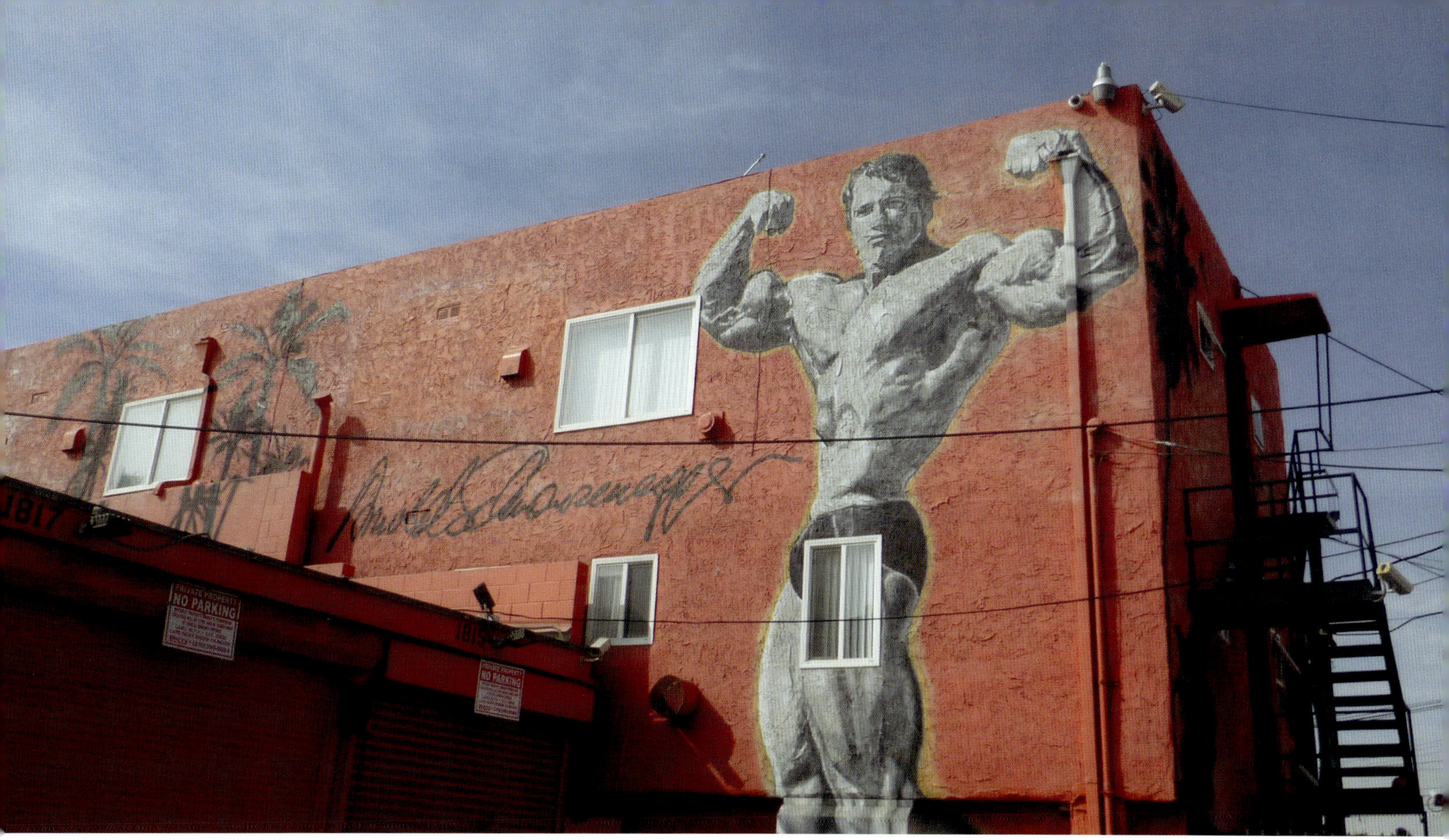

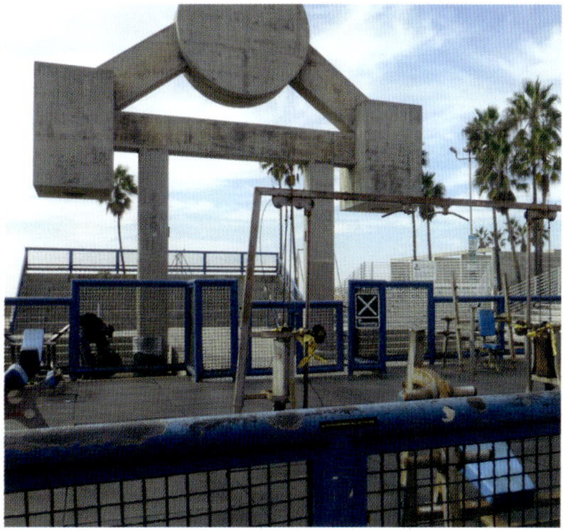

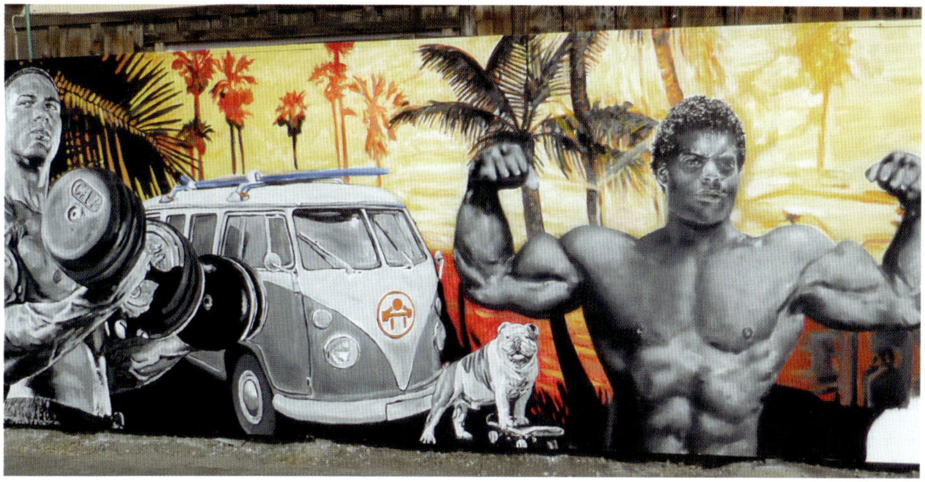

California's beachside workout culture finds expression at the renowned Muscle Beach, where pumping iron by the Pacific became an obsession to achieve the pumped-up body perfect.

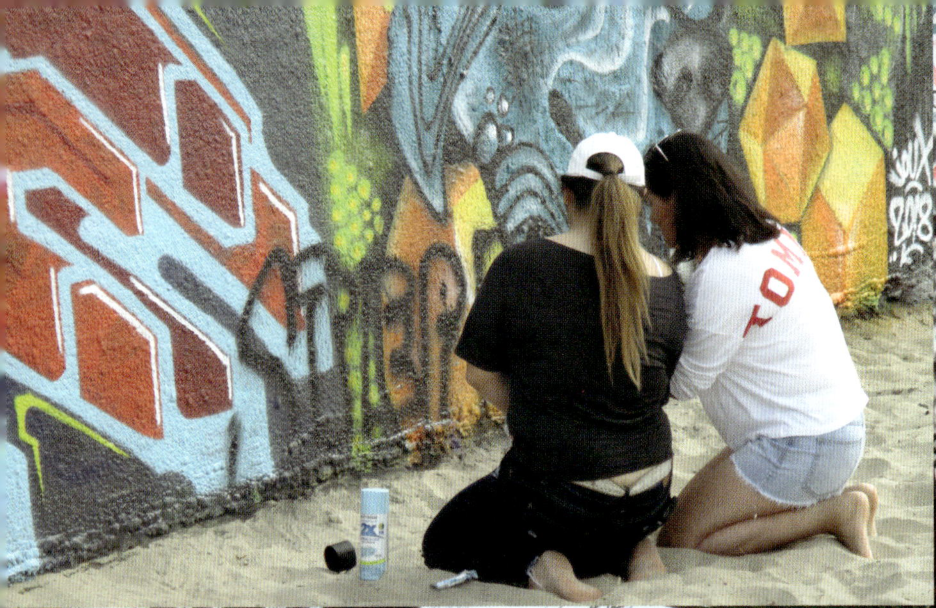
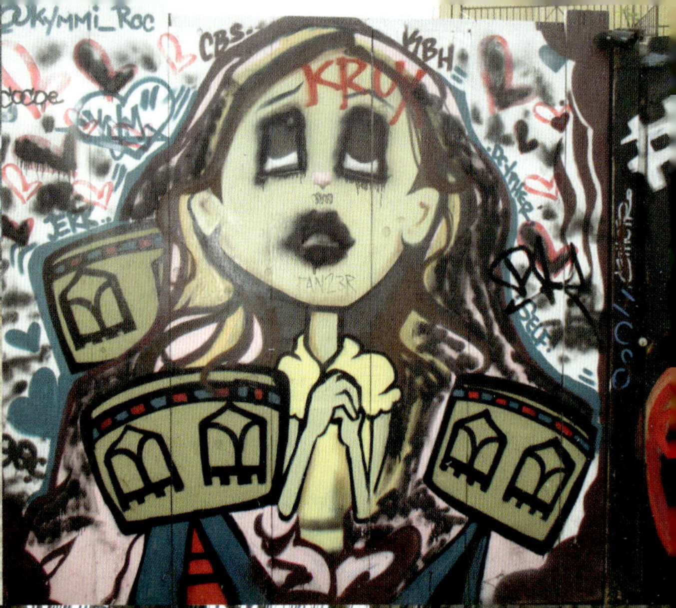
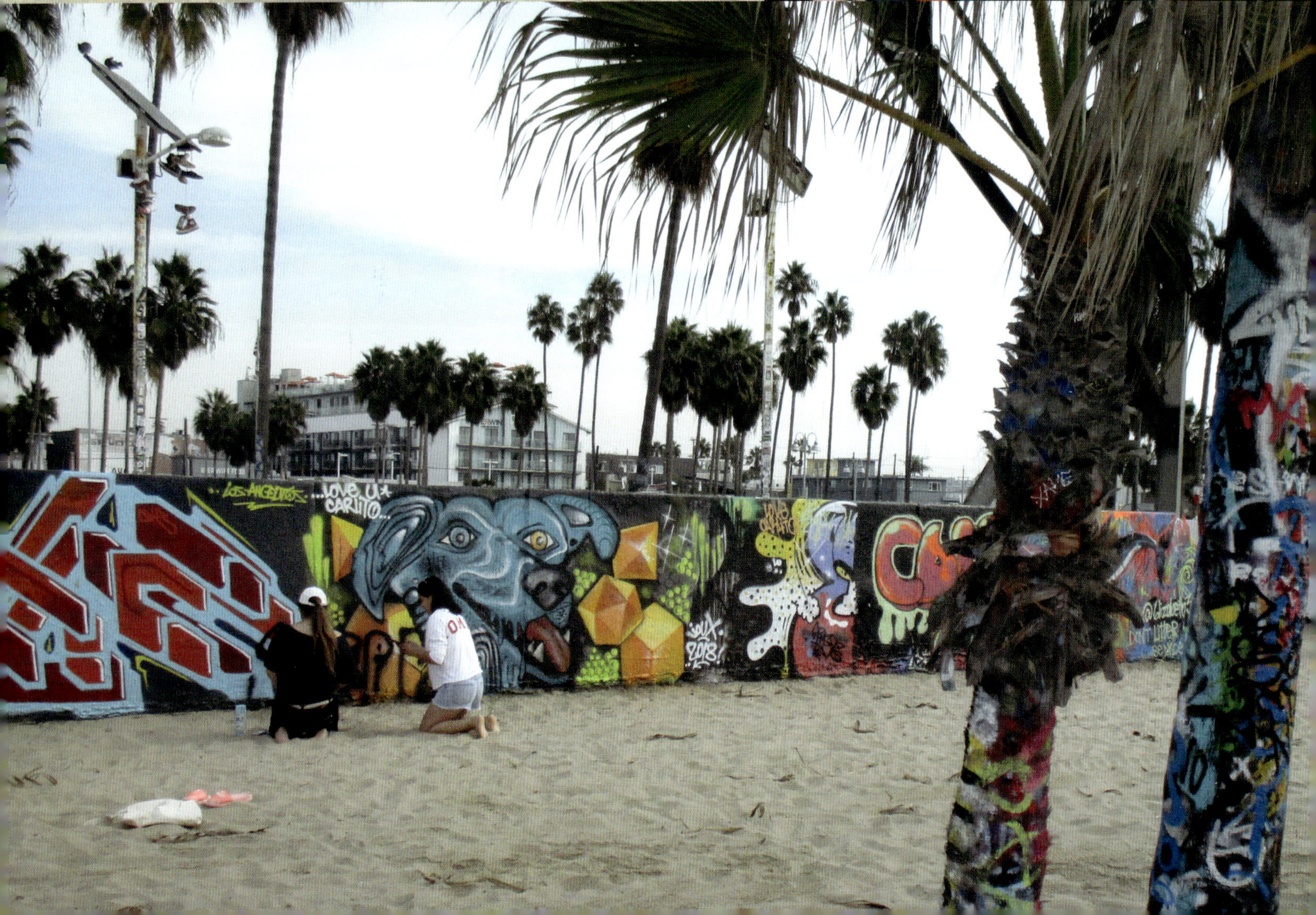

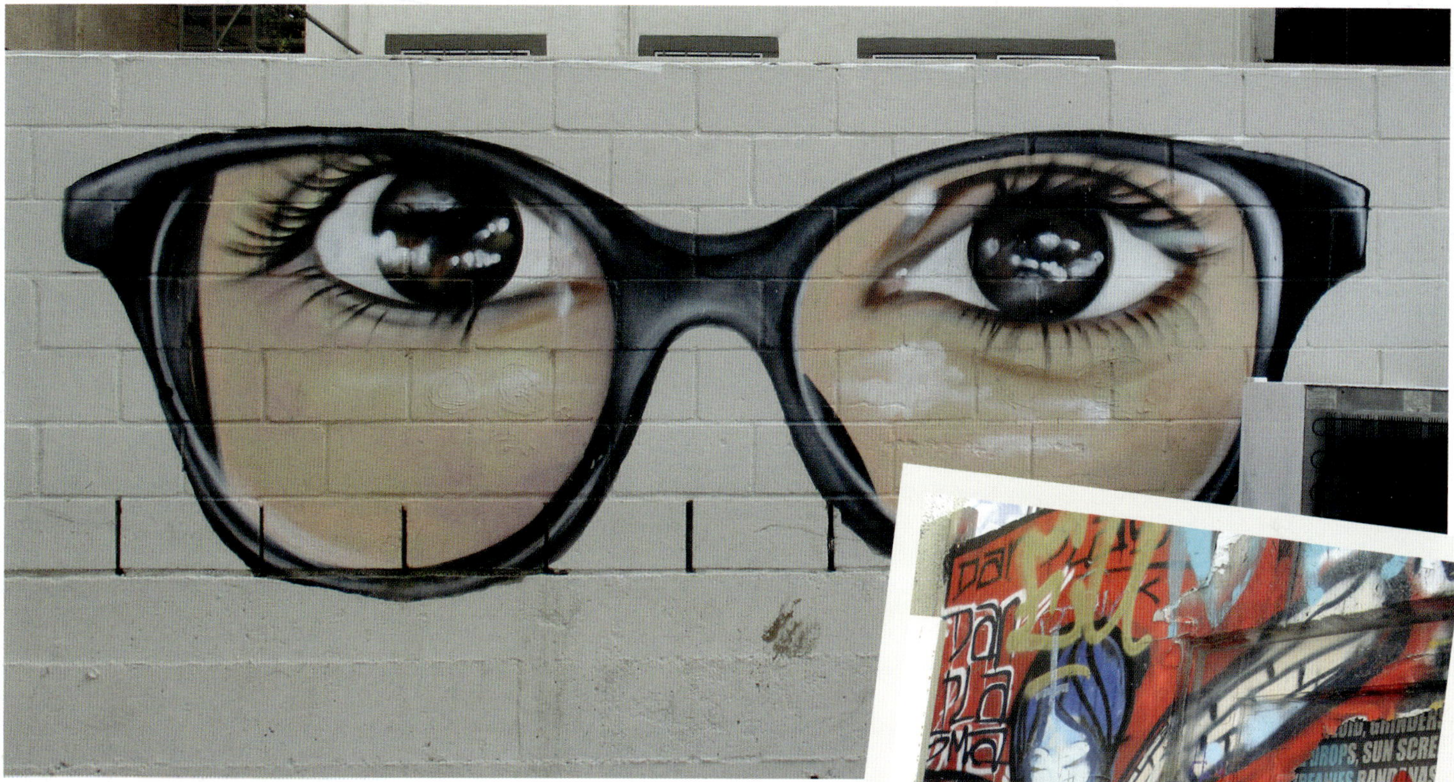

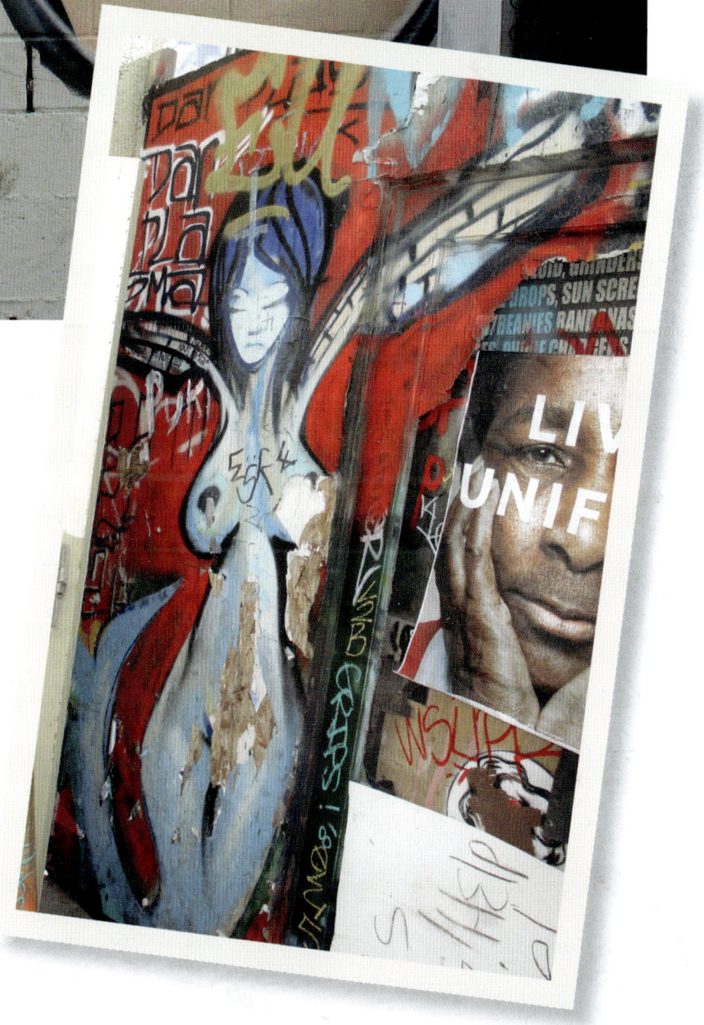

As we leave the tourists and the beach behind, we enter a new interpretation of women on the wall practiced by an artist who grew up painting the walls of her bedroom in East LA, a world away from the tourist sidewalks of Venice.

OPPOSITE *Venice Beach displays the whole gamut of wall art, from amateur tagging to throw-ups next to the boardwalk. There are even places along the boardwalk where budding women muralists can practice their own tags on an open wall near the Muscle Beach workout pen where Arnold Schwarzenegger built himself into Mr. Universe.*

Venice Beach wall art looking back at you

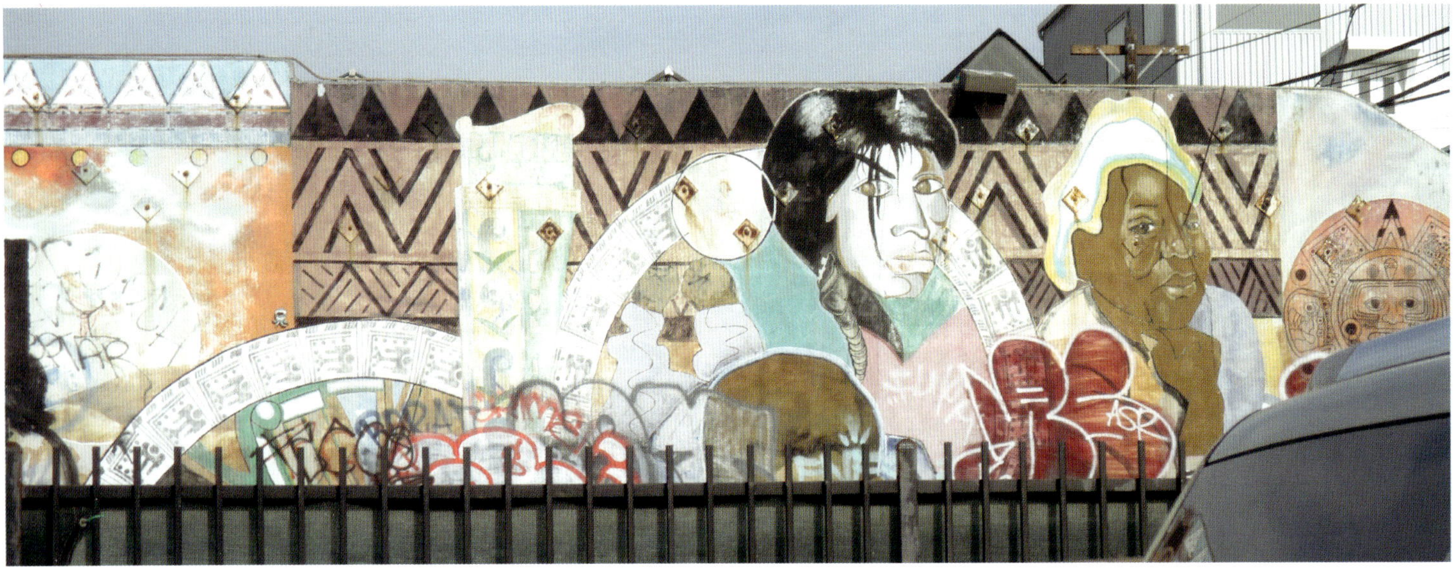
ASR

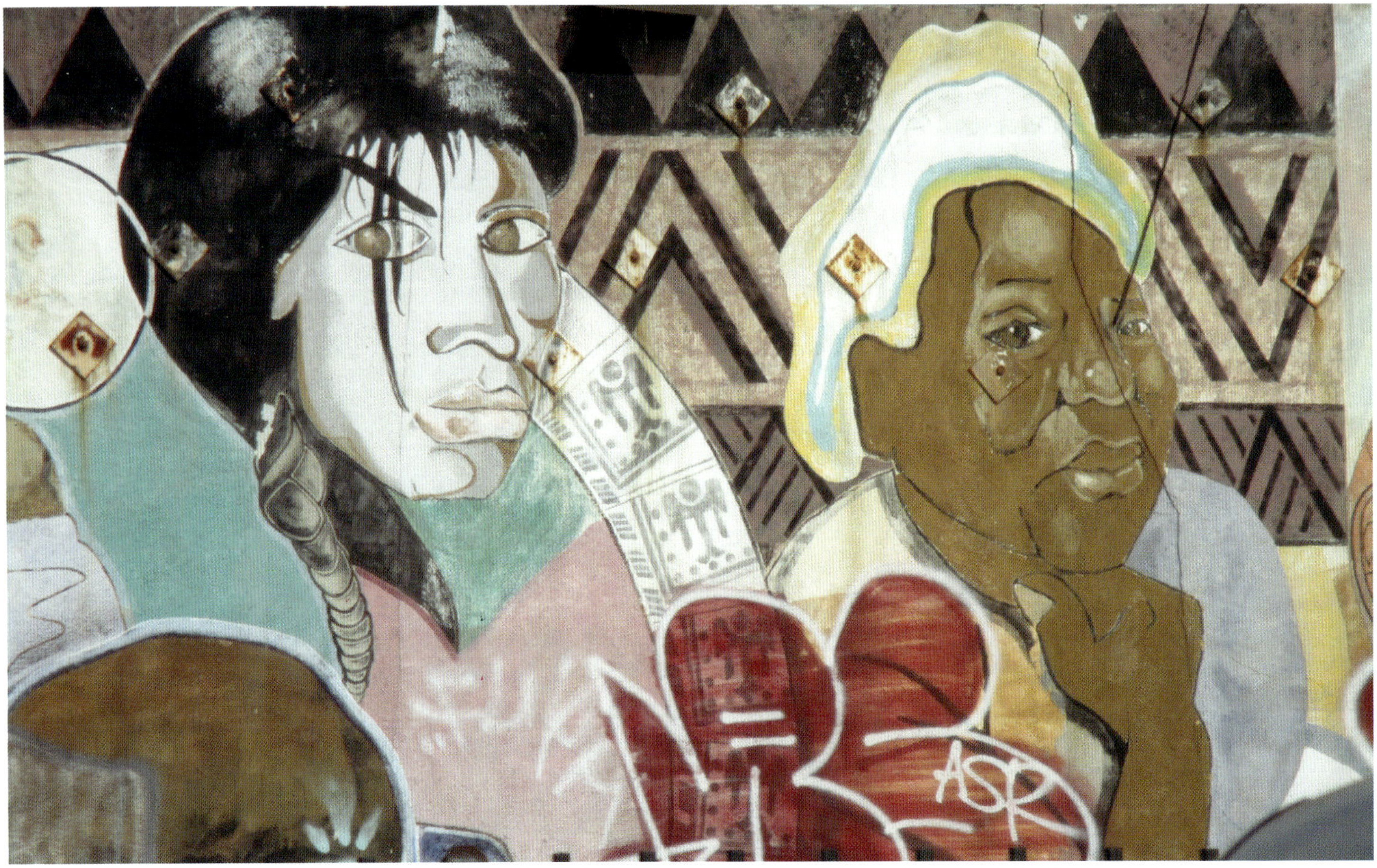
ASR

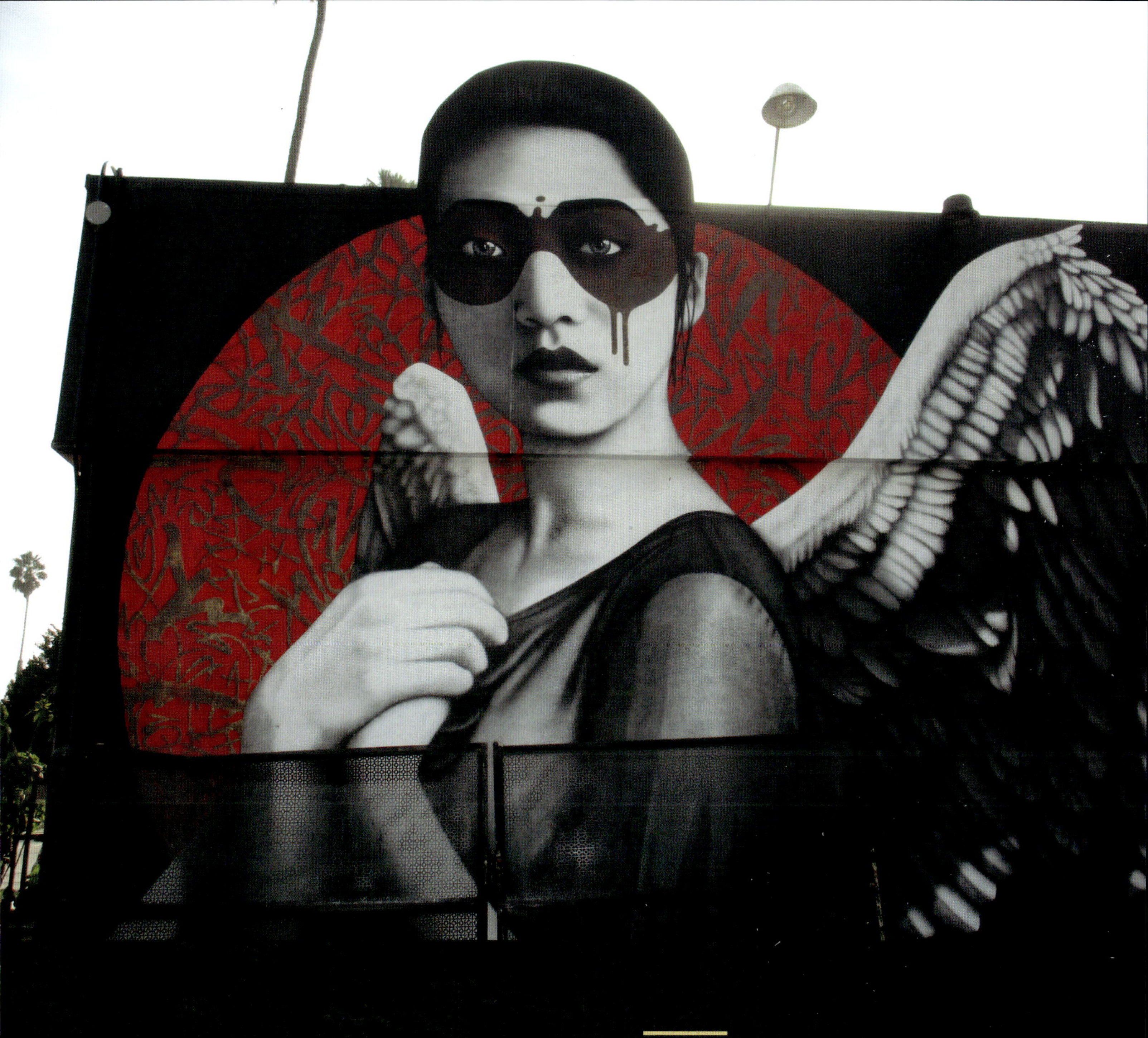

As you leave Venice you are followed by the gazes of women, like this one with a mask and angel wings that overlooks a pop-up coffee shop.

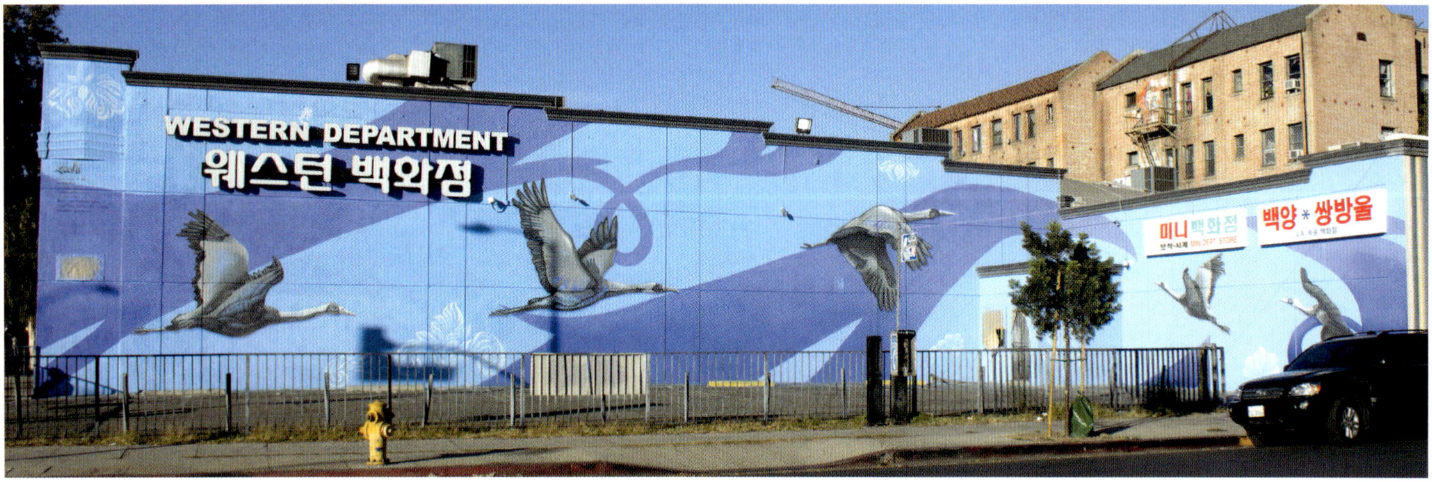

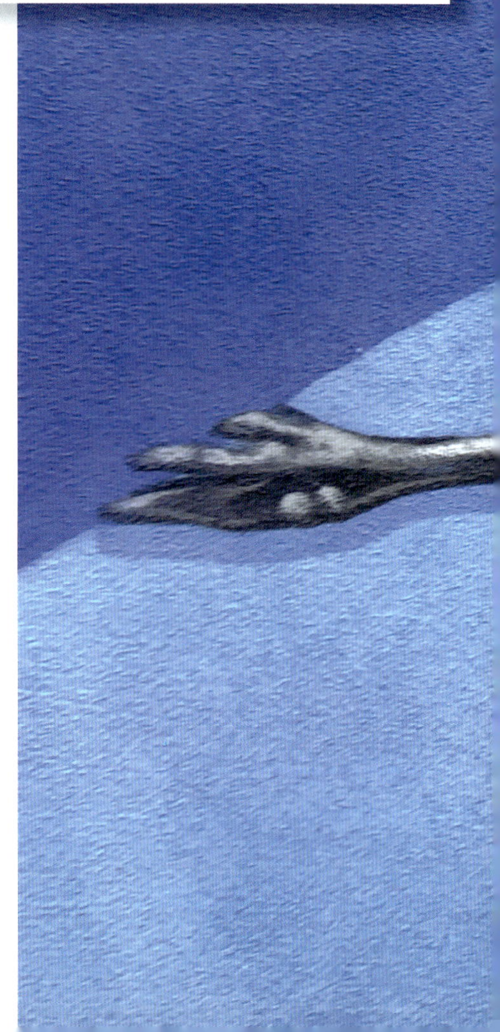

ERIN YOSHI Tapping into Nature and the Wisdom of Women Elders

Erin Yoshi was one of the artists featured in SPARC's 2018 showing of young women street artists. We met Erin at the SPARC building, sitting near a former jail cell, where she spoke enthusiastically about her past work and her current inspirations. The jailhouse was a good metaphor for her early experience as a street artist, where she risked imprisonment in Colombia while painting a mural commemorating the assassination of anti-government activists. Yoshi is relaxed and confident, and she exemplifies the new generation of women wall artists whose subject matter counters that of male street artists whose highly sexualized versions of women resemble tattoos on walls. Instead, Yoshi features older women whose wrinkled faces project an inner wisdom. Yoshi's inspiration to become a wall artist started with a dangerous passage in Colombia and is now expressed in her latest work in LA's Korea Town, reflecting a message of peace by painting flying cranes.

Erin Yoshi at work on her latest mural of a peace crane on the side of building in LA's Korea Town. Photos: Carlos Sosa

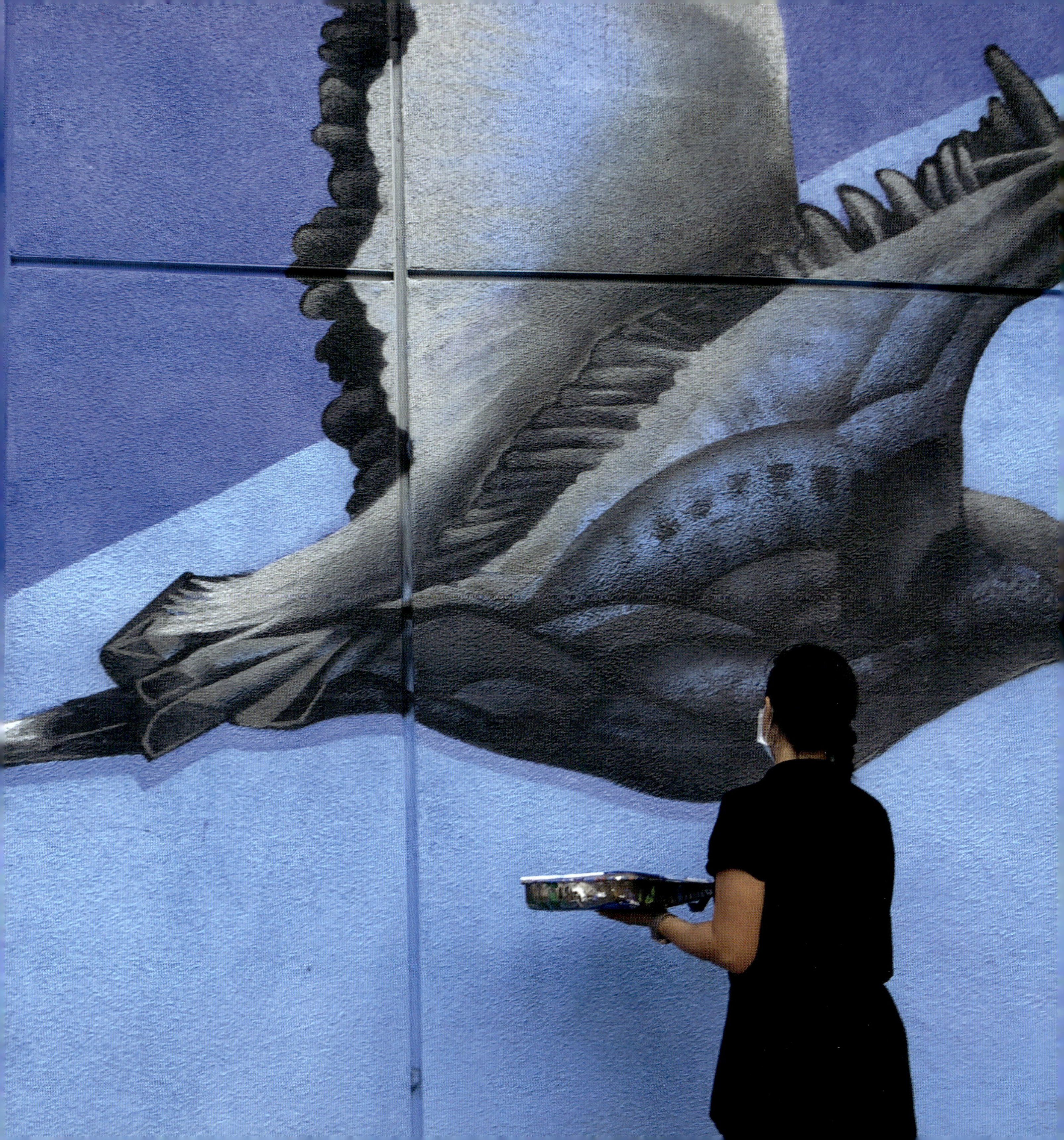

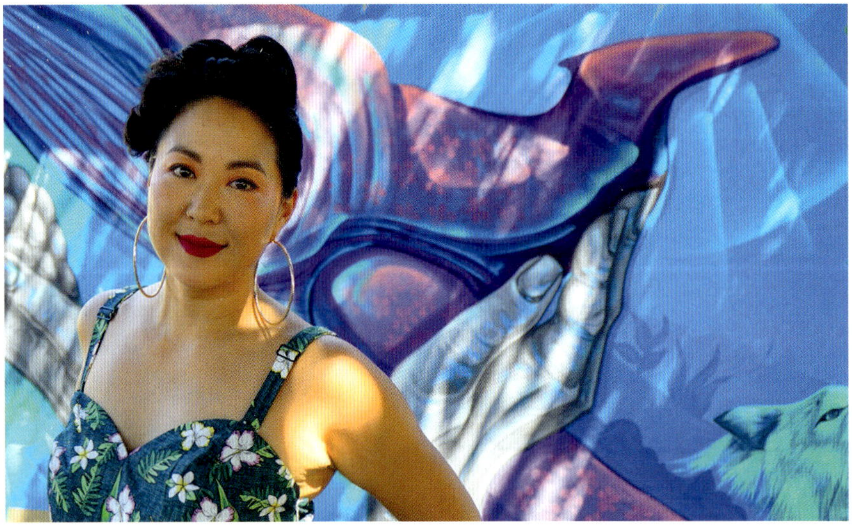

INTERVIEW WITH ERIN YOSHI

Memory to the Fallen

Erin Yoshi.
Photo: Melinda Sanchez

RIGHT *The Meta mural that Yoshi painted in Colombia at a university, commemorating the memory of assassinated political leaders. The mural launched Yoshi's career and put her in the way of danger. Photo: Pablo Serrano*

I did a project that really kicked me off into "This is what I want to do with my life." I was in my mid-twenties and I was living in Colombia at the time, and I was sponsored by this law firm, and they had the court case against the Colombian government in the Inter-American Court of Human Rights for a genocide that happened from the '80s to the first few years of the 2000s. The genocide was of the members and leaders of the leftist party called the Unión Patriótica (UP), which was a legitimate political party. [The UP was founded by FARC and the Colombian Communist Party in 1985. Colombia security forces, drug cartels, and paramilitary groups were behind the assassinations that led to the party's elimination.] So it was kind of something that at the time was still very tense to talk about. I knew I had a foreign passport that didn't give me that much freedom, but it gave me a little more leeway so I could go into cities and paint on this topic; I had so many people tell me that this is "crazy," like, "What you're doing is really dangerous."

One of the murals, which was on the front of this university, portrayed a town called Meta with a military base right next door. Nine days before I got there, a teacher had been assassinated on his way home from school. Shot in the head. They said it was because of his political alliances. They said this is very, very dangerous for you to do this. There was a military checkpoint right in front of the school while I was putting up the mural. So they were kind of watching me. I was supposed to write this dedication under the mural through my sponsor that said, "Dedicated to the victims and survivors of the Unión Patriótica." The principal called me at four in the morning the night before I finished it, and at eight in the morning, when I showed up, he said, "We can't have that here . . . you understand the context of the climate here. We love the mural on the face of the school, but we can't have those words, Unión Patriótica, because we're taking a side and we just can't do that."

So he kind of went back and forth, and I said I understand. I don't live here. You live here. There's obviously a lot of tension. I don't want to put you guys in any jeopardy. So we came to an agreement graying out the words Unión Patriótica. So you knew that there was something there, but you didn't know it was there. It was censorship, but it was completely understandable, and actually afterward we were kind of assessing its message honoring of all the victims and survivors.

The Wisc Women

> Do you know I never paint men? Occasionally if they're in a scene I'll paint a man, but I never paint them as the main forefront. Because I feel men always get the shine.

I feel as women we're a step behind in accessing opportunities, so why would I use this space that's like a billboard to give a man a shine? It's not going to happen. He might be in there, but he's not going to be at the forefront.

> I think women are muses. Women are amazing. I think their interior wisdom is what they bring to the table.

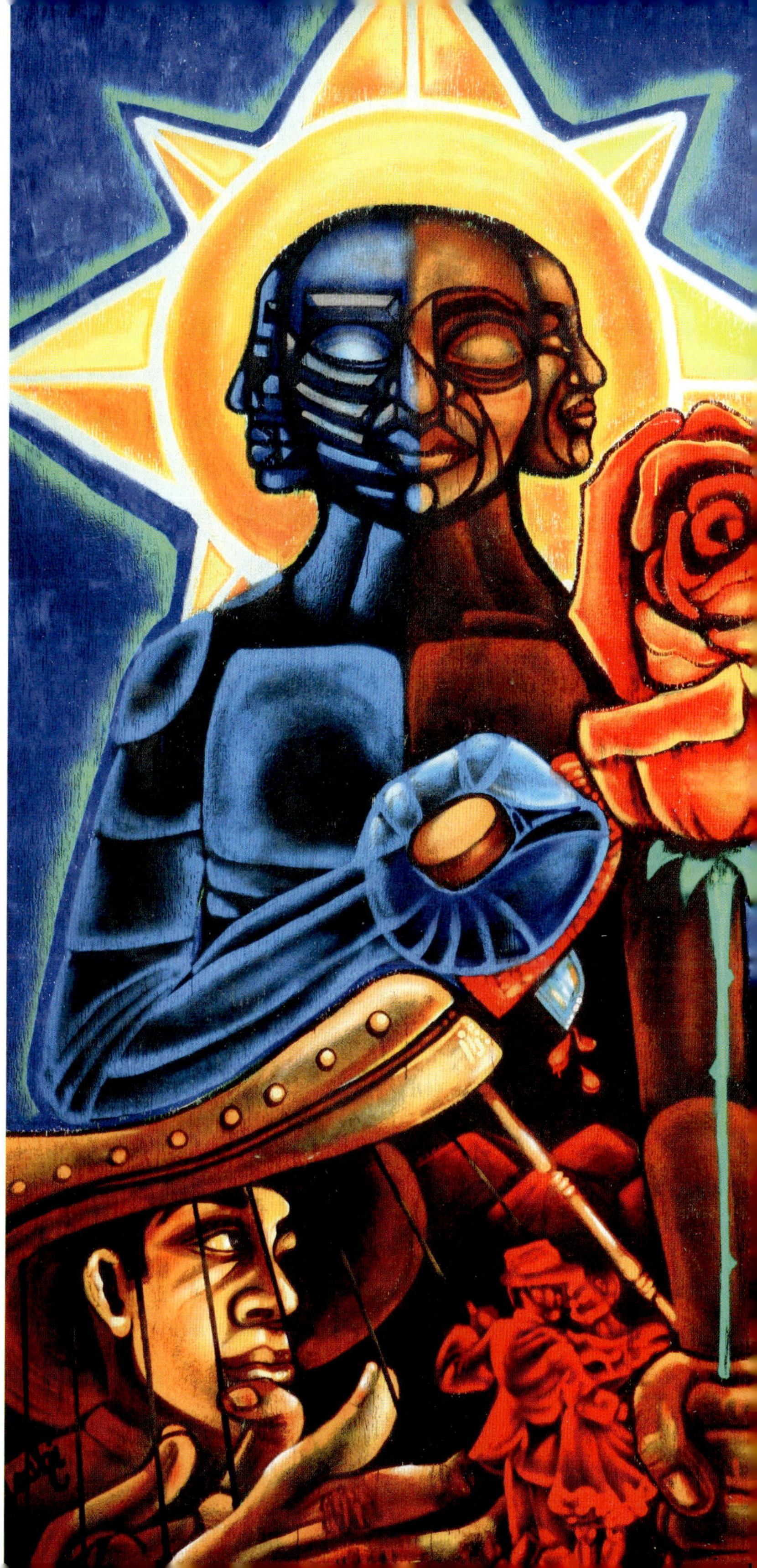

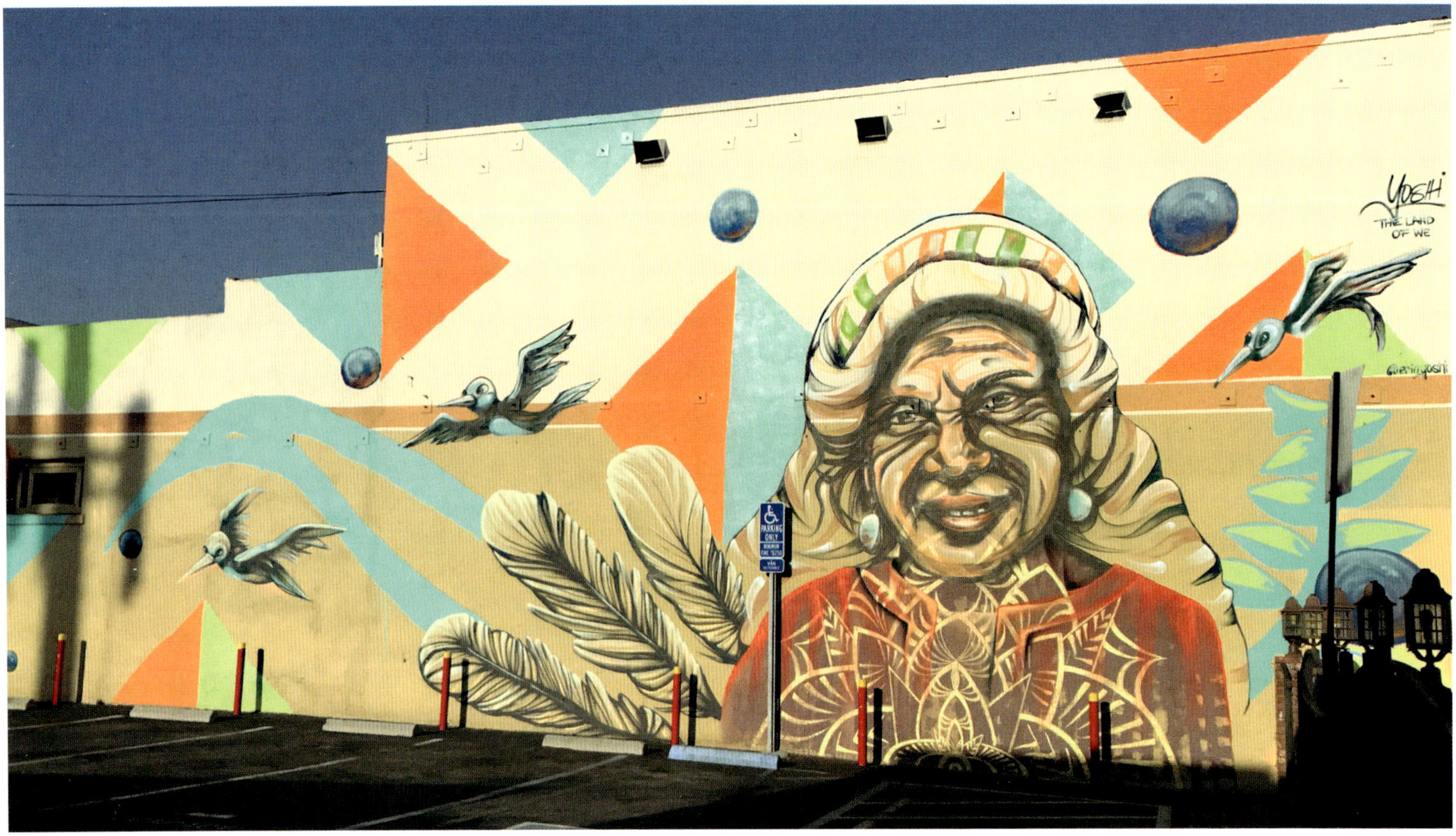

The Land of We celebrates the wisdom of elders. Mural and photo: Erin Yoshi

Light in My Eye. Mural and Photo: Erin Yoshi

I kind of came from a matriarchy in my family where women are in charge absolutely. Somehow they let the men think they're in charge, but we all know the women are running the show.

How can you not look up to women and not want to paint them? A lot of times I paint women with very crooked teeth, a lot of wrinkles, and gray hair because to me that is beautiful. I try to highlight that on the same platform of men who are highlighting the sexy women.

> A lot of the women I paint, I want to highlight elders and the women I've looked up to over the years. I feel there is real beauty and wisdom that comes with age, and when people fully accept who they are, I try to capture that through my murals.

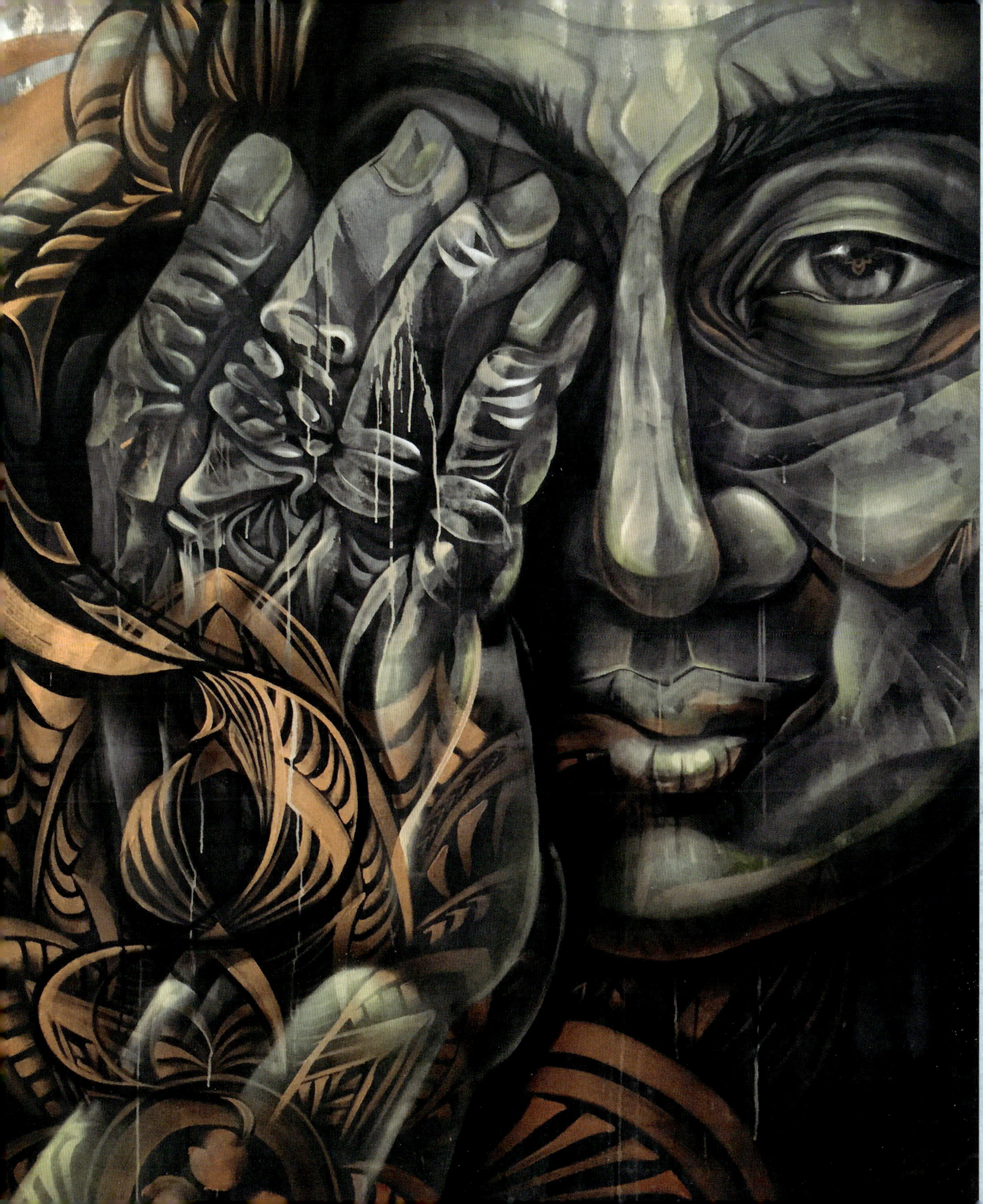

I found that when I was younger, painting murals with a lot of men, they would always paint these very sexy women, and I would kind of push back against that. I'd say, "There's other women out there." And they'd say, "You're painting, so why don't you paint them?" So that would kind of push me, so I would paint my grandma next to their sexy women, and it would change the dynamic and feel of the location, and that kind of kicked it off for me to paint women I looked up to.

I have a lot of elder crushes. I love highlighting women that really embody what it means to be a woman through grace, through the way they're loving to their community; a lot of time I highlight women who are really great community workers or give this feeling of something your own grandma would have.

I try to capture that feeling because I feel as I get older, that's what I'm trying to achieve in my own life too. I definitely love to highlight it; it does change dynamics of space. I've actually had people tell me, when I've painted like a grandma character in an office building, and they say, "Gosh, every time I'm sitting there I feel my grandma is watching me, so I feel I better behave." A lot of my murals highlight things that are not being recognized in today's modern times. I like to do things around the environment because of climate change and also around women.

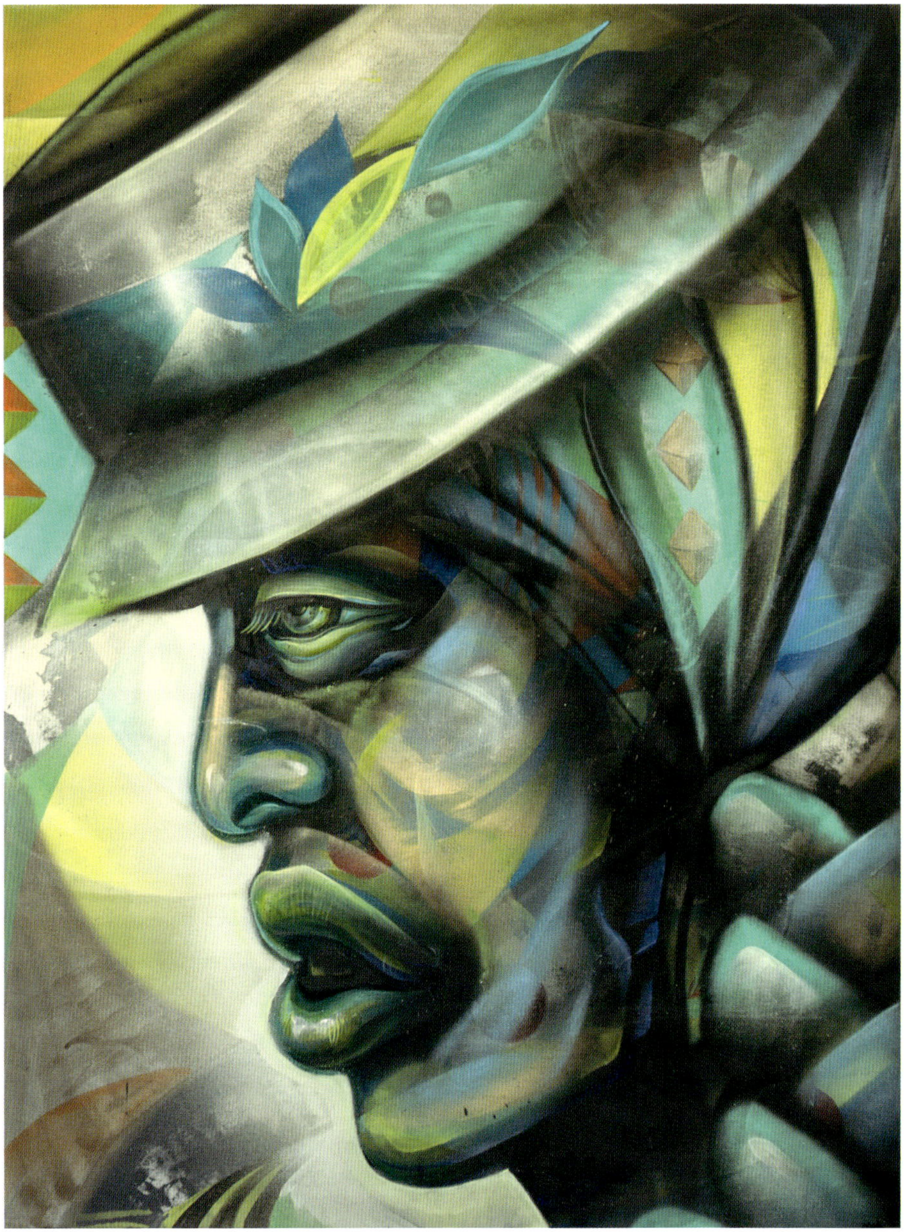

The Rise of the Protectors. Mural and photo: Erin Yoshi

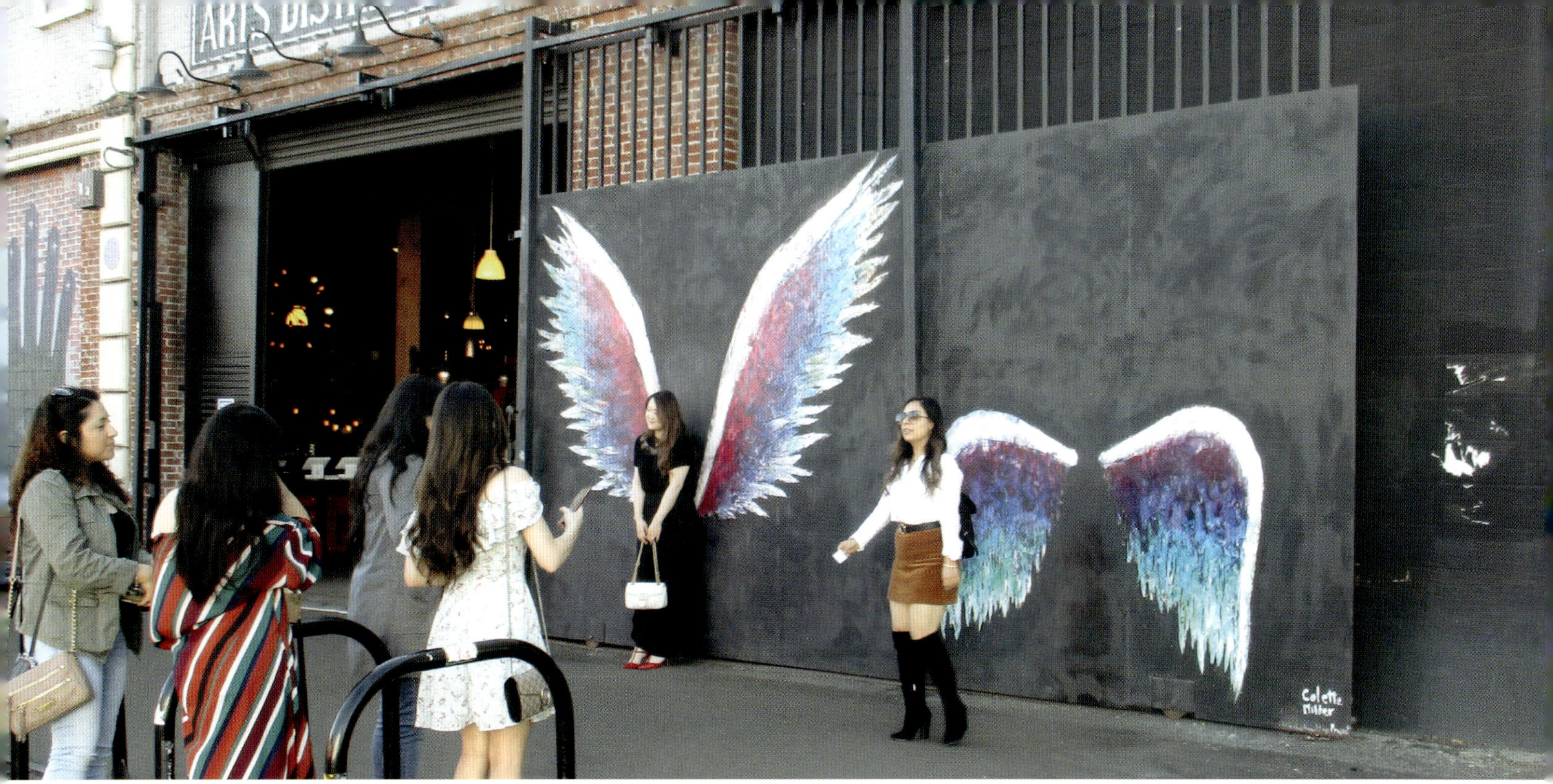

COLETTE MILLER: The Better Angel in All of Us

Colette Miller's Angel Wings have become the subjects of selfies from visitors to the LA Arts District.

Unlike Judy Baca, who has a strong political view in her wall art, and Erin Yoshi, whose vision now encompasses saving the natural world and features elderly women, our next wall artist has taken off on a journey inspired by wings. Colette Miller is known through her Global Angel Wings project. She works out of a studio near downtown LA in a ramshackle house stacked with her large-scale canvases. Miller emerges from her studio in stiff, paint-covered jeans, the living portrait of an artist at work. Colette Miller rocketed to recognition following social media postings of her work by celebrities who posed for selfies in front of her Angel Wings. Her work is self-described as "interactive street art" because people stand in front of the wings and usually take selfies; the interaction with the wings becomes part of the viewer experience, which can be uplifting.

When you first encounter the large wings, you can understand why Miller rejects the notion of being labeled a "feminist" wall artist. In some ways she represents an apolitical view of street art that is a means to communicate a highly personal vision. When we caught up with Colette Miller, she was about to travel to Dubai to paint her Angel Wings on a window inside the world's tallest building.

INTERVIEW WITH COLETTE MILLER
Humanistic Wall Art on the Wings of an Angel

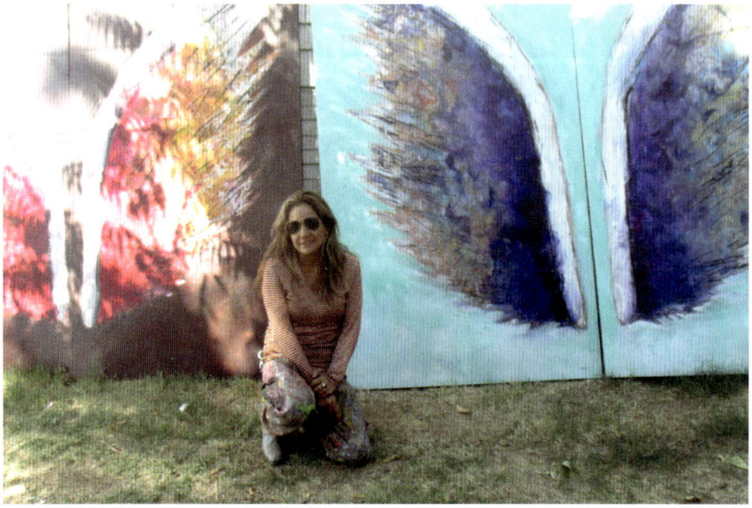

I try not to leave a piece until I feel a certain kind of love for it. That's when I call it finished. Particularly for the Global Angel Wings project, my inspiration was reminding humanity that we're and can be the angels of this earth. This was the Global Angel Wings' original core purpose.

I never had the same feminist slap in my face where I had to go, "I'm a woman and need to do this too!" I grew up with parents who never made me aware or hindered because I was a female or weaker. I just saw myself as human, and if my art was successful or it was good, then it would be not about whether I was a male or a female.

I think we are human first and might be in a female form or male form, but I never felt I had something to prove because I was a female. I already thought I was there.

Universal Images

What has happened with the Global Angel Wings project, and this has been discussed with some of my clients, is that it is a unification image that crosses politics, religions, poor, rich, male, female; it's kind of like a universal symbol that reminds us of our humanity first. I want to do the wall in Israel/Palestine—where both groups are standing back to back with their wings, and maybe I can film it by drone. I'm trying to organize that to remind us of our humanness and our differences.

The Outlaw Days

In the early days when I first got to LA, I did it all rogue and subversive, and I did these native American animals like a buffalo with a handprint on it. And some Native American images I did with a friend of mine named Becca who was another street artist. That was the very early days in LA, and it was illegal. The first few pieces were anonymous—I didn't sign them.

Colette Miller's humanistic approach to her wings goes beyond sexual identity politics.

With the Global Angel Wings, I felt like I had this vision come to me of wings everywhere about the divinity of humanity. The divine self. So I acted on it, and it was illegal, but the very first pair got very popular.

There was a street art festival; there was a line right away. Some developer downtown had seen them, and he gave me permission to put them up on Main Street. And then this LA photographer took pictures of all the politicians in front of the wings, and then it was on the cover of *Downtown News* and he got a show of his photographs. And then I started getting commissions . . . it was all organic and word of mouth. The original Angel Wings paintings were illegal.

I also did a pair in East Harlem. All these ballerinas took photos with the wings, which were not legal. It's under a bridge and gets graffiti around it. New York City wanted to preserve them, and they painted over the graffiti and left the wings. That was huge compliment. I did a pair in Baltimore after the Freddie Gray riots that were illegal too, but now they're mostly commissioned, mostly requested. I'll do the wings sometimes for money or commissioned prices and expenses—if an area is really destitute or impoverished.

I will paint the wings under my own auspices or use monies from some of the products I sell. I also put aside money for some of the more charitable locations like orphanages or the slums of Africa. Those are actually my favorite to do.

Men vs. Women Street Artists

I don't think female artists are better than male artists or vice versa. I think women have gone down different paths in the past, and their voices are becoming more relevant and probably even more peaceful. I don't think about someone if they're a female or a male first. I think about whether I like it or find the art successful or moving.

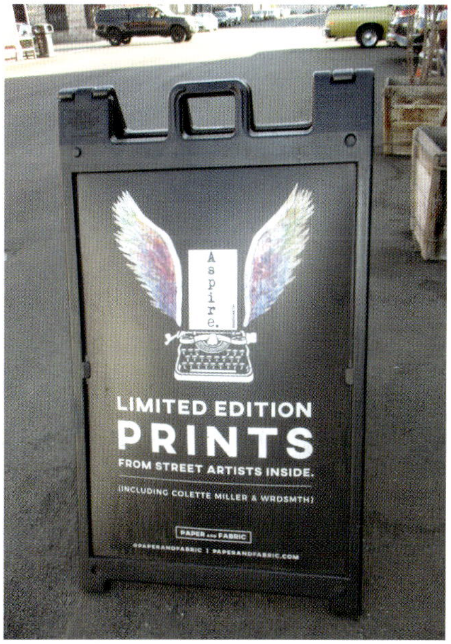

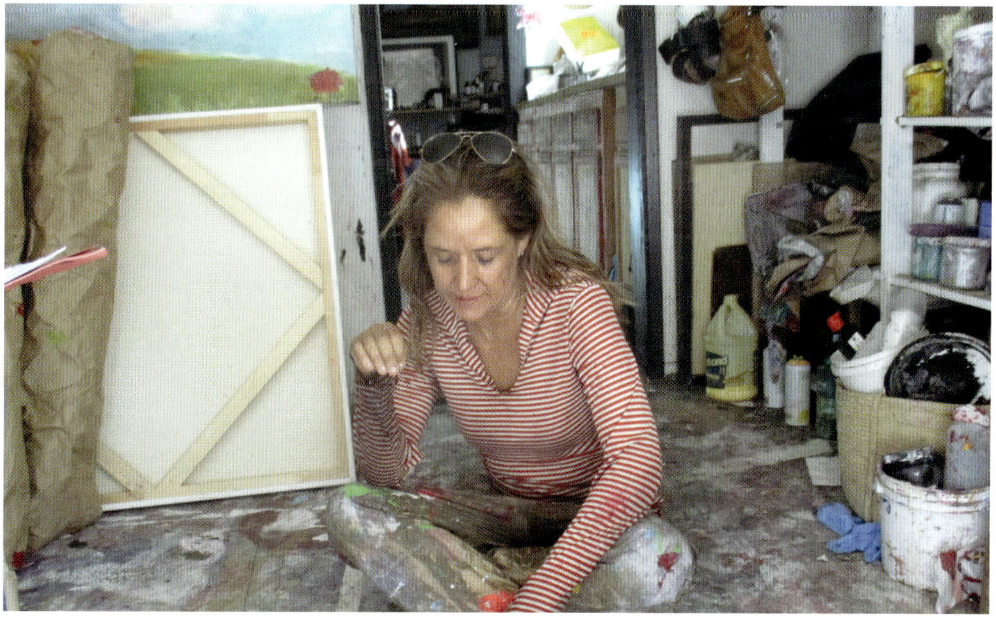

I know some girls who say, "Women are warriors too!" Of course, they're warriors. We always were warriors. Why do we have to say it?

I always knew that, so I just don't have that same battle to fight. You know it's not my battle. It might be a battle for some other people, but it's not my particular one. I just grew up with pretty liberal parents, I guess. They never stressed, "You're pretty" or whatever when we were little. I was basically raised when those things weren't that important. What was important was integrity and authenticity and traits from both sexes. Good traits.

Why Wall Art Is a Male Vocation

I think that a lot or most wall art is made by men because sometimes it's at night you do it if it's illegal, which it is sometimes, and maybe some males are more aggressive like in sports.

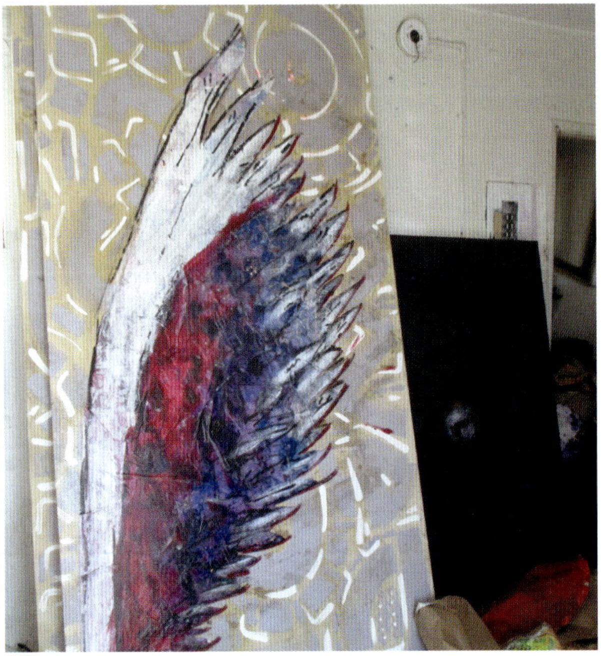

They're cultured to be a little bit more assertive, and I don't know if it's nature that males will go out and become soldiers first, because street art is kind of like the "soldiers of art." They're the troops on the ground. You put yourself out there. You don't get paid most of the time. It's an act of your voice. And often it's anonymous. I guess males might be cultured to do that more. You know, like they play more rugged sports or something. Because I think street art is a little rugged. There's a lot of climbing; there's a lot of nighttime work.

Social Media Fame

I've had some famous people in front of my wings—like Halle Berry, Annie Lennox, Gerald Butler, Meghan Markle [the Duchess of Sussex]. The coolest ones always tag me, like Halle Berry tagged me, and Annie Lennox. I know how busy they are, and I'm always humbled when they do. Like Gerald Butler did and it's cool. I don't have hashtags on my wings. I just have a feather that says Global Angel Wings project. That's like my signature.

When I started, I really didn't have Instagram; I didn't do Twitter. I did Facebook for friends, but when I did the wings, I intentionally wanted them to be human sized so people think, "It's us. It's always been us." It's up to us to step up to the plate and be the good on this planet. It was an activation piece. And because of technology with smart-phones and cell phones, that just jump-started it. It wasn't intentional, and it's been a really good thing. It put the project on steroids.

Social media can really be used for the good. I don't think it's just selfies. A lot of people doing interactive art now have a hashtag.

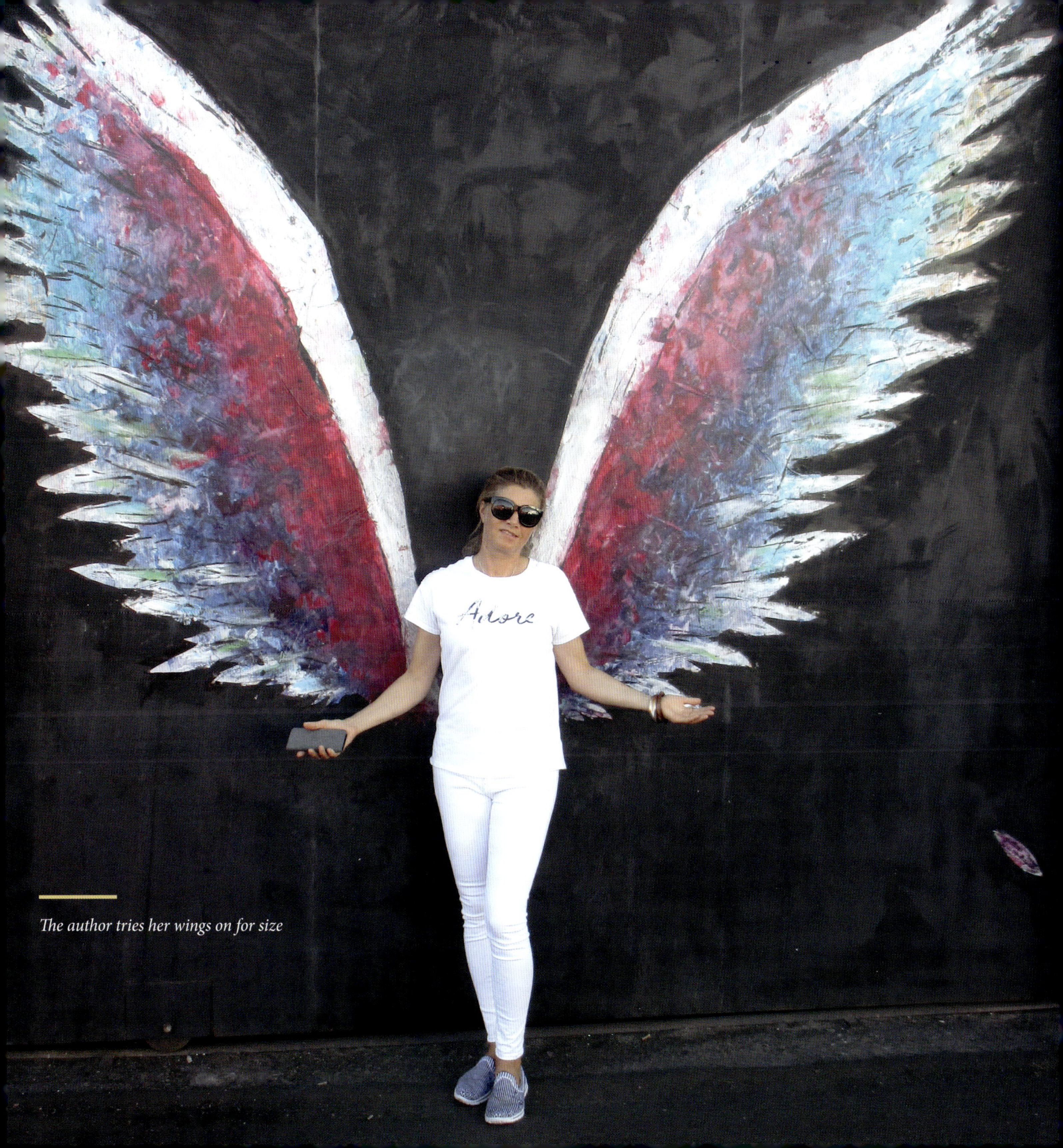

The author tries her wings on for size

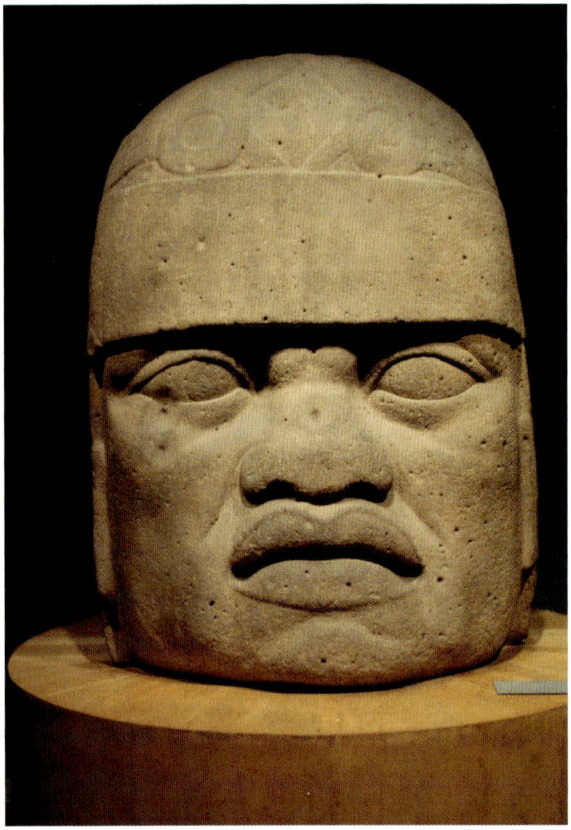

Next Stop: Mexico

We now strap on our wings and fly due south to Mexico, which perhaps laid the foundations for modern muralism with strong connections to California. Mexico's wall art of women is politically charged while at the same time incorporating the symbols of its ancient past, when the Olmecs, Zapotecs, Aztecs, and Mayans built great civilizations long before the arrival of Europeans. Today wall artist collectives work their magic with women subjects in the long shadows cast by the Big Three.

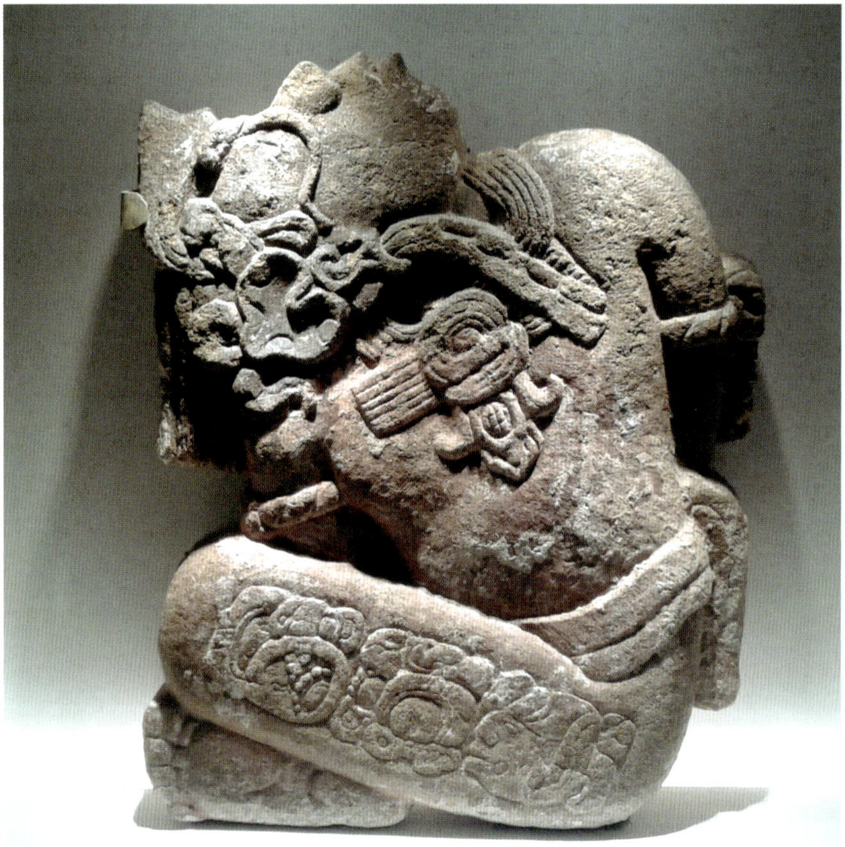

Olmec colossal head, San Lorenzo, Veracruz, Mexico, 1,200–600 BCE. Photo: Gary Lee Todd, PhD, Creative Commons CC0 1.0 Universal Public Domain Dedication

A bound and captured slave carved in stone, from the Museum of Anthropology, Mexico City

3

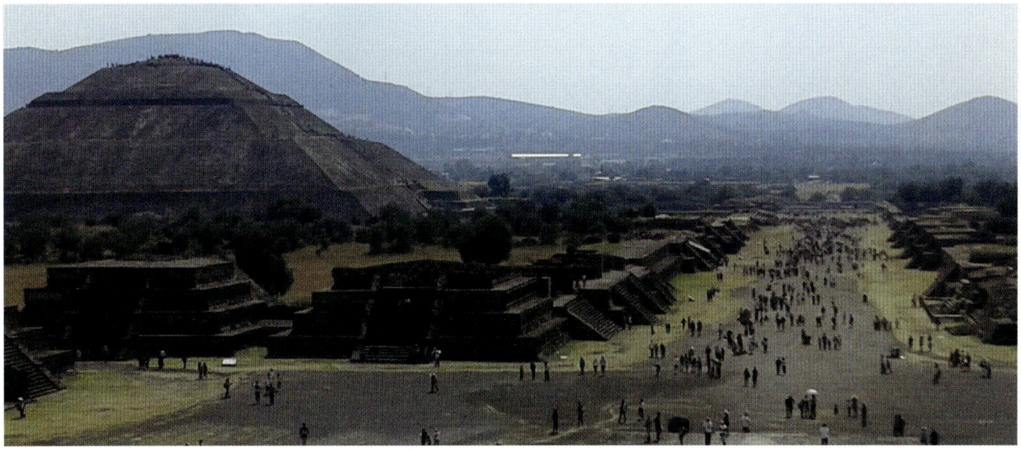

Teotihuacan pyramids outside Mexico City, predating the Aztecs by a thousand years. The main road was called the Street of the Dead.

NEW WORLD ARTISTS

Mexican Monumentalism and Animism

The Mexico most people know today was the cradle of advanced civilizations that gave the world spectacular art and influenced wall artists around the world.

Wall art was sculptural in Mesoamerica civilizations, where life was dependent on corn crops, rainfall, and the power of unforgiving celestial gods. There is a monumentalism about this art reflected in the stairstepped artistic symmetry of the ancient pyramids. The Mesoamerican cultures, with deep roots in the natural world, are found in the stone carvings of animist gods on pyramid terraces and the quotidian objects like gourds and pots, which assumed the form of sacred animals like jaguars and serpents. From this rich soil of visual symbolism, springs Mexico's impressive portfolio of muralism, which reached its apex in the works of Rivera, Orozco, and Siqueiros. The giants of Mexican muralism painted with bold colors, often confronting images and an unmatched structure and vision to convey their political messages. That unparalleled artistry and craftsmanship is found in the astonishing sculptural works carved eons ago by the pre-Columbian Olmecs, whose giant heads made from basalt boulders demonstrated a preternatural sense of design and execution.

The Olmec civilization's sculptural sophistication found much different expression in Mayan and Aztec cultures. The Aztecs enshrined the power of rulers and their shamanic priests, who held the power over life and death. In the Aztec world, women, men, and children were sacrificed on stone altars to appease the sun god Huitzilopochtli, who kept darkness at bay.[1] The Mayans also had their sacrificial rituals, where evidence lay entombed underwater in the cenotes (underwater grottoes) of the Yucatán Peninsula.[2] There is also a tradition both in the Aztec and Mayan civilizations to paint walls and pottery with intricate designs and carve stories of conquest out of stone.

This monumentalism is also found in South America, where the Incas built their civilization in the cradle of the Andes. These are lands dominated by a restless earth, prone to earthquakes and volcanic eruptions both in politics and artistic vision.

Tapping into this rich historical vein, today's wall art in Mexico, Central America, and South America reflects a tradition of the mythical and legendary stories ingrained in the faces of its inhabitants and painted onto its walls, particularly in the depiction of women and the staple crop of these ancient peoples—corn.

Spanish colonialism and religious imperialism never quite took root in its rigid, Gothic form in the New World. This blend of Catholicism and pantheistic and animist beliefs is still found today in places like Oaxaca (wuh HAA kuh) in Mexico, where locals celebrate the lives of dead as though they are still living among us. The holiday's origins may be disputed by historians, but the Day of the Dead symbolism of skulls and flowers is one of celebration, unlike Halloween, which has a more macabre association.

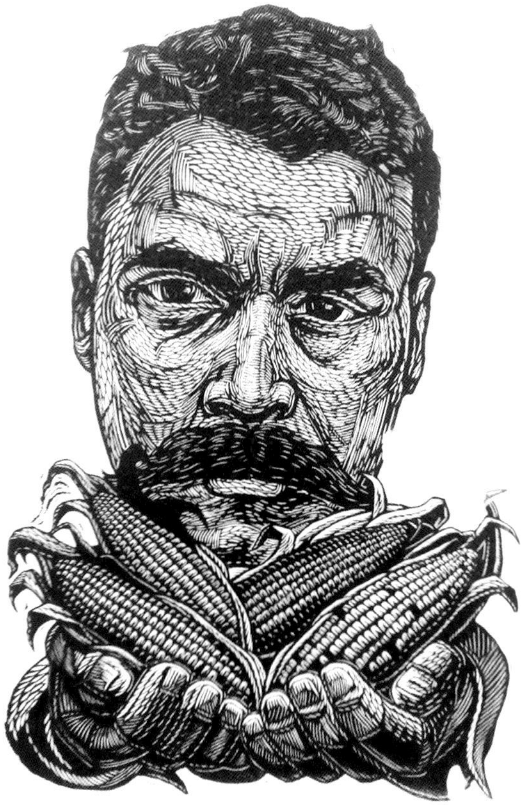

Emiliano Zapata, a key leader in the Mexican Revolution who fought for agrarian reform, cradles an armful of corn, a symbol of sustenance in Mexico in this Urtarte poster.

Mexican Muralism and Marxist Musclemen

A student of murals cannot begin a survey of women on the wall in Mexico without stopping to admire the patron saints of Mexican muralism, who worked on big ideas on big walls in commissioned projects. The monumental murals by Diego Rivera, David Alfaro Siqueiros, and José Clemente Orozco are on full display at the Palacio de Bellas Artes in Mexico City.[3] Their work is a testament to compositional brilliance, power, and use of color, but the murals are also traditional in their portrayal of women.

The Mexican muralists celebrated the Mexican Revolution by using striking symbols, and in the case of Diego Rivera, a decidedly Marxist theme emerged while Mexican women were presented in traditional *campesina* roles. The pantheon of

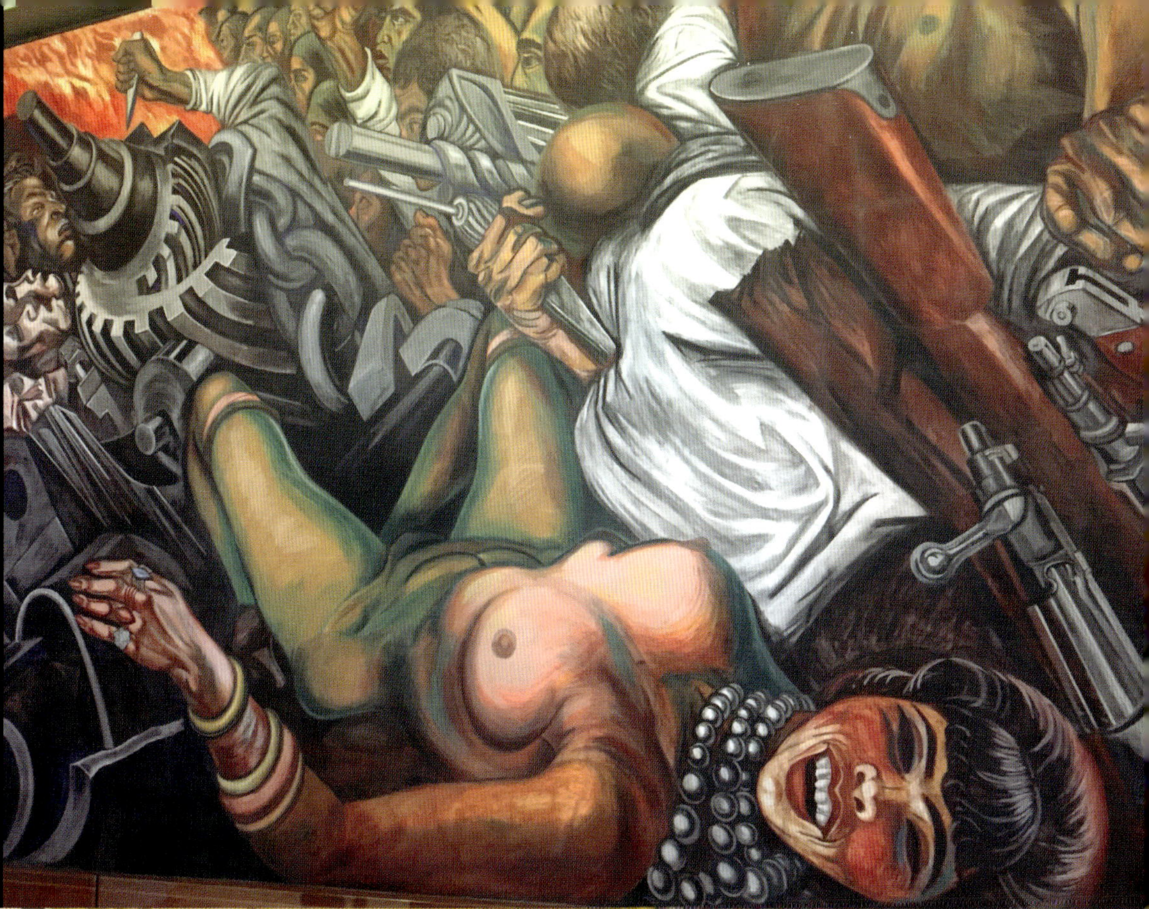

José Clemente Orozco, La Katharsis, Palacio de Bellas Artes, Mexico City. Photo: John Harris

Diego Rivera mural, Man Controller of the Universe, Palacio de Bellas Artes, Mexico City by dnunz is licensed under CC BY-ND 2.0

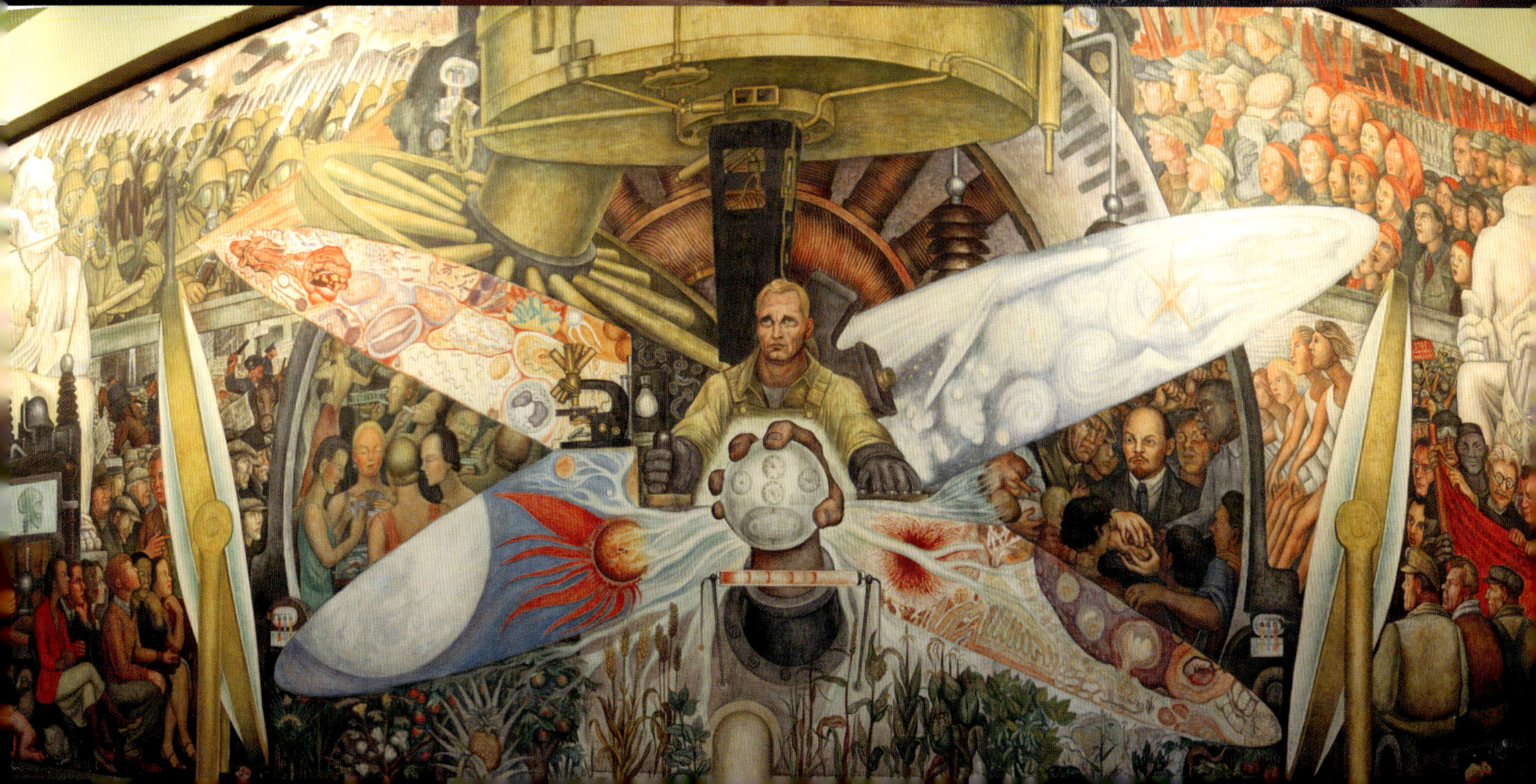

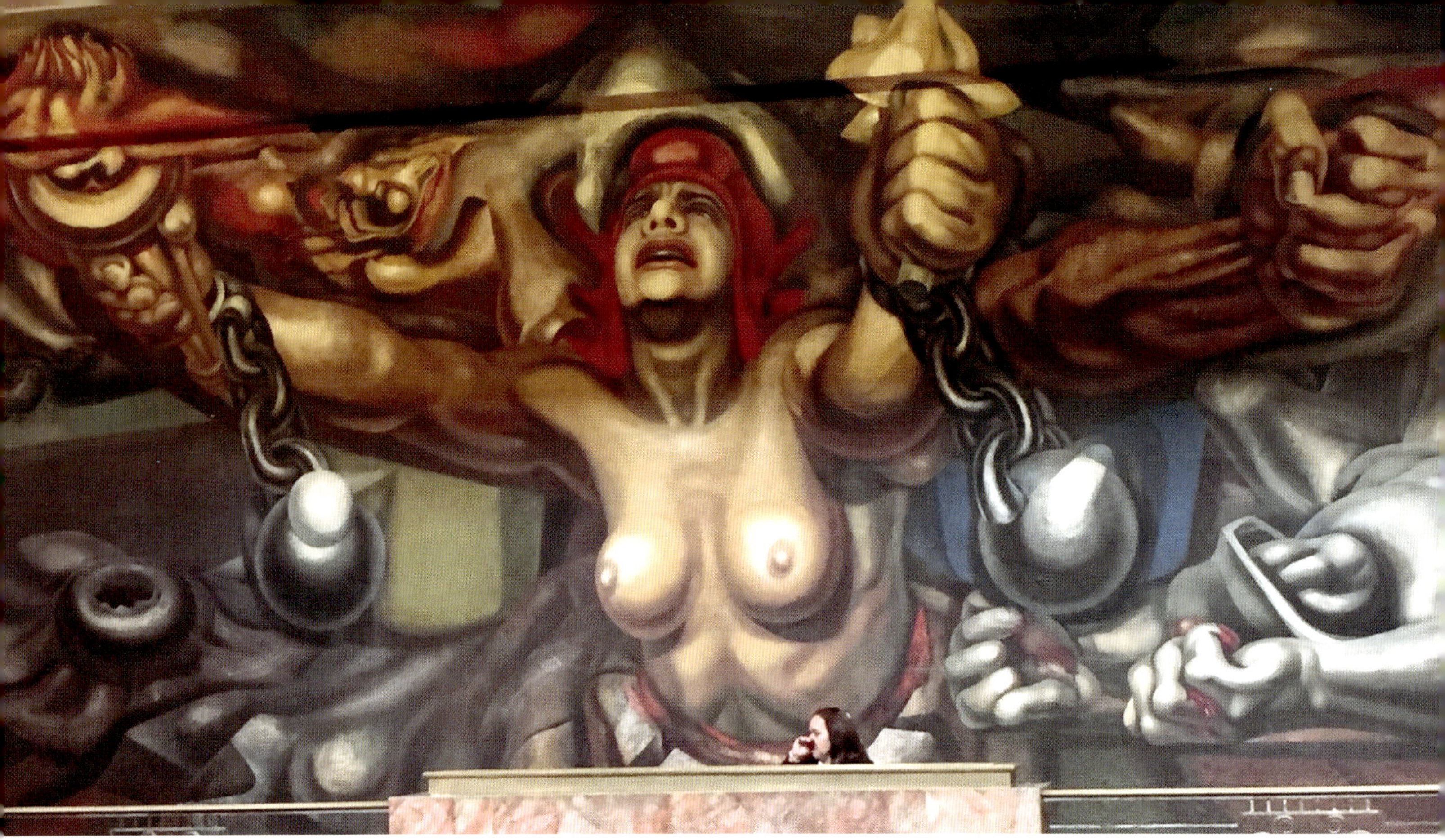

Marxism's founders—Lenin, Marx, and Trotsky—makes cameo appearances in Rivera's murals, leading the working class to a Utopian future occupied and dominated by Promethean symbols of science and industrial progress. In Orozco's *Katharis*, a laughing, debauched woman lies at the bottom of a ruined world plunged into war and disorder by the venal ruling class, while in a nearby Siqueiros mural, democracy breaks her chains in a powerful gesture of freedom. The Mexican muralists created their vibrant interpretations of revolution without the two-dimensional symbolism and trappings of political propaganda associated with socialist realism.

Mexico City's murals have always been must-sees on the tourist itinerary as symbols of an era when muralism gave birth to a powerful political expression of revolutionary ideology, which has since been adopted and reshaped by such wall artists as Judy Baca and Faith47, a South African muralist whose feminist viewpoint is featured in chapter 7. There is no doubt why the Big Three influenced generations of wall artists with their bold and original artistic vision. But you have to leave the heaving city founded by the Aztecs and fly into Oaxaca to experience women on the wall who reflect a different form of revolutionary zeal and symbolism.

David Alfaro Siqueiros, Democracy Breaking Her Chains, Palacio de Bellas Artes, Mexico City. Photo: John Harris

Oaxaca—a UNESCO-listed city—is also a mecca for mescal drinkers. Like tequila, mescal is made from agave cacti, but its handcrafted production involving fire pits is different, and its flavor is smoky, spicy, or savory depending on the type of agave being used.

Oaxaca also rates five stars on the culinary trail with its moles, a rich sauce of spices most famously mixed with bitter chocolate; in Oaxaca you also can enjoy guacamole garnished with smoked crickets before discovering wall art that is a potent mix of politics, paganism, and social justice messaging.

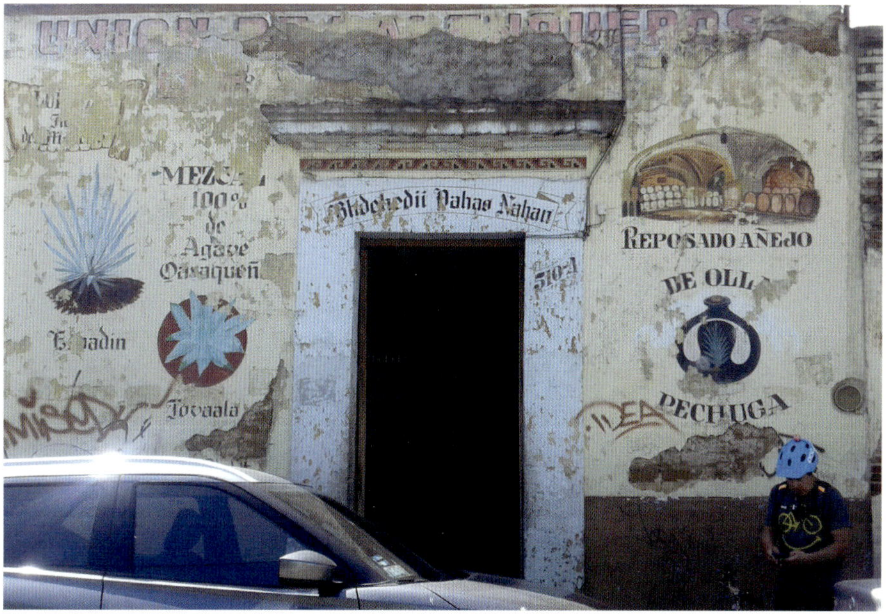

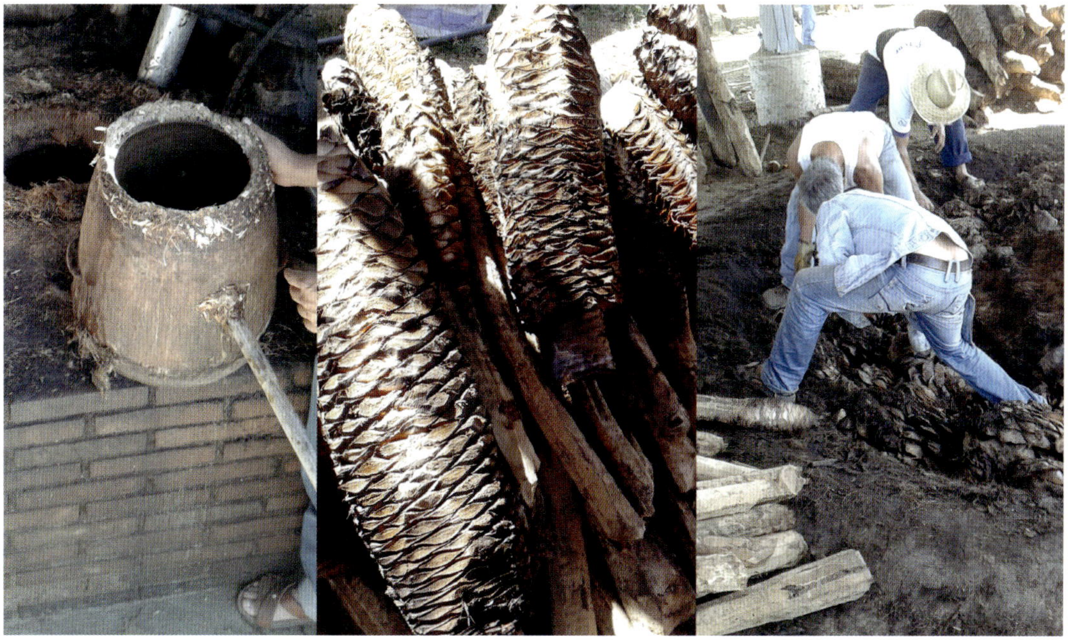

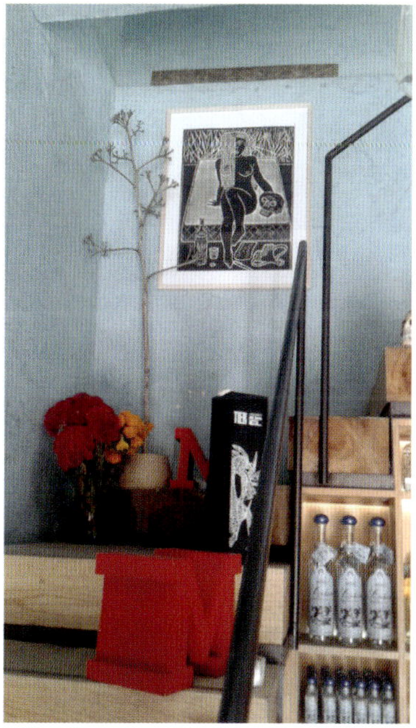

Oaxaca is known for its mescal bars and culinary inventiveness.

Mescal production in full swing outside Oaxaca

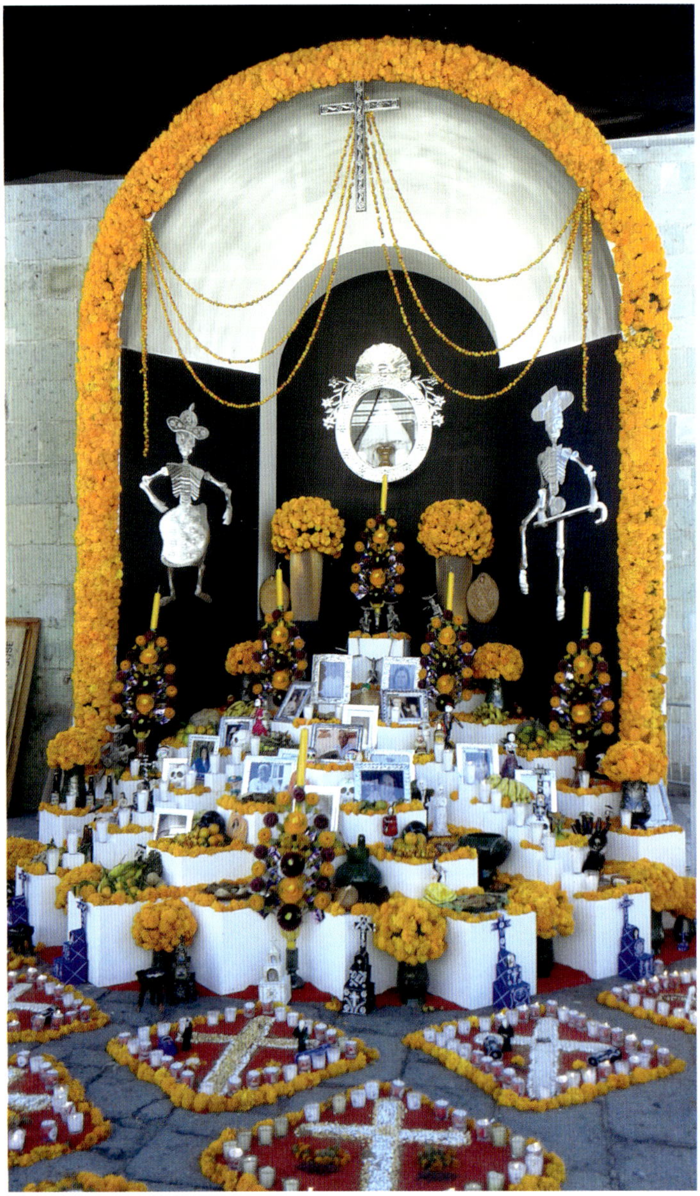

Day of the Dead Symbols and Oaxaca's Spicy and Rebellious Wall Art

This celebration of death is woven into the traditions of the Mexican Día de los Muertos (Day of the Dead), and Oaxaca is arguably its spiritual center. The ubiquitous La Catrina, the tall, elegant skeleton woman with a feathered hat, has become a globally exported icon that has made its way into tattoo parlors and logos on sweatshirts and sometimes morphs into street art involving women. The Aztecs had a god of the dead, and the Catrina is part of that heritage, as are the intricate altars or *ofrendas* constructed of marigolds, photographs, sugary skulls, and other Mexican delicacies, including mescal. In graveyards, the food, drink, and music are offered to the memories of the dead and shared with loved ones who still inhabit our world.

Oaxaca is also home to a vivid street art culture that is nurtured by a tradition of protest wall art that is often the work of artist collectives. In Oaxaca, the ASAR-Oaxaca (ASARO, Assembly of Revolutionary Artists of Oaxaca) has been using their protest art to deliver ideological messages for more than ten years. ASARO is still actively campaigning for teacher's rights with silkscreened posters plastered in the city. The ASARO posters cry for justice, revolution, and recognition for the Indigenous peoples of the region. Their artwork also calls for the recognition of teachers as bearers of truth.

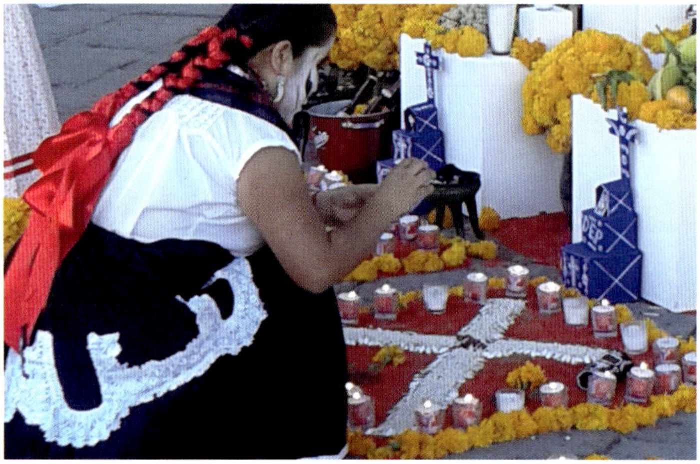

Day of the Dead ofrendas or altars, a children's parade in Oaxaca, and mythical beasts created for the Mexico City parade. Lower right, ofrenda at Casa Azul, Frida Kahlo's former home and museum.

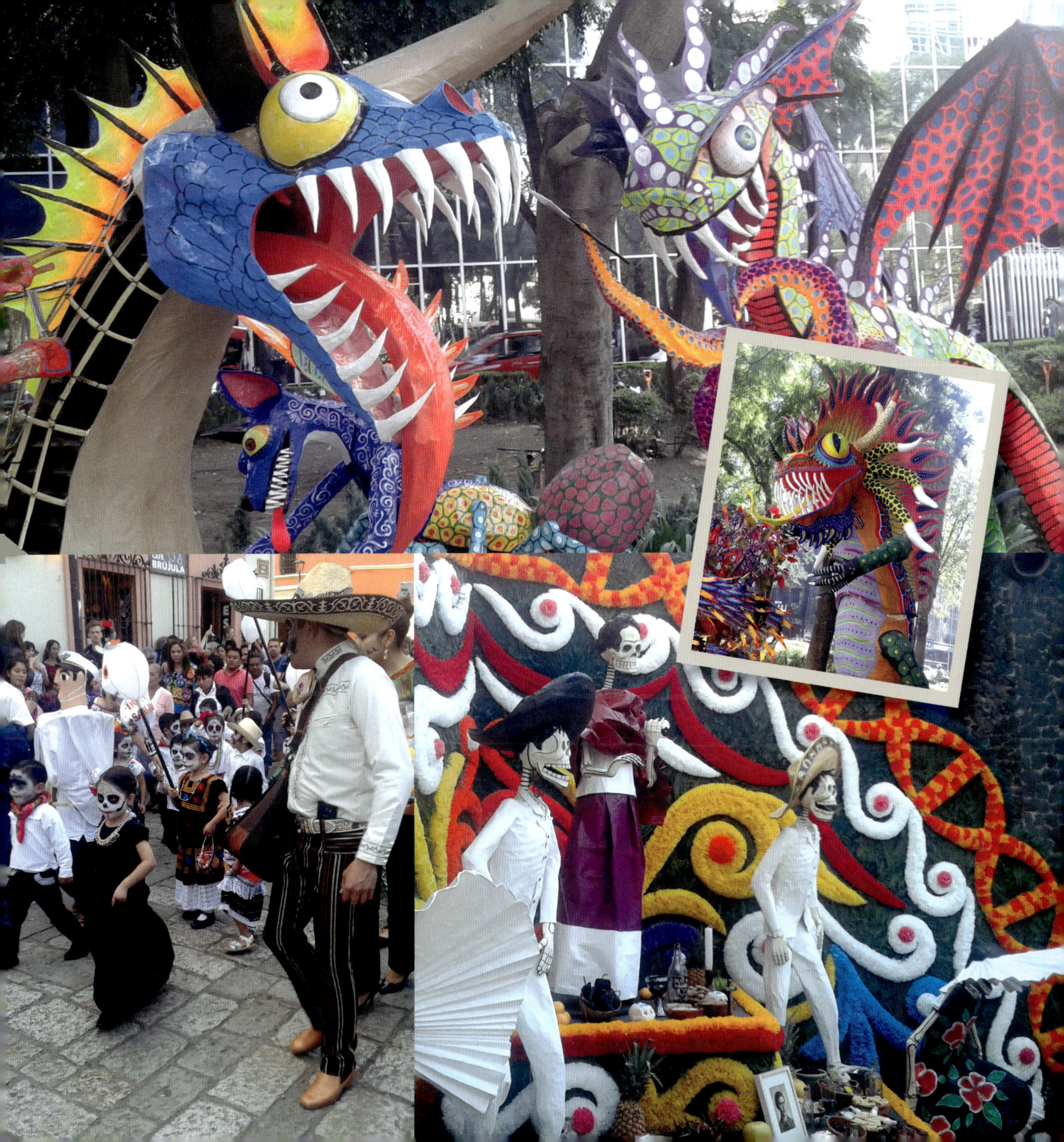
BRÚJULA

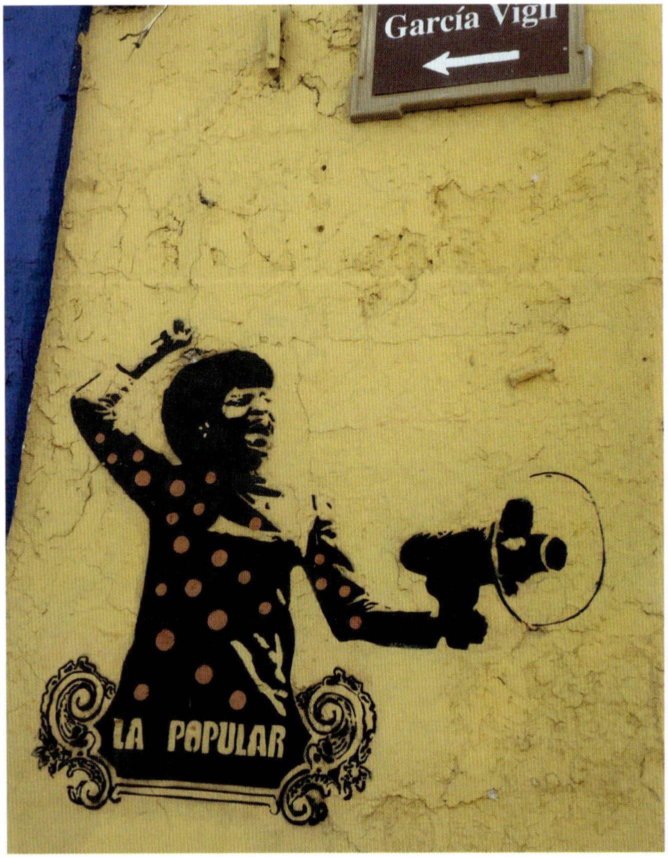

A stencil depicting a revolutionary woman, by an unknown artist in Oaxaca. Photo: John Harris

Another revolutionary wall art collective, Urtarte, is also well represented in Oaxaca. In one artwork, a child clutches a heart in a call for justice or revolution. The heart is a beating symbol in the Urtarte paste-ups, which are inspired by woodcuts depicting the influence of the Indigenous culture. Oaxacan wall art also transforms women into hybrid creatures representing the earth and sea.

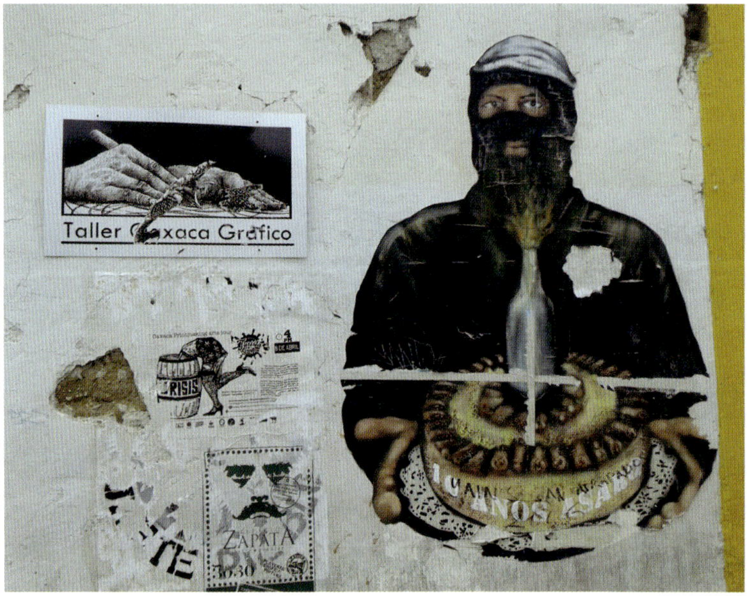

Wall art celebrating the tenth anniversary of ASARO, showing a masked rebel holding a birthday cake

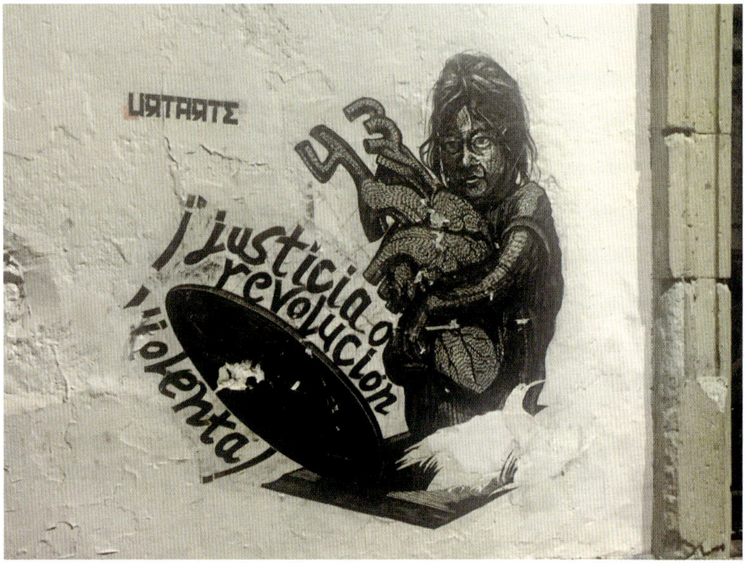

Urtarte, an artist's collective that bases its paste-ups on woodcuts, sends a message calling for justice or violent revolution, symbolized by a child clutching a heart.

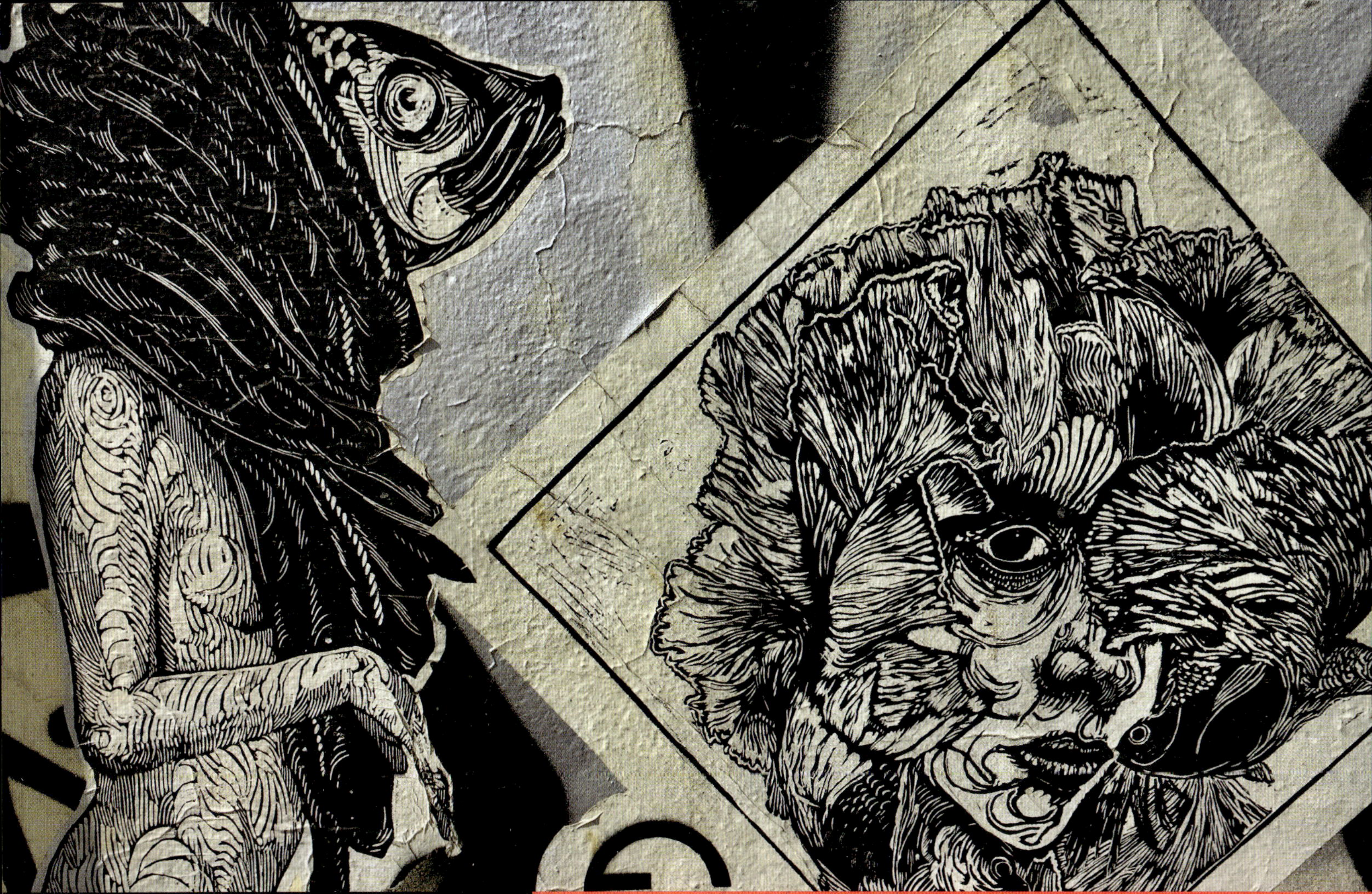

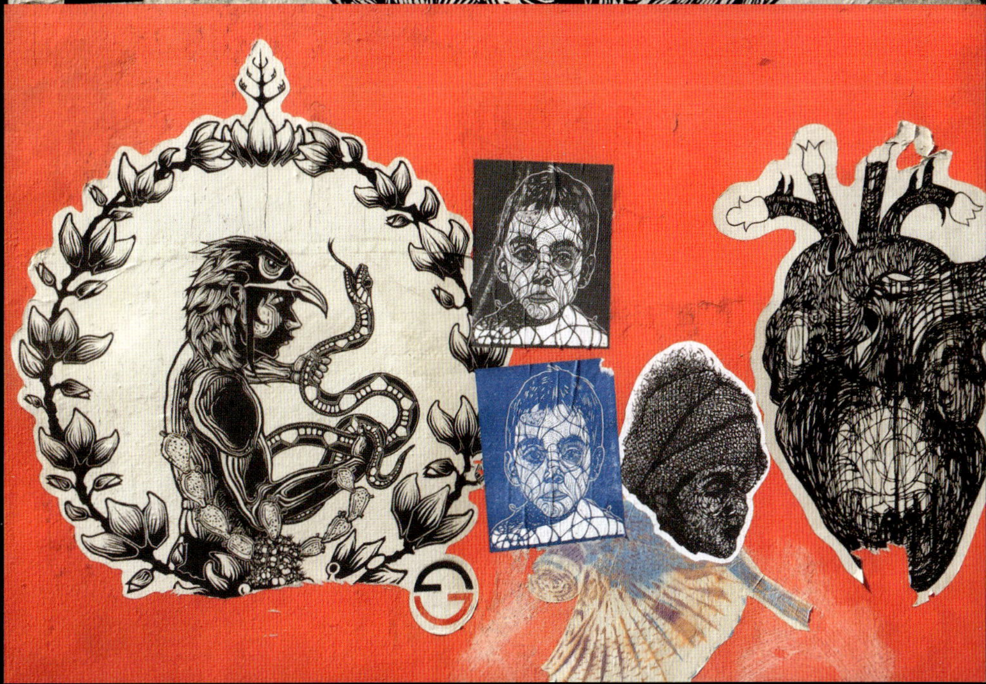

These works are unknown but most likely associated with the Urtarte artist collective. One features the heart that the collective uses, while the other depicts its women as hybrid creatures with natural connections to the sea and crops. Photos: John Harris

Market Town's Prized Produce and Women on the Wall

Outside Oaxaca, not far from mescal, moles, and Mayan ruins, you'll find the market town called Tlacolula. The market here is full of beautifully colored local produce and flower stalls, and its walls are adorned with women.

Two unique examples of women on the wall, both in black and white, are located next to one another. The contrasting interpretations of Zapotec women depict a seemingly humble and shy subject in a headscarf, and the other a defiant woman, whose tattoos on her upraised left arm symbolize the coming of the Spanish and their religion. Her hand clutches a bottle of mescal labeled with a skull, perhaps

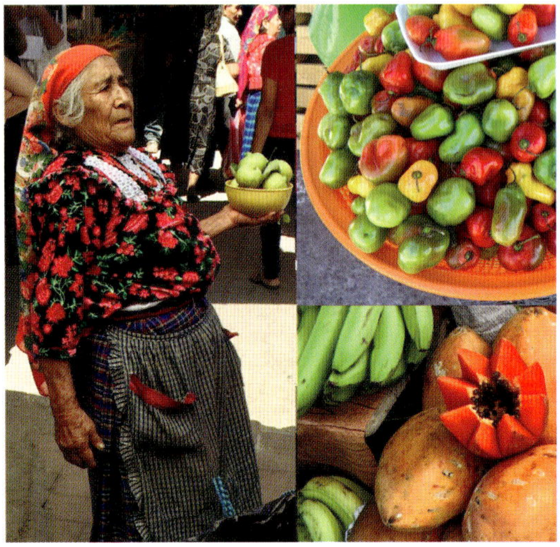

Tlacolula's market abundance on display. Photo: John Harris

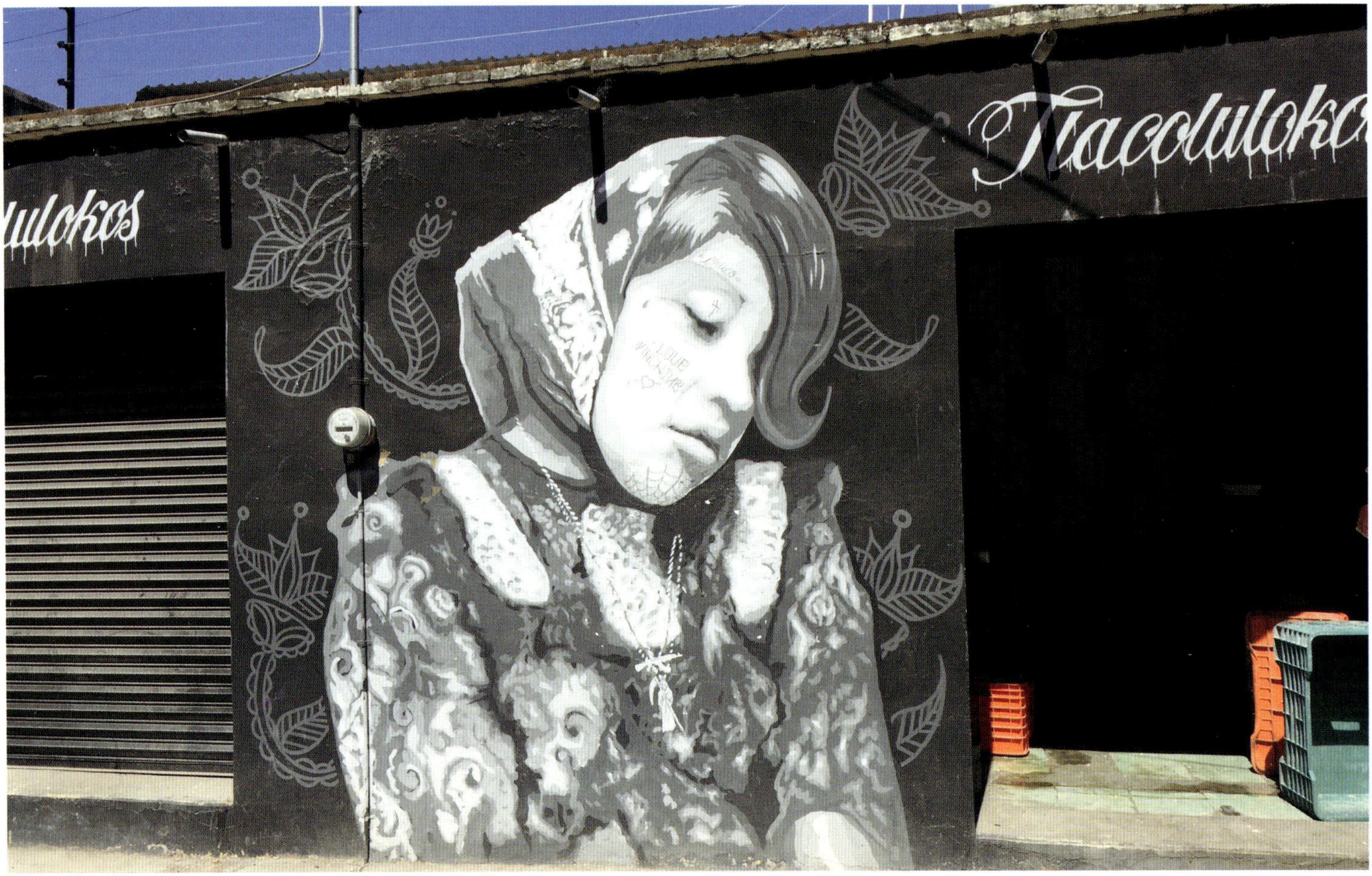

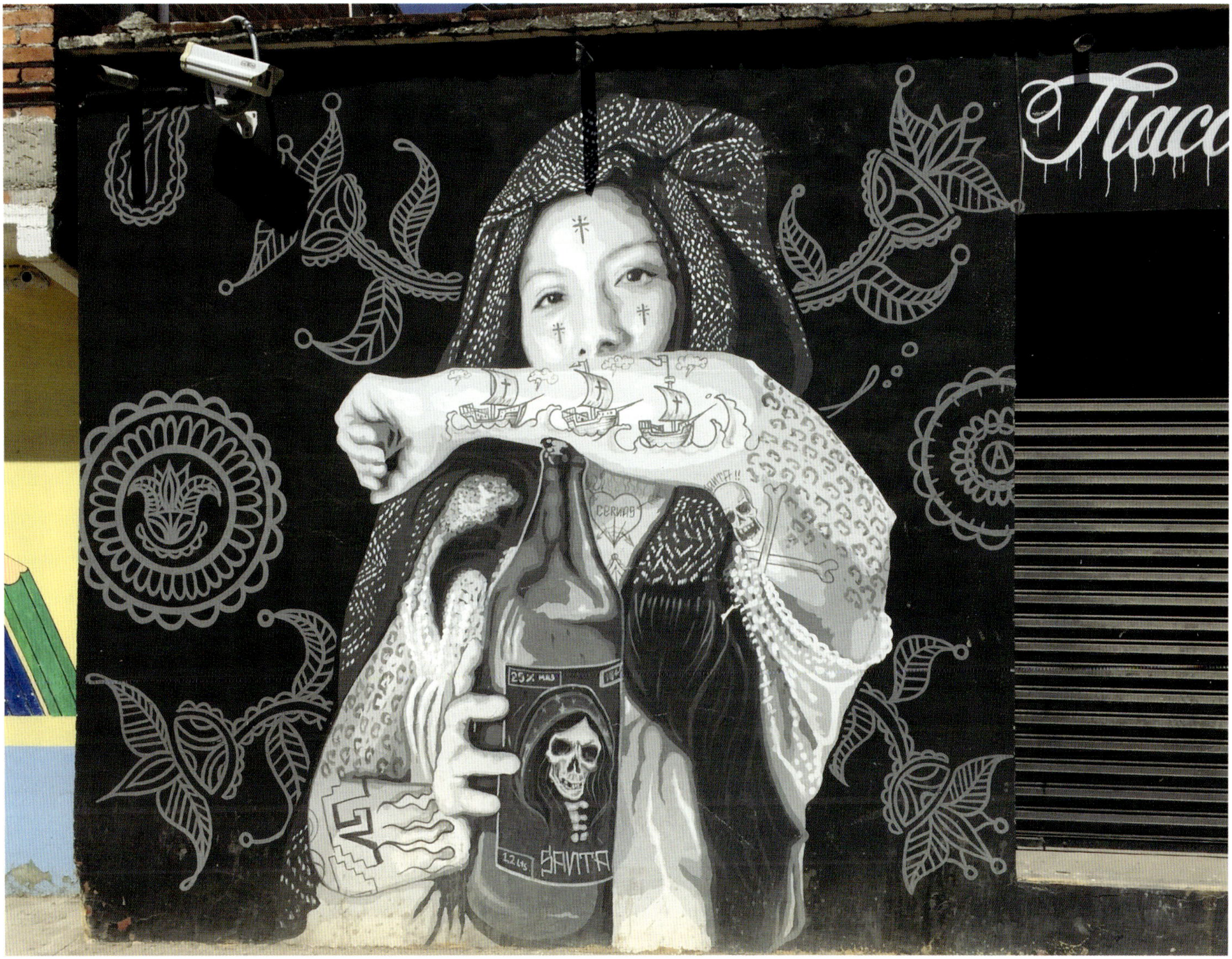

Tlacolula women on the wall by Dario Canal and Cosijoesa Cernas. The two are the Tlacolulkos hometown art collective, whose work focuses on how the Spaniards impacted the local Zapotec communities. Photos: John Harris

symbolic of its poisonous attractions, or perhaps it is a way of dealing with the enforced servitude brought by the conquistadors. The woman's skin also shows off jaguar spots, marking her with a symbolic and fearless animal spirit. Both works are signed works by the Tlacolulkos Zapotec artist's collective, who were also invited to paint the Los Angeles Public Library's rotunda. The collective also has a permanent installation at the Museum of Latin American Art in Long Beach, California. The connection with California is strong; Oaxacans from this region have lived and worked in the LA region for generations.

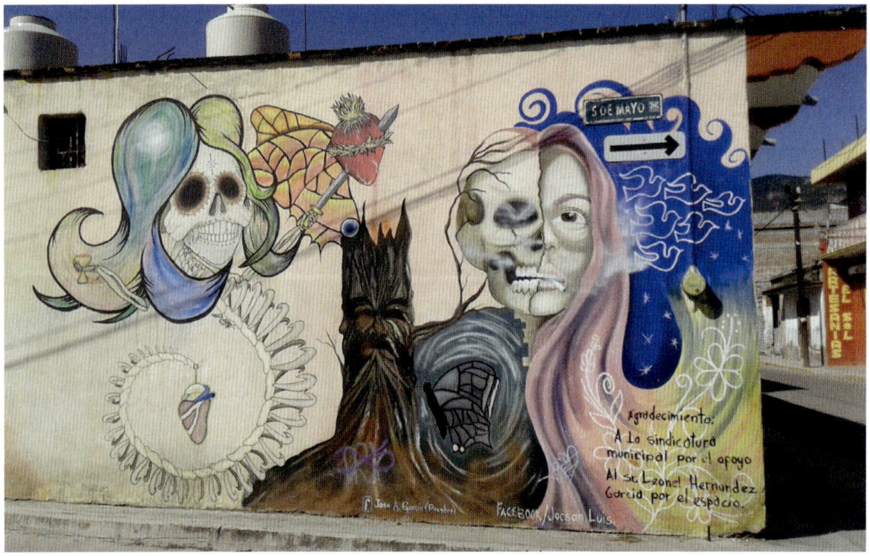

Animist symbolism lies below the surface of the women on the wall in this region of Mexico. The duality is evident—the face on the right shows a modern, smoking woman who has one foot in the world of death. The sacred heart pierced with the sword is a religious symbol found throughout Oaxaca, and represents the compassion of Jesus for humanity.

Close to the ruins of Mitla is a wall covered with women who reflect this connection with the land and the Zapotec civilization.[4]

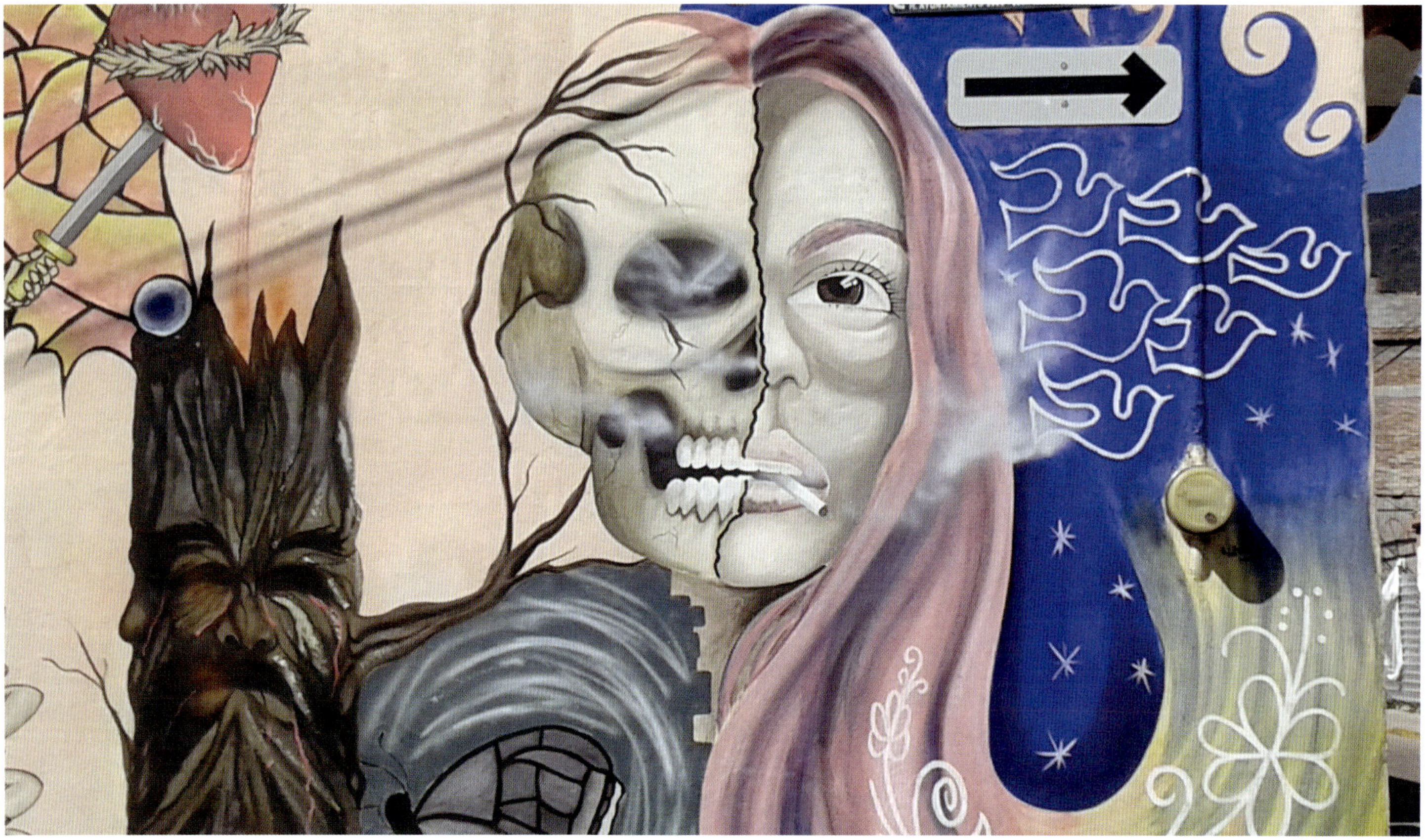

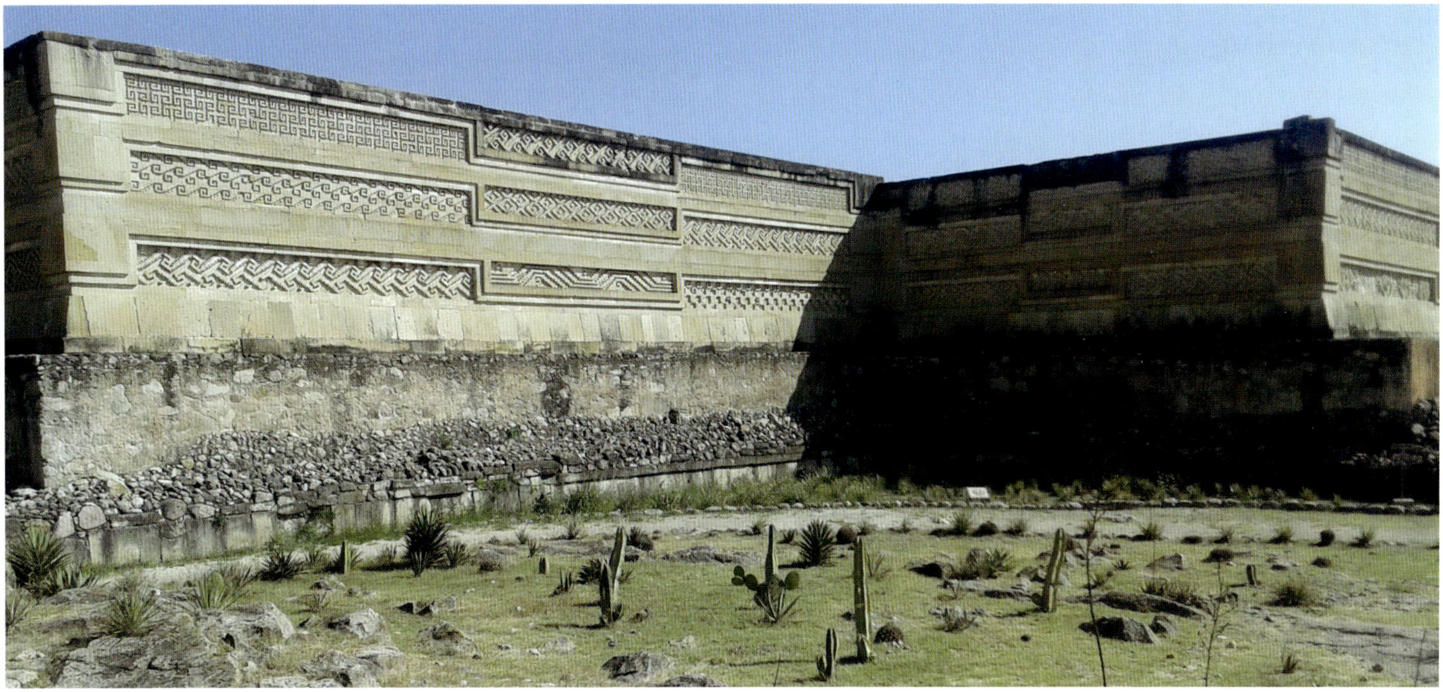

One of the paintings is the work of a group of Mexican wall artists called the Derrumbe Colectivo. The artists' goal is to paint work commissioned by local governments to create outdoor galleries for local residents. It is a chance to help locals feel proud about where they live, and to bring color to rundown streets and otherwise broken walls.

The following examples of women are from a long wall adjacent to a dirt parking lot. Many of the paintings portray Indigenous women: one is practicing her weaving; another highlights the symbolism of corn.

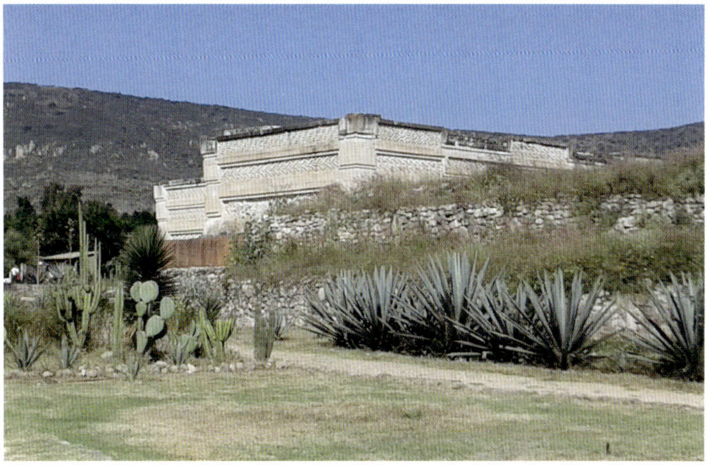

The artist, who painted the dual-faced woman, thanks the city for the support and Leonel Hernandez for the space on the wall. The work is signed by Jose A. García and Jocsan Luís.

Mitla ruins, a Zapotec religious center whose name means "place of the dead." It is one of the few archeological sites in Mexico where the geometric carvings are well-preserved features of the ruins. The Zapotecs are the largest Indigenous group in the Mexican state of Oaxaca.

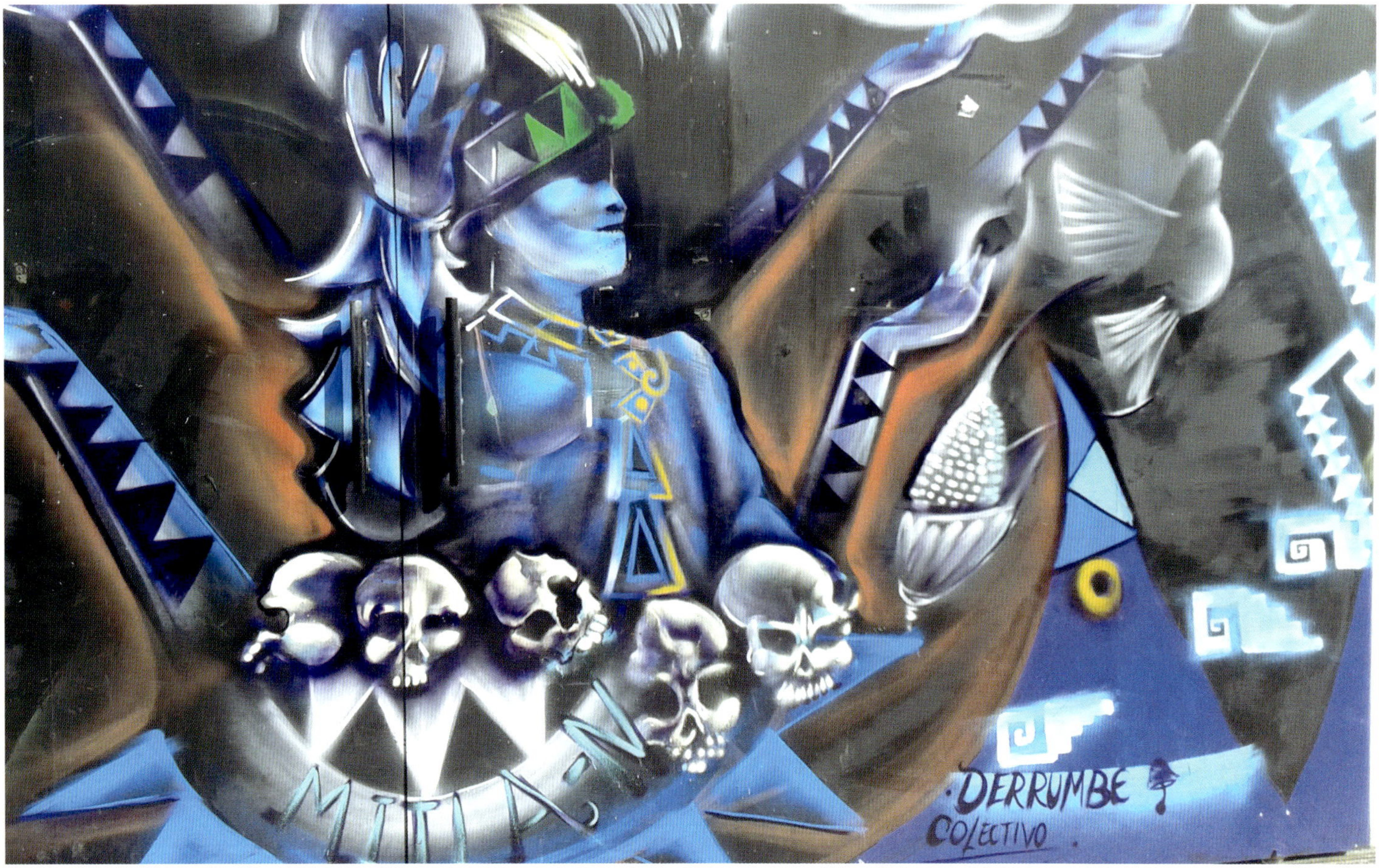

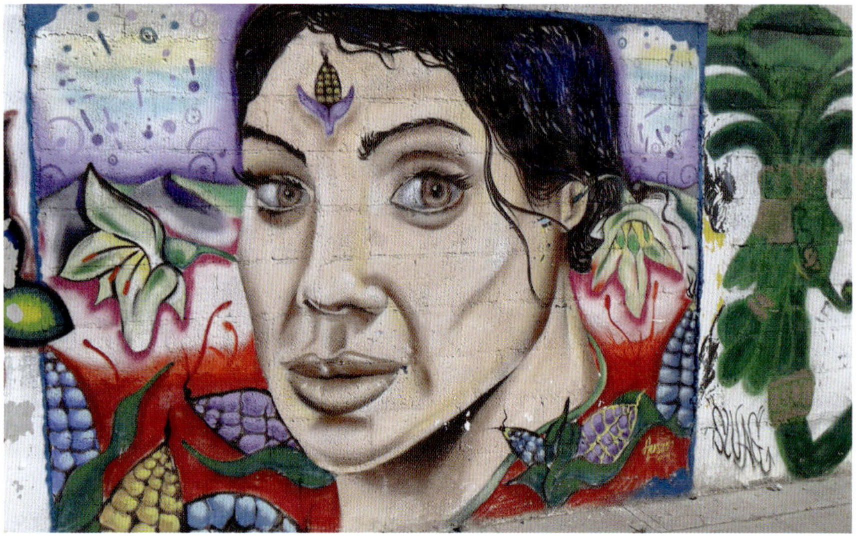

The Derrumbe Colectivo has signed the piece in blue, depicting ancient culture and skulls. A woman displaying the all-important symbol of corn on her forehead goes to the heart of Indigenous Mexican culture.

Oaxaca's cultural richness is everywhere to see both in the city and in its outskirts. Its women on the wall reflect a combination of defiance and tradition, using symbols that date back to Mesoamerica. But our tour found another unusual place for women on the wall in the heart of a tourist island in the Mexican Caribbean, with artwork that is not rebellious in content but instead consists of murals promoting ocean health.

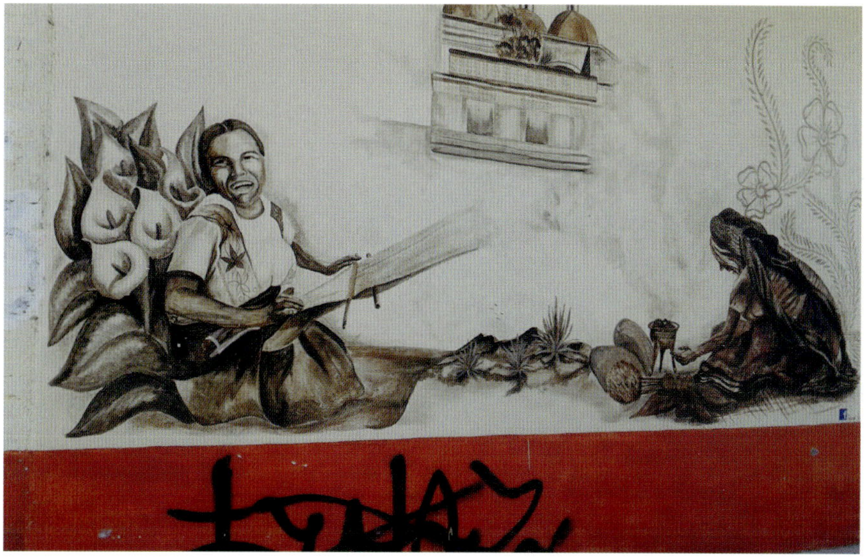

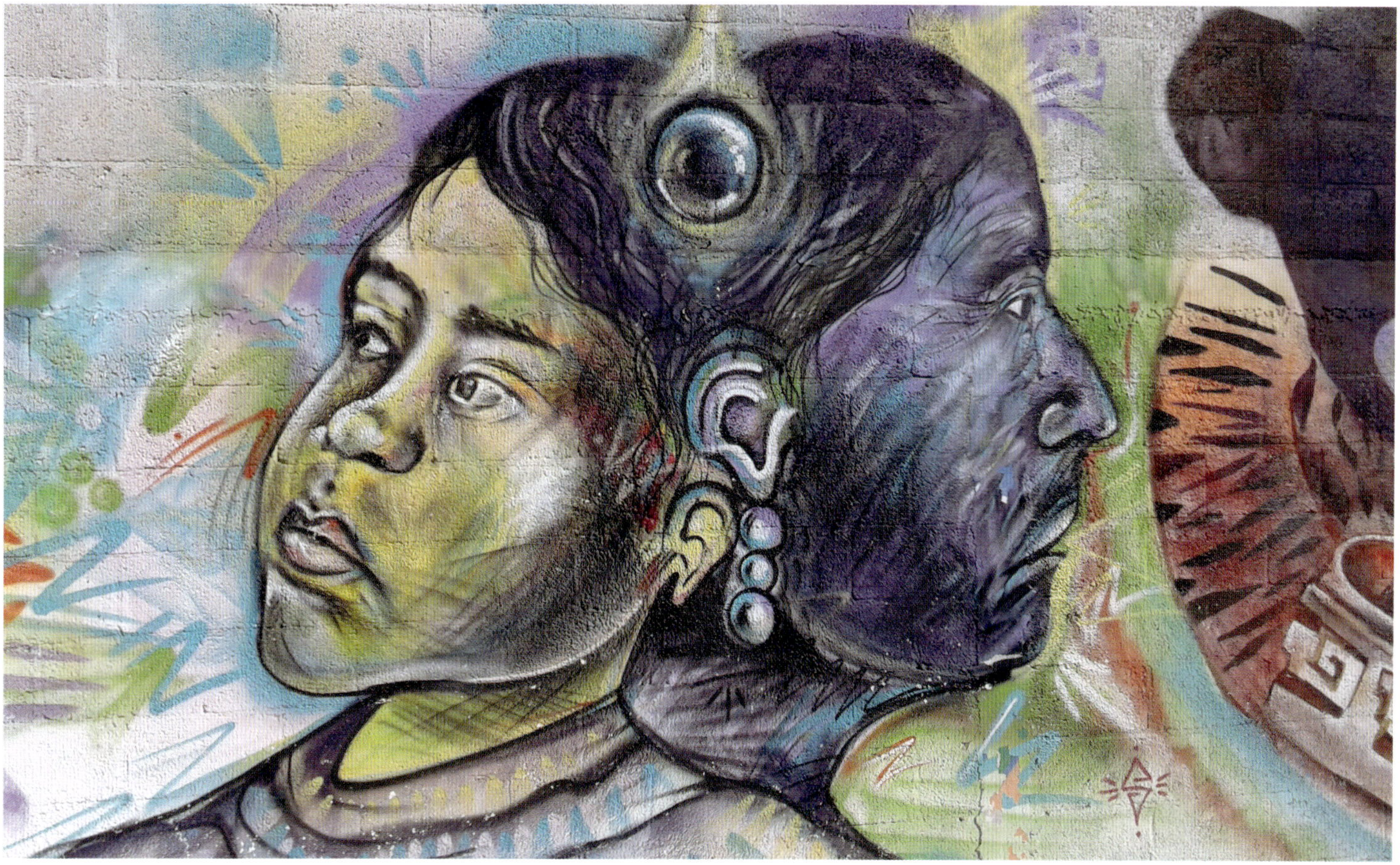

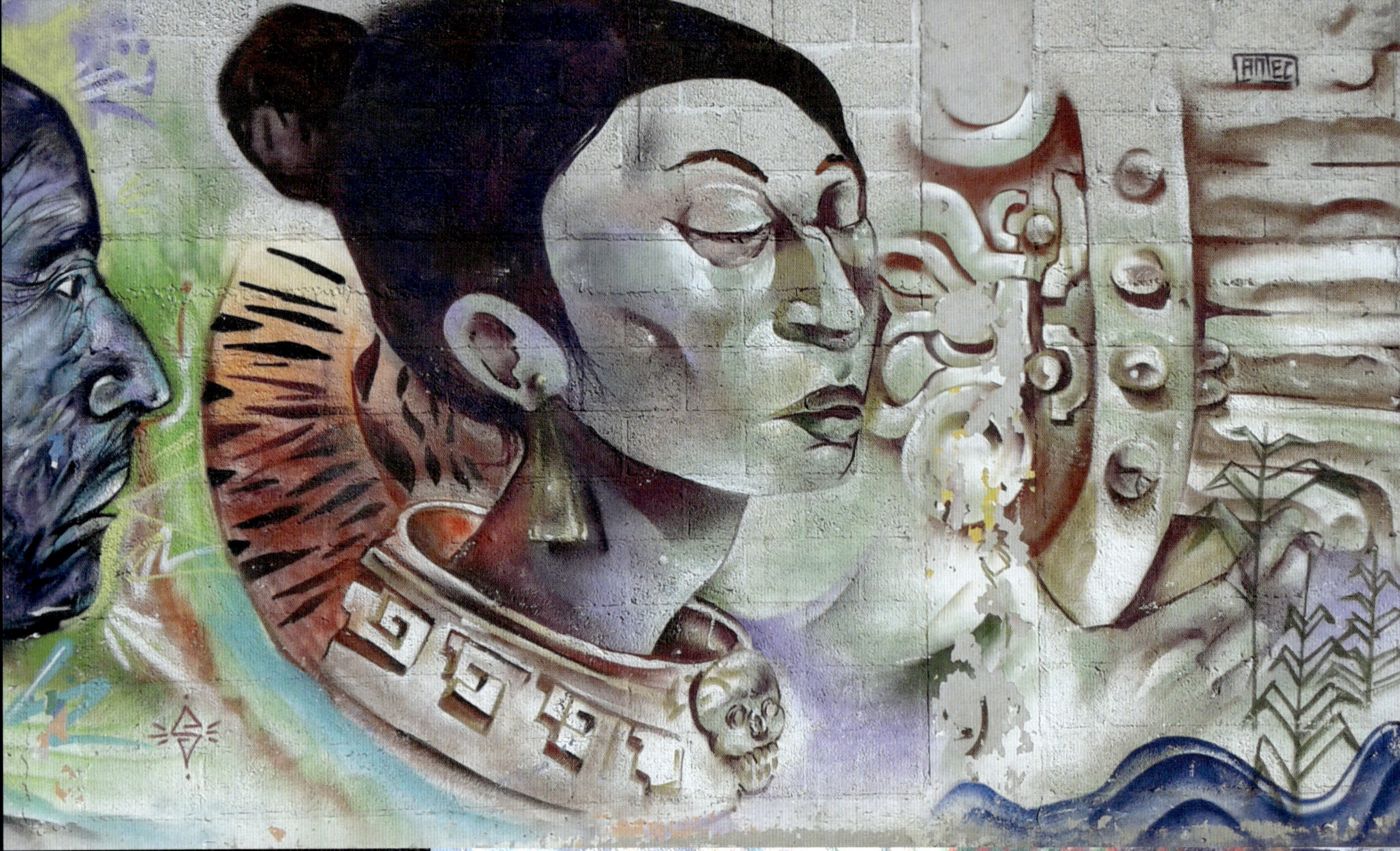

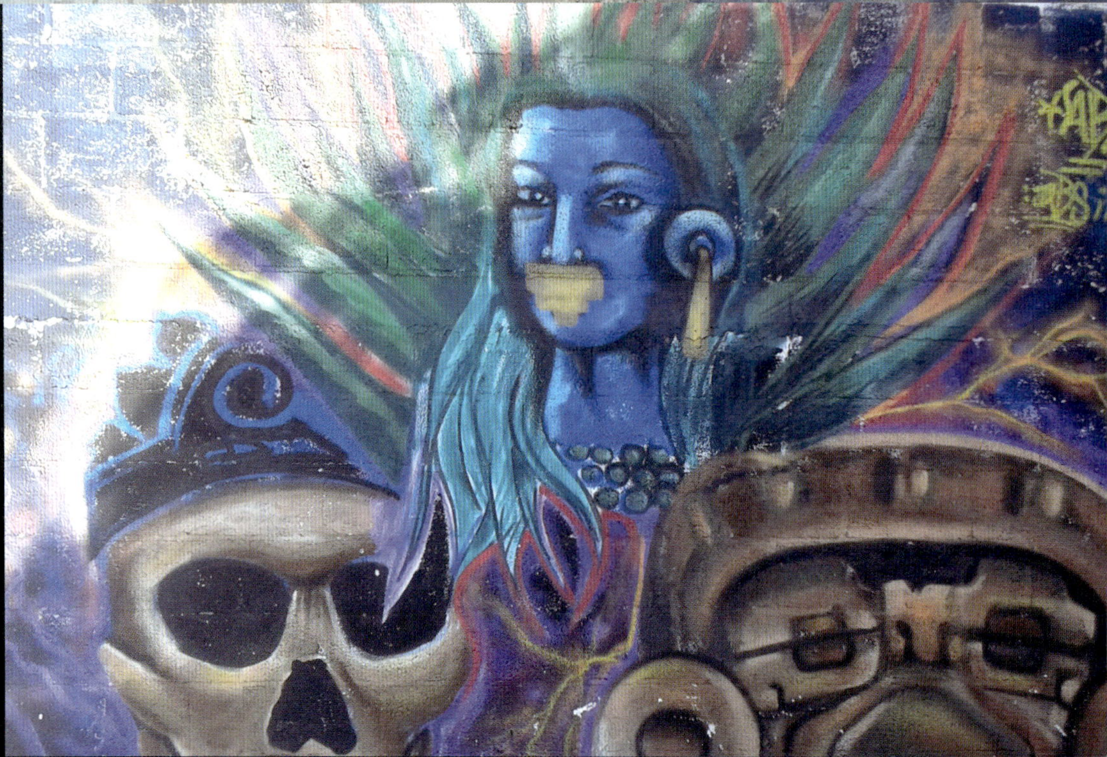

All these images of women run on a wall alongside a dirt parking lot outside Oaxaca.

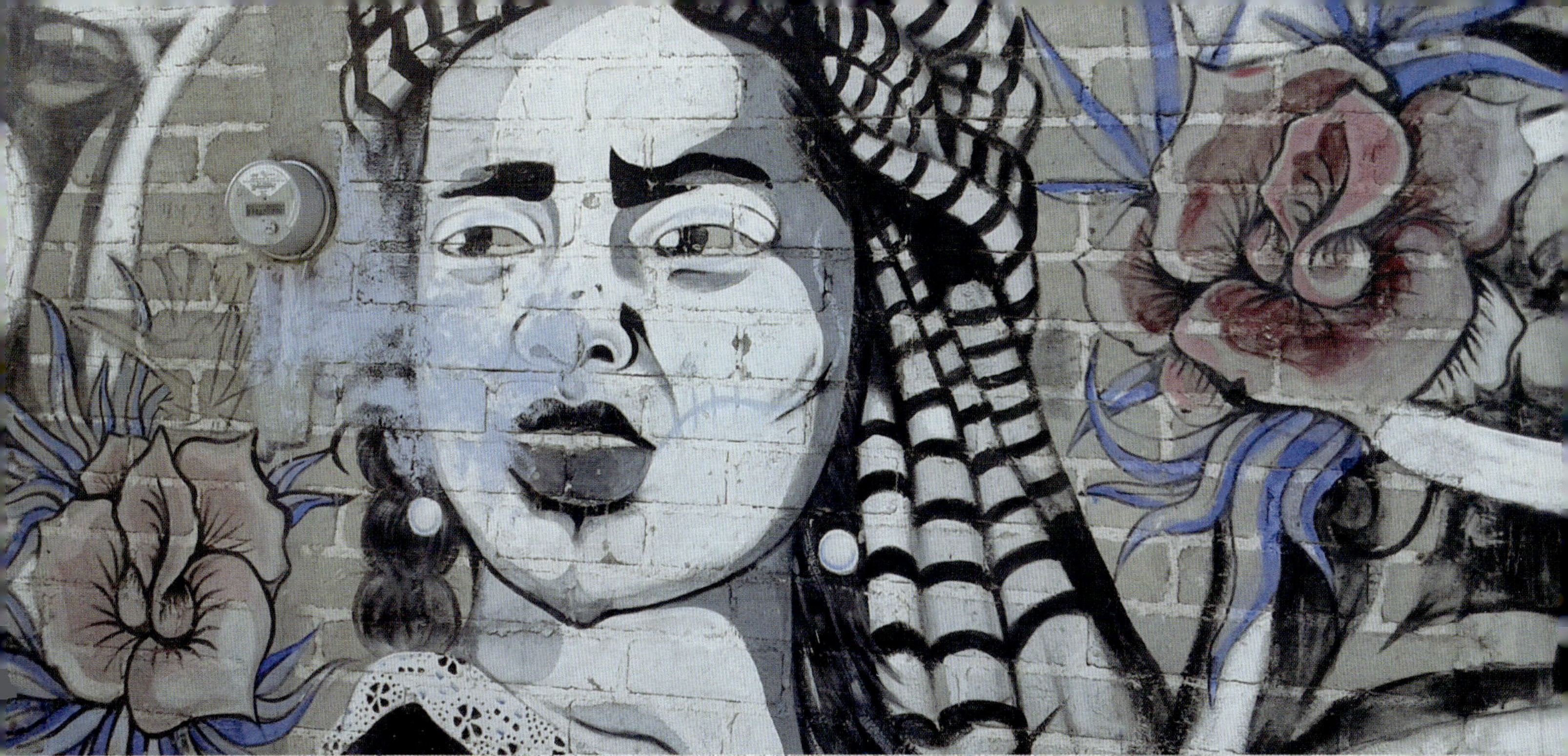

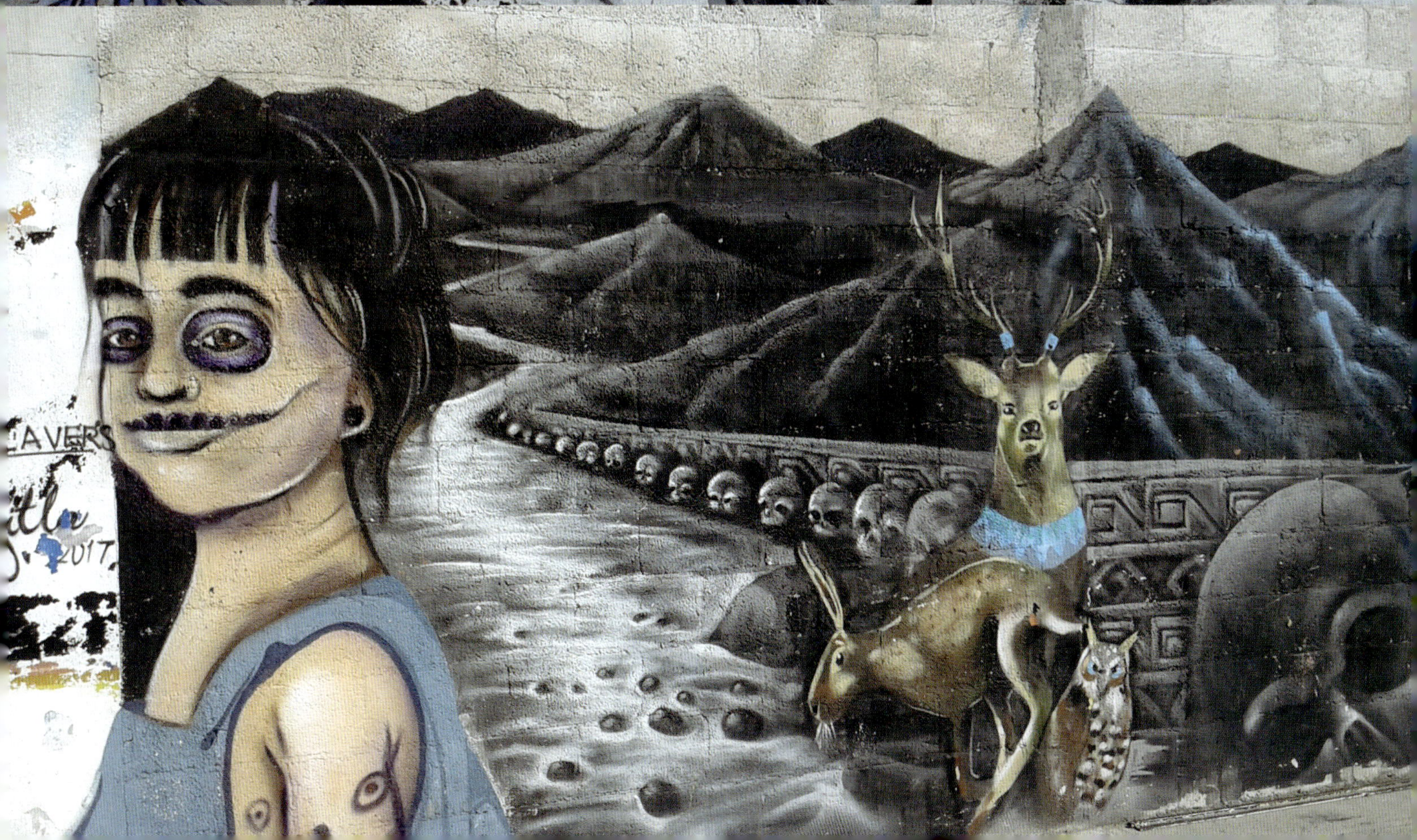

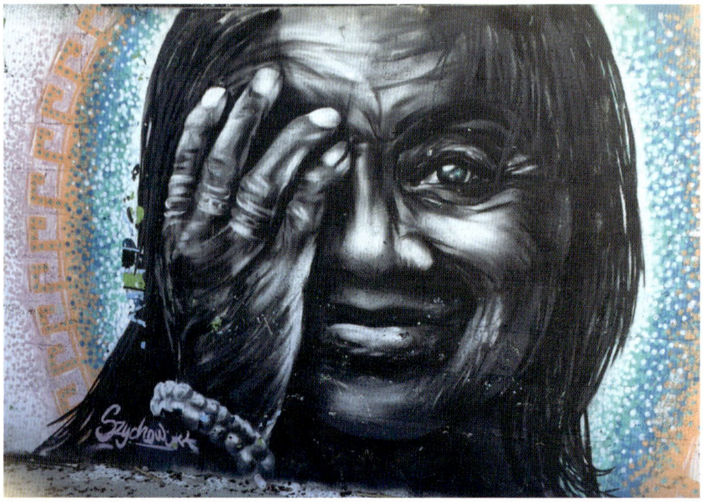

Maria-Rosa Szychowska is a Canadian wall artist who painted this descendant of a Zapotec woman covering her eye in a market town outside Oaxaca. Photo: John Harris

Cozumel's Cruise Ship Camp and Ocean Walls

Street art of women is an essential part of Mexico's landscape, even in tourist hotspots like Cozumel, a popular port of call on the Caribbean cruise ship and scuba-diving itinerary. Partygoers who disembark from cruise ships can purchase from duty-free shops or swim with captive dolphins. When tourists wander the back streets, they encounter women on the walls who are part of an international effort to increase awareness about saving the ocean from exploitation and pollution, called Sea Walls. It's a cause that is a bit ironic, given that the controversial cruise ship terminal in Cozumel has negatively affected the area's magnificent underwater reef system.

Sea Walls is part of the PangeaSeed Foundation public art program, which counts more than three hundred artists as members practicing what the group calls ARTivism. The group's stated goal is to "revitalize and beautify once-decaying neighborhoods and districts" and to bring awareness about the oceans.[5]

If you walk down the backstreets of Cozumel's oceanfront promenade, full of tourists with balloon hats and beakers full of booze, you run into colorful examples of Sea Wall's ARTivism, such as the depiction of the modern mermaid supported by sea turtles.

A short walk away from the Sea Wall women are two murals framing the entrance of Cozumel's City Hall building. They are the work of Argentinean artist Ever and were painted in 2019. The supine woman is next to the Sacred Heart; the other, draped in a Mexican flag bunting, seems to float over a swordfish with her feet planted in a field of grain and the ocean, perhaps signifying the abundance of this part of Mexico.

The Mexicans have been a source of incredible fertility when it comes to producing images that capture nature and women entwined in an intricate dance. It is a country firmly rooted in creative and visually stunning Indigenous cultures that worshipped the gods, the stars, and the shared connection between death and life. These Mesoamerican cultures built great pyramids by hand, were inventive astronomers, were the first civilizations to cultivate corn, and gave the world its great Mexico City muralists, Mesoamerican symbolism, and Cozumel's sea goddesses.

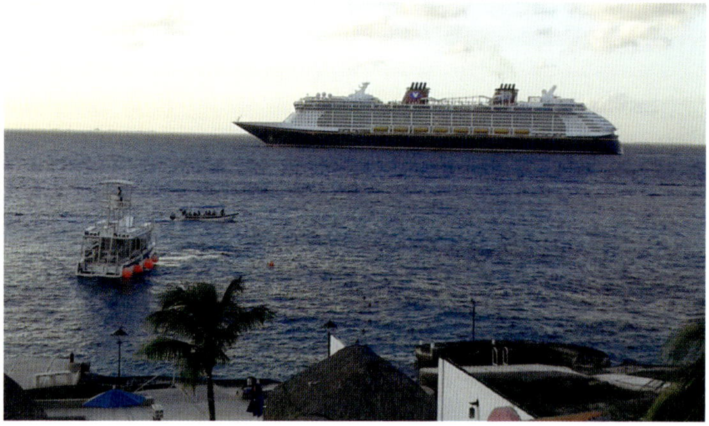

A cruise ship off the coast of Cozumel, Mexico

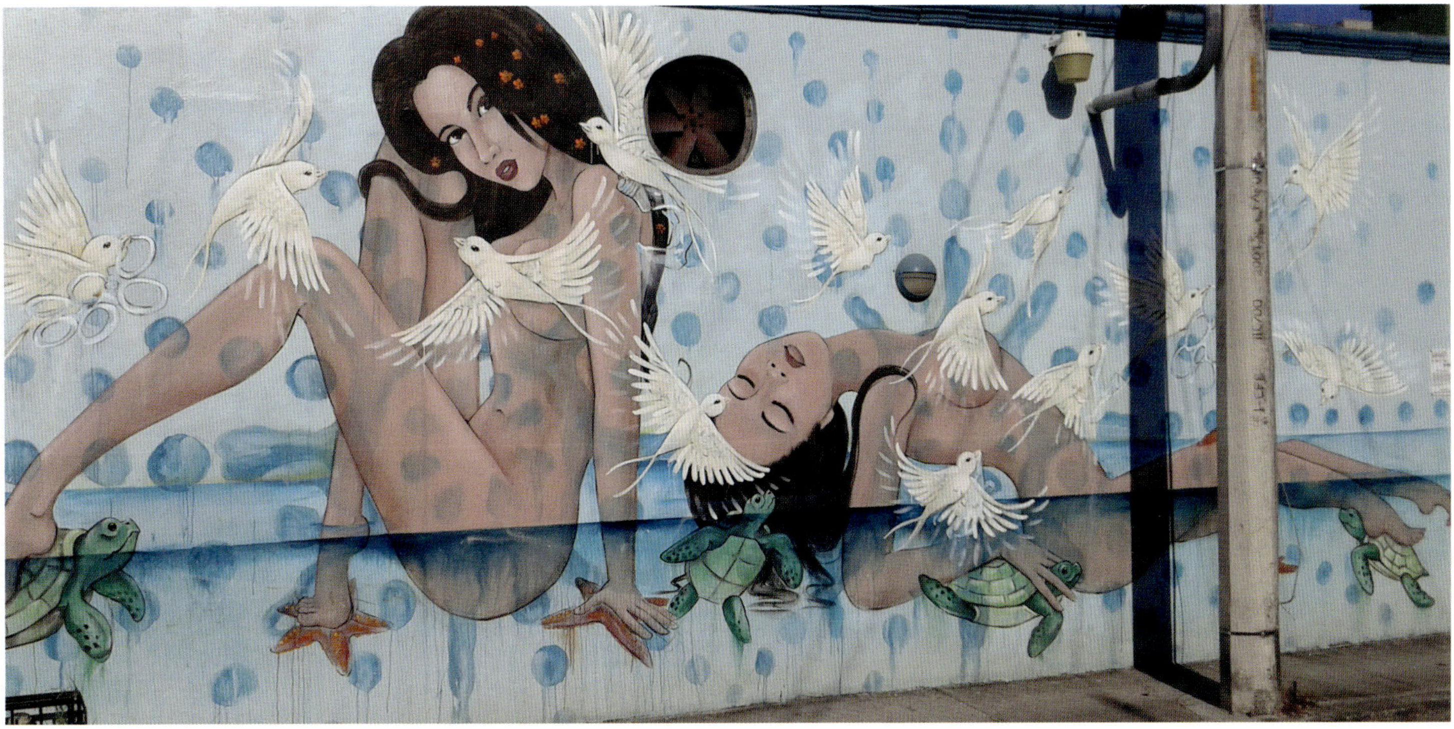

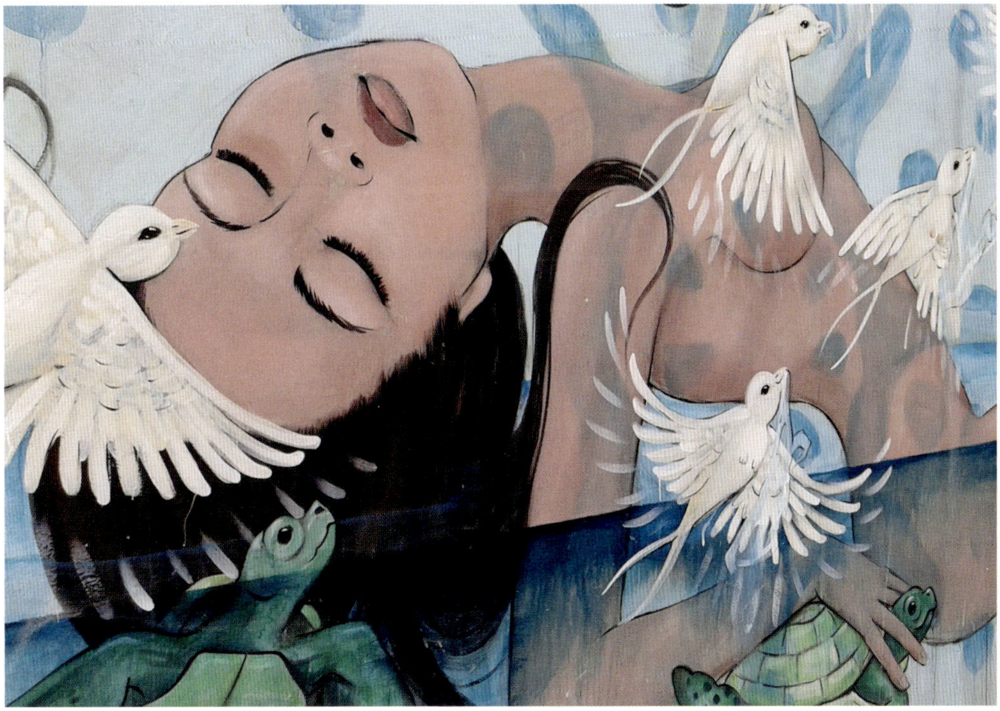

Sea Wall mural by Amanda Lynn, San Francisco muralist

Unknown Sea Wall artists (next page) depicts a woman whose hair is surrounded by octopus tentacles, while a snorkeler enjoys the underwater marine environment.

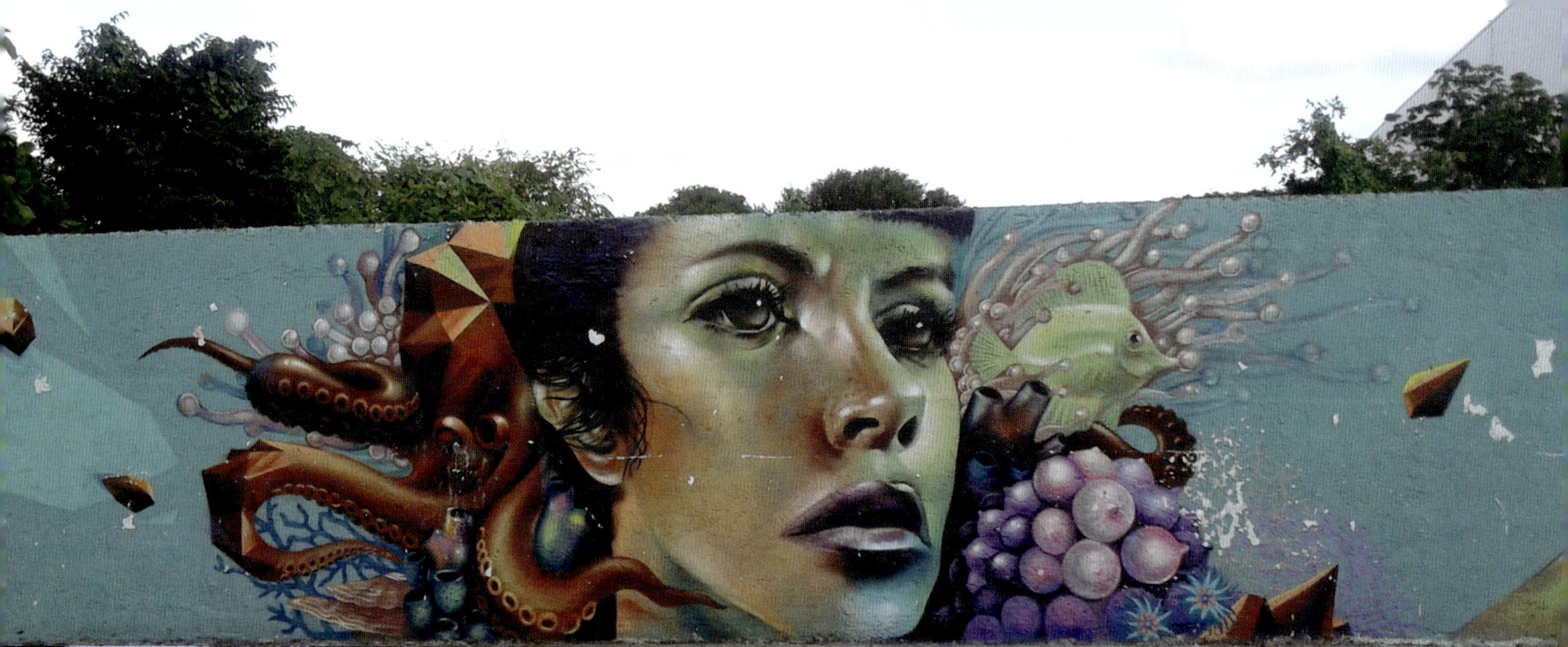

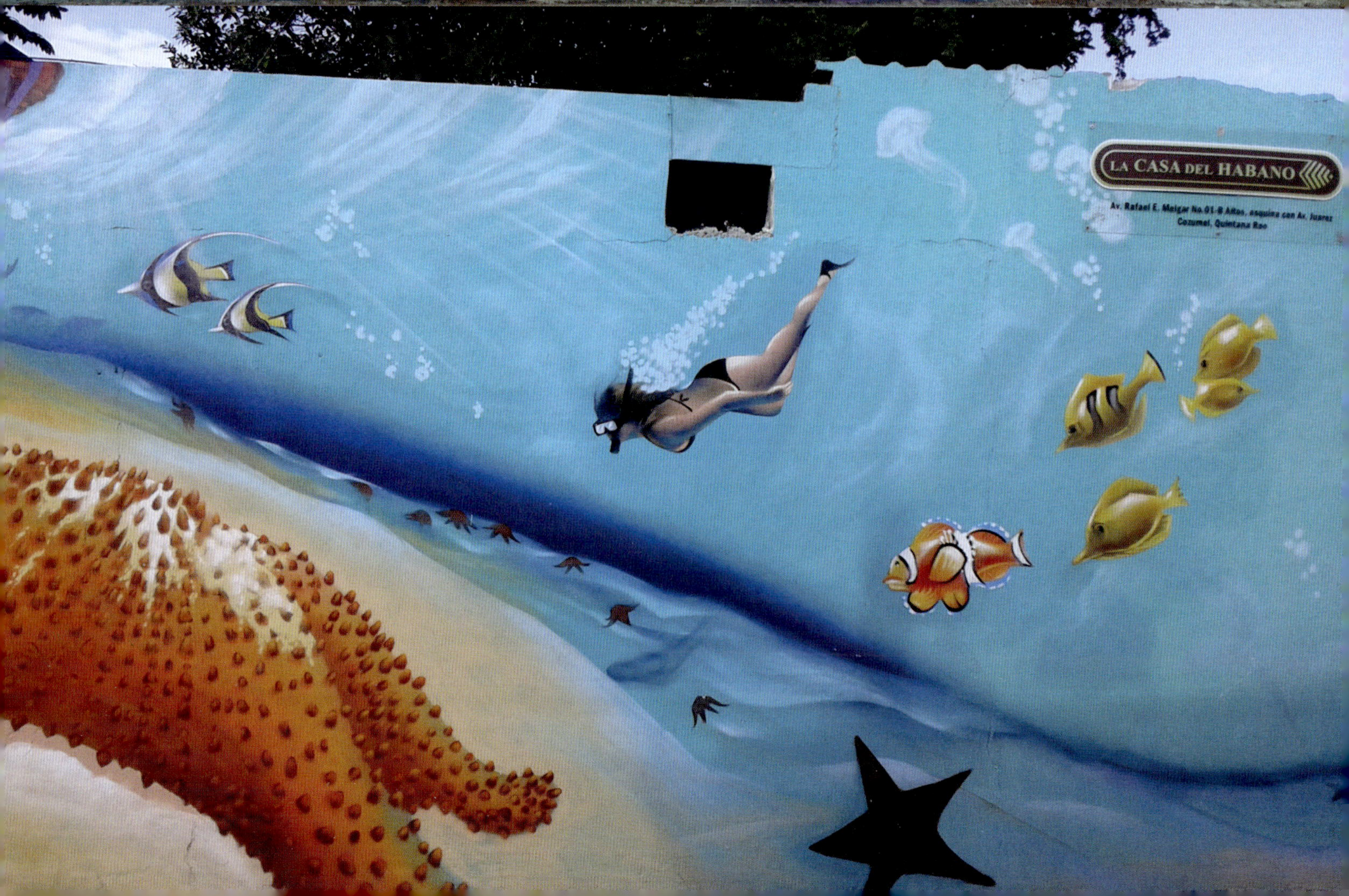

LA CASA DEL HABANO
Cozumel, Quintana Roo

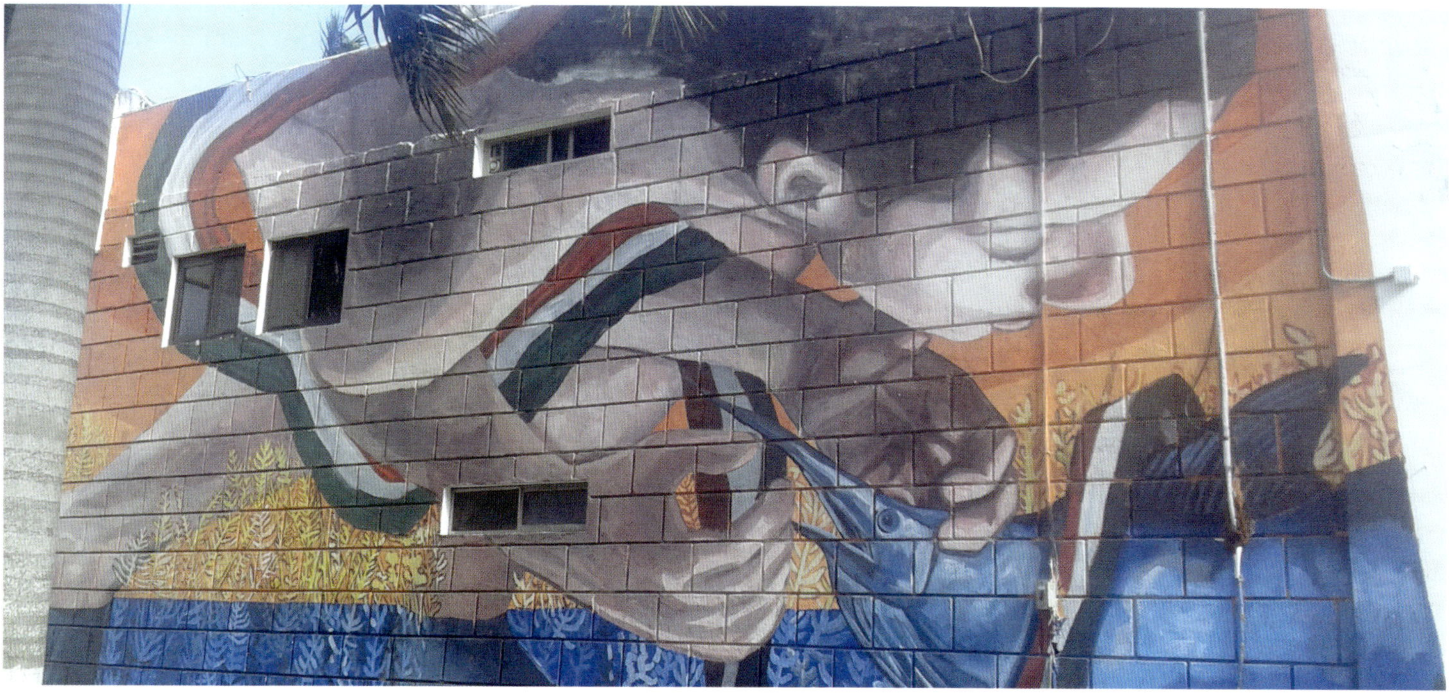

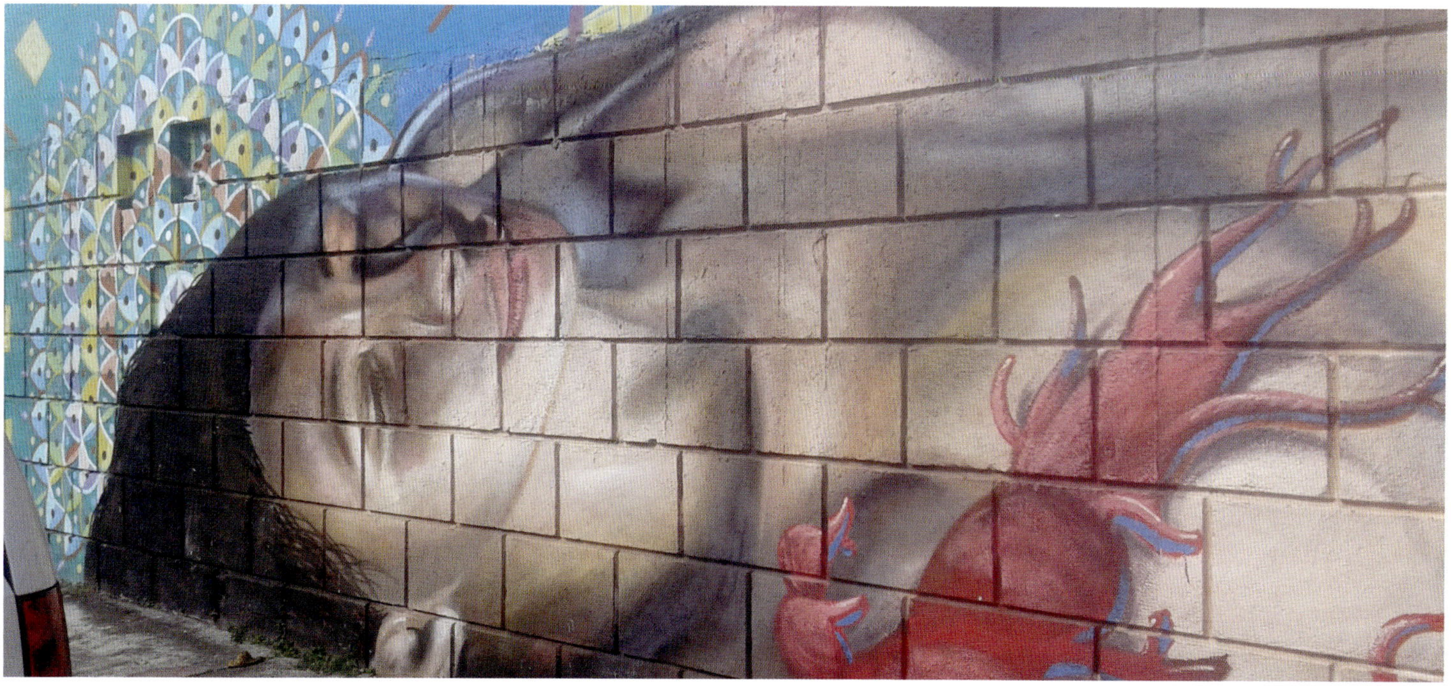

Cozumel City Hall's women on the wall by Argentine wall artist Ever

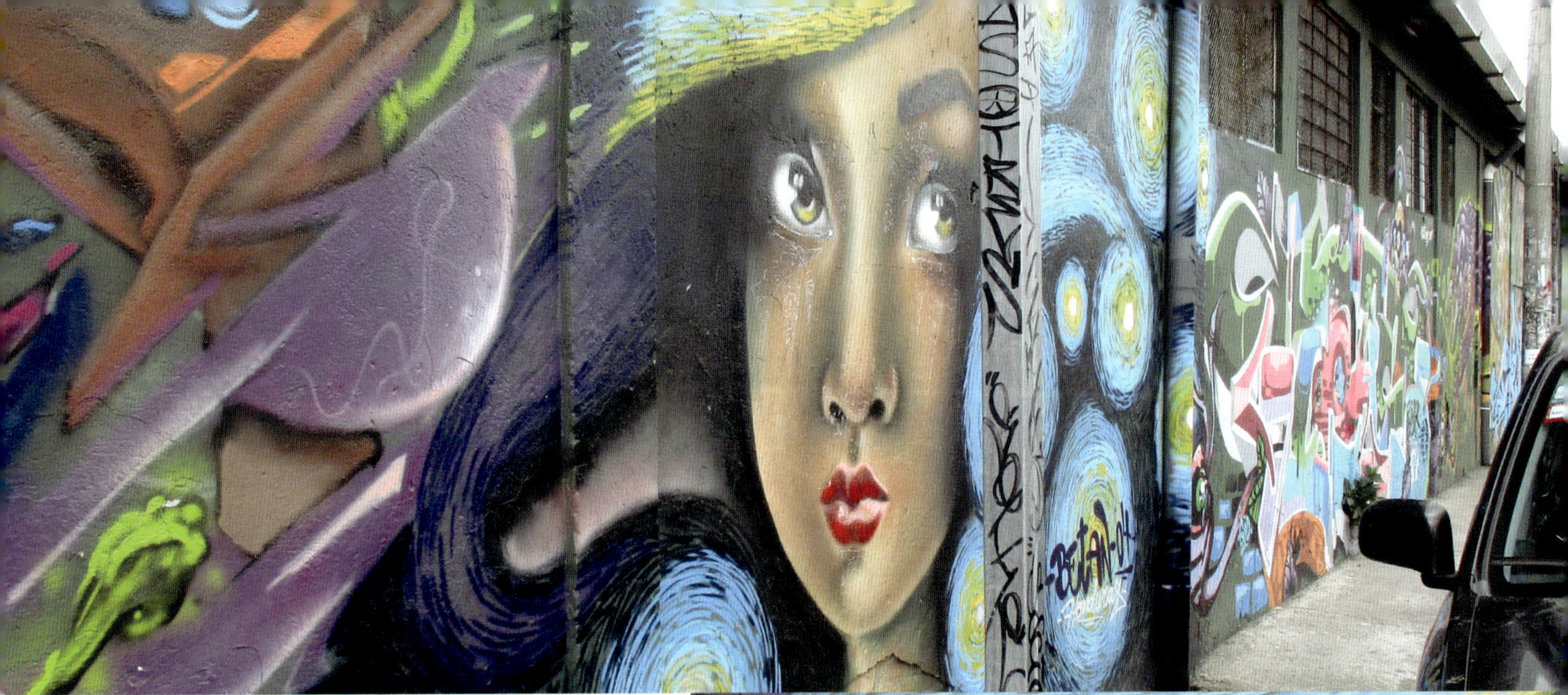

Next Stop: Costa Rica

Mexico's rich tradition of painting women on the wall is admired in Costa Rica, our next stop on the women on the wall itinerary. Costa Rica is a country where street artists labor in obscurity, in a country known as an ecological paradise where coffee grows on the side of volcanos. The Costa Rican practitioners of wall art the authors interviewed are doing all they can to put food on the table. One of them is living with his mother while inking tattoos on the side; the other is a t-shirt designer and sign painter. Their street art has an innocence linked with awareness about the natural world, and their portraits of women reflect that openness to their land and culture.

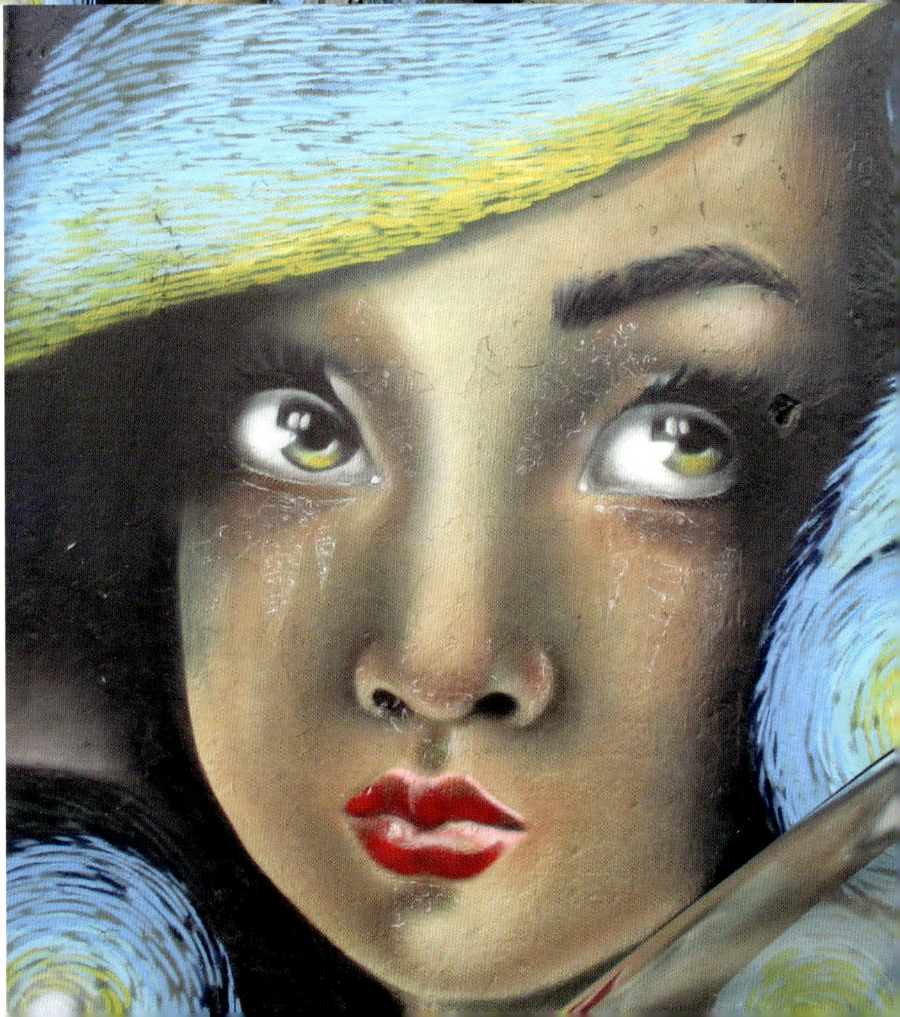

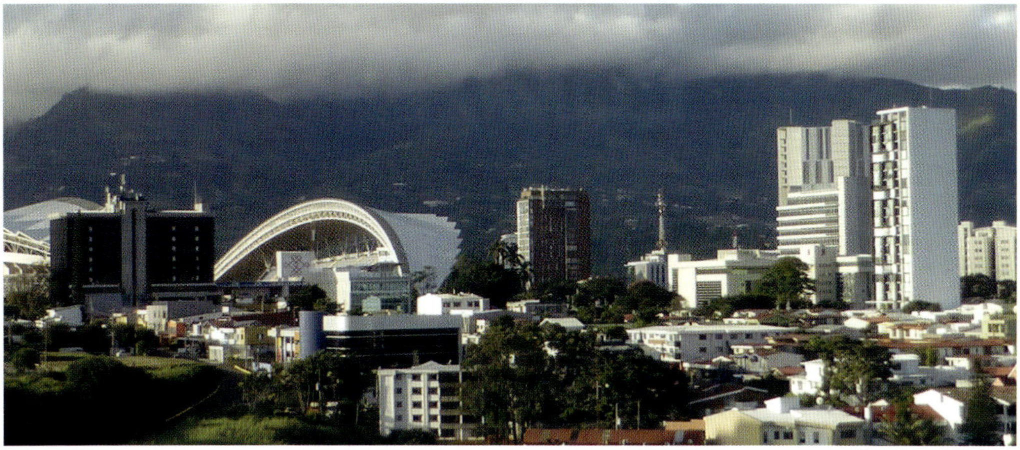

4

A view of the cloud-covered mountains surrounding San José, Costa Rica

COSTA RICA

Land of Volcanos, Rainforests, and Local Street Cred

Toucans in cloud forests, the resplendent Quetzal, hummingbirds, jungles, and caimans in waterways of mangrove swamps. This is the Costa Rica of ecotourism, but for street artists, it's a much different story.

South of Mexico, in the heart of Central America, Costa Rican street artists are scraping by to be able to practice their public declarations. These artists, most of them young men, have created a visual style that venerates the beauty of women in a youthful way, often tied into Costa Rica's commitment to preserving its natural heritage and link to its Indigenous past. Interviews with Costa Rican wall artists display a humility not found in the glitzy world of street art in LA or Paris, where "making a statement" is part of standing out from the crowd. The street artists we encountered in and around San José, Costa Rica's capital, work in urban spaces like concrete playgrounds or abandoned car parks. Their color palette is bright, and their women subjects often reflect Costa Rica's connection with the natural world, Indigenous culture, and a young man's idea of feminine beauty.

We tracked down the wall artists "JUST" and "PUCHO" by word of mouth and recommendations from the filmmaker we interviewed. The contacts were made via social media, which is how many street artists in Costa Rica communicate. JUST and PUCHO were very open to speak about why they paint women on walls and what informs their vision of women. The third interview took place under a tree with a documentary filmmaker and hip-hop DJ—Federico Peixoto—who has surveyed and filmed street art throughout Central America for many years and has found an emerging and original Central American street art identity.

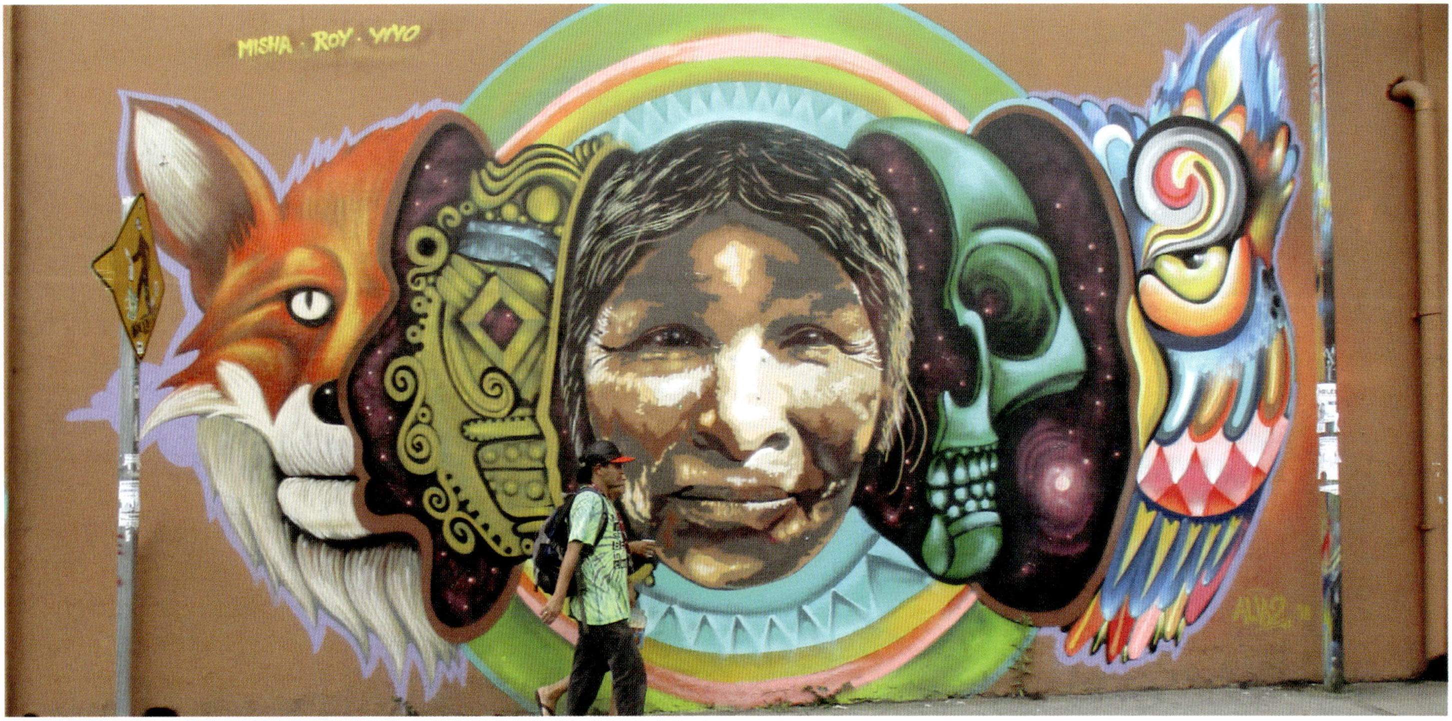

Negotiating Ticoville

By any measure, San José is a modern Central American city. And like many big cities, it is difficult to negotiate by any form of transport. The streets and its few highways are congested, involving dicey lane changes on one-way, twisting roads, requiring a certain faith the other driver will give way before you crash into a building or oncoming traffic.

To get to the interviews, there were many false starts, lots of stops, and lots of "Do you know where I can find . . . ?" questions to friendly strangers. And there were many helpful directions given to amend Google maps and directions on WhatsApp.

The city's University District, where we met our first interview subject, features a heavy concentration of street art of women that was part of an international gathering of street art in March 2018 called the Aliados International Latin American Graffiti Festival. Fifty wall artists from Chile, Guatemala, Panama, Brazil, Mexico, El Salvador, Honduras, Panama, Nicaragua, and, of course, Costa Rica were featured. The walls around the Calle de La Amargura in the San Pedro neighborhood became their playground to showcase their striking and colorful wall art of women.

The Aliados Graffiti Festival in San José in 2018 brought together street artists from throughout Central America to exhibit their works of women on the walls. Artists whose works appear on the walls include ROY, Misha, Yiyo (Costa Rica, collaboration), Betan-04 (Honduras), and Ted.

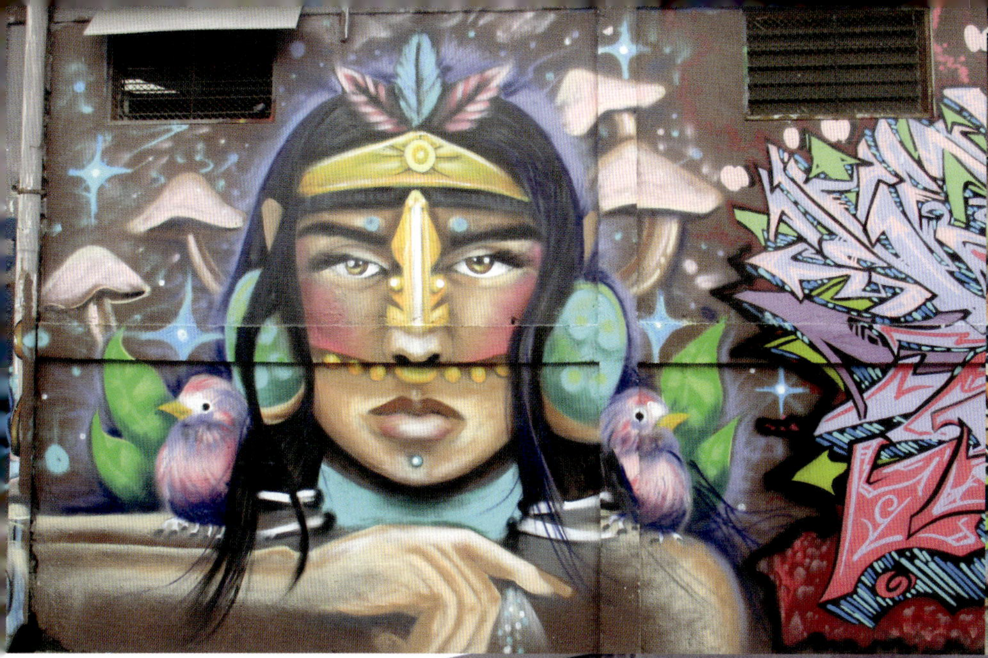

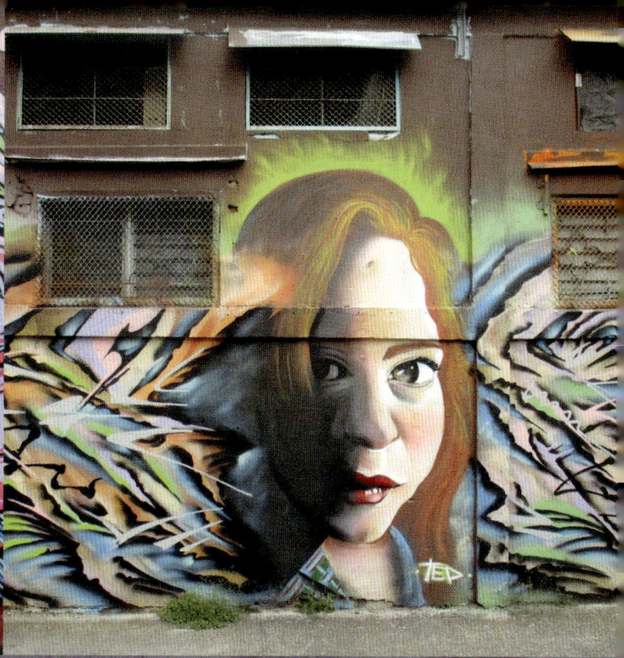

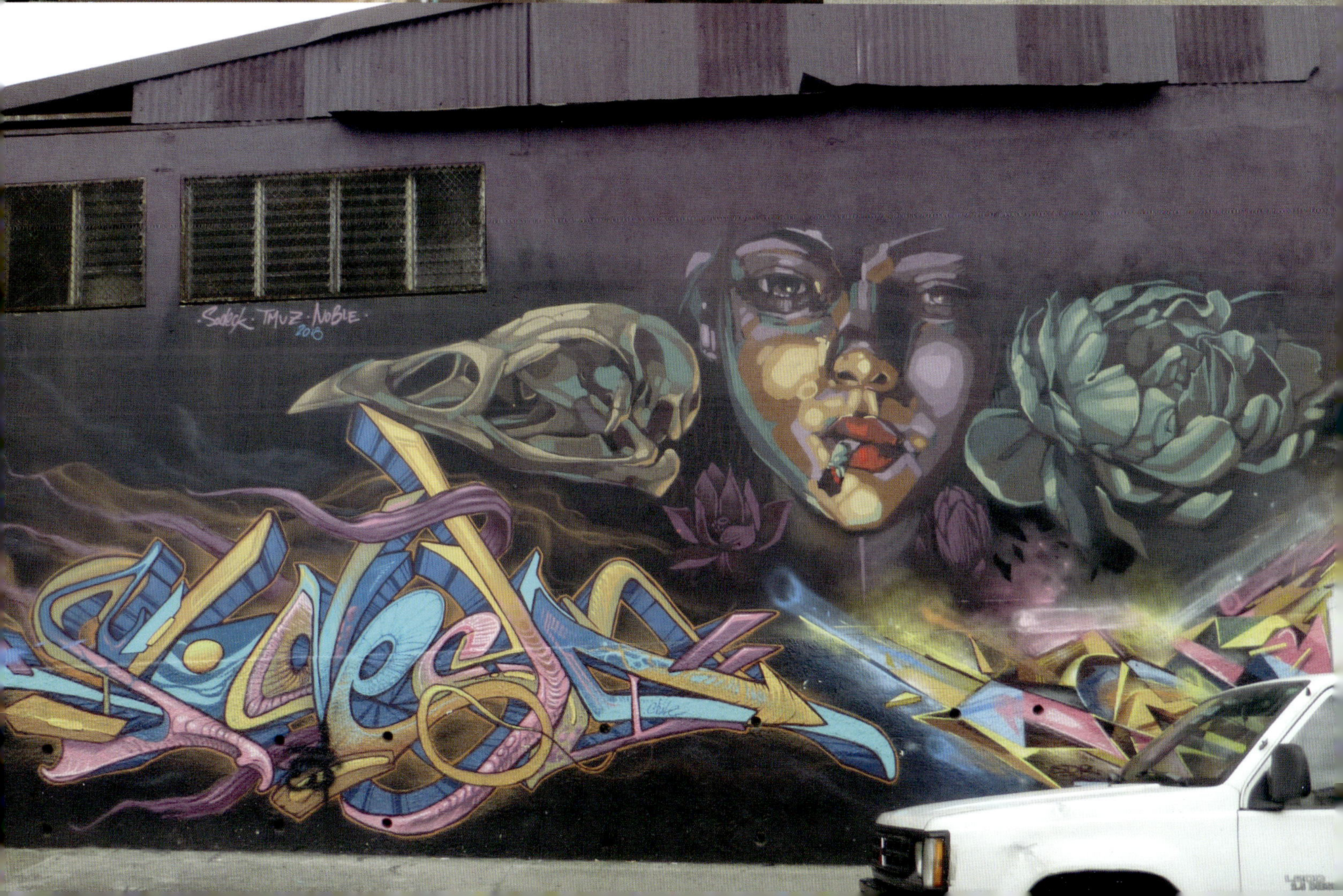
TMUZ · NOBLE
2010

FEDERICO PEIXOTO Toward a Regional Identity

The Aliados artists are part of the colorful fabric of the world traversed by Federico Peixoto, who has a unique view of the development of street art in Costa Rica and Central America. Peixoto's life bridges Europe and Central America. Born and raised in Berlin, Peixoto moved at an early age to Costa Rica, his mother's home. Peixoto started off in the early street scene of San José, learning graffiti in a trial-and-error way, always looking north to Mexico, the US, and New York for inspiration.

He turned his love for the underground heavy metal music and art scene into a passion for film and produced a documentary about graffiti artists in Central America that debuted in New York City at an international film festival in the Bronx. His documentary *Tlacuilos* is born from his celebration of a regional way of looking at wall art. The title of the documentary is taken from ancient Mexico, where a *tlacuilo* was a writer, a painter, a wise man.
The meeting with Federico Peixoto took place on a retaining wall underneath the spreading branches of a rainforest tree at the University of Costa Rica, near a labyrinth of walls full of street art.

Peixoto is comfortable in this environment, where student string quartets practice in open-air rehearsals. The ferment of a university is where ideas are hatched, and Peixoto is an ideas man—someone who straddles the arts and appreciates self-expression. His documentary is a travelogue through Central America backstreets, with a thumping Spanish hip-hop accompaniment that tracks the works of wall artists seeking to define their part of the world. Peixoto's greeting was warm and welcoming, and he was wearing a t-shirt promoting his documentary. Our conversation was punctuated by his animated hand gestures.

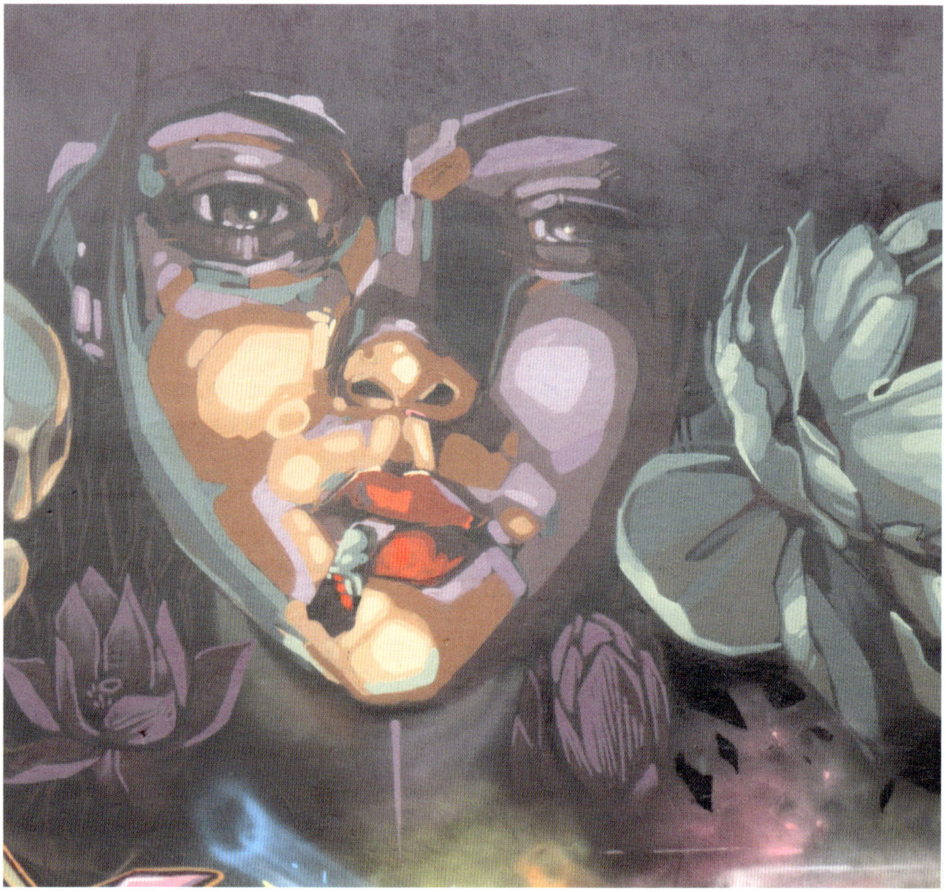

Another unknown wall artist displays a moody example of a woman smoking.

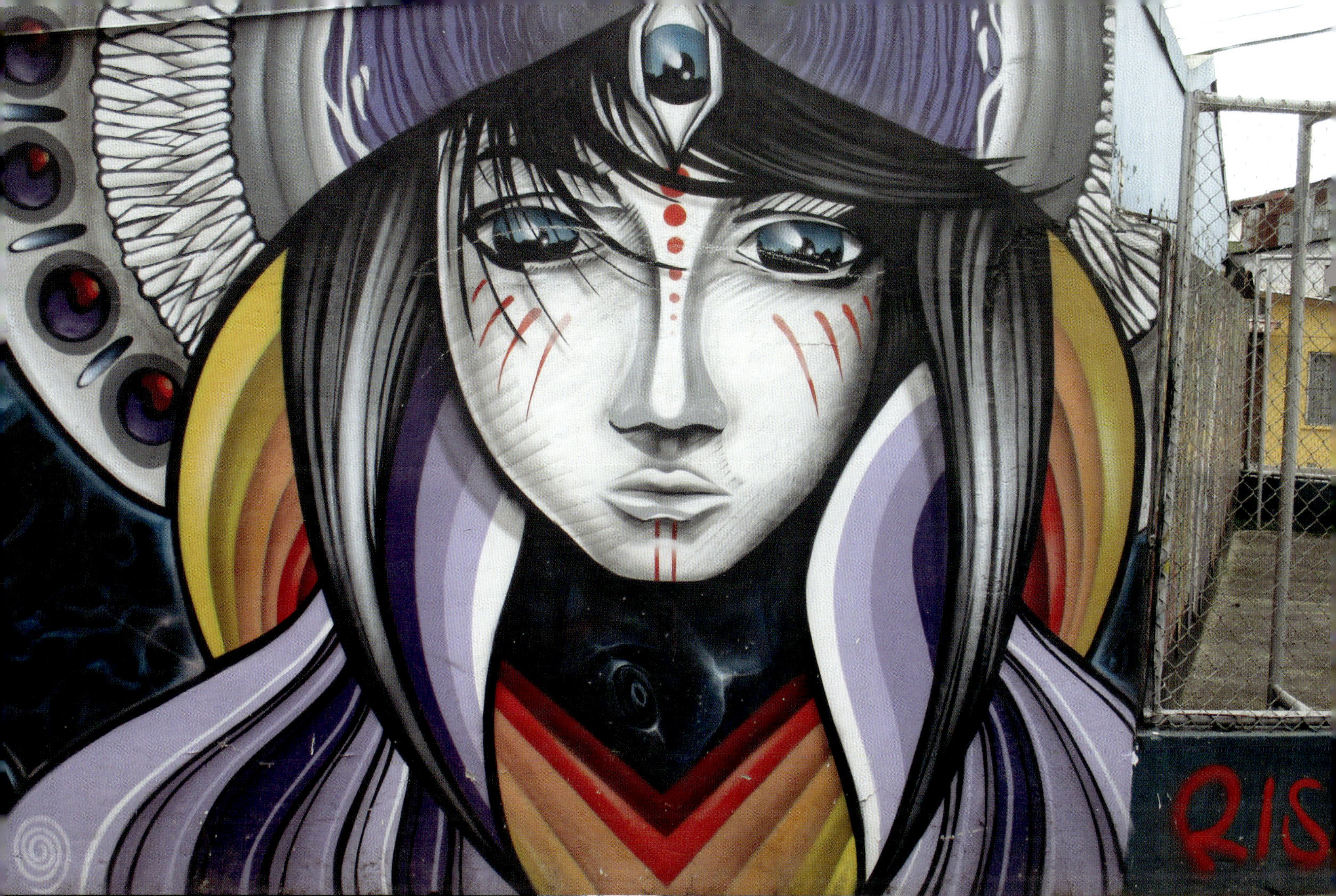

The obscurity of the wall artists is evident in this example, which may be the work of Risas (which means "laughs"), but it is unclear if that is the artist from the placement of the signature.

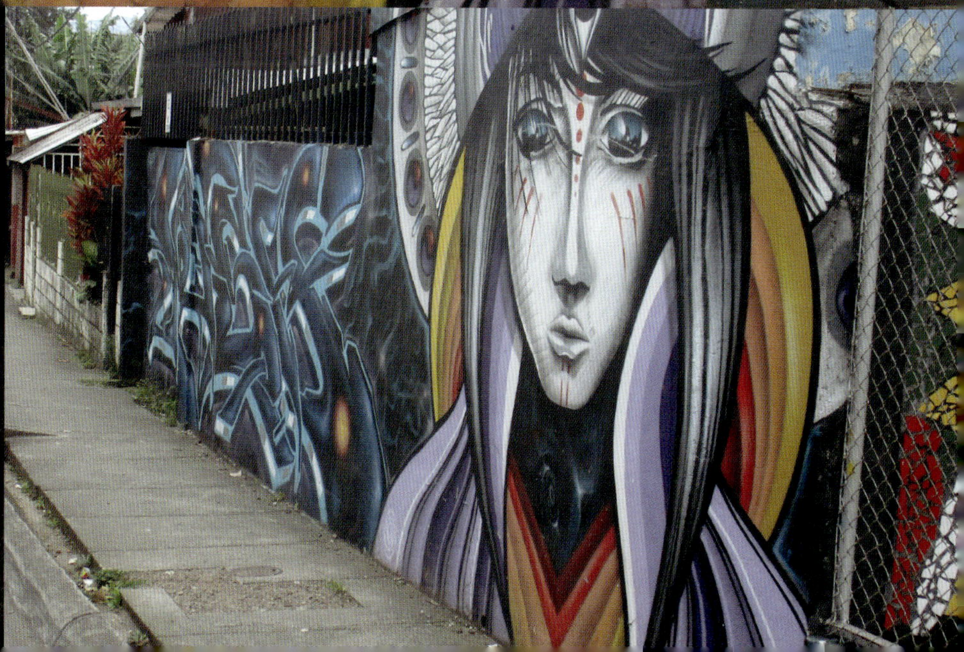

INTERVIEW WITH FEDERICO PEIXOTO

In Search of a Cultural Identity through Wall Art—Starting from Ground Zero

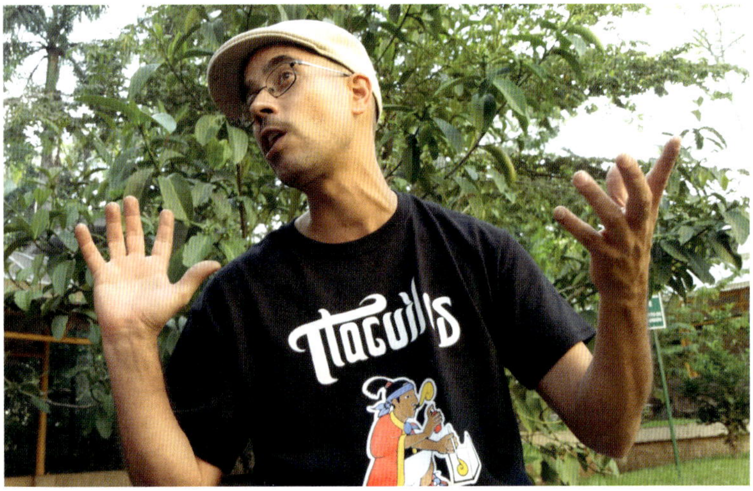

I was part of all these movements, these urban movements, like the metal music scene in San José, and I began to shoot videos of what we were doing. I began to study to get more professional to record this punk movement; I began to do hip-hop.

And one of my friends, who was a skater when we were fifteen, was one of the first to try his hand at graffiti. The only graffiti at that time was what people would paint on the walls about local football teams. It was more of a flag for football. Or some of it was political graffiti from a leftist party or the right, or poetic graffiti where you wrote something. But there wasn't graffiti like we know from the New York style or more finely painted murals. So my friends and I were the first generation that began to do this kind of graffiti because we were influenced by hip-hop music and skateboarding.

At first we were copying much of the graffiti from Europe or the US. One of the things that makes me proud of the artists in my region is that artists are now doing their own thing. They're finding their own styles—they're copying less.

And we had to learn from scratch. Everything was a mystery, because we didn't have the internet. Nobody knew how to use the caps or nozzles. We had to invent everything from zero because there was nobody to learn from. It was Third World graffiti here, with poor-quality materials, but the artists were still doing good work. For a long time, there wasn't good paint here for graffiti. The paintings were of poor quality. Necessity is the mother of invention. People were inventing their own caps (spray can nozzles). Guys in Mexico were painting incredible things by mixing colors to get special tones.

Federico Peixoto is a documentary filmmaker and hip-hop DJ who has recorded the development of Central American graffiti artists.

Looking North

The US has had more time to evolve. There are a lot more artists with a lot more skill levels. The styles, the colors, the themes are different. The color palettes are more alive. There's a lot of connection here with the US, because there are a lot of Latinos there and a lot of diverse Latino cultures from Central America.

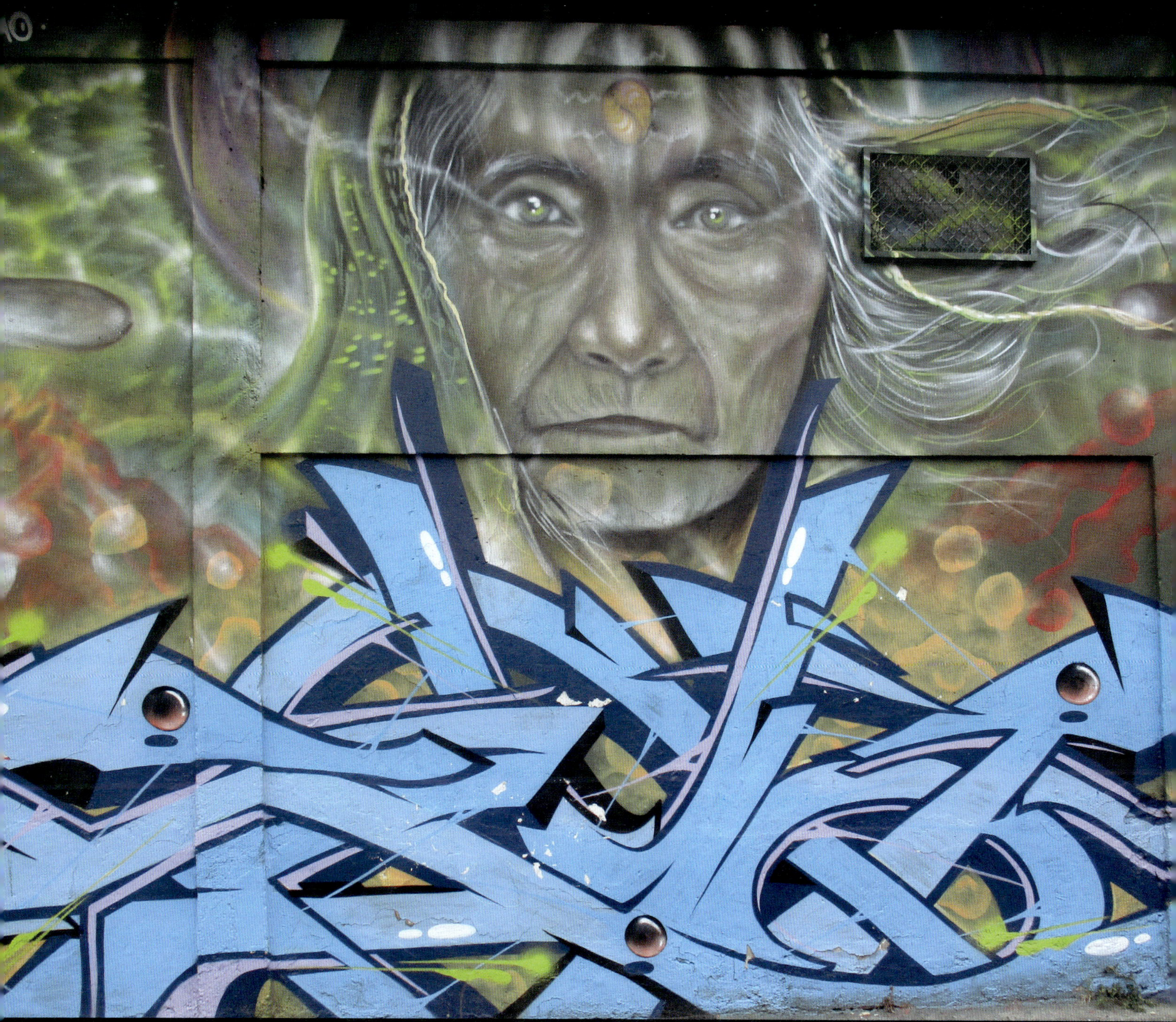

The face of an elderly woman peers through a veil of tagging in this work by PUCHO and SEYOR.

It's part of the evolution, right? They might say, "I want to do that; how do I do it?" They say I can do this or that. There's been enough time to see the evolution of interesting styles that include the point of view from other people around the world. It's like finding your voice. It's not easy in art or in music to have an original style.

Also, there wasn't information either on the evolving street art scene. There came a moment when I wanted to document all this, and we began to connect with the rest of Central America.

> We knew what was happening in Los Angeles and New York—this was the start of 2000—but we didn't know what was happening in Managua, or Guatemala. Because there wasn't communication, only in certain scenes like punk and skateboarding, etc., and only with Panama and Nicaragua. But there wasn't much exchange of information.

So I started to do my underground videos of these scenes. I started to realize the whole Central American movement was starting to connect. That was my intent, what I was trying to do—the history of this movement.

Getting the Vision Together: A Question of Scale

I started organizing festivals, going to festivals to play or film, whatever. For me it made a lot of sense because Central America countries are small, with small scenes compared to Mexico, Colombia, or Brazil or Argentina, which are monsters in the break-dance scene or whatever, with thousands of people participating. For us it was always difficult because we were a few people. We're so small in Central America, and the rest of the countries are really big.

So I had a sense of a regional movement where you can travel between each country and there are more people practicing wall art or graffiti. I was able to go to Nicaragua and Panama. We began to do that because it was closer.

> I wanted to document the story of how the graffiti movement evolved in each of the countries in Central America. And how this regional movement came into being. For me it was really interesting because I spent a lot of years in these scenes. And it was a very special moment in history, and it was an important moment in history

The goal of the documentary is to let everyone know about the artists that are here and the history of the country, the wars and revolutions. All this is from the viewpoint of graffiti artists. I interviewed a lot of people who were there. There are some veterans who remember the war in El Salvador and in Nicaragua. The war continues today. It's a different war. Now, the drug highway goes through here. The *narcos* come here and do whatever they want. Central America is very beautiful and magical, but it's dangerous. We are also a strategic point in North America with the Panama Canal. The gringos want to control this area through coups. Central America is damned. And the documentary is a way of seeing this area. I've given access to people who can't come here and experience this.

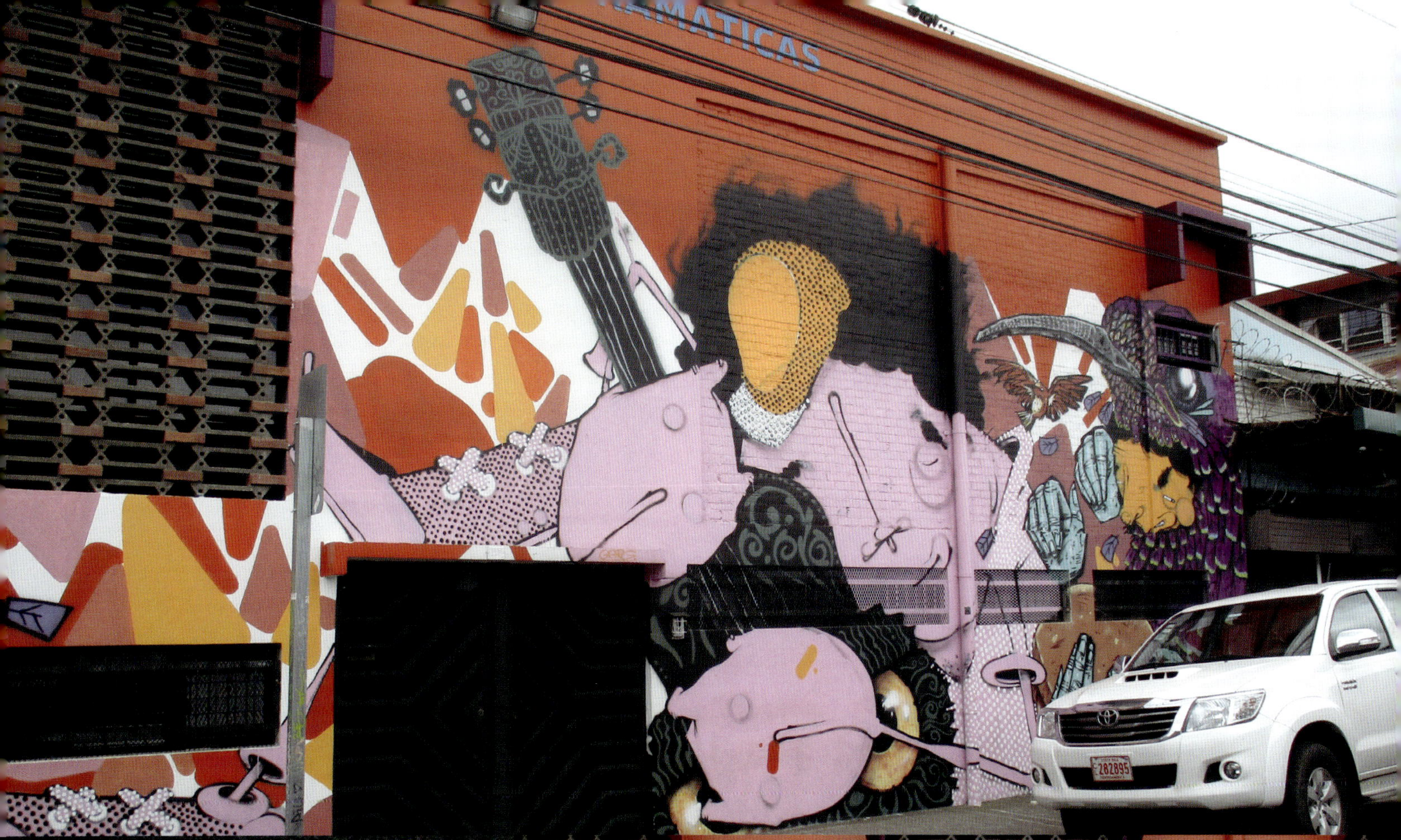

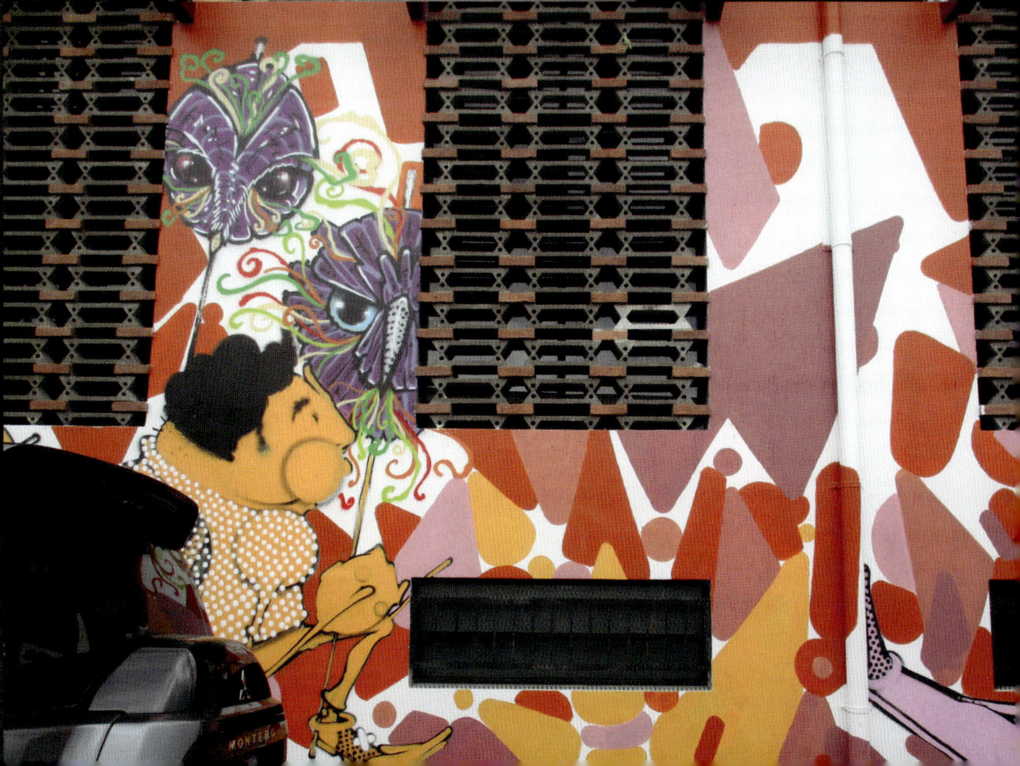

Works by Onesto Birdaz, who has a unique style that borders on caricature. Another Birdaz example is on the following page.

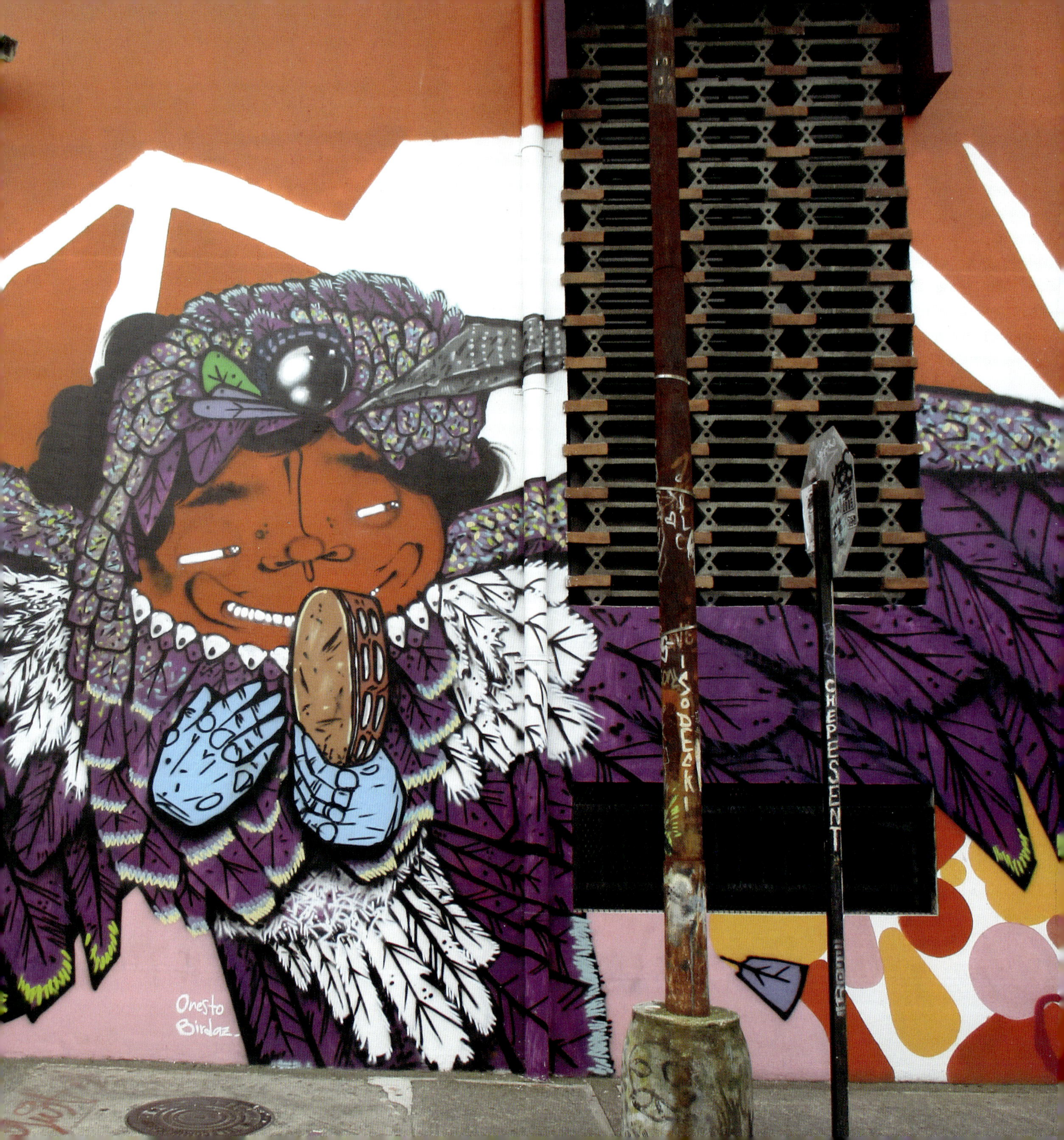
Onesto
Birdaz

The Central American Style

> Each country and style is different. There are countries in Central America that have more connection with their pre-Columbian culture, some with less. Some paint according to their gangs, others with references to Mayan culture. In Panama it's more Caribbean, more Black culture. All these influences show up in the art.

The people of Central America are different ethnically. In Guatemala the people are Mayan. They paint their women with Mayan features. In Costa Rica it depends on the region. In San José it's more white or mixed race. The people here are distinct. It also depends on the artist. There aren't that many artists who paint women either. I know artists who paint women's faces, but not everyone. Many paint letters and other things. In Panama they paint faces of women. I like women, so I like seeing them as subjects. I don't know if I'm being macho saying this. It depends on the person who sees the art.

Women Wall Artists in a Macho Culture

There are more women entering the wall art field now. But at the start, it was the men who started it. It was a little violent. . . . That's what I think. I know a lot of women who started doing graffiti but haven't continued for whatever reason.

The macho culture also has something to do with it. Women would limit themselves for what other people are thinking or what their boyfriend would think.

> The macho culture affects all women at all levels. There are a few women who have dedicated their lives to graffiti and are continuing, but there are only a few. I would love it if there were more female wall artists, right?

They have a different mentality. There's a new generation of young women who are coming along. But it takes a number of years to arrive at the point of achieving a high level. In Mexico, there are a lot of women painting on big walls in big formats more than in Central America. But this is changing rapidly. There's no reason why not.

The Political Tilt to the Right and Wall Artist Response

I think Costa Rica has the reputation of being a country at peace, but people express their political views on the wall in graffiti like "Oscar Arias, corupto." It's one of the ways the people can express their discontent on the wall. It reflects the state of being of the people in that city. If you don't see any graffiti, that says a lot too. Sometimes you can wake up other people if my vision is different than the knowledge I have and the references I make. Art can open your eyes. That's what surprises me. I find a work of art, I say, "OK, it opens my mind."

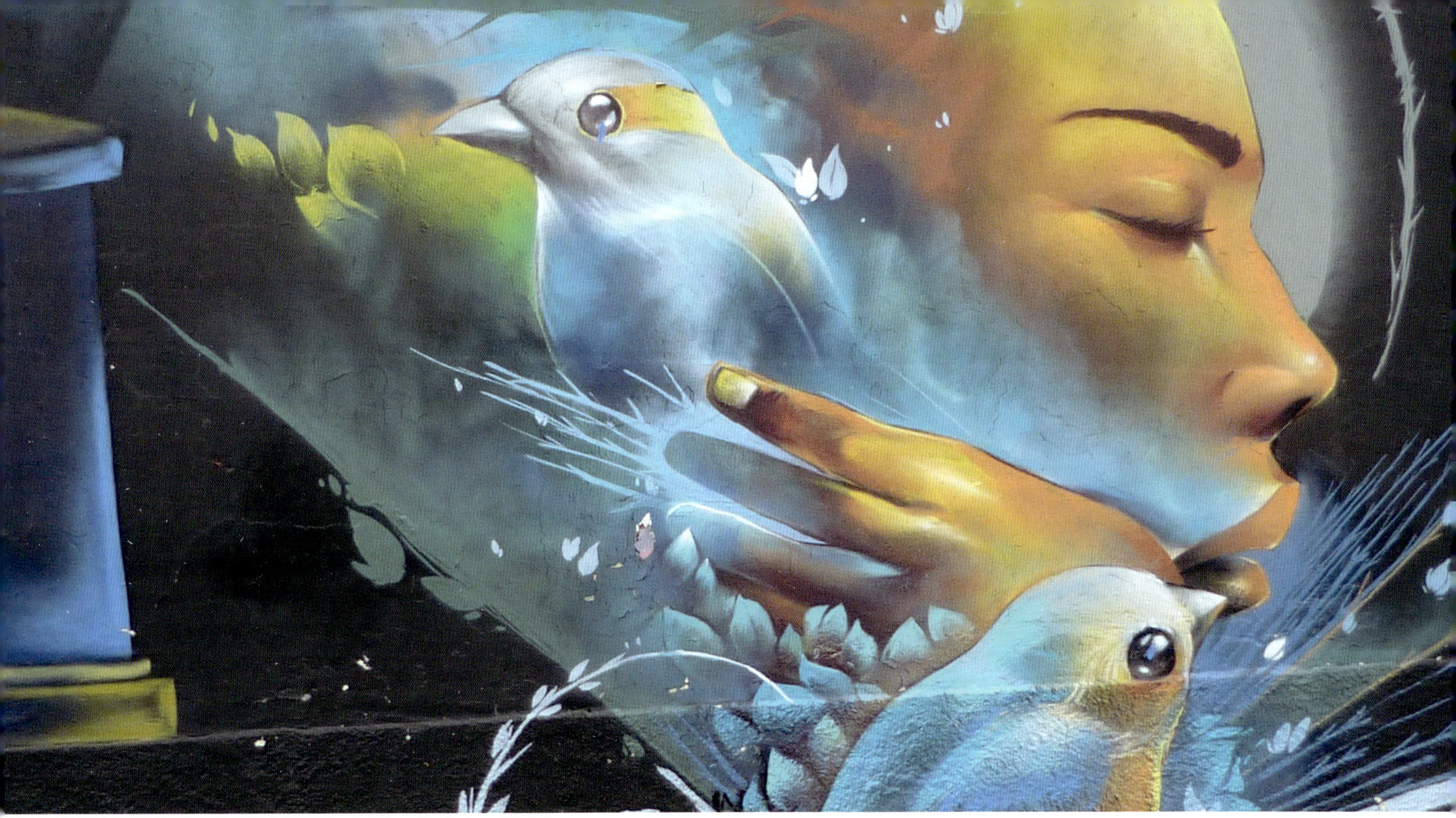

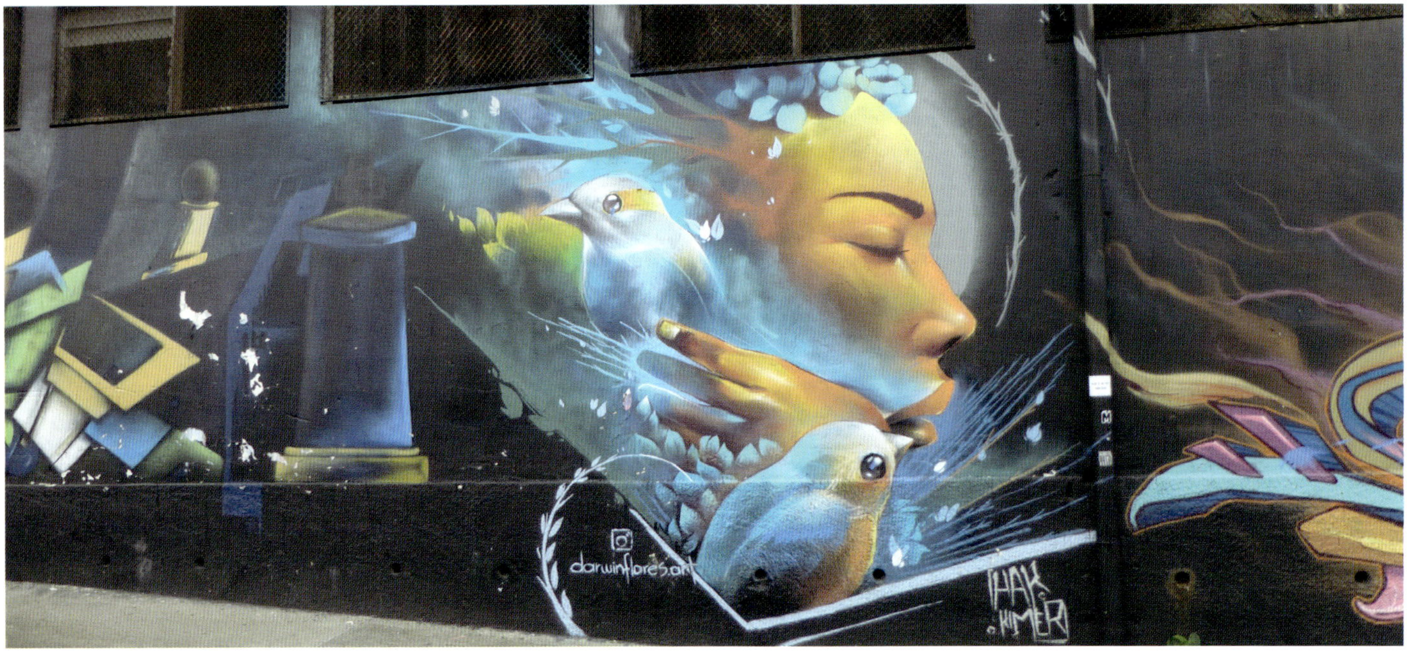
darwinflores.art
IHAK
KIMER

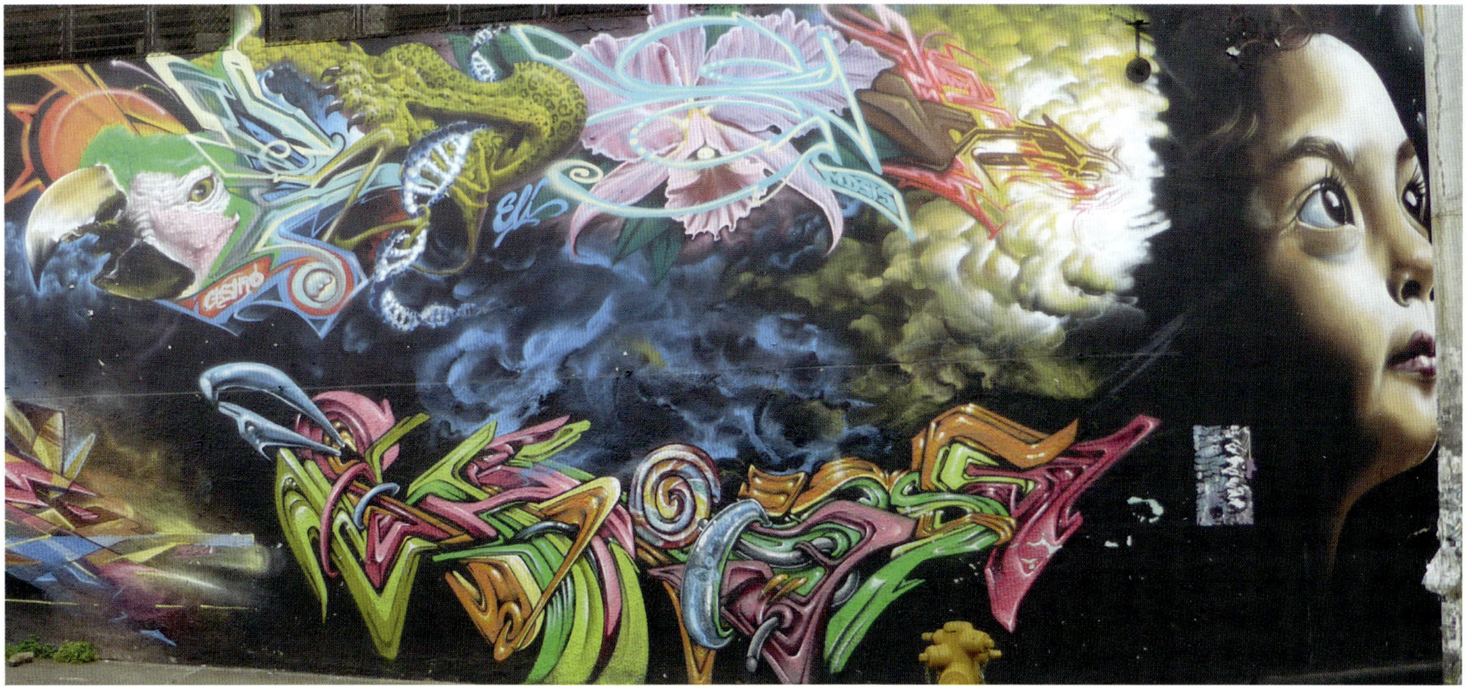

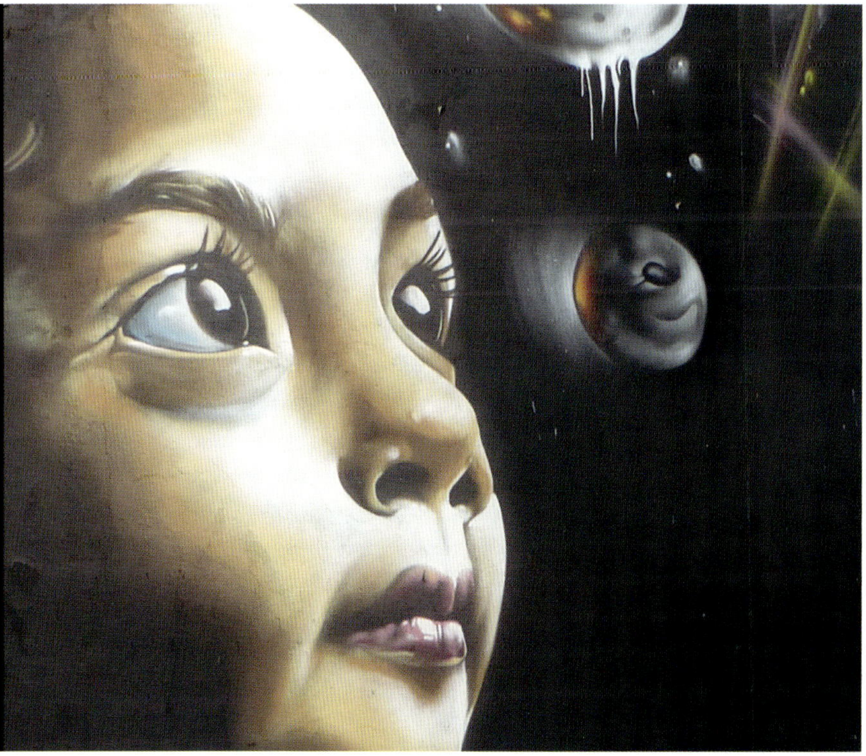

A striking example of how street art of women can convey movement, color, and introspection. Wall art by darwinflores (left).

Artist Sinless from Panama captures the curiosity and wonder of a young girl.

JUST: Tattoo-Inspired Wall Art of Women

After a hair-raising drive, the small suite of shops comes into view in a working class neighborhood of the city. That is where we found JUST, whose street handle isn't used in the tattoo parlor where he makes his living, so he can paint his wall art in San José. Like all our interviewees in Costa Rica, JUST embodied a humility and pride about his work and his development as an artist. His output on the wall and on the skin is prolific. The lanky, bearded artist is genuine and straightforward and tells his story in a reflective way.

Like many tattoo artists, JUST's portrayal of women as body art involves women as idealized objects of beauty, often in clichéd guises. But that's what most male customers want, and accordingly JUST provides his male clients with a bookful of drawings of women he can ink into tattoos.

Before he turned to tattooing as a way to make a living, JUST was tagging and bombing walls with his friends. It is clear that JUST looks the part of the wall artist, even down to his tattooed leg, which features spray cans.

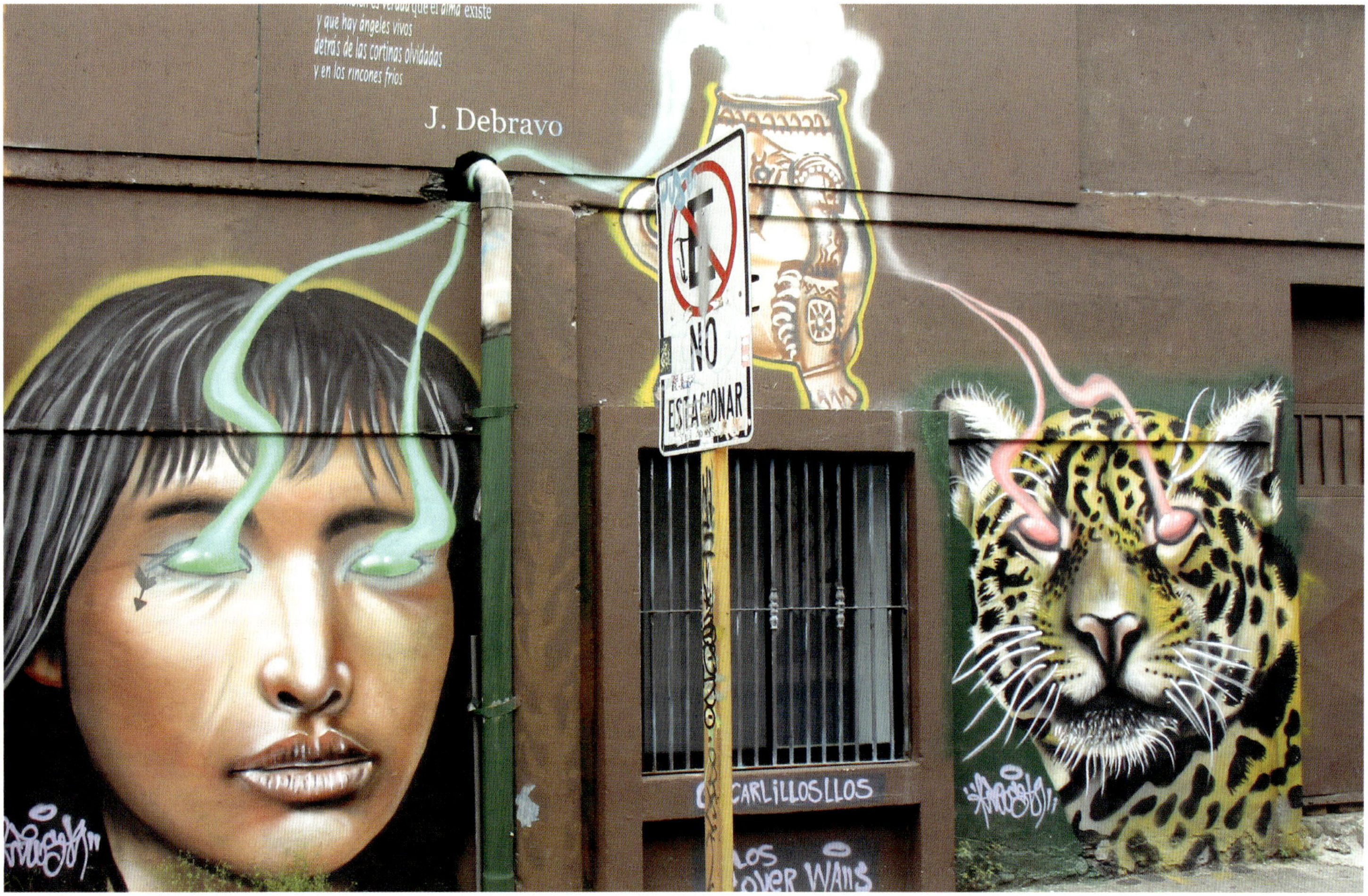

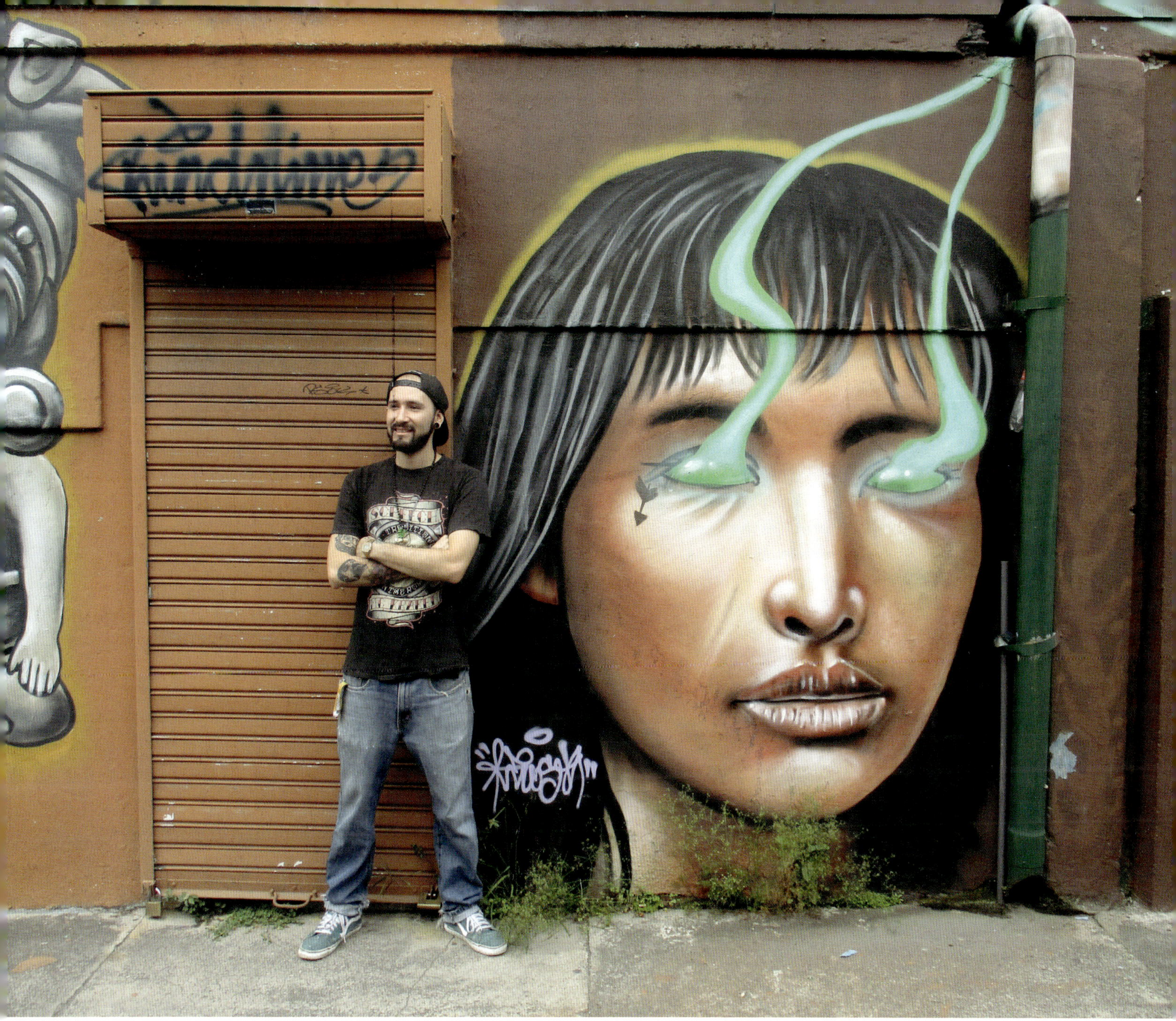

JUST (Carlillos Just) poses in front of his work in the University district of San José.

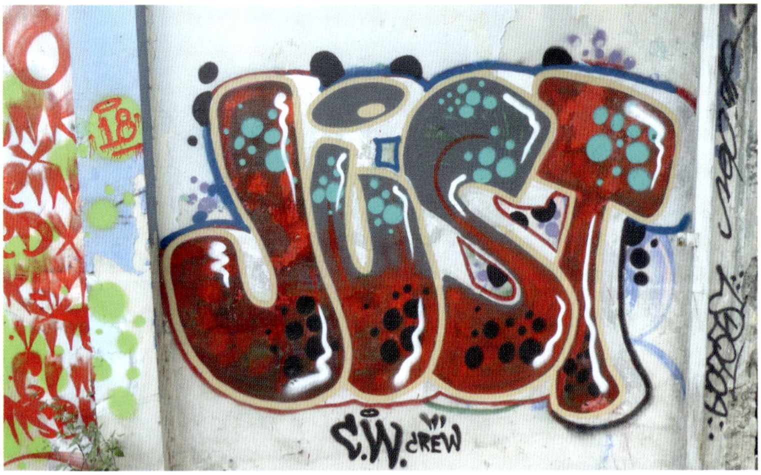

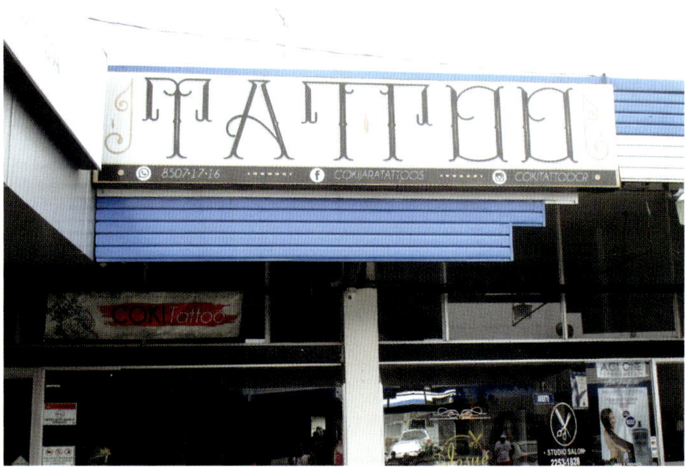

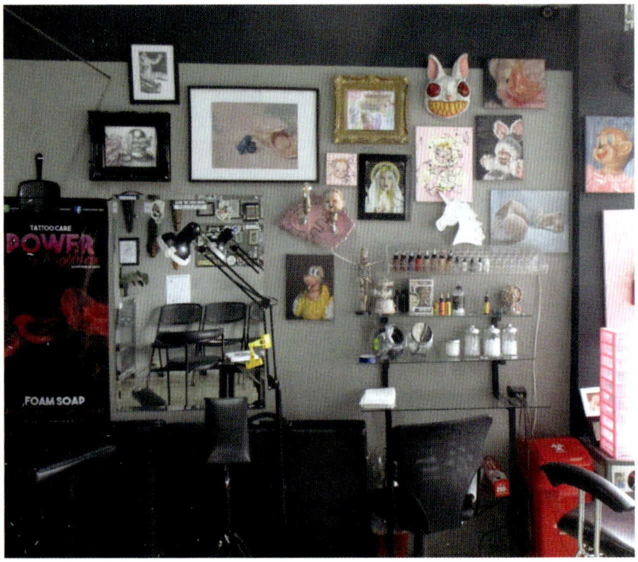

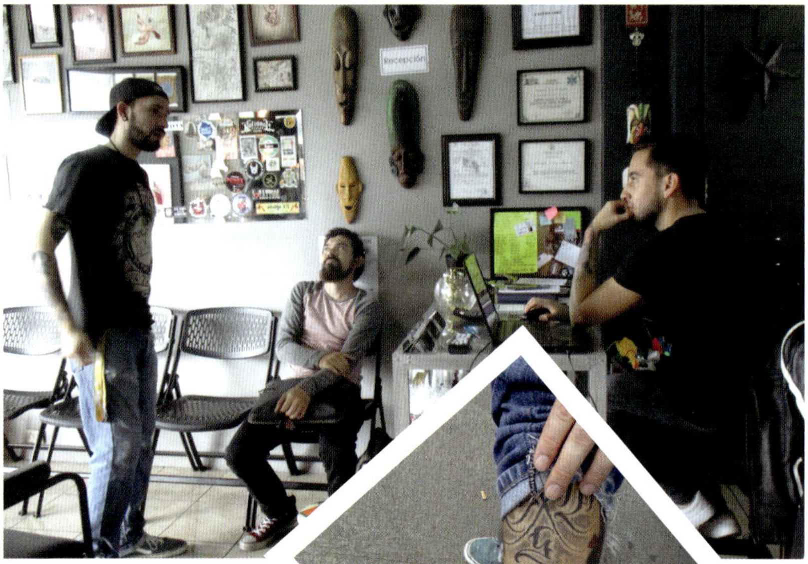

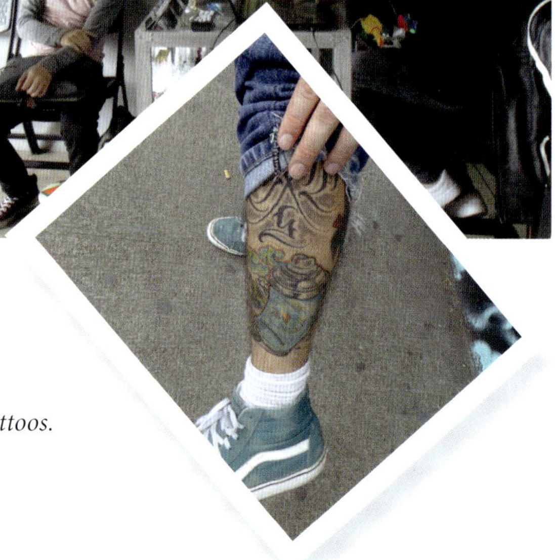

JUST's tag at an abandoned parking lot

The tattoo shop where JUST earns the money he needs to paint walls

The interior of the tattoo shop is full of portraits of women JUST uses to ink his tattoos.

JUST discussing his work as a client waits

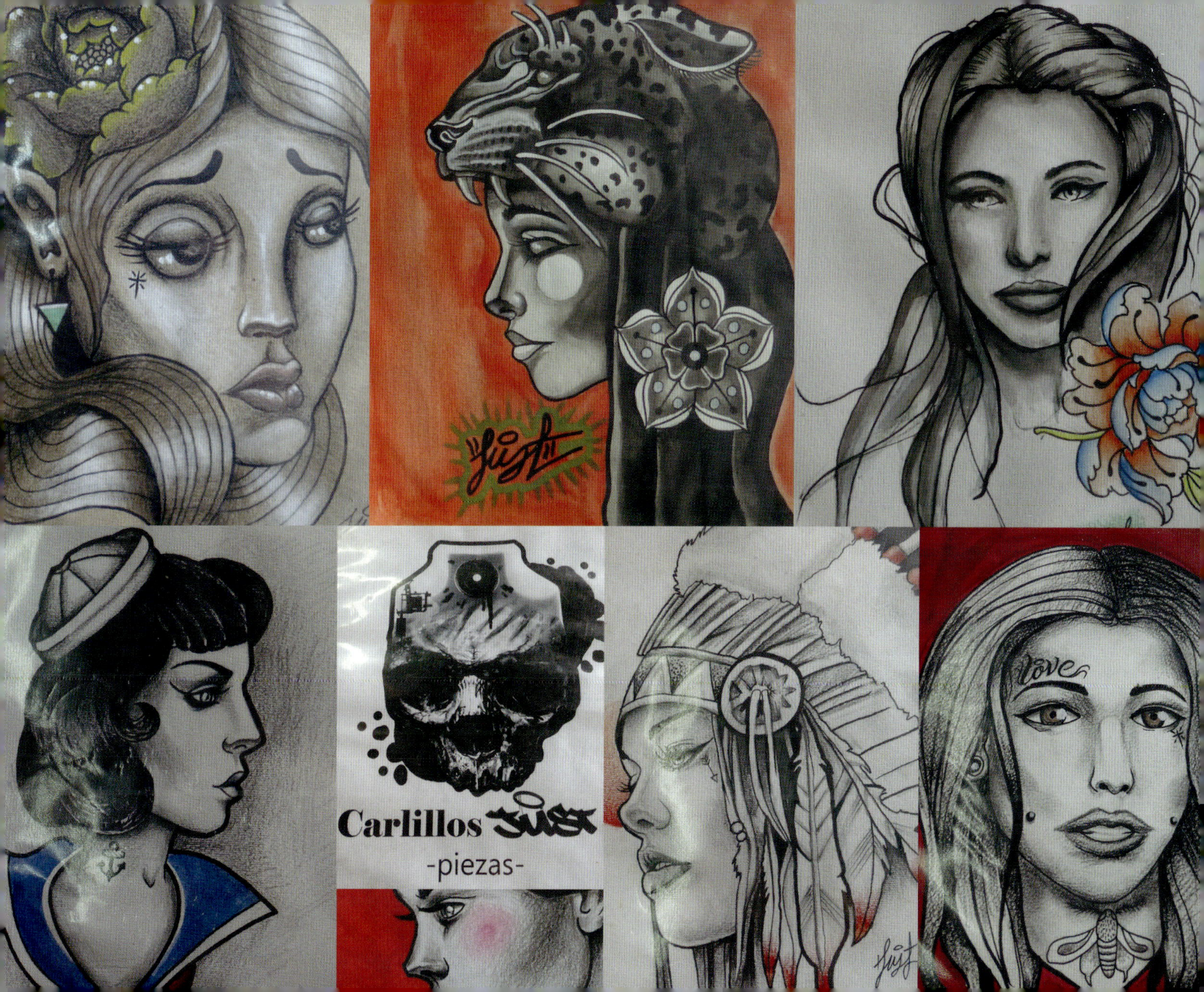

Carlillos JUST
-piezas-
love

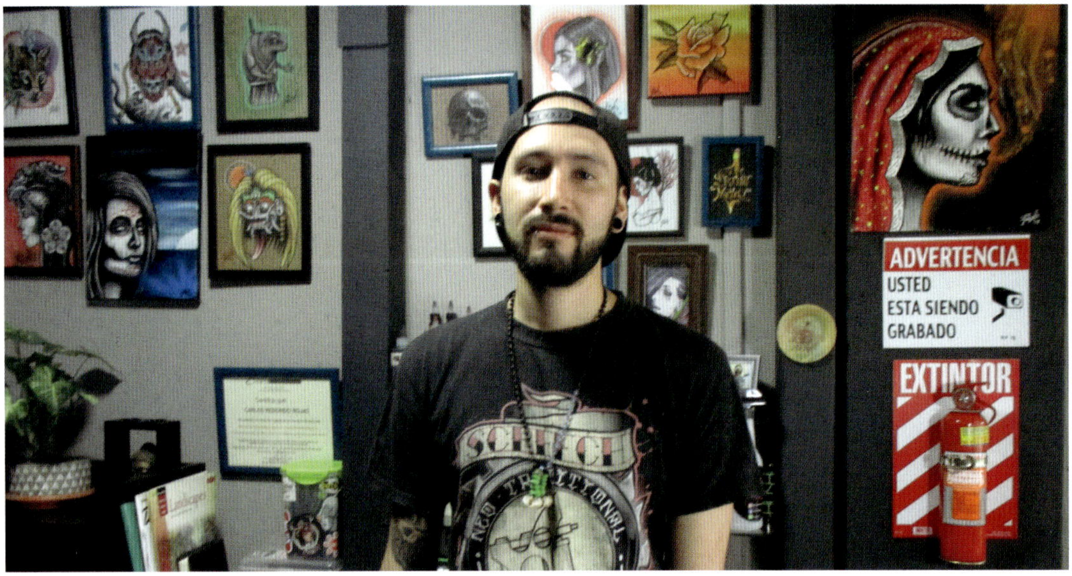

INTERVIEW WITH JUST: Just a Kid from the Streets

Why women? Obviously, they're more attractive than men in all ways. A woman is more beautiful than a man. They're more delicate; the shape of their faces is more attractive, right?

I've always liked photos of women in my art, and I also think the art draws more attention. But I also realized that's not everything. I always tattoo "Catrinas," animals, the countryside. I've done a lot of graffiti using the countryside as a subject with mountains in the background.

I began when I was sixteen doing graffiti in the neighborhood. I still do graffiti and have my crew. I began with two friends from my neighborhood who were doing graffiti. They taught me a little, and I got a bit of money and bought some spray paint cans. Then I was evolving from what they were teaching me. Then one of them died. He was a coke head and drinking a lot and getting really screwed up in the head, and he was living on the streets and he was hit by a car. It's been two years since he died. The other guy was lazy and had no job, a super-simple life, and he's got a daughter who is twelve years old now. He always brought money to his daughter, doing odd construction jobs. These two taught me: One of them is dead and the other is living a very poor life. The guy who died was a very good friend of mine, and I went with him all the time to the football stadium when we were sixteen or seventeen years old. When I went to his burial, I was talking with his mother, and in her pain she told me, "At least my son accomplished something good by teaching you about art."

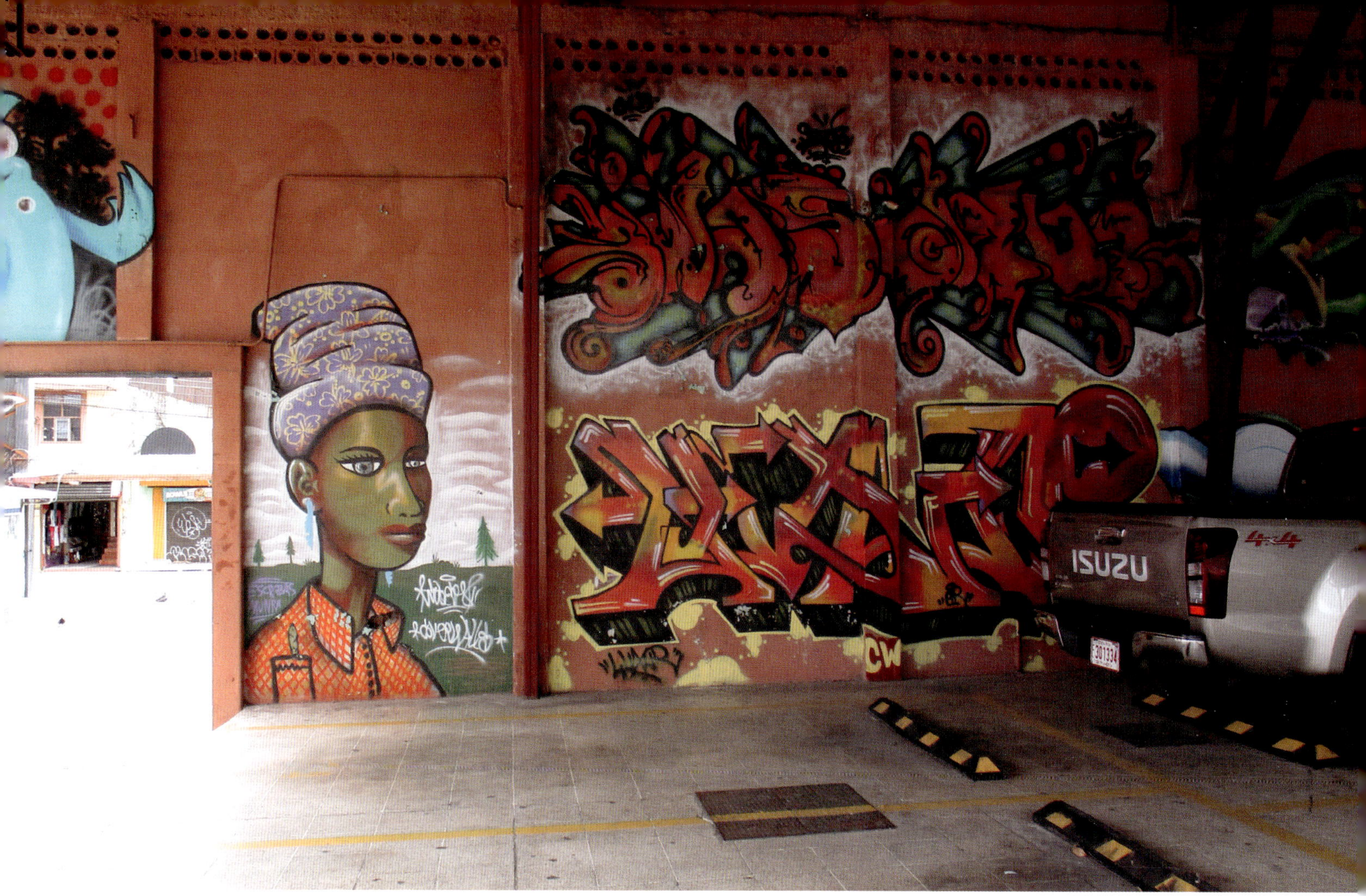

On Painting Women

When I studied art, I was taught artistic expression is what informs all art. I don't have a particular point of view. Sometimes I draw a woman, and people say she's happy or is having sad thoughts. Or another person regards the portrait from a nostalgic point of view. It all depends on the point of view of the person who is looking at the art.

JUST's portrait of a good female friend of his

What attracts me are women, which is why I paint women. Artistically, they're more beautiful. One feels an attraction for women. When people see art of women, their reaction is "Wow, how beautiful." The art impresses them. It's beauty and attraction. And it's matter of a good reception for the art.

On Making it as a Wall Artist

My tattoo business helps pay bills, and that's it. Most people can't make a living from what they like doing. And my mother supports me a lot. I pay her a little money in the house to cover costs like food, water, and electricity. She has her pension and she's supporting me now. She tells me, "Go to the studio and draw!" She's always supported me. She's very active and eats super-healthy food. It's a super-nice relationship I have with her. If it wasn't for her, I'd be doing tattoos at night, and I would work locally and live alone. My mom knows that at some point I will leave, but I don't want to leave now because I don't have the income yet.

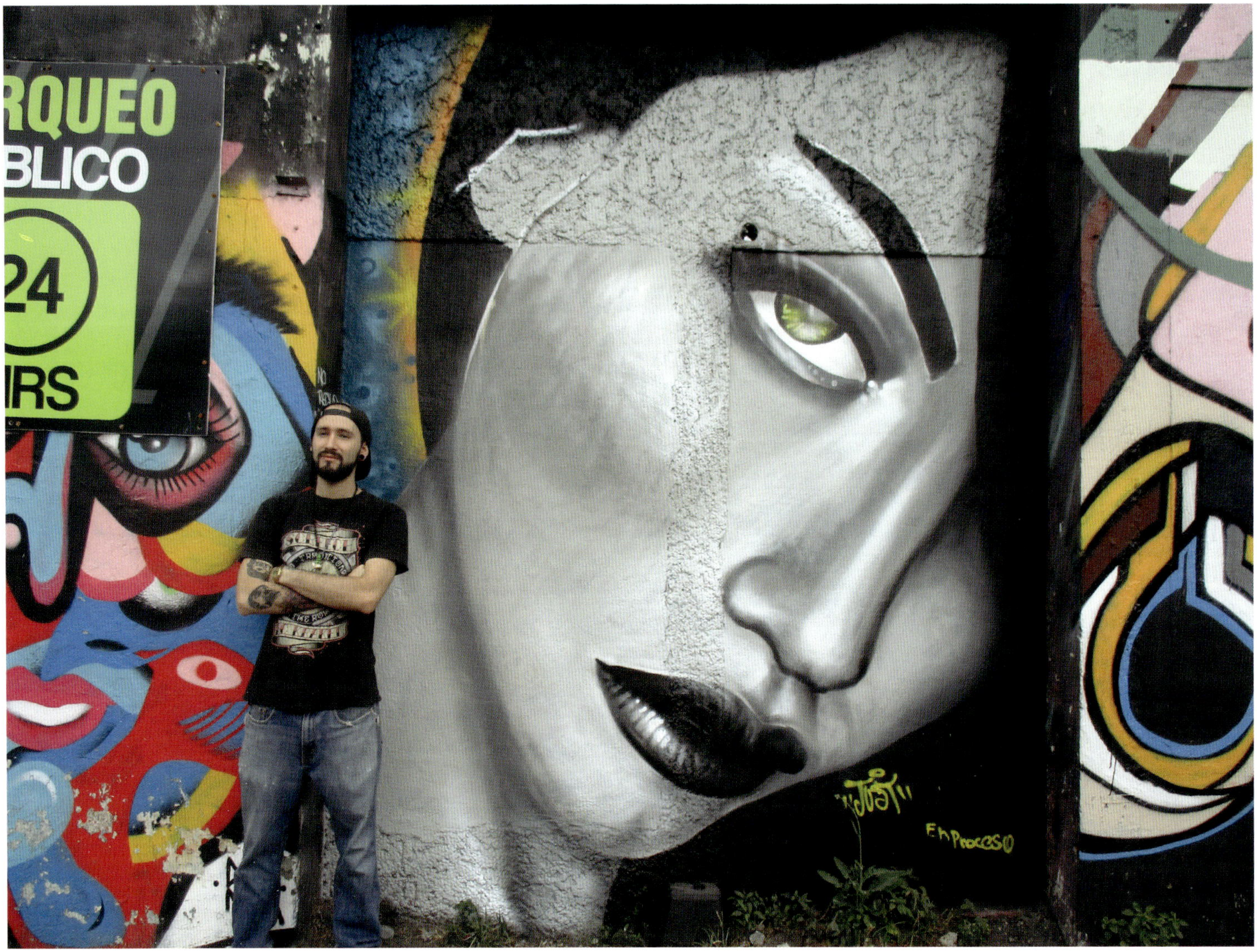

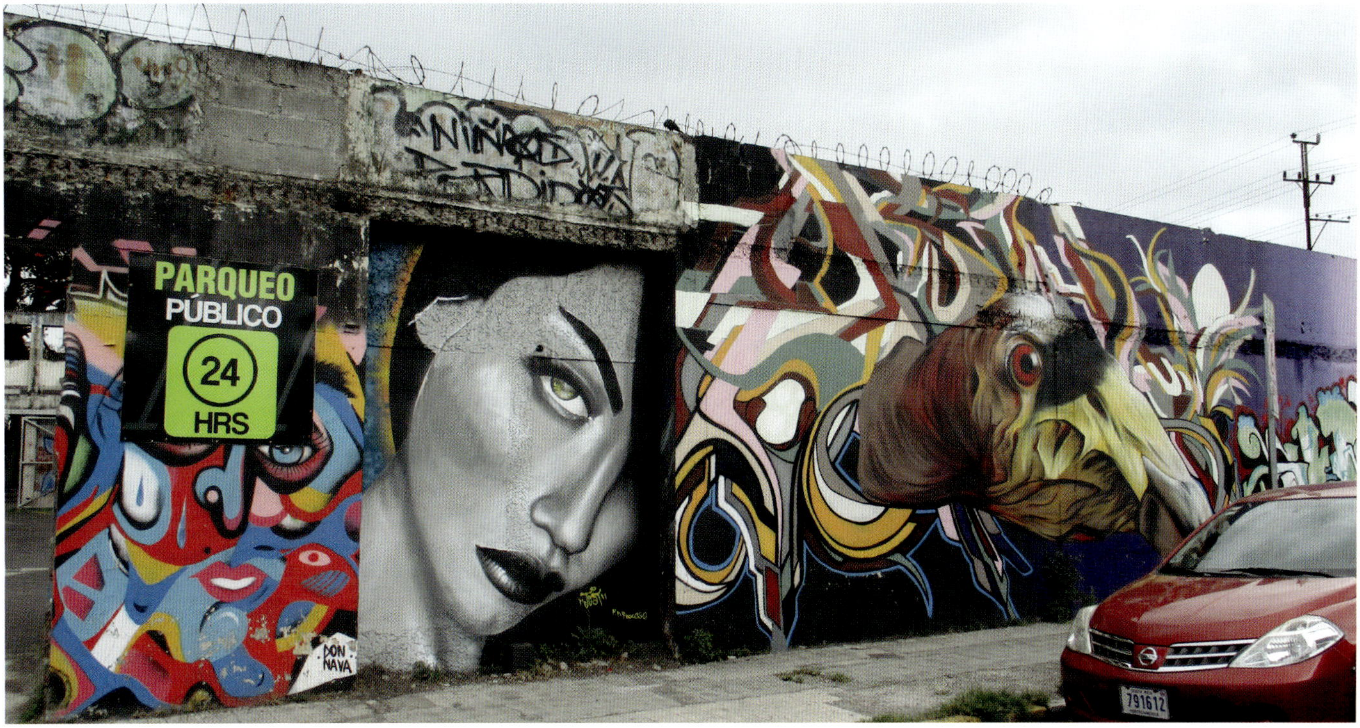

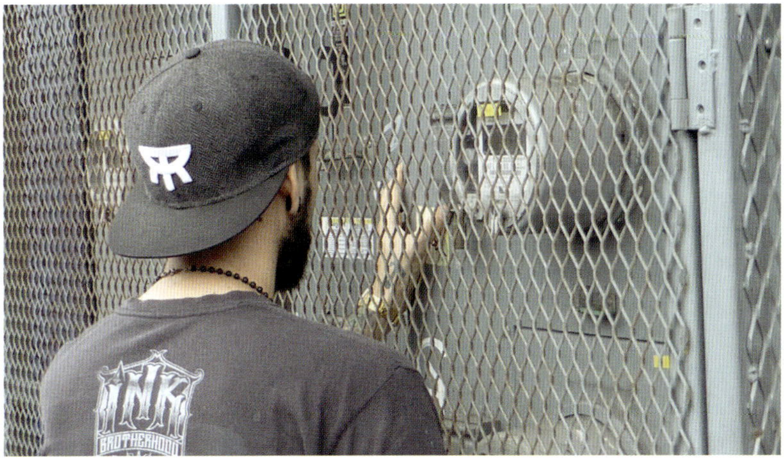

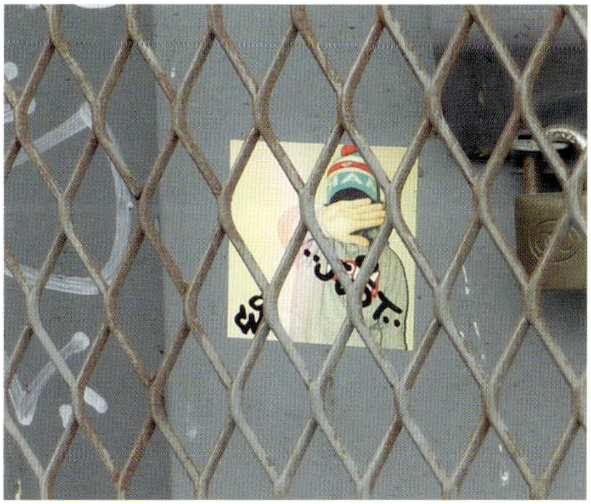

JUST's intimate portrait of a woman brightens up an otherwise dull urban wall.

JUST pastes up stickers advertising his wall art.

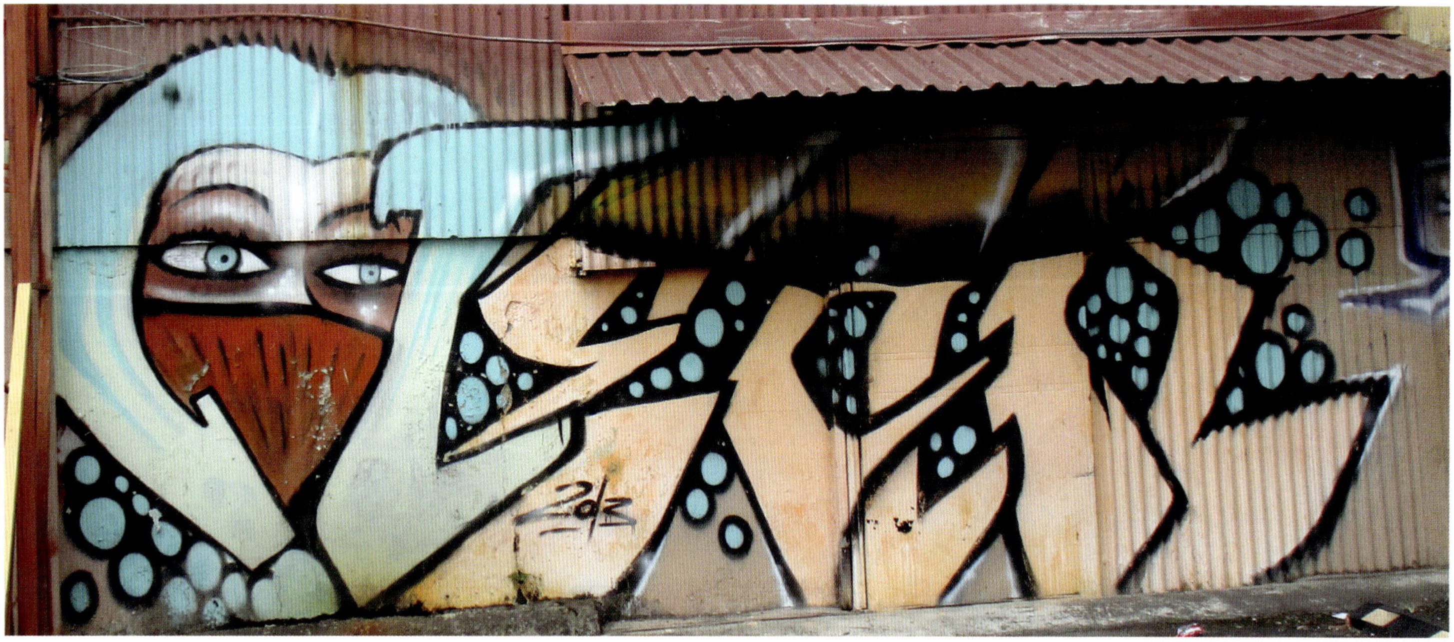

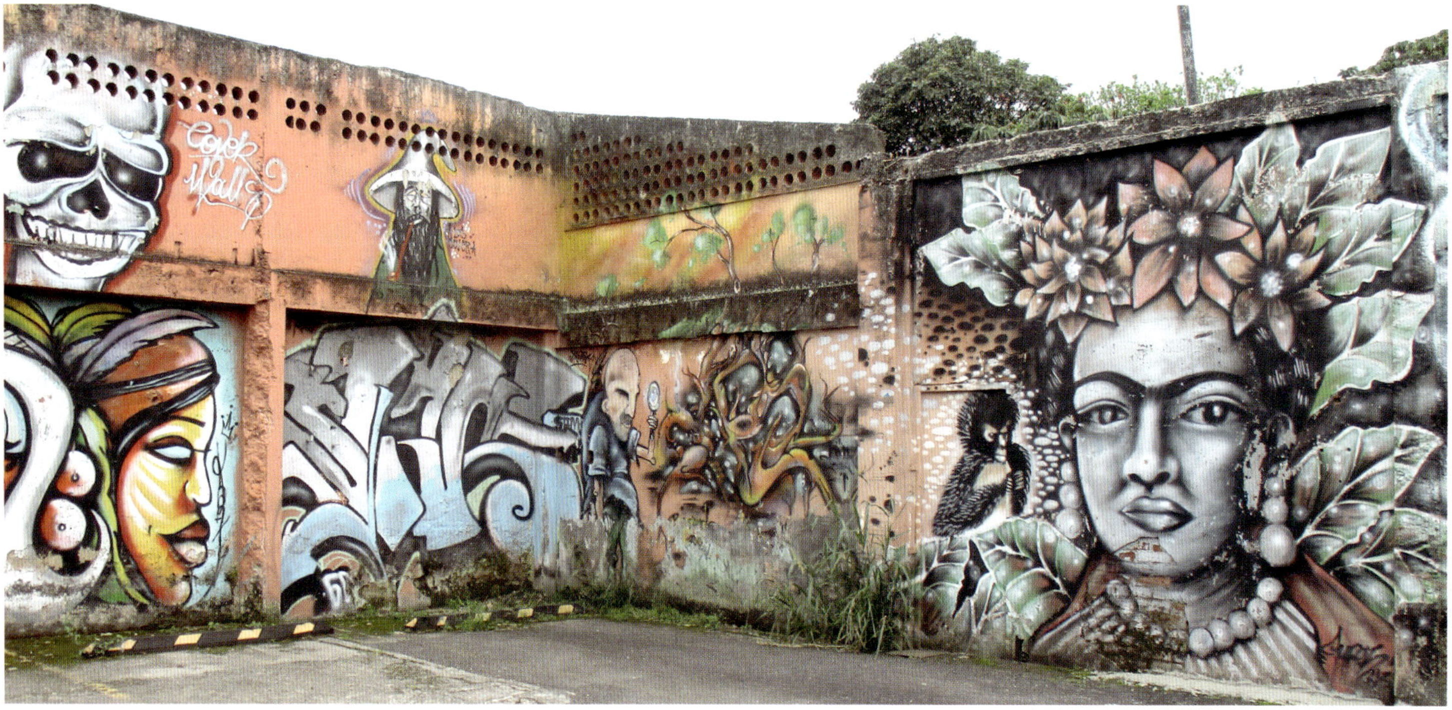

JUST took the time to show the authors a little known space where wall artists in San José practice their craft of women on the walls at an abandoned parking lot.

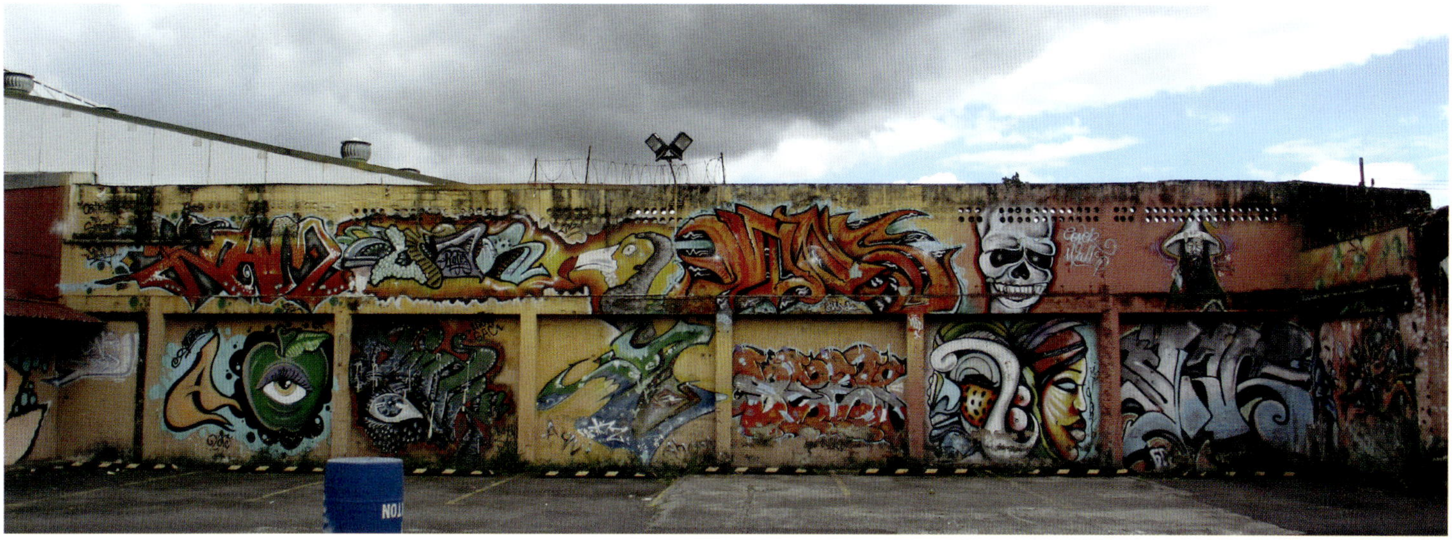

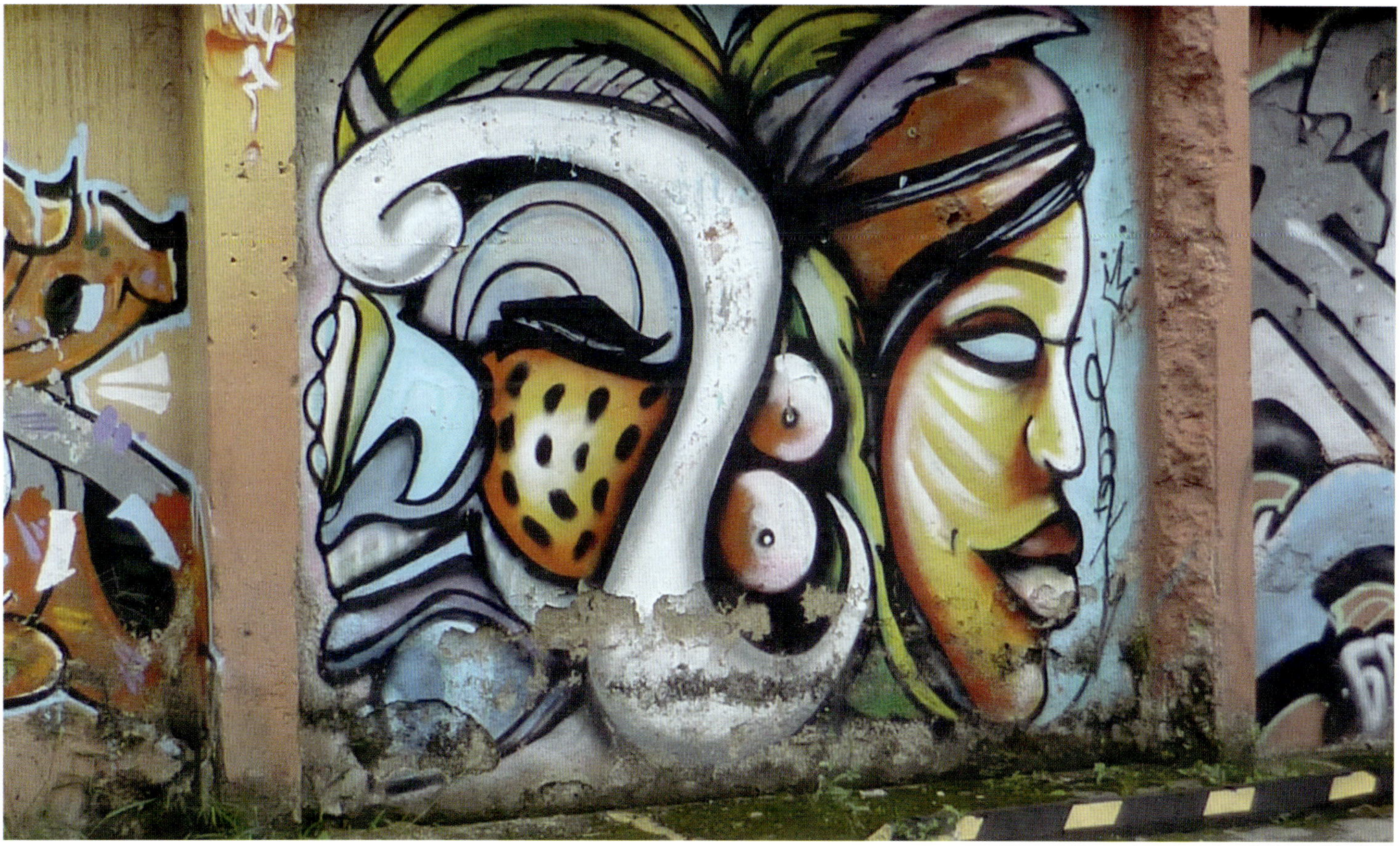

PUCHO: Making a Name for Himself outside San José

The hour-long drive to San Ramón de Alajuela takes you outside the often claustrophobic streets of San José. In this small, quiet town pushed against the mountains, you'll find PUCHO and other street artists who paint women who reflect the natural world. The walls of San Ramón feature many portraits of women, some of them by ROY, a friend and collaborator of PUCHO. The works of PUCHO include walls focusing on the natural heritage of Costa Rica. PUCHO is surviving with his sign painting, tattooing, t-shirts, and commissioned work. He had just returned from painting a commissioned mural in a nearby mining town when we caught up.

Many wall artists in this abandoned garage have painted women subjects to practice their skills.

The wall artist PUCHO, who is the subject of our next interview, is on the wall here with his surprised boy and bird.

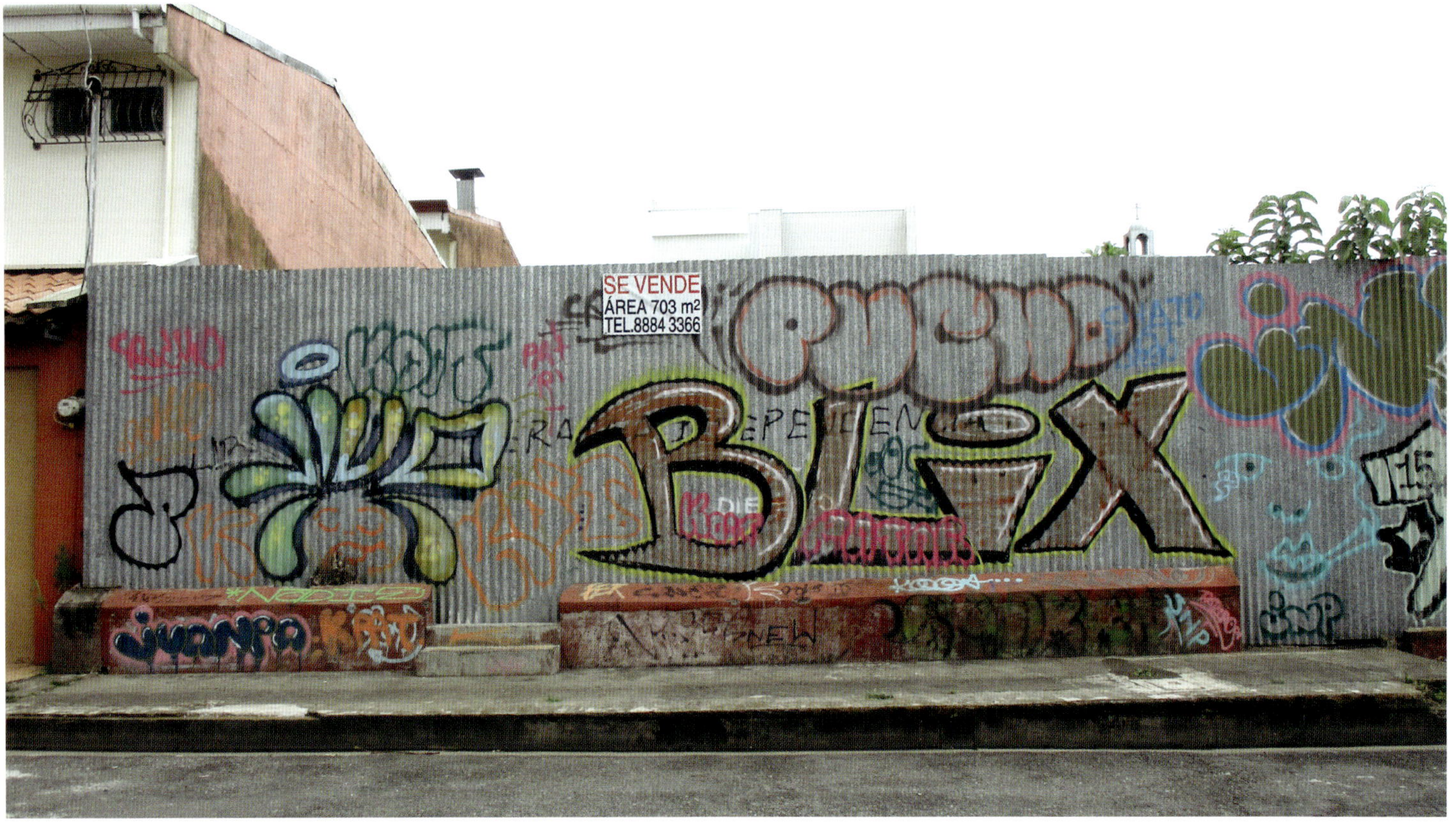

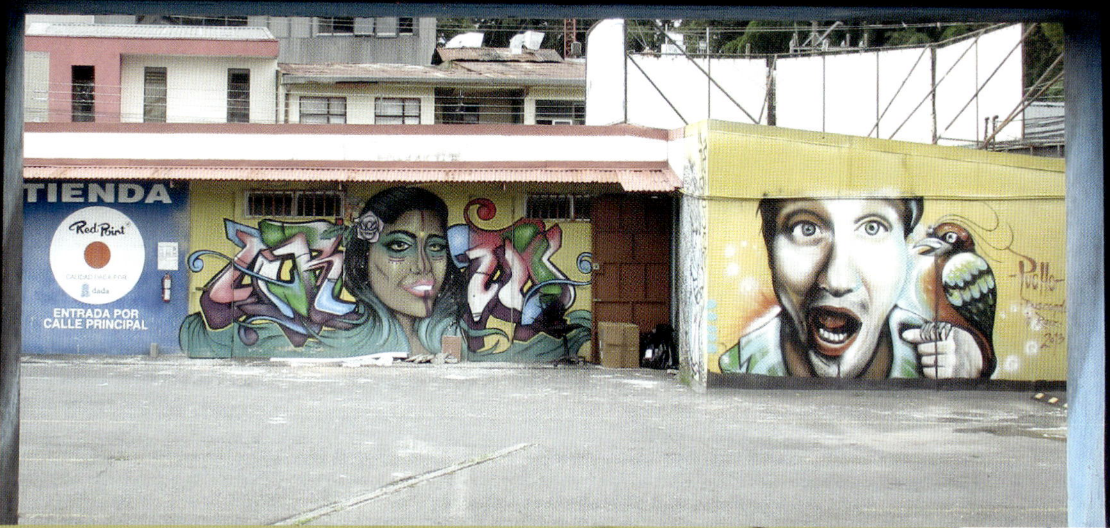
TIENDA
Red Point
ENTRADA POR
CALLE PRINCIPAL

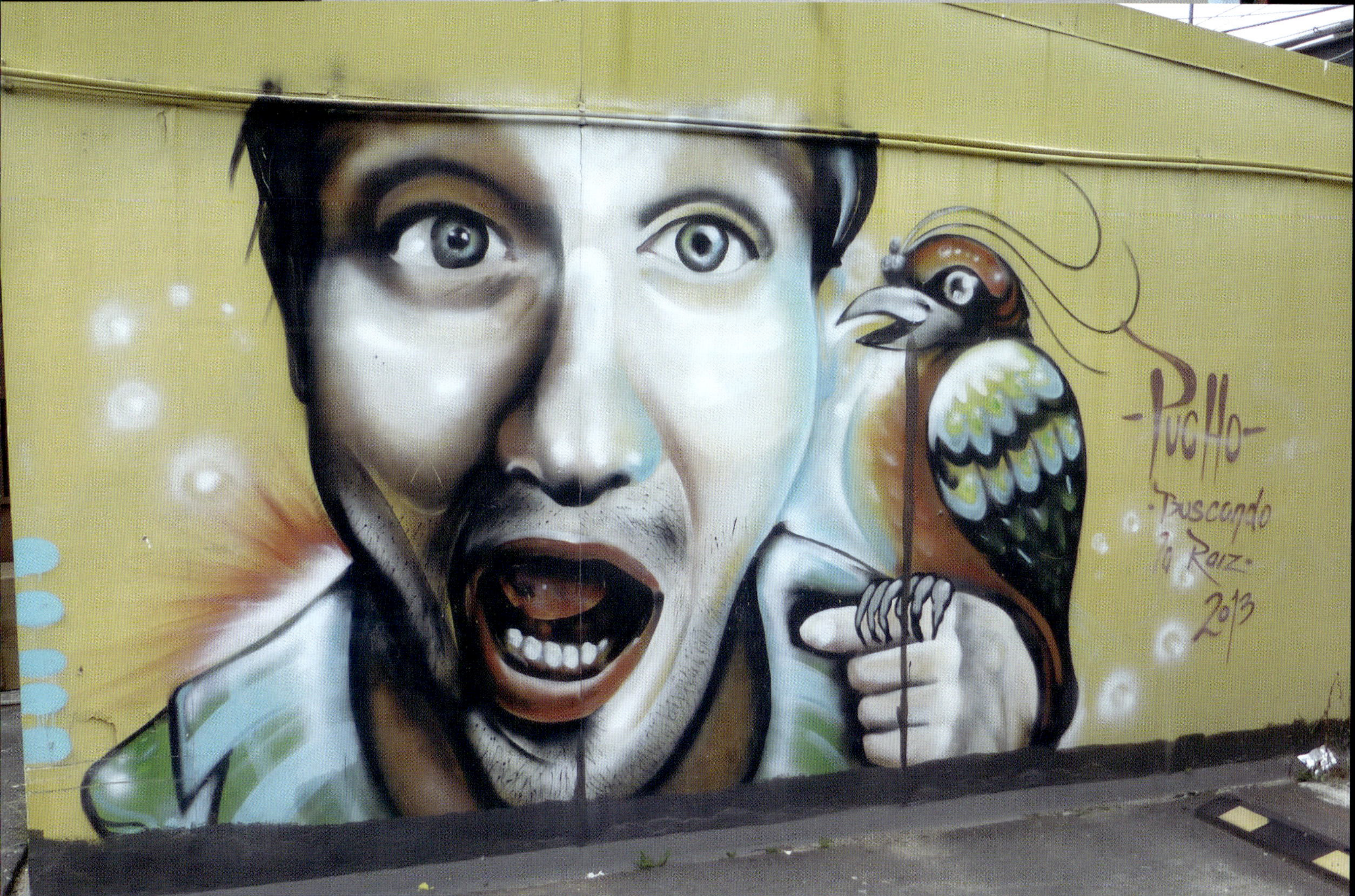
-PucHo-
-Buscando
la Raiz-
2013

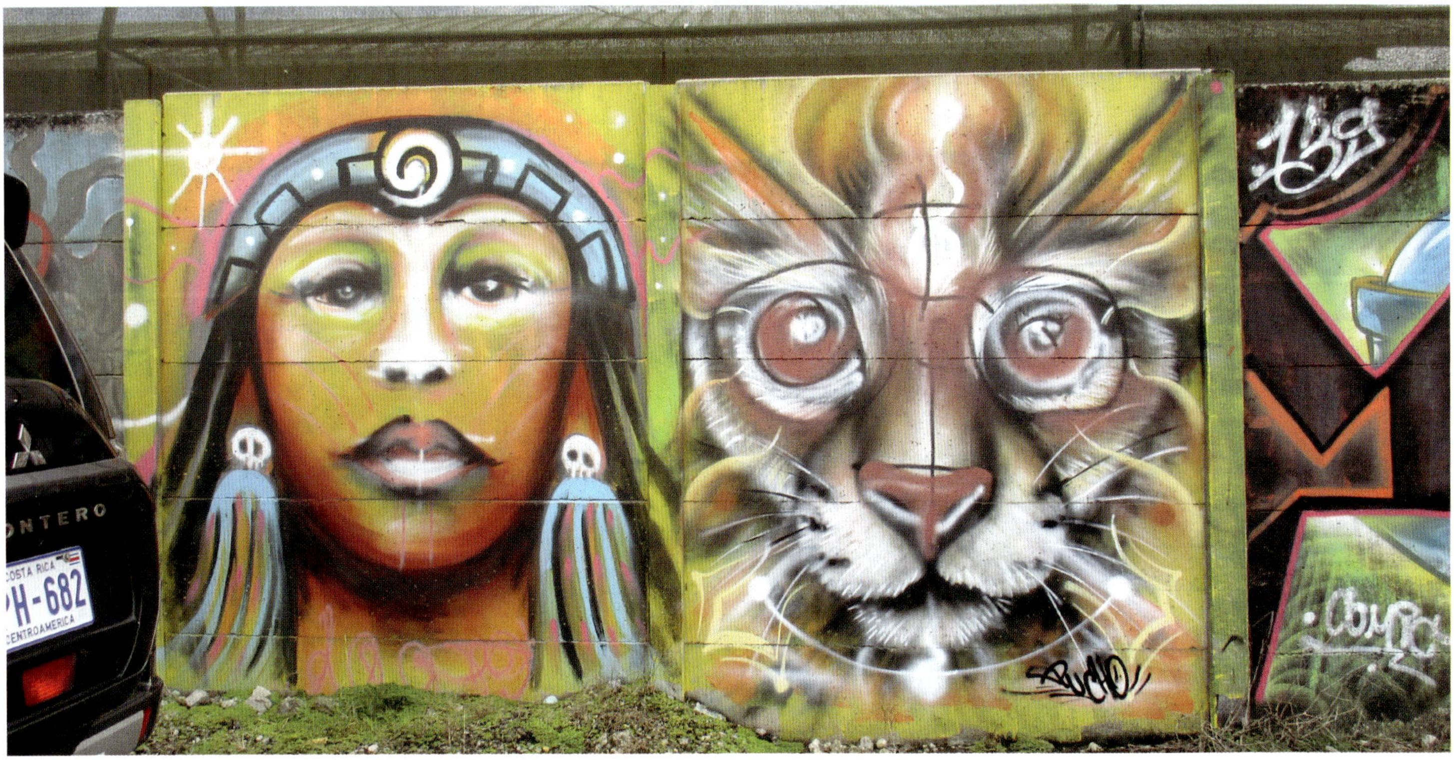
COSTA RICA
CENTROAMERICA

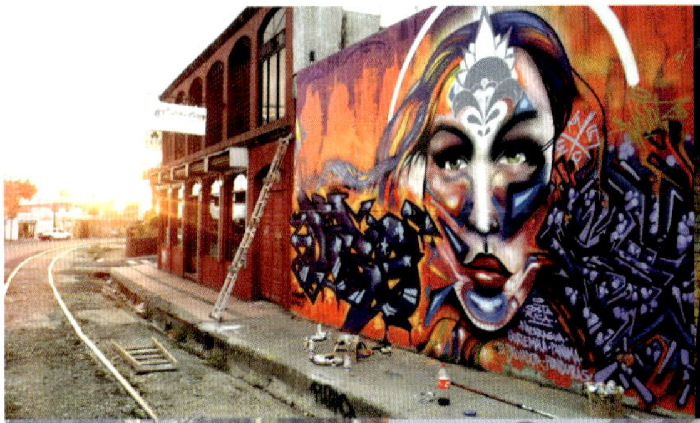

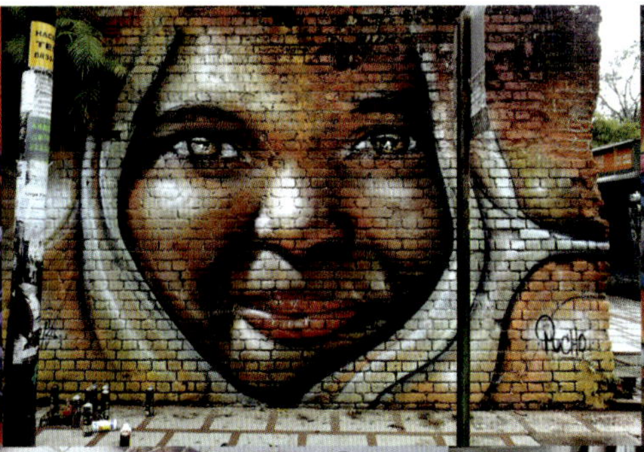

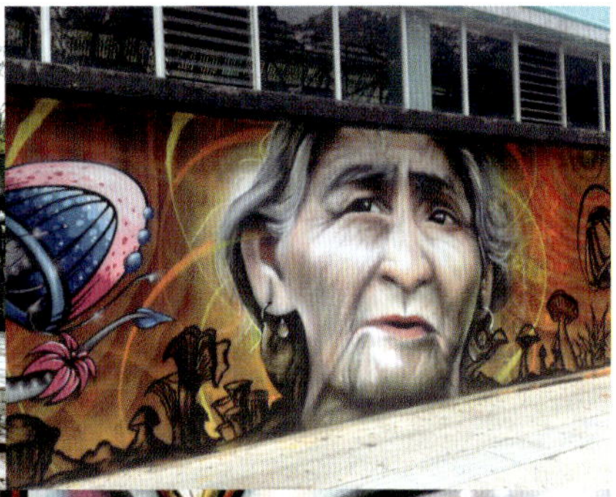

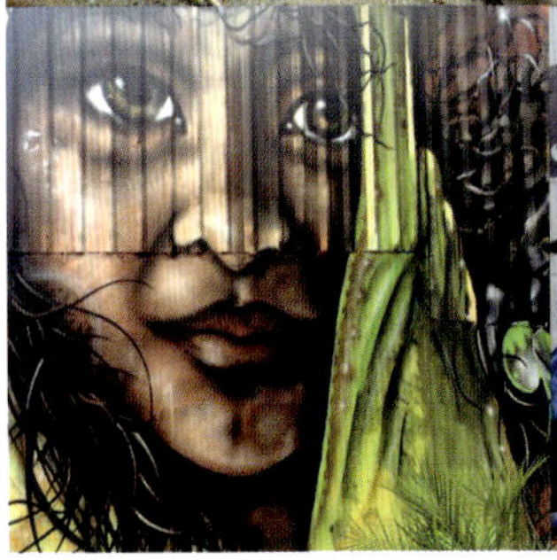

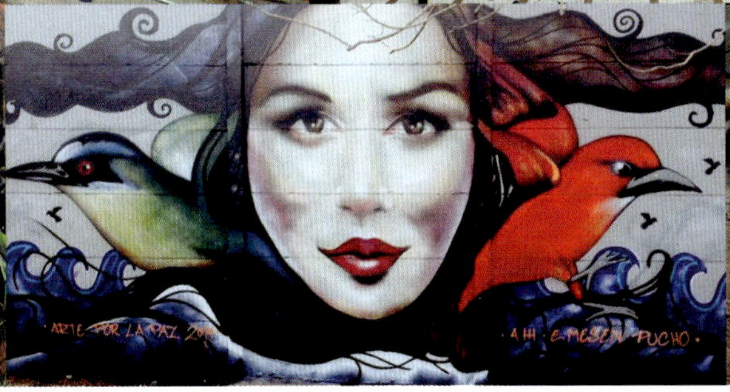
ARTE POR LA PAZ

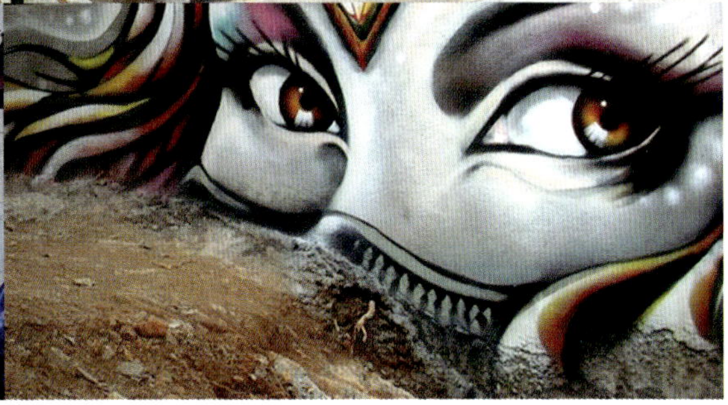

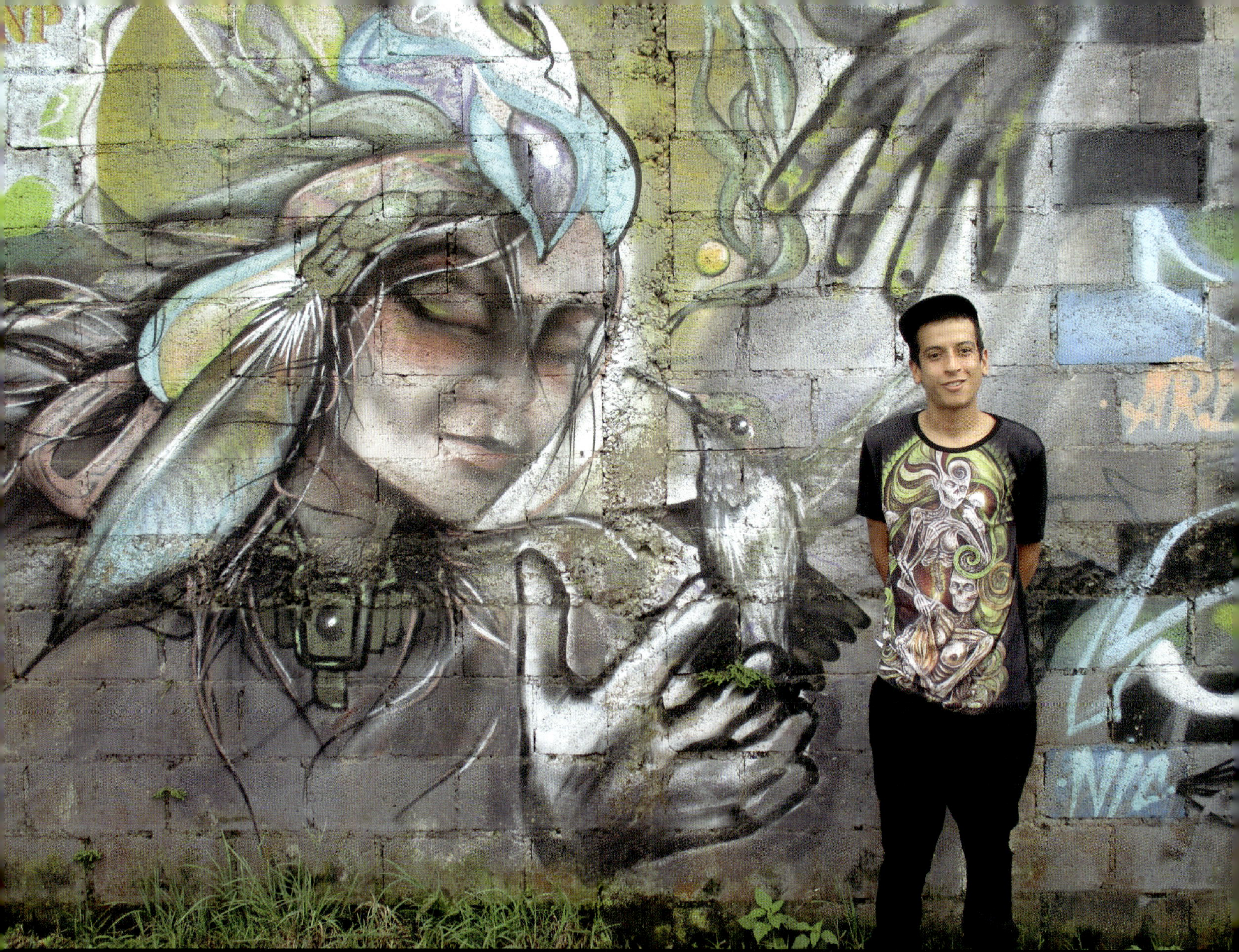

PUCHO's artistic talents are on full display in this montage.
Photos: PUCHO

PUCHO poses in front of one of his works.

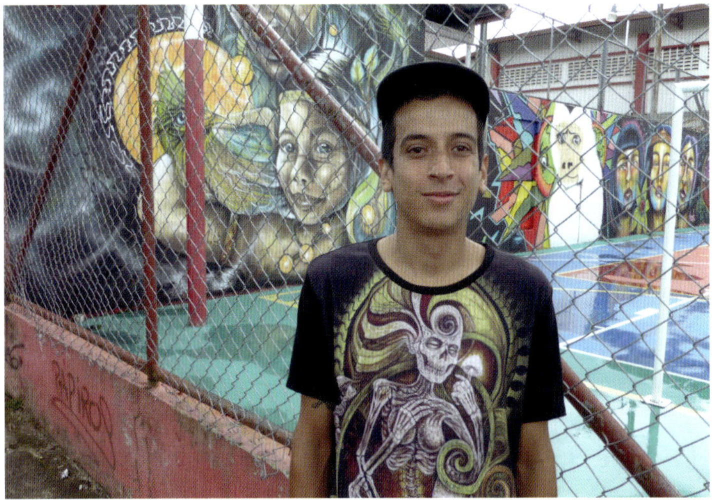

PUCHO is a slight young man with fine features who began his art career at the age of seven. His small frame hides large-scale ideas about the natural world expressed in his murals.

INTERVIEW WITH PUCHO: A Need to Draw

Ever since I was a little kid I had an interest in drawing. I started when I was seven years old. I was doodling on tables at school or bathrooms. When I was going to high school, I began bombing with a stencil. I looked at the bombs when I was little and said to myself one day I would paint graffiti. The first graffiti I did was a bomb that was small, and at this point I told myself that I would become a graffitist.

Ten years later I was buying my first spray cans. I was doing painting at my house that I wanted to bring out to the street. The first five I did was at a contest painting a couple of walls. They chose me for the prize, and then I encountered a lot of people doing the same. I began slowly and then started using more and more cans, and I ended up painting a room and I began experimenting. And a lot of people wanted it. Now I'm making a little money at it, painting walls. I just did one in Guanacaste. I live from those paid works and tattoos. With walls I had a lot of space to work with. I like doing work with a bit of magic or something cosmic. We come from everything. We're all one.

PUCHO's work shines on the walls of a basketball court at a local school, where you have to scale a fence to access it.

If you fancy a game of hoops, you'll be doing so next to PUCHO's wall art.

The most interesting part of graffiti, right, is to give a gift. If it's commissioned, it's not like that. When you do graffiti you arrive with your materials, and you do what's yours.

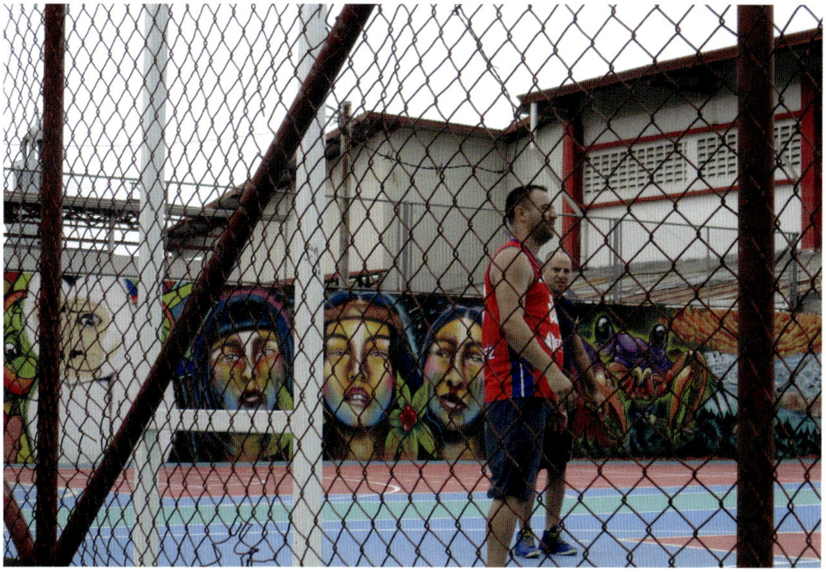

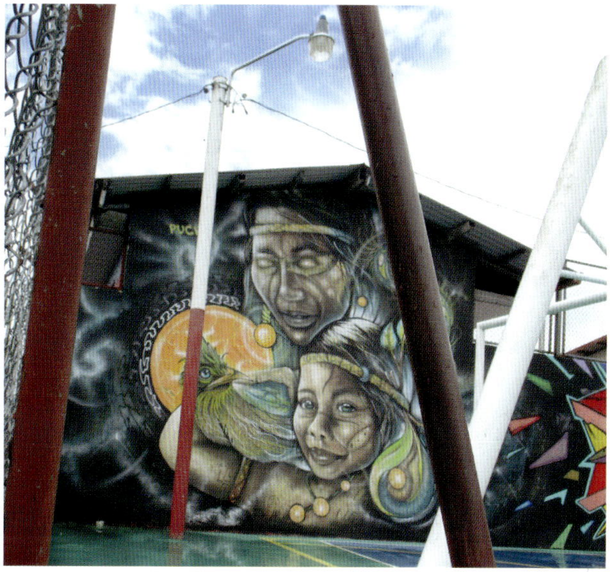

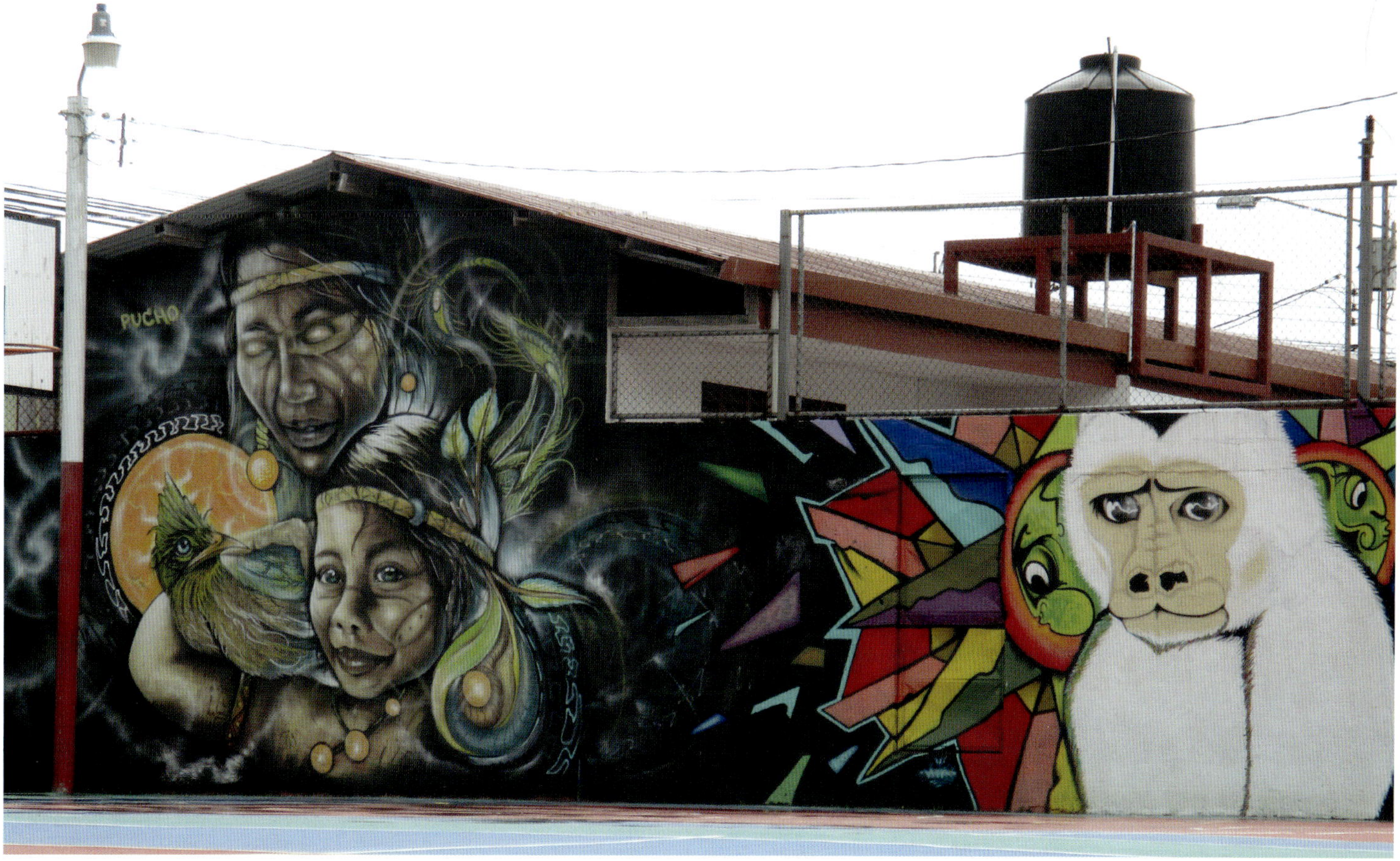
PUCHO

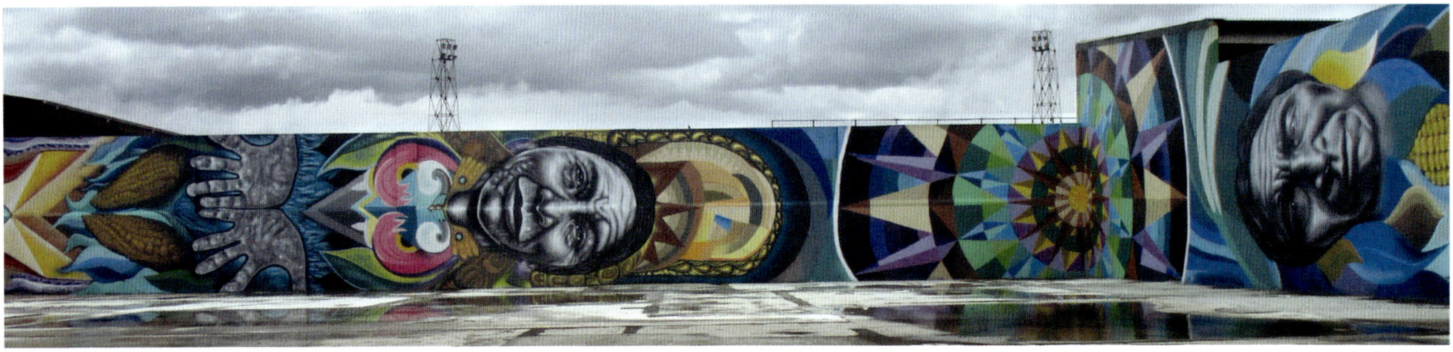

The Feminine Side of Nature

I'm always looking for the experience of nature. For me, nature is an infinite inspiration. There's always something to paint from the natural world. With a magnifying glass, a sharp eye, you discover a new world. Principally, I look for nature.

> In nature you find the feminine presence. Life is the presence of women, the water, fruits; it's part of a process.

With the faces of women, you can find the presence of nature, whether it's a painting in a town square or a photo like the source of a river or an animal; it's spiritual.

> Women are such an inspiration to men, which is why most of the art of women is painted by men.

Personally, I consider women are more aesthetic. They're more magic. They're more visually attractive. I don't know. If I have to decide between painting a boy or a girl, I'll paint a girl, of course. They appear more interesting on a wall, right? They reflect the concepts I want to explore.

Politics on the Wall

You can have political themes, but I don't like to focus on that a lot. It's not my field of interest. If there's a political theme that I run into, then I might take it up because I like to tell the truth. The murder of Jairo Sandoval was a shocking event. [Sandoval was murdered trying to protect leatherback turtle nests in Costa Rica, where poachers sell the eggs as aphrodisiacs.][1] The wall I painted demonstrated a truth most people don't know about. Why the mural? Because it demonstrates a reality most people don't realize. Everybody thinks of the green Costa Rica, Costa Rica the ecological paradise, Costa Rica and its nature, when a lot of times that's not the complete reality. His family wrote me and thanked me for painting the tribute, and Michael Collins of Sea Shepherd wrote me and was making a documentary and wanted to include me. The wall demonstrated a truth most people don't know about.

PUCHO's wall art pays homage to the Indigenous culture of his country.

PUCHO takes into consideration the orientation of the wall, which makes for interesting challenges of perspective and scale. This piece demonstrates his celebration of Indigenous culture.

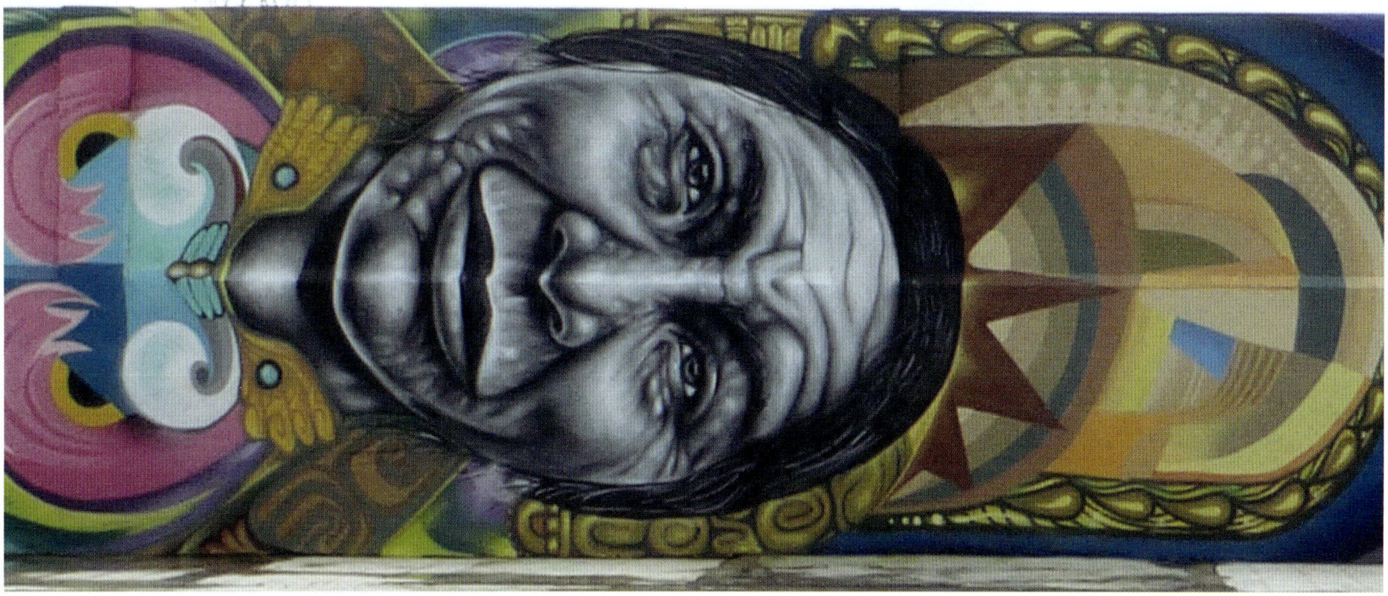

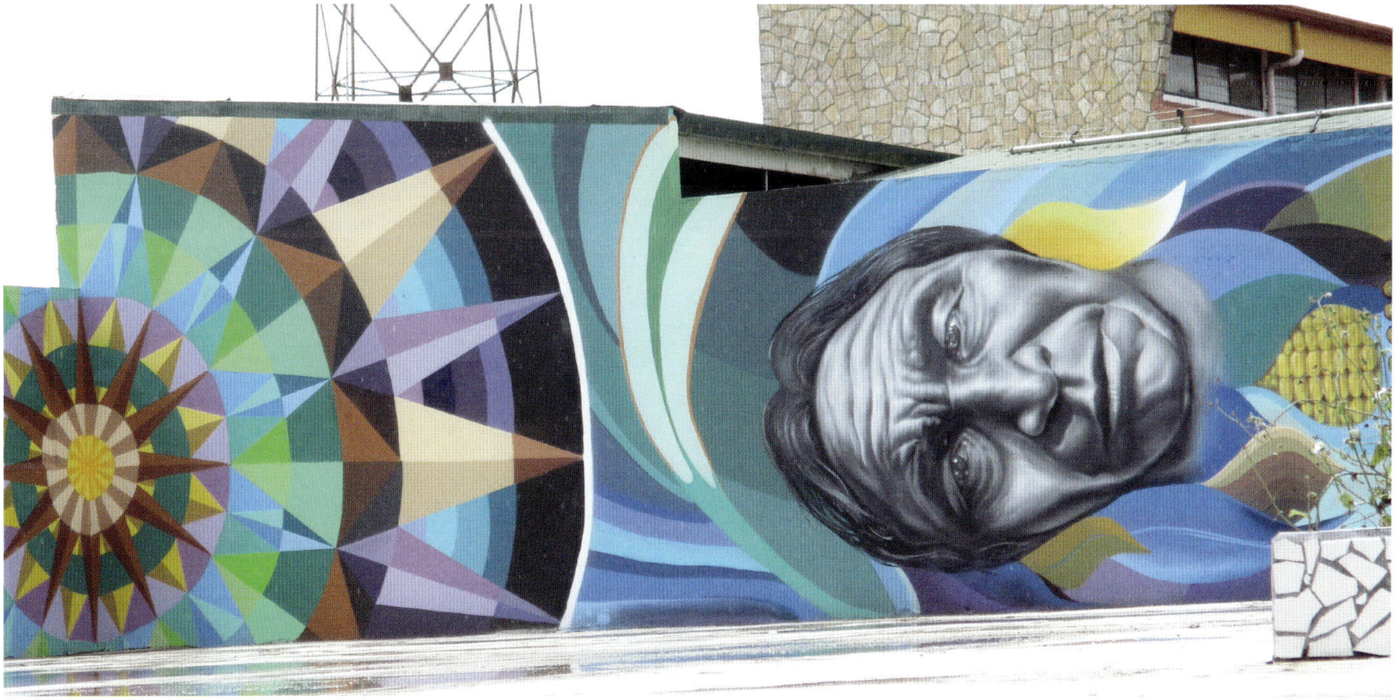

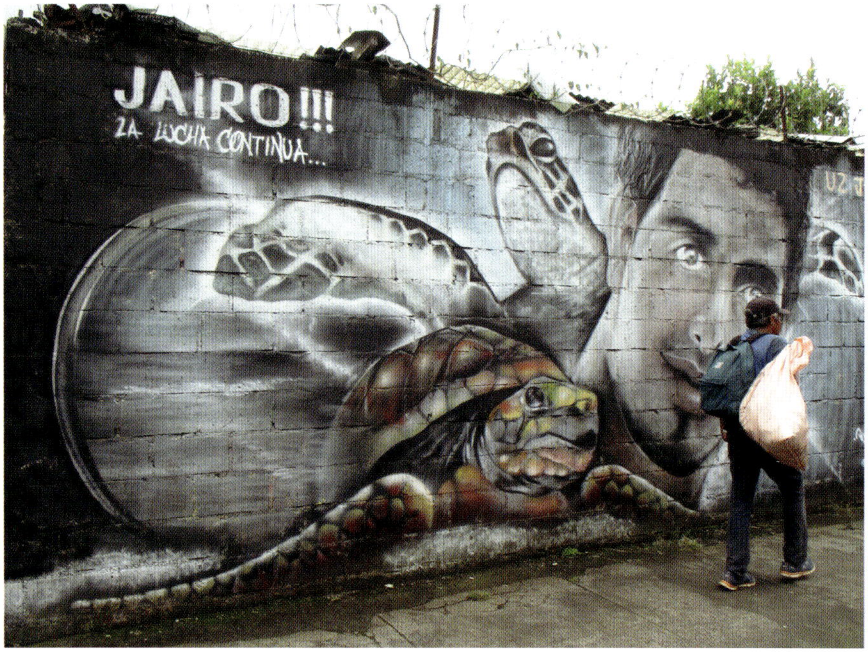

Women Wall Artists in Costa Rica

There's not many women wall artists in the country, maybe a handful. There are about five women wall artists in the whole country. Maybe there's one who is doing walls. The others are doing bombing. They're very well known for that. Their work is everywhere. It's really good. The role of women is important in Central America. We're more inclusive now. A lot of the fight is there.

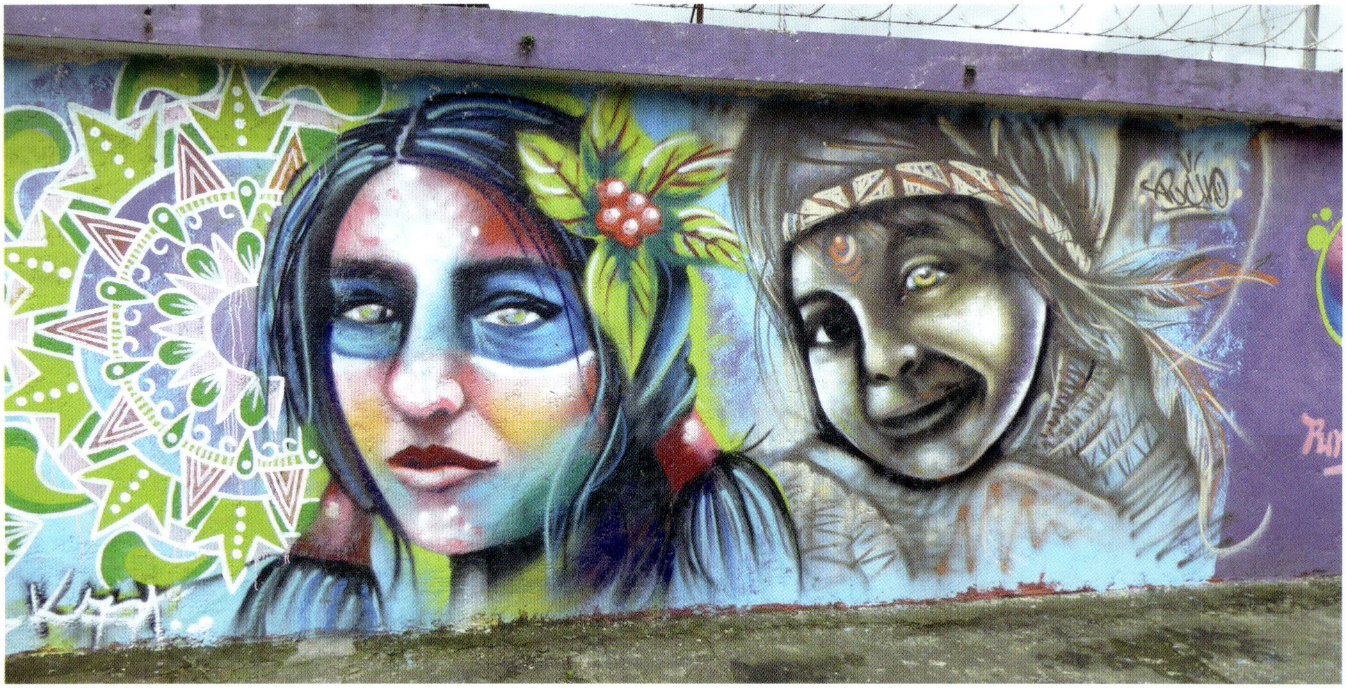

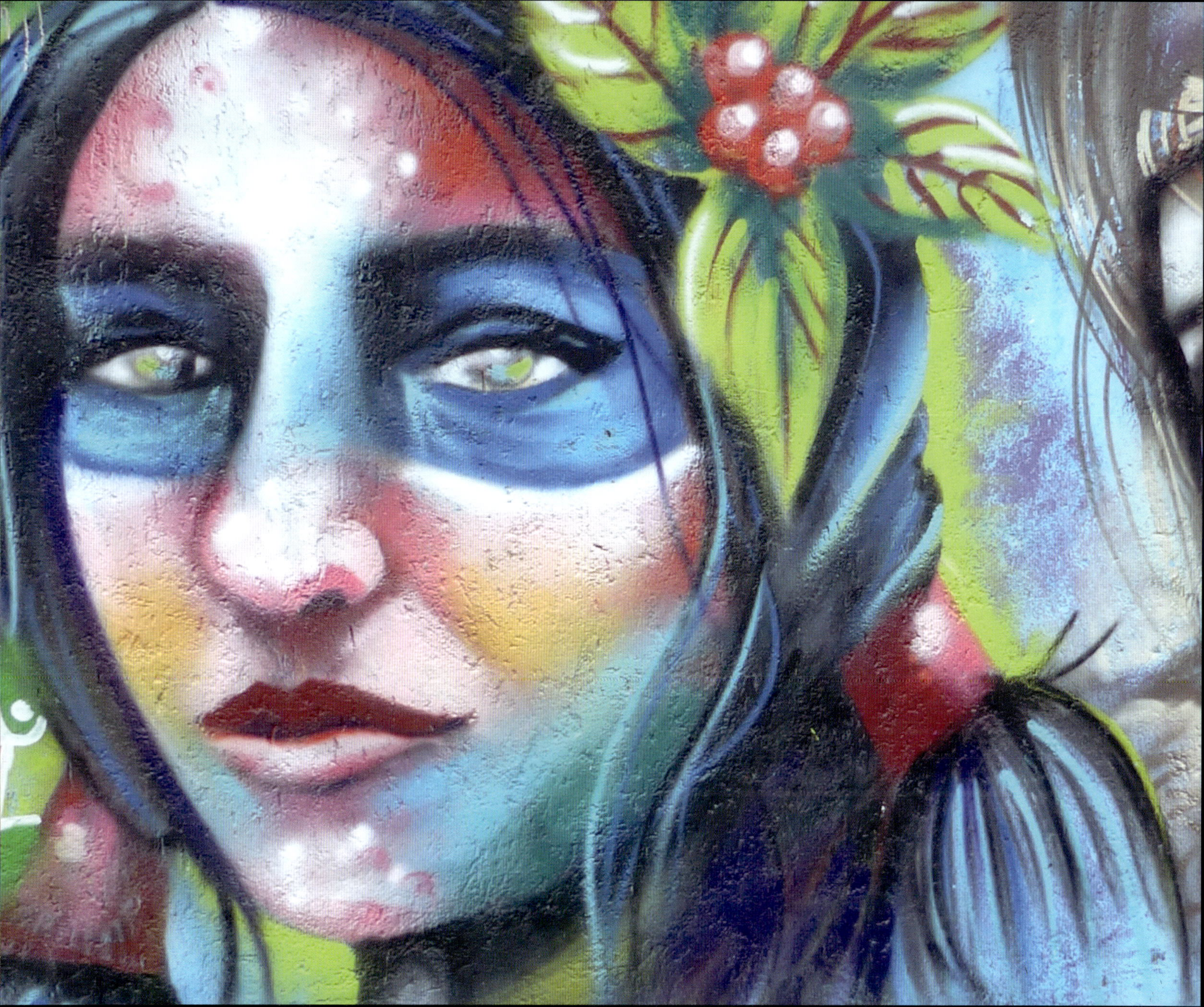

Politics are rarely found in PUCHO's work; however, he did make an exception in dedicating a wall to the memory of Jairo Sandoval, who was murdered in Costa Rica for trying to protect the nests of sea turtles.

PUCHO's collaborative work with Kaat, one of a handful female wall artists working in Costa Rica.

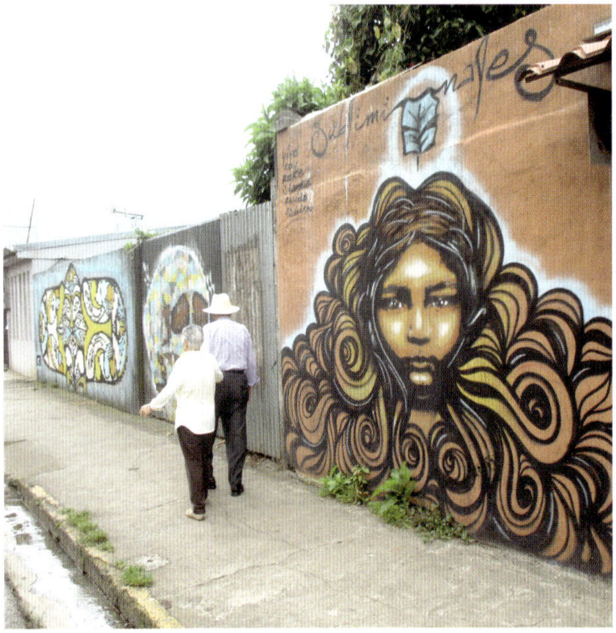

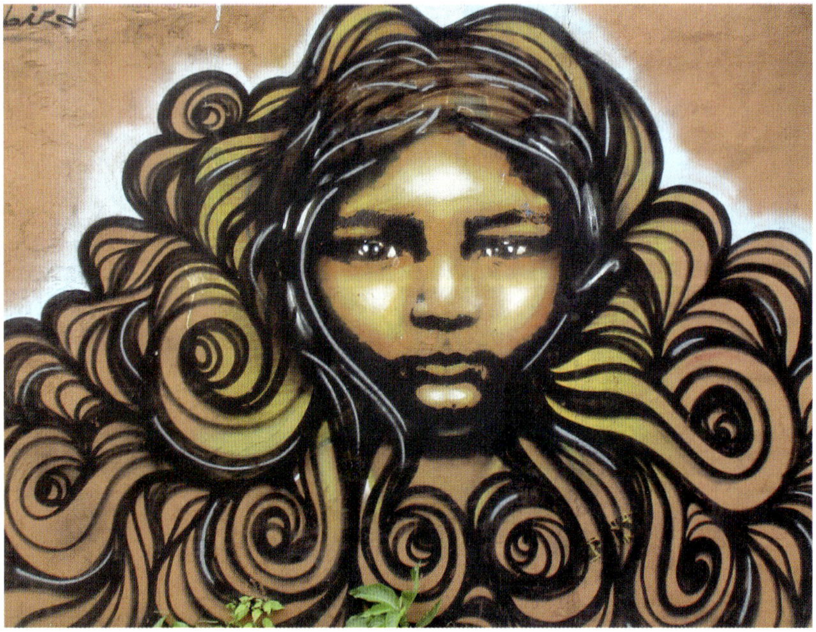

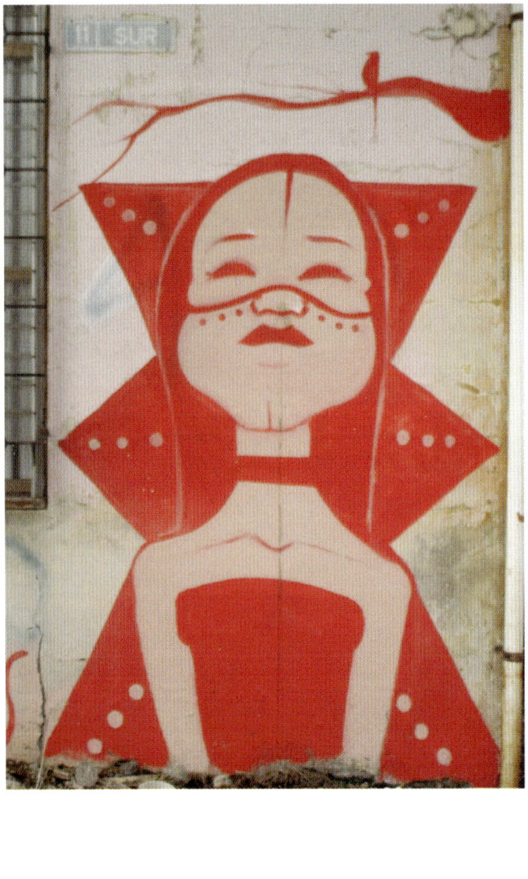

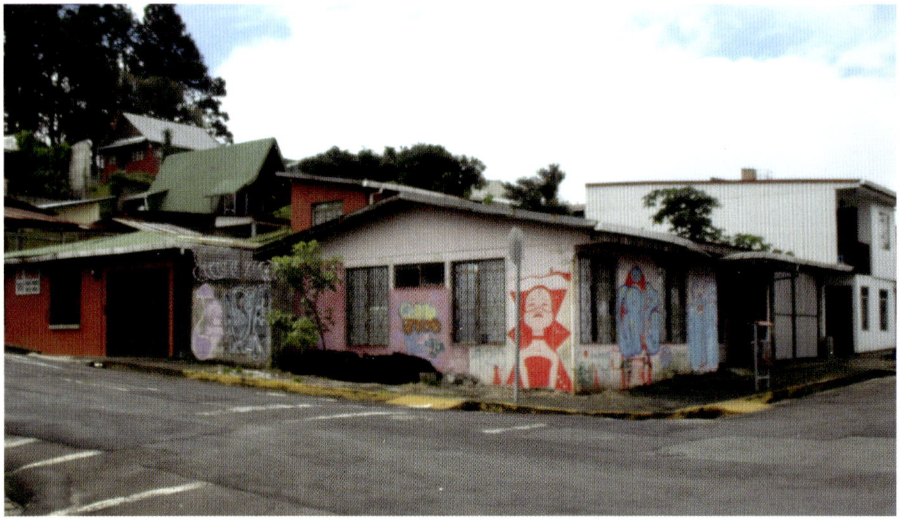

PUCHO's connection with other street artists in San Ramón unfolded during a tour of his city. Among the artists was ROY, a fellow graffitist whose portrait of a woman with flowing hair features on the cover of this book. Street artists flourish in this peaceful valley outside San José.

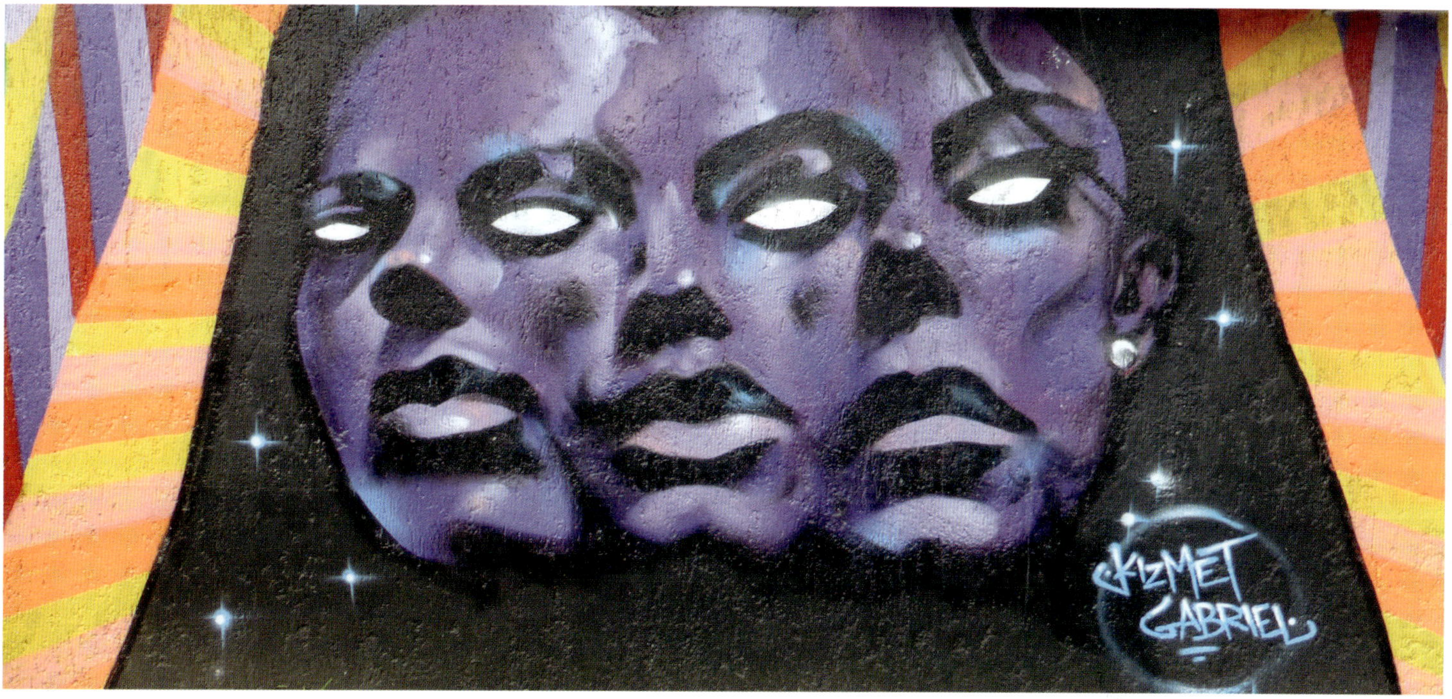
KizMET
GABRIEL

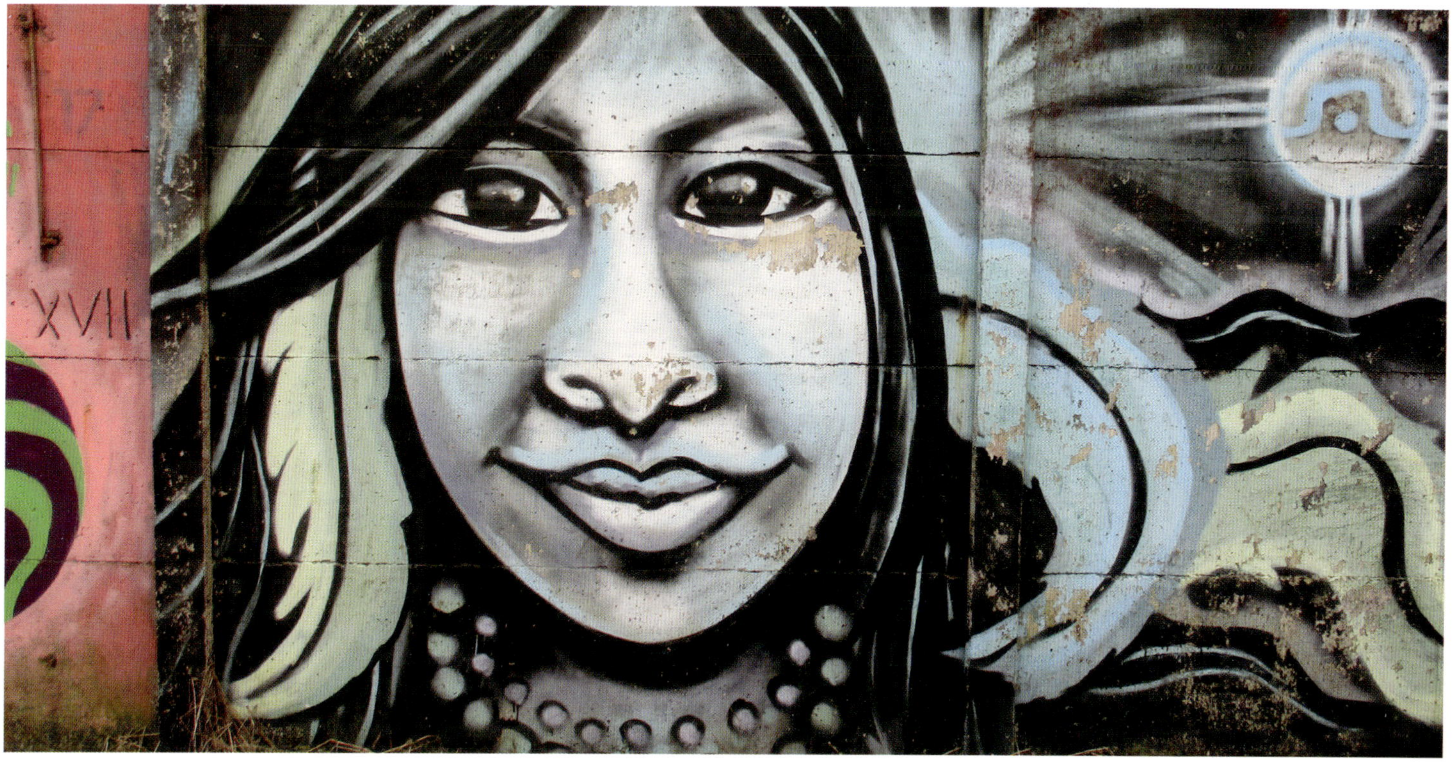
XVII

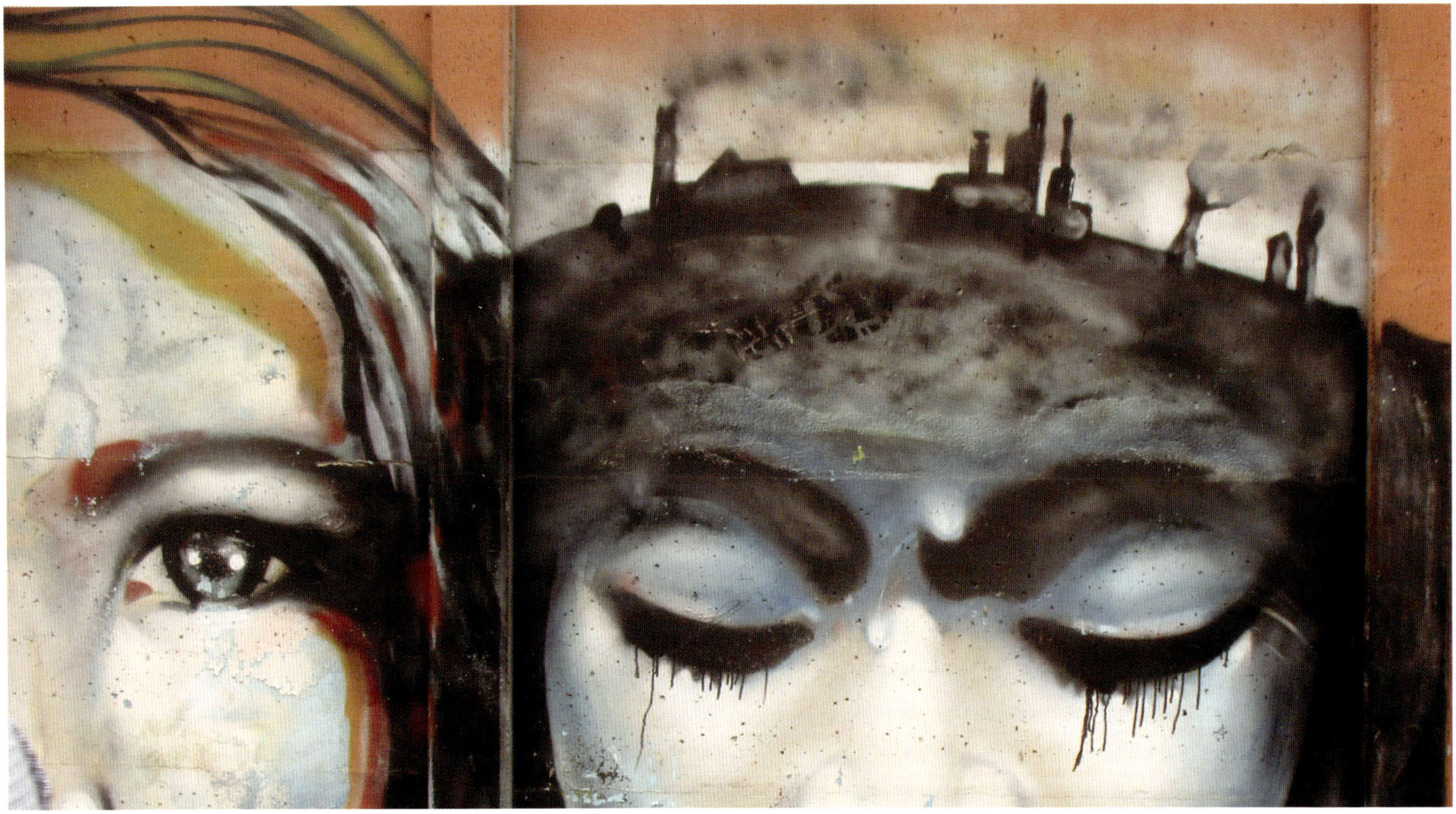

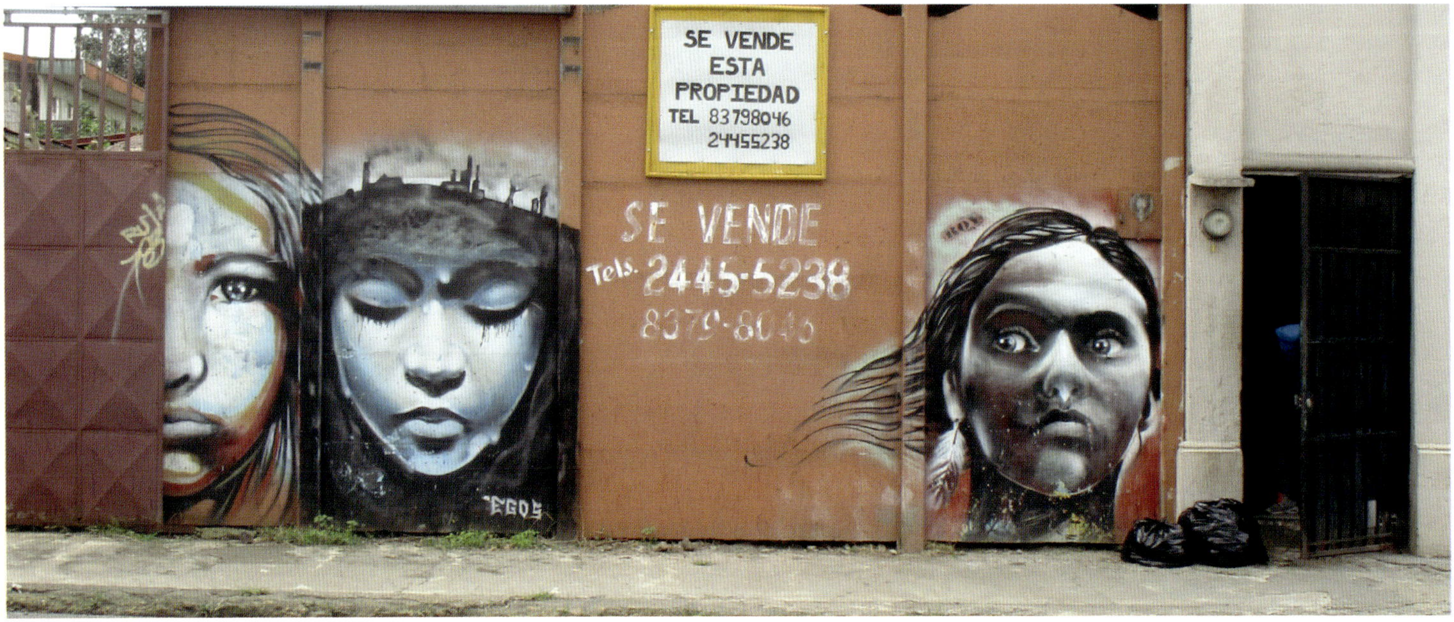
SE VENDE
ESTA
PROPIEDAD
TEL 83798046
24455238
SE VENDE
Tels. 2445-5238
8379-8046

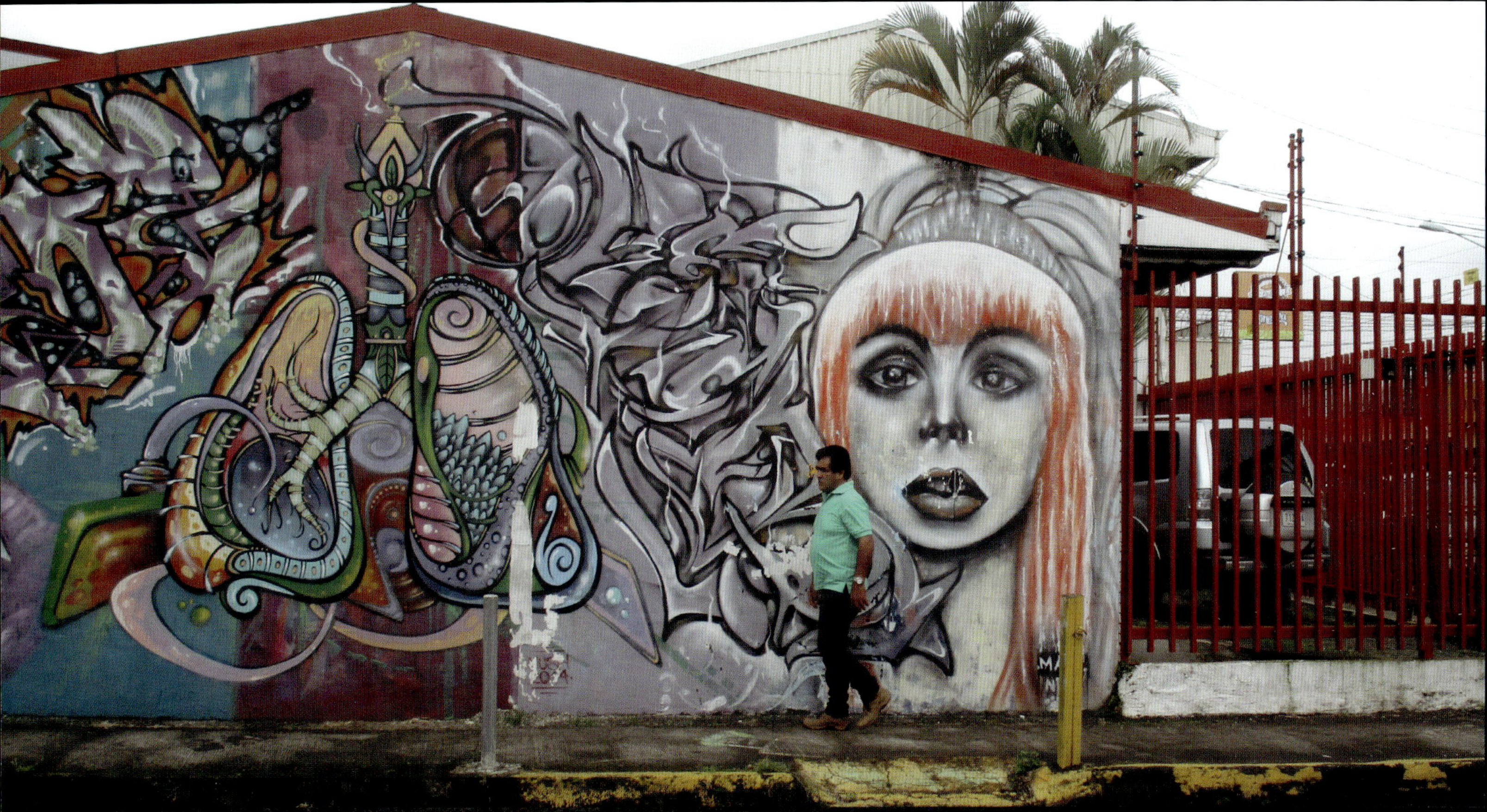

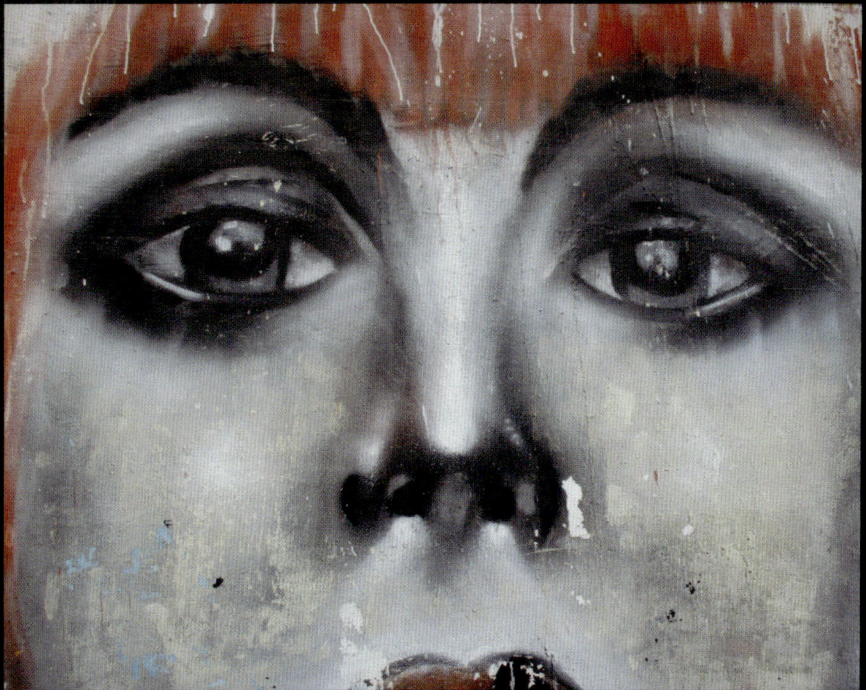

ROY is the street handle for one of San Ramón's most productive and evocative muralists (left and next page).

Women on the walls feature prominently on many corners in San Ramón. The straight haired woman is signed by Mac and Nic. The purple triplets portrait is signed by Kizmet Gabriel.

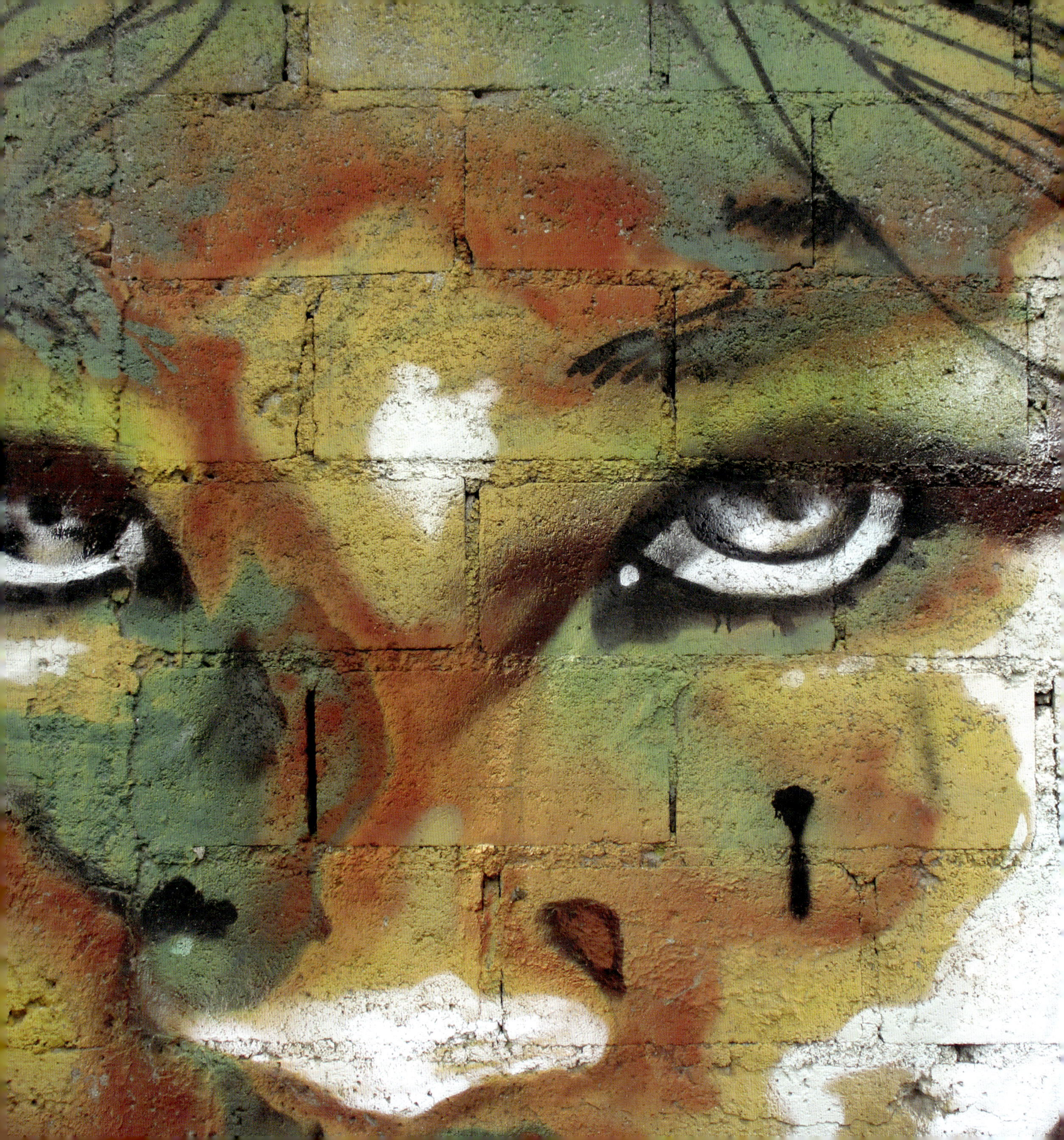

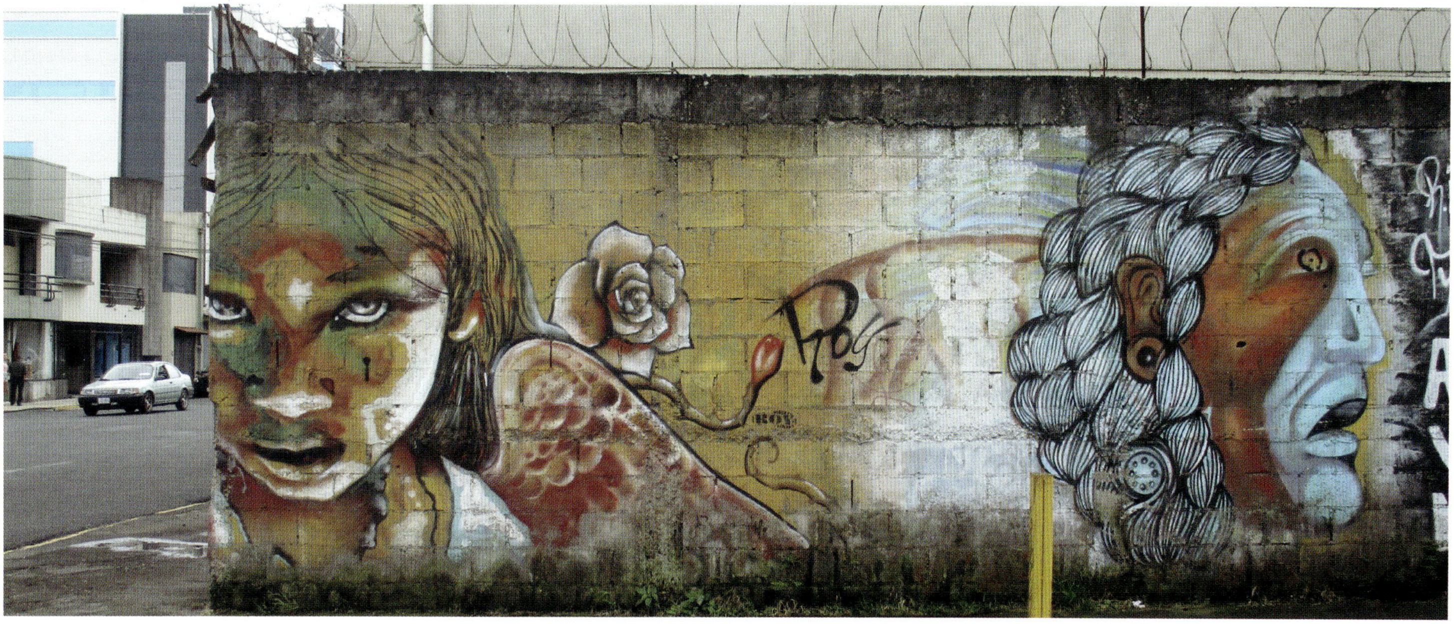

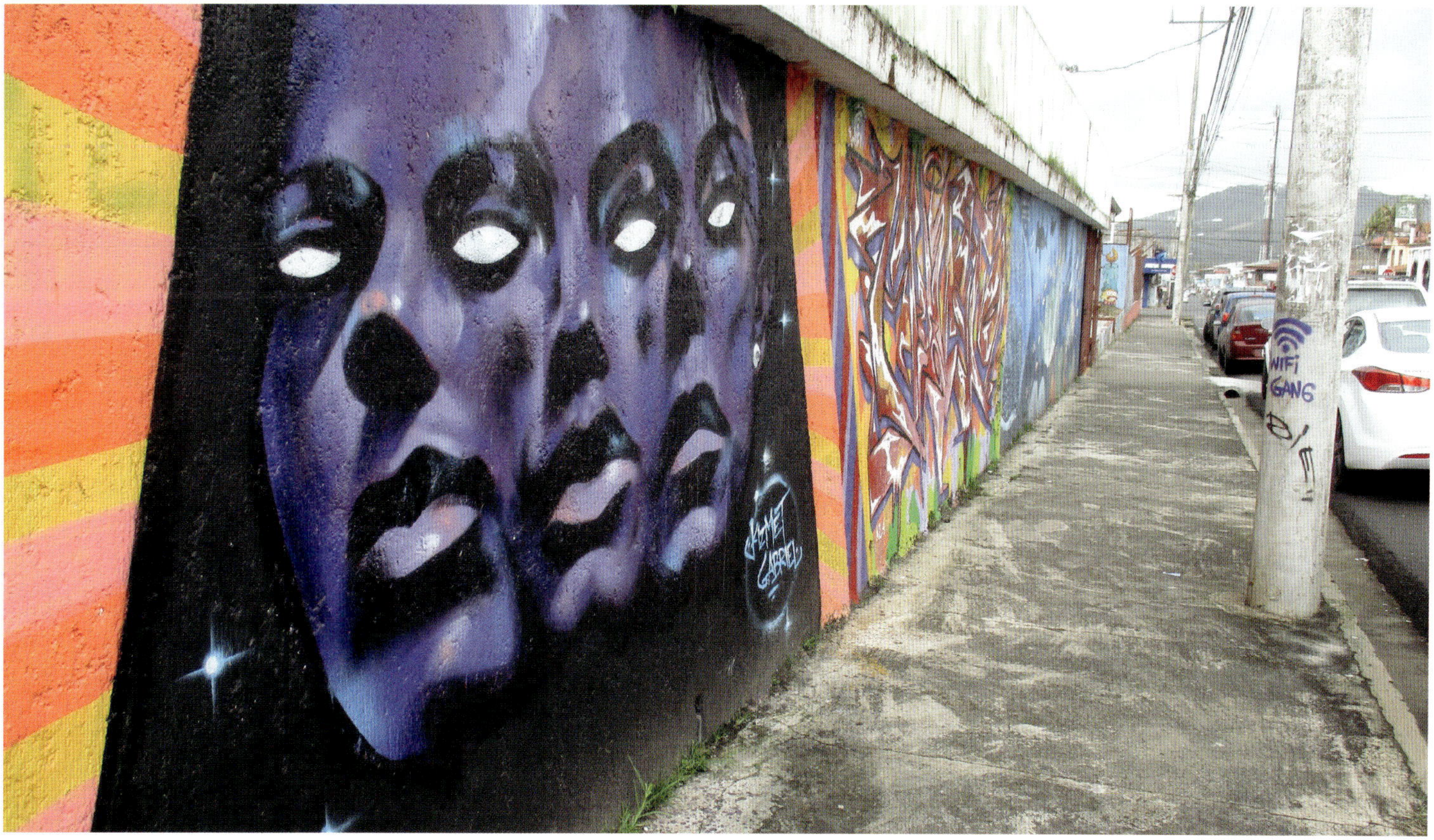
WIFI
GANG

Next Stop: Chile and Peru

The Costa Rican artists project a youthful enthusiasm that has also made its mark in South America, where depictions of women on the walls also display a young attitude. In the Chilean port city of Valparaíso, much of the wall art features a colorful interpretation of young women. In Huanchaco, Peru, a surf destination, we found women on the wall who inhabit an often surreal, cubist-influenced world. In both places, wandering the backstreets provides its own rewards, and surprises await the keen observer around every corner.

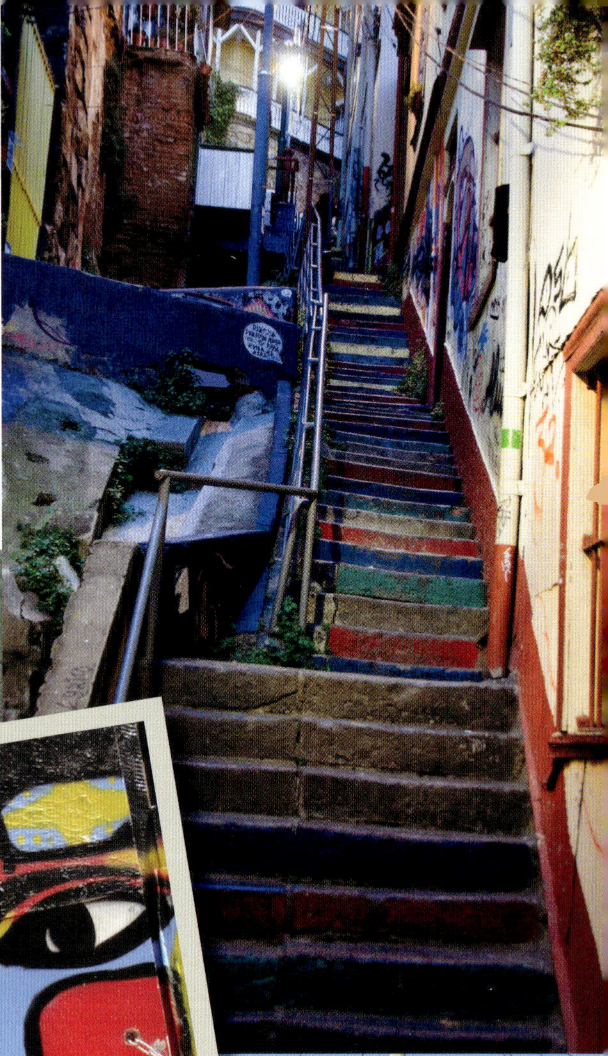

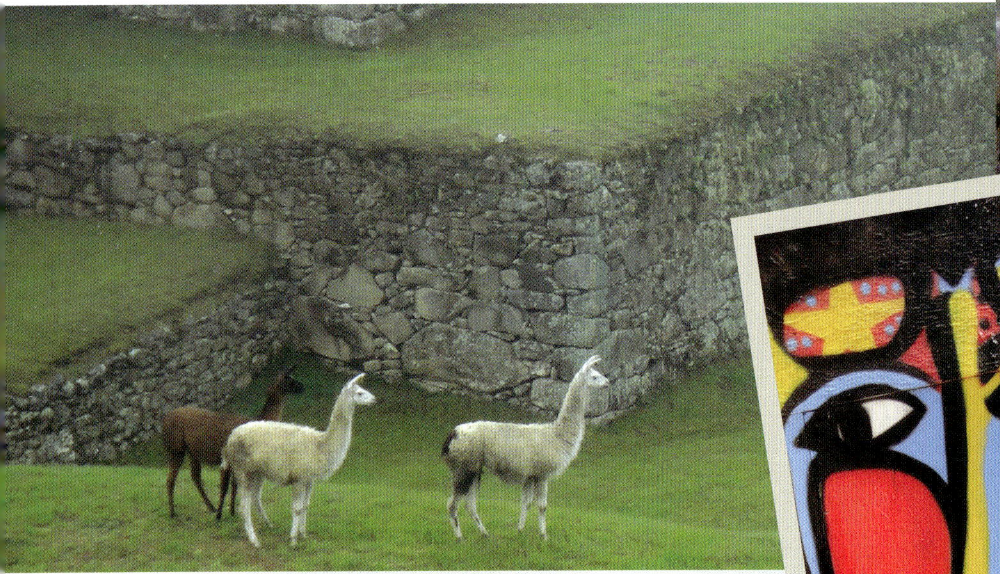

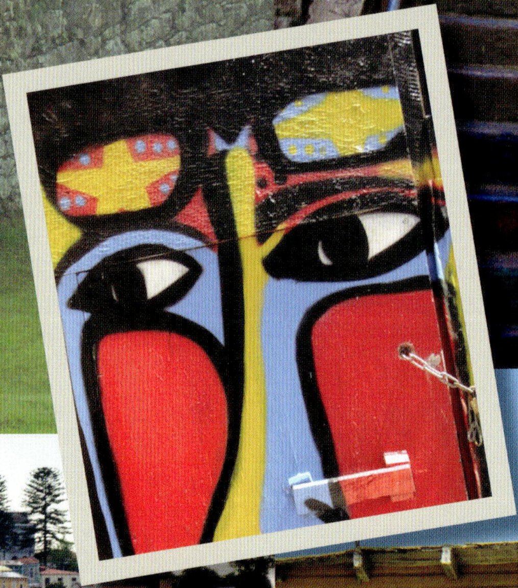

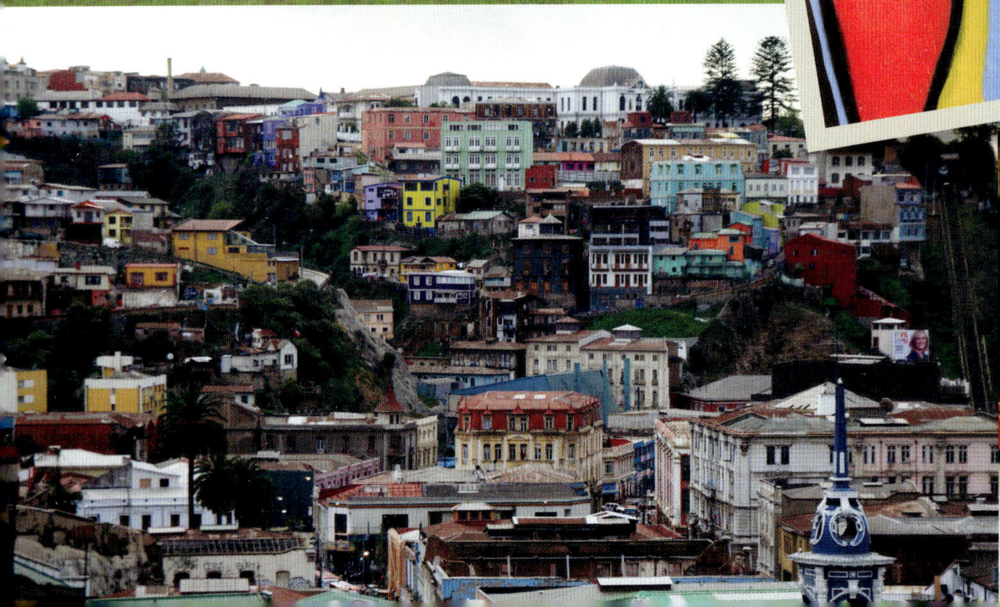

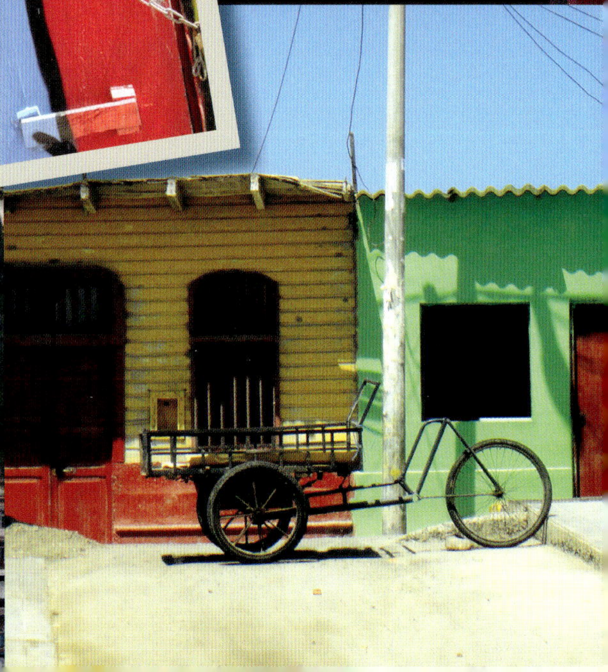

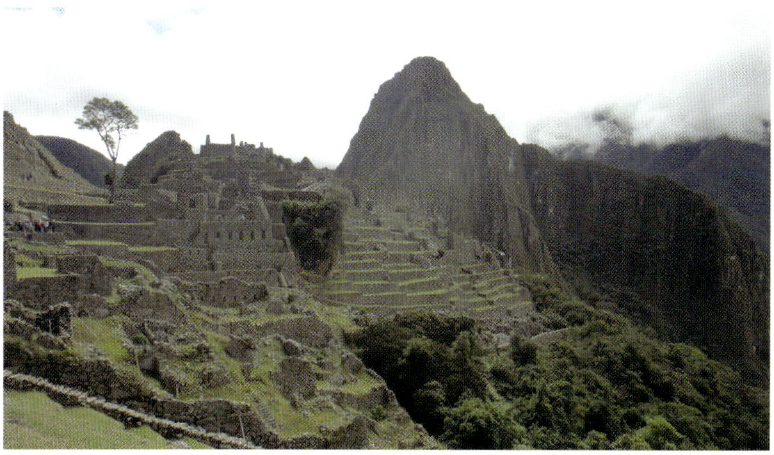

Machu Picchu.

5

CHILE AND PERU

The Spine of the Andes and a Wild Beach Culture

Like Costa Rica, Chile and Peru appeal to wanderers who want to experience natural wonders.

Cities and towns in South America, like Valparaíso and its colorful staircases and homes produce a dramatic backdrop for street art of women. The same colorful backdrop is the canvas for surprising street art in Huanchaco, Peru. This is a world born in the ruins of Machu Picchu where sacred llamas wander freely.

Valparaíso, Chile, September 2013. Photographs by Mitch Altman, licensed under CC BY-SA 2.0

In South America, the restless Andes form a rampart that shapes this continent's Pacific coast, topping the list of majestic nature with Machu Picchu as its crown jewel. The Andes gave rise to the Incas and their incredible citadel nestled in the spine of jungle-clad peaks and towering mountains. When you first encounter this royal estate with its magnificent terraces in the clouds (built in 1450), you have to pinch yourself. Yes, it exists, as do the sacred llamas who wander and graze its verdant grounds. Machu Picchu is a marvel of architecture and engineering that is part of a long chain of Incan temples and towns that are still being uncovered along 25,000 miles (40,000 kilometers) of Incan trails and roads stretching from Chile to the border of Ecuador and Colombia.

Chile is also a geologically young and unstable country, built on a sloping alluvial plain that nestles against the Andes, where earthquakes rattle the affluent suburbs and any assumptions of solid ground. Chile's history has been shaken by political turmoil, yet politics did not color the wall art of women the authors encountered in its fabled port city, Valparaíso. At times almost naive and innocent, the wall art in Valparaíso has childlike qualities. In Peru, the authors uncovered an amazing diversity of wall art of women in an unlikely town put on the map by its ancient, crescent-shaped reed fishing craft, which are surfed into shore.

Our examples of women on the wall from Chile and Peru occupy a kind of hybrid world where myths, eros, surrealism, photorealism, and science fiction intersect. The ambiguity of subjects combines traditional subjects and themes with often wild, unusual imagery. There is no single style that represents the women on the wall in this part of the world, only a sense that personal expression is influenced by geography and a subconscious reflection of ancient cultural influences as well as avant-garde art.

In this chapter we will walk the streets of Valparaíso, the artistic Chilean port on the coast near the capital, Santiago, where Pablo Neruda once wrote his sensual poetry overlooking the rocky, cold, and turbulent Pacific. Then we will stroll the street galleries in the small Peruvian beachside town of Huanchaco, a fishing village and home to an active surf culture. As will be seen, there are definite connections of feminine symbols that cross the equator.

Valparaíso Street Gallery

In English, its name means Paradise Valley. Perched on hills overlooking the Pacific, Valparaíso, Chile, was home to one of South America's most influential and sensual poets, Pablo Neruda, who wrote an ode to his home in the coastal hills. Neruda's words tumble and cascade to the sea over the city's slanted streets, crashing by the women on Valparaíso's walls. The homes in this legendary, seaside port are brightly colored, like much of the wall art of women. Valparaíso is like many ports of the world that cling to the edge of continents, with their own artistic milieu and commingling of cultures and ideas.

Women on the walls have found a home in Valparaíso, and some express a salty tang of independence. Our first example expresses that simplicity of erotic freedom. It is a hasty spray painted line drawing that has a sensual rhythm of sexual freedom. The only writing next to the nude is "Libre," which means "free" in Spanish. This throw-up celebrates a woman's sensual freedom to stand naked to the world with confidence, like the city itself.

The liberated woman contrasts sharply with a striking woman on a workshop door who captures the essential female quality of Valparaíso.

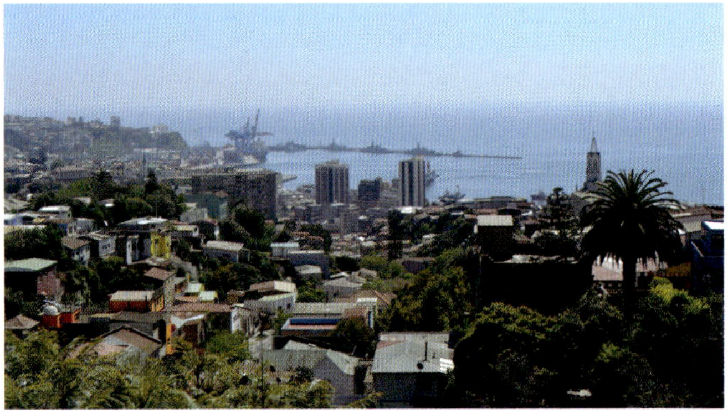

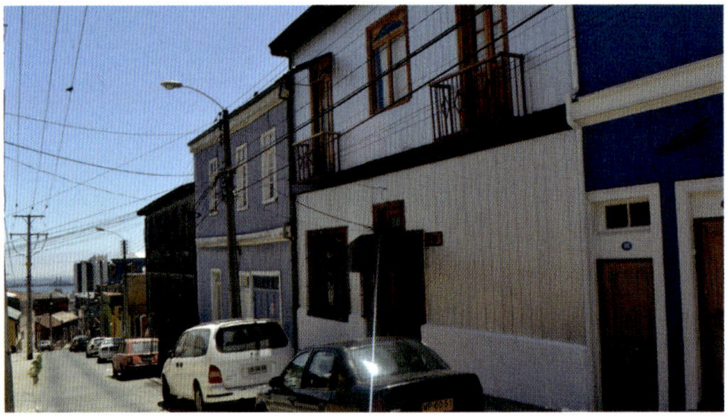

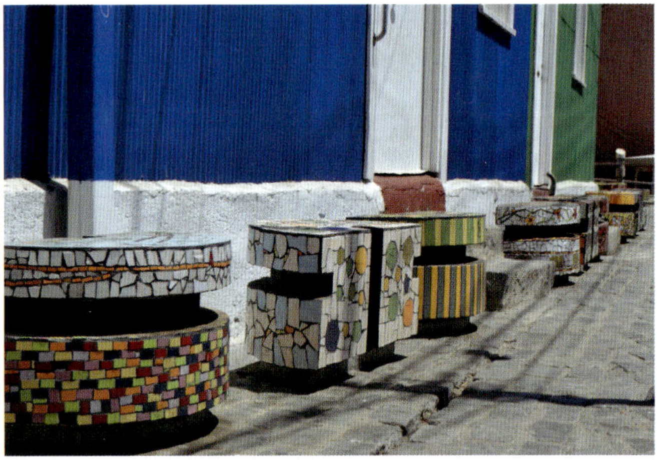

Valparaíso's steep streets reveal hidden street art gems of women on walls and an artistic sensibility that forms part of the city's character. Photos: Beatriz Navarro Soto

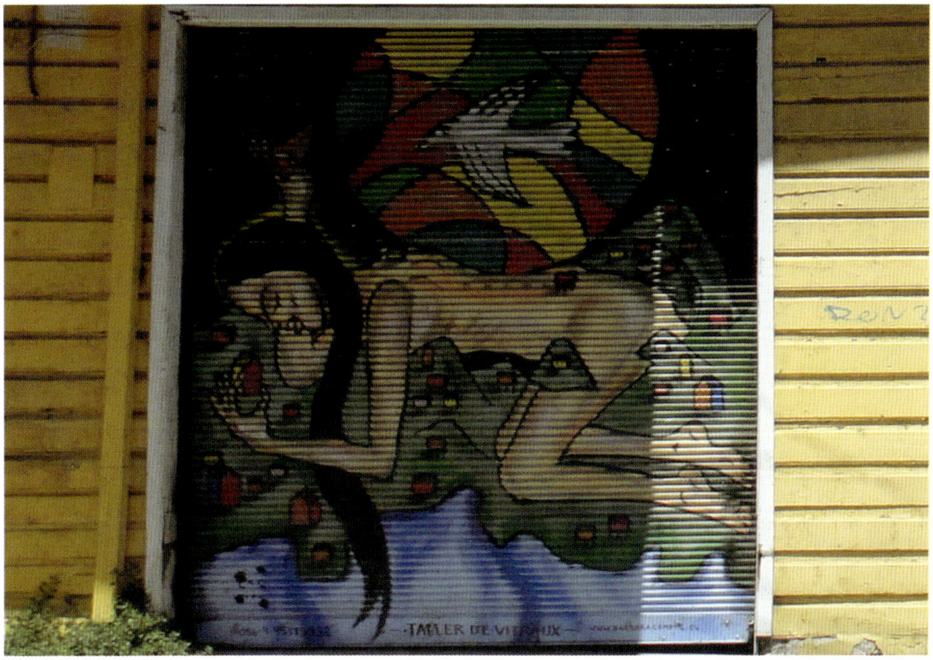

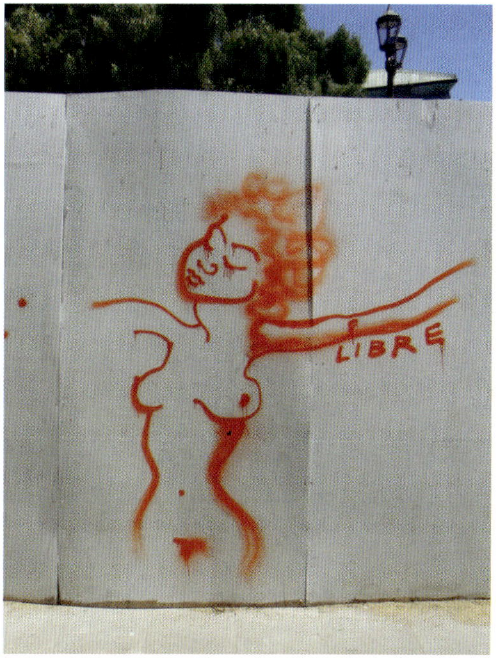

This symbolic representation of the feminine quality of Valparaíso assumes the form of a woman straddling its hills and holding one of its homes in her hand. Her well-defined spine is like a mountain range.

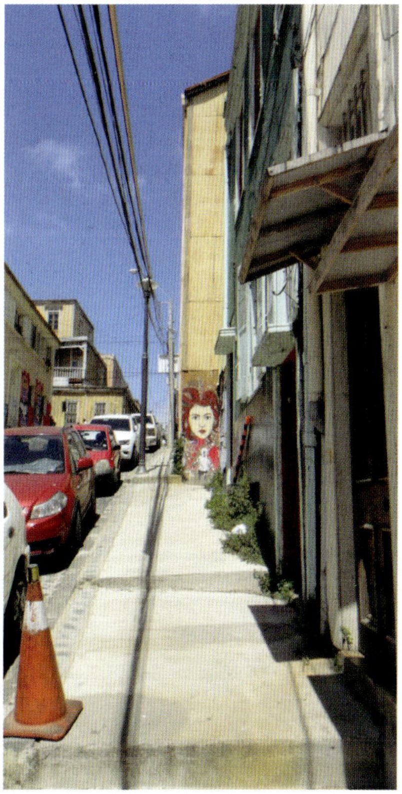

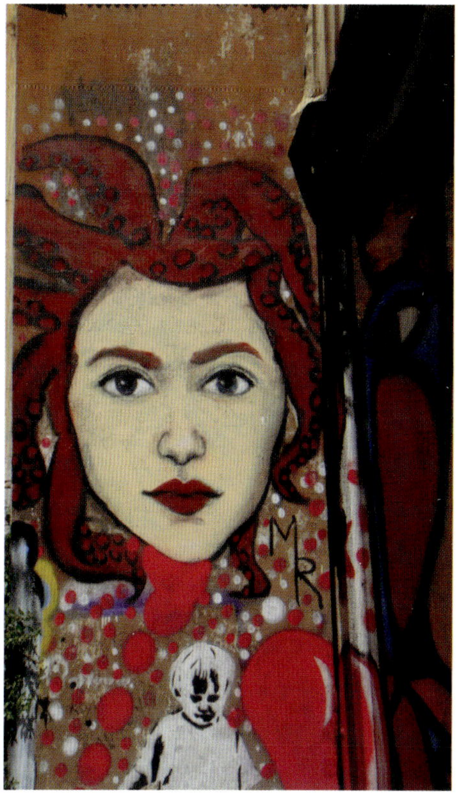

The nude woman is tagged with the word "libre," which means "free."

MR's portrait of a red-haired woman suggests an ancient goddess overlooking a hill.

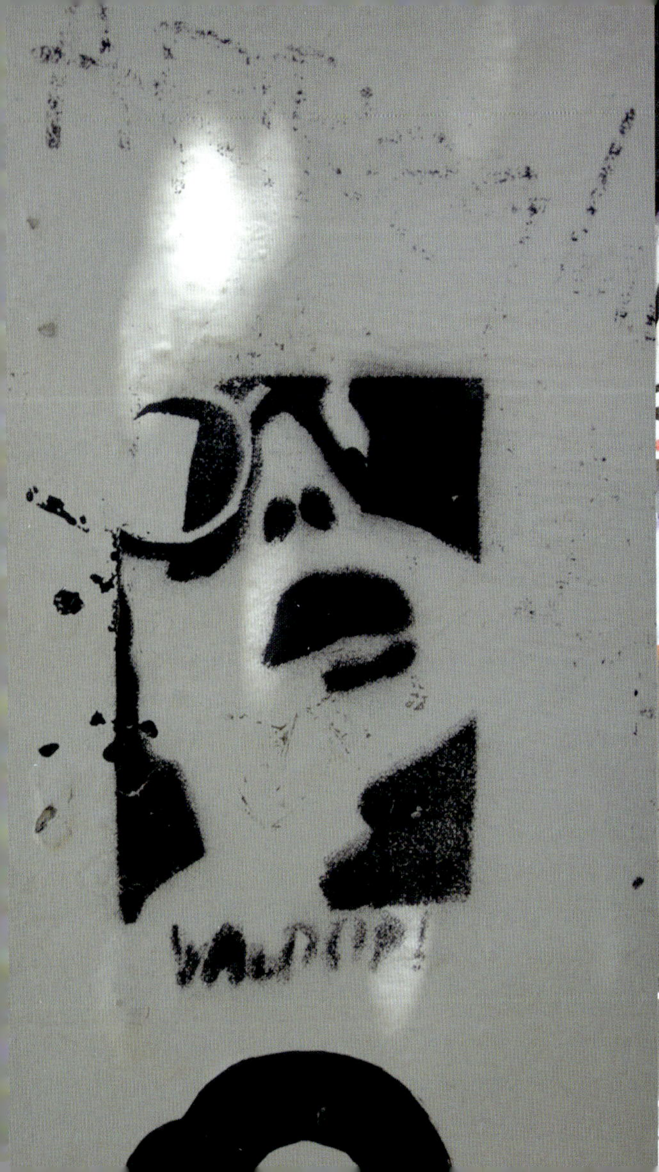
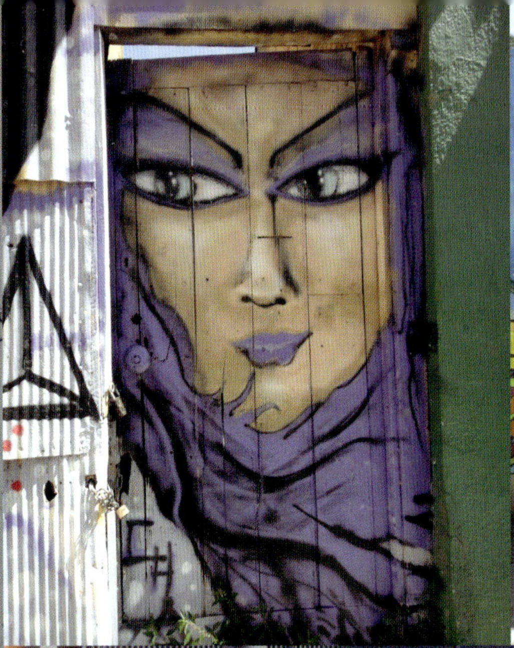
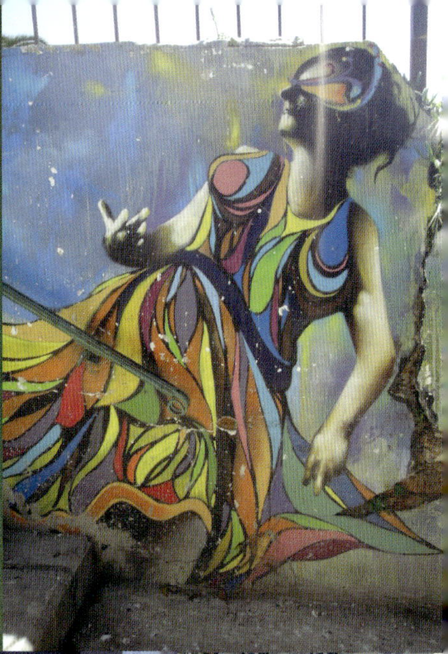
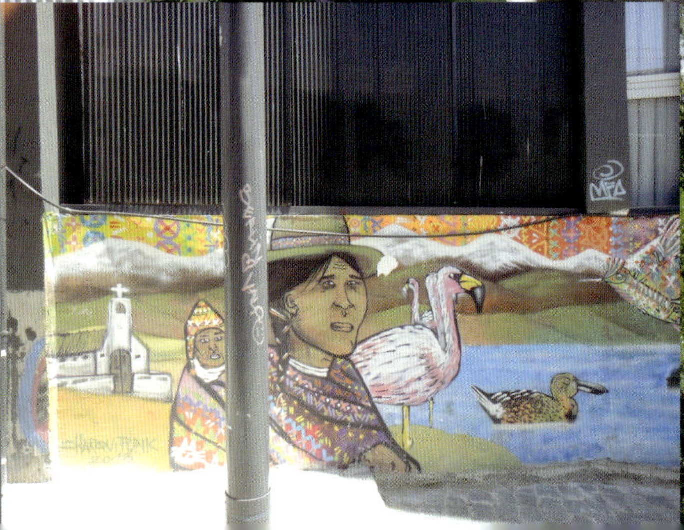

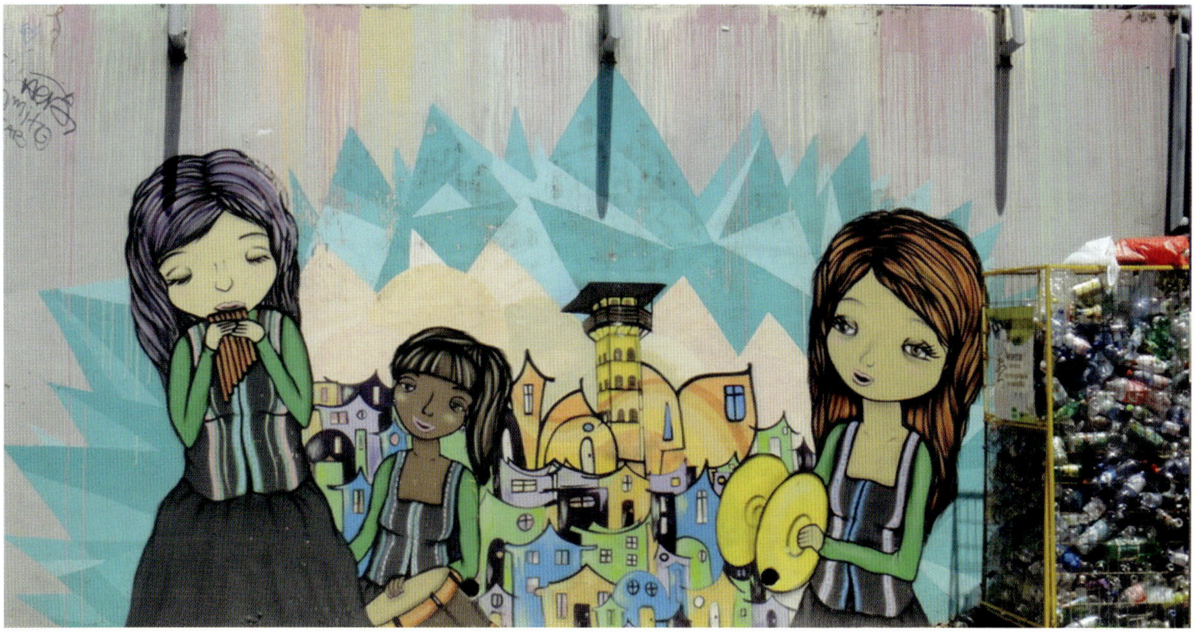

"The Girls"

Exuberance is at the heart of these next two examples from the streets of Valparaíso. The young girls in the band embody creativity by playing traditional Andean instruments like the pan flute and drums. Next to this mural is a bin full of recycled aluminum cans, which provides an urban counterpoint that shows how women and girls on the wall can enliven an otherwise bland wall.

The figure painted by French muralist Mr. Papillon embodies unbridled energy. The young girl's smile captures her pleasure as she runs her fingers through her thick, black hair. Her movements are delightful and produce an energy that can bring the viewer back to the joy of youth. Both pictures take a different approach to the developing women inside the girls.

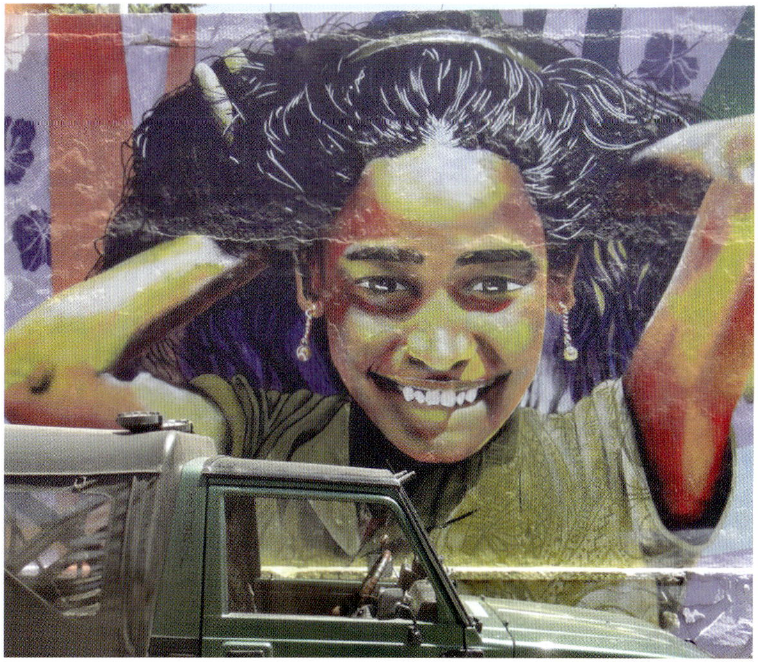

The young girls in the band play on while Mr. Papillon's photorealist portrait on the right exudes youthful joy.

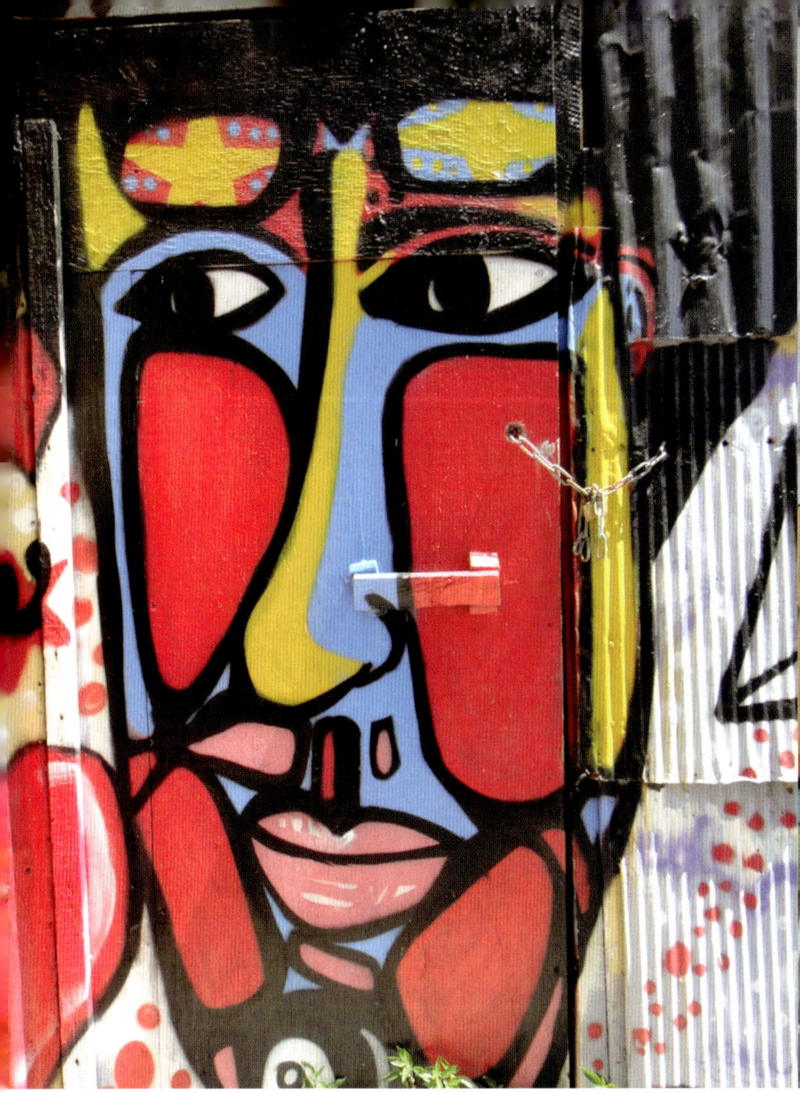

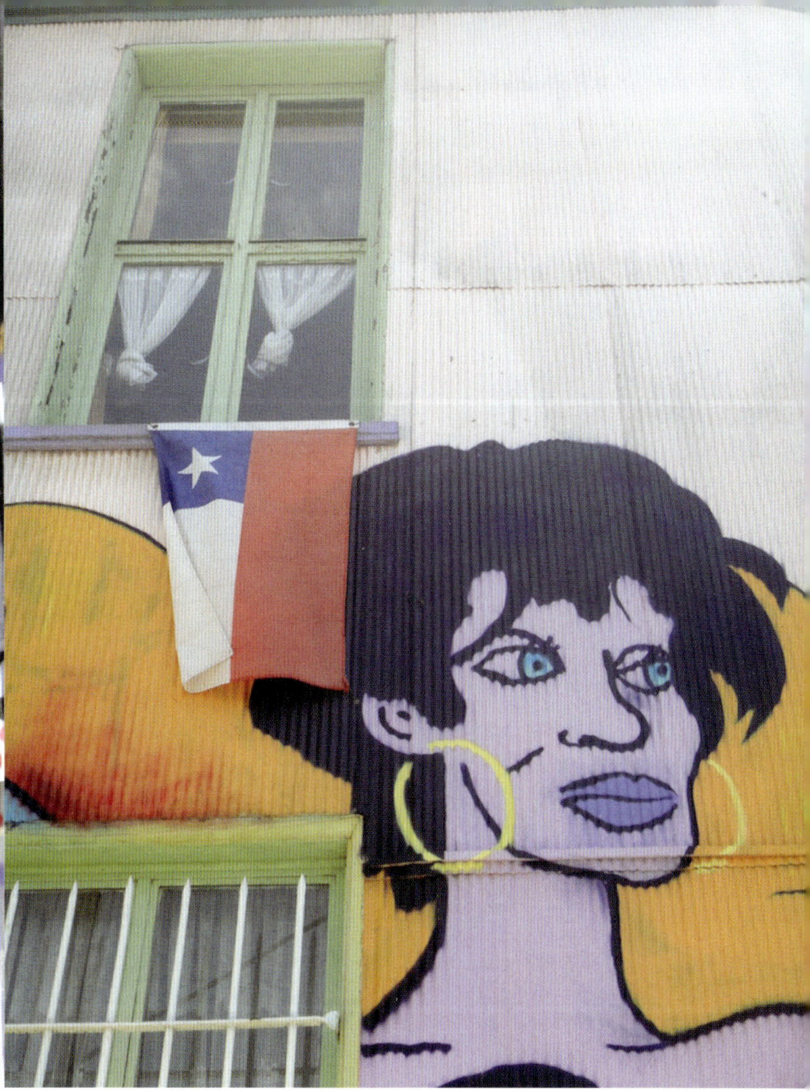

This abstract design and execution on corrugated iron are the essence of street art language, where found spaces become the backdrop and add texture to the work. In this example, there are vague references to cubism in a unique use of color and form, without an easily identifiable gender. The ready-made metal canvas is emblematic of street art's found surfaces.

There is no mistaking the gender of this woman on the wall. This larger-than-life portrait on the side of house also features the lavender lips and limpid blue eyes of the purple woman presented before. In this case we see the expression of a Chilean woman in full bloom rather than our sly woman under a head covering.

The sheer playfulness of movement is what comes across in these paintings, which enliven the wall. They may be sisters or a young mother and daughter. Whoever they are, these examples of wall art connect the city with its joy of life. The importance of family is a given in Chile and reflects in its wall art of women.

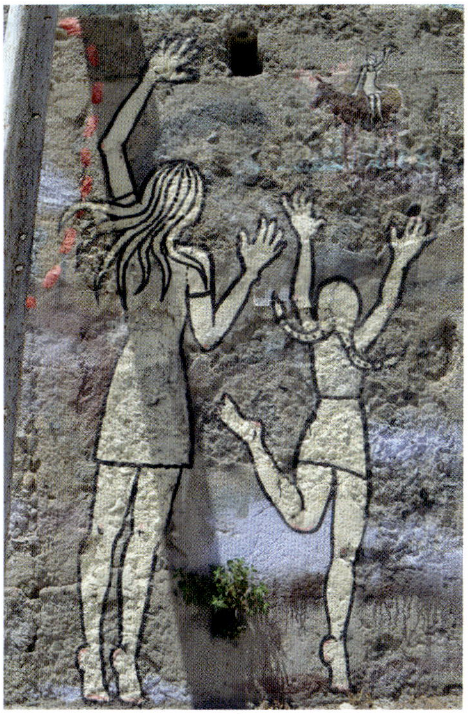

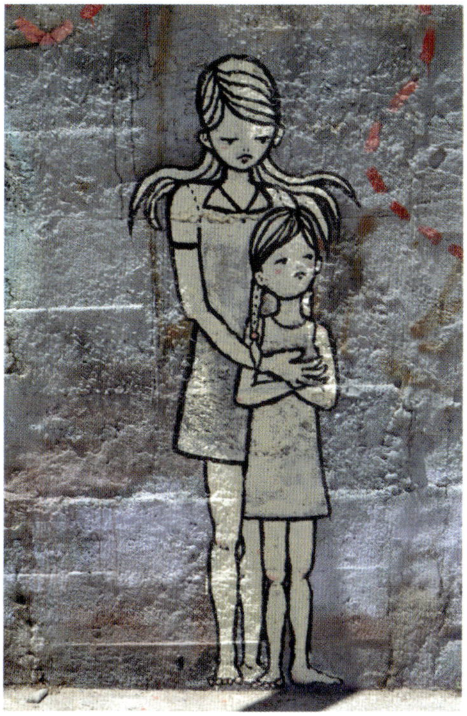

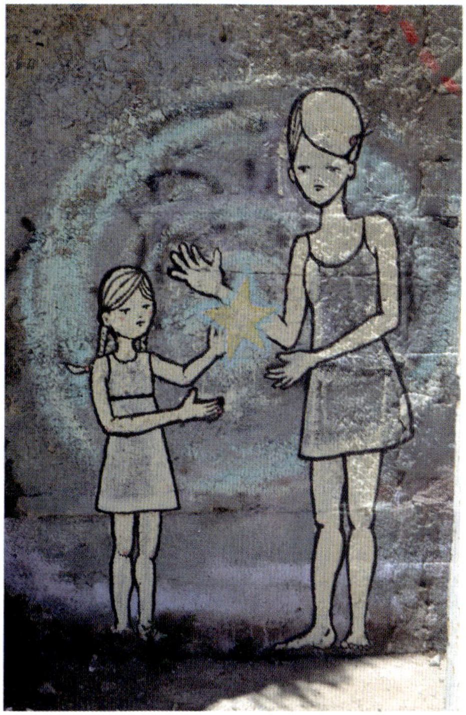

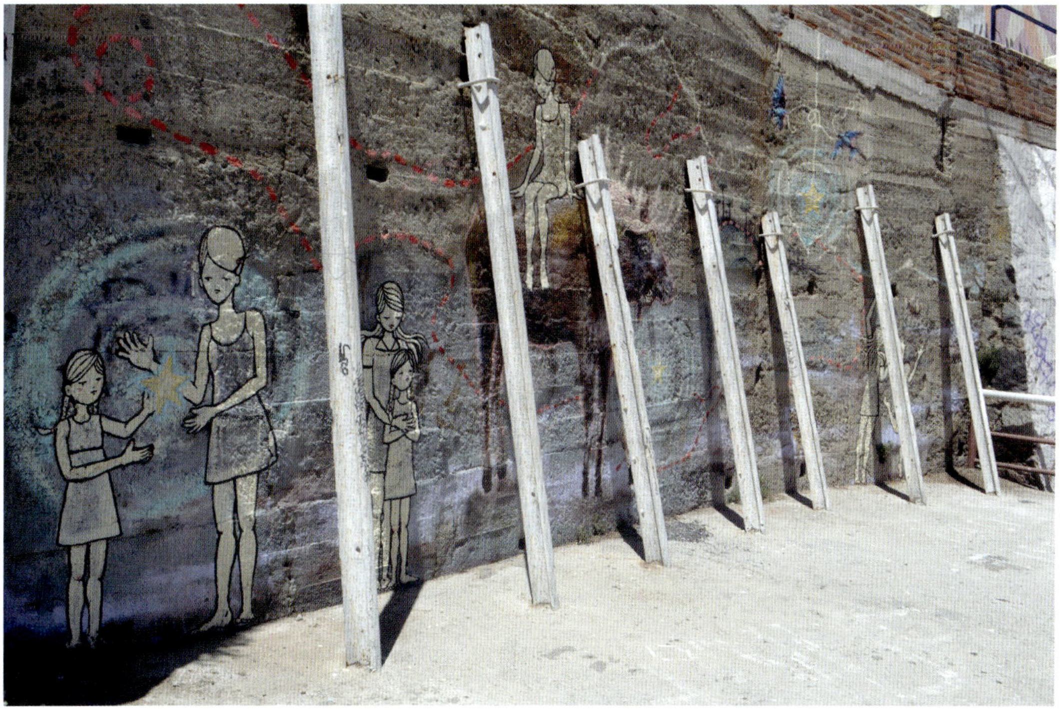

One of the joys of wandering the streets of Valparaíso outside the boundaries of an organized tour is the hidden gems not on the "must see" list of wall art.

The style may be simple, but there is no mistaking the message of feminine tenderness and energy in this piece by an unknown wall artist (right). Photos: Beatriz Navarro Soto

HUANCHACO: Peru's Surf Town

The next stop on our tour of women in outdoor galleries takes us to Huanchaco in northwestern Peru. On the desert coast of Peru sits this unlikely outdoor gallery of women on the wall. Those interested in Incan ruins visit nearby Chan Chan, which is a cheap bus ride away. The city has a kicked-back, slow-paced feel of rural Peru, and tourists enjoy the al fresco restaurants that serve the Peruvian specialty, ceviche (raw seafood salad marinated in fresh citrus juice). Huanchaco also caters to the surf crowd, with surfing classes on offer for first-time riders, although there are better places to ride Peru's powerful Pacific swells for the more experienced. Huanchaco is also home to the *caballitos de totora*, the reed-fishing and surfing boats lashed together and still used by locals as a different way of wave riding that dates back some three thousand years. You would think that Huanchaco would feature the occasional piece of wall art, mostly having to do with surfing. But its street art is surprisingly diverse. In fact, the backstreets of Huanchaco feature women on the walls who are surreally modern.

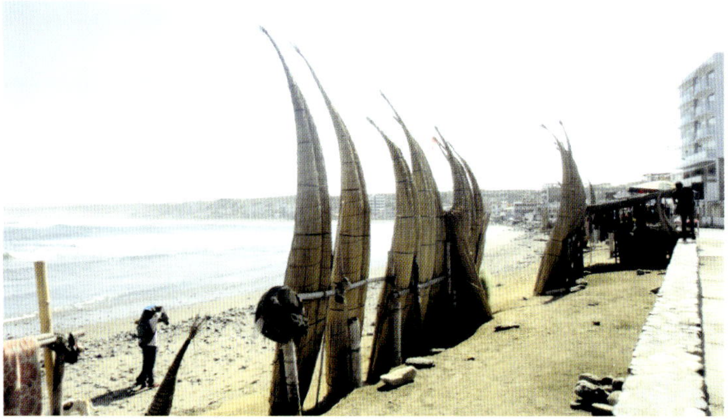

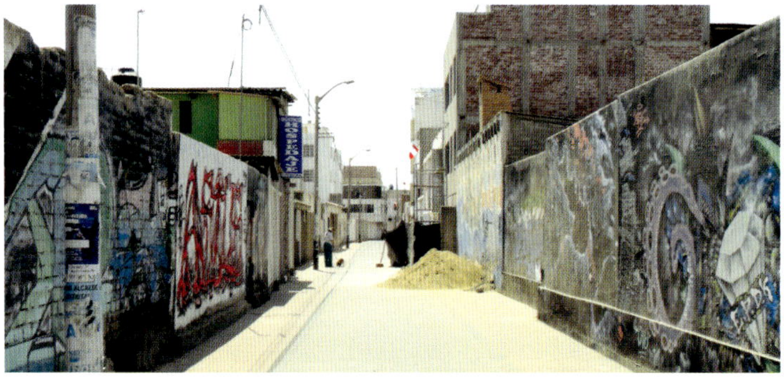

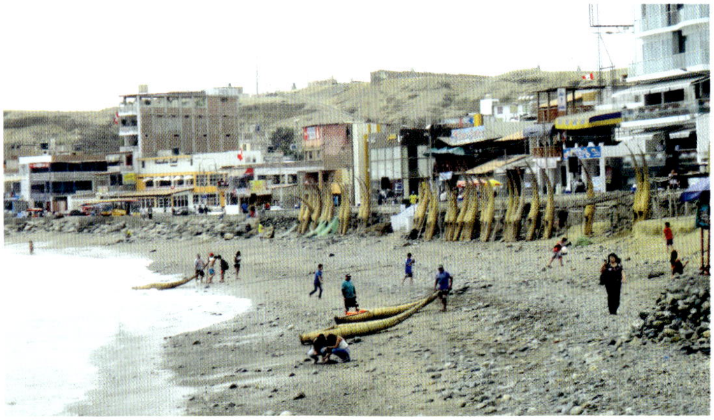

Huanchaco's reed fishing/surfing craft, caballitos de totora, are still used for fishing and to ride the town's waves.

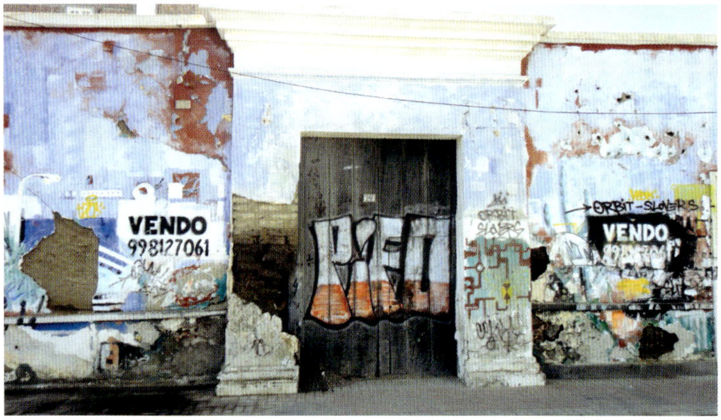

The backstreets of Huanchaco host an unusual gallery of bizarre and striking wall art of women and display the overlaid texture of the walls.

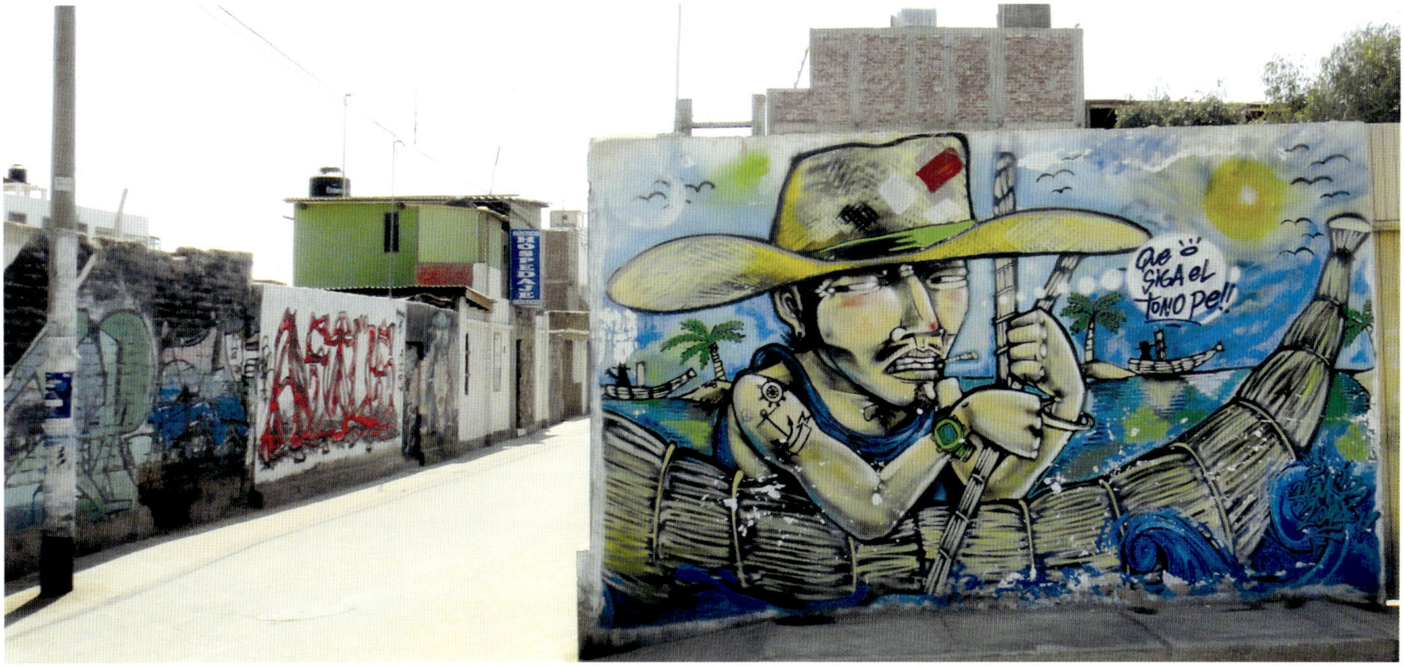
Que SIGA eL TONO Pe!!

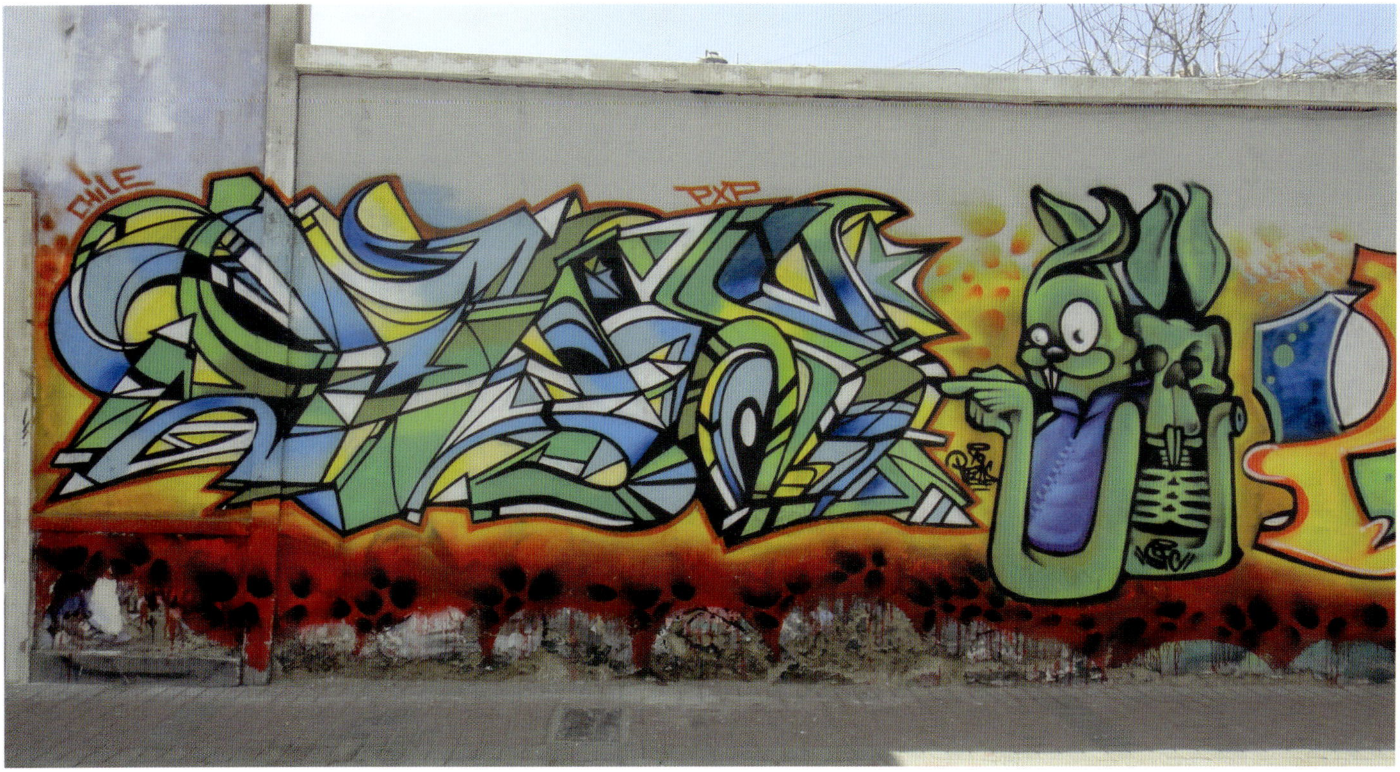
CHILE
PXP

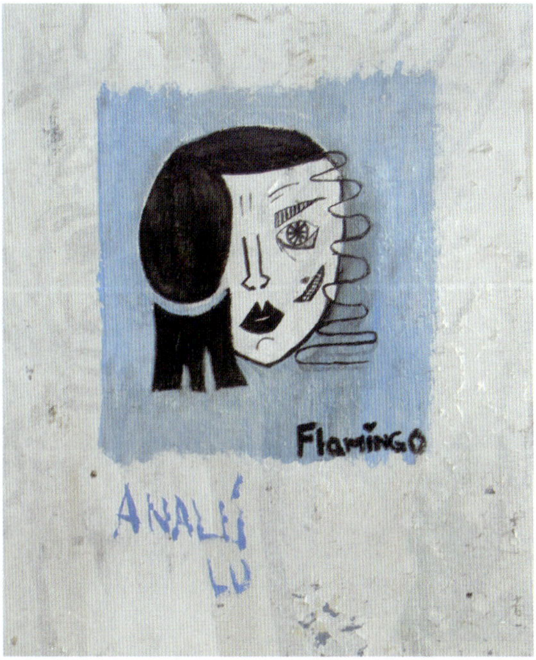

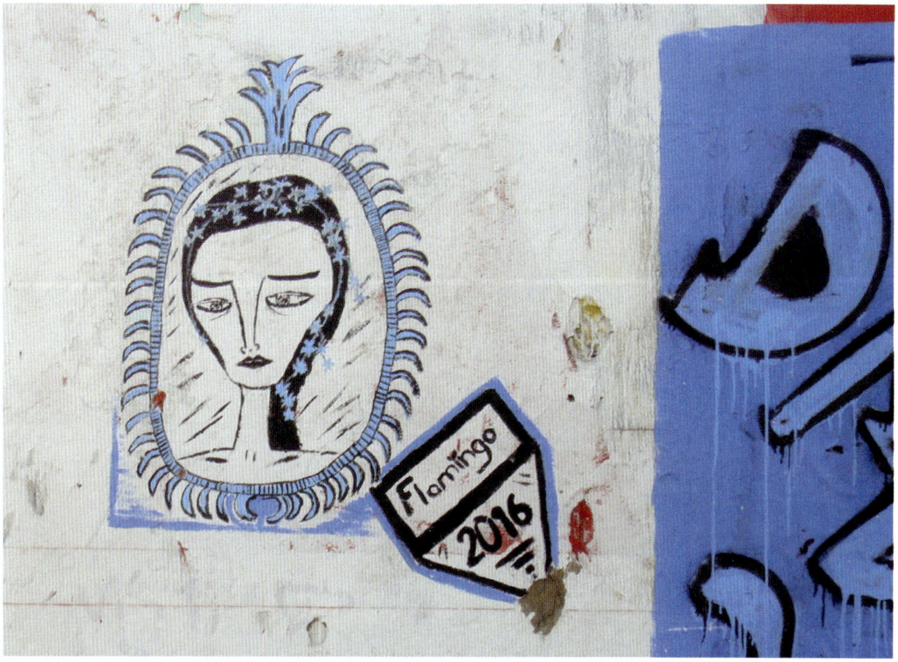

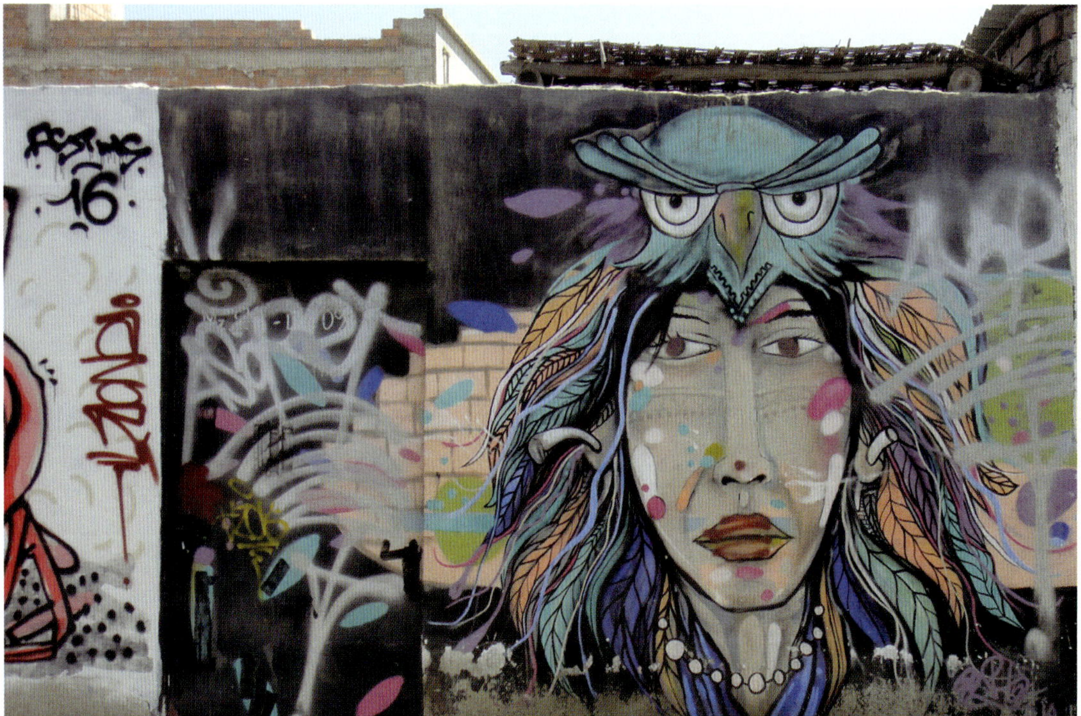

Flamingo's portraits in blue

Peru's connection with nature and ancient symbols is evident in much of its street art. Artist unknown.

HUANCHACO'S WOMEN:

Seeing Eye to Eye

The women on the wall in this surf town have little in common with the surf culture. There are no idealized paintings of waves or surfers that you often find on surf community walls. The women are curiously abstract, more befitting a gallery with one foot in surrealism, cubism, and the "other" planted in the digital world. And then there are examples of the feminine power of ritual symbolism in nature. See for yourself.

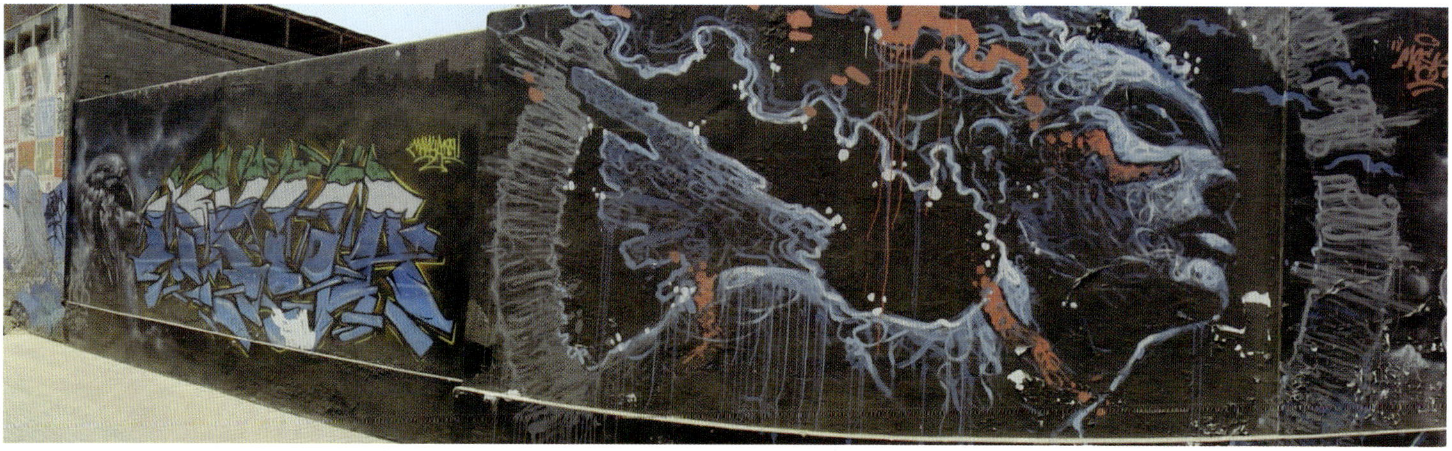

Flamingo's two portraits of a woman in blue display a minimalist style. The more formalized portrait is framed by a mirror and is more detailed and intimate. The other is a mechanist portrait of a woman whose right eye is covered by a single strand of falling hair zigzagging from her scalp like a loose thread. This portrait shows little signs of intimacy, but almost a robotic sense of distance. The eye is an expressionless wheel revealing nothing in this masklike portrait.

This next painting suggests a priestess connecting with her animist past. The owl is a symbol of wisdom, good fortune, and death in Andean culture and features prominently in this portrait. The owl headdress covers her face, and her hair reveals a strong connection with the natural world and its potent myths.

This grounding in nature resides at the opposite end of the symbolic spectrum from our next two examples of Huanchaco's women on the wall. The first has more in common with time traveling and science fiction than it does with cultural/historical references. This woman appears to be passing through a time portal, her electric visage dominated by a hypnotic expressionless look. The image confronts the viewer with its mysterious symbolism, which refers to Victor Frankenstein's creation.

Walking down Huanchaco's alleyways reveals a futuristic portrait of an electrified woman on the wall.

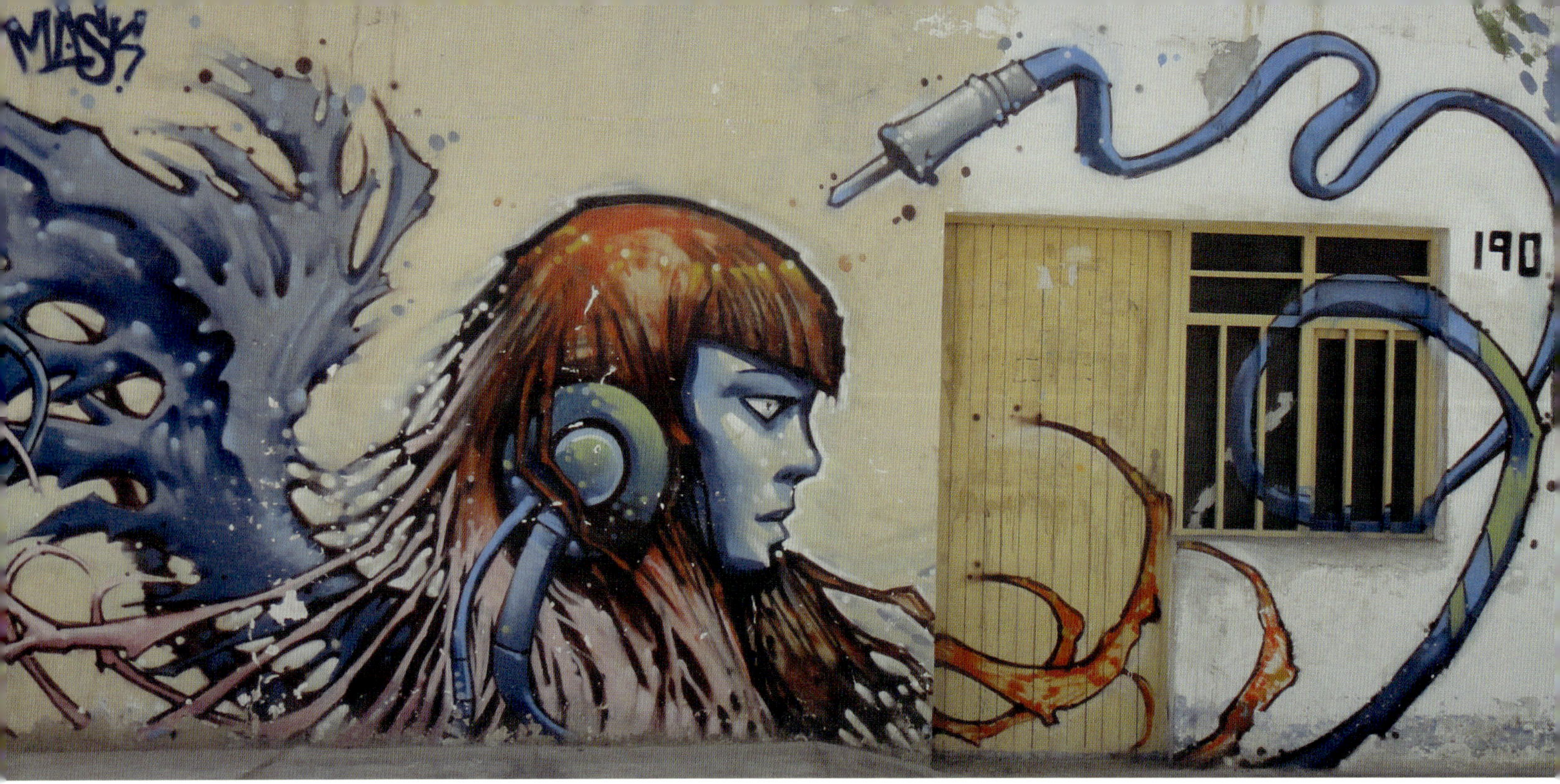

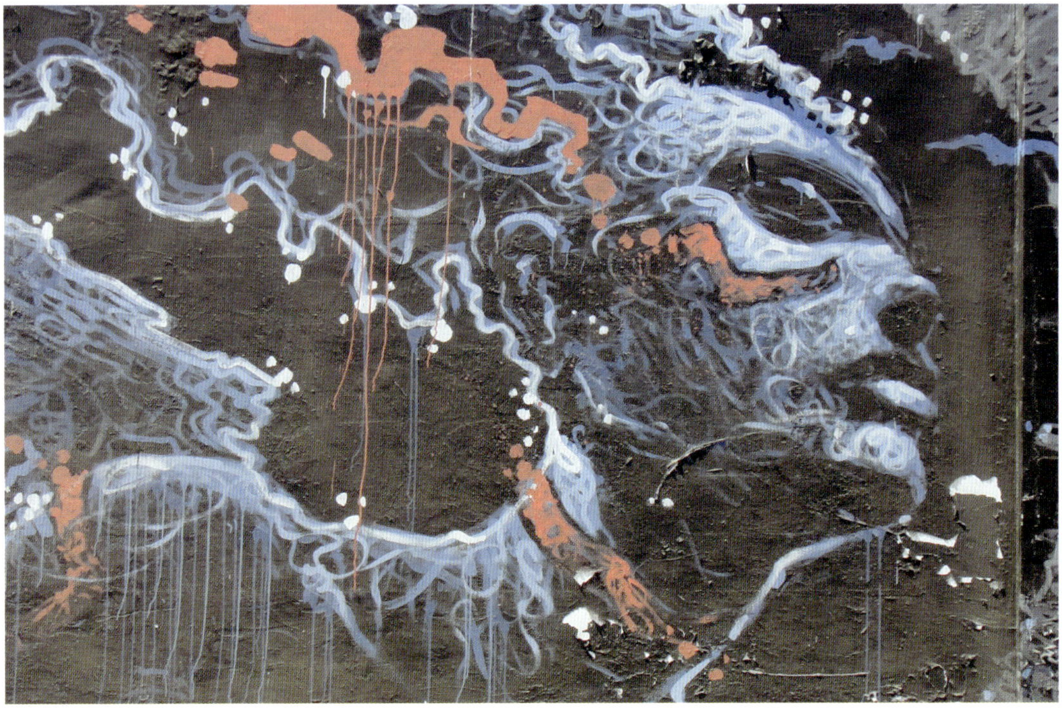

TOP *Science fiction meets street art in this portrait, while the digital woman connects to her isolated world. Artist unknown*

BELOW *Detail of the electrified woman.*

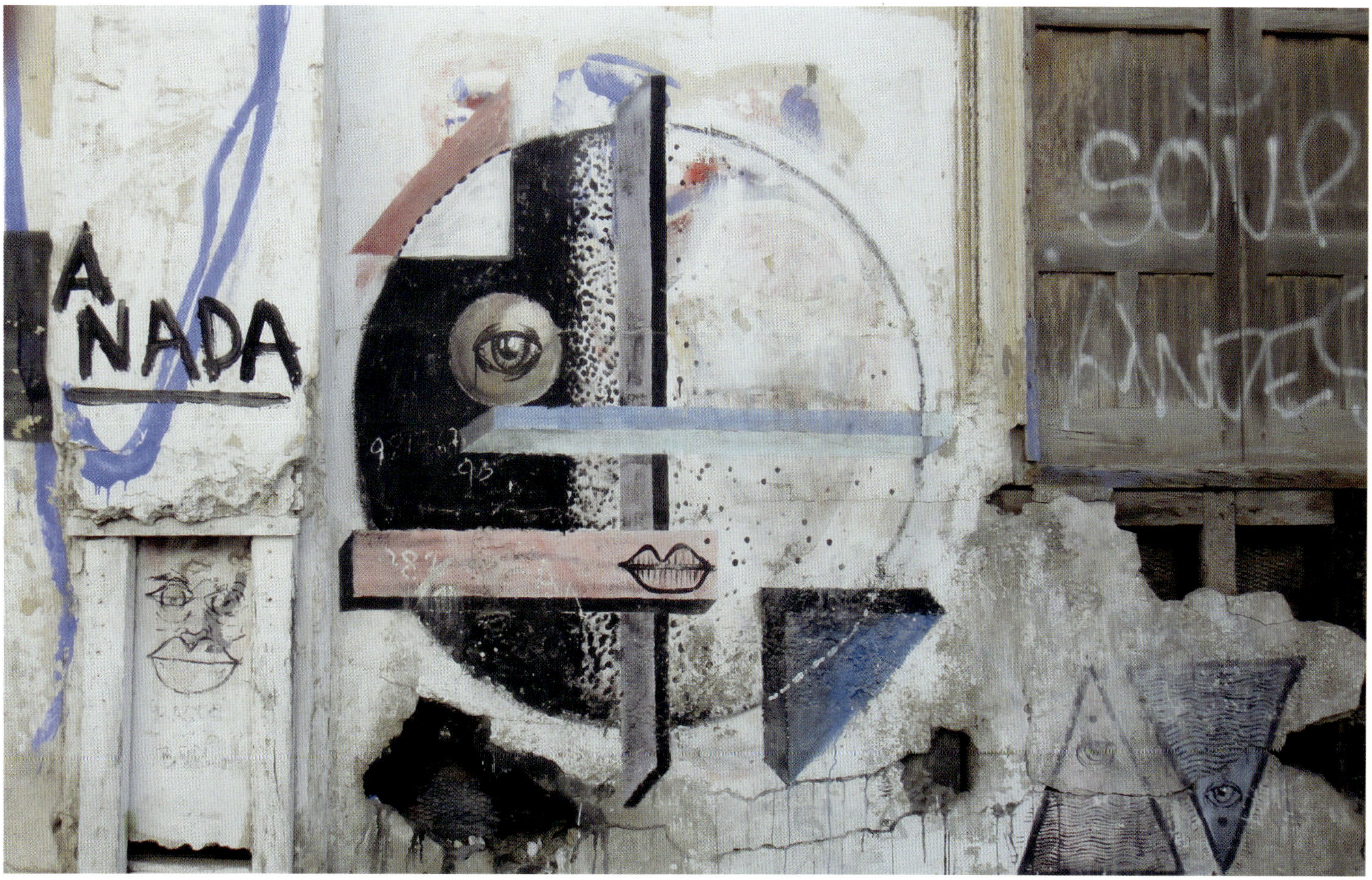

In a companion piece, the woman with expressionless eyes is plugged into a digital world, with a sound cable snaking near her head. It is almost as if she is being swallowed alive by a digital creature that cuts her off from everything that isn't plugging into her senses. This is a commentary on our digital-world isolation as much as a portrait.

A single eye takes center stage in the following homage to surrealism and cubism. The artist uses wooden planks and a disc to literally frame the face of a woman who looks through a planular keyhole. We focus our attention on her eye floating in this scaffolding construction of geometric shapes.

Much of wall art of women can be found on walls like this, with layers of work that have peeled off, leaving room for new growth.

This artist relies on a reference to René Magritte's floating lips. Artist unknown.

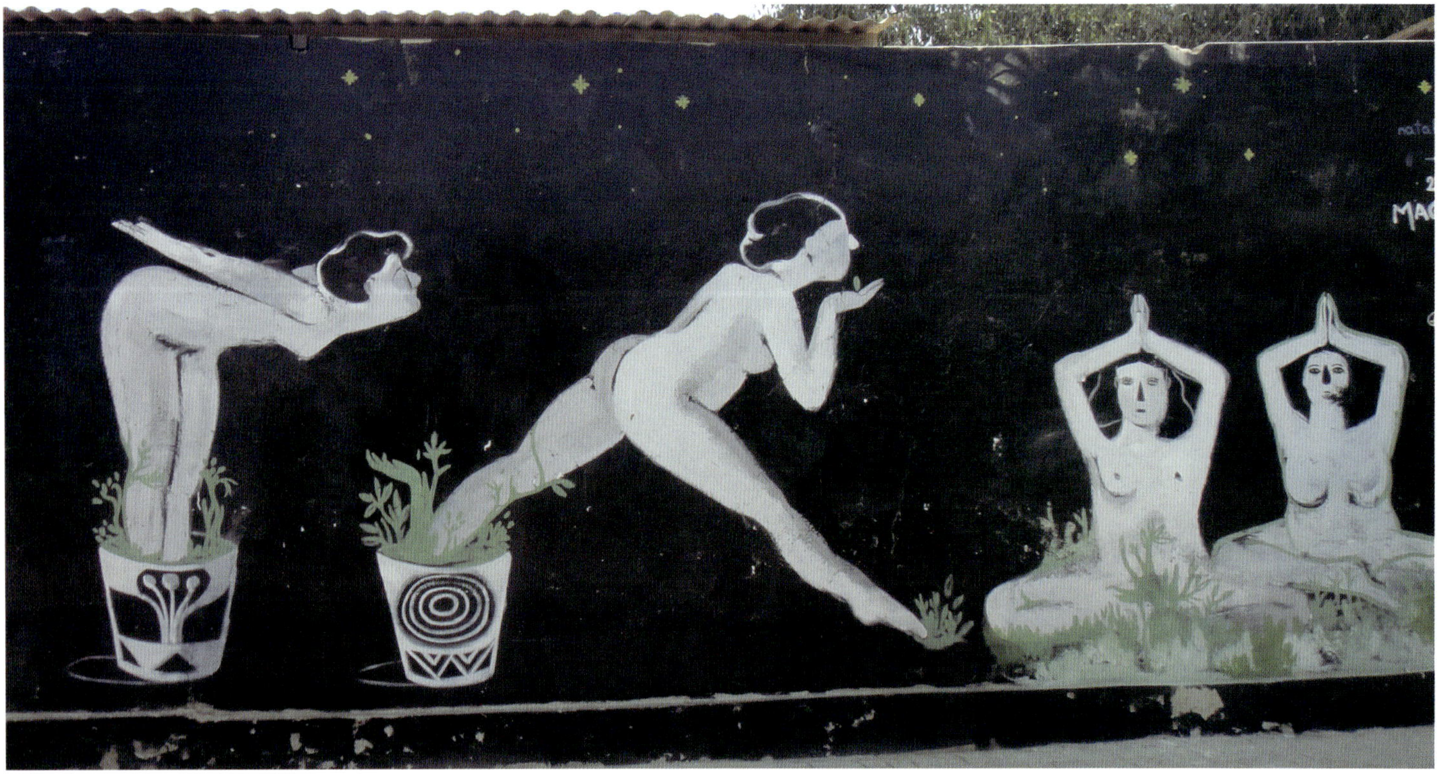

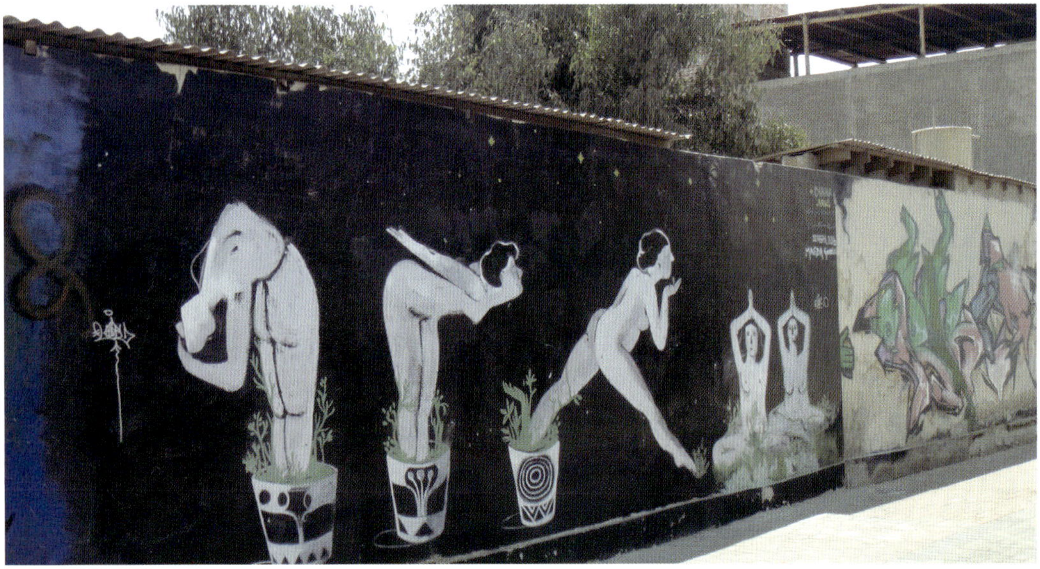

The path to enlightenment is tackled in this piece of wall art.

The colored feathers of nature are a beautiful counterpoint to this portrait of a young Peruvian girl.

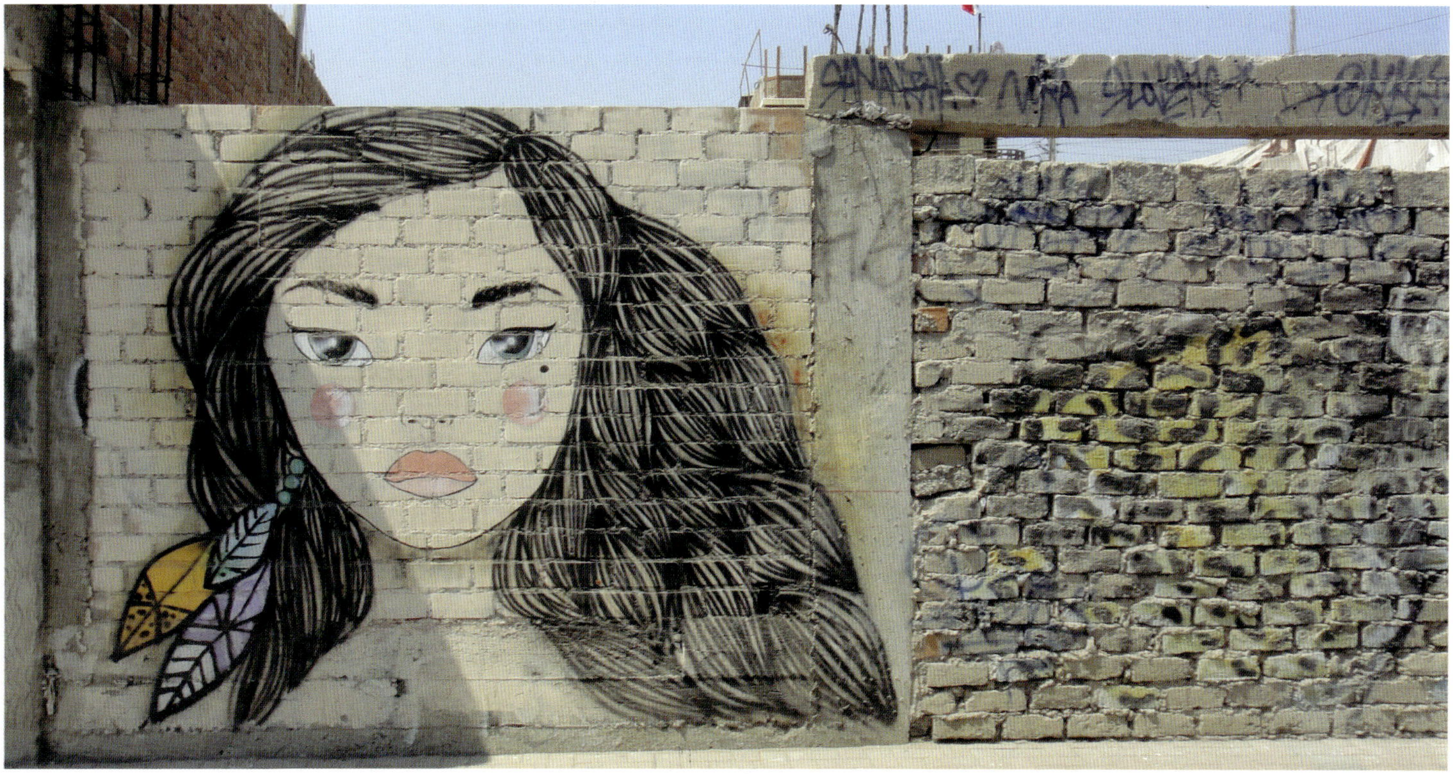

In contrast, ancient Greek vases inspire our next example of wall art. The women on this wall are growing out of pots like plants as they emerge and transition to an enlightened state. This piece is a reference to becoming one with the world around us, possibly through yoga and enlightenment.

Our final example of street art from Huanchaco on a brick wall is another young woman who is adorned with colored bird feathers. She is like a younger example of our animist priestess wearing the owl headdress.

"Keeping it real" is an expression often used to remind ourselves not to betray our vision or intent. In the examples of New World women on the wall, there is definitely a grassroots, real feeling to representation of women far from the trendy commercialization of wall art. With long roots entangling the past, the women on the wall from Mexico, Costa Rica, Peru, and Chile reflect the diversity of subject matter and historical antecedents found in its women on the wall. The practitioners of wall art in the Southern Hemisphere are generally not well-funded commercial ventures. They paint their art from the heart, which beats to the rhythm of women who often symbolize justice, beauty, animism, protest, nature, and the simple joy of being alive.

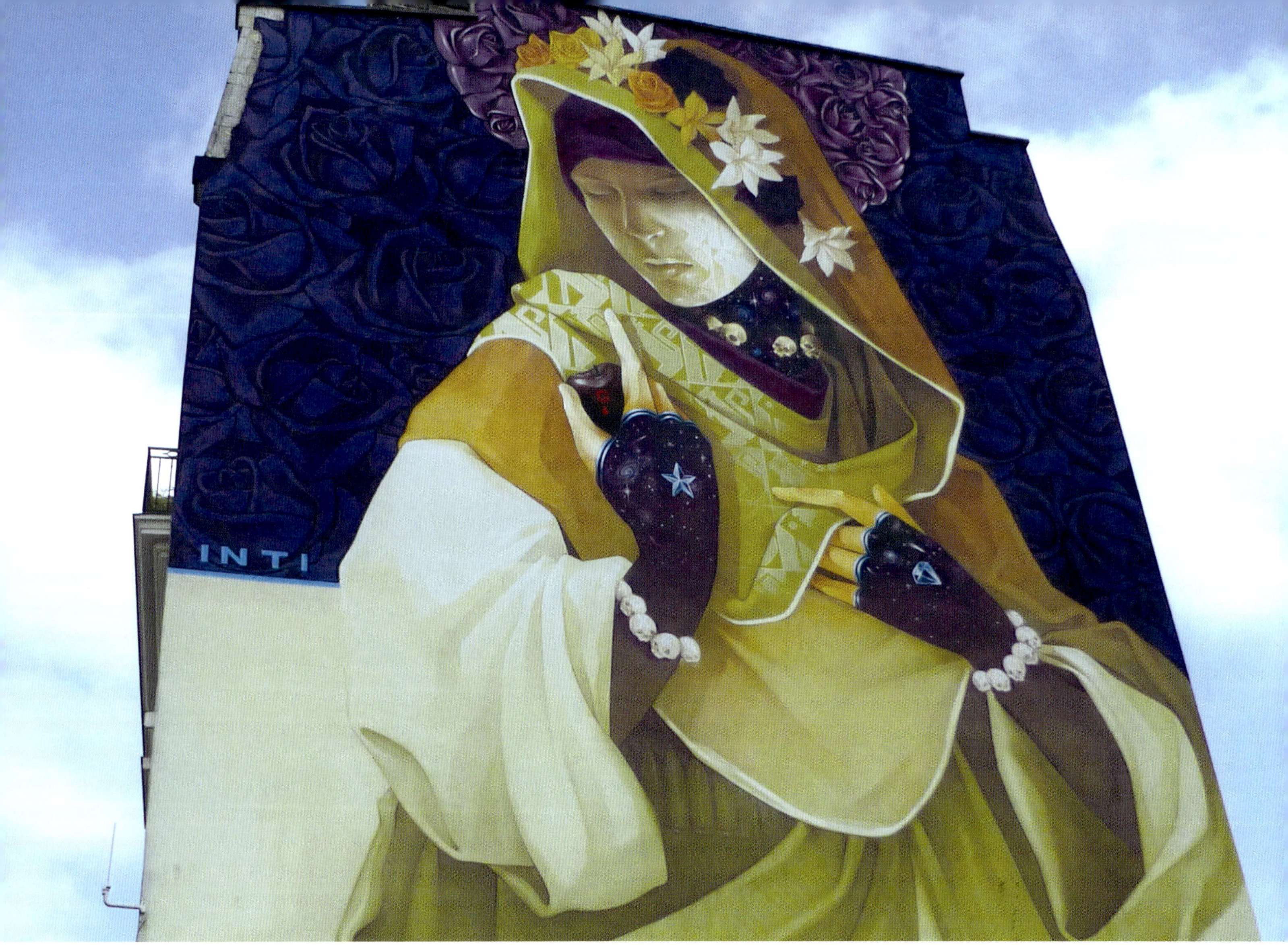

Next Stop: Europe

The next stops on our itinerary are the busy streets of Europe, where wall art of women takes center stage in Paris, while the backstreets of Berlin and Palermo offer surprisingly raw examples of women on the wall that incorporate satire and acerbic political commentary. We also speak with a street artist of women based in Europe who works with a hammer and chisel instead of a spray can. Like many of the wall artists you encounter in Europe, Vhils has a broad perspective of the role of his work in representing the humanist identity in the world's cities.

Inti's portrait takes up the side of an apartment block in the Thirteenth Arrondissement of Paris.

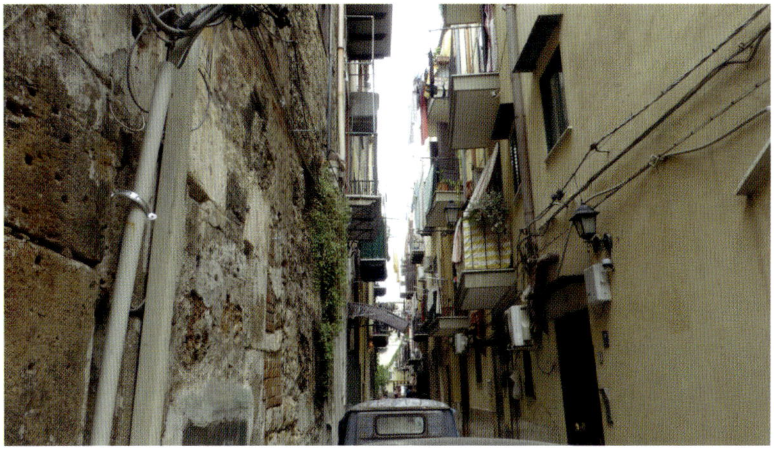

6

Alleyway in Palermo, Sicily

EUROARTISTS

Big Walls, Big Ideas in Small Spaces

Throughout western Europe, women on the walls have taken center stage. In some cases, it is difficult to separate what may be an act of personal advertising or the work of an anonymous street artist making a highly personal statement about women

In Paris, women subjects often symbolize larger-scale political movements linked to female empowerment. The scale of their artwork can be breathtaking, like the large-scale work by Inti Castro, a Chilean wall artist born in Valparaíso whose first name is the Quechua word for "sun." His work combines Indigenous influences from Chile with an accomplished graphic sensibility.

Street art in Europe is a cultural touchpoint and urban experience that is now just as much a part of a cityscape as famous museums and cathedrals. The difference with street art is that the canvas keeps changing. A new visit to a European city will yield new pieces of wall art; the way women are portrayed varies with neighborhood location as much as artistic temperament and style.

In this chapter we walk the streets of Paris, Berlin, and Palermo to sample the unique characteristics of women on the wall. In Paris, two distinct neighborhoods celebrate women as a way to broadcast on a massive scale the vibrancy of an immigrant neighborhood (Thirteenth Arrondissement); by contrast, the upscale inner-city neighborhood (Marais District) approaches wall art of women as borderline advertising and almost-hidden messages of defiance and social commentary. Both neighborhoods illustrate on a large and a small scale how wall artists are becoming more like celebrities than outlaws.

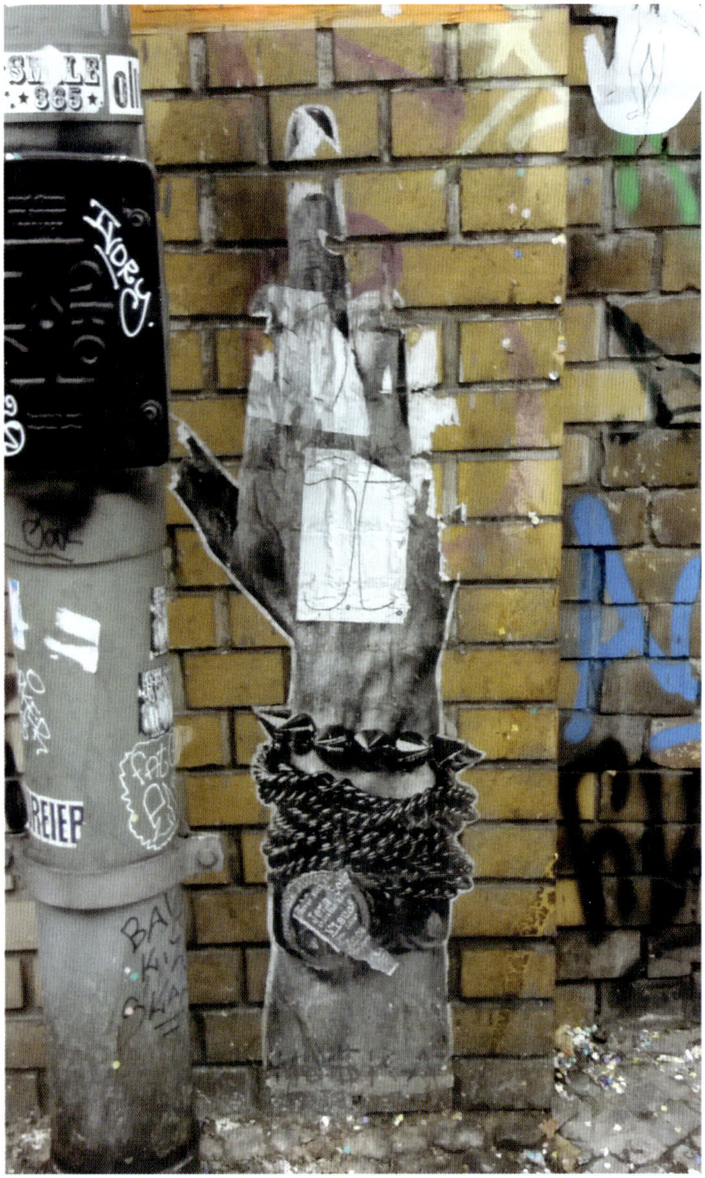

In Palermo, Sicily, another European stopover, wall art maintains its raw appeal far away from the stylized and fashionable streets of inner-city Paris. Nothing is polished on the walls or back alleys of Palermo, just a fast energy that may be lacking in the more considered and planned pieces of Paris. The examples in this chapter do not follow a particular trajectory, but they compose far ends of the visual spectrum based on the walls that often host their ephemeral pieces.

Then we take a walk on the wild side in Berlin, with its wicked sense of humor and vision. Wall artists from around the world showcase their strong political views and take their cultural cues from this city known for its outspoken visual grammar. Berlin's women on walls often rebel against cultural norms and reflect the edginess born from a city that was divided by war but now reveals its anger in parody and protest in wall art of women.

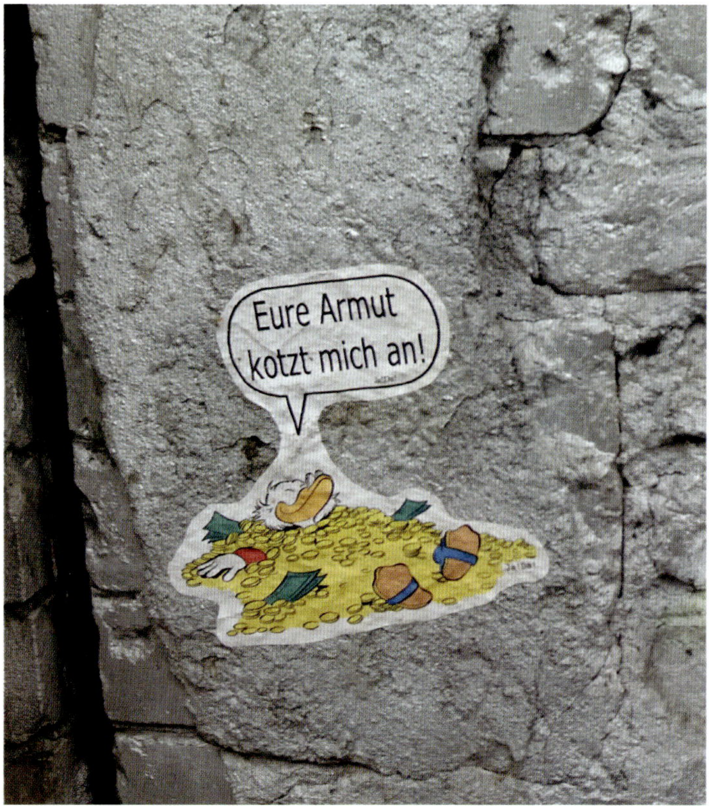

The middle finger gets the Berlin wall art treatment, while Disney's Uncle Scrooge's message is "Your poverty gets on my nerves." Artists unknown.

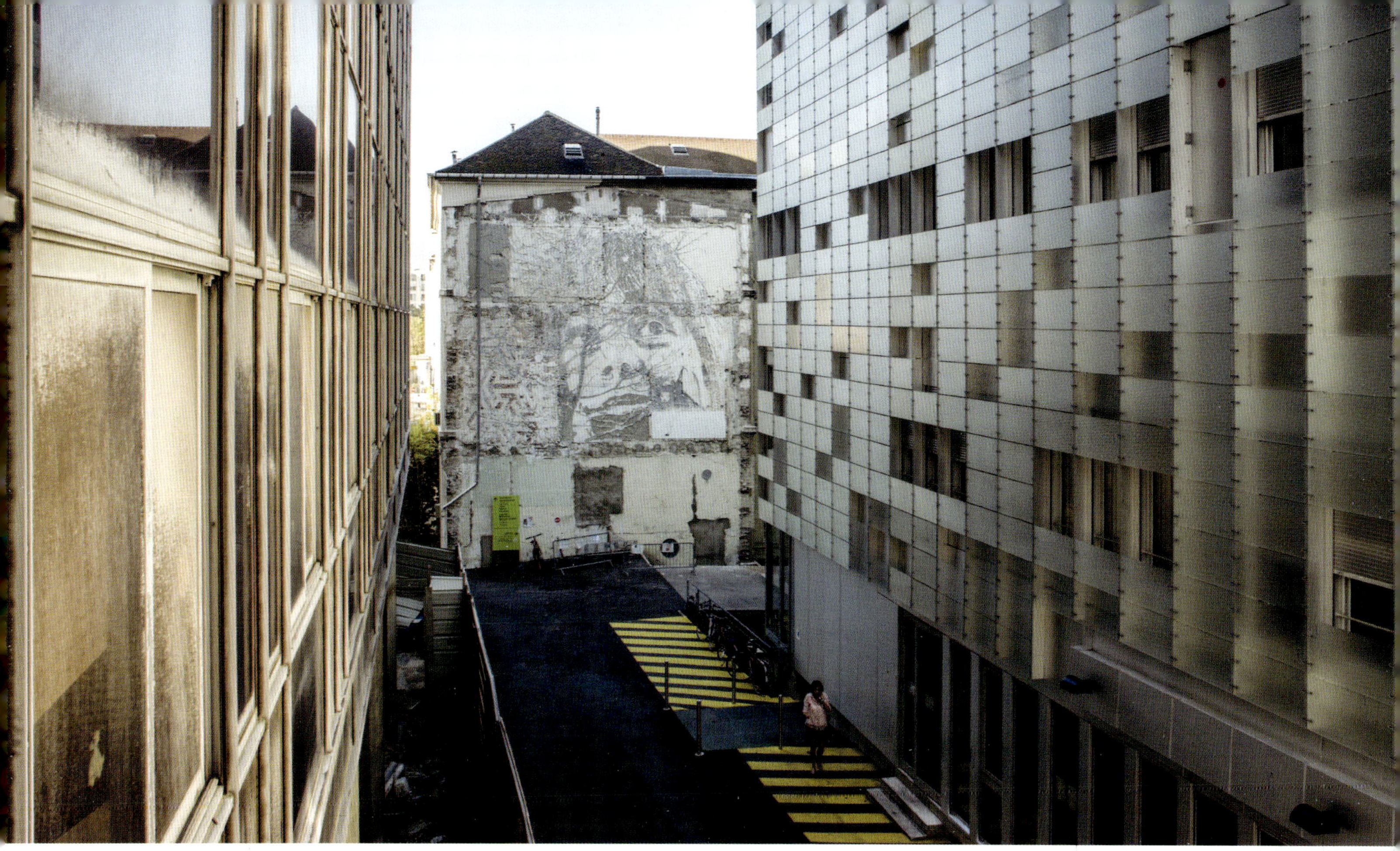

Untitled—Scratching the Surface project. Bas-relief wall carving and paint. Paris, October 2014. Photo: Vhils Studio

VHILS: International Star with Feet Firmly Planted on the Ground

If there is one thread that joins the European wall artists, it is that many of them work on a global scale. Although they may be based in London, Paris, or Portugal, they travel the world practicing their craft, often in collaboration with other wall artists. Vhils (Portuguese-born Alexandre Farto) is an example of this globetrotting wall artist. He is based in Lisbon and London, yet his work can be seen in Los Angeles and Brazil. Vhils is essentially a wall art sculptor. He coaxes the images out of walls with hammer and powered chisel, chipping away at the hidden images brick by brick, instead of covering them with paint. His is a thoughtful, considered approach to street art that highlights how street art has become much more than graffiti and instead has become a way of humanizing the urban landscapes with portraits that reflect their place. The interview with Vhils was done via the internet, when a series of questions were posed to him through his agent.

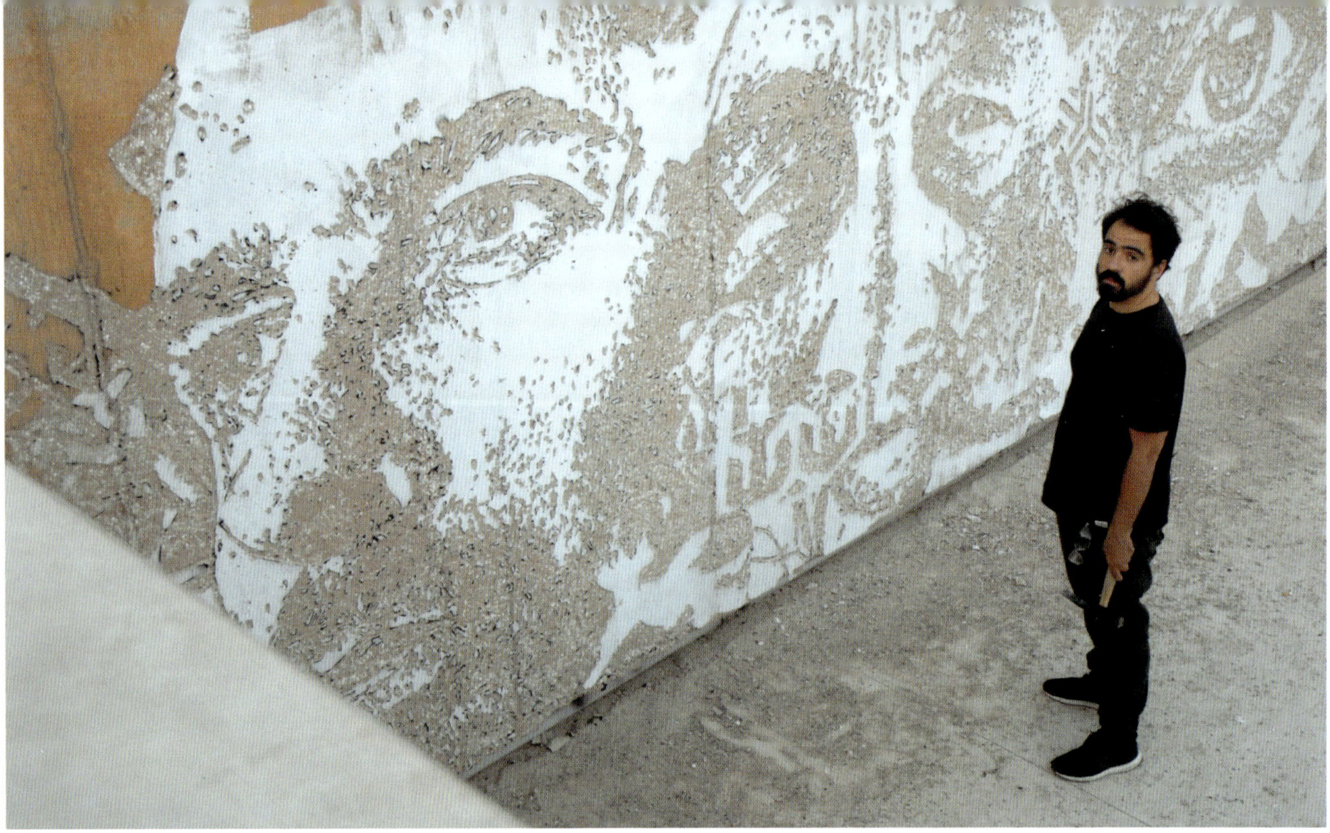

The best thing about working in the streets is the freedom, the way it allows you to operate at will in the city space and put up work that has the potential to reach and touch a vast, heterogenous audience.

Vhils at work in Beja, Portugal, in 2017. Photo: Nicola de Nunzio, licensed CC By-SA 4.0

INTERVIEW WITH VHILS:

Early Days as a Tagger

I started out on this path painting illegal graffiti when I was a youngster. After spending a few years focused on painting letter-based graffiti, I reached a stage when I began questioning what I was doing and where I wanted to go. I came to the conclusion that I wanted to keep on creating work in the public space but directed toward a broader audience, beyond the closed community of graffiti writers.

Inspired by what was taking place with the new street art scene and my discovery of the stencil technique around 2003, I began shifting toward more figurative work. I had already learned from graffiti how to move about the city and when and where to put up work, so I simply put this knowledge to use with a different line of work that enabled me to explore the urban environment's full potential. Sometime later I began questioning the use of stencils in the classical way.

From my observations of how city walls seem to grow thicker over time, as they are repeatedly covered with new layers of paint, graffiti, posters, etc., I realized that instead of adding yet more layers to them, I could work with what was already there by reversing the stencil technique and subtracting some of these layers. I began using this approach to cut through the layers of advertising posters I removed from the streets, and eventually started experimenting with walls and other mediums.

And to do so in a very direct way, without any intermediaries. Public space should be open to everyone's participation. If it's public, people should be allowed to use it freely and take part in its management and embellishment. Art should be a priority in public space. To me personally, it has always been important, since most of my work deals with the realities of our contemporary urban societies, so it makes sense that the city is both subject and material.

I believe that the relationship between a city and its citizens is like a complex network of reciprocal stimuli, of cause and effect, and that art in general can contribute to create a better environment for the city, its people, and its communities.

The Sources of Inspiration: Photography, Interviews, and Peeling Back the Walls of Identity

Regardless of their gender, inspiration for my portraits comes from my travels and work experiences in different cities, from photographs I take myself, from photographs I find while researching historical archives related to a particular location, or even from glimpses of images that somehow become ingrained in my memory.

When I work in the public space, the idea is to fundamentally humanize it in some way.

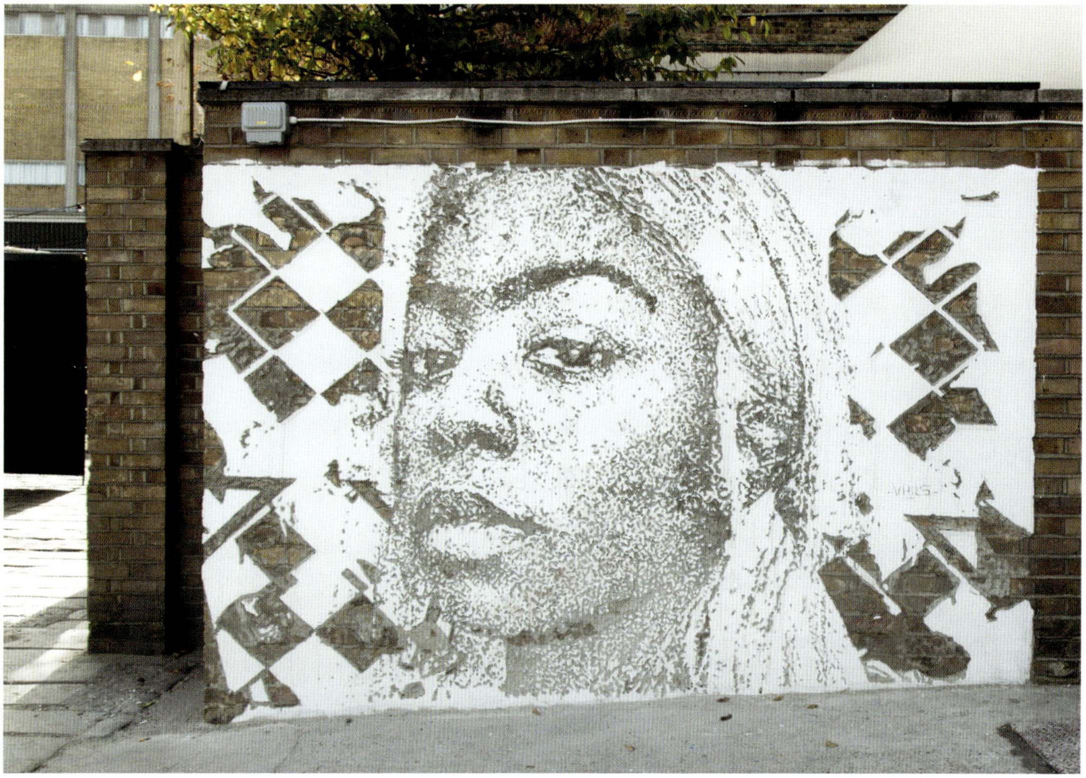

Portrait of Siobhan Bell—Scratching the Surface project. Bas-relief wall carving and paint. London, October 2018. Photo: Alexander Silva (@ as.analogic) / Vhils Studio

Sometimes I also use composites, creating a new image that can represent people in general while not depicting anyone in particular. It all depends on the nature and scope of the project. Some of the real people I depict have a particular connection with the location.

In some of the larger projects, especially those involving a community, this involves getting to know them, sharing experiences, listening to their stories and concerns, photographing them in their environment, and then carving their portraits in a place they have a particular connection with. In other cases, I might walk around the streets when I arrive in a city and simply ask people if I can take their photo. I explain to them what I want to do with it, and ask them a few questions. Even if it's a short conversation, I always like to have a sense of who this person is, where they come from, what they do, what they like, but also if their city and culture have changed much over the years, and things like that.

A portrait speaks of identity and human nature, and my pieces in particular seek to explore poetically the intimate relationship between the city and the people who live there, how both are locked in a cycle of reciprocal shaping, each contributing to the other's character. The city is fundamentally the people who help shape it, but while doing so, the people are also being shaped by the city.

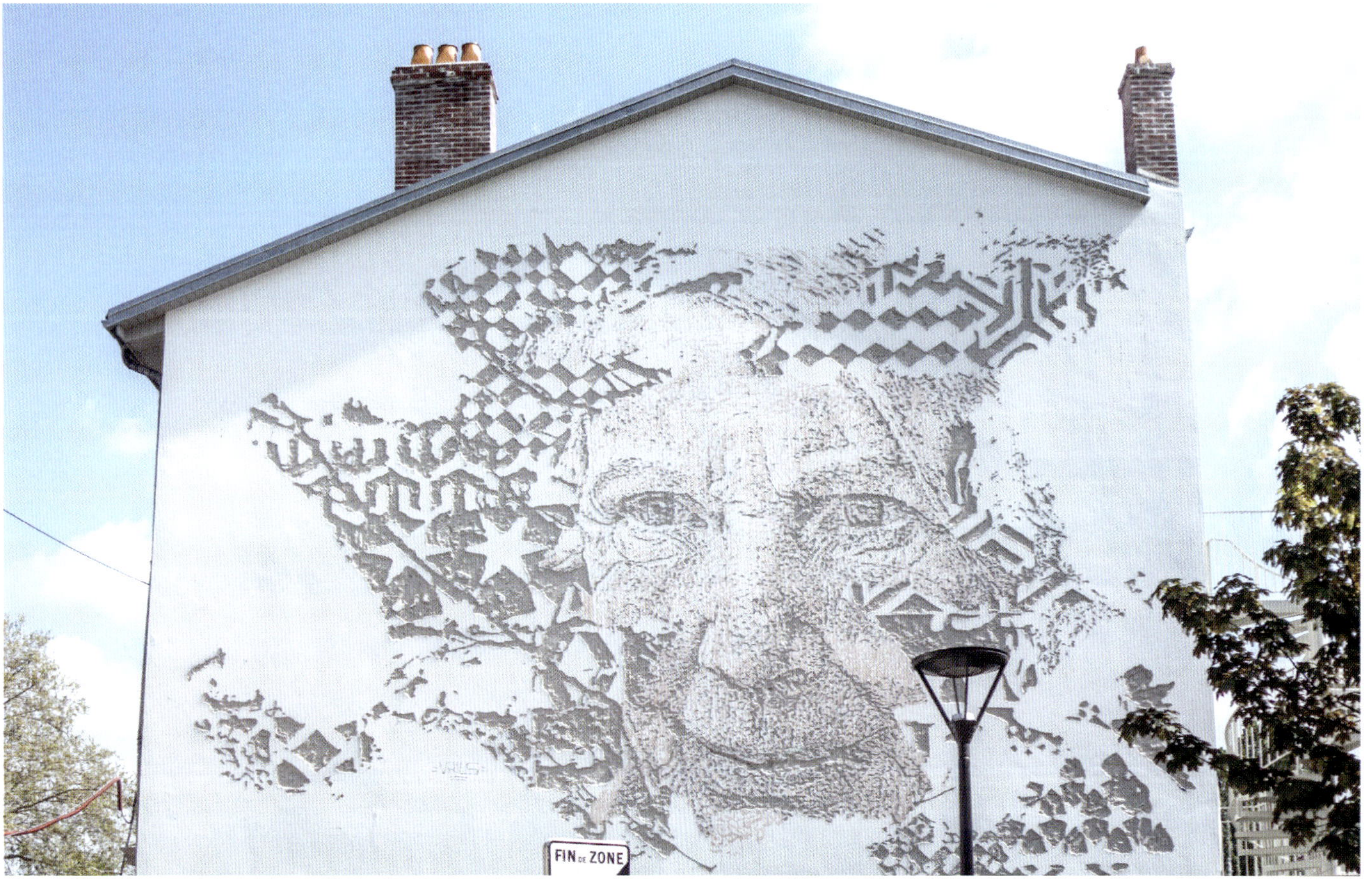

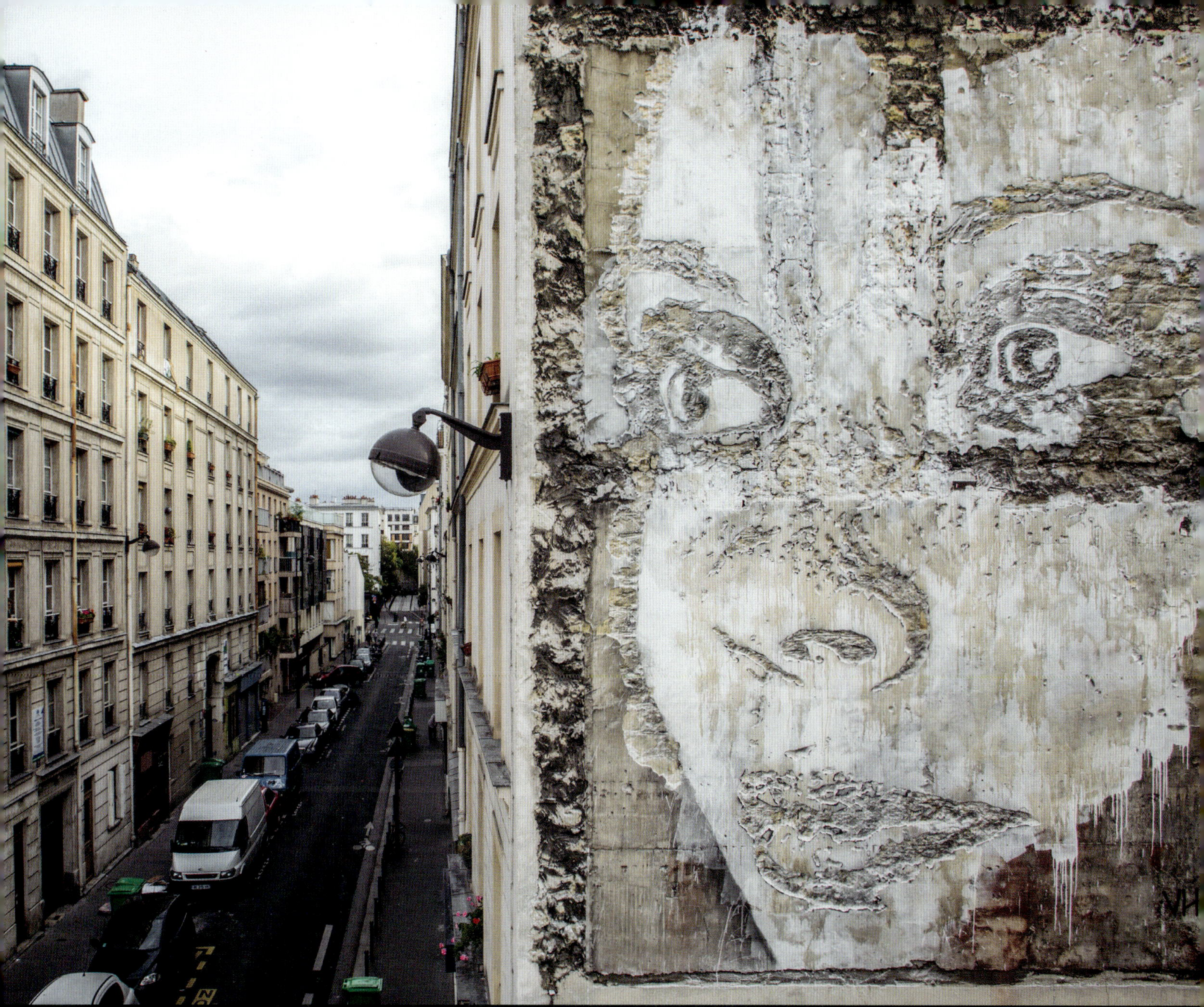

Untitled—Scratching the Surface project. Bas-relief wall carving and paint. Nancy, France, April 2019. Photo: Vhils Studio

Untitled—Scratching the Surface project. Bas-relief wall carving and paint. Paris, October 2013. Photo: Vhils Studio

By carving a portrait on an old wall, I try to reveal some of its older layers, making them part of the piece. While expressing something of the history and the life of a given place, these contrasting textures also speak of our own layers, our own wrinkles, our own personal history.

The Power of Wall Art in a Globalized World

Over the years my work has evolved into a reflection on human identity, especially in connection with contemporary urban societies exposed to a model of globalized development that is making the world an increasingly uniform environment, eroding the elements that once made each culture unique. Traveling and working in different contexts around the world has become pivotal to understanding the phenomenon, as I'm interested in witnessing and experiencing this process firsthand in as many locations as possible.

The aim is to interact with different people, to listen to their stories and experiences, to gather images and capture something of this unique moment the world is experiencing now. I like to help raise questions and help people think about this process, while also helping to put the focus on places and communities that are undergoing huge transformations that are detrimental to the safeguard of their identity. I believe that tackling these issues in public is very important. I want to contribute toward people's awareness by pointing them out as being worthy of reflection.

You can say that my work speaks of human identity, of effacement and resistance in the face of these radical transformations affecting all of us, while it explores the connections and contrasts between global and local realities. In essence, it aims to help make visible the invisible that lies buried beneath the surface of things. I have been

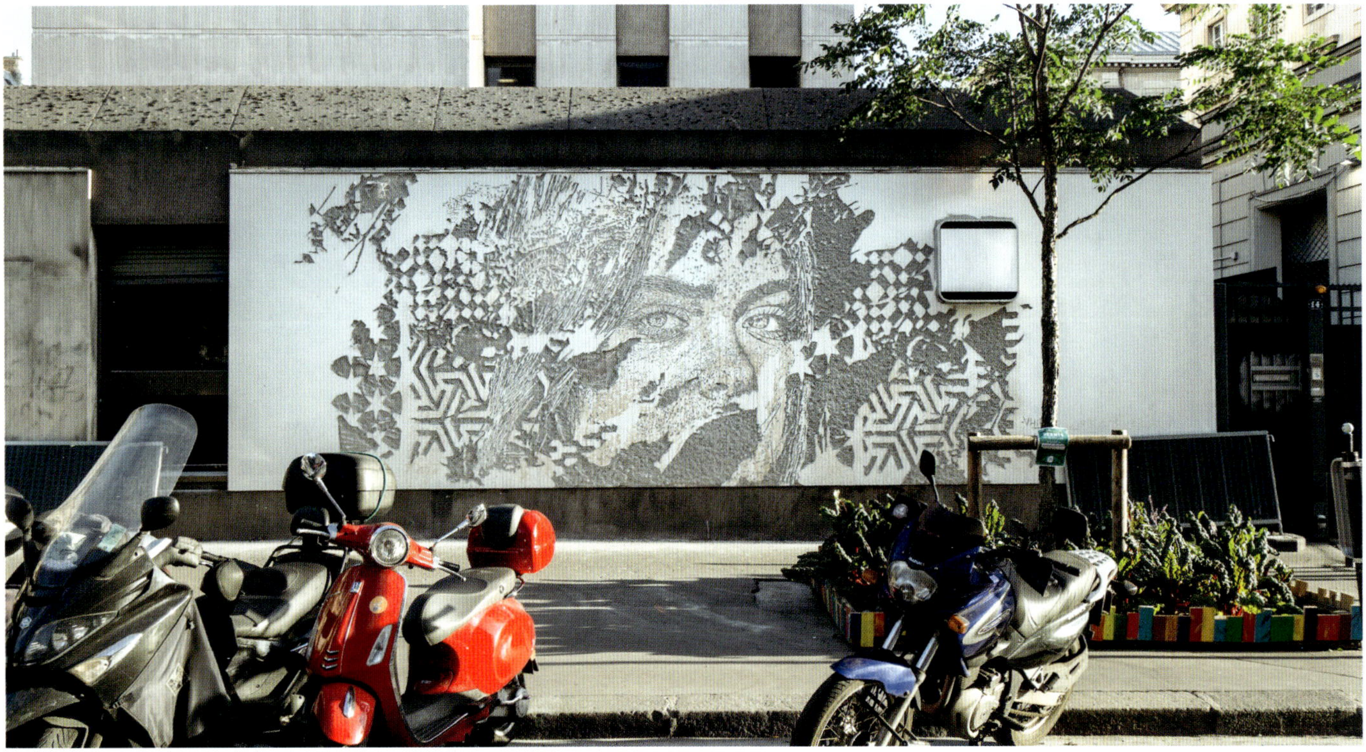

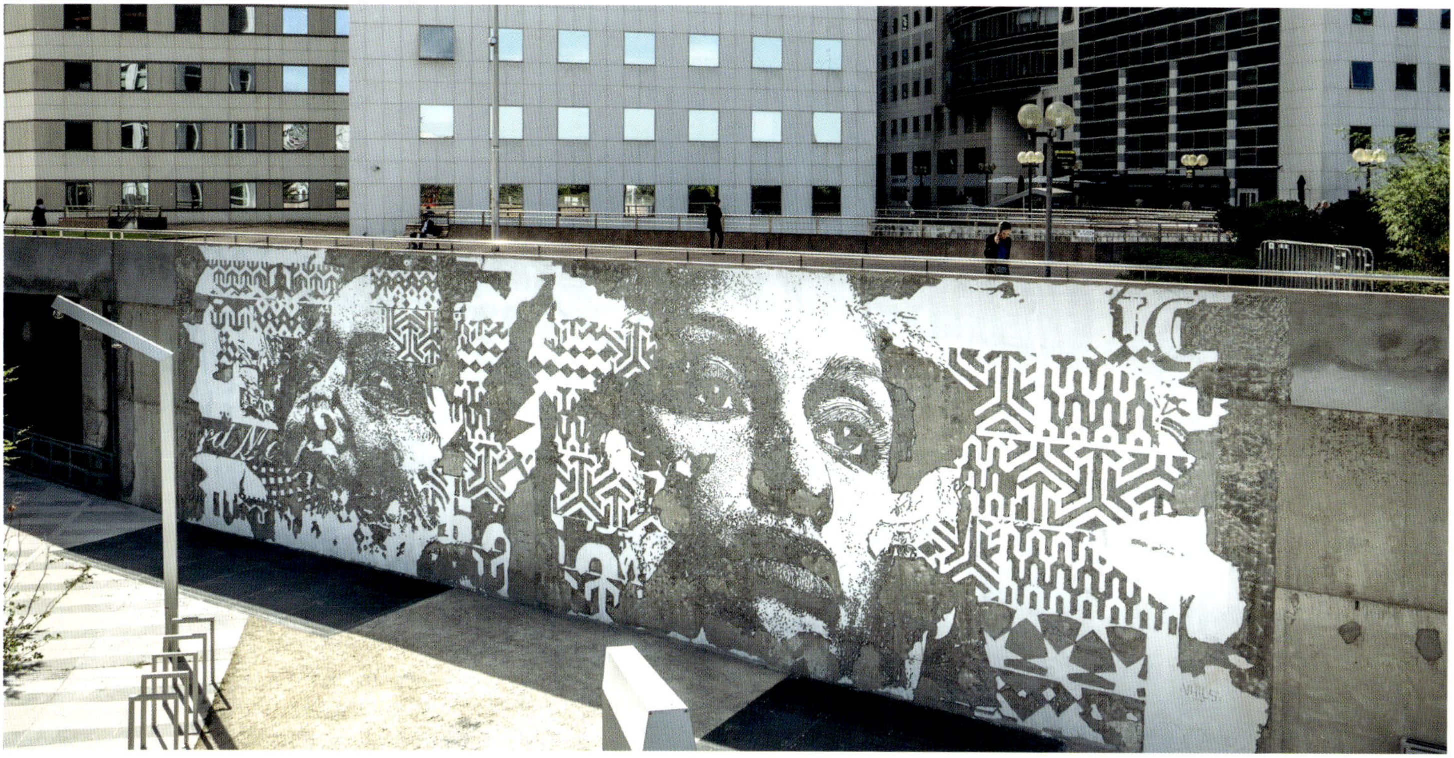

materializing this reflection in the public space through the portraits I create in the scope of the ongoing Scratching the Surface project, which also tries to humanize the overbuilt urban environments most of us live in today. In most of these, the important thing is to represent human beings in general and not a specific gender in particular, but there are particular projects where I have focused on women I wanted to give visibility to.

An example can be seen in the portrait I carved in Lisbon of Brazilian councilor and activist Marielle Franco, who stood out for denouncing human rights violations, especially against Black youth, women, and LGBTI people, and was brutally assassinated in Rio de Janeiro. This project in particular was done in collaboration with Amnesty International's Brave Walls initiative, which aims at celebrating the courage of women such as Marielle who are fronting the struggle for human rights.

I have depicted many other women of courage, most of them ordinary yet brave women who stand up against oppression and the violation of the rights of individuals and the communities they live in.

I portrayed these women in Rio de Janeiro's Providência community in 2012 and in the community of Ladeira dos Tabajaras, in the same city, in 2013, among many others.

TOP / RIGHT *Untitled—Scratching the Surface project. Bas-relief wall carving and paint. Paris, France, September 2019. Photo: Alexander Silva (@as.analogic)/Vhils Studio*

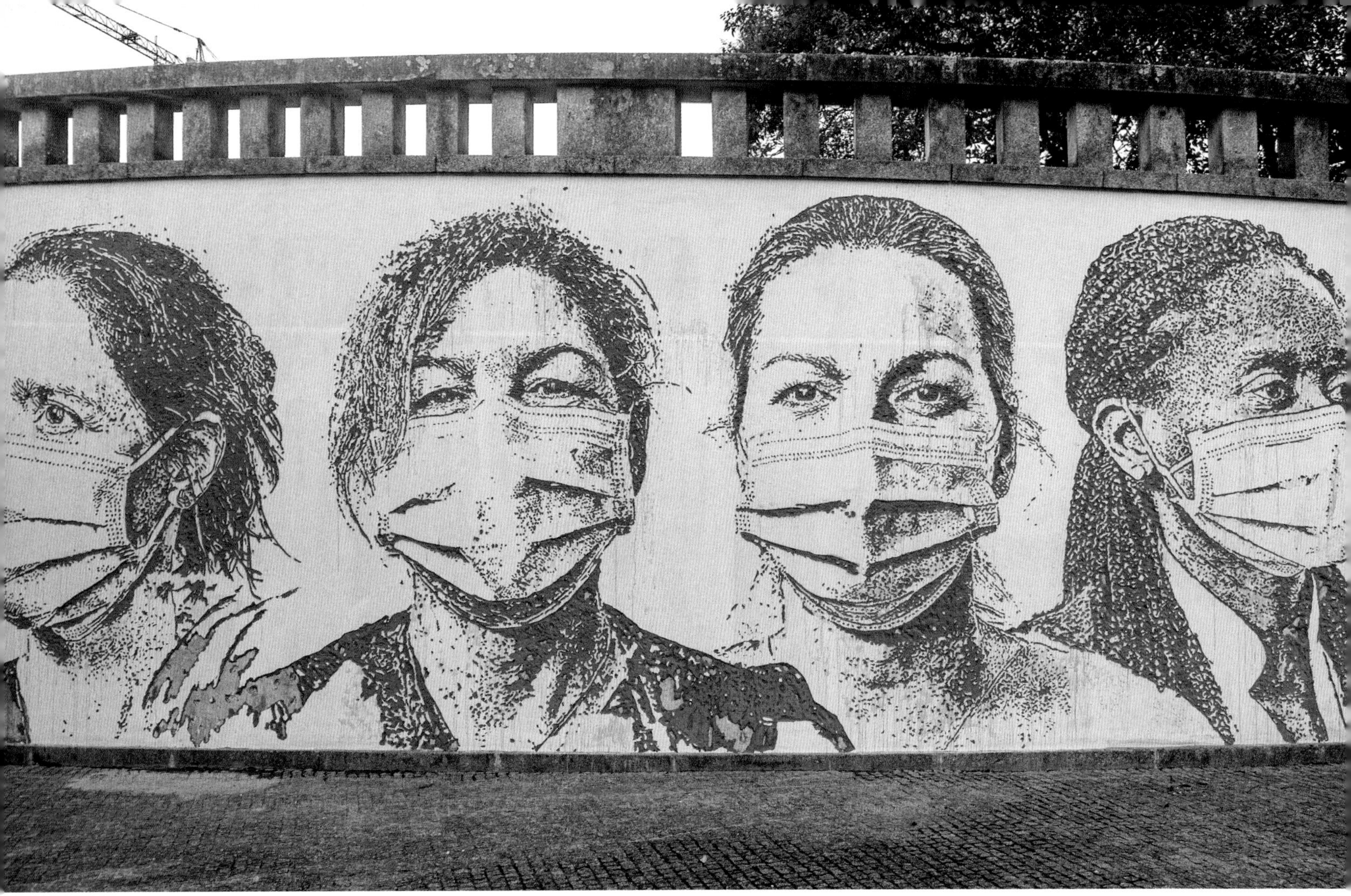

Frontline–Scratching the Surface project to honor health care workers. Bas-relief wall carving and paint. Porto, Portugal, June 2020. Photo: Expanding Roots

An Activist View

I strongly believe that art has the power to draw attention to important issues that represent the times we live in. I feel that most of my art is socially committed, trying to reflect on realities that usually don't get the visibility they deserve, but I believe the concepts behind it are more politically charged than the art itself. It is political insofar as it offers a statement on life in contemporary urban environments, which I see as an expression of the current model of socioeconomic development. I like to question things, and in doing so I offer a critical reflection, but I have no pretension of thinking I have the right answers or magical solutions to these problems. I'm not anti-entrepreneurship in any way, and I'm not against development or even consumption. I believe in rewarding people for their efforts and I also believe in profit, but I believe development and profit should be ethically oriented. I believe in social responsibility and the inclusion of the people who are directly concerned with or affected by these transformations. Development has to be made for the good of the people, not the good of a few.

My work looks into the excesses of this model of development—its emphasis on overconsumption and overmaterialism, its culture of obsolescence and fast replacement of goods, its practice of waste . . . I just try to juxtapose different realities through the creation of images, by delving into the layers of matter and exposing what has been buried by these fast-paced transformations.

I like to interact with the people who I believe really matter, the people who make up the cites, who live in their spaces, who lead undervalued lives. In this overglamorized, media-saturated environment where the value of image is everything—be it personal, social, corporate, etc.—there seems to be no respect for ordinary individuals, the people who really make the world work, who keep it clean, who provide us with food and clothing and other essential goods and services . . . I celebrate these people and their daily efforts in eking out a living in this complex, dog-eat-dog environment. By celebrating this notion of "unknown icons" or "everyday heroes," I offer a contrast with the people we are meant to aspire to become, unlike these photoshopped vacuities we are confronted with daily in advertising and the media. When I came up with the idea of carving people in city walls to humanize these gray, derelict spaces, I realized I could only complement it with this celebration of the anonymous.

Women Wall Artists Balancing the Equation

I'm not sure that most representations of women in this field are created by men. I know many women artists who are focused on representing women in their wall art, as well as many artists who, regardless of their gender, are focused on depicting people (both men and women) in their wall art. It can be argued that there might be more men working in this field than women, and therefore there might be more representations of women created by men, but this is a general perception, I can't back it up with hard facts.

> There are lots of women working in this field, and I tend to believe that there is a more balanced representation today, and in this field in particular, than there has been historically, but again, this is solely based on my own perception. Yet, if art reflects society at large, it is inevitable that it reflects something of the overall unbalance between the representation of genders that has been, and still is, fundamentally systemic.

Things are definitely changing, and I believe that the openness we find in this field is contributing positively toward a more balanced inclusiveness and representation, but the key still lies with a system that doesn't take these issues as a priority. It is up to all of us, both artists and viewers alike, to address them and contribute toward a greater balance, providing girls and women with the visibility and opportunities they deserve as human beings.

Street Art's Wide Canvas

It seems natural for street art to have become increasingly accepted and popular as it really has made a mark on cities around the world. It's become a phenomenon for this age, and I think it owes most of its popularity to the fact that it is both readily accessible and easy to understand. It's simply there for all to see, and there is so much of it today that you can't miss or ignore it.

Like all phenomena that grow popular and become absorbed into the mainstream, it has both positive and negative aspects: on one hand, you have lots of talented artists out there interacting with their cities and creating fantastic artwork; on the other, the growing popularity inevitably attracts those who seek to profit from it through commodification and commercial exploitation.

The present urban art scene seems to be split along the legal and illegal seams, and in both contexts people are creating very interesting and valid work. Illegal street art will always be rough and vibrant, and as the root of the movement it's important for it to continue to exist and retain its vitality. Then, over the last decade or so we have witnessed a huge increase in the number of large-scale mural works being produced in cities around the world. This has been a tremendous change, added to the fact that the majority of these are legal, commissioned works that can be viewed as a new form of public art.

I think that both this development and the ongoing coexistence between legal and illegal street art are the main differences from what the scene was like ten or fifteen years ago. This reflects a growing maturity in the movement itself but also in the way institutions, authorities, and the public at large have come to view, accept, and promote it. In this sense, I believe that urban art projects have become a positive tool for cities to rethink their approach to and their management of public space. Just to give an example, they can contribute directly to help renovate neglected areas of a city by embellishing them, which in turn can create new interest for outsiders who are mobilized to come and see the new art. This interest can help draw attention to the communities and generate a new respect and acknowledgment for these areas and their people and ultimately help foster the local economy.

Untitled—Scratching the Surface project. Bas-relief wall carving and paint. Los Angeles, November 2014. Photo: Vhils Studio

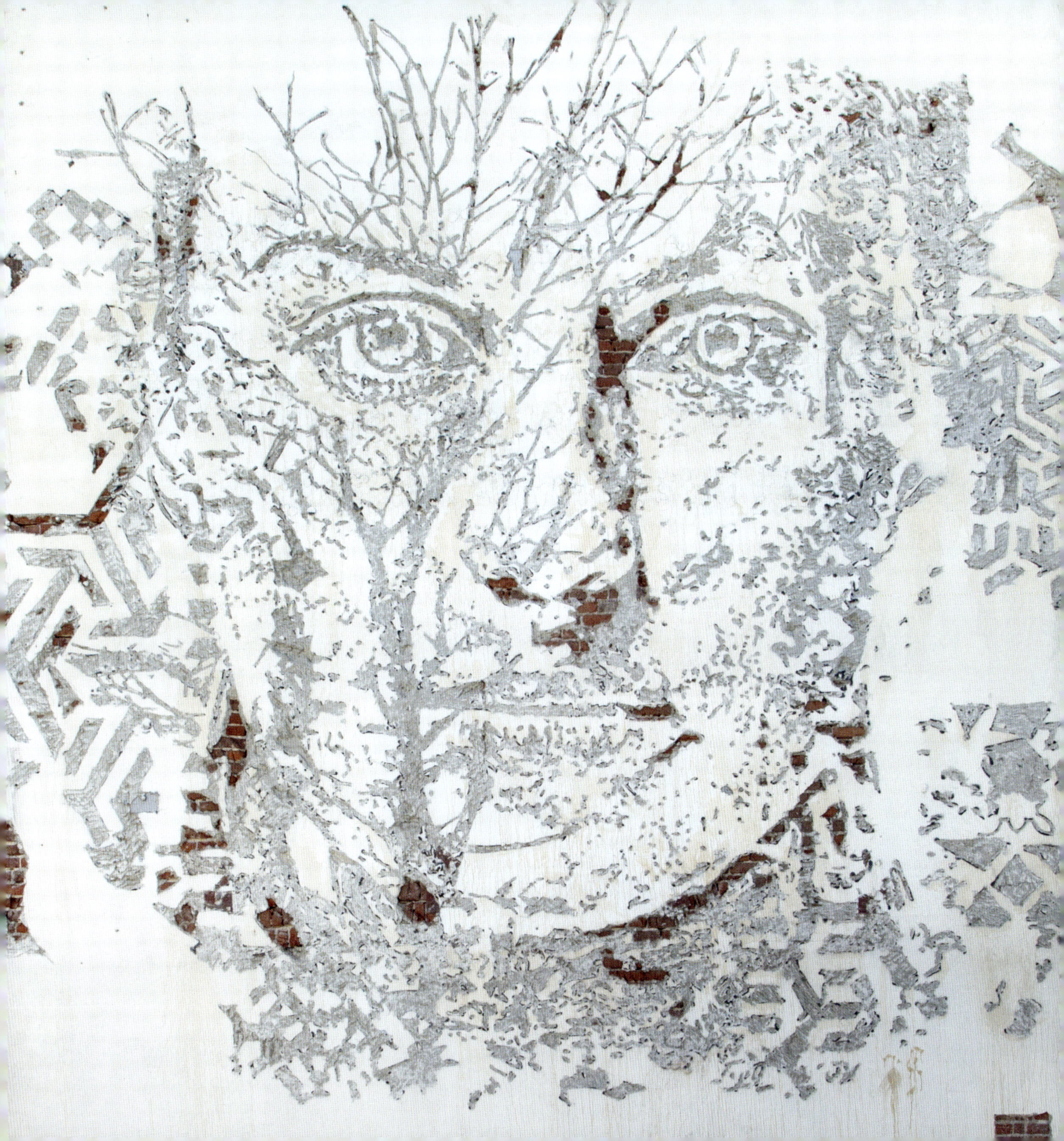

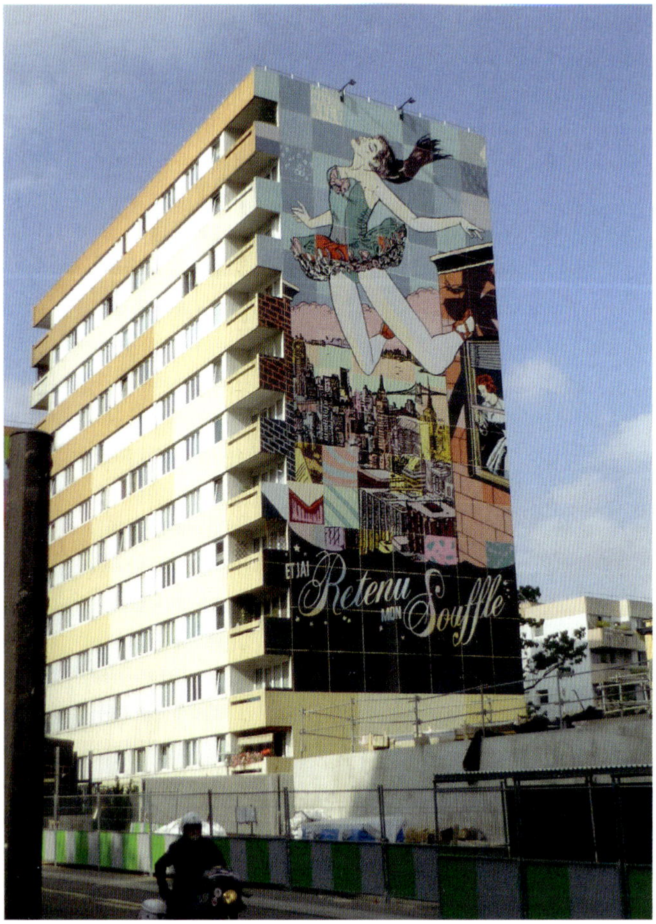

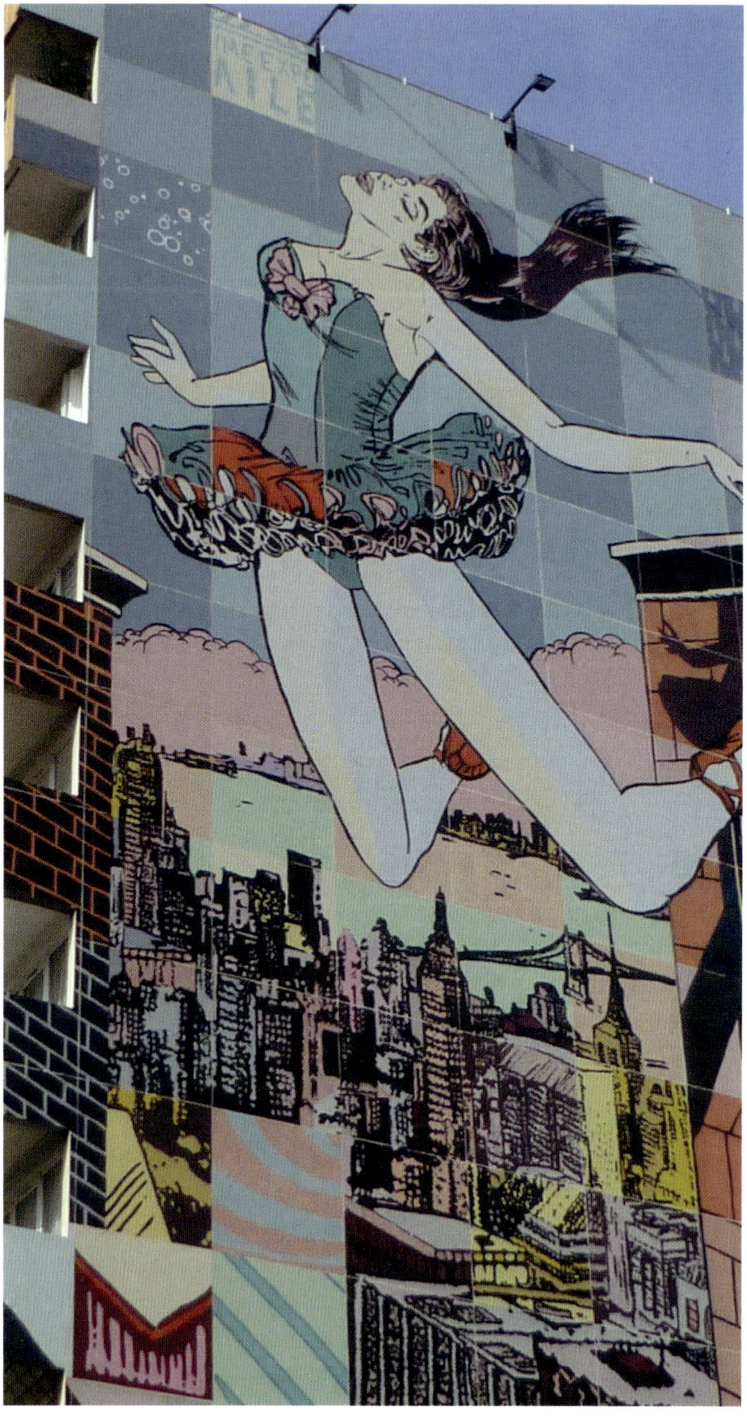

ELEVATED PARIS

Things Are Looking Up in the Thirteenth

Perhaps more than any other urban European city, Paris illustrates the wide diversity of subject matter, style, and painterly execution common to all wall art of women. Paste-up posters feature in small alleyways where an entire wall may resemble its own gallery. Along narrow streets, you'll find bizarre retro examples from renowned artists like Invader, who takes his pixilated inspiration from early computer games.

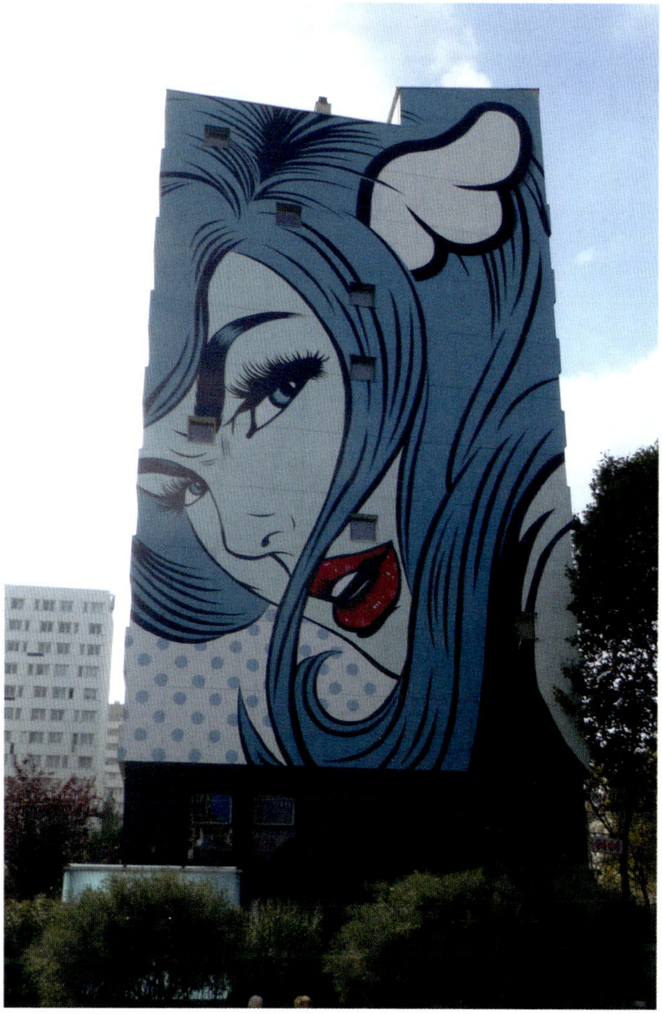

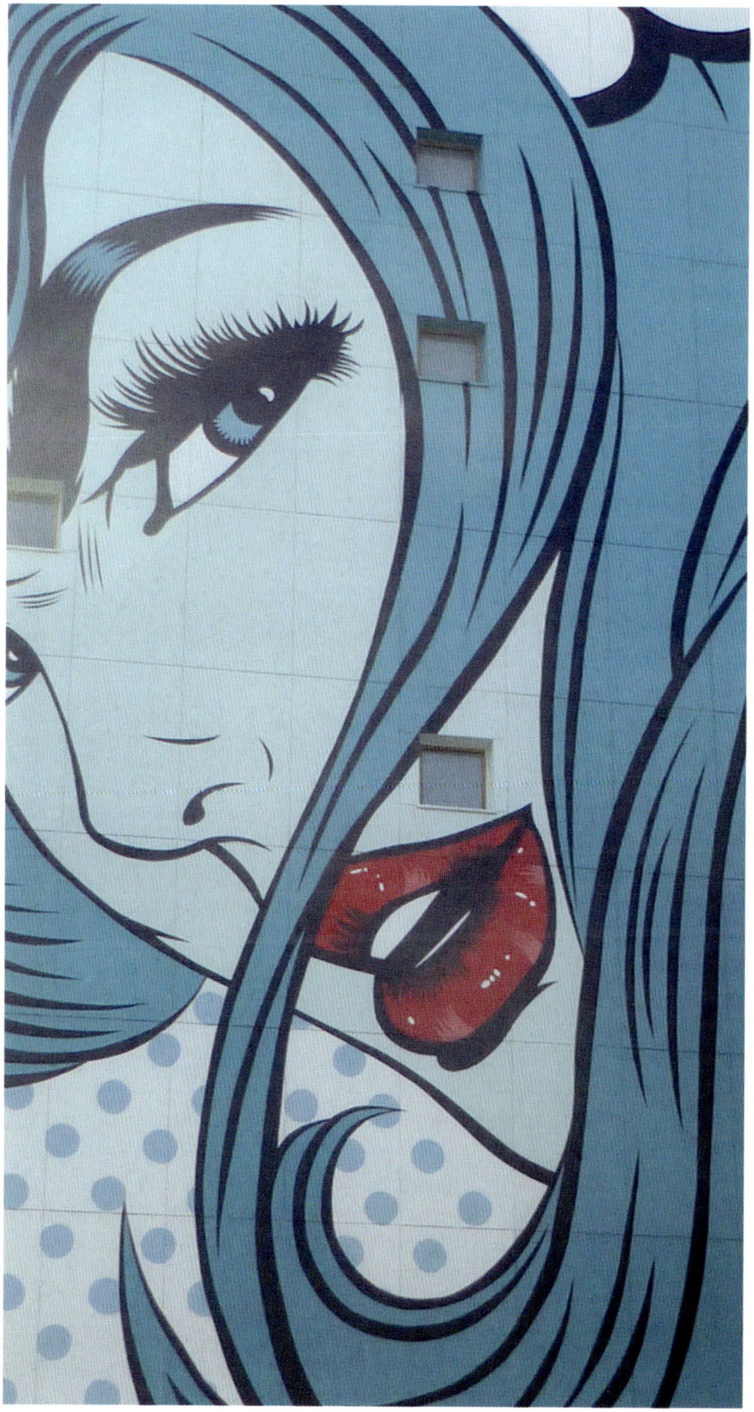

FAILE are two multimedia artists from the US, Patrick McNeil and Patrick Miller, who created a building-size mural of a ballerina with the tagline "I held my breath."

*This portrait by d*face, titled Turncoat, next to a playground, references the work of pop artist Roy Lichtenstein.*

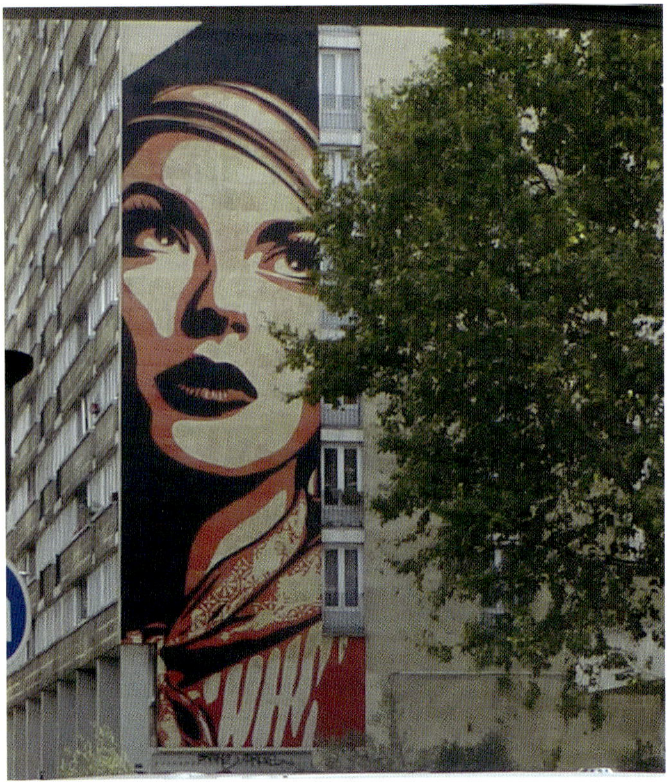

As you pass through the Thirteenth Arrondissement on Line 6 on the Paris metro, the grandeur of street art of women is on full display from the metro's elevated tracks. When you disembark and walk under the tracks, you really appreciate the huge scale of the murals and how women on the wall can transform an otherwise ordinary neighborhood of apartment blocks into an awe-inspiring display of artistic prowess. Sanctioned street art clearly flourishes in the Thirteenth Arrondissement and qualifies as a public-works project fashioned by political will.

The minute you get off the Paris Metro, the woman with the upturned eyes greets you. Shepard Fairey is the artist. Shepard Fairey is not only a wall artist but a clothing entrepreneur. He has also collaborated with Vhils.

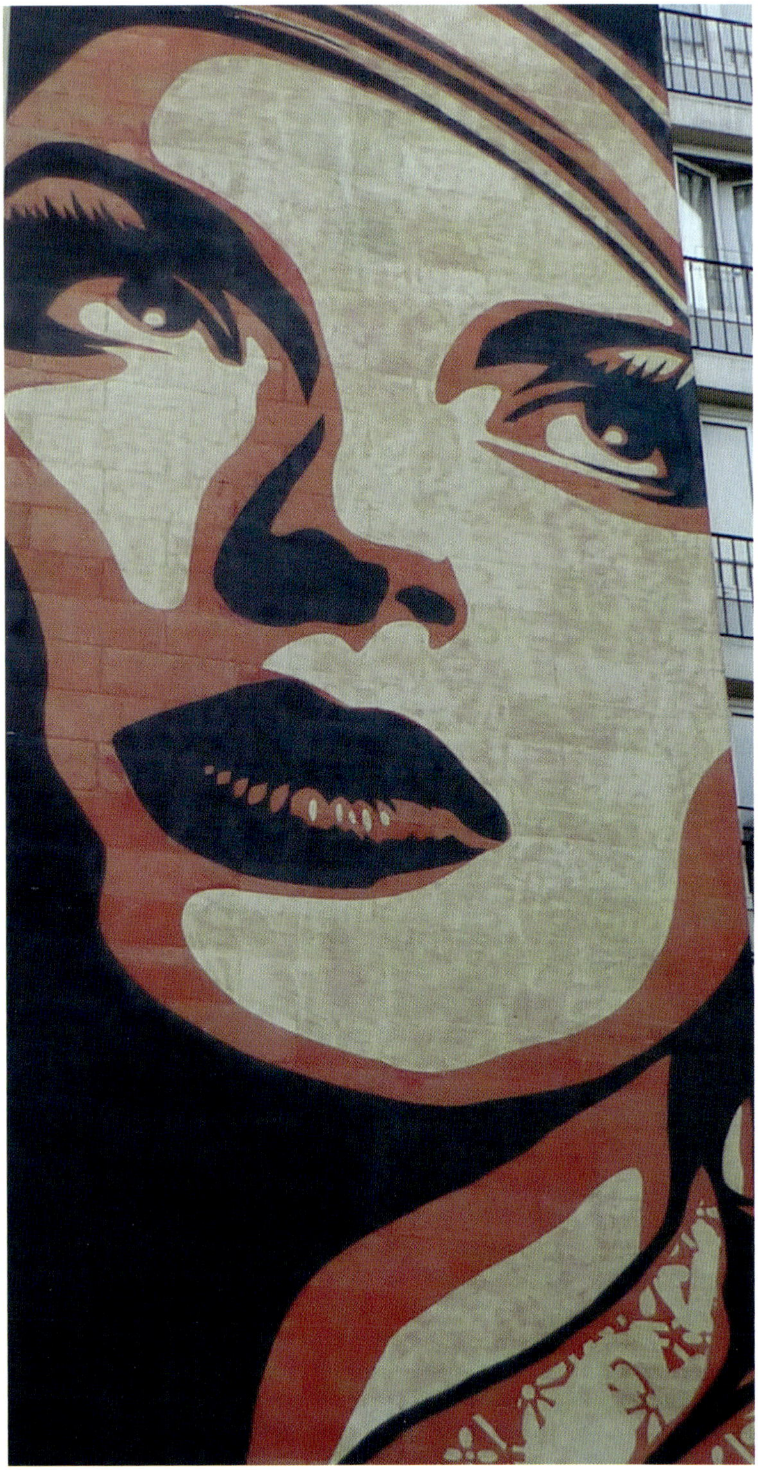

These large-scale works did not appear by accident. Most of the wall art here was commissioned by the local major Jérôme Coumet, who financed the works of fifteen well-known street artists from around the world in 2009.[1] As you wander among the nondescript apartment blocks, your gaze moves upward to these monumental portraits, and you become aware of the power of street art to transform a multicultural neighborhood. Strip away the art, and the neighborhood becomes a dull stopover on a metro line with fast-food cafés and small urban parks.

Shepard Fairey is one of the artists represented on these buildings. His undeniable skill as a wall artist is found in this bold portrait of a woman with upturned eyes. The American artist is one of the muralists who has crossed over into the world of entrepreneurship with his Obey clothing line and recent association with Adobe software to honor heroes of the COVID-19 pandemic.

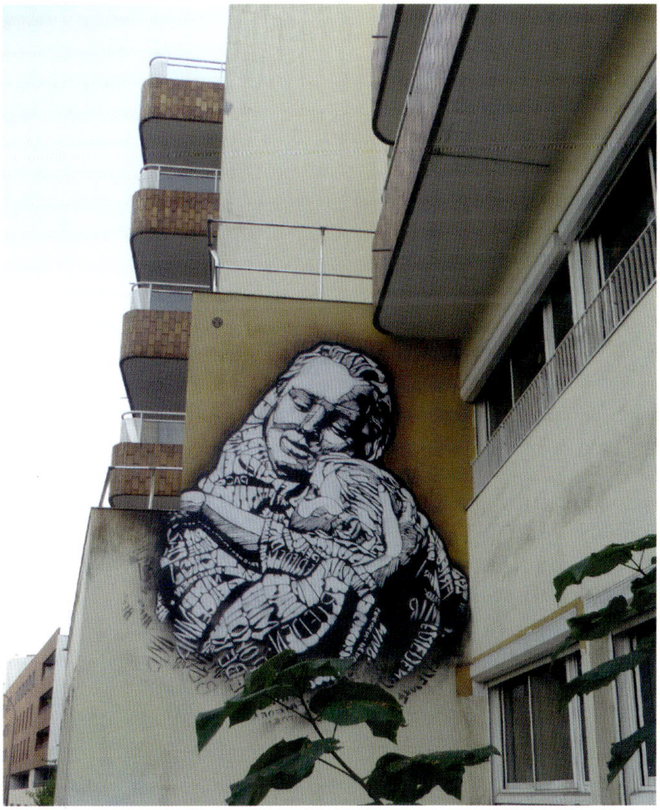

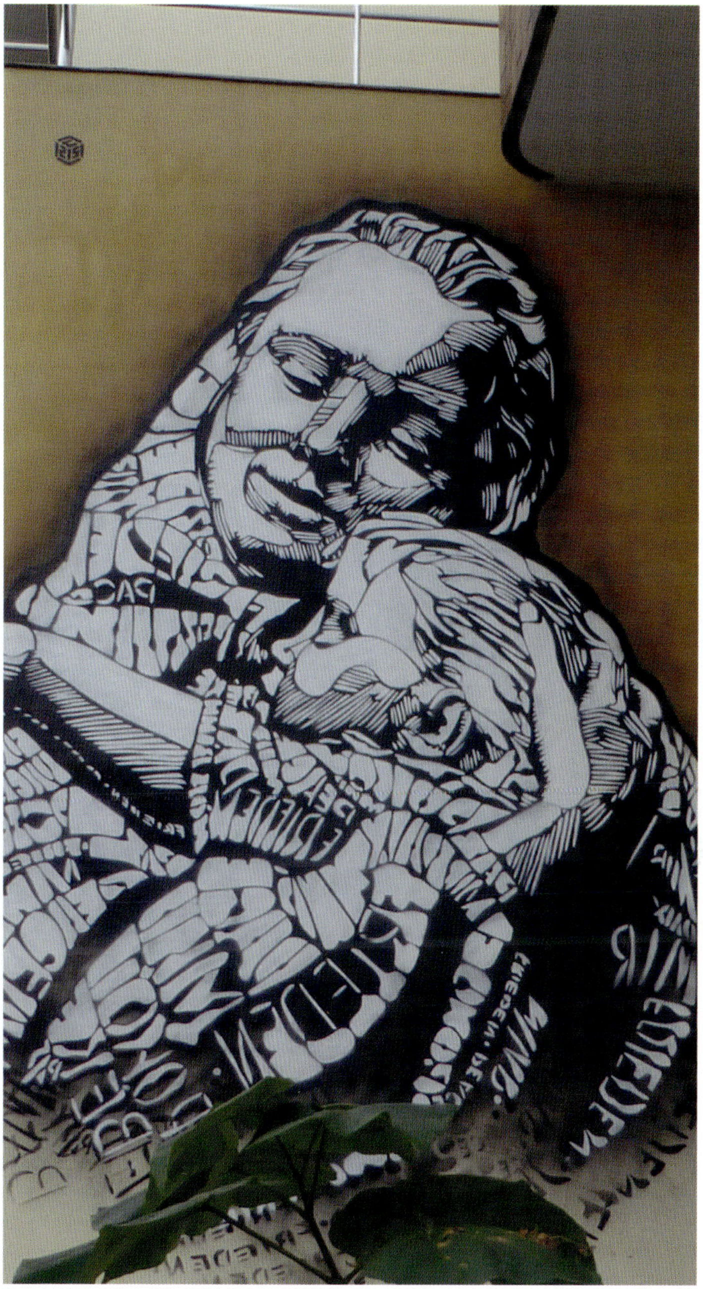

C215's intimate portrait of a mother and child reflects the immigrant neighborhood where it is found.

C215 is the street handle for French artist Christian Guémy, who has been described as the French answer to Banksy. He has been a graffiti artist for more than twenty years, and his intimate portrait of a mother and child down a side street displays a sensitivity to the huge immigrant population that calls Paris home. His street handle came from the prison cell he once occupied.

Fairey's, Guémy's, and FAILE's works illustrate three examples of how scale can embolden the presentation of women on the wall and completely transform a neighborhood.

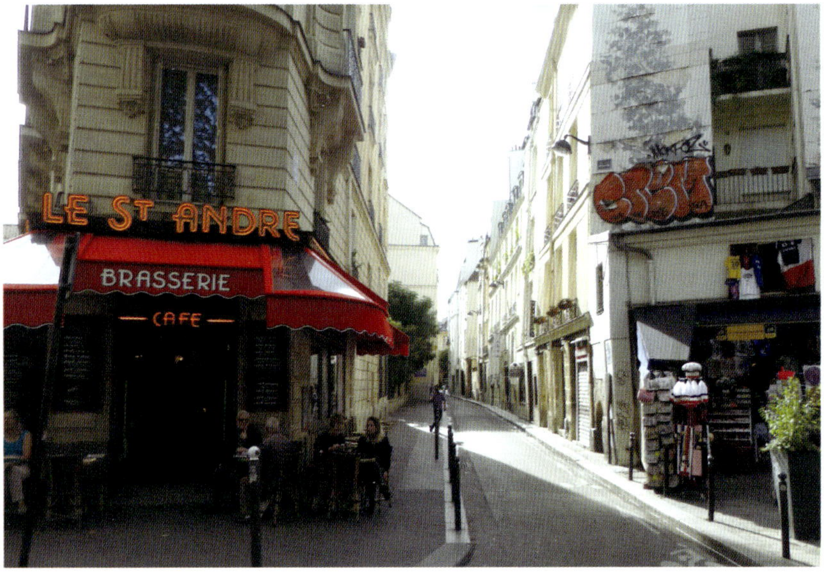

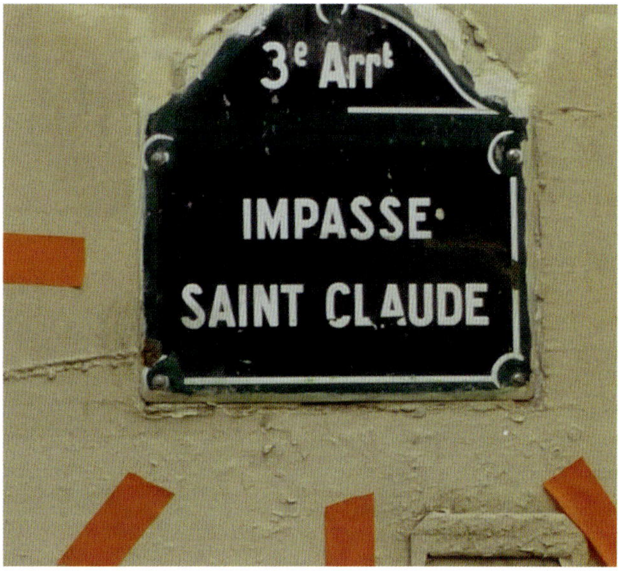

The Marais District of Paris is full of narrow streets and daring wall art of women.

RIGHT *Puissante Femme. The translation of this example of a striking paste-up (a poster affixed to a wall) is Powerful Woman. The artist is unknown.*

THE MARAIS

Women Art Galleries Everywhere You Turn

While large-scale portraits define the Thirteenth Arrondissement, the Marais District of Paris presents a smaller, more specialized gallery. The old Jewish Quarter of the city now qualifies as one of the trendiest in the City of Light, home to the Picasso Museum, the beautiful Place de Voges (where Victor Huge once lived), and small winding streets that delight in their charm. This trendy neighborhood showcases street art that is more intimate in appeal and yet more daring in subject matter. In these backstreets and alleyways, women are communicating a much more powerful message of sexuality and power. That idea is clearly summed up in a poster that has been plastered along a small street in the Marais District.

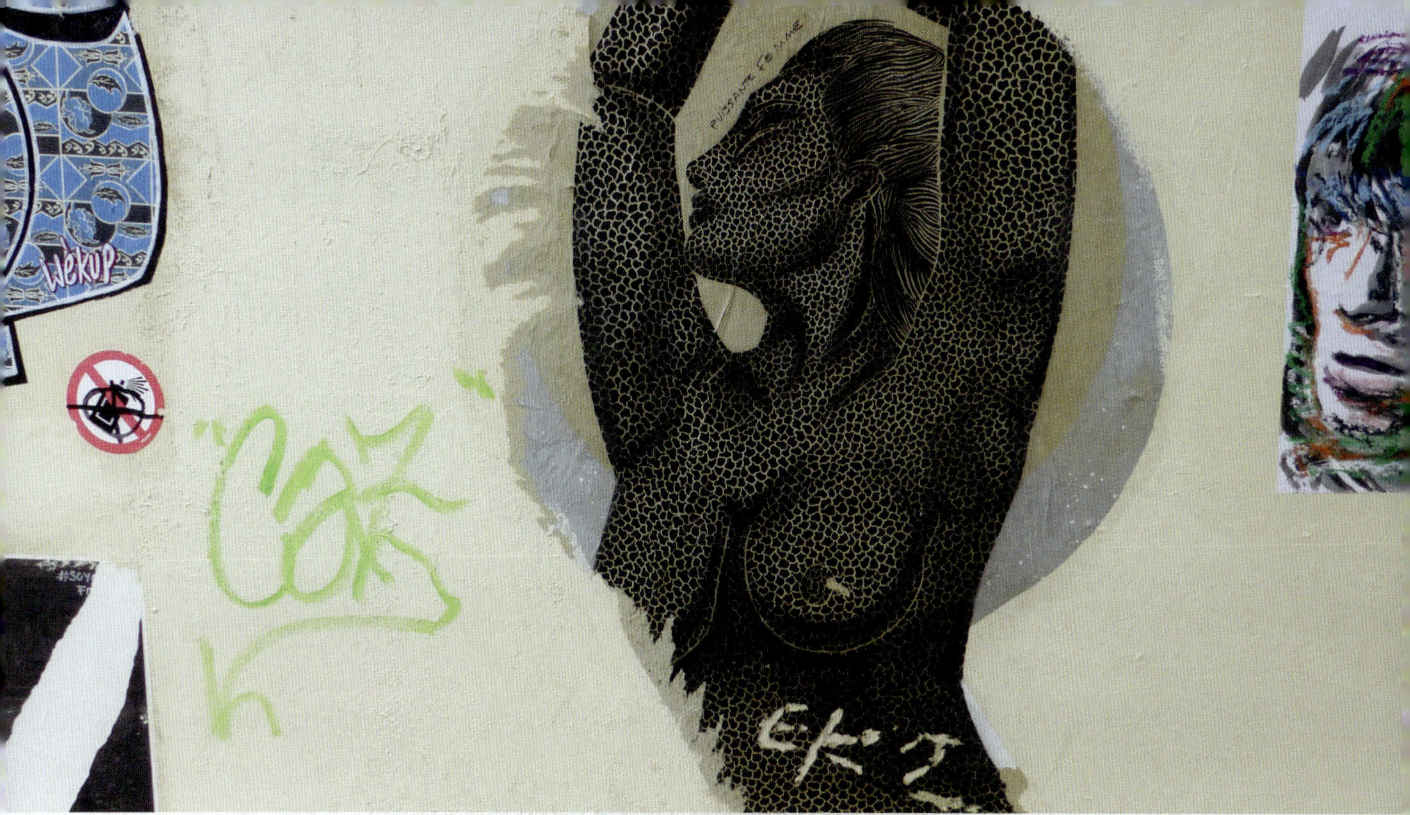
Wekup
PUISSANTE FEMME

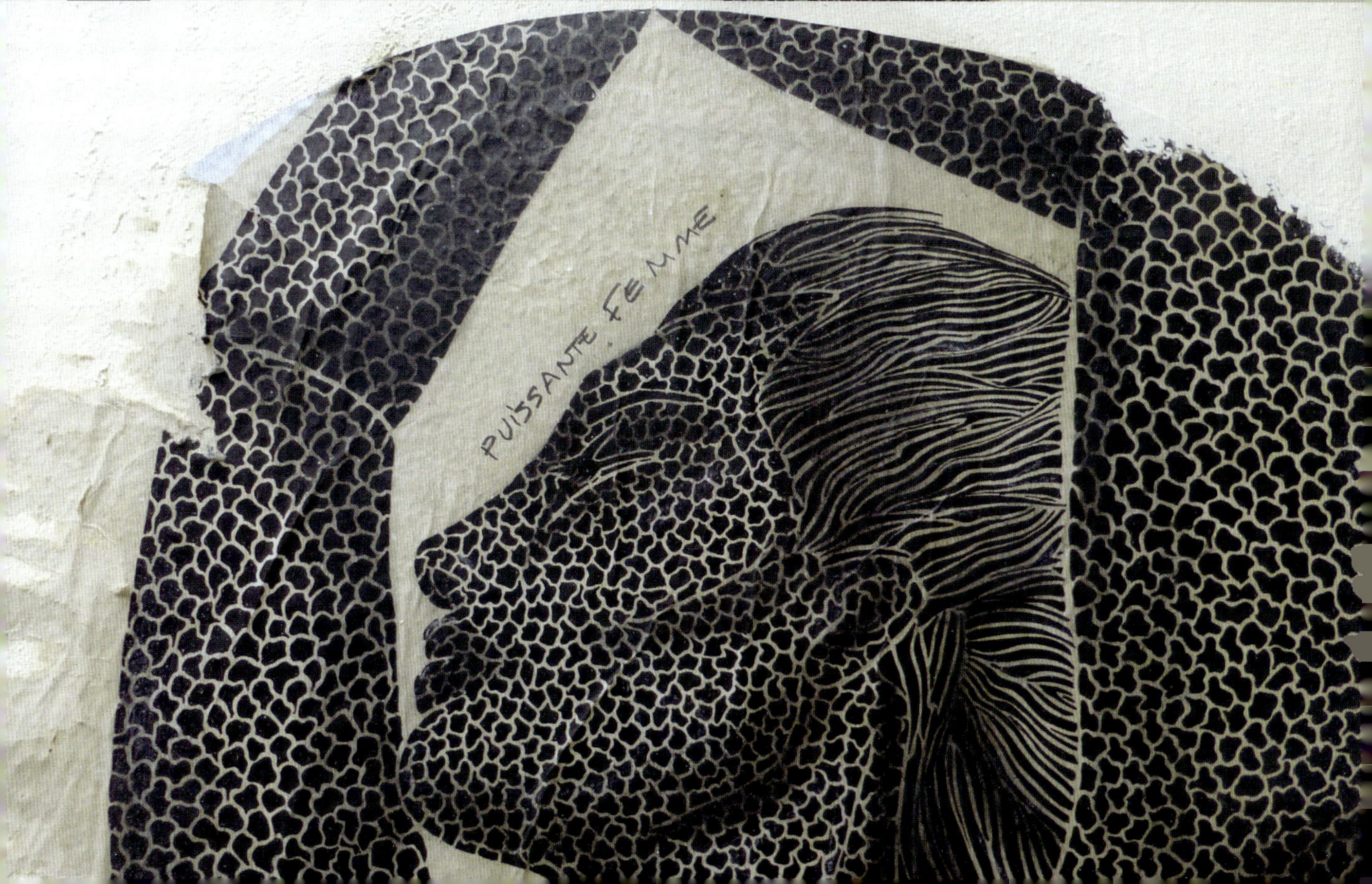
PUISSANTE FEMME

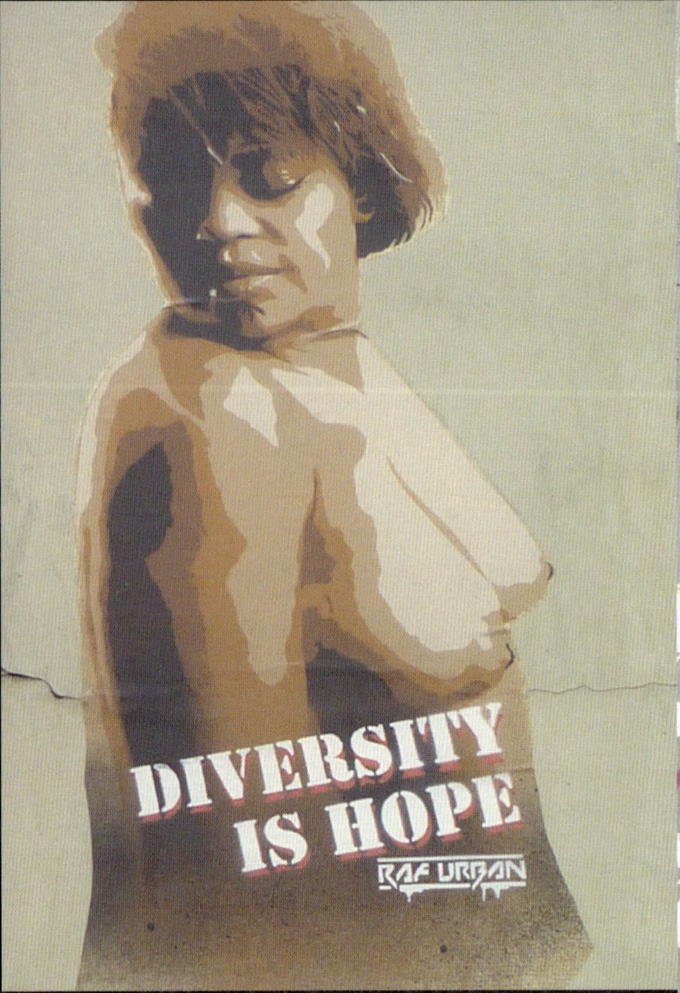

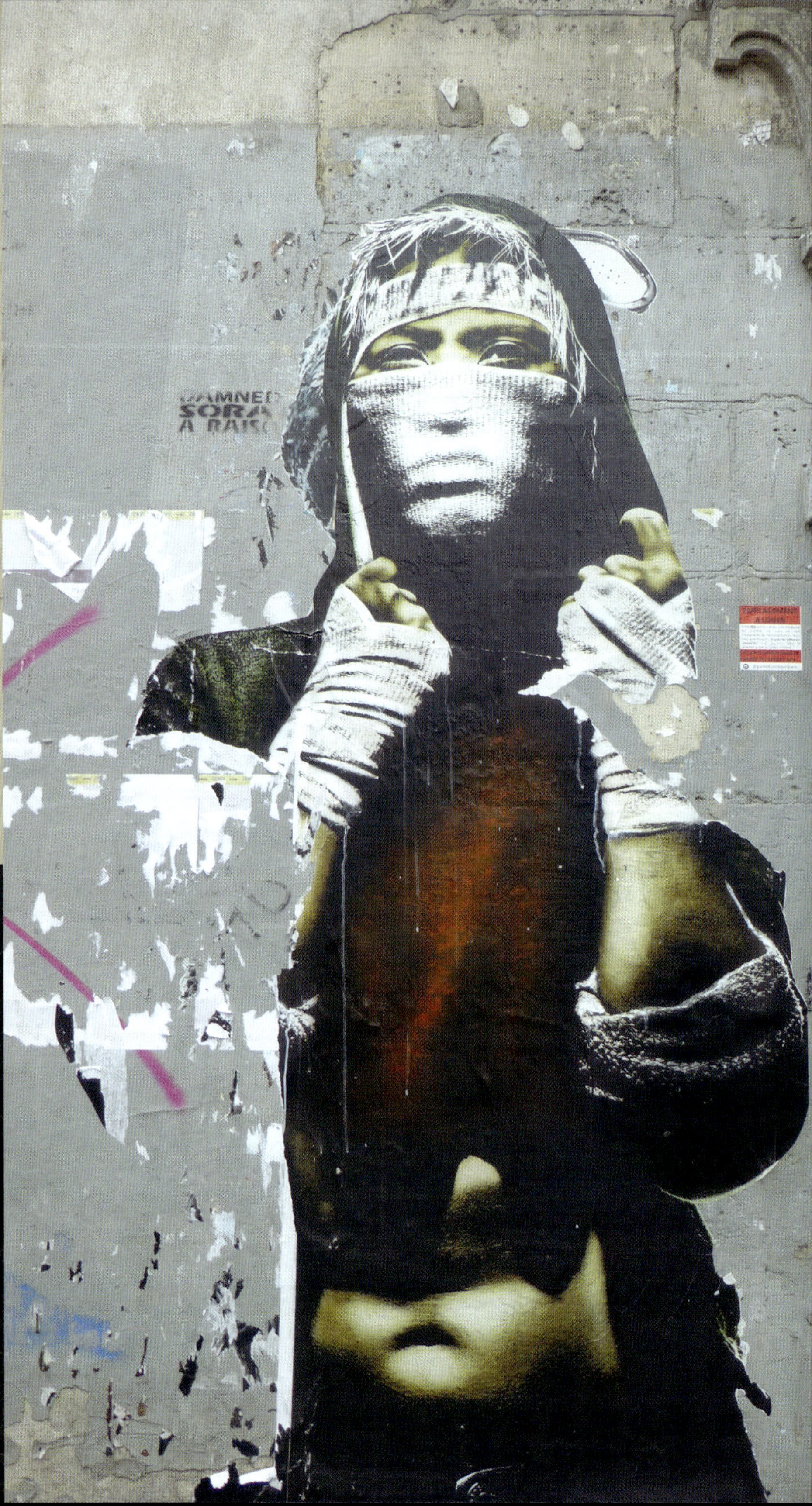

RAF Urban is the street name of an artist born in the 1970s in a Paris suburb, whose work focuses on influential women.

Eddie Colla's women in his Salvage Portrait series are bandaged and covered survivors. Colla's background includes stints in the advertising world as a photographer.

While *Female Power* has an unabashedly erotic, powerful presentation, RAF Urban's *Diversity Is Hope* poster is based on the artist's inspiration of women political activists. RAF Urban, who largely works in the Paris area, uses paint bombs and stencils to portray subjects such as the Black Panther's Angela Davis, singer Amy Winehouse, and education crusader Malala Yousafzai. In this stenciled wall work, RAF Urban's message is clearly presented in this intimate nude portrait.

Eddie Colla's photographic collages contrast sharply to those of RAF Urban. His "paster-ups" are affixed on a wall on the Rue du Prévôt in the Fourth Arrondissement. The bandaged women form a part of Colla's Salvage portrait series. Colla comes from a commercial art background. He attended art schools in New York and Oakland, California, and began his career as a photographer for the *New York Times*, magazines, and ad agencies. Eddie Colla describes himself as a "thief" on his website [2] because he steals space from advertisers with his wall art.

Images from the Salvage Portrait series can now be found on T-shirts, which are marketed as celebrations "in the face of adversity."

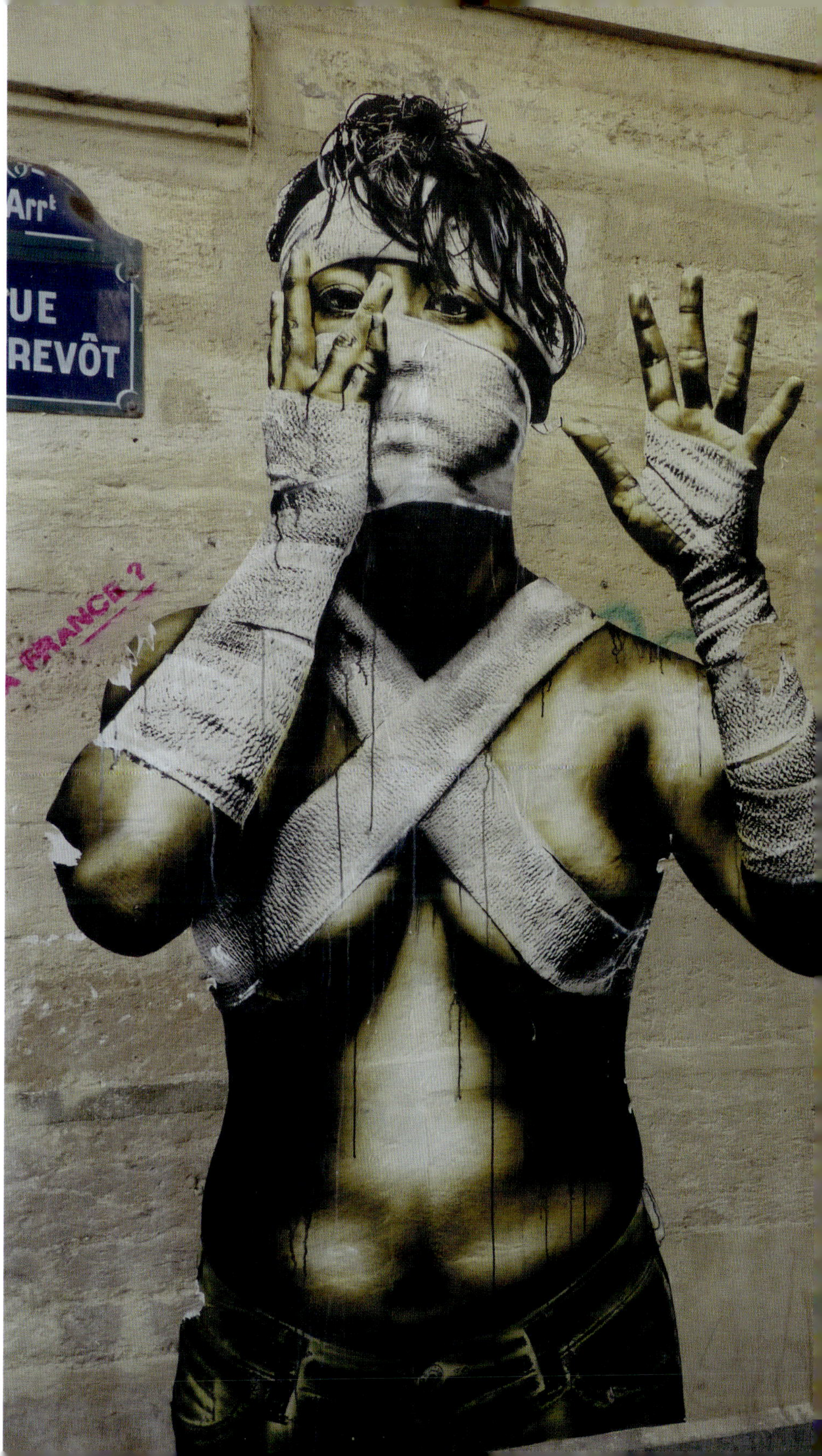

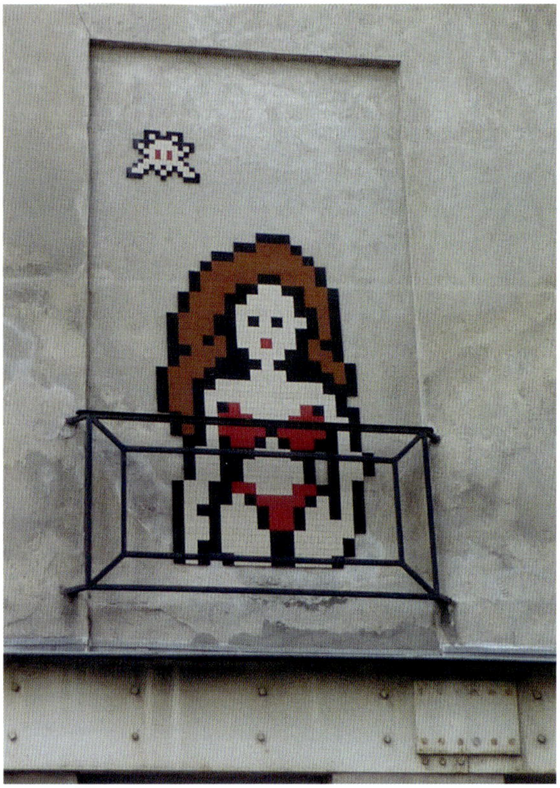

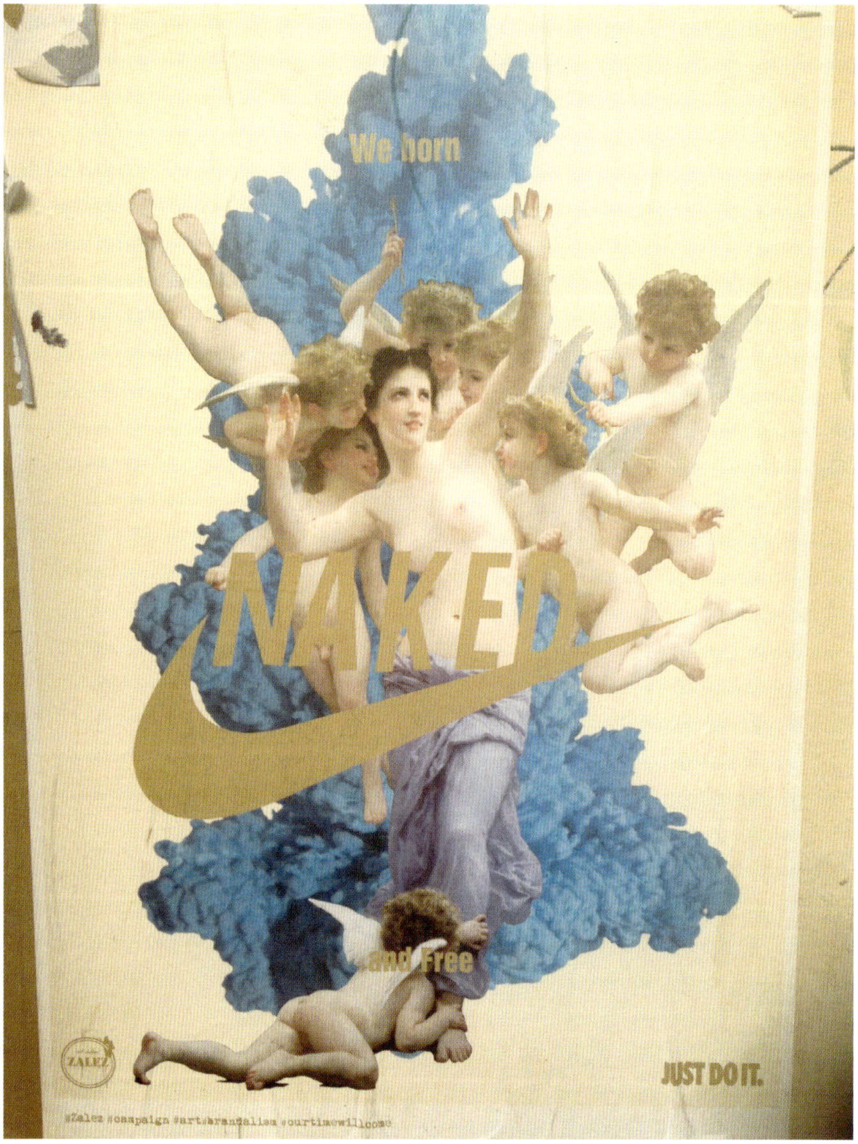

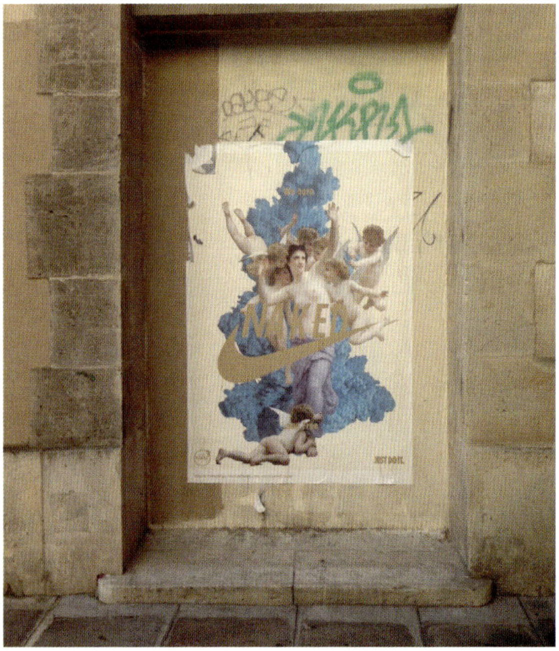

French artist Invader uses small mosaic pieces to create his work of Wonder Woman.

This work of cultural jamming is found in an alcove in the Marais District of Paris. The paste-up is thought to be by Zalez.

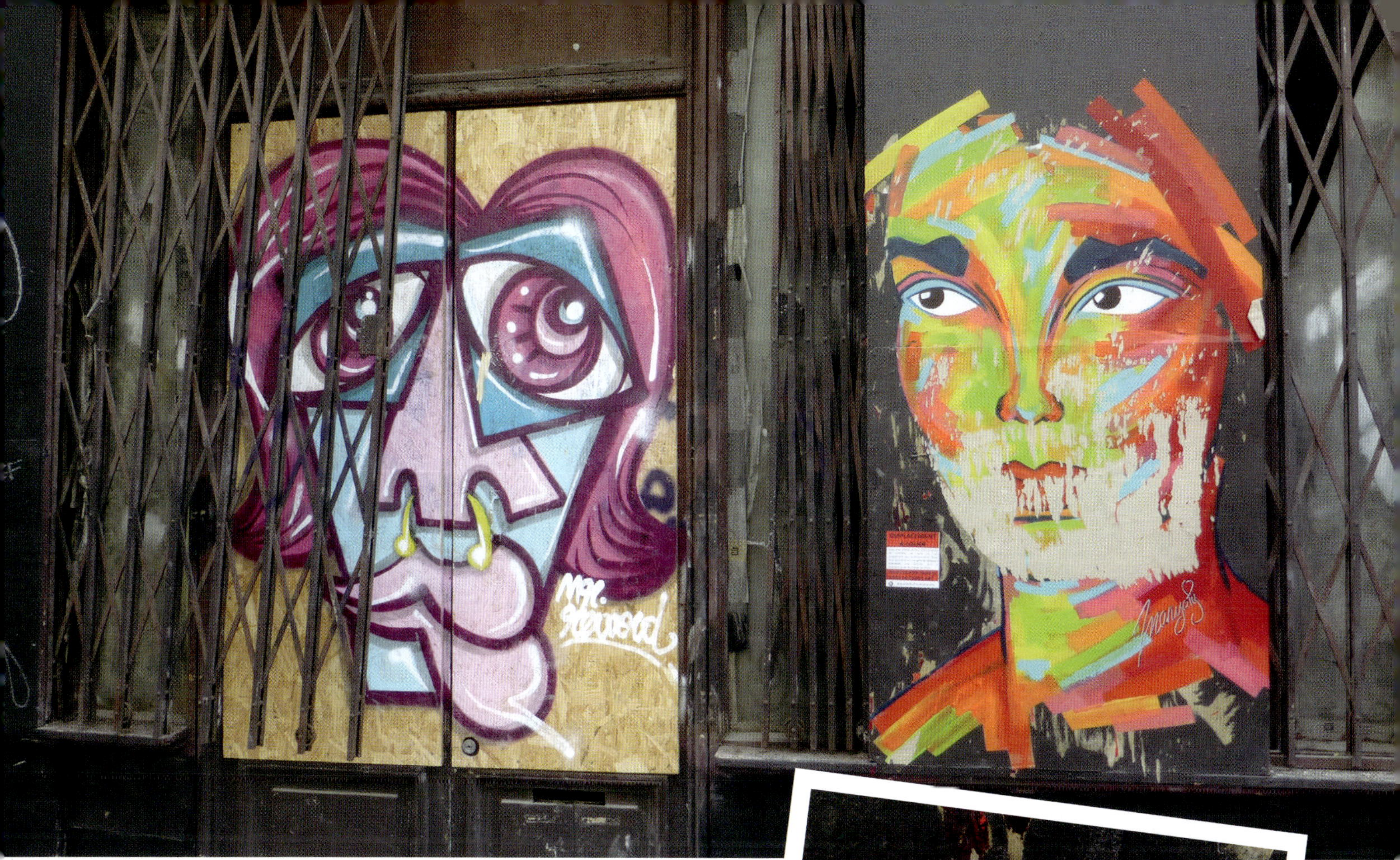

The art of cultural jamming can be found in the works of Invader, who turned to old video games of the 1980s to present his pixilated mosaics found throughout Paris. He is an internationally known street artist whose work can be found in thirty-three countries. His interpretation of Wonder Woman in this recessed window alcove is a satirical jab at the ill-fated attempt by the United Nations to use the image of Wonder Woman in a social media campaign to promote women's rights. Other examples of cultural parody include this example from Zalez found in the Marais District which marries the Nike tagline "Just Do It" with a borrowed idea of Eugène Delacroix's *Liberty Leading the People*.

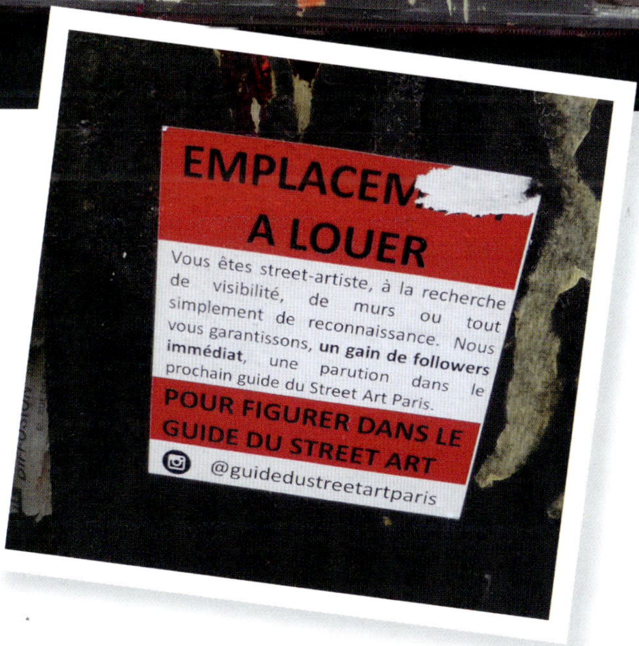

In the Marais, you can even rent space on a wall to do your art of women. This sign advertises that service.

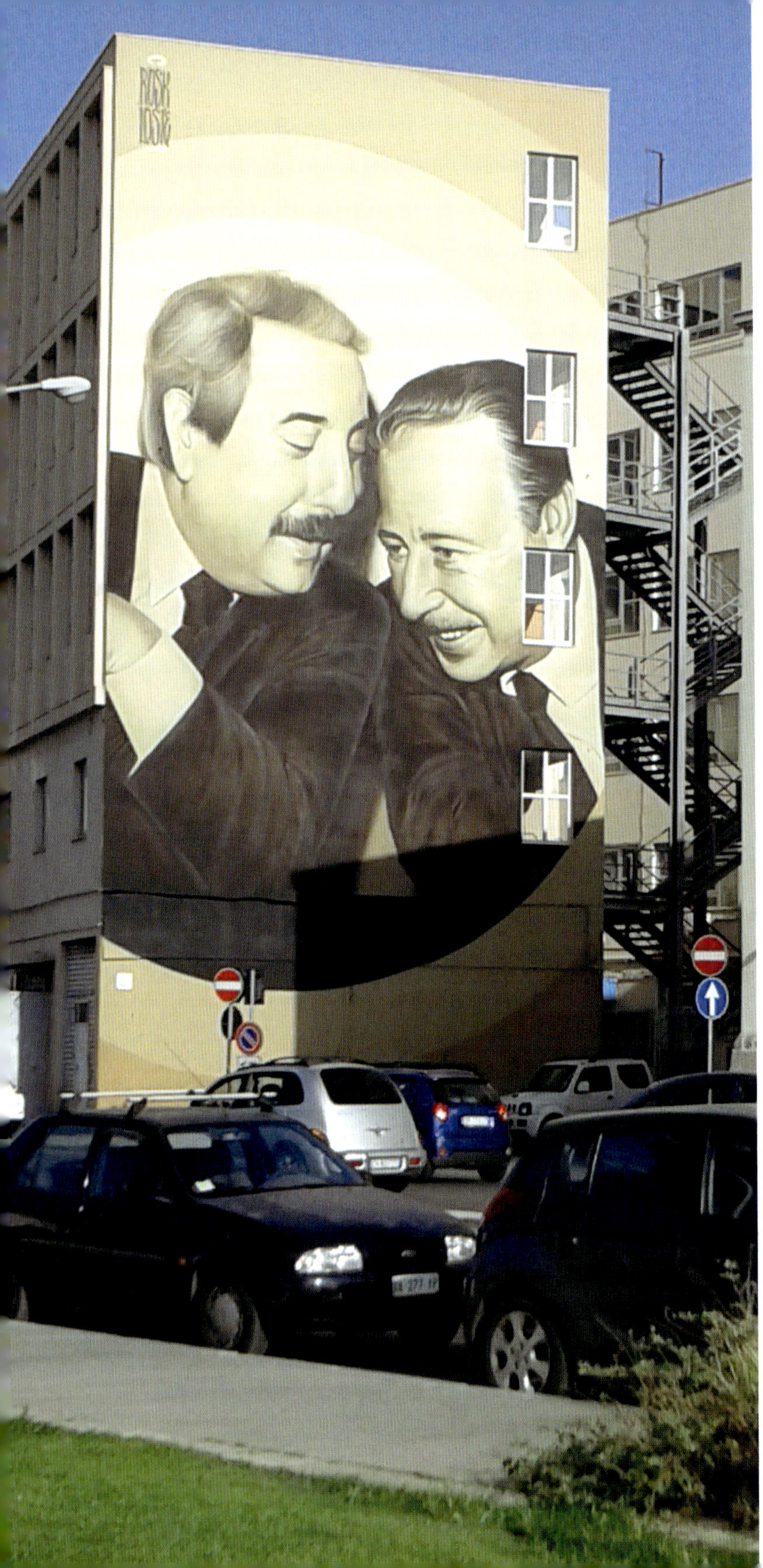

PALERMO, SICILY

Where the Mob Meets the Sea

On Palermo's waterfront by the boat harbor there is a building with a large photorealist mural based on a famous photo of Giovanni Falcone and fellow magistrate Paolo Borsellino. The two judges spent their professional careers trying to take down the Sicilian Mafia. Both paid with their lives when they were killed by car bombs thought to be planted by the Sicilian Mafia.[3]

The legacy of the Mafia is part of Palermo's bloody history, and this wall portrait of Falcone and Borsellino serves as a kind of gateway to backstreets of Palermo, which is home to a very different type of women on the wall. None of the artists are clearly identified by their tags or signatures. Their often haunting style can be overtly political. Many examples are stencils, while some are paste-ups. All share a rawness in their execution and often an intensity from their women, who stare at you intently, like they can see through you.

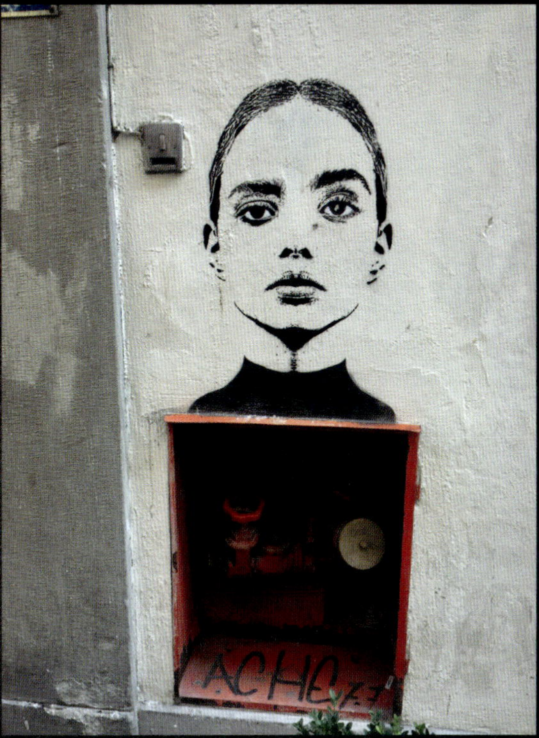

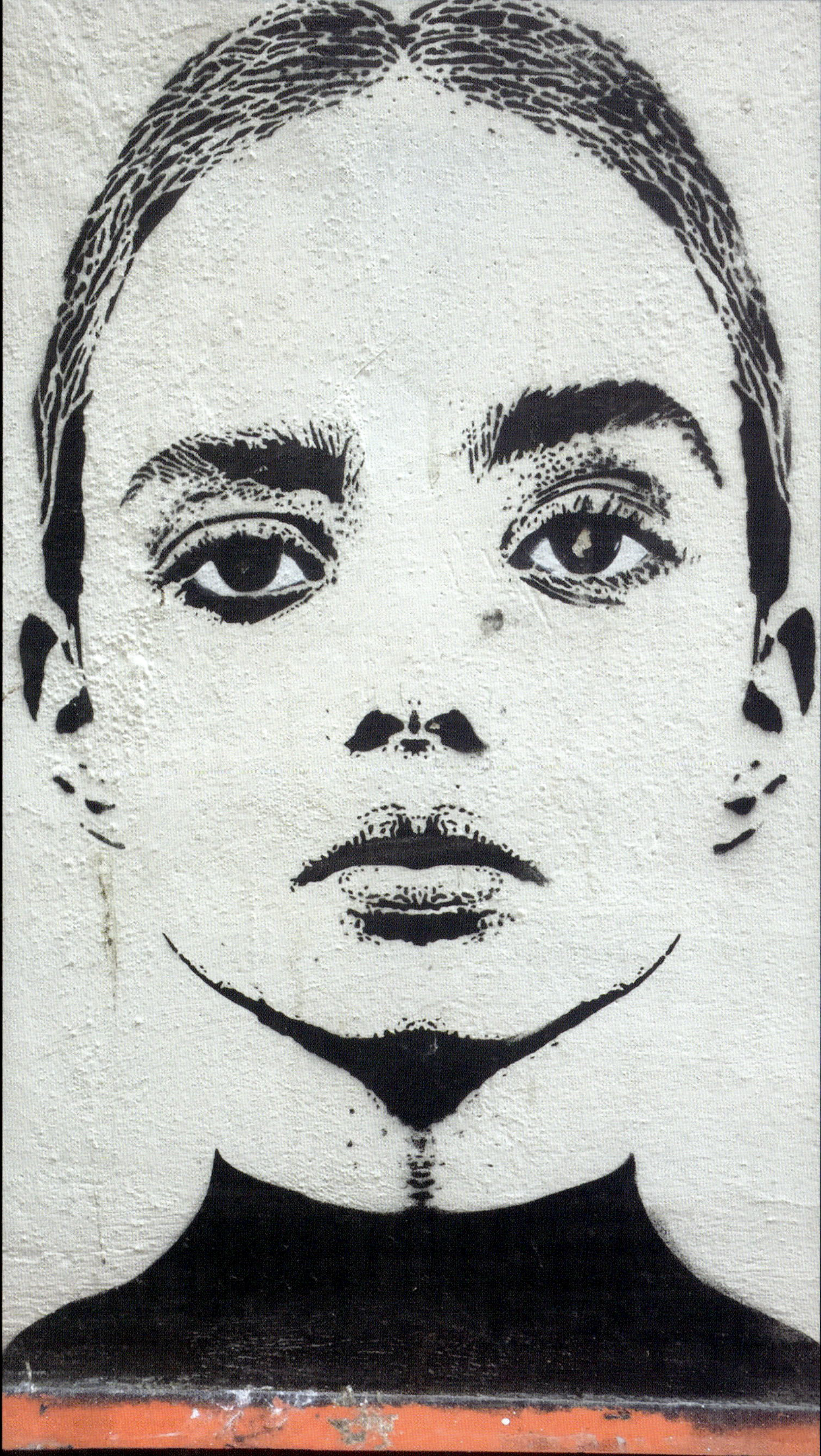

This large-scale mural near the waterfront depicts two assassinated judges in Palermo, Sicily, who went after the Mob.

The wall art of women in Palermo is often stenciled and found in out-of-the-way places. Photos: John Harris

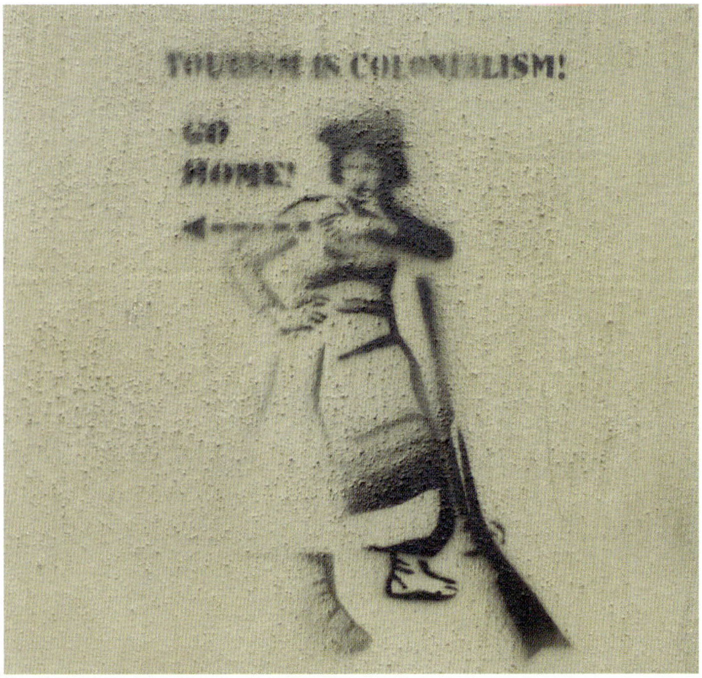

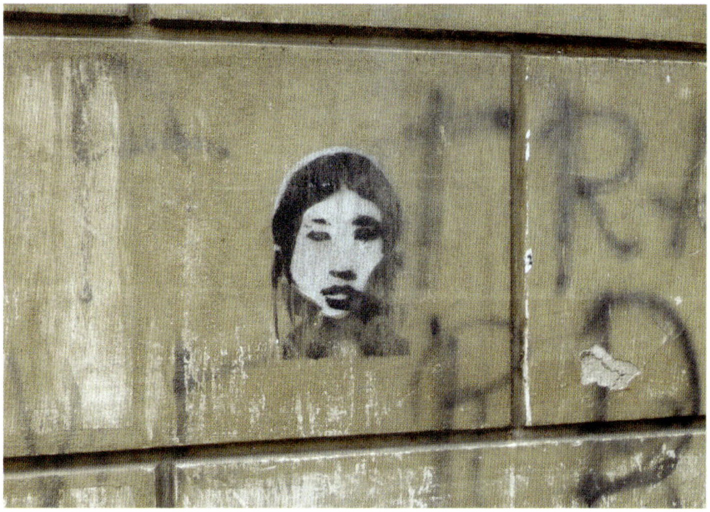

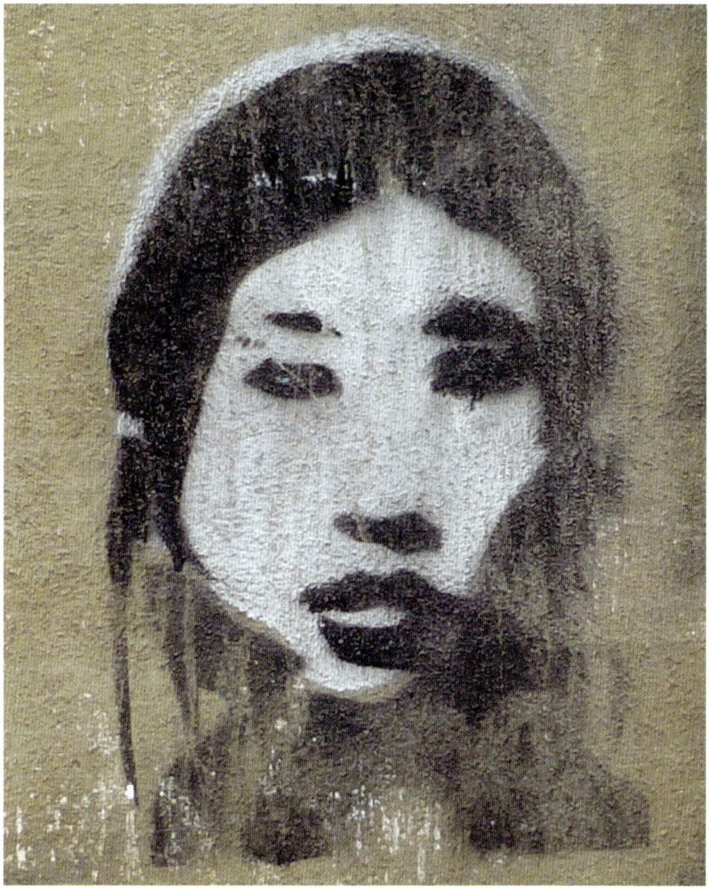

In these examples from the alleyways of Palermo, the viewer is witness to an anonymous gallery of street art of women that is subdued in color but is vibrant in its hasty depictions. These are not famous works destined for the pages of blogs or instant art books. They come from a darker place of the heart, not the world of well-publicized artists with commercial pedigrees. This is street art of women at its most expressive, without embellishment.

The stencil work in Palermo often delivers a politically freighted message, like this one that uses the iconic image of Annie Oakley to deliver a lethal message to tourists. Was it tongue in cheek?

The women on the wall of Palermo do not follow any prescribed style and are generally throw-up stencils.

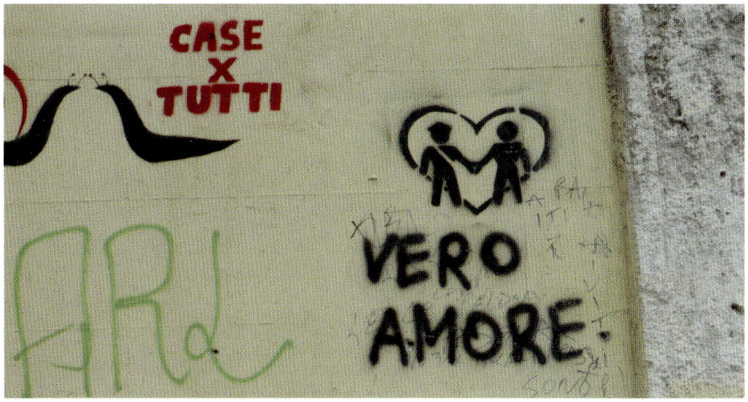

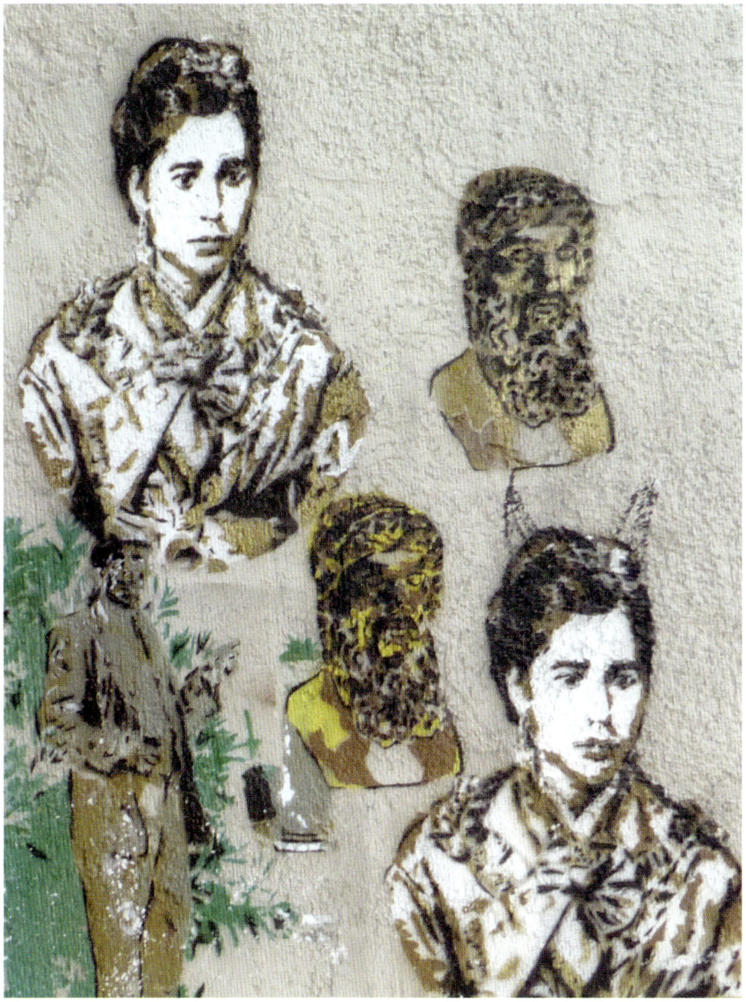

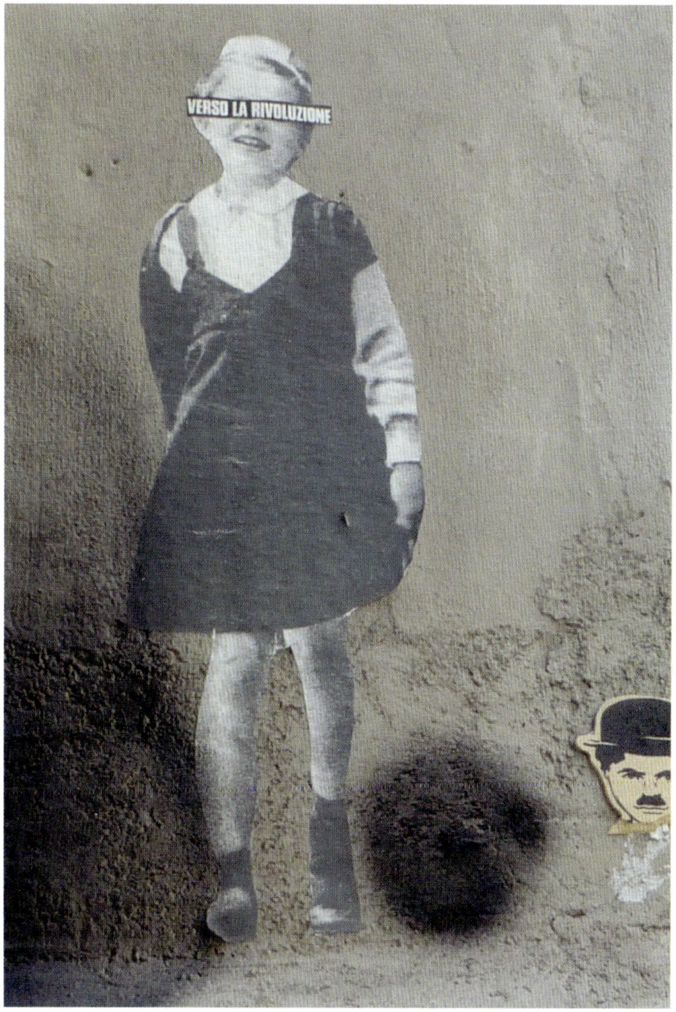

The stenciled pieces demonstrate a humorous twist, one showing hand holding between a *carabinieri* (police) and a citizen with the caption "True Love." In its simplicity and in the context of Palermo, there is a sardonic quality to the subject matter. It is far removed from the fashionable streets and neighborhoods of Paris and goes to the heart of wall art with its raw quality.

Photos: John Harris

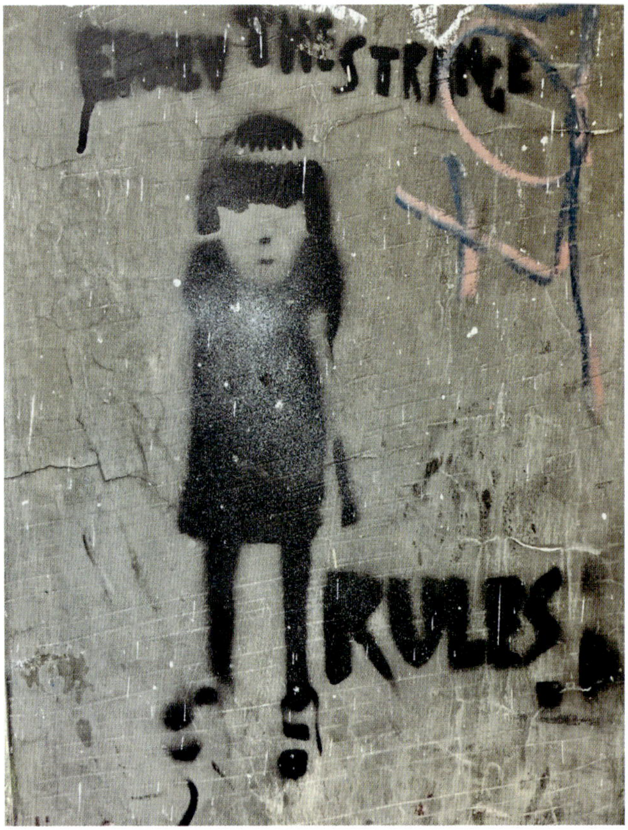

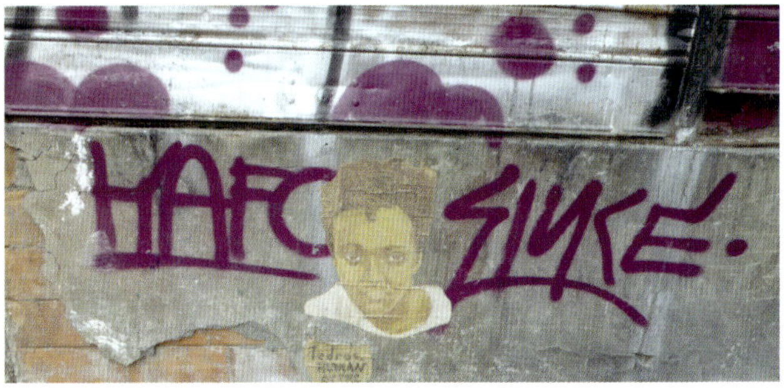

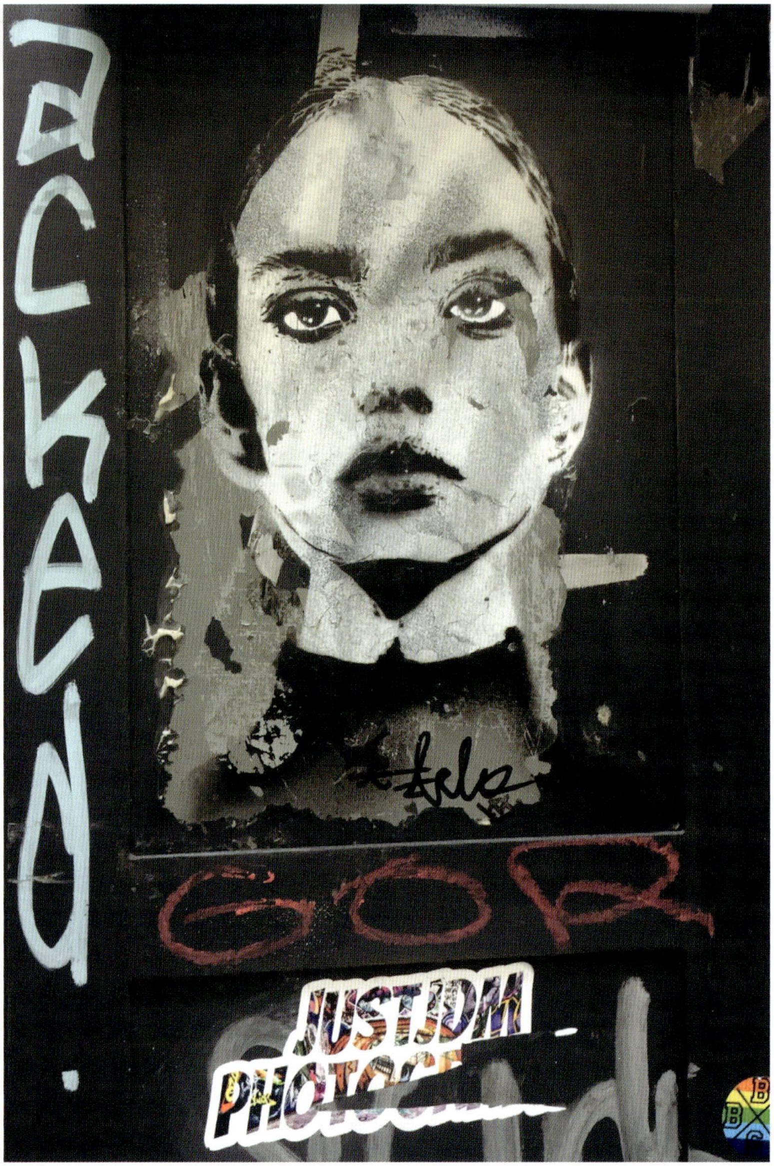

One thing is certain about Palermo's wall artists of women—their subjects often communicate a great intensity and have the hardened look of someone who has seen too much. Photo: John Harris

There are many other European capitals, such as Berlin, that feature a panoply of wall art of women that can be appreciated when wandering the streets. It is up to you, dear reader, to take the first steps toward discovering these hidden portraits of women that reveal more about who we are as individuals in how we react to the art. And Berlin is just the place that demands observer participation and reflection. There is no sitting on the sidelines.

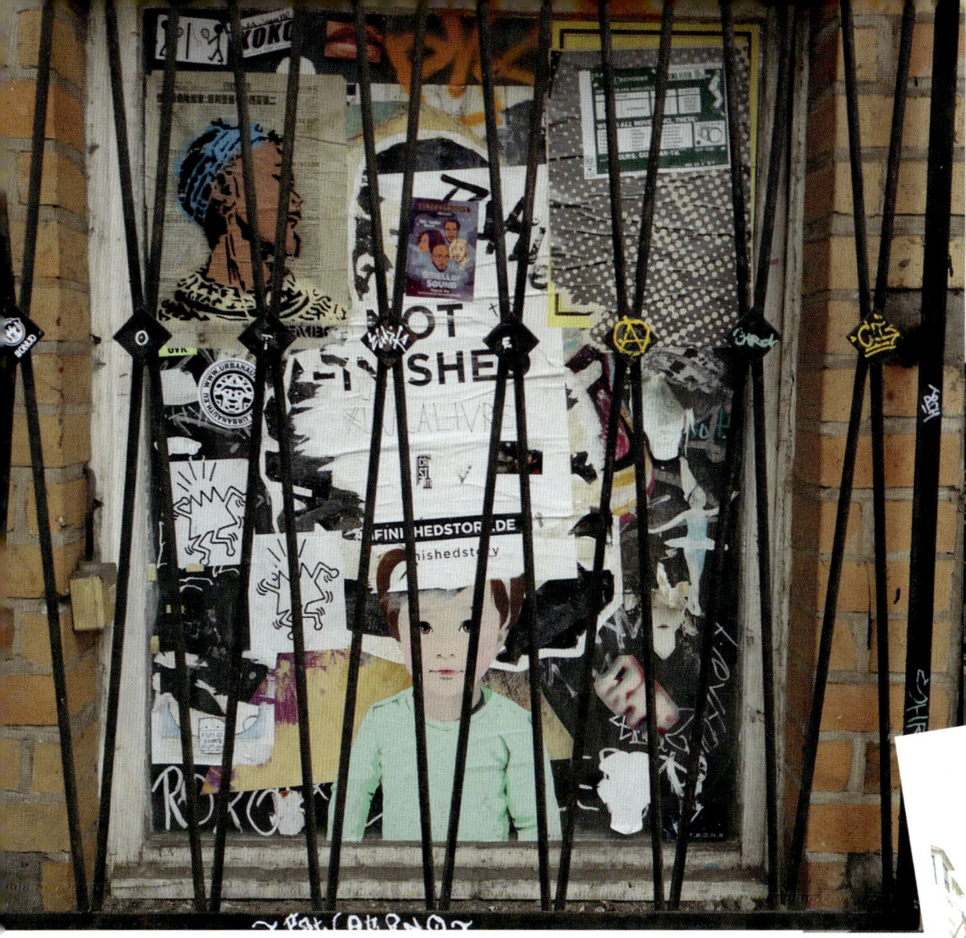

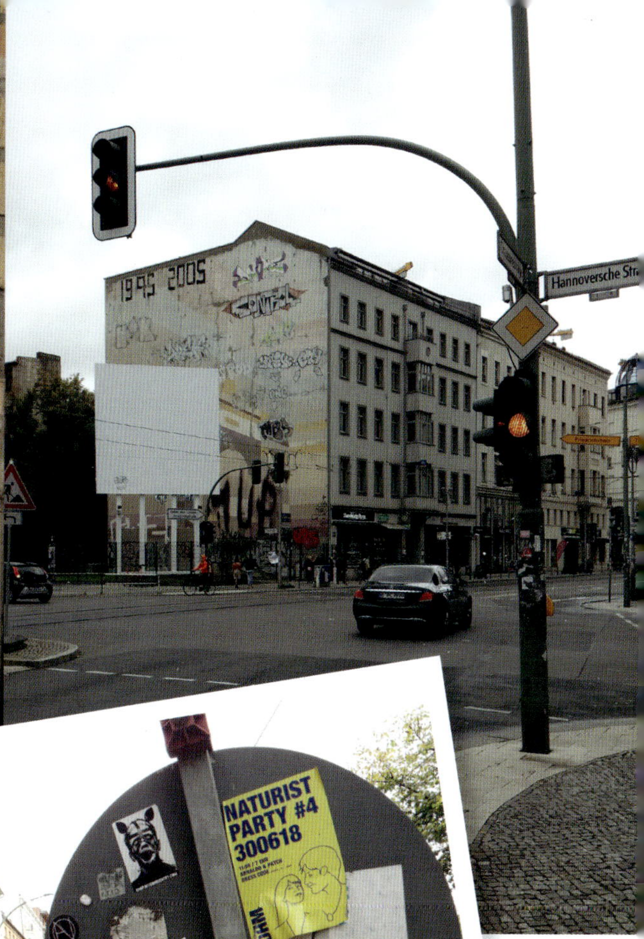

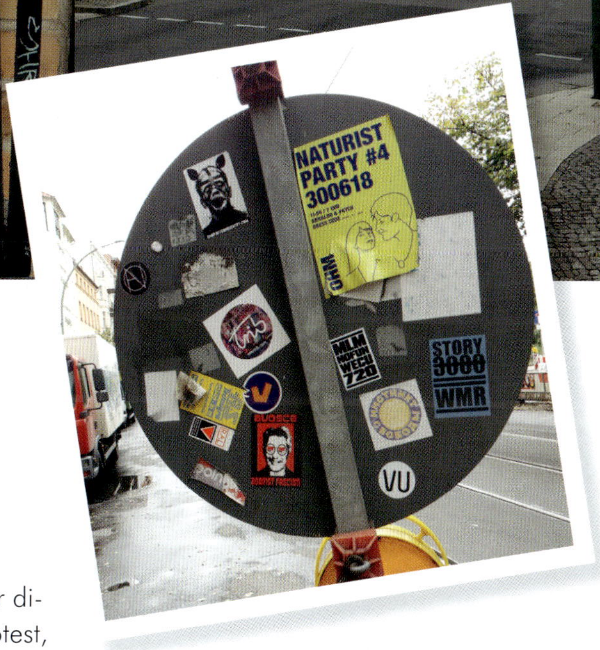

BERLIN

An Edgy Coexistence with the Past

Berliners view themselves as free thinkers. The former stage for Cold War divisions has always practiced a form of street art as visual puns, political protest, commentary, and expressions of defiance when a wall divided the city. Berlin's sense of self can be found on its walls, which are outward expressions of an inner strength born from wartime and ideological survival.

The streets of Berlin have seen devastation wrought by war and a slow rebuilding process that has covered the scars of the past with a thick skin of tolerance. Percolating below the surface is an edginess found in the city's wall art that reflects its turbulent history.

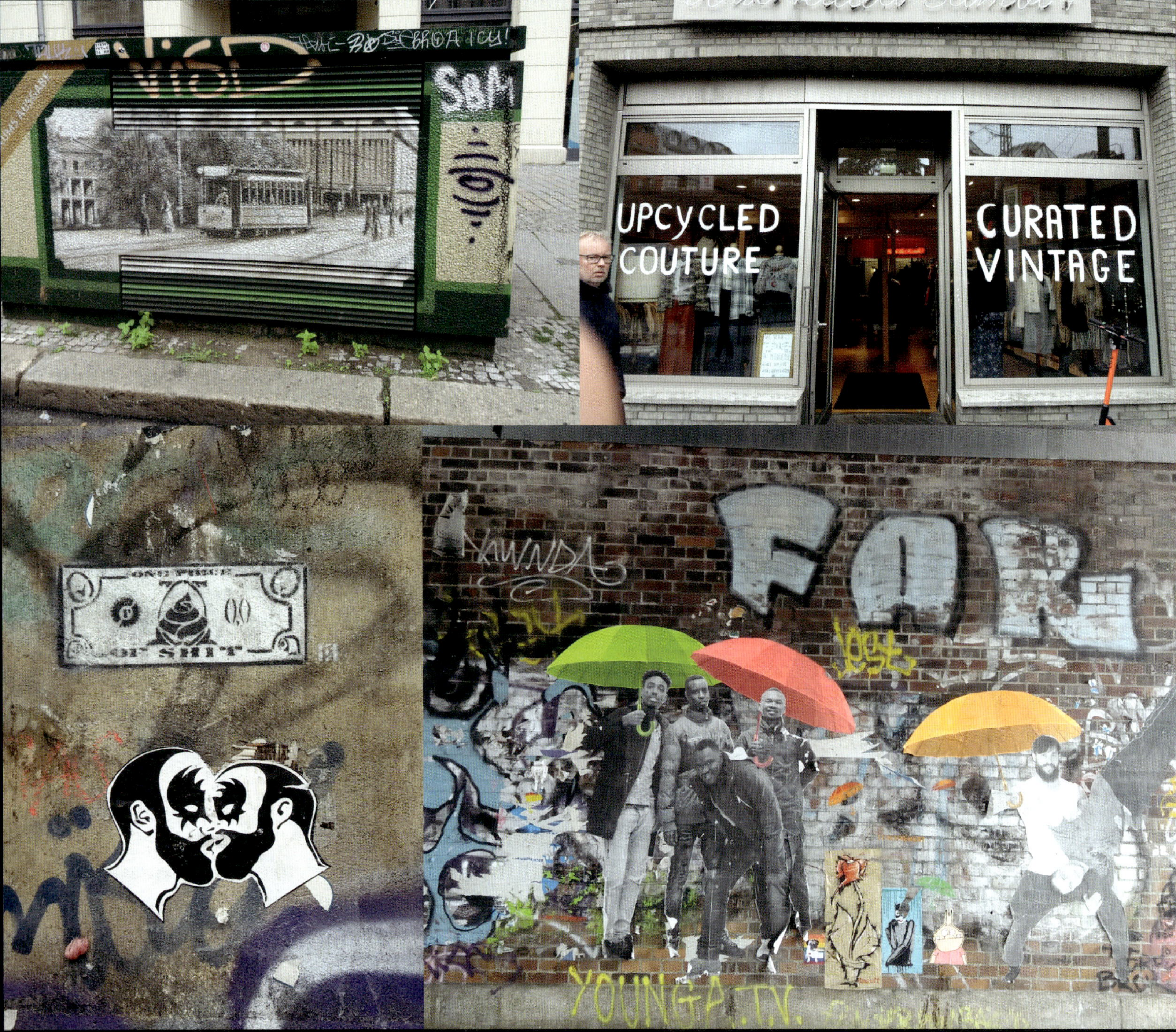

Berlin defies the search for a label that ties together its distinct neighborhoods. The city has an edgy quality resulting from its mix of government bureaucrats, students, immigrants, clubbers, and tourists. The best way to discover the city's diversity is to take the underground and trams and just hop off.

East vs. West in Berlin's Wall Art

A wall art observer cannot visit Berlin without stepping into its troubled modern history as a symbol of the Cold War between socialism and capitalism, which divided and imprisoned German families and friends behind barbed wire and a guarded wall. The East Side Gallery celebrates the wall's collapse under the weight of its own ideology, caused by geo-political shifts in the world order.

The remnants of the Berlin Wall became an outdoor gallery painted by wall artists from around the world who were invited to create their impressions of the fall of the wall in 1989.

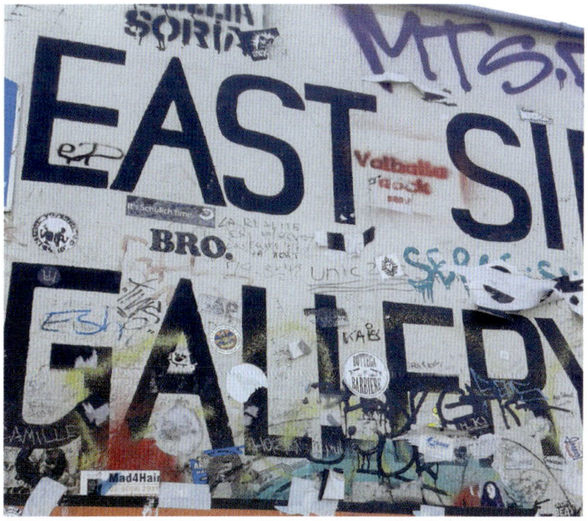

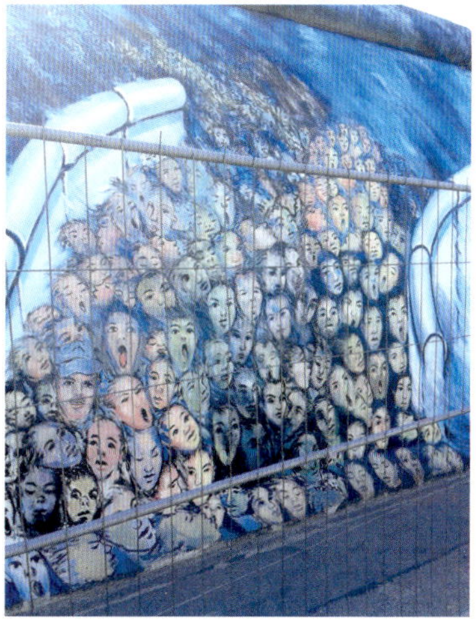

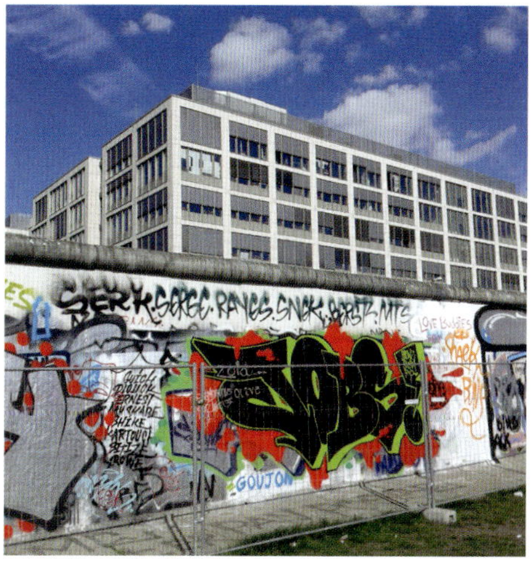

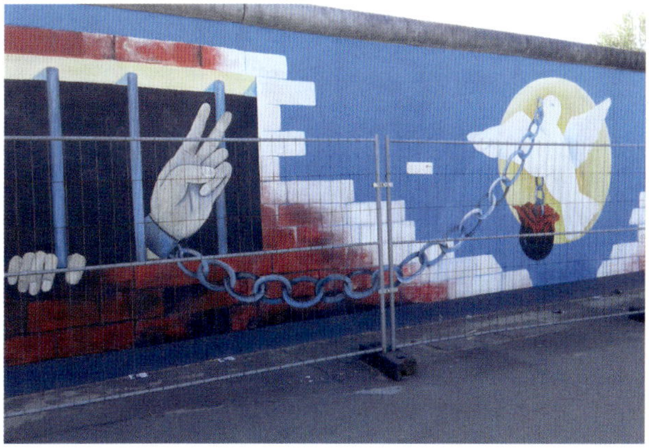

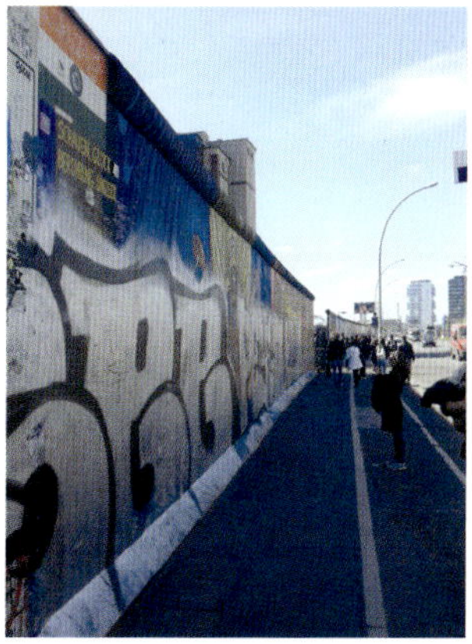

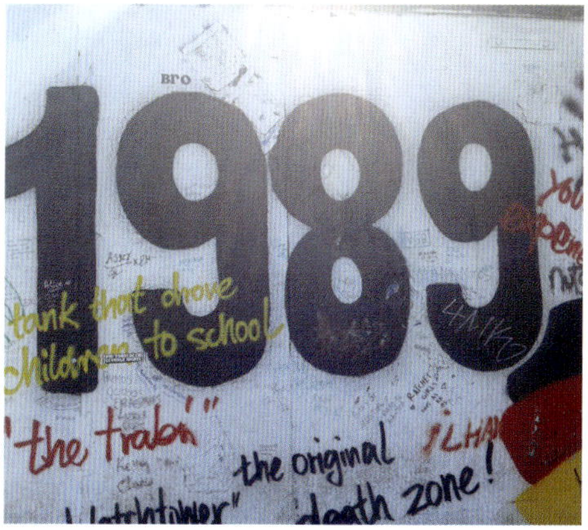

Most visitors to Berlin sample the remnants of the wall that divided the city between East and West until its fall on November 9, 1989. In 1990, artists from around the world were invited to paint their interpretation of the fall of the Berlin Wall on panels of the wall that were preserved as a concrete canvas that stretched for blocks on Mühlenstraße in Friedrichshain and Kreuzberg, about 8 km from the center of the city. The East Side Gallery is emblematic of the wall's deep divisions in Berlin, and the depictions of freedom when Germany was unified after the wall came down. The wall panels were under restoration, which is why the fence was put up to protect the wall art, which has, ironically but somehow appropriately, become the target of graffitists.

One of the East Side Gallery's most famous images is the socialist fraternal kiss between Soviet leader Leonid Brezhnev and the German Democratic Republic's Erich Honecker, general secretary of the Socialist Unity Party of the GDR. The work is by Dmitri Vrubel, a Russian artist who titled the piece *My God, Help Me to Survive This Deadly Love*. The painting is taken from a photo in 1979, during the celebration of the founding of the German Democratic Republic in 1949. On the right, Birgit Kinder's Trabant, an East German–made car, crashes through the wall on its journey to the West. The Trabant was called a "spark plug with a roof" and was seen as a symbol of the GDR.

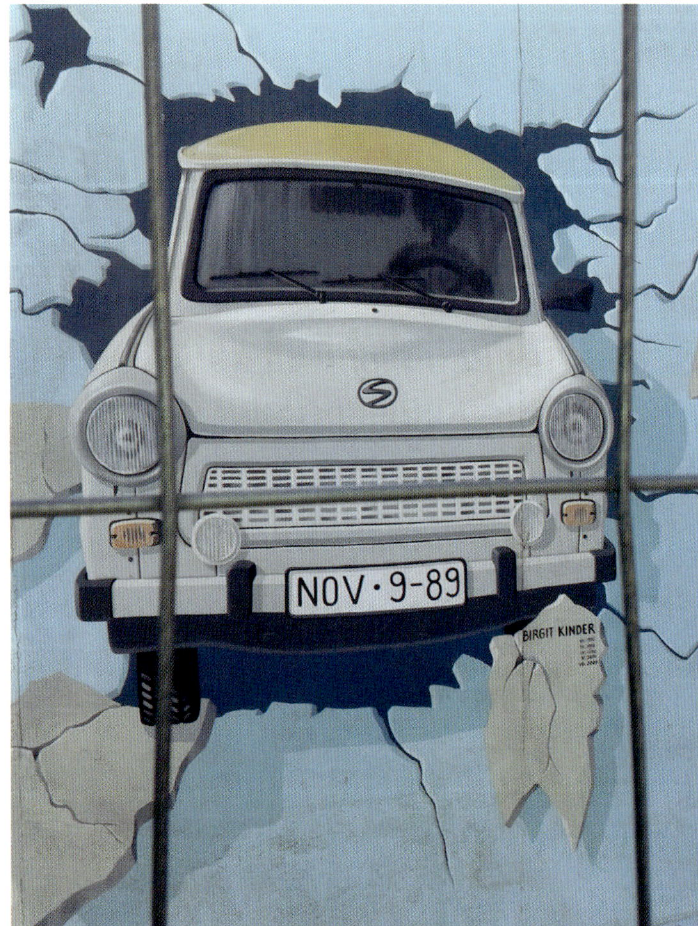

The Underbelly of Berlin's Street Art: Dircksenstraße

If you look from the top of Berlin's TV tower on Alexanderplatz, you see a 360-degree view of a modern city that rose from the ashes of war. The TV tower itself is a symbol of defiance built by the government of the German Democratic Republic to overlook the West, in a kind of thumb-in-the-eye gesture showcasing the engineering prowess of the East. West Berliners couldn't avoid looking at it. The tower overlooks an elevated train overpass with brick galleries that feature women and a confrontational, humorous version of street art. It is a much more graphic and sardonic version of the East Side Gallery.

Dircksenstraße, in Mitte, Berlin, connects Alexanderplatz and Hackescher Markt and is dominated by the Berlin TV Tower, which was the shiny example of GDR ingenuity.

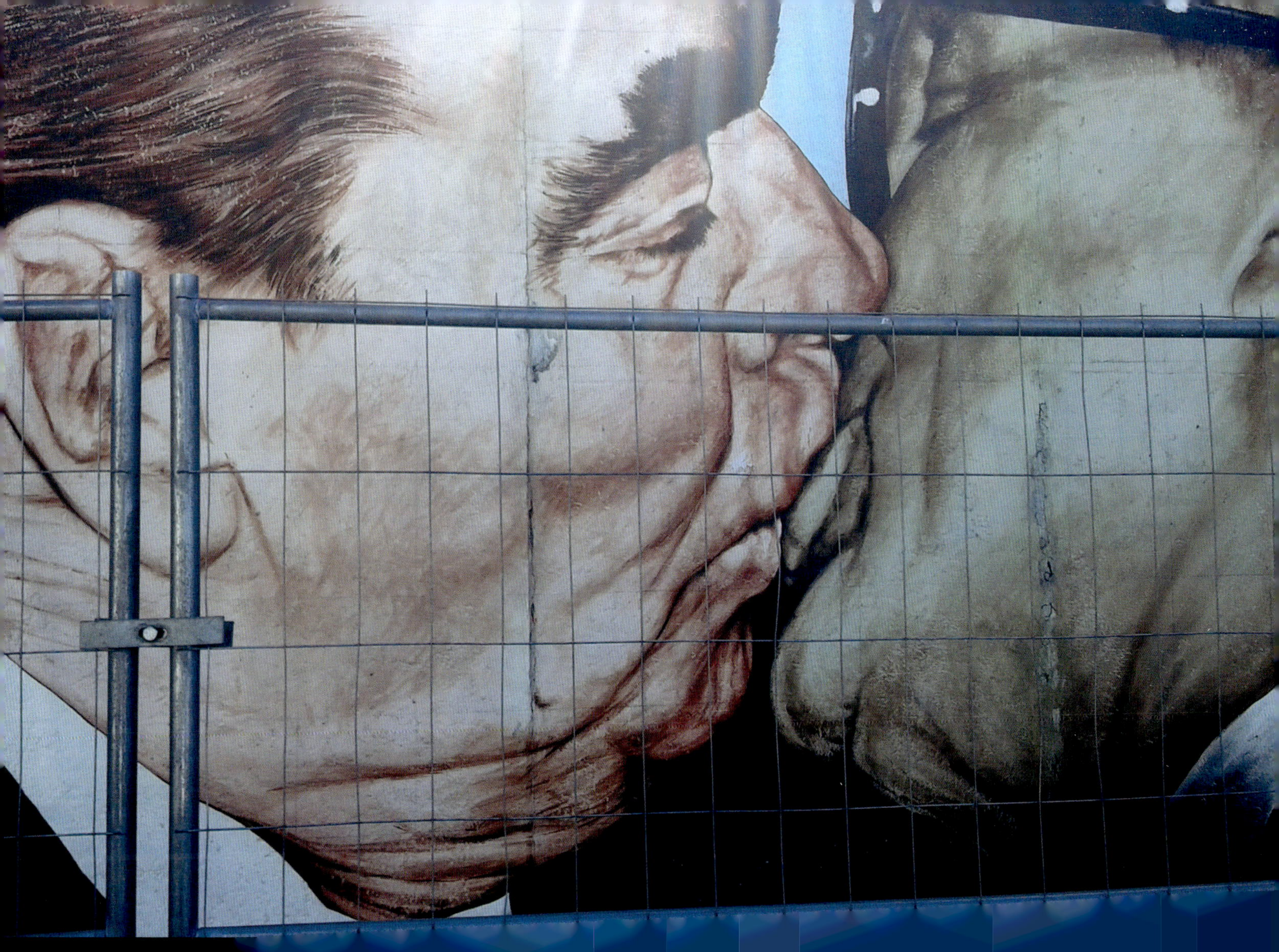

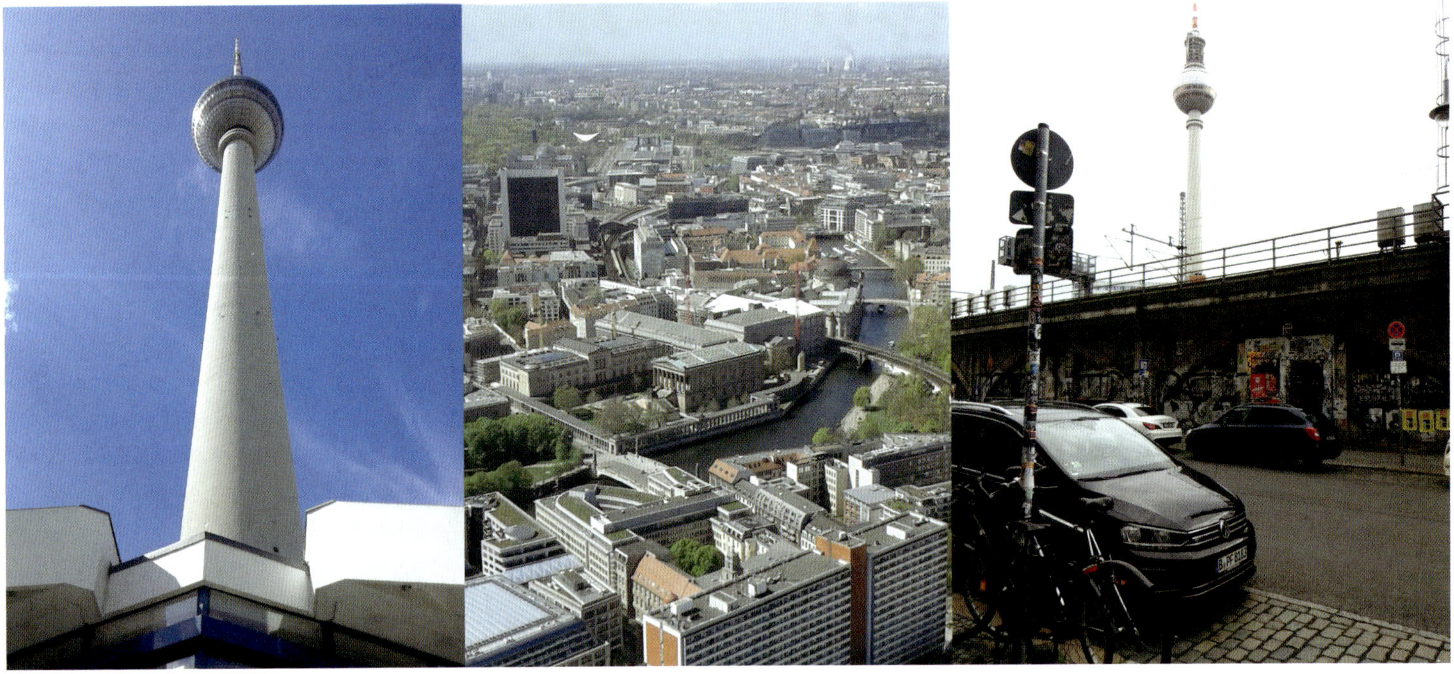

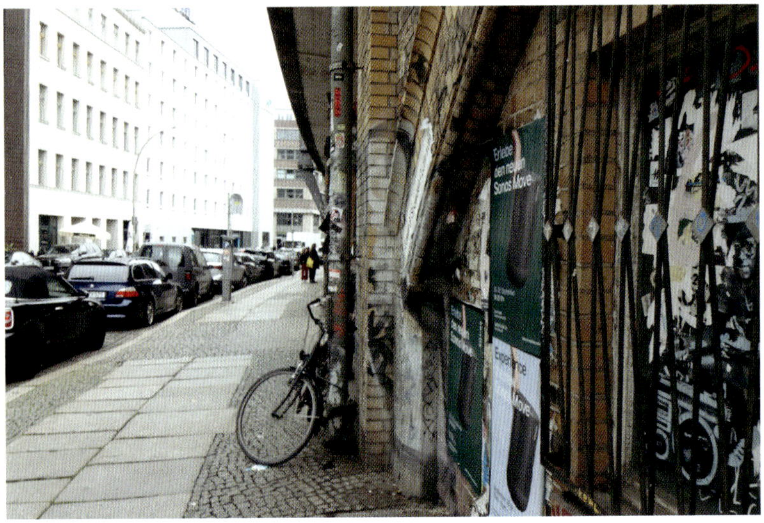

Women on the wall in this area of Berlin are part of a complicated, multilayered gallery both by well-known and unknown artists. There are wild examples of tagging, paste-ups, and stencils that reveal a sensual and often chaotic display that takes time to study. Some of the same artists who work in Paris surface in Berlin, like Sobr and his dancing women. Berlin's wall artists also set out to shock observers with candidly sexual and satirically crude images. But through all the layers of posters and graffiti, imaginations are burning brightly. All you have to do is point the camera and you will come away with a sometimes controversial but always interesting view of women.

Berlin TV tower from Alexanderplatz and the view from Dircksenstraße

Dircksenstraße from the street-eye view

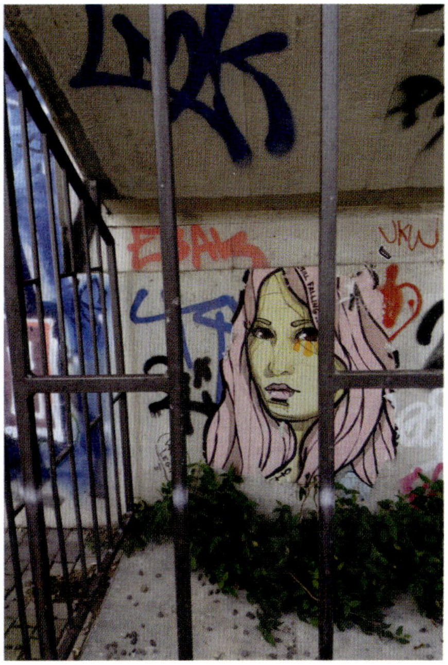

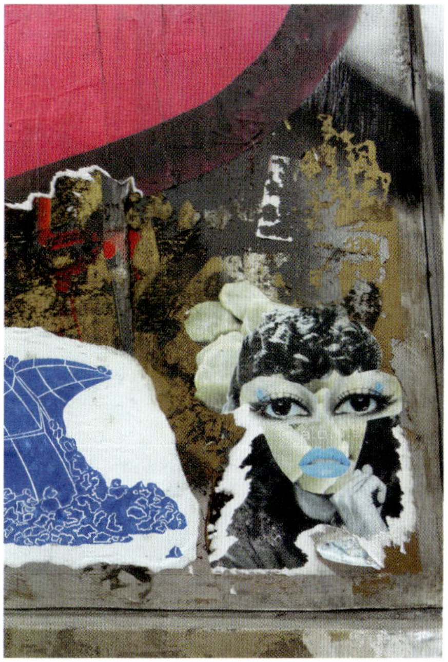

Walking around Dircksenstraße requires concentration, not only to avoid cars but to really study the walls, because much of the art of women is small and often hidden, sometimes behind iron bars like this pink-haired woman.

There are also historical references, illustrated in this portrait of Rosa Luxemburg, a Polish Marxist philosopher and antiwar activist who was venerated in the GDR. Rosa Luxemburg had a realistic and embracing approach to life and was a fierce advocate for human rights. She was quoted as saying, "Women's freedom is the sign of social freedom," a fitting epitaph to her life memorialized on the walls of Berlin. The Luxemburg portrait is signed by marycula.

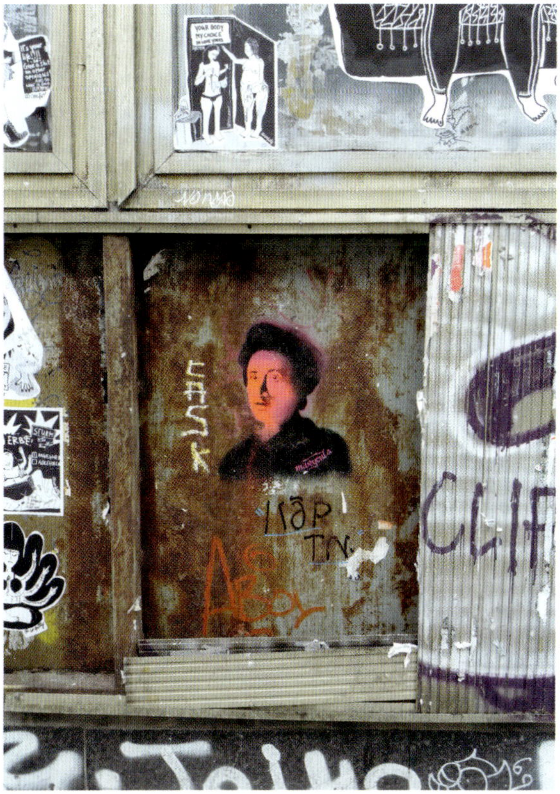

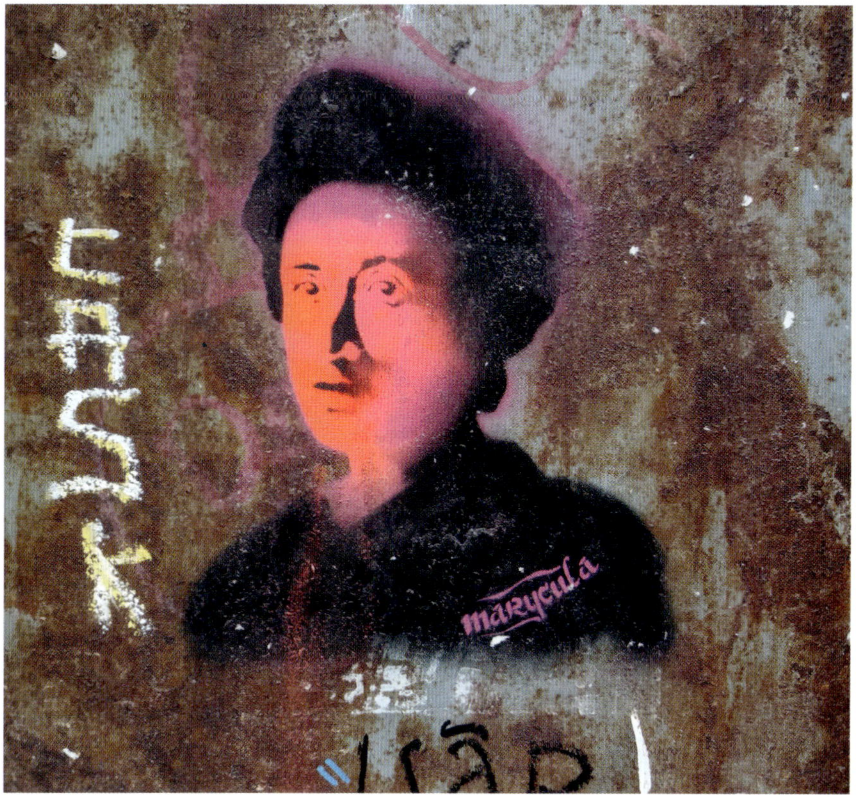

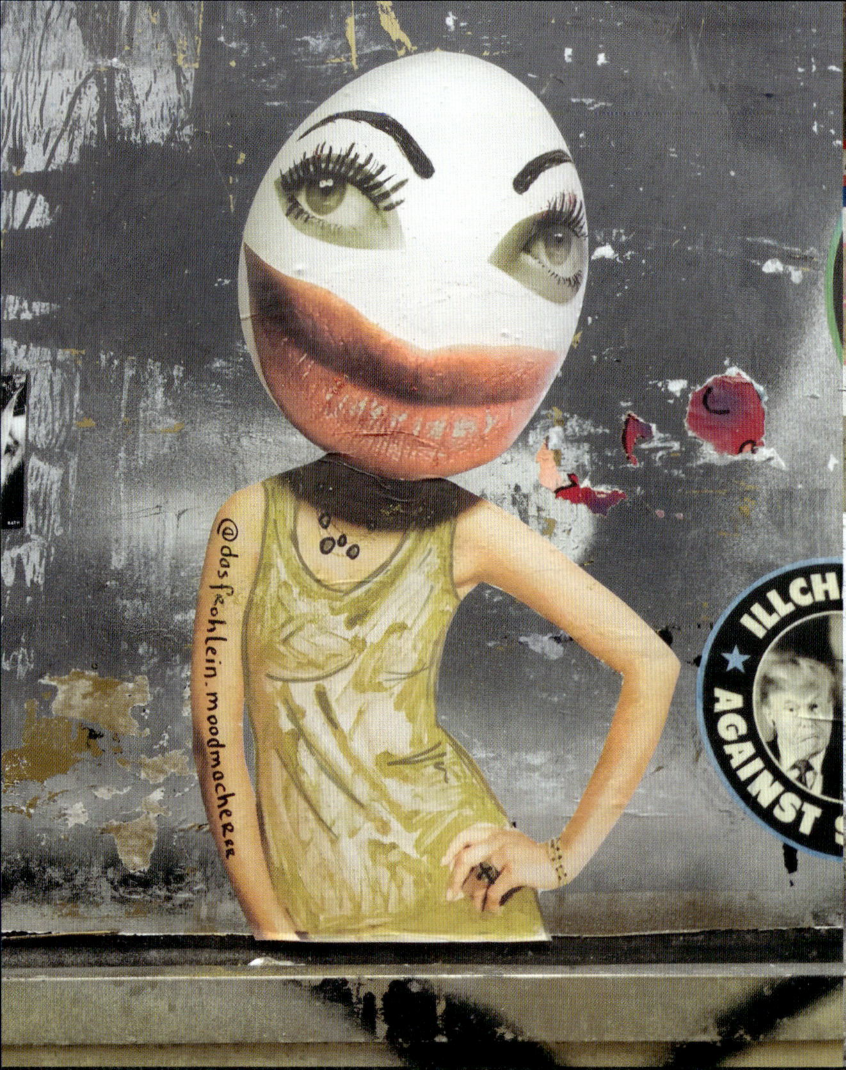

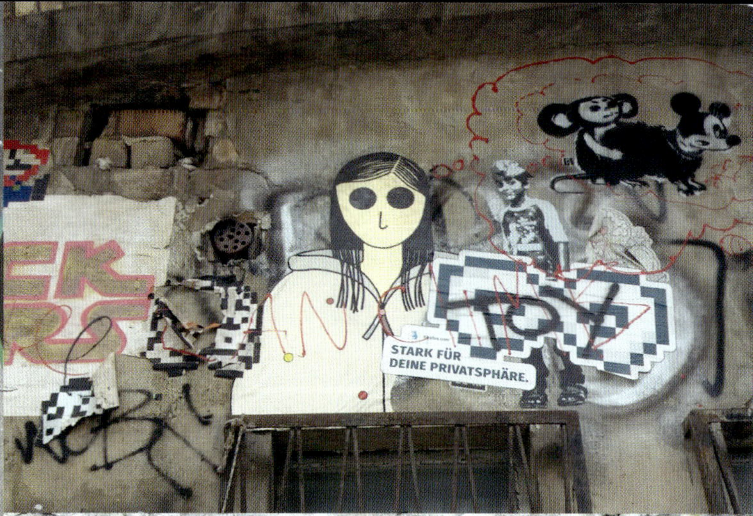

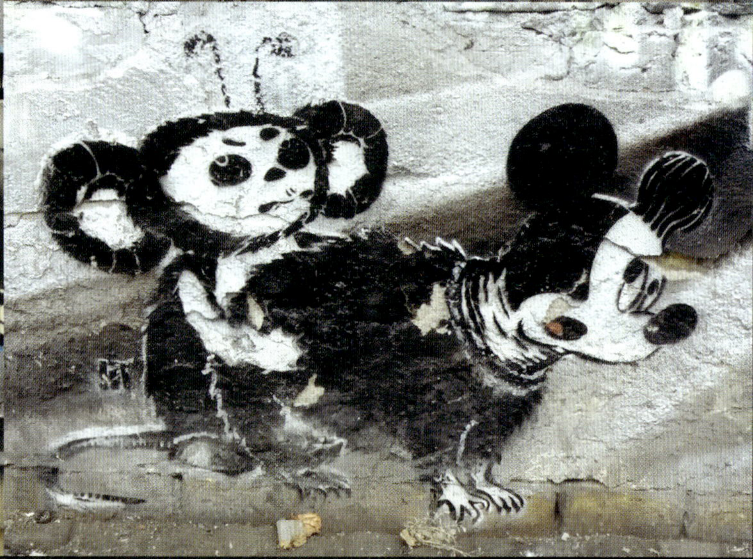

Sometimes as a wall art observer, all you can do is appreciate the imagination of the artist, who in this case feminizes eggs with giant eyes and inflated lips. The artist goes by the handle @dasfrohlein.moodmacherrr, which is a play on words that roughly translates into the "happy mood maker."

There is often a sense of humor at play in wall art of women, who use double entendres and puns to make a point. Disney characters appear on Berlin walls, but few like in this image of Mickey Mouse being dominated by a Russian children's book character, Cheburashka, in this stencil by Ukrainian artist Ostap. These types of graphic satire are not uncommon on the walls of Dircksenstraße.

The eye-patched woman sitting in an overstuffed easy chair is celebrating "Fat Power" in a work by Confatty, whose Instagram page labels her work as "Fat Feminist Artivism."

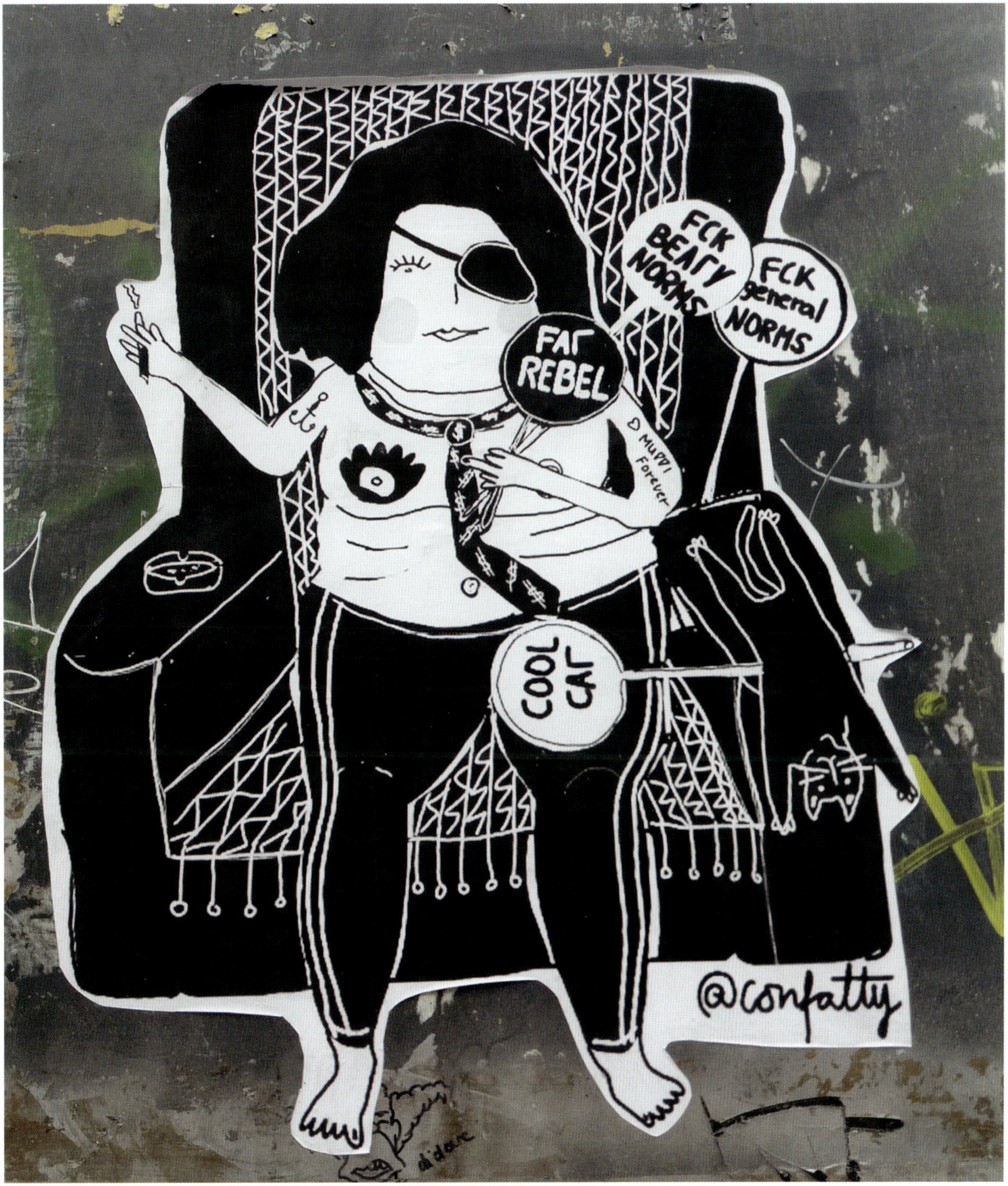
FCK BEAUTY NORMS
FCK general NORMS
FAT REBEL
COOL CAT
@confatty

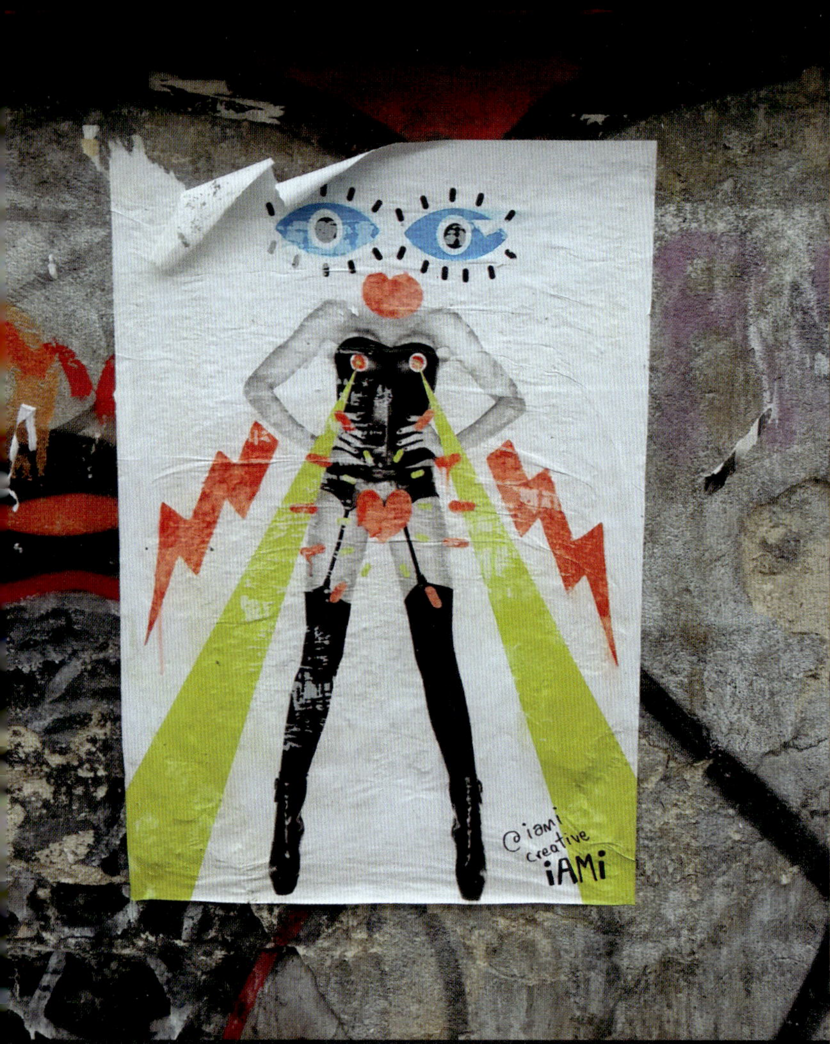

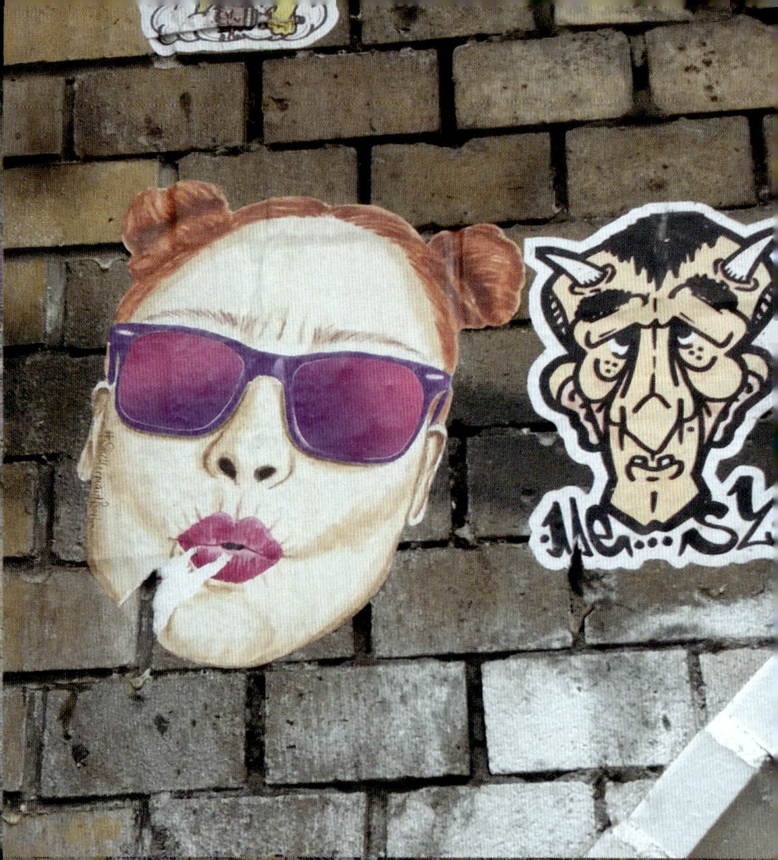

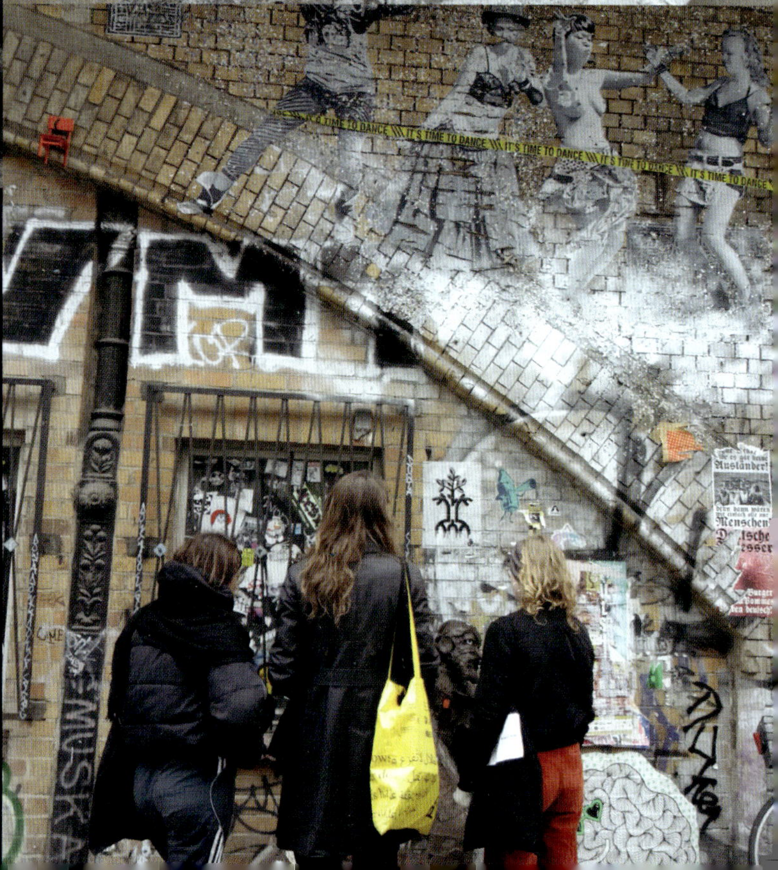

The idea of a superhero colors this interpretation of gay feminism by iAMi.

The freedom to be who you want to be and to project whatever style you want is part of the gestalt of being a Berliner, and it's clearly evident in this paste-up of a woman.

Sobr's dancing women can be found pasted up all along Dircksenstraße. Sobr's Time to Dance series of paste-ups are getting more faded as the years march on.

Sobr again makes appearances on these Berlin walls, topped by a woman with a tight hairdo hiding her eyes behind her shades, sending you an air kiss next to a devil-like man. Sometimes the wall art of women is just strange and interesting to look at, and you think, "What was the artist thinking?"

A young girl in a red dress walks off into the unknown, one of the few examples of a forward-looking perspective.

The subversive street art of women found in the backstreets of Berlin coexists with the big names of wall art. Away from the busy walls of Dircksenstraße, you can find quieter examples of women on the walls, as seen on the next page.

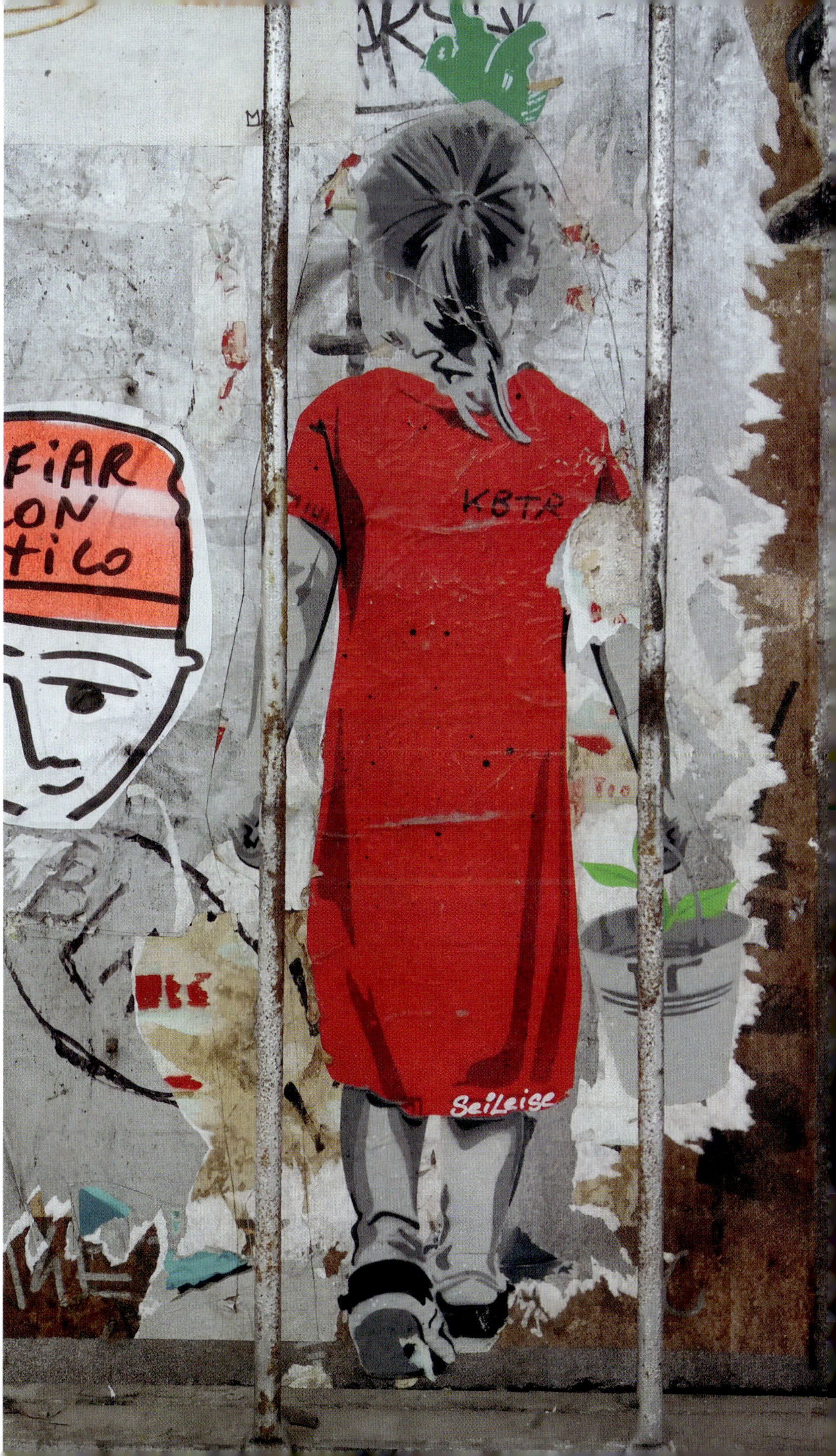

Mondmädchen by seiLeise is an artist based in Cologne, Germany, whose subjects are usually walking away from viewers.

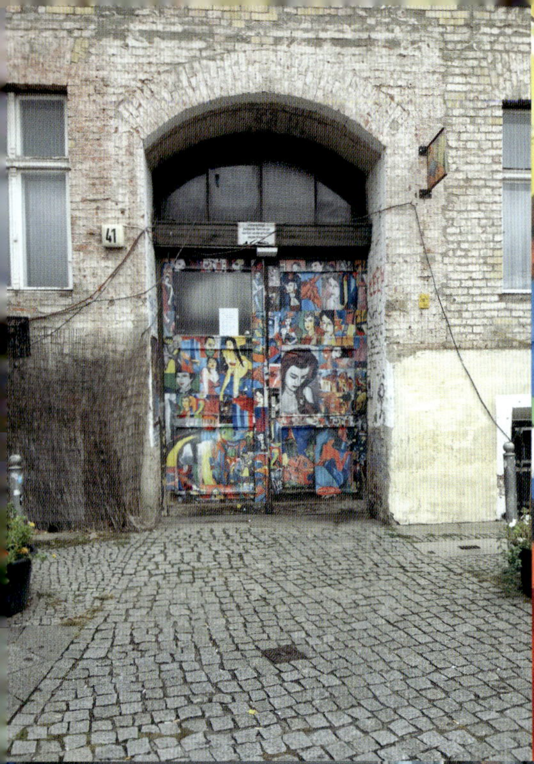

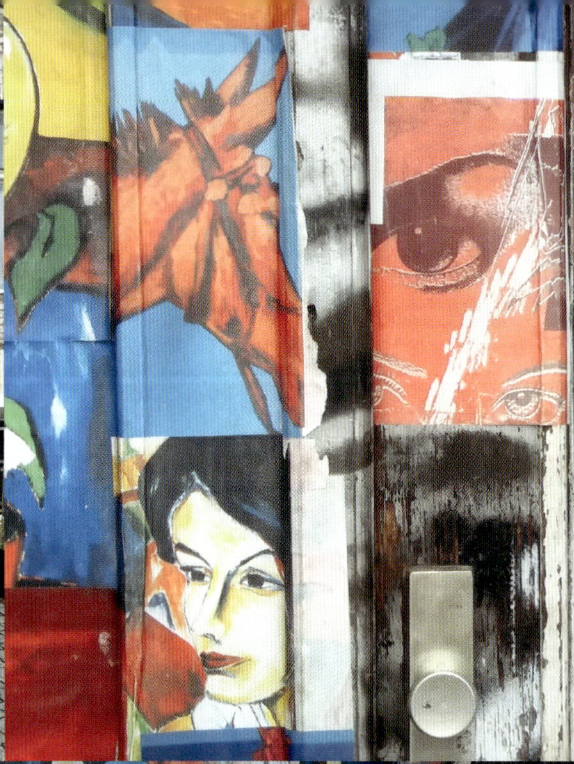

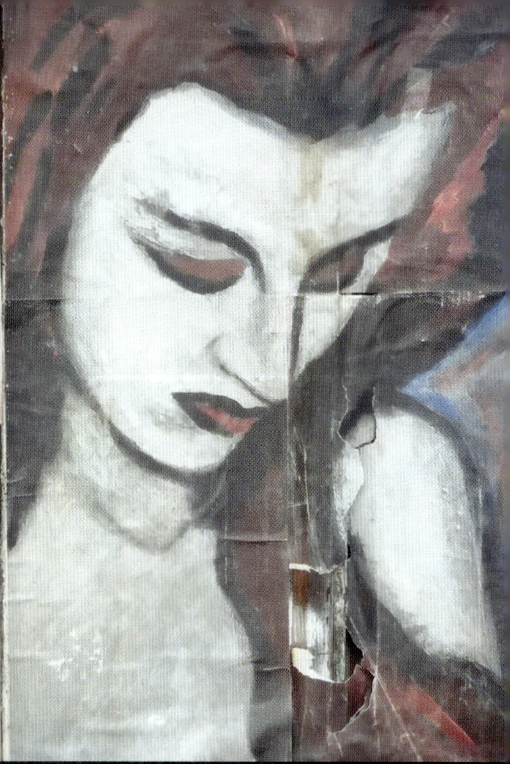

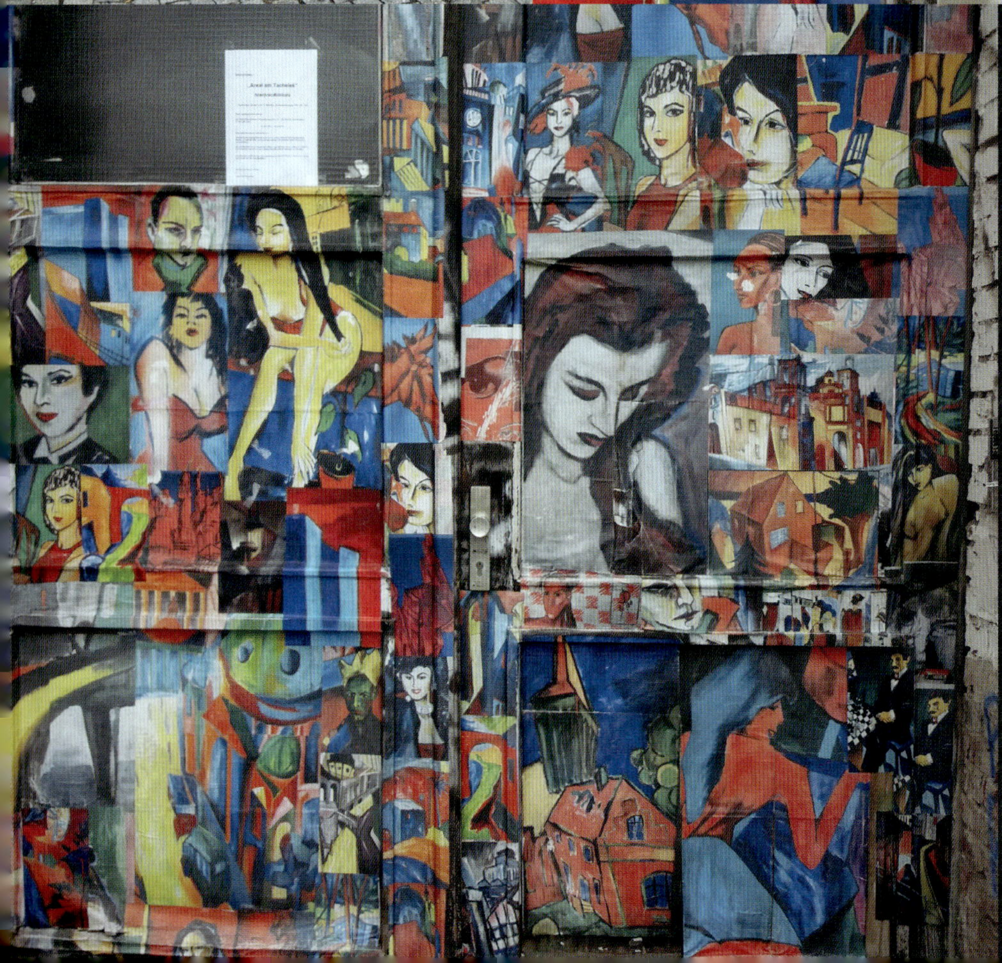

This doorway has become a gallery unto itself. And away from the concentrated images, you can also observe a circumspect portrait of a woman by Greek artist DEM.

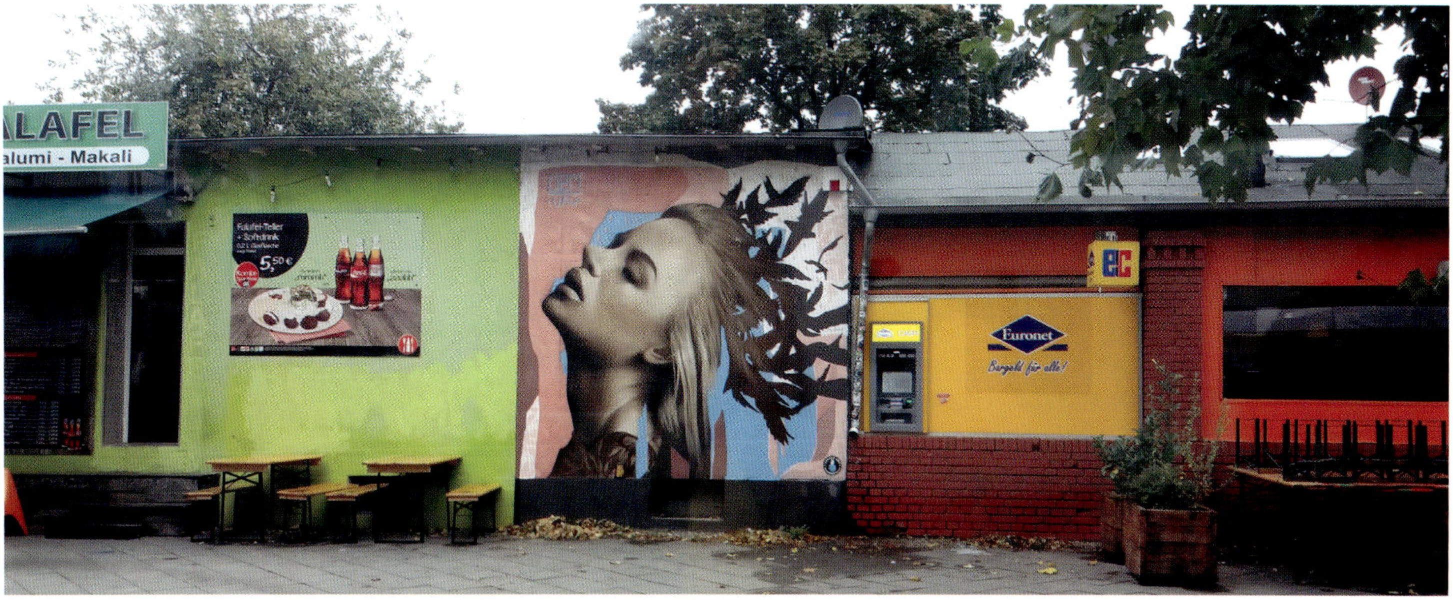
ALAFEL
alumi - Makali
Falafel-Teller
+ Softdrink
5,50 €
Euronet
Bargeld für alle!

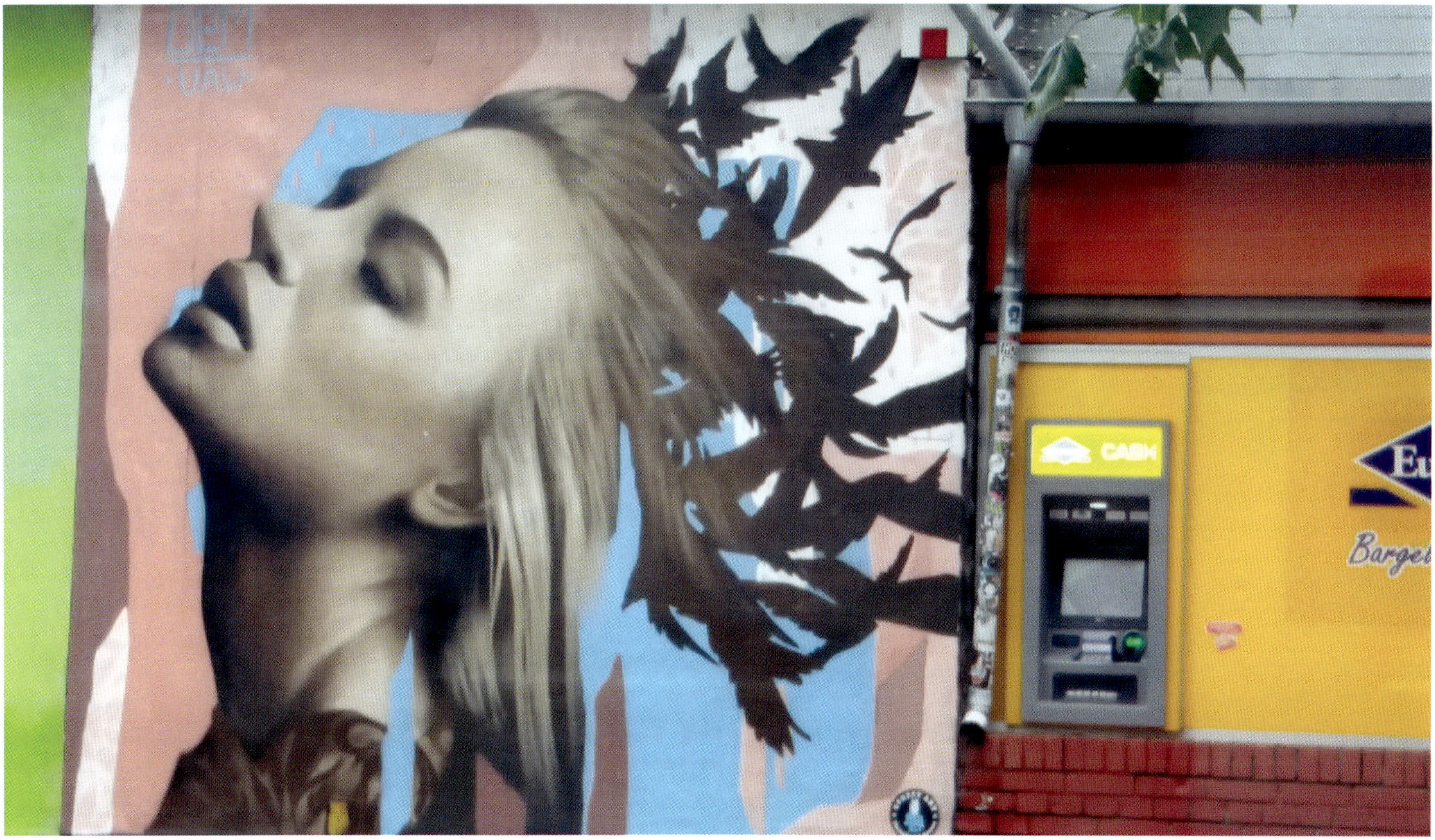
CASH

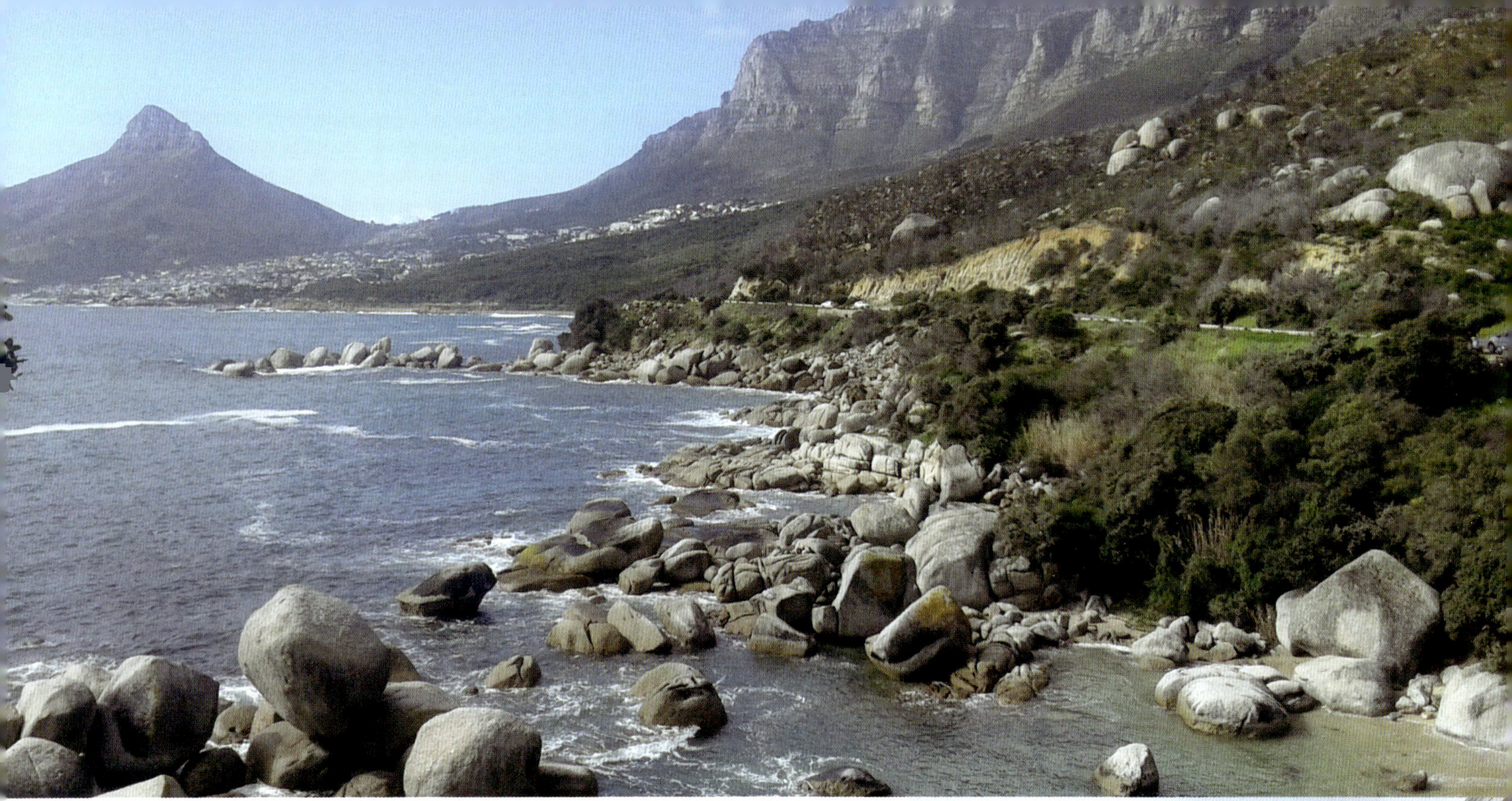

Next Stop: Cape Town and the Digital World of Women on the Walls

What does it take to become a successful wall artist? In our next chapter, we'll examine that question by introducing you to one of the most well-known woman wall artists in the world, who cut her teeth in the dangerous streets of Cape Town, South Africa. Faith47's work has become a powerful voice for women. We will also explore the idea that some wall artists have less to do with rebellion and more in common with selling their brands. We also look toward the future of digital wall art of women.

A view toward Lion's Head from the coastline south of Cape Town, South Africa

Woodstock neighborhood of Cape Town, where street art thrives. Photo: John Harris

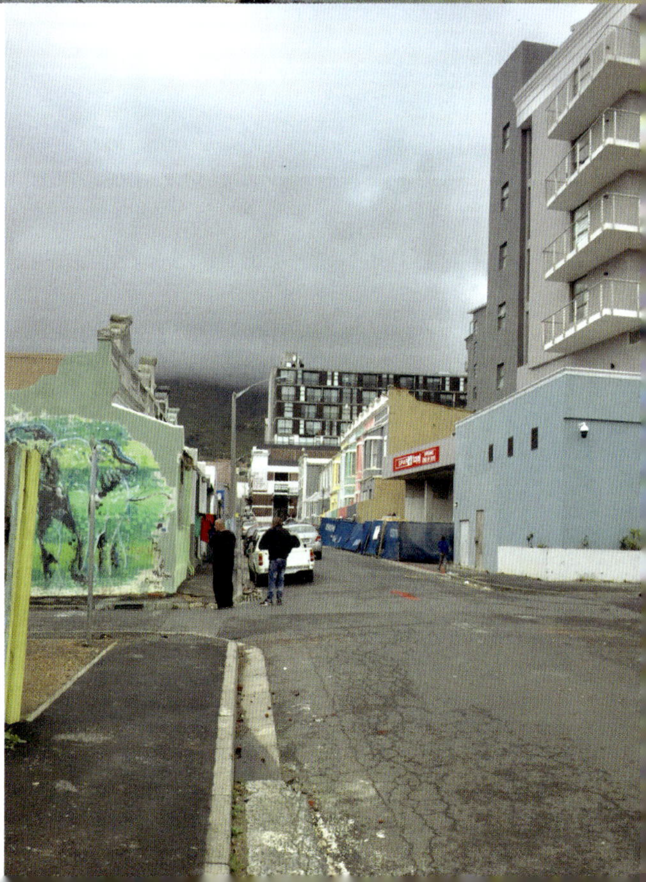

7

CLIMBING OVER THE WALL FROM OBSCURITY TO RECOGNITION

Faith XLVII's Journey from South Africa to LA

Wall art of women is often born from deeply personal places of the artists and helps us understand who we are as individuals.

As you have seen, street art of women encompasses a huge array of styles and creative approaches that go well beyond tagging. To label the street art in this book as simply "graffiti" would be doing it a disservice and ignoring its value as a cultural and historical art form. Easy labels also ignore the hard journey many street artists have made to gain a modicum of recognition and financial success.

Although many of the well-known wall artists featured in this book are formally trained and accomplished graphic artists and designers, some are self-taught and honed their vision on the walls of their neighborhoods. One of those artists goes by the street name of Faith XLVII or Faith47, whose women on the wall are intimate portraits in muted colors, often conveying an ethereal and spectral quality. Women on her walls embrace, and their arms and hands focus your attention, wrapping their subjects in tenderness; others are shrouded and emerge from broken surfaces, projecting strength in their vulnerability even as they hide their faces. Hers is a unique interpretation of women on the walls born from her country of birth and its violence against women.

Faith, born Liberty Du in Cape Town, South Africa, started out—like many street artists—working on the run in the violent neighborhoods of her birthplace. In a long journey with many detours around the world, Faith XLVII has since moved to LA and is now selling her studio work; she has become well known as South Africa's greatest street art export, whose subject matter comes from a feminist viewpoint. In a large part because of her work, Cape Town is now on the street art map for artists who work in the city's Woodstock district, near the harbor. Cape Town now hosts an international festival for street artists, and you can, as in many cities we introduced in his book, take street art tours along what were some of the most dangerous streets in the city in the Woodstock district.

Faith's forthright responses to the authors' written questions are confronting in their honesty and give even more depth to her extraordinary work.

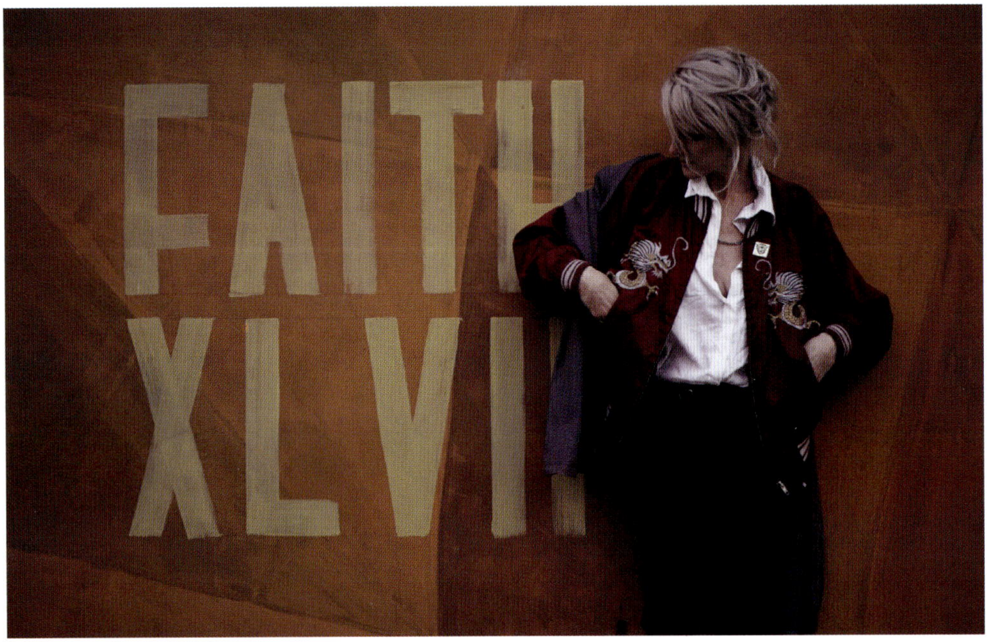

Portrait of Faith47. Photo: Zane Meyer, Chop 'em Down Films

INTERVIEW WITH FAITH XLVII
A Feminist Message Extending a Hand to Men

I come from a country where gender-based violence is five times higher than the global average. With some of the highest incidents of feticide, corrective rape, and child and infant rape in the world. I was raised by a single mother and raised my own child when I was eighteen. So I have seen and know the weight of what females bear.

I am very much a feminist and want to see a world where women not only are safe in cities with men as allies but also have access to abortion and are free to choose their sexuality without judgment. Where women are respected and upheld as the powerful beings that they are.

I paint men too, just less frequently. We are living in societies that have an inherent male perspective. So I'm interested in bringing the feminine perspective more power. This is why my natural tendency is to represent the female figure.

580–265 BCE, Athens, Greece. Photo: Zane Meyer, Chop 'em Down Films

1200–900 BCE, Cape Town, South Africa. Photo: Faith XLVII

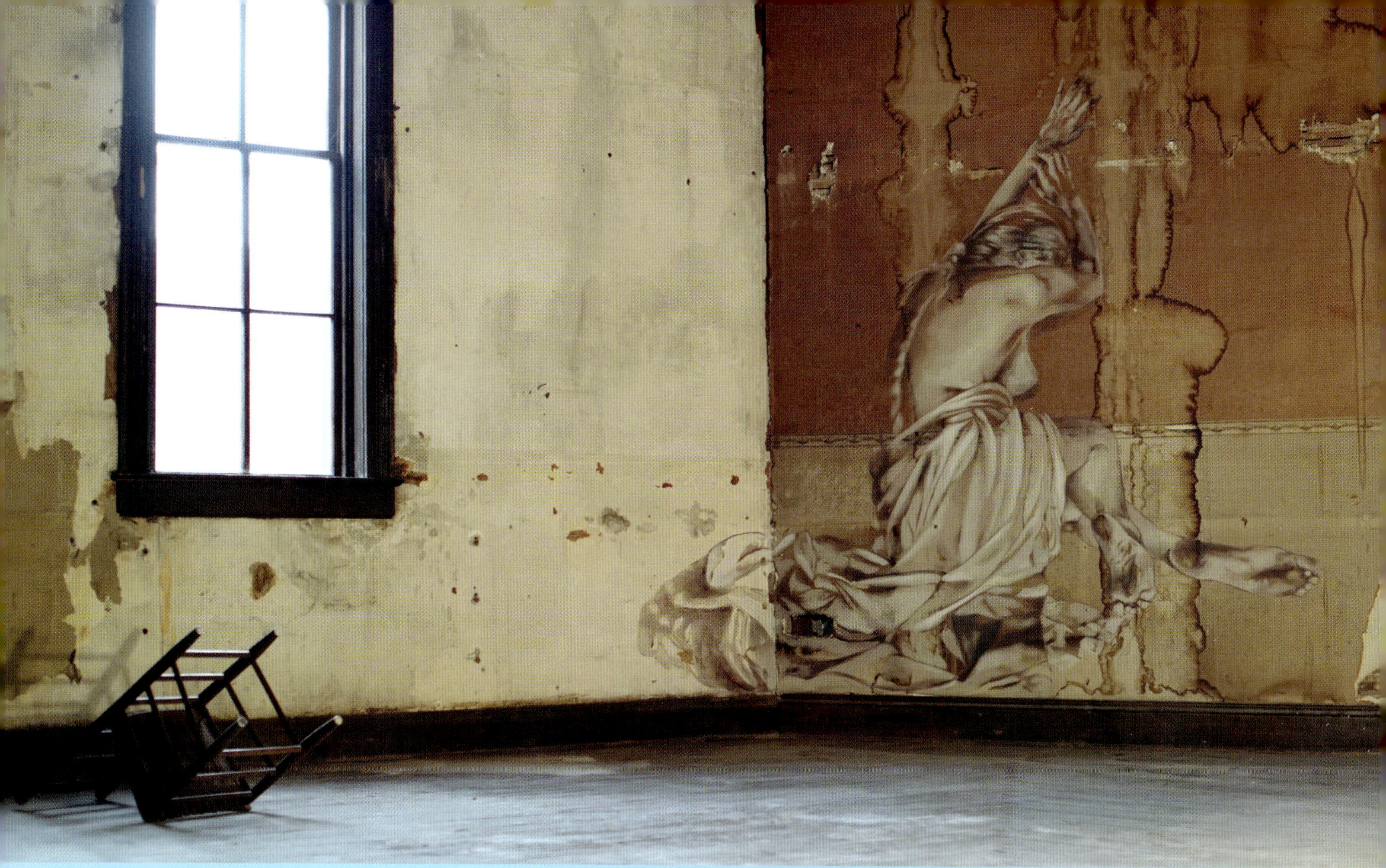

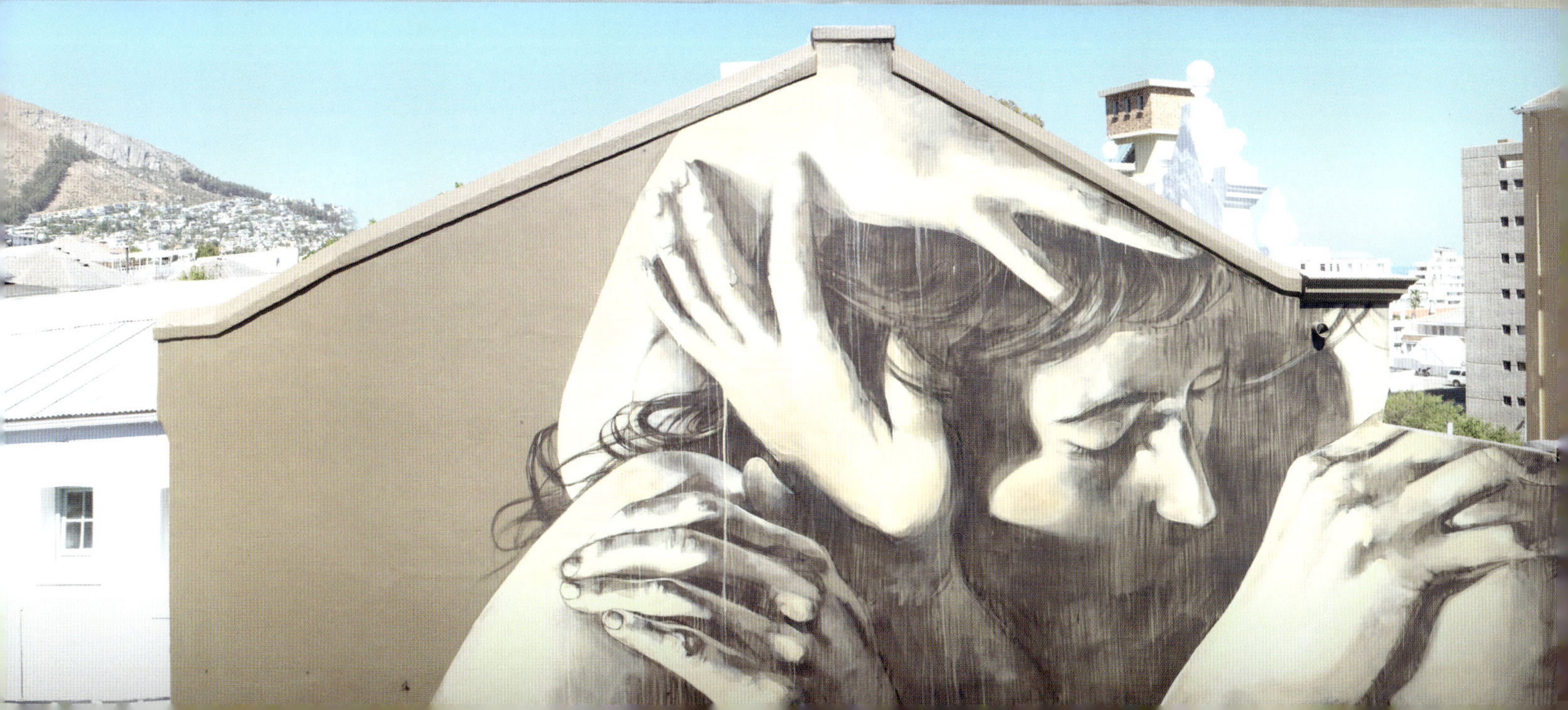

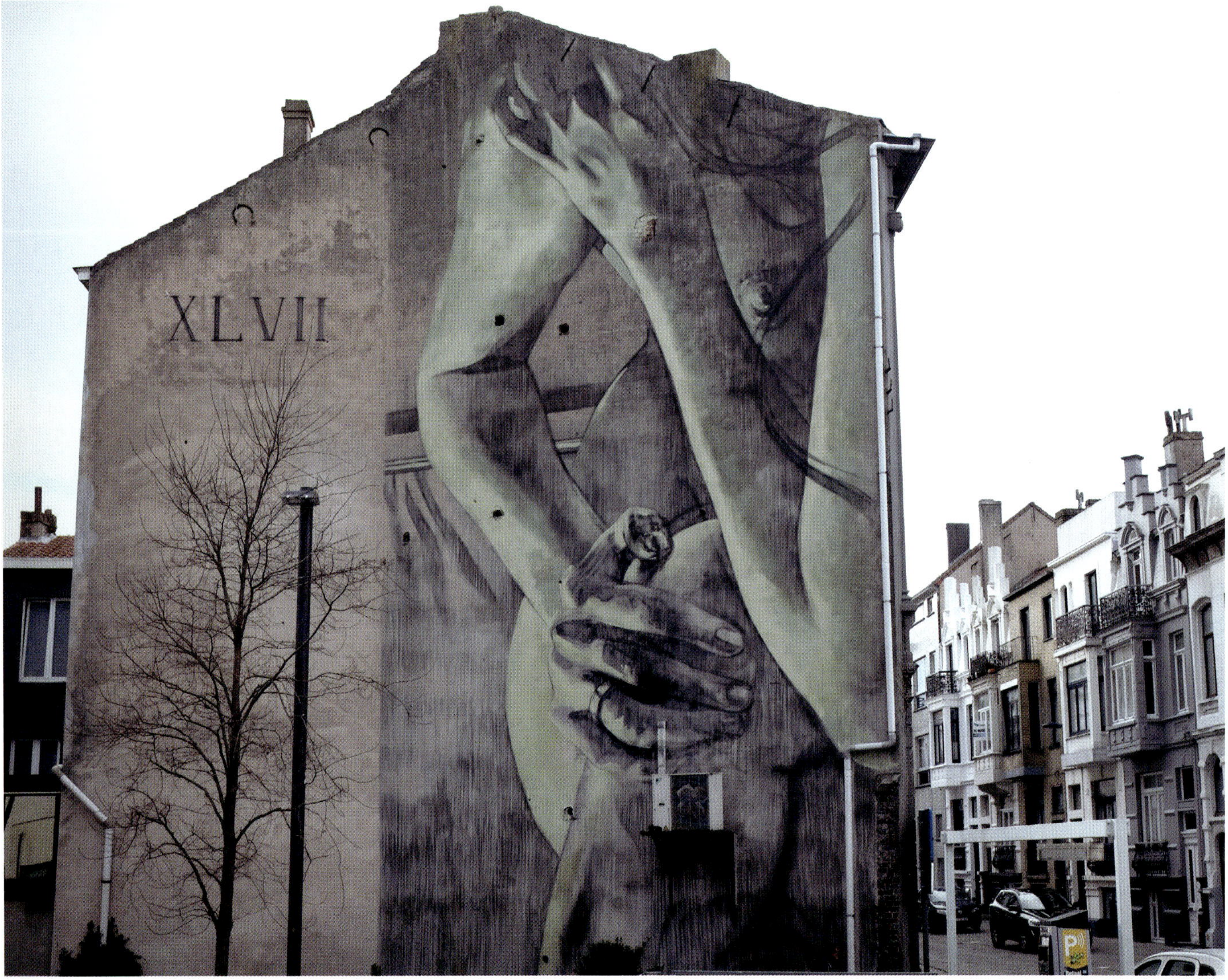

1430–1350 BCE, Belgium.
Photo: Faith XLVII

The subjugation of the feminine is an integral part of the religious patriarchy, which is part of the inherited colonial legacy. By eradicating, raping, and pillaging all the deep wealth and wisdoms from traditional cultures. We have lost vital understanding about what it means to be human. I do believe that balancing our feminine and masculine energies and rethinking our roles is a way in which to heal. This is also linked to sustainable ways of living on the earth and in seeing the ecosystems as part of us.

Art is reflective of its time. Whether it's intentional or not, I think that the artistic community mirrors the consciousness of the age it is born in. Aesthetics, space, and environment are all very important to me; medium is integral; and content, reflection, intuition, data, research, emotion, rawness. Being still. Being wild. All of this contributes to the final sounds uttered.

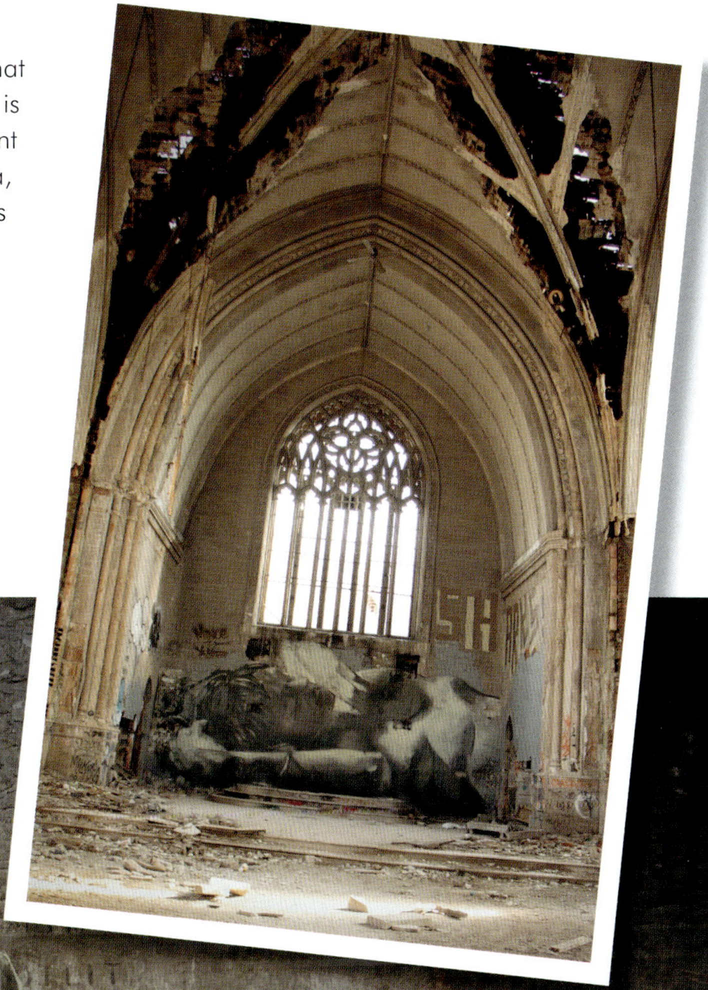

315–307 BCE, Detroit, USA. Photo: Faith XLVII

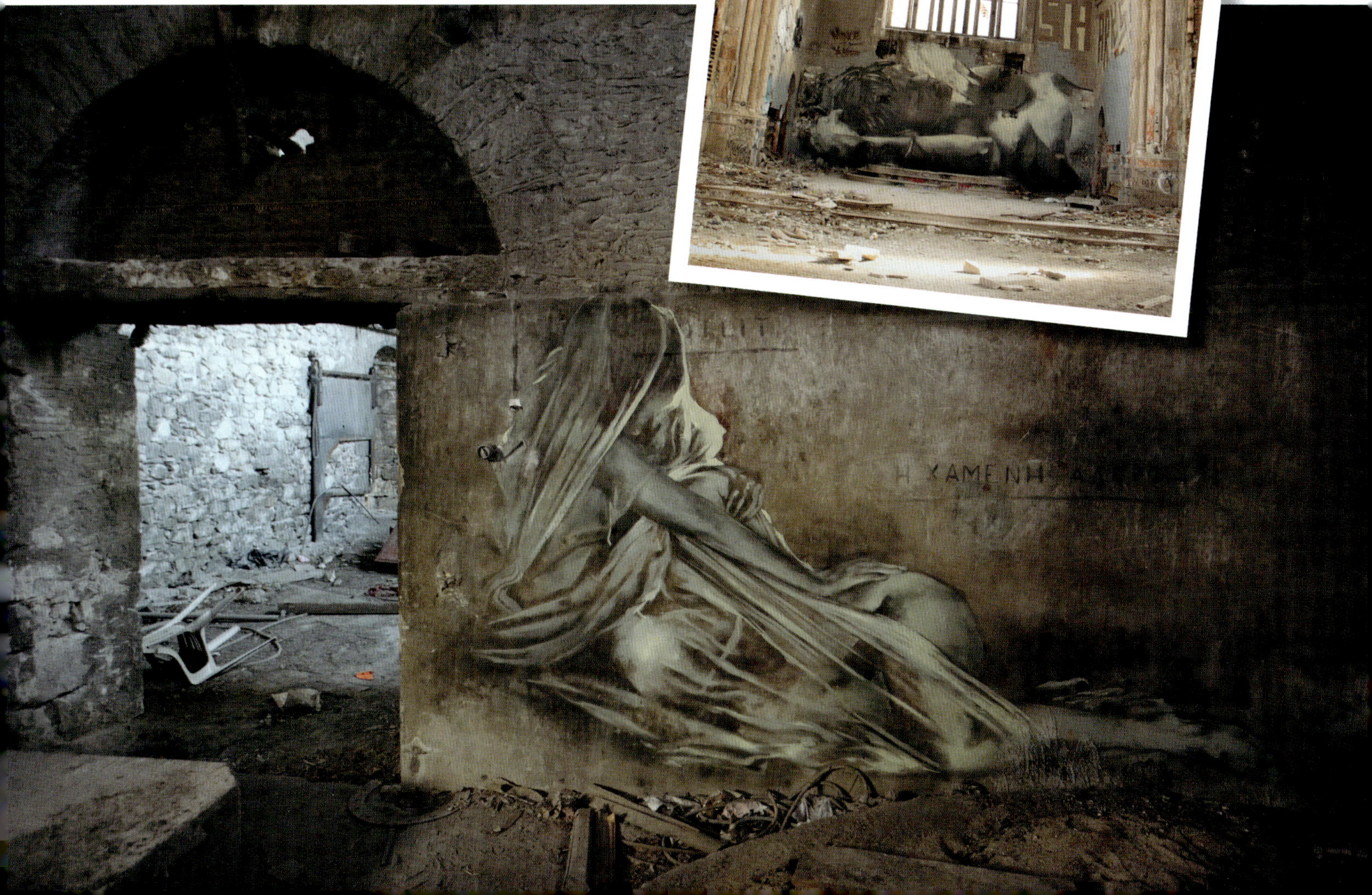

580–265 BCE, Athens, Greece.
Photo: Zane Meyer, Chop 'em Down Films

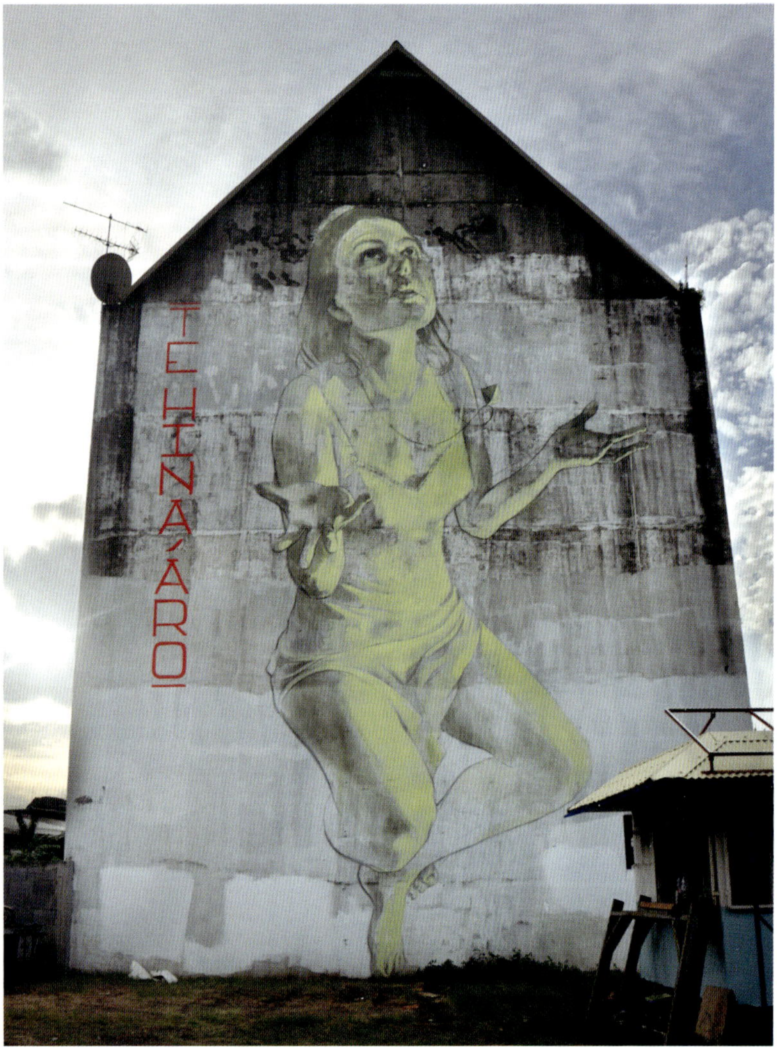

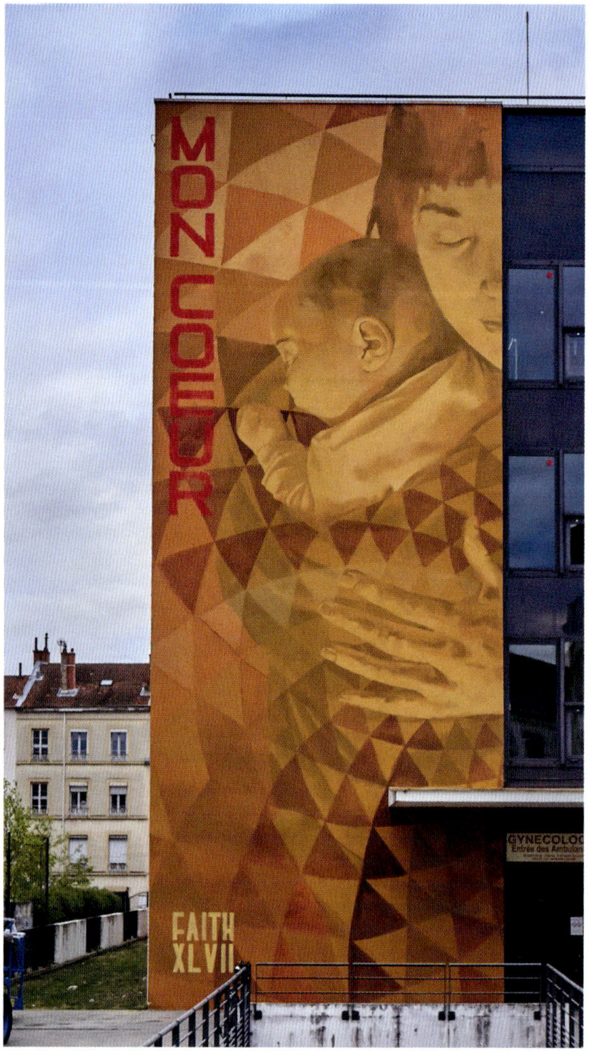

I love the conversation between my work and the environment around it. I am interested in the contribution of art within societies as something that can add a certain depth of thinking, feeling, reflection, appreciation to the everyday life.

Te hina'aro, Tahiti. Photo: Faith XLVII

MON COEUR, Lyon, France.
Photo: Zane Meyer, Chop 'em Down Films

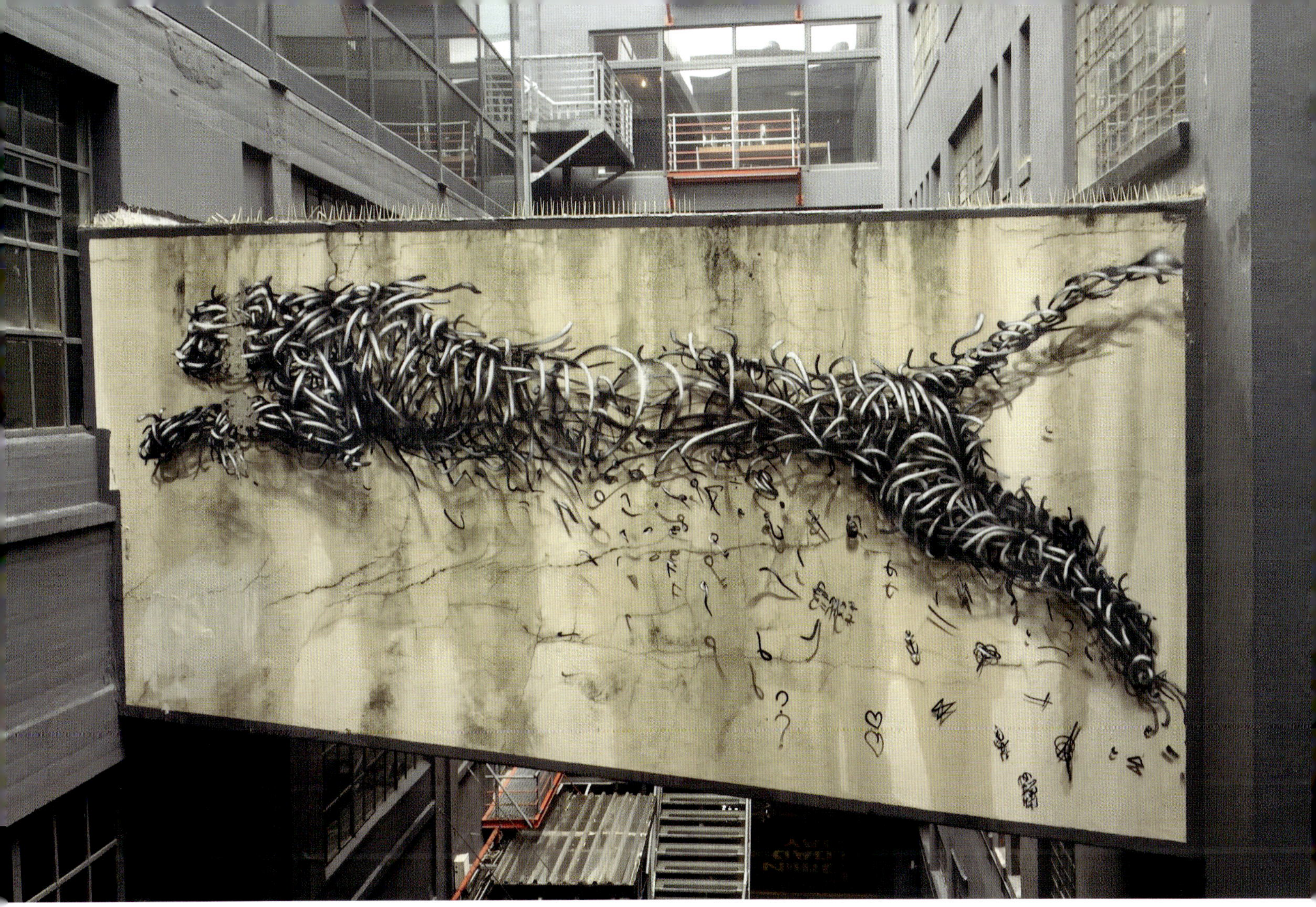

Back over the Wall in Cape Town

Faith's belief in the power of wall art and her influence can be discovered in Cape Town, like the striking works by Chinese artist DALeast, who doesn't focus on women but movement in the natural world. DALeast was born in Wuhan, China, and has painted his unique animal walls throughout the world.

DALeast's strip-art technique creates a unique 3-D effect, like this leaping leopard that seems to be made of intertwining metal or paper strips. This work spans two wings of a Woodstock arts and media center that is part of Cape Town's gentrification of the neighborhoods by the port. In the Woodstock neighborhood there are also anonymous portraits of women on the wall that reflect the culture and place of Cape Town.

DALeast is a Chinese artist who found a home in Cape Town for his dynamic interpretations of animals in motion. Photo: John Harris

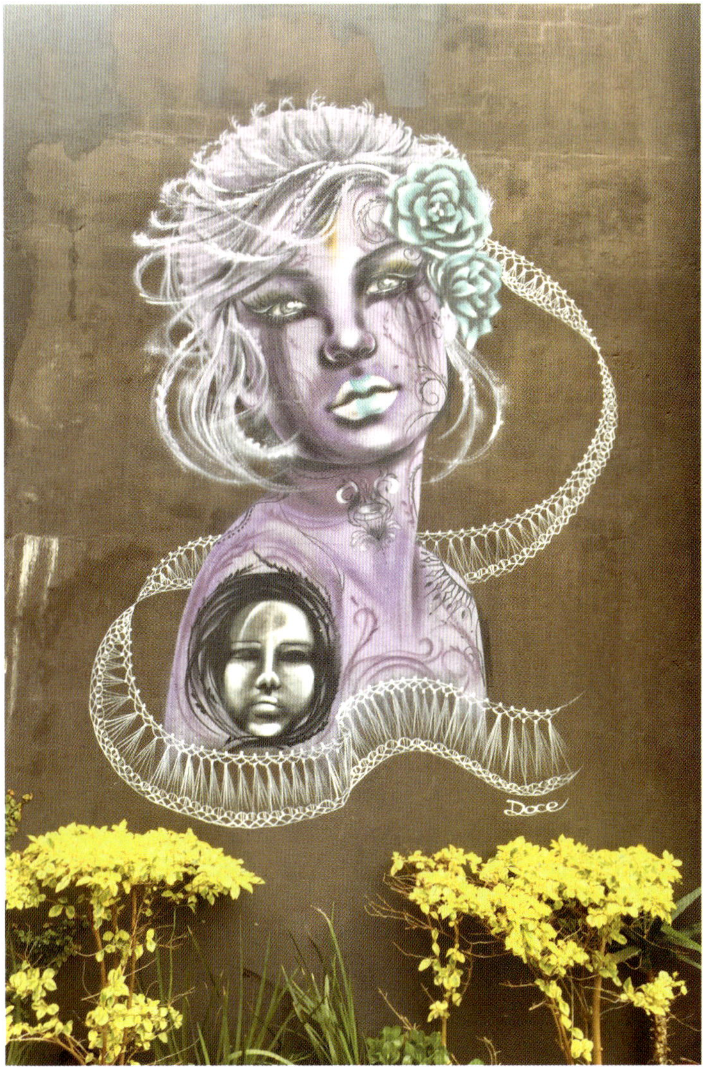

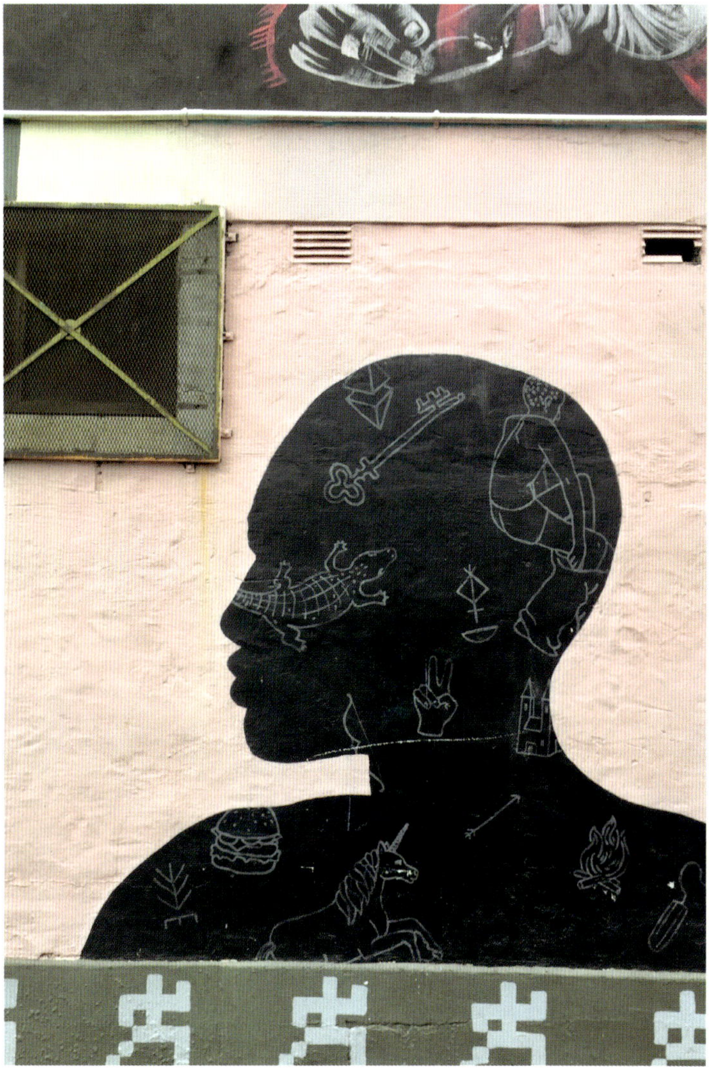

The neighborhood, which is now a well-known street arts district, has become something of a gathering point for budding artists who are using walls and even small homes to practice their skills, while corporations have turned to wall art as a bonding experience.

The walls in Woodstock feature African women and reflect the multicultural side of Cape Town. Photos: John Harris

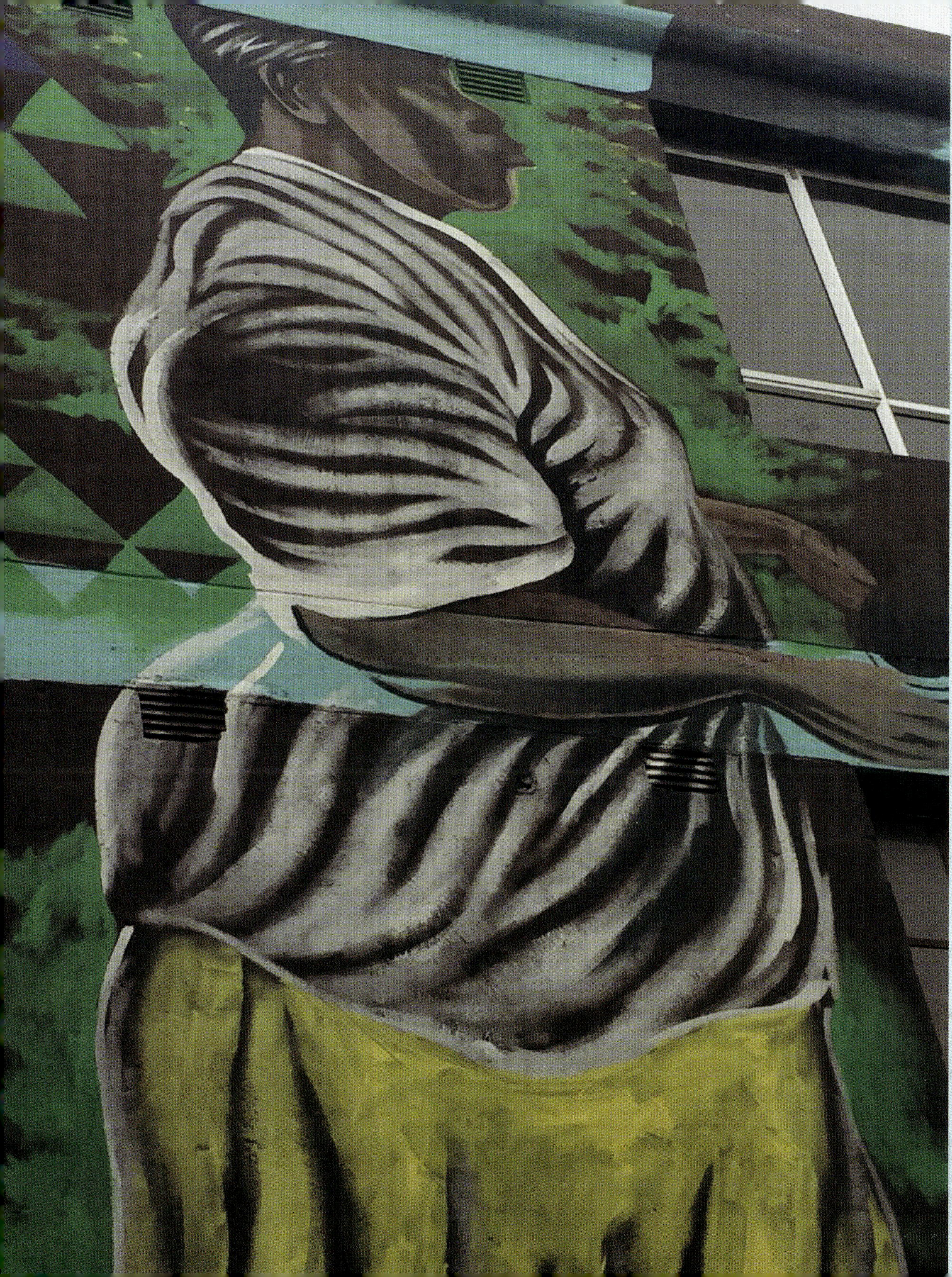

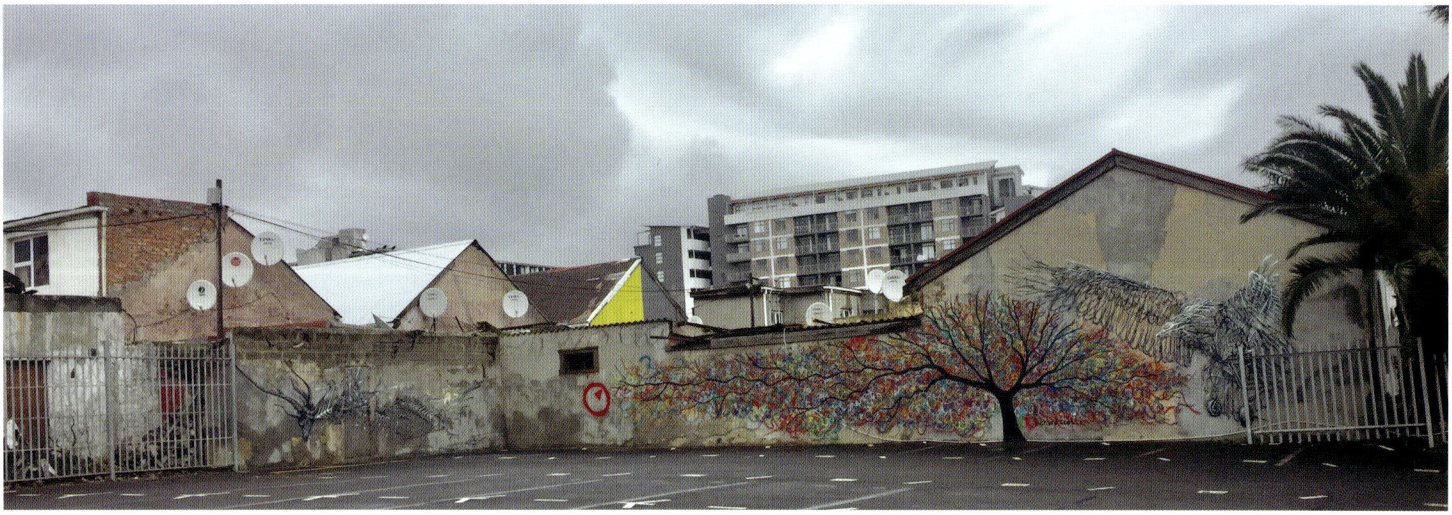

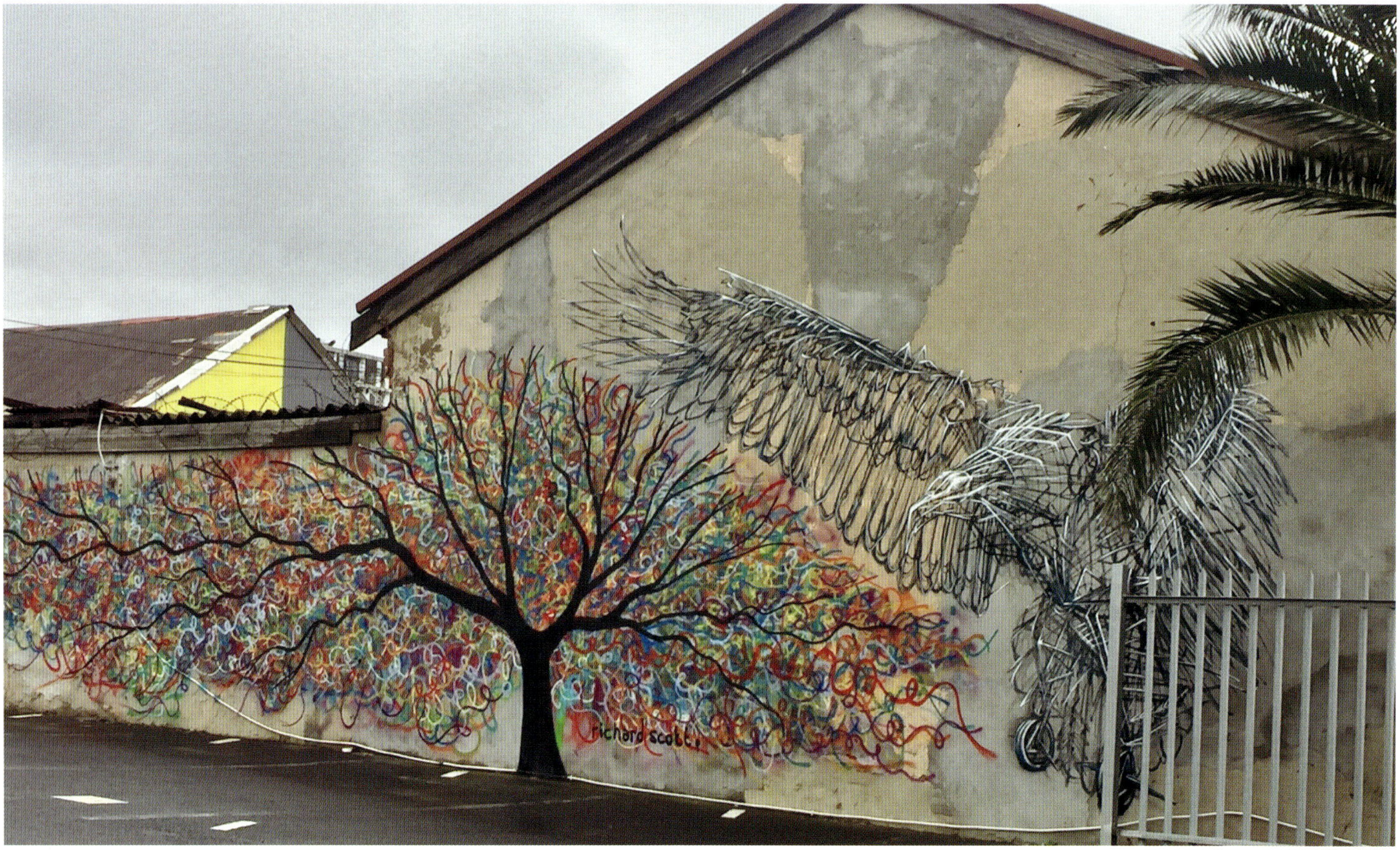
richard scott

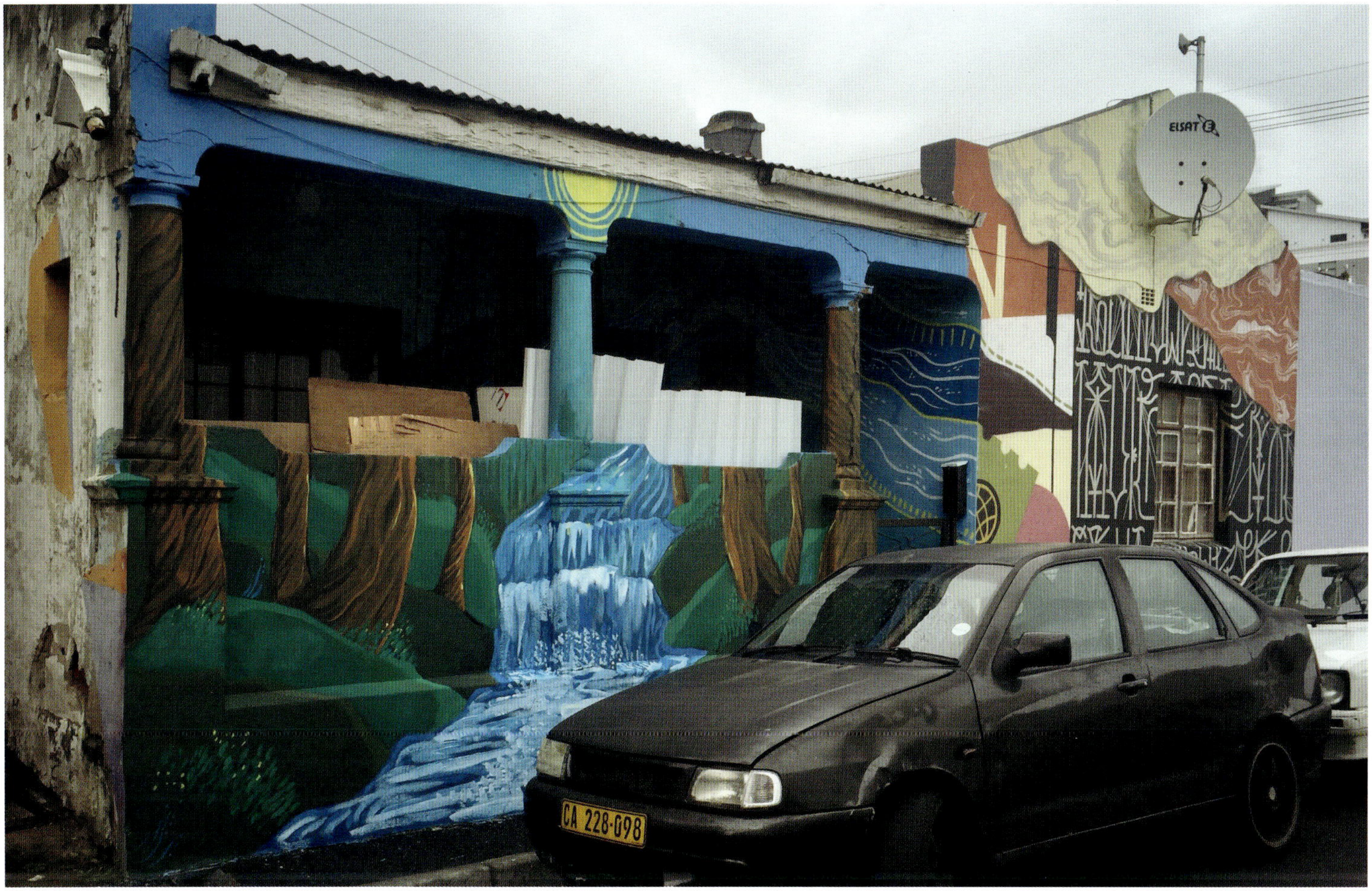

DALeast's eagle spreads its wings next to a rainbow tree, which was the result of a corporate team-building exercise. Photos: John Harris

A small home next to the neighborhood mosque becomes a canvas for a Finnish woman street artist who is using trompe-l'oeil techniques to create a woodland scene. Photo: John Harris

Cape Town's wall art is being preserved on rundown buildings in what used to be one of the most dangerous areas of the city, which is dominated by the Sulaimania Masjid mosque on Williams Street. Not only are there street art tours, but the neighborhood is also home to the International Public Art Festival, where twenty local and international street artists will be painting murals this year.

While LA and Paris attract the stars of the wall art scene, in Cape Town you'll find a world that still shines with raw possibility and energy. If you look at the young South African street artists, wall art is a passion that is not fueled by money, because, with rare exception, wall artists can't make a living at it.

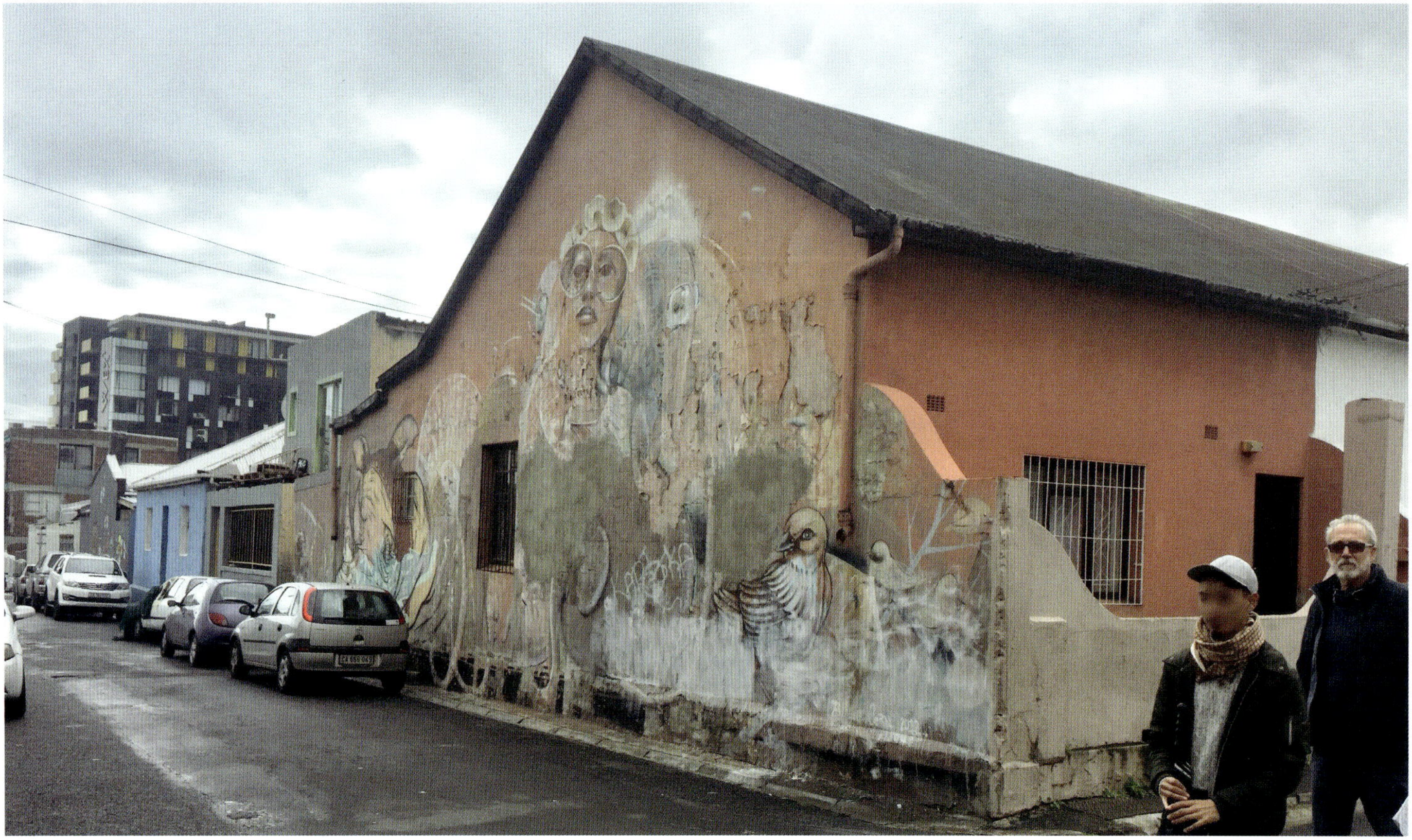

As told by the street art guide, this unfinished mural was a present to Faith47. Photos: John Harris

Even some well-known wall artists who have made a name for themselves on social media are not getting rich. Angel Wings painter Colette Miller, for example, sells some of her work online, but her vision remains hers, and the brand she has built does not go to the highest bidder. Her interactive pieces have an element of fun in them, which is not lost on anyone who stands in front of her oversized wings. The proceeds of some of her work go to charities. But there are some artists who have broken through the hand-to-mouth barrier through their art because they have created a famous brand and make news that now travels very fast on the internet.

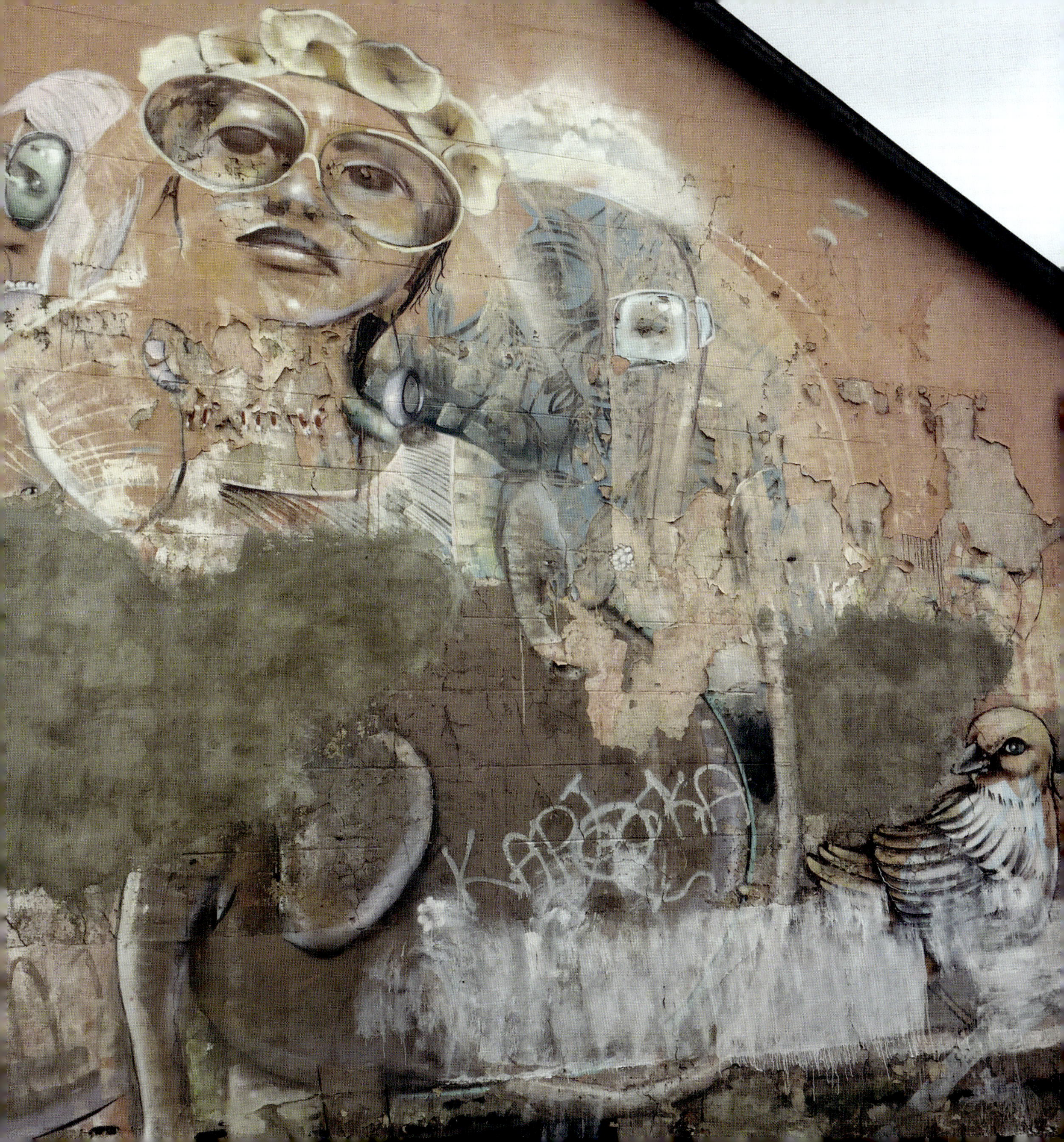

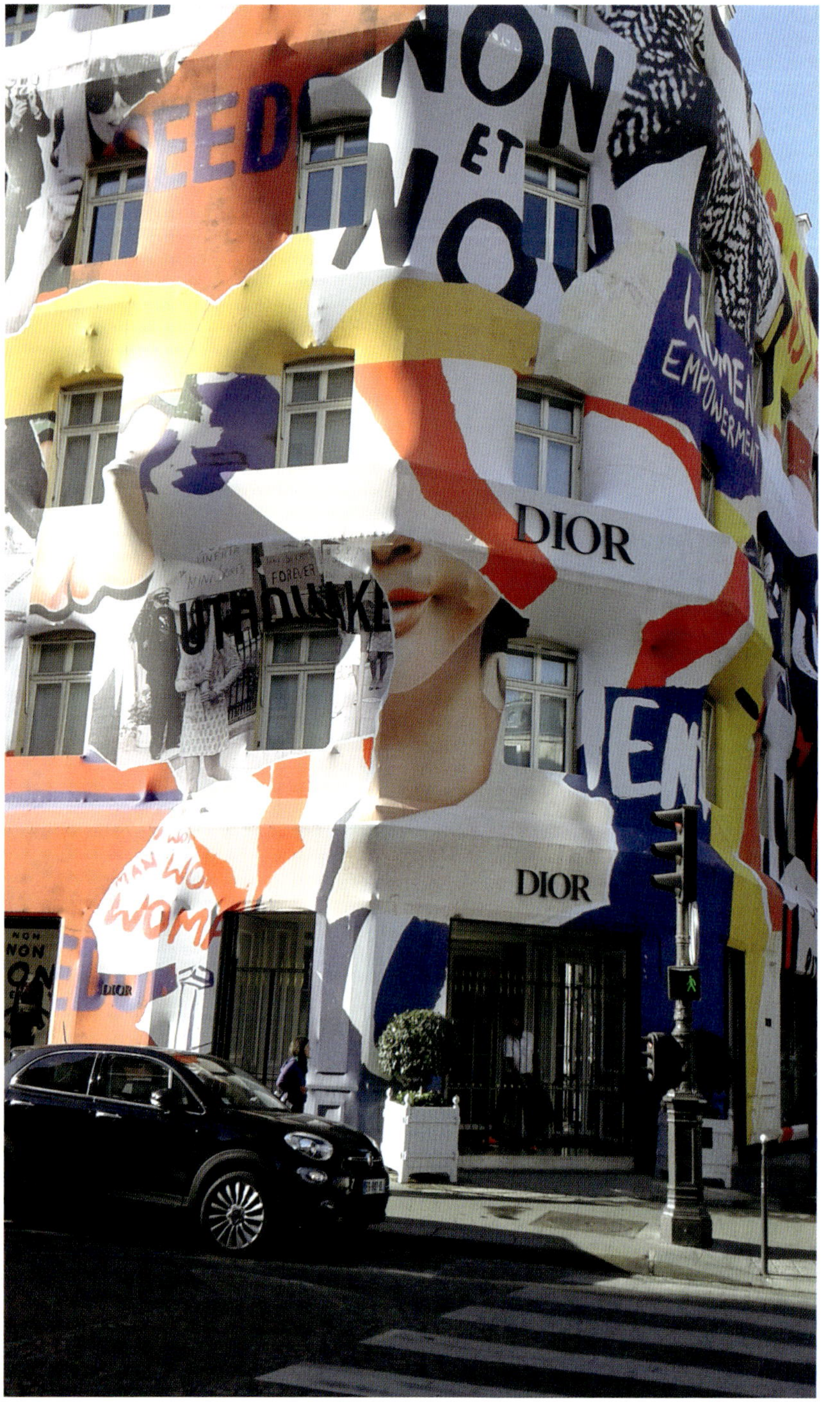

BIG NAMES, BIG DOLLARS:
Street Art as Business

The transition from the early subway taggers to the "star" street artists has been gradual and has gained momentum largely because of social media, which is driving the commercial machinery that often trades on artist street cred. If you plug in the name of a street artist on Google, chances are you'll be directed to websites that sell reproductions of street art suitable for framing. Some street artists have also picked up the pen—biographies often trace their humble beginnings and hard-won ascent into the celestial kingdom of success and recognition. Luxury brands such as Gucci have hired street artists to be part of ad campaigns, while other big-name companies like Mercedes got into legal hot water for using a piece of street art by Adrian Faulkner (a.k.a. Smash 137) as a backdrop at a Detroit parking garage to promote a car. The photo triggered a copyright lawsuit that was later settled.

Brands like Dior in Paris have been incorporating street art into their outdoor marketing. This outdoor ad on the Dior building in Paris features a woman and the words "Women Empowerment" framed by shapes and colors reminiscent of Catalan artist Joan Miró. The theme of women empowerment has recently been adopted in Dior's corporate ethos and brand, and the building advertisement borrows from wall art to emphasize its message.

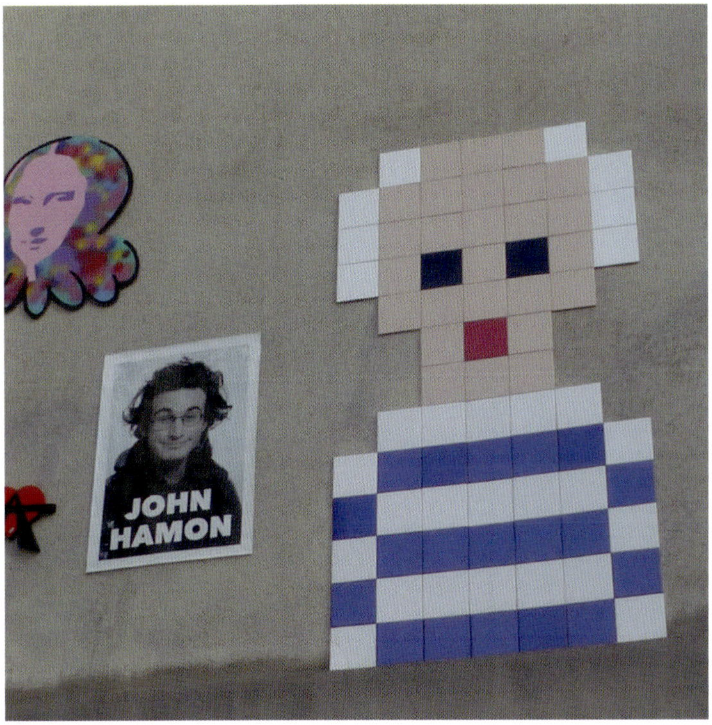

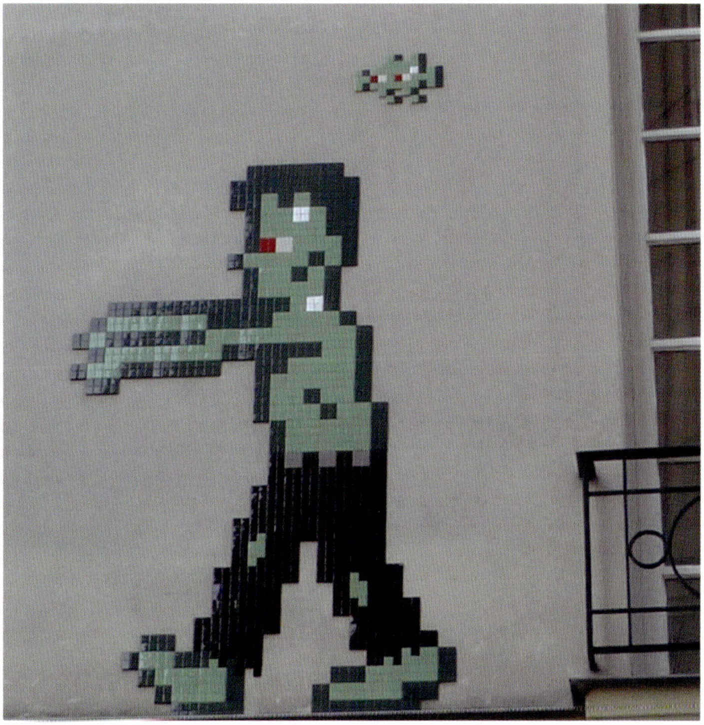

The contextualization of street art as a commodity is best illustrated by Banksy, who has taken his art into the realm of absurdity with his self-shredding painting that sold at auction for $1.4 million. Despite his fame and wealth, Banksy still works in the shadows, stenciling his arch, anti-authoritarian views while protecting his identity. Local governments have gone to great lengths to protect their Banksy wall art, even erecting a Plexiglass barrier around one wall. And some businesses are cashing in on his reputation. The public can now buy custom-cut stencils from a UK company that replicates Banksy's work, so you can practice being Banksy on your wall of choice.

Shepard Fairey is another wall artist who is doing well financially. Launched into the international spotlight with his *Hope* poster to support the election of President Barack Obama, Fairey used his considerable commercial and graphic art skills to create an iconic image of then candidate Obama based on a photo by the Associated Press, which resulted in a copyright lawsuit settled out of court.

Invader's work is found all over Paris, including his humorous digital Frankenstein.

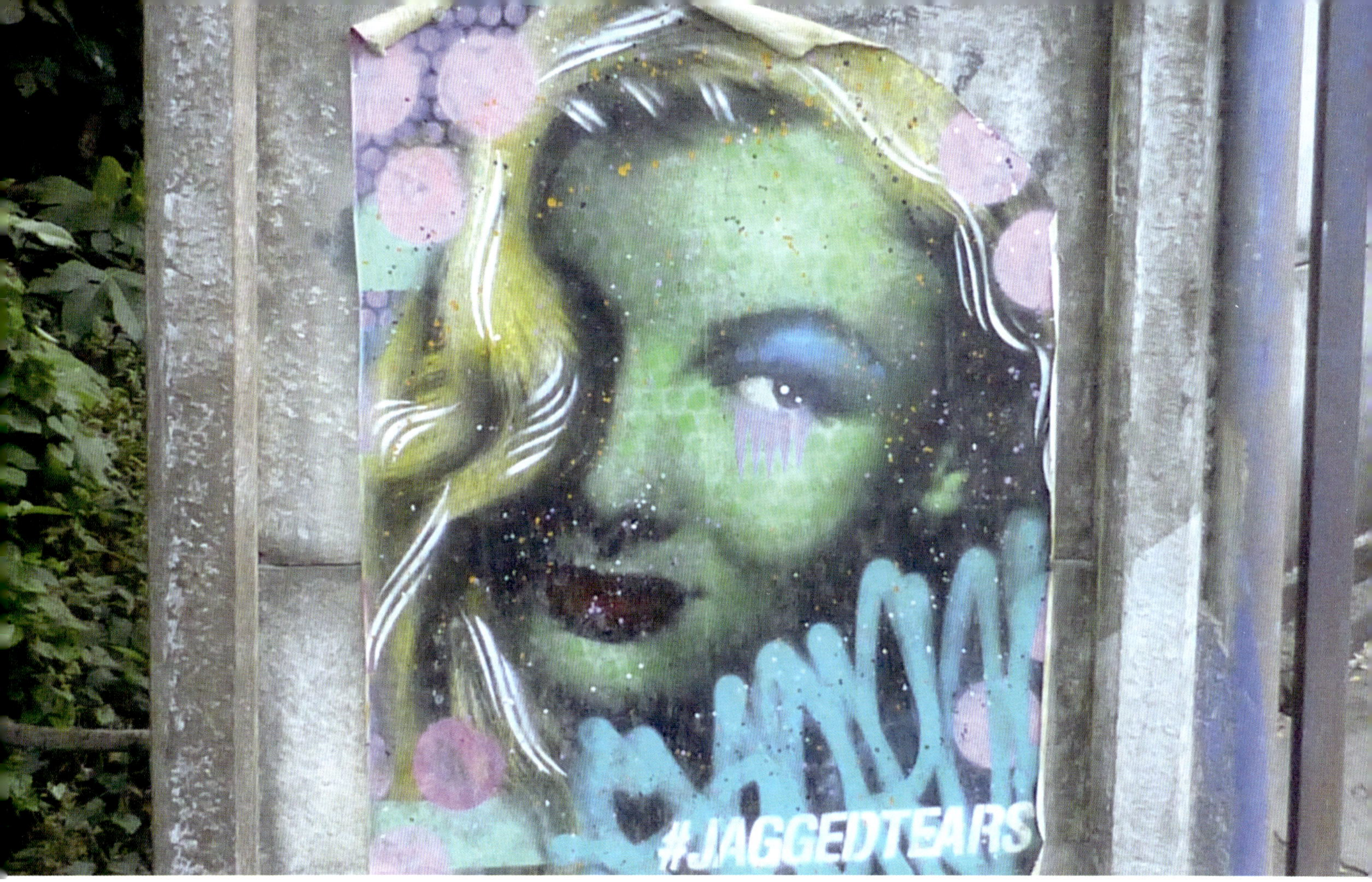

Even in the narrow, unpoliced streets of big urban areas, street artists can perform acts of defiance and still make money of their brand of art. For example, the works of Invader can be found throughout Paris. He works in small teams to install his mosaics. The team invades a public space and affixes their mosaic creations without permission, using cement and glues. Invader conceals his identity with a mask and cheekily calls himself an Unidentified Free Artist (UFA). Invader's work is commanding high prices to finance his clandestine street art and promote his brand. On his online store, Invader was selling one of his pieces for 3,900 GBP, around 5,100 USD. Despite its dubious legality, Invader's work can be viewed throughout inner Paris, which has become his de facto outdoor gallery; city law enforcement has not touched Invader's pieces, but some thieves have stolen them.

There are no billionaire street artists, as far as the authors know. But there are certainly multimillionaires, which raises the question of whether street art credibility goes down when the till starts filling up. One list of the world's richest street artists compiled back in 2014 included Banksy ($20 million), Shepard Fairey ($15 million), Retna ($5 million), Mr. Brainwash ($10 million), and David Choe at a whopping $200 million, because he was paid in Facebook shares to paint a mural at the then start-up company.[1] Not a woman among the top five, yet.

> Clearly, wall art has become big business. Museums hang paintings by wall artists, and galleries are featuring wall art prints as prized collector's pieces, which is anathema to the wall art ethos. Or is it? This move to legitimize what was once a secretive practice is essentially what happens when the wider culture absorbs subcultures. And this is exactly what is happening to the wall art "genre." Renegade artists are now "contextualized" by the art market.

Some street artists, then, have become something like celebrities who still cultivate the image of outlaws working on the fringe of mainstream art. You won't find most street artists on talk shows, but some have agents now, which would have been unheard of fifteen years ago. The authors stumbled onto an example of this cultural and financial shift in the LA Arts District, where a well-known wall artist was starting to spray paint a large-scale mural. It was revealing to see the care he put into his mural. As he sprayed, glancing down and referencing a printout of his work, his crew was watching approvingly from the sidelines with wooden carriers full of new spray cans to give to the master artist. Normally, street artists shun the spotlight to practice their craft, but not in this case. Here was a street artist practicing his art in full daylight while a camera drone flew overhead. It was like stumbling into a movie production.

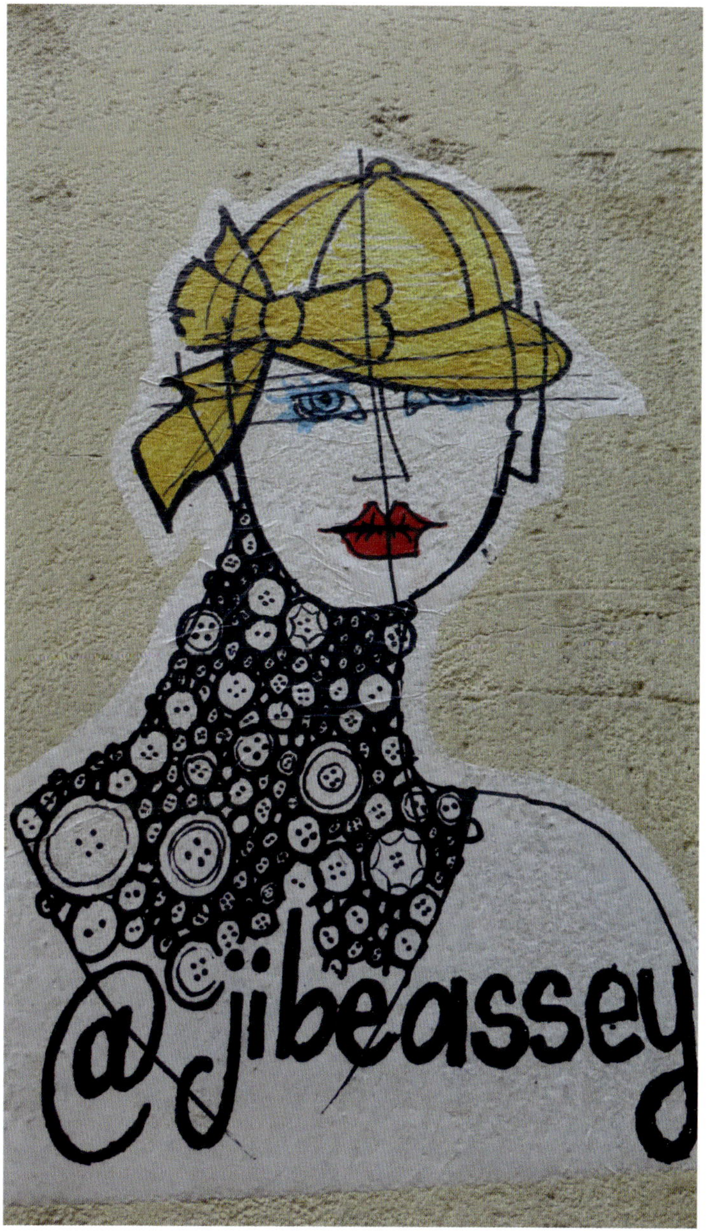

Two examples of social media tags found on wall art of women from Santa Teresa, Costa Rica, by #Jagged Tears and @jibeassey in Paris

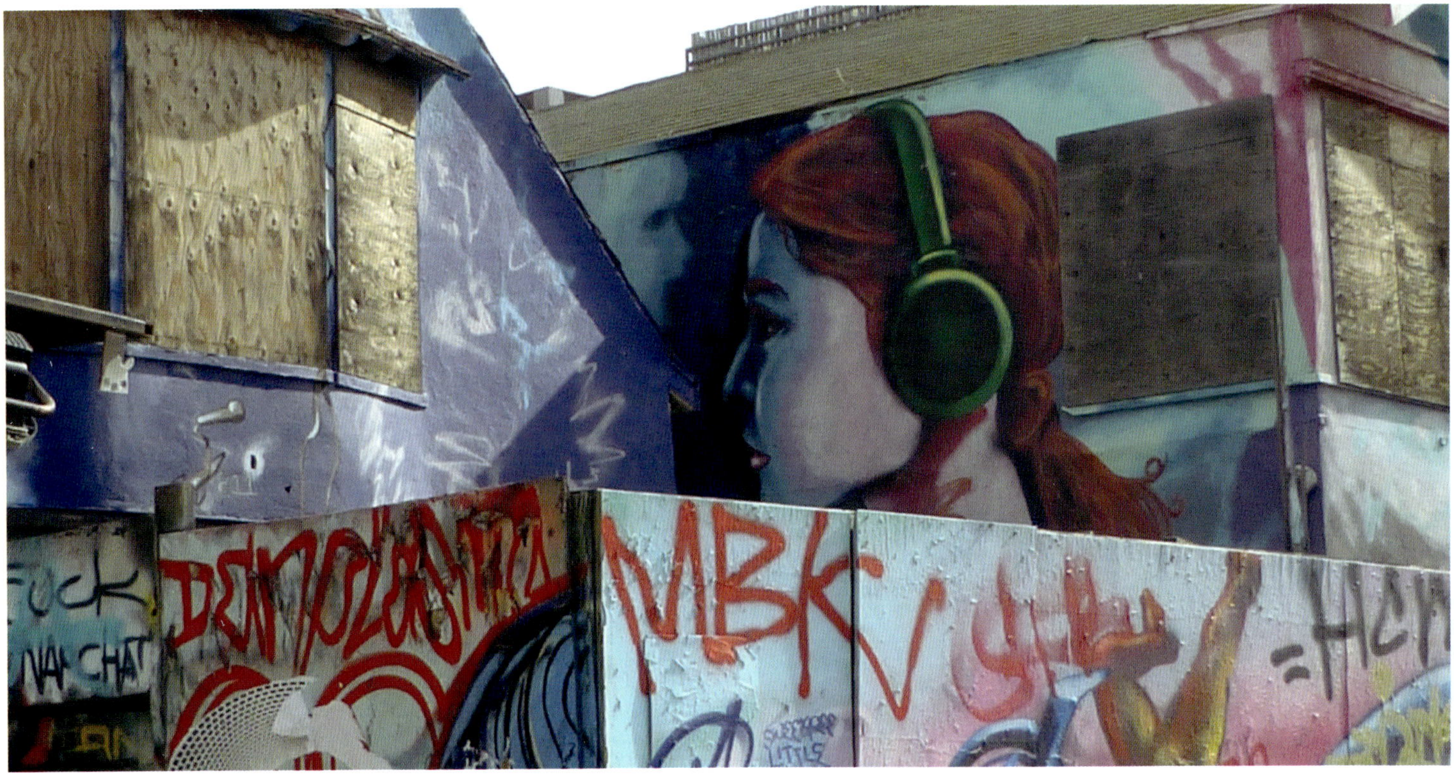

In the case of getting interviews for this book, it was not uncommon for the authors to contact artists' agents and be told that they were too busy to answer a few questions about why they paint women on the walls. In some cases, the more well known the artist, the harder it was to get twenty minutes of their time to explain the ideas behind their wall art of women. Not all of the artists were elusive. Well-known street artists, like those featured in this book, were freely available and willing to be interviewed, despite a project that was in its early stages.

One thing is certain: social media is the digital megaphone amplifying street artists and their work. Absent an agent, Instagram, Pinterest, and Facebook are used by budding wall artists to develop a following and profile. The reality is that the financial rewards of painting women on walls are elusive for most wall artists. The vast majority of the artists live on the side of the fence where getting paid for your passion is out of reach. Some street artists can barely afford paint, while a small group of well-known artists are making money off their vision. A few are successful entrepreneurs, such as Shepard Fairey, whose clothing brand Obey has earned him money and acclaim for street wear based on his social activism.

Street art of women now occupies an interesting space between commercial acceptability and the struggle that first defined it as an outlaw game of hide-and-seek with the police. As Vhils pointed out in his interview, there is a place for entrepreneurship in street art as long as it includes what he calls "social

Venice Beach, artist unknown

responsibility." An example of what Vhils is talking about is found in Paris, where a neighborhood of faceless apartment blocks in the Thirteenth Arrondissement is now a massive outdoor mural gallery used to give a neighborhood pride of place and recognition on the street art map. The move raised the profile of the neighborhood internationally, judging from the articles that feature its murals.

Few would disagree that street artists invest time, money, creativity, and their hard labor to create their artworks, and they should be compensated. They have to make a living like anyone else. The commissioned mural is now a means to an end for many street artists. Mural artists such as PUCHO count on his commissions to make money. The commissioned work is not a new concept. Patrons of the arts have always been in the background of some of the world's greatest artists. During the Italian Renaissance, the Medici family were great patrons of such masters as Leonardo da Vinci and Michelangelo. Today, you don't need to be a wealthy banker from Florence to commission a mural. You can commission artwork or a mural done by graffiti artists through multiple websites. Just google "commission a mural" and you'll be surprised by all the links to artists happy to make your mural a reality.

The wall artists of women featured on our tour generally honor their women subjects as symbols of power and grace, and it comes across in their art despite the Disneylandification happening with some wall art. Arts districts, like in Los Angeles, are carefully controlled environments, where painters are doing their work in broad daylight instead of sneaking around with spray cans. It is wall art as performance art in a regentrified warehouse district that used to be the sleeping quarters for bums pushing shopping cart homes. But the art of women there is striking and magnificent. In Paris, the alleyways and winding streets of the Marais District offer a more discreet canvas for women subjects, while in Costa Rica, Chile, Mexico, and Peru, wall artists often labor in obscurity on forgotten, deteriorating walls.

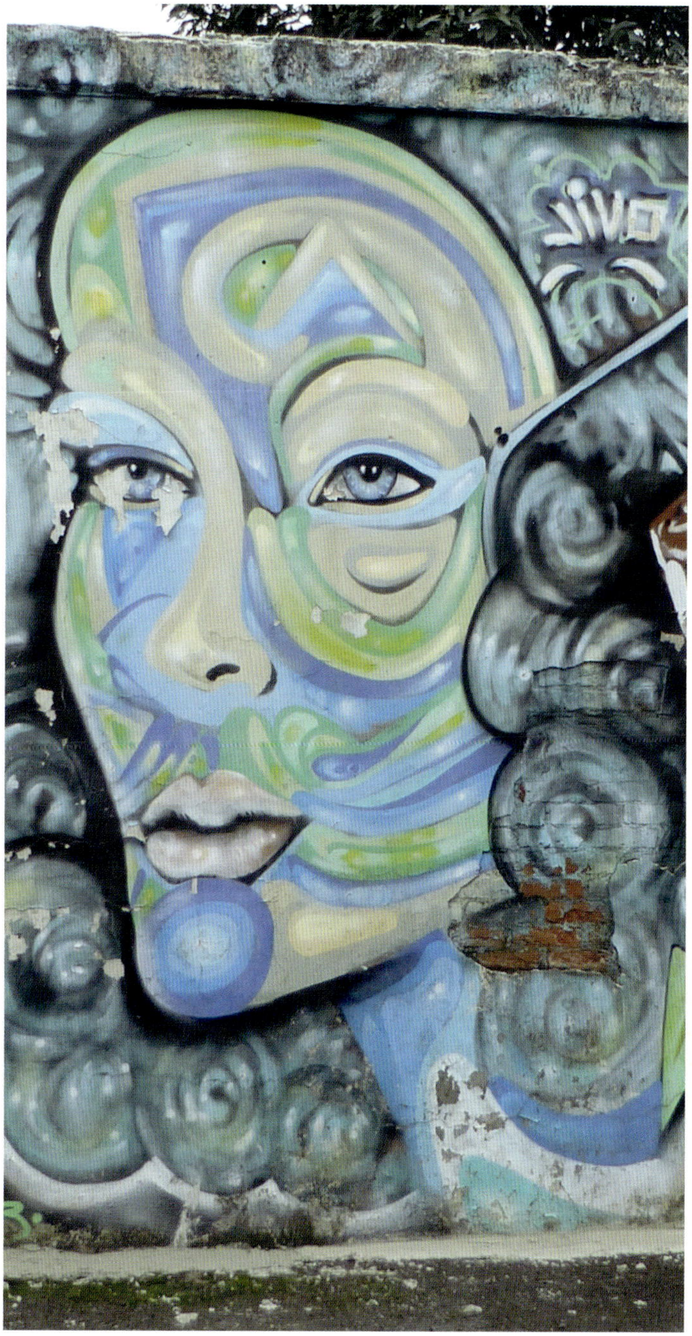

Where to from Here? Walls for Women in the Digital Age

The world of social media is redefining how wall art is regarded. Angel Wings artist Colette Miller rocketed to recognition because of social media photographs showing celebrities like Meghan Markle and Halle Berry posing in front of her wings. Even the most obscure of street artists are now signing their pieces with social media tags.

And it's not just publicity being changed by the digital world; it's also the process of making wall art of women. The Digital Mural Lab2 at the Social and Public Art Resource Center (SPARC) in Venice Beach, California, is an example of combining traditional muralism with digital-printing techniques. The lab offers courses to create digitally generated murals and experiment with "emerging technologies." The results are on display at SPARC.

SPARC's first digital image of an Indigenous Californian woman was created using an archival photo, digitizing it, and printing it by using a technique called dye sublimation, which is a computer printer that uses heat to transfer dye onto materials such as a plastic, paper, or fabric. According to Judy Baca, her collaborators are now using this same method to create digital murals 16 feet across at a 1,000 dpi resolution.

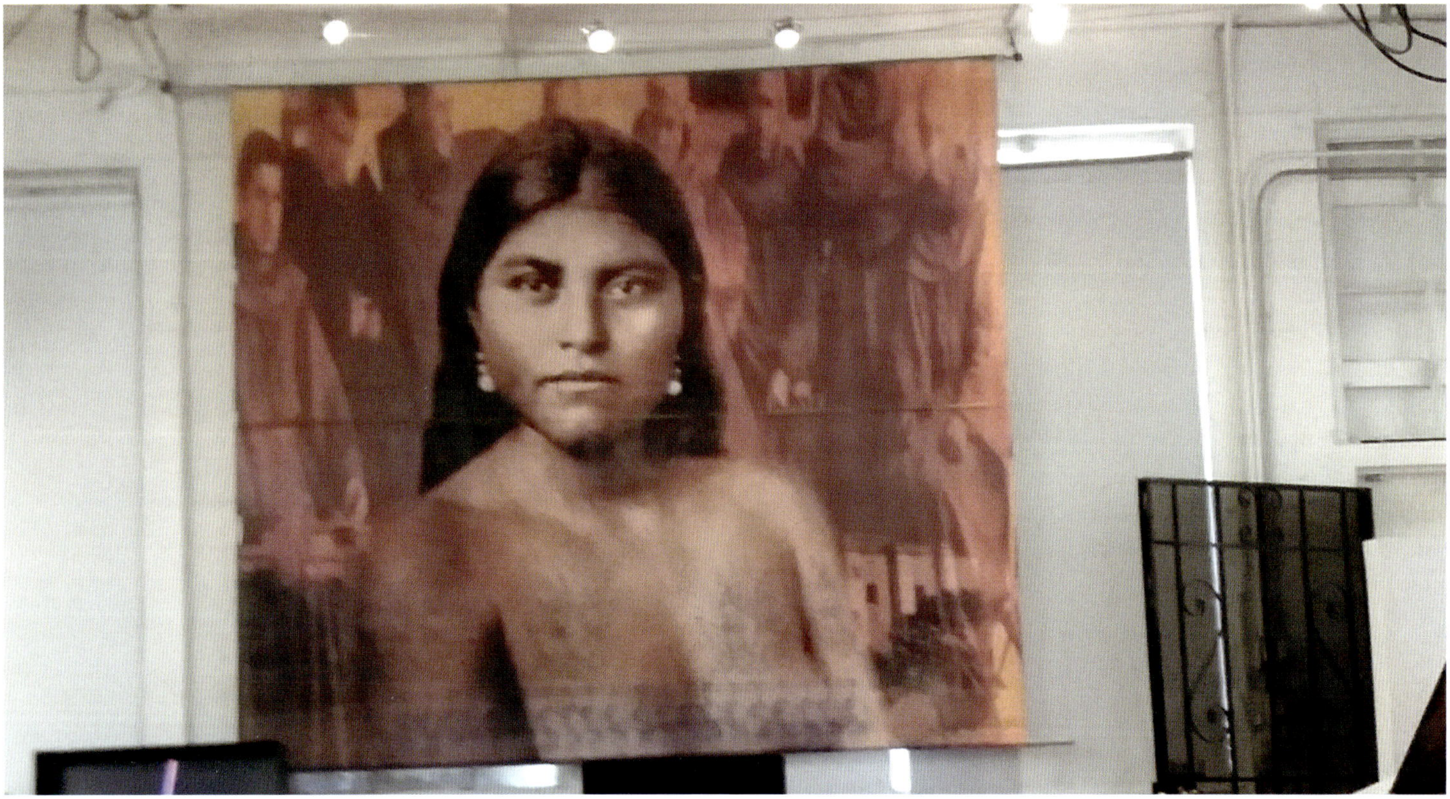

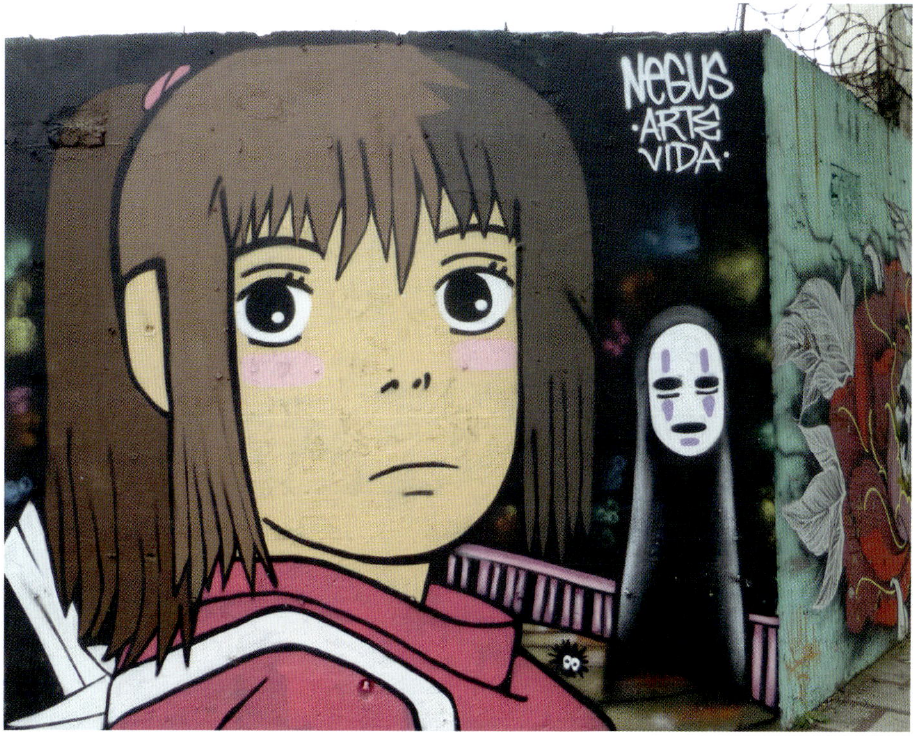

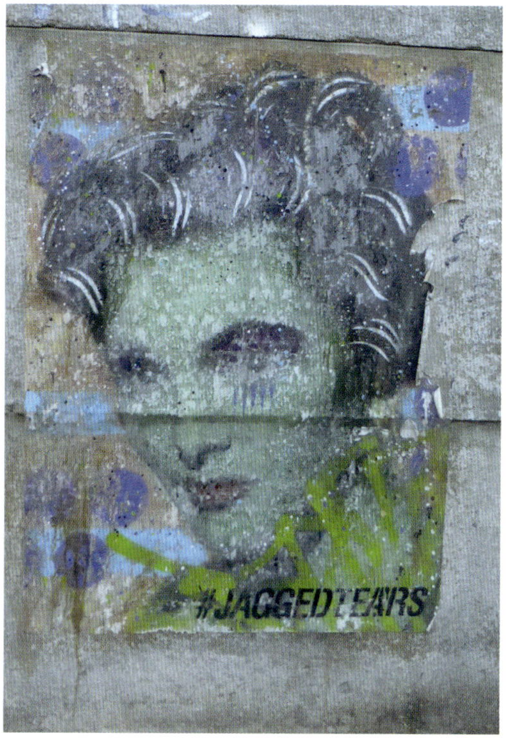

The original photo is of a Tongva Indian, one of the original inhabitants of the Los Angeles area. The photo of the woman was discovered by Judy Baca at the archives of the University of Southern California. The Tongva woman is surrounded by the ghostly images of Mission San Gabriel fathers who established their church on the Tongva lands and who tried to convert them to Christianity. The artists in the SPARC Digital Lab added the tattoos and Spanish pearl earrings to suggest the Spanish sublimation of the native Angelinos. Professor Baca thinks her facial characteristics suggest a mixture of Native American and first generation mestiza.

"It's the future and we're doing that now," Judy Baca commented during our interview. Baca also explained how one of her murals that hangs in the Denver International Airport was imprinted on a holograph-like surface of a metallic-coated surface.

No matter how it is practiced—with paint or digital printers—the wall art of women is gaining momentum in our cities and towns and is part of the social fabric uniting the world. The authors have just scratched the surface of this world, but it is our hope that we peeled back enough of that surface to pique your interest. We sincerely hope you have enjoyed the journey and will regard women on the walls with wonder. And a small piece of advice before you head out: Be sure to wear good walking shoes when you explore the alleyways of this world.

Works by Negus and Jagged Tears

NOTES

CHAPTER 1:
Welcome to the World of Women on the Walls

1 Marguerite Johnson, "The Grim Reality of the Brothels of Pompeii," *The Conversation*, 13 December 2017, accessed 29 November 2020, https://theconversation.com/the-grim-reality-of-the-brothels-of-pompeii-88853.
2 "What Are Pompeii's Frescoes?," *Sightseeing Tours Italy*, last modified 30 November 2020, accessed 30 November 2020, https://www.pompeiitours.it/blog/what-are-pompeiis-frescoes/.

CHAPTER 2:
Los Angeles and Celebrity Power: The Real Deal in a Land of Make-Believe

1 "Indigenous Peoples," Wikipedia, last modified 30 November 2020, accessed 30 November 2020, https://en.wikipedia.org/wiki/Indigenous_peoples.
2 "California Missions," History.com editors, last modified 21 August 2018, accessed 29 November 2020, https://www.history.com/topics/religion/california-missions.
3 "Treaty of Guadalupe Hidalgo," History.com editors, last modified 28 September 2020, accessed 29 November 2020, https://www.history.com/topics/mexican-american-war/treaty-of-guadalupe-hidalgo.
4 "Arts District, Los Angeles," Wikipedia, last modified 14 November 2020, accessed 29 November 2020, https://en.wikipedia.org/wiki/Arts_District,_Los_Angeles.
5 SPARC — Social and Public ART Resource Centre, accessed 29 November 2020, https://sparcinla.org/.
6 "Great Wall of Los Angeles," Wikipedia, last modified 20 November 2020, accessed 1 December 2020, https://en.wikipedia.org/wiki/Great_Wall_of_Los_Angeles.

CHAPTER 3:
New World Artists: Mexican Monumentalism and Animism

1 Daves Roos, "Human Sacrifice: Why the Aztecs Practiced This Gory Ritual," *History*, 11 October 2011, accessed 29 November 2020, https://www.history.com/news/aztec-human-sacrifice-religion.
2 Carly Miller, "Skulls Analyzed from the Maya Sacred Cenote Show That Human Sacrifices Were Sourced from Far and Wide across Mexico," *Forbes Magazine*, 9 August 2019, accessed 29 November 2020, https://www.forbes.com/sites/carly-miller/2019/08/09/skulls-analyzed-from-the-mayan-sacred-cenote-show-that-human-sacrifices-were-sourced-from-far-and-wide-across-mexico-in-1000-ad/?sh=409cd040e8b7.
3 "Mexican Muralism," Wikipedia, last modified 26 November 2020, accessed 29 November 2020, https://en.wikipedia.org/wiki/Mexican_muralism.
4 "Zapotec," Cengage, last modified 22 December 2019, accessed 29 November 2020, https://www.encyclopedia.com/history/latin-america-and-caribbean/mesoamerican-indigenous-peoples/zapotec.
5 "A Drop of Paint Can Create an Ocean of Change," PangeaSeed Foundation, accessed 29 November 2020, https://www.pangeaseed.foundation/sea-walls/.

CHAPTER 4:
Costa Rica: Land of Volcanos, Rainforests, and Local Street Cred

1 "Death of Jairo Mora Sandoval," Wikipedia, last modified 21 November 2020, accessed 29 November 2020, https://en.wikipedia.org/wiki/Death_of_Jairo_Mora_Sandoval.

CHAPTER 6:
EuroArtists: Big Walls, Big Ideas in Small Spaces

1 "Boulevard Paris 13," accessed 29 November 2020, https://boulevardparis13.com/.
2 Eddie Colla, "Bio," Eddie, accessed 29 November 2020, https://www.eddiecolla.com/pages/bio.

3 "The Life and Death of Sicilian Anti-Mafia Judge Paolo Borsellino," *The Local*, last modified 19 July 2020, accessed 29 November 2020, https://www.thelocal.it/20180719/italy-commemorates-via-damelio-paolo-borsellino-mafia-massacre-26-years-on.

CHAPTER 7:
Climbing over the Wall from Obscurity to Recognition: Faith XLVII's Journey from South Africa to LA

1 Maximilian Braun, "5 Wealthiest Street Artists Who Know How to Earn Their Living," *WIDEWALLS*, 1 March 2014, accessed 29 November 2020, https://www.widewalls.ch/

magazine/5-wealthiest-street-artists.
"About the Digital Mural Lab," SPARC Digital Mural Lab, accessed 29 November 2020, http://digitalmurallab.com/dml/about-the-dml/.

ARTIST INFORMATION

What follows is more information on the artists who feature in *Women on the Walls*. Included are web addresses that at the time of this writing were current; however, some may have changed since publication. Also listed are books about the wall artists.

CHAPTER 1: Welcome to the World of Women on the Walls

Jovial, the Hula-Hooper. Stencil artist whose work was photographed on sidewalk in Venice Beach, California. More information: https://www.instagram.com/jovialstreet/?hl=en.

Sobr, the Paris fan dancer. The French artist whose *Time to Dance* paste-up posters in Paris and Berlin are based on photographs of dancers at European rave parties. Sobr told an interviewer that the yellow tape in the work is inspired by the repetitive rhythms of techno music, although it resembles police tape at crime scenes. More information: http://www.paristreetart.com/2014/10/its-time-to-dance-project-by-sobr.html; https://www.iheartberlin.de/2016/01/28/following-the-dancing-street-art-girls-in-berlin/.

Loretto, The Dominatrixes. Loretto is a London-based wall artist who uses a spray-and-stencil technique to lampoon those in power. His identity is unknown. More information: https://www.graffikgallery.co.uk/collections/loretto#.

Rip Cronk, Venus on Venice Beach building wall. Cronk's arch work can be found throughout this Southern California beachside community known for its wall art. This work is a boardwalk landmark that was painted in 1989. More information: https://www.visitveniceca.com/2014/05/31/rip-cronk-venice-artist/.

CHAPTER 2: Los Angeles and Celebrity Power: The Real Deal in a Land of Make-Believe

Royyal Dog, LA women in traditional Korean robes. Royyal Dog is a South Korean street artist (given name is Chris Changyang Shim) known for painting women in traditional Korean robes called *hanbok* to reflect the cultural diversity of LA. More information: https://en.wikipedia.org/wiki/Royyal_Dog.

Christina Angelina, *Her eyes are like emotional sensors*. Also known as Starfighter, Angelina collaborated with other artists for her work in the LA Arts District. More information: https://en.wikipedia.org/wiki/Christina_Angelina.

Tristan Eaton, A well-known creator of toys who employs a multilayered and colored approach to murals and paintings. Tristan Eaton is an easily recognized LA street artist whose work also hangs in the Museum of Modern Art (MOMA) in New York. More information: https://tristaneaton.com/about; https://thehundreds.com/blogs/content/the-life-and-times-of-tristan-eaton (interview, 2016).

Jules Muck, the green wall. The work of Jules Muck, a UK transplant, can be found in the alleyways of Venice Beach with her signature monochrome interpretations of women. More information: http://julesmuck.com/ https://en.wikipedia.org/wiki/Jules_Muck.

Syntek, a street artist who remains incognito while painting his vision of a mysterious, caped woman in LA More information: https://www.pinterest.com.au/pin/328551735311755259/.

Carley Ealey has a fondness for celestial objects combined with women. More information: https://en.wikipedia.org/wiki/Carly_Ealey.

Dr. Judy Baca, *Great Wall of Los Angeles* and co-founder of the activist Social and Public Art Resource Center (SPARC) in Venice Beach, California. Judy Baca has made a life out of social activism and promoting young wall artists, particularly women, who diverge from the cookie-cutter images of women on walls as fetishized male fantasies. Her *Great Wall of Los Angeles* mural was painted by young wall artists with a police record, who turned a storm channel into a national monument. Her digital murals are also part of SPARC's reshaping of how wall art is made. (Featured Interview)
Further reading: *Judith F. Baca* by Anna Indych-López (Minneapolis: University of Minnesota Press, 2018). More information: https://sparcinla.org/.

Erin Yoshi, *Memory to the Fallen*. Yoshi's vision of women is inspired by older women whom she portrays on walls in large-scale portraits. Her background includes politically dangerous work in Colombia, where she painted a wall dedicated to the memories of a political group targeted by the Colombian military. She continues to work in the LA area. (Featured Interview) More information: https://www.erinyoshi.com/.

Colette Miller, interactive angel wings. Founder of the Global Angel Wings project, Miller has painted her large-scale wings throughout the world to inspire all people. Her goal is to bring out the humanity in everyone. (Featured Interview) More information: https://colettemiller.com/; https://en.wikipedia.org/wiki/Colette_Miller.

Emily Winters, *Endangered Species*. A mural depicting the results of gentrification and its impact on Venice Beach's poorer residents. More information: https://sparcinla.org/projects/venice-boardwalk-mural-endangered-species-by-emily-winters-to-receive-needed-more info.

Levi Ponce, whose mural on the Venice Beach boardwalk features influential women from history. His murals are often done with the help of volunteers. More information: https://en.wikipedia.org/wiki/Levi_Ponce.

LA ARTS DISTRICT

There are many guides and organized street art tours for the LA Arts District, which can be found by browsing the internet. More-general information can be found here: https://en.wikipedia.org/wiki/Arts_District,_Los_Angeles; https://www.international-traveller.com/north-america/usa/california/los-angeles/meet-the-heroes-and-the-villains-of-the-wondrous-l-a-arts-district/.

CHAPTER 3: New World Artists: Mexican Monumentalism and Animism

Mexican Big Three: Diego Rivera, José Clemente Orozco, and David Alfaro Siqueiros have largely been acknowledged as the founders of the Mexican muralist movement, which inspired generations of wall artists from around the world. Their bold use of colors, technique, space, and theme broke new conceptual ground. Further reading: Desmond Rochfort's *Mexican Muralists* (London: Laurence King, 1997) is a good place to start to learn more. More information: https://en.wikipedia.org/wiki/Mexican_muralism; https://mxcity.mx/2018/07/sobre-los-asombrosos-murales-del-palacio-de-bellas-artes/; https://en.wikipedia.org/wiki/Mexican_muralism.

MEXICAN WALL ART COLLECTIVES

ASARO (Asamblea de Artistas Revolucionarios de Oaxaca). This group has long been agitating for educational and social reform in Oaxaca, which has seen violent clashes between protestors and police. They have been active in Oaxaca for more than ten years. Further reading: *Getting Up for the People: The Visual Revolution of ASAR-Oaxaca* by ASARO, Mike Graham de la Rosa, and Suzanne M. Schadl (Oakland, CA: PM Press, 2014). More information: https://jsma.uoregon.edu/ASARO.

Urtarte (La Unión Revolucionaria de Trabajadores del Arte / The Revolutionary Union of Art Workers). Inspired by woodblock prints, this group of social activist wall artists pastes up their work throughout Oaxaca. Their work often features images that includes symbols of Mexican tradition, like the sacred heart and corn in the context of social protest. More information: https://www.facebook.com/urtarte.oaxaca/.

Derrumbe collective. A group of wall artists who voluntarily paint murals on neighborhood walls to give locals a pride of place and connection with Indigenous and historical roots. More information: https://www.youtube.com/watch?v=ggB7EoBKlSA.

Tlacolulokos collective. These two Oaxacan street artists, Dario Canal and Cosijoesa Cernas, paint detailed wall art of women from Mexico to LA. Their subjects often feature Zapotec women who display tattooed arms. More information: http://tlacolulokos.blogspot.com/; https://www.latimes.com/entertainment/arts/la-et-cm-tlacolulokos-visa-revoked-20180829-story.html; https://www.facebook.com/Tlacolulokos/; https://www.nytimes.com/2018/01/27/opinion/sunday/immigrants-protests-art-culture.html.

COZUMEL

Amanda Lynn. A San Francisco–based muralist, Lynn received her bachelor of fine arts from the San Francisco Academy of Art. She has painted her street murals of women from Miami to Cozumel, where she contributed to the SeaWalls project. More information: https://www.juxtapoz.com/news/street-art/live-outside-sf-an-interview-with-amanda-lynn-and-lady-mags/.

Ever. A wall artist from Buenos Aires, Argentina, whose large-scale work is on display at the Cozumel city hall. His real name is Nicolás Romero, and his work often features women. More information: https://streetartnews.net/2015/07/seawalls-15-ever-creates-new-mural-in.html.

CHAPTER 4:
Costa Rica: Land of Volcanos, Rainforests, and Local Street Cred

Federico Peixoto, DJ and filmmaker. Peixoto has followed the development of the street art scene throughout Central America and has documented its artists at work. (Featured Interview) To view his documentary *Tlacuilos*, visit https://vimeo.com/ondemand/tlacuilosgraffitidoc. More information: https://www.facebook.com/BronxWorldFilm/videos/costa-rican-filmmaker-federico-peixoto-in-nyc-for-us-premiere-of-tlacuilos/594326127793907/.

Aliados Festival Artists. The 2018 Graffiti Festival in San José, Costa Rica, brought together wall artists from throughout Central America. Festival background information: https://ticotimes.net/2018/03/11/photos-graffiti-festival-unites-latin-america-in-costa-rica; https://www.pri.org/stories/2015-06-26/worlds-deadliest-city-graffiti-artists-use-their-weapons-good. Those artists represented at the festival include darwinflores, Los Chacuas (Nicaragua), Sinless (Panama), Betan-04 (Honduras), Topan, Negus, Onesto Birdaz and Yiyo, ROY, Roke, Simer, and Ruido.

Onesto Birdaz creates bizarre cartoonlike people on the walls he paints. He has achieved an unmistakable style with his wall art in Costa Rica. More information: https://www.behance.net/gallery/71649029/Alia2-Costa-Rica-Onesto-Birdaz.

Darwinfloresart paints women on the wall in dreamlike background. More information: https://www.instagram.com/darwinflores.art/?hl=en.

Negus, whose works often feature fanciful animals and people with masks in an alternative mythos of bright colors. More information: http://globalstreetart.com/negus-arte-vida.

JUST, a tattooist from San José, Costa Rica, whose focus on women subjects is part of his skin and wall art. (Featured interview)

PUCHO, a muralist from San Ramón de Alajuela, Costa Rica, a small town outside the capital whose wall art of women connects with the natural world. (Featured Interview)

ROY. Costa Rican wall artist whose evocative and intimate portraits of young women feature on the cover of *Women on the Walls* and in the Costa Rica chapter.

CHAPTER 5:
Chile and Peru: The Spine of the Andes and a Wild Beach Culture

Mr. Papillon. Using a photorealistic technique, this French muralist celebrates the joy of youth. More information: https://www.facebook.com/mpapillon.page/.

CHAPTER 6:
EuroArtists: Big Walls, Big Ideas in Small Spaces

THIRTEENTH ARRONDISSEMENT

General information: https://en.parisinfo.com/discovering-paris/walks-in-paris/street-art-walking-tour-in-the-13th-arrondissement.

Inti. A Chilean artist, Inti Castro works globally to portray the culture of his native land in large-scale murals. Inti, whose first name means "sun" in Quechua (the language of ancient Peru), often portrays women in his works. More information: https://www.streetartbio.com/artists/about-inti-biography; https://www.vayaadventures.com/blog/inti-the-chilean-street-muralist/#:~:text=The%20two%20kitty%2Dcorner%20walls,a%20portrait%20created%20by%20INTI.

Vhils. This Portuguese artist does not work in the shadows or try to conceal his identity. He is the only street artist featured in this book who sculpts his art by removing bricks on facades to reveal the wall-sized portraits hidden in the walls (Featured Interview). Vhils has worked around the world, including in LA, where he collaborated with Shepard Fairey. Further reading: *Pentimento*, Vhils Studio, limited edition, https://www.under-dogs.net/products/pentimento-alexandre-farto-aka-vhils-special-edition. More information: https://www.vhils.com/.

Shepard Fairey. A globally recognized name, Fairey does a great deal of collaborative work with other wall artists. Fairey founded the Obey clothing line and has achieved financial success. His works in this book are found in LA (collaboration with Vhils) and Paris. Fairey came to international recognition for his poster *Hope* for the Obama presidential campaign. Further reading: *Post No Bills* by Shepard Fairey (Corte Madero, CA: Gingko, 2002). More information: https://en.wikipedia.org/wiki/Shepard_Fairey.

d*face. His real name is Dean Stockton, and he grew up in London, where he developed a taste for graffiti. The artist uses a multitude of techniques for his street art, including spray cans, stencils, and stickers. Stockton has had many gallery shows and exhibitions, and his large-scale mural in Paris references the pop art of Roy Lichtenstein. More information: https://en.wikipedia.org/wiki/D*Face http://www.dface.co.uk/about.

C215. This French street artist's handle is based on the prison cell in which he was once locked up. His real name is Christian Guémy, and his stencil work can found throughout the world, usually in locations where he does not have permission to do his work. Much of his work focuses on subjects who are often marginalized by society, including refugees and homeless children. More information: https://www.streetartbio.com/artists/c215/.

RAF Urban is a French street artist whose subjects, particularly women of color, are his main inspiration. He grew up in a suburb of Paris. Urban uses paste-ups and stencils to quickly get his work on the walls. More information: https://www.artsper.com/en/contemporary-artists/france/8527/raf-urban.

FAILE. Patrick McNeil and Patrick Miller are FAILE. The two Brooklyn-based artists specialize in multimedia exhibitions and projects, including their large-scale wall art in Paris. They've been working together since 1999. More information: https://en.wikipedia.org/wiki/FAILE.

Eddie Colla. Colla began his artistic career as a photographer and worked for a number of high-profile publications and ad agencies, whose street art bites that hand that once fed him. His attitude toward wall art and its place in society is taken verbatim from his website: "There is a visual conversation that takes place on the streets of urban environments. This conversation is dominated primarily by advertising and utilitarian signage and assumes passive participation. Whether invited or not I am going to participate in this conversation. Public spaces were never intended to be coated from top to bottom with photos of consumer products. These spaces should, in some manner, reflect the culture that thrives in that space." More information: https://www.eddiecolla.com/.

Invader. His mosaic wall art is assembled without permission and is modeled after the Space Invader video game, which featured heavily pixilated symbols in a virtual shooting gallery that emerged in arcades in the late 1970s. Invader's work is found down many Paris streets. More information: https://en.wikipedia.org/wiki/Invader_(artist); https://www.space-invaders.com/home/.

EAST SIDE GALLERY (BERLIN)

Dmitri Vrubel. What is perhaps the best-known and most photographed piece of wall art from the East Side Gallery is this work by Russian painter Vrubel. It is the fraternal socialist kiss between Leonid Brezhnev and Erich Honecker titled *My God, Help Me to Survive This Deadly Love*. The painting is based on a photograph taken October 7, 1979, when Brezhnev was in East Germany to mark a ten-year agreement between the German Democratic Republic and Russia. More information: https://en.wikipedia.org/wiki/Dmitri_Vrubel; https://theculturetrip.com/europe/germany/berlin/articles/5-things-you-should-know-about-dmitri-vrubel-a-must-read-artist-profile/.

Birgit Kinder. In her somewhat satiric work, East German artist Birgit Kinder's Trabant, a GDR-made car, smashes through the Berlin Wall. The often-ridiculed Trabant was manufactured in the GDR up until 1990. More information: https://www.theguardian.com/world/2011/may/03/berlin-wall-artists-sue-city; https://chnm.gmu.edu/1989/items/show/718.

Kani Avali. An Iranian immigrant living in Berlin; painted this flood of humanity flowing through Checkpoint Charlie border crossing. More information: https://edition.cnn.com/style/article/east-side-gallery-berlin-trnd/index.html.

Ostap. Disney characters appear on Berlin walls, but few like this image of Mickey Mouse being dominated by a Russian children's book character in this stencil. These types of graphic satires are not uncommon on the walls of Berlin. More information: https://selfmadecrew.com/cheburashka-banksy-streetart/.

DEM. This intimate portrait is by the Greek artist whose work demonstrates a refinement in the rough walls of Dircksenstraße. More information: https://www.facebook.com/streetartthessaloniki/videos/791392734651394/.

Confatty. The work by Confatty, an advocate of Fat Power, has a humorous quality that makes the viewer question its message as satire or serious. More information: https://www.instagram.com/con_fatty/?hl=en.

iAMi. The paste-up by iAMi reaches into the future to promote its message of gay feminism. More information: https://www.facebook.com/iAMicreative/.

Marycula. Her works skew toward leftist politics and its heroes. More information: https://www.instagram.com/explore/tags/marycula/top/; https://salzig.berlin/marycula/.

CHAPTER 7: Climbing over the Wall from Obscurity to Recognition: Faith XLVII's Journey from South Africa to LA

Faith47, born Liberty Du in South Africa. Faith47 / Faith XLVII (who adopted her nom d'rue from her grandmother's numerological beliefs) began her street art career in 1979. She has created works in thirty-nine countries, including wall-size portraits of women that are intimate in style and spectral in shading and color. (Featured Interview) Further reading: biography *Faith47* (Berlin: From Here to Fame, 2011). More information: FAITH47.com.

DALeast. Using a black-and-white palate and unique brushstrokes, DALeast's animal action wall art has a unique three-dimensional quality that also looks like it coalesces before it blows away like a party streamer. More information: https://www.streetartbio.com/artists/about-daleast-biography/.

Further reading on Banksy: *Banksy: Wall and Piece* by Banksy (London: Random House Penguin, 2006).

STREET ART GLOSSARY (a Quick Reference Guide)

The following is a pocket-sized glossary to street art terms. You can find many references to the argot of wall artists. One is www.mentalfloss.com/article/51583/14-street-art-terms; another good source is Wikipedia's Glossary of Graffiti: https://en.wikipedia.org/wiki/Glossary_of_graffiti.

bombing: Painting a large number of surfaces at one time
caps: Spray cans that can have specialized nozzles
crew: Your gang of wall artists who often work together to bomb an area
legal walls: Walls where artists have received permission to do their work
murals: Usually large-scale painted pieces on buildings
paste-ups: Usually posters created in a studio and glued to walls, often with wheat paste
stencils: Cutouts that are placed against a wall and sprayed, resulting in a fast result. Banksy does stencils.
stickers: Small advertisements for wall artists that can be put in public places, such as street signs
tagging or writing: A quick signature on a wall or any public surface
throw-ups: Fast graffiti done without much planning or time investment. Can be bubble letters with one filler color.
yarn bombing: Using yarn to wrap public objects

About the Authors

Dr. Katja Fleischmann

grew up in Berlin, where edgy street art is part of the local landscape. She has always been a student of the global language of design, especially expressed on the walls in signage and wall art. She was the youngest professor of design in Germany and was also awarded a Fulbright scholarship. Her profession took her to London, New York, Miami, and Australia, where she currently works as a researcher and design educator. Dr. Fleischmann's interest in wall art of women has occupied her travels in many out-of-the-way locations.

Robert H. Mann

is a journalist and writer who grew up in LA, where he was first exposed to street art. While living in Barcelona, he collected political posters that were proliferating following the death of Generalissimo Francisco Franco. His interest in politics and propaganda piqued his curiosity about why women are the favorite subjects of street artists.